THE MENTALLY RETARDED CHILD

McGRAW-HILL SERIES
IN PSYCHOLOGY

Consulting Editors
NORMAN GARMEZY
LYLE V. JONES

LAZARUS, R.   Patterns of Adjustment
LEWIN   A Dynamic Theory of Personality
MAHER   Principles of Psychopathology
MARASCUILO   Statistical Methods for Behavioral Science Research
MARX AND HILLIX   Systems and Theories in Psychology
MILLER   Language and Communication
MORGAN   Physiological Psychology
MULAIK   The Foundations of Factor Analysis
NOVICK AND JACKSON   Statistical Methods for Educational and Psychological Research
NUNNALLY   Introduction to Statistics for Psychology and Education
NUNNALLY   Psychometric Theory
OVERALL AND KLETT   Applied Multivariate Analysis
PORTER, LAWLER, AND HACKMAN   Behavior in Organizations
RESTLE   Learning: Animal Behavior and Human Cognition
ROBINSON AND ROBINSON   The Mentally Retarded Child
ROSENTHAL   Genetic Theory and Abnormal Behavior
ROSS   Psychological Disorders of Children: A Behavioral Approach to Theory, Research, and Therapy
SCHWITZGEBEL AND KOLB   Changing Human Behavior: Principles of Planned Intervention
SHAW   Group Dynamics: The Psychology of Small Group Behavior
SHAW AND COSTANZO   Theories of Social Psychology
SHAW AND WRIGHT   Scales for the Measurement of Attitudes
SIDOWSKI   Experimental Methods and Instrumentation in Psychology
SIEGEL   Nonparametric Statistics for the Behavioral Sciences
SPENCER AND KASS   Perspectives in Child Psychology
STAGNER   Psychology of Personality
STEERS AND PORTER   Motivation and Work Behavior
VINACKE   The Psychology of Thinking
WALLEN   Clinical Psychology: The Study of Persons
WARREN AND AKERT   Frontal Granular Cortex and Behavior
WINER   Statistical Principles in Experimental Design

THE MENTALLY RETARDED CHILD
A PSYCHOLOGICAL APPROACH

SECOND EDITION

NANCY M. ROBINSON, PH.D.
HALBERT B. ROBINSON, PH.D.
University of Washington

With Contributions by
GILBERT S. OMENN, M.D., PH.D.
University of Washington

JOSEPH C. CAMPIONE, PH.D.
University of Illinois

McGRAW-HILL BOOK COMPANY
New York   St. Louis   San Francisco   Auckland
Düsseldorf   Johannesburg   Kuala Lumpur   London
Mexico   Montreal   New Delhi   Panama   Paris
São Paulo   Singapore   Sydney   Tokyo   Toronto

To Charles R. Strother,
friend, humanitarian,
and distinguished leader
dedicated to the welfare of
handicapped children everywhere.

And to Lois Rae.

THE MENTALLY RETARDED CHILD

Copyright © 1965, 1976 by McGraw-Hill, Inc. All rights reserved.
Printed in the United States of America. No part of this publication may be reproduced, stored in a retrieval system, or transmitted, in any form or by any means, electronic, mechanical, photocopying, recording, or otherwise, without the prior written permission of the publisher.

4 5 6 7 8 9 0   DODO   7 9 8 7

This book was set in Times Roman by Rocappi, Inc.
The editors were Richard R. Wright, Janis M. Yates, and Phyllis T. Dulan;
the cover was designed by Joseph Gillians;
the production supervisor was Charles Hess.
The drawings were done by Eric G. Hieber Associates Inc.
R. R. Donnelley & Sons Company was printer and binder.

Library of Congress Cataloging in Publication Data

Robinson, Nancy M
    The mentally retarded child.

    (McGraw-Hill series in psychology)
    Order of authors' names reversed in 1965 ed.
    Bibliography: p.
    Includes index.
    1. Mentally handicapped children. 2. Mental deficiency. I. Robinson, Halbert B., joint author.
II. Title. [DNLM: 1. Mental retardation. WS107 R663m]
RJ506.M4R62   1976   618.9'28'588   75-30903
ISBN 0-07-053202-8

CONTENTS

FOREWORD TO THE SECOND EDITION

The term "mental retardation" covers a multitude of sins of omission, commission, and transmission with a resultant range and complexity of behavioral manifestations which makes unitary consideration out of the question. No segment of intellectual handicap is neglected in this text; but the extent of the problems leads the authors to focus on the large, gray borderline area between low-average human mental achievement and the deficiency of the severely retarded. The reader is made well aware even within this range that there exist tremendous individual differences in behavior, in appraisal of the cause, and in the efficacy of possible treatment. The authors recognize the fact that all forms and all degrees of mental retardation do not offer equal promise of improvement. They concentrate their attention on evaluating the voluminous and often contradictory literature concerning those individuals with whom the greatest degree of progress is possible, the mildly retarded.

The historical background of treatment and diagnosis, often in that order, emphasizes the longtime hopelessness of attempts to utilize the resources of children who did not measure up to the intellectual achievement of their peers. The authors' thorough knowledge of the resource material reveals the continued existence of this difficulty, the advances made in recent experimental studies, the ever-present need for further research toward better understanding of mental retardation, and further refined methods of treatment.

Toward the goal of unraveling the web of mental impedimenta, various theories of intelligence and their educational significance are discussed in depth and in breadth. Piaget's studies of cognition, if thoroughly digested, offer valuable developmental information on levels of comprehension and an opportunity to assess variances between concrete and abstract cognitive capacities. The differential behaviors of the retarded child in mastering concrete and abstract learning is of special interest to recent research.

The chapters on memory and learning report research which has direct and effective application to improved learning techniques with the intellectually slow or impeded. Extensive recent research, on both short- and long-term memory, offers specific cues and clues which have already produced measurable improvement in the learning of retardates.

The advantages and disadvantages of institutional versus home care for retarded children are presented throughout the book in different contexts. Presently, the institution has been in considerable disrepute as the dispenser of inadequate or nonexistent affectional bonds for the children involved, regardless of their intellectual capacity. This failing has in some measure been overcome in such custodial situations as the kibbutzim of Israel. The children there spend fixed periods with their mothers regularly during each week and absorb enough maternal contact comfort and other attributes of motherly love to prove the saying that "a little love goes a long, long way." The authors of this text, on the other hand, document some exceptional cases in which the home situation may be so unalterably evil in effect that "hell is where home is." The modified and modulated institution becomes a heavenly haven.

The fundamental facts as presented in the text concerning causes and cures of mental retardation, accurate appraisal of academic achievement, and scientifically sacrosanct theories of intelligence are important. More important, however, is the authors' appreciation of the double-barreled handicap of children who cannot satisfy their parents' expectations and at the same time are constantly ridiculed and prodded by their peers and playmates. It is difficult for parents to choose effective methods of discipline and encouragement with the most model members of the youngest set. How then should parents choose for children who seem to do nothing as well as they should? Probably, in the majority of cases, negative conditioning of the infant is being conveyed even before the family is authoritatively aware of the condition of the child. Caustic comparisons with the baby next door or with brother Don or sister Deni at the same age may seem innocuous, but they have started the chain of unfortunate interpersonal reactions. By the time that communication and language develop the child cannot tell taunts from truths or failure from functioning, so frequent may be the negative reinforcements.

Recent studies at the Wisconsin Primate Laboratory have utilized a new type of therapy for the rehabilitation of rhesus infants who have been raised in total isolation from six to twelve months. This technique is based on a new type of therapist. As we believe therapists should be of the same breed as the patients, the therapists are monkeys, but monkeys from three to ten months younger than the isolates, termed "junior therapists." Being younger and smaller, these animals pose little threat and, very gradually, together in a playroom, ease the frightened and depressed strangers into acceptance of contact, acceptance of others, and finally into the first steps of play. Play proceeds to further ease and ameliorate the plight of the isolate. The concept of the junior therapist might have meaning in aiding and abetting researchers in the field of mental retardation. Over a period of years does the retarded child with younger, normal siblings fare better than the child with older brothers or sisters? Would younger playmates at an early age lessen the chance for negative reinforcement? This is but a single sample of the type of challenge posed by a book full of challenges.

The authors portray vividly and absorbingly the historical and recent developments in special education of the mentally retarded children. When realizing the ever present need for increased facilities and more refined techniques, the reader feels a profound, personal relief to find that when these needs are met, these children can become adults who, on the whole, are a happy group and who more than fulfill the promise of youth.

The Robinsons' monumental book is not only comprehensive but definitive. It serves present needs in a vital field and will be a guideline to scholarly efforts far into the future.

HARRY F. HARLOW
University of Arizona

FOREWORD TO THE FIRST EDITION

What makes a book both good and great? There must be a conjunction of need and excellence to produce the phenomenon, as it may here be produced.

Excellence in a serious book has its origin in several sources. Scholarly competence is surely one, perhaps the first, and the Robinsons have this richly. They know mental retardation, in depth and range, from cytogenetics to social action programs. They know when they can be confident and when they must be tentative; they are thorough and careful, yet willing to commit themselves to a position. Clarity is a second requisite. This book is lucid from sentence to paragraph to chapter to the structure of the whole. They have let pass no fuzzy thought, small or large. Engagement and compassion are requisite too; the Robinsons obviously care about the problem of mental retardation and about people who are retarded. They care enough even to discipline themselves to an appropriate measure of detachment.

Greatness is something that can happen to a really good book, as I think it may to this one, when need is pressing. Today there is a lively national concern with mental retardation, but no adequate introductory book on its psychological aspects exists; or, more accurately, there has not been one until now. At a time of great need the Robinsons have done a great service. Because of their scholarly effort, laymen can work with more intelligence, and professional people with more competence. The ultimate benefactors will be those who may, as a result, suffer less impairment of intellect, that most human of functions.

NICHOLAS HOBBS
Vanderbilt University

PREFACE

In the eleven years since publication of the first edition of *The Mentally Retarded Child,* the field has changed dramatically. Programs providing prevention, diagnosis, education, medical treatment and therapies of many kinds, community residential care, financial aid, vocational rehabilitation, employment, and recreation have been undertaken by many private and governmental groups. No longer is concern for the retarded found only among those whose lives have been touched by a retarded relative. There is widespread commitment to the goal of optimizing the development of all retarded children, enabling them to live amicably and with dignity as participating citizens in supportive communities.

At the same time, research has increased phenomenally. Many disciplines contributing to the prevention of mental retardation and the amelioration of its consequences have mounted energetic efforts to expand their knowledge base and to refine their investigative methods. The present degree of sophistication about mentally retarded individuals far exceeds that of the previous decade. The first edition of this book attempted to summarize most, if not all, of the research bearing on mental retardation. Such an ambition is totally out of the question now. We have attempted only to indicate major research investigations and their findings, referring the reader elsewhere for more detailed reviews.

The audience to whom the present edition is addressed remains much the same as that for the first edition. The book is intended as an introduction to the field for several groups of persons involved in central as well as peripheral ways with the mentally retarded. First, it is addressed to upper-division and graduate students in colleges and universities who seek information about the retarded as part of a general major in such fields as education, sociology, or psychology. Second, it is meant to serve as an introductory text in specialized programs preparing students for careers within the field of mental retardation. Those in training as special education teachers, clinical and rehabilitation psychologists, pediatricians, social workers, speech pathologists, public health and pediatric nurses, and occupational and physical therapists will, we hope, find this text suited to their needs. Third, the book may be useful to professionals who are already engaged with mentally retarded individuals or their families and who wish to gain a more accurate and contemporary perspective on the field.

We are psychologists and this book clearly reflects our professional orientation. Psychological theory and research and the procedures involved in psychological appraisal and psychotherapy have been given a prominent role. It is our conviction, however, that the members of all concerned disciplines require a widely conceived background in this area. The book extends, therefore, considerably beyond the boundaries of what is ordinarily considered the province of psychology.

Because the appropriate material has expanded so rapidly and broadly, we have sought the help of colleagues in preparing this revision. We were fortunate indeed to have the collaboration of two experts who have contributed generously. Gilbert S. Omenn, Associate Professor of Medical Genetics of the University of Washington, prepared by far the major portions of the revisions of Chapters 3, 4, 5, and 6, which deal with the genetic and medical aspects of mental retardation. Joseph C. Campione, Professor of Psychology of the University of Illinois at Champaign-Urbana, prepared the first drafts of Chapters 13, 14, and 15, which discuss learning and memory in retarded persons. In order to preserve the unitary character of the text, we have attempted to ensure that these chapters are well integrated with the presentation as a whole. We assume full responsibility for any errors which may have occurred in the process.

In addition, we have had the aid of a number of professionals who have reviewed sections of the book. We are indeed grateful for the honest criticism and assistance of Alfred A. Baumeister, Irv Bialer, Lee J. Ehrman, Norman R. Ellis, Herbert Ginsburg, Earl B. Hunt, Elizabeth Loftus, Clifford E. Lunneborg, Joseph D. Matarazzo, Albert Reichert, Dorothea M. Ross, and David W. Smith. Most particularly, we are indebted to Harry F. Harlow, whose careful review of most of the manuscript was extremely helpful.

A number of the exceptional photographs in the original edition, all of them taken by John and Marian Menapace, have been retained. Additional photographs were taken by the Media Staff of the University of Washington Child Development and Mental Retardation Center and by Wayne Barclay. Dr. David W. Smith and the W. B. Saunders Company generously permitted us to use nine illustrations from *The Child with Down's Syndrome* by David W. Smith and Ann Asper Wilson, published in 1973. The many other publishers and authors who permitted us to reprint excerpts from their publications are acknowledged in the reference list or, at their request, in the text.

Our children seem to have managed extremely well for the past two years during our preoccupation with this manuscript. It will be very pleasant for us to become reacquainted with them.

NANCY M. ROBINSON
HALBERT B. ROBINSON

PART I
INTRODUCTION

1
Theories of Intelligence

The observation that individuals differ in their intellectual abilities certainly antedates recorded history. The earliest writings contain thoughtful references to such differences. More than 2,000 years ago, for example, in a discussion with a particularly modern ring, Plato suggested in *The Republic* that individual variations in intelligence must be a basic determinant of the social and political order in any workable society. Even though man has pondered the nature of intelligence and its importance in human affairs since the beginnings of civilization, no single definition of intelligence has ever satisfied all or even a majority of those who have dealt with the concept. Indeed, it would be difficult to cite any concept which has remained more confused or more controversial.

In spite of centuries of speculation about the nature of intelligence, the beginnings of scientific concern can be traced back no further than the nineteenth century, to revolutionary concepts in biology and statistics, and especially to the new conceptions of the individual differences among men attributable to evolution and genetics. A case can be made, in fact, that the concept of intelligence as it is used today was unknown before the striking breakthroughs of Alfred Binet and Theodore Simon in 1905. Before that time, "no one had differentiated the attribute of intelligence as today conceived from the excess meanings and embellishments with which . . . philosophers . . . and . . . psychologists had adorned it" (Matarazzo, 1972, p. 25).

During this century, there has been an explosion of interest in this facet of human development. Scholars of the life sciences and professionals in the disciplines concerned with the human condition have attempted to unravel the mysteries of this most crucial of man's attributes. The layman's concern with individual differences in intellectual ability has been developed chiefly since World War I. The achievements in psychology, particularly in the development of tests of mental abilities, together with the growth and improvement of public education, have been largely responsible for the expanding public interest. Since the world's entry into the Space Age in the late 1950s, particular impetus has been given to the study of intellectual development. The proper utilization of intellectual resources has come to be seen as vitally affecting national progress.

Even in the midst of popular interest in intelligence and of vast expenditures of private and public funds for studies concerned with its enhancement, substantial confusion about the nature of intelligence still exists. Indeed, the concept is almost as obscure now as it was many years ago. Paradoxically, greater and greater efforts are being made to develop information about intelligence, although few can agree on a definition of what they consider it to be.

In 1921, at the height of efforts to achieve a definition of intelligence, fourteen leading specialists in the psychology of individual differences presented their views in the *Journal of Educational Psychology*. Each defined the concept somewhat differently. Because of the difficulties in formulating a widely acceptable theoretical definition, such attempts diminished in number, and the concept of intelligence has only recently again become the subject of widespread and vigorous debate. For almost half a century, a general though imperfect consensus of the criteria of intellectual behavior was tacitly accepted, bypassing concern for the nature of the concept itself. Because of the importance of education and because almost all children in the developed nations go to school, intelligence to a large extent became—and in many ways still is—equated with the abilities underlying scholastic achievement.

It is easy to understand why concern for a definition tended to give way to an applied orientation. During the early days of the study of individual differences in intelligence, applied research and theoretical speculation went hand in hand, and test construction seemed to most workers to require an explicit and well-developed theoretical basis. It soon became clear, however, that scores on tests based upon widely varying theoretical orientations tended to be highly correlated. Theoretical differences evidently had little practical effect; intelligence tests differed a great deal less in their relation to outside criteria than in the rationale of their authors. Gradually, an emphasis on devising good tests superseded attempts to develop a theoretical rationale.

No one can deny that the mental testing movement has flourished under an applied orientation. There are today an almost unbelievable number of tests which purport to measure one aspect or another of mental functioning. Normative data based on respectably large, if not altogether representative, samples are available for many of these tests. In the process of its rapid development, however, the mental testing movement became somewhat removed from the mainstream of psychological theory. Consequently, most of the major theoretical issues were either subordinated to practical necessities or cast aside as irrelevant.

Many psychologists would argue that no other branch of psychology has contributed so much to human welfare as the field of intellectual assessment. Certainly, no other has enjoyed such widespread acceptance, although at the same time critics abound. It seems clear, however, that the early abandonment of the theoretical for the practical was premature. Without theoretical guidelines, there developed an atmosphere in which straw men were set up to fight straw men and in which studies abounded but could not be compared because they were established within quite different frames of reference. Although psychologists obviously cannot and should not delay practical work while awaiting perfect theoretical agreement, there is little wisdom in forsaking theoretical discussion altogether. It is hoped that theory and its application will in the future move forward side by side, each enhancing the richness of the other.

EARLY DEFINITIONS OF INTELLIGENCE[1]

Although a great many diverse ideas about the basic nature of intelligence were proposed by early theorists, a few themes are common to most definitions: (1) the capacity to learn, (2) the totality of the knowledge which has been acquired, and (3) the ability to adjust or to adapt to the total environment, particularly to new situations. These definitions were not necessarily meant to be contradictory. The points of view differed primarily in emphasis. Indeed, several authors at one time or another defined intelligence in each of the three ways. They recognized that the ability to learn must underlie the acquisition of information and that both learning ability and knowledge assuredly provide the foundation for adjustment to new situations.

According to definitions which emphasized the *capacity to learn,* an individual's intelligence was seen as a matter of his educability, using this term in its broadest sense. Colvin argued that "intelligence is equivalent to the capacity to learn" (1921, p. 136). Similarly, Woodrow maintained that "intelligence . . . is an acquiring-capacity" (1921, p. 207).

The definitions which emphasized the amount of *knowledge* possessed by an individual considered that intelligence should be equated with the information which had been acquired as well as with the ability to acquire it. Henmon, who defined intelligence as "the capacity for knowledge and knowledge possessed," argued that the "untutored savage . . . may have high intellectual capacity, but without knowledge we should not ordinarily call him an intelligent man" (1921, p. 195).

The most common theme in the early definitions was one which pointed to the *adjustive* or *adaptive* aspect of intelligence. The majority of theorists seemed to agree that there is a general attribute of mental functioning which involves the ability of the individual to adapt to his or her environment. Binet and Simon, for example, wrote: "It seems to us that in intelligence there is a fundamental faculty, the alteration or the lack of which, is of the utmost importance for practical life. This faculty is judgment, otherwise called good sense, practical sense, initiative, the faculty of adapting one's self to circumstances" (1905, p. 197).

Some prominent theorists, although agreeing that intelligence was related to learning, knowledge, and the adaptability of mental processes, were sharply critical of broad, all-encompassing definitions. Terman, for example, maintained specifically that "an individual is intelligent in proportion as he is able to carry on abstract thinking." He argued that those who cannot see that "intelligence is the ability to think in terms of abstract ideas" have "a disturbed sense of psychological values." "It cannot be disputed," he continued, "that in the long run it is [those who] . . . excel in abstract thinking . . . [who] eat while others starve, survive epidemics, master new continents,

---

[1] The interested reader is advised to consult Cronbach (1975), Matarazzo (1972), or Tuddenham (1962) for a more complete discussion of the historical aspects of the long struggles to define and measure intelligence.

conquer time and space, and substitute religion for magic, science for taboos, and justice for revenge." Those who "excel in conceptual thinking could, if they wished, quickly exterminate or enslave all those . . . notably their inferiors in this respect" (1921, p. 128).

Some psychologists proposed that we distinguish between several kinds of intelligence. They agreed with Terman that the traditional definitions were too broad, but they advocated that we subsume under the term more than the capacity to deal with abstractions. E. L. Thorndike, for instance, set forth a scheme in which intelligent activity was divided into three types: "namely, (1) social intelligence, or ability to understand and deal with persons; (2) concrete intelligence, or ability to understand and deal with things, as in skilled trades and in working with the appliances of science; (3) abstract intelligence, or ability to understand and deal with verbal and mathematical symbols" (as quoted by F. S. Freeman, 1955, pp. 69–70).

Although these definitions seemed to indicate a fair degree of agreement among groups of theorists writing about such qualities as "adaptation," "learning," and "abstract thinking," the concurrence was more apparent than real. Each theorist interpreted the terms in his own fashion. This underlying divergence prevented the development of concrete, behavioral guidelines by which theories might be tested or refined. Although these early attempts had considerable heuristic value, further developments were needed.

CONTEMPORARY APPROACHES TO DEFINING INTELLIGENCE

Four distinct approaches to the problem of intelligence enjoy considerable support today: (1) There are attempts to combine and extend the definitions we have already considered, often in addition viewing intelligence as inextricably intertwined with the total dynamic functioning unit called "personality." (2) There are approaches which emphasize the factorial structure of intelligence, the existence of one, several, or many independent components or traits. (3) There are definitions which emphasize the processes of mental functioning, some of which are oriented toward the progression of intelligence from infancy to adulthood. (4) There are definitions which present intelligence simply as a hypothetical construct which has enabled the behavioral scientist to conceptualize and to discuss an aspect of behavior about which we know very little. This last approach denies that the construct need be precisely defined, since our ideas about intelligence change as our knowledge increases. It is closely related to the view that intelligence is a normative phenomenon which should be defined in quantitative terms such as test scores. As before, these approaches frequently overlap in the writings of contemporary workers. A single writer may at one time or another emphasize points of view which might easily fit into several of these interdependent categories.

The most prominent of those who have combined and extended the types of definitions previously discussed is David Wechsler, who has defined intelligence as "the aggregate or global capacity of the individual to act purposefully, think rationally, and to deal effectively with his environment" (1944, p. 3). Elaborating on his definition, Wechsler either specifically mentions or clearly implies capacity to learn, knowledge acquired, ability to adjust or adapt, and capacity to conceptualize on an abstract level. In addition to these familiar themes, he introduces several new ones. First, intelligence is seen as "global" because "it characterizes . . . behavior as a whole," and it is an "aggregate" because "it is composed of elements or abilities which, though not entirely independent, are qualitatively differentiable." Second, Wechsler places some emphasis on the purposiveness of behavior. Intelligent actions are viewed as goal-directed. Third, behavioral manifestations of intelligence are seen to be greatly influenced by factors which are not primarily intellectual. Wechsler says that "Factors other than intellectual ability, for example, those of drive and incentive, enter into intelligent behavior" (1944, p. 3) and are a proper part of any attempt to measure general intelligence.

Factorial Theories of Intelligence

This discussion of intelligence so far has emphasized differing ideas about the attributes which should be included in a concept of general mental capacity. We shall now consider the relationships among the various components of mental ability. Simple enumeration does not reveal the dynamic nature of intelligent activity, relationships among the components or their relations to nonintellectual aspects of human behavior such as achievement motivation and anxiety.

Factor analysis is the name applied to a number of statistical methods designed to identify relatively independent determinants or unitary traits involved in a set of observed data. There are a variety of such techniques, almost all of them requiring some subjective judgments on the part of the statistician. Each of these techniques yields slightly different results and, in consequence, there is a fertile field for debate. The techniques are applied to correlational matrices, all the intercorrelations of a group of tests given the same subjects, and *not* to an individual's scores. Examples of the factors related to intellectual performance are verbal fluency, quantitative reasoning, speed of reaction, and rote memory. In principle, these "pure" factors, or building blocks of mental capacity, should not be highly correlated with one another but should operate independently. Factor analysis, ideally, offers an appropriate tool to discover whether mental capacity is determined largely by an overall, pervasive general factor or whether it is composed mainly of several more specific factors. The differences among the statistical techniques tend, however, to obscure the issues as much as to clarify them.

Interest in the factors which should be included in the concept of intelligence and their relationships to one another is not new; it antedates the development of the factor analytic methods themselves. In fact, this has been a central area of concern for the better part of the century. During the latter part of the nineteenth century, attempts to measure intelligence—largely through the use of psychophysical tests of rather simple functions of discrimination, memory, perception, reaction time, and susceptibility to illusions—had been unsuccessful. Such tests proved to be, for the most part, unrelated to one another and were most certainly uncorrelated with independent practical estimates of intelligence. Many were willing to conclude that there is no such thing as intelligence but only a large number of independent mental activities connected solely by this common and misleading term.

G-factor Theory   Charles Spearman, a noted English psychologist and statistician, challenged this view in a classic paper published in 1904. Following an analysis of the relationships among children's proficiencies in a variety of school subjects and their scores on tests of visual, auditory, and tactile discrimination, Spearman argued for "the hierarchy of the Specific Intelligences." He concluded that the "observed facts indicate that all branches of intellectual activity have in common one fundamental function (or group of functions) [the general or *g* factor], whereas the remaining or specific elements of the activity [the specific or *s* factors] seem in every case to be wholly different from that in all others" (p. 292).

Spearman's two-factor theory proposed that there is a "general intelligence," a fundamental, unitary, causal attribute of mind which is more or less revealed in all cognitive activities. This *g* factor, he asserted, was present in both the discrimination tasks and performance in school. Although others subsequently refuted his contention that discrimination abilities and general intelligence were closely related, Spearman's *g* factor was found to be related to complex functions involving reasoning and judgment.

Multifactor Theory   E. L. Thorndike of Columbia University was perhaps Spearman's most effective and formidable critic. He rejected the notion of "one sole common element" in intelligence and proposed instead a very large number of elementary abilities intertwined in different intelligent acts. These abilities, he thought, might correspond with neuronal connections in the brain. At one point, he wrote,

> . . . in their deeper nature the higher forms of intellectual operations are identical with mere association or connection-forming, depending upon the same sort of physiological connections but requiring *many more of them.* By the same argument the person whose intellect is greater or higher or better than that of another person differs from him in the last analysis in having, not a new sort of physiological process, but simply a larger number of connections of the ordinary sort (1925, p. 415).[2]

Sampling Theory   A somewhat similar view formed the basis of the sampling theory of G. H. Thomson (1916, 1948), a Scottish psychologist, and of R. C. Tryon (1935, 1959), Professor of Psychology at the University of California at Berkeley. Thomson viewed tests as *samples* of the kinds of bonds which the mind could form, correspondences between tests thus resulting from the sampling of common bonds. He maintained that some tests were richer than others in the number of bonds they sampled, the more intricate tests sampling a wider number of bonds. These complex tests tended, therefore, to be more highly correlated, since they were more representative samples of the bonds individuals possessed. "Like the tests, some men are rich, others poor, in these bonds. Some are richly endowed by heredity, some by opportunity and education, some by both, and some by neither" (1951, p. 315). Thomson was able to show that the *g* and *s* factors of Spearman's hierarchy could be produced by pure chance on artificial arrays of data generated by throwing dice.

Group Factor Theory   T. L. Kelley (1928), an American psychologist, held a view intermediate between those of Spearman and Thorndike. He maintained that certain mental operations have in common a primary or group factor which differentiates them from other mental operations. Most prominent among the followers of Kelley was L. L. Thurstone, a factor analyst who conducted extensive research concerning the nature of intelligence (1934, 1938, 1947). Together with Thelma G. Thurstone (1941), he developed a theory of intelligence later called the "multiple factor theory." They proposed approximately a dozen group factors, of which the following were most frequently corroborated by their own research and that of others: verbal

---

[2] For a recent critique of Thorndike's position, see Estes (1974).

comprehension, word fluency, numerical reasoning, associative memory, spatial reasoning, perceptual speed, and induction or general reasoning. Undoubtedly of greater importance was Thurstone's method of factor analysis, which served as the first major statistical breakthrough in this area. He provided a method which, although laborious prior to the advent of computers, enabled one to extract, from the matrix of intercorrelations among tests, successive levels of factors such that each one has high correlations with some tests and low correlations with others. The meanings, or labels, of the factors must, however, be supplied by the statistician through examination of the apparent commonalities of the tests so clustered. In these analyses, group factors assume considerable importance, but something like Spearman's g also turns up again and again, though redrawn in a much more sophisticated and precise way than Spearman had been able to do.

Factor analysis can reveal only those factors derived from tests fed into it. What is not put in cannot come out. The range and variety of the tasks analyzed determines not only the nature of the factors identified, but the relative importance of common (g) and secondary factors. For example, if one chooses to include tests of gross motor skills in a matrix of intelligence tests, one is very likely to derive a factor subsequently labeled "gross motor skill," and its inclusion is also likely to reduce the importance of a general cognitive factor in accounting for the intercorrelations of the matrix.

Guilford's Three-dimensional Theory   The factorial theory of J. P. Guilford (1968; Guilford & Hoepfner, 1971; Meyers & Dingman, 1966) illustrates a somewhat different approach. As a preliminary step, Guilford and his collaborators made extensive use of factor analytic methods to determine the content of a wide range of ability tests. Guilford found it unnecessary to assume a general factor of intelligence but, like Thorndike, posited instead a large number of primary factors. His scheme, which extended far beyond the factors which actually could be derived from existing tests, is an attempt to incorporate simultaneously all the known primary factors of cognitive behavior, point up some principles which unify and elucidate the total list, and help to identify and define factors which are as yet undiscovered. His theoretical model for the complete structure of intelligence was first presented in its present form in 1959(a). The model can be represented by a three-dimensional rectangular solid, as shown in Figure 1-1.

Like three-dimensional space, Guilford's model can be described and organized according to three schemes of classification. Each of the many primary factors of human intelligence (each "cell" in the model) can be thought of as possessing a unique combination of three different dimensions: one referring to the content of the material dealt with, a second to the operations performed on the material, and a third to the products achieved by the operations.

Guilford described four categories of content of the materials dealt with by the subject. These categories represent classes of stimuli, or general informational variables. Operations, which Guilford divided into five types, represent the major kinds of intellectual activities or processes by which individuals handle raw information. Finally, Guilford identified six categories of products which are achieved as the result of processing information. Guilford's scheme thus postulates the existence of $4 \times 5 \times 6$, or 120 different primary intellectual abilities. Through a monumental effort, Guilford, his students, and his colleagues have identified or devised tests for approximately one hundred of these intellectual abilities, each of which is regarded as a generalized skill which is affected by the individual's experience and may be further developed by

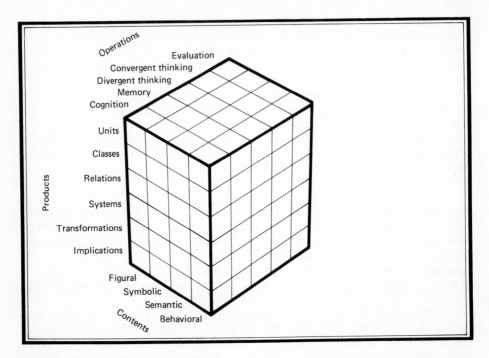

Fig. 1-1   A cubical model representing the structure of intellect. *(From Guilford, 1959, p. 470)*

means of special exercise. Although this extensive body of work is extremely systematic, it has not greatly affected the conceptualizations of other researchers in the area of intelligence, with one major exception: the distinction between convergent thinking, arriving at a problem solution requiring a simple best or correct answer, and divergent thinking, related to production of new information or ideas, flexibility, and originality. Divergent thinking is very poorly represented in the mental tests currently in wide usage, but has been the basis for and catalyst of the very active area of investigation of creative thought (Guilford, 1967; Torrance, 1965; Wallach & Kogan, 1965).[3]

Fluid versus Crystallized Intelligence   An equally extensive body of work has been produced by R. B. Cattell (1964, 1968, 1971) over the past several decades, more recently in collaboration with a former student, J. L. Horn (1968). Cattell's theory has much in common with a theory proposed by Hebb (1942), although it is much more elaborate and has been more extensively tested. Cattell has proposed the existence of two major components of intellectual activity, *fluid intelligence* and *crystallized intelligence*. Fluid intelligence is a general relation-perceiving capacity which represents one's potential intelligence independent of socialization and education. It comes to include, however, the kinds of incidental learning which occur as the result of unplanned experiences with basic aspects of the environment which are relatively common in all cultures. Fluid intelligence "flows" into a wide variety of intellectual abili-

---

[3] Because mentally retarded children typically demonstrate very restricted creative skills, this topic has not been considered in the present volume. See Meeker (1969) for an introduction to Guilford's work as it can affect educational theory and practice.

ties because it is a fundamental response capability. Crystallized intelligence is much more reflective of one's cultural exposure, including formal educational experiences. Of paramount importance are knowledge and skills of the type normally taught in school, including, for example, vocabulary, numerical skills, a rich memory store of facts, figures, and concepts, and habits of logical reasoning. The adequacy of crystallized intelligence depends upon several factors: one's underlying fluid intelligence, the intensity and duration of one's exposure to effective educational experiences, and one's motivation to learn. Crystallized intelligence is not quite the same as scholastic ability; crystallized abilities, in fact, continue to increase long after the period of formal schooling has ended. Fluid intelligence, on the other hand, peaks at about age fourteen, then plateaus, and begins to decline in the decade after age twenty.

Crystallized intelligence is relatively easy to assess by the ordinary achievement tests and most of the widely used intelligence tests. Cattell proposed that to assess fluid intelligence, one must emphasize aspects of functioning which are much more independent of one's specific culture and formal educational experiences. He therefore was instrumental in an attempt to devise "culture-fair" tests which would circumvent these influences (Cattell, 1964). Unfortunately, he found, as have others, that it is almost impossible to develop truly culture-fair tests, since even such basic attributes as the attitude toward taking the tests is highly dependent on one's cultural heritage.

Jensen's Two-level Theory   The hue and cry which occurred in response to A. R. Jensen's (1969a) presentation of evidence suggesting a very high degree of heritability of intelligence and his assertion that there are substantial racial differences, has almost overlooked his proposal of two types of intellectual capacity, both largely inherited. Jensen (1969a, 1970a) differentiated between what he termed Level I intelligence, which is essentially associative in nature, and Level II, which is more directly cognitive. In the abilities represented by Level I, the response form is essentially similar to the form of the stimulus. One learns, for example, that $2 \times 2 = 4$, or that *c-a-t* spells *cat*. To some extent, this type of learning can be thought of as the acquisition of a bond between the stimulus and the response, of "S-R" learning. In the abilities represented by Level II, however, much more complex functions are demanded, in the sense that the stimulus input is acted upon and transformed or elaborated. The kinds of abilities required to reach problem solutions, to define abstract words, or to understand proverbs are examples of Level II functions.

It is difficult in practice, however, to separate these two functions. As we shall see in Chapter 13, even apparently simple learning tasks, such as paired-associates learning, can be accomplished much more efficiently if the individual transforms the task or adds to it some means of mediating the connections he or she is trying to acquire. Measures of Level I and Level II functions tend to be correlated in a given population, according to Jensen, because (1) even though they depend on independent genetic factors, assortative mating tends to produce individuals high or low in both abilities, (2) the behavioral expressions of the two are functionally interdependent as some threshold amount of Level I ability is necessary, for example, for Level II functions, and (3) the acquisition of certain Level I skills, such as reading, makes much more efficient the operation of Level II ability. Even though the two are positively correlated, Jensen maintains that Level II ability tends to differ by social class, whereas Level I does not. He sees cultural-familial mental retardation as primarily a deficit in Level II functions.

Age Changes in Factorial Composition of Intelligence   Before we leave the topic of factorial theories of intelligence, we should mention at least a few of the numerous studies which indicate the presence of important age changes in components of intelligence. For example, Hofstaetter (1954) studied data from the Berkeley Growth Study in which children were tested repeatedly from birth to age eighteen. She suggested that the functions measured during the first two years could best be described as "sensorimotor alertness," those measured between two and four years as "persistence," and those measured after age four as "manipulation of symbols." Hofstaetter was looking for g-factor characteristics. So was McNemar (1942), who factor analyzed Stanford-Binet items at fourteen age levels from years two to eighteen. In general, his results indicated that a single factor explained a large part of the performance at each separate age, but that the factor changed in nature over this age span, becoming increasingly verbal at the upper ranges.

Other psychologists, convinced of a multifactorial theory, interpret test scores quite differently, even though they may work from the same data. One of McNemar's students, L. V. Jones (1949, 1954) carried his professor's analysis further, using different techniques, and identified several group factors at various ages from seven to thirteen, without any important general factor at these ages. He found, moreover, that within this age range, group factors became more distinct at the higher age levels, presumably showing progressive differentiation of ability. Similarly, Bayley (1970), working primarily with data from the Berkeley Growth Study but also with analyses of other investigations, concluded that the evidence supports the presence of multiple mental abilities, each with its own pattern of development. Some are more continuous in growth than others, some more consistent over time. She concluded that the most stable general class of abilities, verbal facility and knowledge, is least bound to the stages of development. Abilities more variable over time include arithmetic and verbal reasoning, speed, and perhaps attention span or short-term memory.

During the past several decades, the most vigorous debates about the nature of intelligence, its components, and their organization, have occurred among theorists who have employed a factorial approach. The reader may be tempted to conclude that all these efforts have only muddied the waters, producing more heat than light and consuming enormous numbers of man-hours and, more recently, computer time. To some extent, this is correct, but there have also been revolutionary changes in the quality of the conceptions of intellectual functioning. The growth of theory and proposals about mental testing have also become more coherently related. Furthermore, a great deal of information has been acquired about the development and nature of human differences, and the means of scientific investigation have been greatly refined. As Tuddenham (1962) said, "To be sure, [factor] research has sometimes yielded contradictory results—but time and the accumulation of knowledge usually resolve matters, and it often turns out that the confusion arose not from conflicting answers, but from improperly phrased questions" (p. 151). We may not have found "the answers," but few would contend that we are not able to ask better questions now than we could when Spearman began his inquiries into the factorial nature of human intelligence.

Process-oriented Theories of Intelligence

A number of theorists have asked a series of questions of a kind different from any we have considered. Concentrating on the processes rather than the results of cognitive functioning, these theorists have not tended to be very interested in individual differences, but rather in the normal progression of the development of human abilities.

Jean Piaget   By far the most prominent among these theorists is Jean Piaget. Because Chapter 12 has been devoted to his work and its relevance to the field of mental retardation, we shall only introduce it here. On the most general level, Piaget conceives of intelligence as an adaptive process. As have other biologists, he asserts that adaptation is the most fundamental characteristic of all activity and that the basic adaptive properties of intellectual activity constitute only a special case of this all-important unifying principle. Adaptation, in Piaget's terms, involves the establishment of an equilibrium between the organism and its environment. The process of achieving this equilibrium is a very active one; the organism is constantly being molded by and is molding the environment. The single most important attribute of Piaget's theory is that it is truly developmental in orientation. At the very core of his system is the proposition that the intellectual functioning of an individual is both quantitatively and qualitatively different at different stages of life. He asserts that we "cannot determine where intelligence starts," but that we can plot its course of development and its "ultimate goal" (1947, p. 7).

Jerome S. Bruner   Representational processes play a much more important role in the writings of J. S. Bruner (1964), who sees cognitive development as essentially the evolving use of modes of representation. For the infant and young child, thinking is closely involved with action. Older preschool and young school-age children tend to be dominated by the vivid perceptual properties of the things they observe, and when asked to classify objects, they do so on the basis of characteristics such as color, shape, and size, using imagery as their primary mode of representation. Children older than six to eight years are able to use symbolic representations much more freely, language being chief among these symbolic systems, and thereby become much more flexible and astute in their classifications. "In effect, language provides a means, not only for representing experience, but also for transforming it" (p. 4).

Soviet Psychologists   Another group of workers for whom language plays a preeminent role in intellectual processes is the Soviet psychologists. Of this group, Pavlov, Vygotsky, and Luria are best known to American readers. It was Pavlov who distinguished the "first-signal system," the physical stimuli of which the world is composed, from the "second-signal system," or language. "A recurrent theme in much Russian research with children is the emergence of this second-signal system. This research is often called the development of 'verbal control.' . . . Language frees the organism from simple, Pavlovian dependence on the immediate events in the environment and allows mental planning and voluntary behavior" (Dale, 1972, p. 219).

Vygotsky (1962) maintained that thought and speech have different origins and lines of development, independent of one another, but that "at a certain point these lines meet, whereupon thought becomes verbal and speech rational" (p. 44). He proposed that *inner speech,* "thought connected with words," is largely unarticulated, highly abbreviated, and unstable, its main element being the meaning rather than the word.

Luria (1959, 1961), whose work has been somewhat influential in modern Western work with retarded children, has emphasized the regulatory or directive function of language. He has been especially interested in the development of the verbal regulation of motor behavior which, he maintains, is basically deficient in mentally retarded, organically damaged, children. His clever experiments with young children

(Dale, 1972), like many other psychological experiments reported in the Russian literature, have been rather imprecisely reported, and American psychologists have had
considerable difficulty in replicating them (Miller, Shelton, & Flavell, 1970; Zigler &
Balla, 1971).

Information Processing Theory   Another important group of theorists who
have attacked numerous problems of cognitive functioning are those who term their
work the study of "information processing." With these workers, we approach the
sketchy frontiers of the new process-oriented approaches to the concept of intelligence.
Representative of this group, and in many ways the most relevant to questions of
individual differences, are Earl B. Hunt, Clifford Lunneborg, and their collaborators at
the University of Washington. In 1973 they outlined a theoretical position with a new
concept of intelligence. Hunt and Lunneborg propose "that intelligence should be
measured by absolute measures of aspects of a person's information processing capacity rather than by measures of his performance relative to the performance of others"
(Hunt, Frost, & Lunneborg, 1973, p. 119; see also Hunt, 1975). The aspects of information processing to which Hunt and Lunneborg refer have to do with such parameters of cognitive functioning as sensory processing, coding strategies, and memory
(short-, intermediate-, and long-term).

Using a variety of tasks devised by experimental psychologists to determine how
people in general receive, store, and retrieve different kinds of information, Hunt's
group (Hunt, Lunneborg, and Lewis, 1975) has demonstrated that there are substantial individual differences in performance on these tasks and, perhaps more impor-
tantly, that these differences are systematically related to the subjects' scores on
standard intelligence tests. Persons who receive high scores on standard measures of
verbal ability, for example, do unusually well on information-processing tasks involving short-term memory. The correlations between the conventional scores of verbal
ability and the scores on the information-processing tasks are, of course, far from
perfect. This is as it should be, Hunt and Lunneborg maintain. The verbal-ability
scores are a function of several independent and more basic abilities, only one of
which is concerned with the effectiveness of the short-term memory system. They
argue that if we can adequately define and measure the basic components of mental
functioning which contribute to the conglomerate scores we now secure, we will be
able to devise tests which will give us a profile of many different mental capacities. It
will then be possible to measure what individuals can do, rather than how they compare in general with other people. A great deal of work remains to be done before the
utility of these proposals are proven, but the theoretical orientation constitutes a provocative and exciting new approach to the concept of intelligence. It is one of the few
efforts which attempts to base a measurement strategy on a theoretical model of
cognitive functioning.

Intelligence as a Hypothetical Construct

Perhaps the most popular view among psychologists has been that intelligence exists
only as a trait or complex of traits grouped not by nature but by theoreticians to
describe a class of behaviors which may broadly be labeled intelligent. Many would
agree with Conger, who stated,

> In the first place, intelligence is not a thing in any tangible sense. We cannot see it,
> touch it, or hear it. It is purely a hypothetical construct, a scientific fiction, like the

concept of force in physics. We invent it because it helps us to explain and predict behavior. That is the first fact to be grasped in attempting to understand the word *intelligence:* namely, that it is a hypothetical attribute of the individual. The second fact to be grasped is that this hypothetical attribute is assumed to vary in amount from one individual to another. In other words, we assume that it makes sense to say that one individual has more intelligence than another (1957).

Conger points to the essential reasons for inventing intelligence in the first place: to explain individual differences and to develop means of measuring them. McNemar (1964) created a fantasy of two identical twins, super-geniuses, marooned on a desert island where there are ample resources to meet all their physical needs. To cope with "the boredom that they foresee as an eternity in this laborless heaven," they pursue the investigation of the living creatures they find, eventually centering upon the most interesting of these, themselves. For years, they study their own mental operations, a fascinating subject since both experimenters and both subjects are super-geniuses. What these identical twins cannot discover, of course, is the concept of individual differences. Will they, questions McNemar, "ever hit upon and develop a concept of intelligence?" Why would they ever have the need?

Among writers who have espoused the view that the construct of intelligence is nothing more than a hypothetical concept requiring a definition in terms of observable phenomena are Pressey, Boring, and Spiker and McCandless. Pressey stated that "the concept of general intelligence is . . . simply a working hypothesis which has been very helpful" (1921, p. 146). He suggested that questions about the ultimate nature of intelligence and its measurement are of considerably less interest than are questions involving what intelligence "tests will *do,* in solving this or that problem" (1921, p, 144). Both tests and theory owe their origins to quite practical problems, and it is their ability to help solve such problems which lends them value.

Two years later, Boring epitomized this point of view in a reply to a series of articles by Walter Lippmann which criticized the mental test movement. He wrote,

> Intelligence is what the tests test. This is a narrow definition, but it is the only point of departure for a rigorous discussion of the tests. It would be better if the psychologists could have used some other and more technical term, since the ordinary connotation of intelligence is much broader. The damage is done, however, and no harm need result if we remember that measurable intelligence is simply what the tests of intelligence test, until further scientific observation allows us to extend the definition (1923, p. 35).

Spiker and McCandless in 1954 stated this view in somewhat similar terms. Their statement reflected the philosophical school of logical positivism or scientific empiricism, which emphasizes the definition of concepts through the operations or measures used to identify them. They pointed out the fallacies inherent in the attempt to discover the "underlying nature of intelligence" when the primary interest lies in empirical findings, such as the ability of a test to predict school achievement. They wrote, "The term "intelligence" is one of a number of words that psychologists have taken from the natural language. Its common sense meaning, like that of many similar concepts, is complex and indefinite. An unequivocal characterization of the common sense notion is probably both impossible and unprofitable" (1954, p. 260).

Writing from a similar point of view but arriving at a different conclusion, Liverant (1960) suggested that the concept be relegated to a merely descriptive role if it is to be used at all. This same limitation of usage had previously been suggested by Guilford (1956). Liverant argued that its applications are far too broad, inexact, and specific to a particular situation to be of explanatory usefulness. He shared the impatience of many with the clumsiness and amateurishness which results when scientists attempt to use a common word in a precise fashion without general acceptance of their redefinition.

A Normative View of Intelligence

The reason for creating a hypothetical construct is a need, in this case, to make some sense of individual differences in competence both on tests and on the criteria one wants to predict. A close cousin, then, of the view of intelligence as a hypothetical construct is the view of that concept as a normative phenomenon, defined in quantitative terms. For nearly a century, it has been recognized that the distributions of most test results approximate a normal curve, given a broad sample of the population and a test of medium difficulty. Each individual's score can be compared with the mean or average of the general population, not only in absolute terms, but also in terms of the breadth or narrowness of the variation about that mean. This conception is particularly relevant in the case of mentally retarded persons, who are categorized as retarded specifically by their place on the distribution of scores. The implications of this view of intelligence will be elaborated at length in the next section, which considers the history, contributions, and limitations of the mental testing movement.

INTELLIGENCE AND THE TESTING MOVEMENT

We have indicated that it was not until the latter half of the nineteenth century that intelligence became the object of scientific analysis. Before this could happen, it had been necessary to rescue the mind from religious dogmas which insisted that it was an entity separate from the physical body. It was also necessary for scientists to turn their attention to individual differences in mental functioning and to devise techniques for dealing with problems of measurement and analysis. All these conditions were present toward the end of the last century, when the first systematic studies of intellectual functioning began.

Sir Francis Galton (1822–1911)

The first great pioneer in the field of mental testing was a remarkable English gentleman, Sir Francis Galton, who became interested in the implications of the theory of evolution proposed by his half cousin, Charles Darwin. On the basis of this theory, Galton strongly challenged the theological dogmas concerning the basic nature of man, and he began the scientific study of individual differences, in particular, the investigation of intellectual faculties. Adapting the work of several mathematical theorists of his day to the study of individual psychology, he established a tradition which persists unabated to this day, the use of statistical methods in psychological research. He is noted in particular for working out the method of correlation.

Galton, a eugenicist, was convinced that mental capacity is inherited, and his first great work, *Hereditary Genius,* published in 1869, was a detailed biographic study demonstrating that genius tends to run in families. In his classification of geniuses, he adopted the work of the Belgian mathematician, Adolph Quetelet, who was the first to apply "the normal law of error" to human data. This law, which we now call the "normal distribution," points to the fact that measures of many variables tend to pile up around the average and to become progressively less dense the more they deviate from it, producing the familiar bell-shaped probability curve. Quetelet found that the heights of French army inductees and the chest circumferences of Scottish soldiers were distributed in accordance with this normal law. Galton proposed that measures of intelligence should be similarly distributed.

To test this hypothesis, he needed a measure of intelligence, or rather several measures of intellectual functioning, for Galton believed intelligence to be a function of a large number of attributes and faculties. As no such measures had ever been devised, he proceeded to develop precise procedures for making a large number of anthropometric and psychometric measurements. He assembled his battery of mental tests at the International Health Exhibition in 1844 and later transferred them to the South Kensington Museum in London. Over a period of six years, data were collected for almost 10,000 volunteers on tests of "height, weight, span, breathing power, strength of pull and squeeze, quickness of blow, hearing, seeing, color sense, and other personal data" (Boring, 1950, p. 487). Although Galton is recognized as the founder of individual psychology, the study of individual differences in human abilities, he never succeeded in producing a useful test of intelligence.

James McKeen Cattell (1860–1944)

The American Galton was James McKeen Cattell, who throughout his long and distinguished career sought to describe "human nature in respect to its range and variability" (Boring, 1950, p. 539). Although he had been a student of Wundt, who had established the first psychological laboratory at Leipzig, Germany, and from him had adopted a habit of precision and experimental control, in his concern for individual differences he was more similar to Galton. He coined the term *mental test* and was the first American to champion the use of tests. He devised a battery of fifty items, mostly measures of sensory discrimination, which he gave to all his students, and from these he selected ten which he offered to members of the general public who presented themselves as volunteers.

Cattell's measures, like Galton's, sought to tap specific mental faculties by sampling elementary capacities through simple, controlled procedures. He included, for example, a measure of dynamometric pressure, a two-point dermal discrimination, and the estimation of a ten-second interval. Cattell was, of course, no more successful than Galton in devising a useful measure of intelligence. He was, however, the first great pioneer of the mental testing movement in the United States, and he excited much interest among the psychologists of his day.

Alfred Binet (1857–1911)

It was an ingenious French psychologist, Alfred Binet, who first devised a practical test of intellectual functioning. Binet, who was aware of the work of Galton, began systematically to observe the development of his two young daughters. By 1890, he had determined that the responses of children to the kinds of measures Galton used could not be differentiated from those of adults. He tentatively proposed that it would be necessary to measure more complex acts of "reasoning, judgment, memory, the power of abstraction" and to recognize intelligence as an age-related phenomenon (1890, p. 74). He spent the next decade refining his "feebly emerging conception of intelligence as a characteristic of global human performance; a unitary characteristic that is present in young children and can be assessed, even in them, by questions which require complex acts of judgment and reasoning" (Matarazzo, 1972, p. 32). In 1896, he and his collaborator, Victor Henri, described an ambitious research program to assess eleven distinct "faculties" or higher mental processes —attention, comprehension, imagery, imagination, memory, suggestibility, esthetic appreciation, moral sentiments, strength of will, motor skill, and judgment of visual space. Results from this program, confirmed by studies by Stella Sharp at Cornell University in 1898, indicated that these tests of complex mental functions were indeed better indices of intelligence than were the tests of specific, simpler functions used by Galton and Cattell. Nevertheless, within a decade, Binet had gone beyond this "faculty" view to a new synthesis.

In 1904, Binet was commissioned by the Minister of Public Instruction in Paris to devise a method to select mentally retarded pupils who might be better educated in separate facilities. In response to this call, Binet and Theodore Simon (1905a) published what is acknowledged as the first real test of intelligence, a scale of thirty tests arranged in an empirically determined order of difficulty, sampling a variety of complex mental functions of judgment, comprehension, and reasoning, which Binet was convinced constituted the essence of intelligence. This scale represented the happy circumstance of a capable scientist whose prior studies had well prepared him to meet a recognized and compelling social need.

An improved scale followed in 1908, which contained fifty-eight tests grouped unequally into clusters at each age level from three through thirteen years. It was this scale which first utilized the important concepts of mental age (MA). With its introduction, Binet and Simon also made the first attempt to give an operational definition of intelligence, couched in terms of assigning an appropriate mental age on the basis of a child's performance on the scale.

The final Binet-Simon scale appeared in 1911. It was a thorough revision, containing five tests at each age level from three through fifteen years and five tests for adults. Both the 1908 and the 1911 scales were meant to be used in classifying the intellectual development of children in the normal and above-average ranges as well as those who were retarded. Their immediate translation into many languages and their enthusiastic adoption by psychologists in Europe and the United States were, however, primarily a function of their utility in objectively assessing degrees of mental retardation.

H. H. Goddard (1866–1957)

The American translator of the Binet scales and their first influential advocate was H. H. Goddard, the psychological director of the Vineland Training School, a New Jersey institution for retarded children. At first rather negative about the utility of Binet's approach, he soon became a dedicated convert. He was amazed at the accuracy of the tests in classifying degrees of retardation among the children at the Vineland School, and he soon became convinced that they provided an objective and valid means of determining intelligence at all mental levels.

As a devoted convert, he went far beyond the claims made for the scales by Binet and his colleagues. He also significantly altered the views of Binet in the process of promoting them in the United States. Binet viewed intelligence as the result of a complex interaction among a variety of discrete higher mental functions and believed that he was measuring an *average* level of performance with respect to these mental faculties. Goddard, however, interpreted the tests as measuring a single, unitary factor, thus substituting Spearman's "general intelligence" for Binet's "intelligence in general." Furthermore, Goddard (1920) proposed that the chief determiner of this unitary mental process was hereditary. Binet had often decried such "brutal pessimism" and had argued that intelligence is not a fixed entity but is a combination of a variety of functions "all of which have proved to be plastic and subject to increase" (1911, p. 143).

Lewis M. Terman (1877–1956)

Goddard was not the only disciple of Binet in the United States. Other translations and adaptations of the scales appeared in the years following their publication in France, but the first thorough and well-standardized revision was the 1916 Stanford-Binet authored by Lewis Terman. This elegantly designed and carefully structured test was to become the standard against which all other intelligence tests were compared. It was the first to use the easy-to-understand index of brightness suggested by Stern (1912), the intelligence quotient, or IQ.

Terman's position regarding the proper uses of intelligence tests and their inherent limitations were parallel with those of Binet. He thought of intelligence as a complex of intellective functions which were manifested in their highest form in the ability to think abstractly. He also disavowed the notion that one could measure innate biological intelligence apart from the complex matrix of learned behavior through which it is expressed.

Terman's version of the Binet scale has been revised several times since 1916. The 1937 revision by Terman and Maud Merrill with significant contributions by McNemar (1942) was again a major improvement. Its standardization was accomplished with a broad, national sample of 3,184 subjects, ages two through eighteen, and it contained many new items, chosen according to a carefully specified set of criteria. One important criterion for inclusion in the final scale was a measure of internal consistency: items of the preliminary pool were retained which correlated best with scores on the overall scale. Two forms, L (for Lewis) and M (for Maud), were constructed. Even by today's strict standards, the procedures consistently employed in constructing and standardizing the scales would be judged of the highest quality.

The 1937 version of the Stanford-Binet remained the basis of the two subsequent revisions which have followed. The 1960 revision, accomplished by Merrill, combined the most effective tests from scales L and M, based on the experience of independent investigators with unselected populations in various parts of the country during the 1950s. The need for an alternate form had been reduced by the publication in 1949 of the Wechsler Intelligence Scale for Children. The most important change was the shift from the use of the ratio IQ to a deviation IQ, which permitted certain important statistical adjustments. (See Chapter 17.)

The most recent revision, accomplished by R. L. Thorndike (Terman & Merrill, 1973), made practically no changes in the items of the 1960 L-M Scale. It did, however, include a complete new standardization, using a stratified sample of children ages two through eighteen in seven U.S. communities. Unlike the earlier standardizations, this population included minority-group children, but the net effect on the norms was small. Intelligence quotients obtained on this test are somewhat lower than would have been obtained had the 1960 norms continued in use.

David Wechsler (1896–   )

The major competitors to the Stanford-Binet scales are now the tests devised by David Wechsler, for many years the Chief Psychologist at Bellevue Psychiatric Hospital in New York City. The original Wechsler-Bellevue Scale for adults appeared in 1939; Form II of that scale appeared in 1944. Wechsler published the Wechsler Adult Intelligence Scale (WAIS) in 1955, which replaced the previous adult scales, and the Wechsler Intelligence Scale for Children (WISC) in 1949. In 1967, he published the Wechsler Preschool and Primary Scale of Intelligence (WPPSI), and in 1973, the revised version of the WISC, the WISC-R.

By any criterion, the standardization and construction of the Wechsler tests have been excellent. The WISC-R, for example, was administered to a stratified sample of 2,200 boys and girls, ages 6½ through 16½. Wechsler introduced several striking innovations in constructing these scales. Unlike the Stanford-Binet, each test is composed of ten to twelve subtests, divided among those which are primarily verbal and those which are thought of as primarily performance scales and require something other than a verbal response. For the WISC-R, for example, the verbal subscales include Information, Similarities, Arithmetic, Vocabulary, Comprehension, and Digit Span (memory for numbers). The performance subscales include Picture Completion (identifying the missing part), Picture Arrangement (requiring a logical ordering), Block Design (copying a model or a printed design by the use of colored blocks), Coding (symbol substitution), and Mazes. Separate IQs are calculated for the Verbal Scale, the Performance Scale, and the Full Scale. Although the unreliability of the subscales is a distinct problem and none of the subscales is a factorially "pure" measure, psychologists have tended to appreciate the opportunity to compare a child's performance on various types of items. This is a more difficult procedure with the Stanford-Binet scale, which includes different types of items at each age level. (See Chapter 17.)

Another innovation introduced by Wechsler was the comparison of each subject's performance only with other individuals of his own age group, including adults. Although the early Stanford-Binet scales had been applied to adults, for want of a better test the MA concept was never really applicable above the adolescent years, and a number of rather shaky assumptions had to be made to derive IQs for adult subjects. The Wechsler adult scales circumvented these problems.

The deviation IQ was also Wechsler's contribution, later adopted by Merrill for the 1960 revision of the Stanford-Binet. The raw scores on each subtest are first changed to normalized standard scores with reference to the subject's own age group and are then added and converted to deviation IQs, standard scores, each having a mean of 100 and a standard deviation of 15.

Wechsler's notions about intelligence were developed from the point of view of the practitioner who had important decisions to make about his clients. Very early it became clear to him that many factors other than mental capacity per se were reflected in performance on intelligence tests. He was concerned not only about such influences as social class, age, and lack of facility with the English language, but also about personality variables such as motivation, anxiety, drive, energy, and impulsiveness. Unlike other theorists who would have preferred to eliminate such "noise" from tests of intelligence, by means of his global definition Wechsler (1950) included them in his concept of mental capacity. He saw intelligence as part of the total personality. He stated, for example,

It is important to realize that intelligence tests do not and cannot be expected to measure all of intelligence, but it is of equal importance to emphasize that they measure a great deal more than the delimited capacities to which contemporaneous theory seems desirous of restricting them. Intelligence tests measure more than mere learning ability or reasoning ability or even general intellectual ability; in addition, they inevitably measure a number of other capacities which cannot be defined as either purely cognitive or intellective. . . . Hitherto, authors of intelligence scales when recognizing this situation, looked upon these factors as disturbing elements and tried as far as possible to eliminate them. Unfortunately, experience has shown that the more successful one is in excluding these factors, the less effective are the resulting tests as measures of general intelligence. What are needed are not tests from which the non-intellective factors have been eliminated (even if that were possible), but, on the contrary, tests in which these factors are clearly present and objectively appraisable. The performance tests are an attempt in this direction (1944, p. 11).

Expansion of the Testing Movement

The tests of Binet, Terman, and Wechsler were immediately successful, not because of their contribution to a theoretical understanding of intelligence, but because they met an urgent social need. With the rapid expansion of the public schools, an objective and convenient method for determining scholastic ability had become vitally necessary. No longer could children simply be excluded who did not do well in an elitist and competitive system; special provisions had to be made. The tests constituted a triumph of pragmatism and were soon thought to be indispensable tools for the classification of talent by school administrators, personnel managers, military commanders, and by the public at large.

America's entry into World War I created the need for an objective test which could be efficiently administered to large numbers of inductees to aid in sorting them out for appropriate training programs. In this setting, group testing became a large-scale reality. Under the direction of Yerkes, and with the cooperation of Terman, Boring, Otis, and others, the Army Alpha was developed as a test for literates, and the Army Beta for those who could not, for one reason or another, read the English language. During World War I, almost 2 million persons were tested with one or the other of these instruments. These were the progenitors of a raft of paper-and-pencil tests designed to measure intellectual ability and scholastic aptitude. A further boost was given this form of testing by the development of the Army General Classification Test (AGCT), given to the next generation, some 4 million American military inductees of World War II. The development of group tests and, even more, the volume of their application, reached tidal proportions after World War II. The tests were not only used in scholastic settings in incredible numbers, but were also applied very widely in industry, often for purposes far different from those for which they had originally been intended.

During the past several decades, it is the rare individual who has not been tested repeatedly with various standardized tests of aptitude and achievement, and millions of adults have, often to their surprise, been asked to take such tests when applying for jobs.

The overwhelming proportion of the tests administered by schools, industry, and the military are quite different from the tests of Binet, Terman, and Wechsler which we have discussed. The group tests are designed to be given to large numbers of individuals, sitting together but working alone with paper and pencil. They are also often administered by completely untrained persons to individuals such as job applicants. The tests indeed are, from some points of view, marvelously efficient. Thousands can take them at one sitting; their answers can be machine-scored, analyzed, and reported without the touch of human hand; and they yield scores with understandable, if not always understood, labels such as "verbal ability" and "quantitative aptitude."

Unfortunately, group tests are inferior to the individual tests in almost every respect. They are particularly inappropriate for individuals unaccustomed to taking tests with equanimity, confidence, and the motivation to do one's best. They are more subject to errors which result from apprehensiveness, situational factors interfering with concentration, poor test-taking skills such as spending too long on one pesky item, and the like. No deviations can be permitted from the rigorous schedule devised for the entire group. No one knows what the subject is experiencing, and no one would be empowered to do anything about it if he knew. Despite these limitations, the entire group tests do correlate on the whole with criterion measures such as school performance or vocational success, but these group correlations conceal individual cases in which the correspondence is poor. Too, the tests are often used in inappropriate situations such as employee selection without proof of their relevance to performance on the job and without reference to other important information about the individual's competence.

Individual tests are more likely to be used and interpreted with sophistication than are group tests. In the individual situation, the examiner can be sensitive to the operation of extraneous factors and is often able to correct them (to wait until outside noise subsides, to calm the fearful child) and to make allowances for them in the interpretation of the results. (See Chapter 16.) They are more often administered by a skilled professional psychologist who has an understanding of the rationale, construction, and standardization of the tests as well as a knowledge of their reliability and validity under different circumstances and for different purposes. The tester is also more likely to have information about the subject from a variety of sources and is thus more likely to consider the test score as but a single index of intellectual functioning. Finally, the tester who has engaged in a face-to-face interaction with the subject is more likely to make recommendations and decisions with the subject's best interest in mind.

Criticisms of the Testing Movement

The authors and publishers of tests have always had their critics, but the range and acrimony of the debate about the proper role of tests in decision-making processes have markedly increased during the past decade. The critics argue that the tests do not measure what their publishers claim, that people are unfairly labeled by the tests, that important decisions are based on these labels, and that these decisions become increasingly difficult to change, in part, at least, because they determine the kinds of opportunities made available. These criticisms are especially pertinent with respect to retarded individuals.

If one thinks of general intelligence as the result of a complex of factors which are best revealed in scholastic performance, the tests do a fairly good job. They seem to measure with reasonable accuracy about half of what we need to know to predict how well individuals will do in school. This is, of course, what they were designed to do. If, however, one conceives of general intelligence as the result of factors which determine adaptation to a broader range of performance areas, the tests do not do a very good job. They measure, for example, very little of what we need to know to predict an individual's performance in various occupations. IQ scores can, of course, be related to the world of work, and occupations can be reasonably well ordered in terms of the degree to which they require the kind of mental attributes measured by the tests. (See Chapter 11). The range of scores within each occupation, however, is typically very large and their relationship to job proficiency is very low or nonexistent.

There can be no doubt that many individuals have been incorrectly labeled and have been adversely affected by decisions based on the faulty assessment of mental level. It is perhaps unnecessary to point out that such errors are almost always the result of misuse of the tests rather than of the tests themselves. There is little doubt that a much higher percentage of individuals were inappropriately labeled as mentally retarded, or, conversely, not retarded, when such labels depended completely on the subjective appraisal of teachers and physicians. (See Chapter 16.)

It seems probable that some of the strong emotion that currently surrounds discussions of mental tests and intelligence is a function of an unrealistic overvaluing of this aspect of human capacity, particularly by those who tend to join the fray. If one is a teacher, a scientist, or otherwise involved in the pursuit and dissemination of knowledge, what attribute of man is valued more highly? To most thoughtful people, however, there are many other human attributes of equal or greater importance— gentleness, sensitivity, compassion, perseverance, loyalty, musical ability, and athletic prowess, for example. Intellectual abilities are doubtless important but they also are overexalted by many in today's competitive and technologically oriented world.[4]

---

[4] The reader will note that a number of important questions have been left unasked in this discussion. Several were omitted because they are discussed elsewhere in this volume. For discussions of the nature-nurture controversy, for example, the reader is referred to Chaps. 3, 7, and 8; for questions concerning IQ constancy, to Chap. 17; for the use of tests when dealing with possibly retarded individuals, to Chap. 16.

2
Definition and Classification in Mental Retardation

In light of the long history of multiple controversies about intelligence, pendulums of opinion swinging from one extreme to another, it is hardly surprising that a single definition of mental retardation has never been completely acceptable to all concerned. Each controversy about the nature of intelligence has had its counterpart in questions about mental retardation, even though most professionals in daily contact with retarded persons and their families have taken a rather practical stance which bypass the theoretical issues.

In recent years, the field of mental retardation has been the center of intense activity. During the 1960s, there was increasing recognition of the multiple problems which even mild intellectual deficit creates for a child or an adult struggling to cope with everyday living in a technologically sophisticated society. Narrow definitions of mental retardation were broadened to include marginal groups with subtle intellectual handicaps, groups which in fact make up a sizable percentage of the general population. There was a concomitant expansion of health programs, diagnostic facilities, compensatory education for children and adults from disadvantaged groups, special classes for mildly retarded children, supportive services for families, and vocational training, counseling, and placement for adults capable of making an adjustment on their own with only limited professional help.

In the 1970s, a somewhat different point of view has emerged. First, the organization of programs and services has come to be guided by a *principle of normalization* which holds that mentally retarded citizens are entitled to services which are "as culturally normative as possible, in order to establish and/or maintain personal behaviors and characteristics which are as culturally normative as possible" (Wolfensberger, 1972, p. 28). Accordingly, a turnabout has occurred in the forms of services being preferred. Many special classes for the mildly retarded are being replaced by programs which enable the children to remain for most or all of the day in regular classrooms, and various forms of community placement are being substituted for institutional care, especially for the mildly and moderately retarded.

Second, there has arisen a *reaction to the earlier enlargement* of the definition of mental retardation which identified as retarded too many children and adults who might otherwise blend unnoticed into the lower social, economic, and educational ranges of the society. Definitions have been redrawn and estimates of the prevalence of mental retardation restricted to individuals with more markedly disabling handicaps. There is, furthermore, greater cognizance of both the benefits and the injuries possible in a social system which singles out deviant children in order to offer them services and in which measures designed to help them and their families are too often inadvertently harmful. In recent years, a series of court decisions has affirmed the legal rights of handicapped individuals to full privileges of citizenship, including equal protection under the law and access to education, treatment, and other services appropriate to their needs and capabilities. Translating these decisions into equitable social action is, however, not accomplished easily.

In this chapter we shall discuss some traditional and contemporary definitions of mental retardation, estimates of its prevalence in various segments of society, classification systems, and issues having to do with labeling. Finally, we shall present a brief review of the recent status of interest and activity in the field of mental retardation.

DEFINING MENTAL RETARDATION

If a concept is to be used, it must of course be defined, but defining the concept of mental retardation has not proved easy. In 1975, the publication of a landmark series of working papers and policy proposals (Hobbs, 1975a, 1975b, 1975c) marked the culmination of several years of study by ninety-three experts from diverse fields relating to the welfare of exceptional children. Recognizing the arbitrary nature of a classification system which defines mental retardation as a category of disability and consequently offers or withholds services from individuals so categorized, the experts concluded that definition and categorization systems serve such practical purposes that they cannot be discarded. A consensus about the definition of mental retardation cannot be left up in the air, for from that consensus there flow a number of practical implications. At all levels of public and private planning and decision making, objective criteria are needed to determine the extent of the population needing services, the kinds of services needed, and therefore the amount and manner of funding. The group clearly distinguished, however, between the function of definition and classification at a policy-making level and the application of these guidelines in individual cases. Unfortunately, the general and the specific use of definitions and their accompanying objective criteria tend to become confused. We shall attempt in this chapter to maintain a separation between a general definition of mental retardation and the application of the label "mentally retarded" to individuals whose disability is so defined.

Some Traditional Definitions[1]

Ever since people have been able to distinguish mental retardation from other forms of mental disability (a task which is far more difficult than one might surmise), a central theme of definitions has concerned the failure of mentally retarded persons to adapt adequately to their surroundings.

The older definitions were couched in terms of adult behavior, requiring those who worked with infants and children to make a number of difficult and often questionable predictions about the hazy future. There was a tendency to avoid precise criteria for deciding in borderline instances who should be labeled retarded, for it was aptly argued that any arbitrary definition would fail to recognize the complexity of the factors which determine adequacy of adjustment. Tredgold (1937), for example, was describing adult behavior in rather general terms when he defined mental deficiency as

> a state of incomplete mental development of such a kind and degree that the individual is incapable of adapting himself to the normal environment of his fellows in such a way as to maintain existence independently of supervision, control or external support (p. 4).

E.A. Doll's definition was somewhat more specific. In addition to the element of social adaptation, he stressed the emergence of the handicap during childhood, its constitutional nature, and its incurability. As we shall see, his last two criteria have been seriously debated. Doll (1941) stated: "We observe that six criteria by statement or implication have been generally considered essential to an adequate definition and concept. These are (1) social incompetence, (2) due to mental subnormality, (3) which has been developmentally arrested, (4) which obtains at maturity, (5) is of constitutional origin and (6) is essentially incurable" (p. 215).

Kanner (1957), in contrast with Tredgold and Doll, defined two classes of mentally deficient persons, though again in terms of their adult status. His definitions balanced the degree of handicap with the nature of the environment to which the individual is forced to adjust. Distinguishing between what he had elsewhere (1948) termed "absolute" and "relative" feeblemindedness, he stated:

> **1** The one type consists of individuals so markedly deficient in their cognitive, emotional, and constructively conative potentialities that they would stand out as defectives in any existing culture. . . . They would be equally helpless and ill-adapted in a society of savants and in a society of savages. They are not only deficient intellectually but deficient in every sphere of mentation.
>
> **2** The other type is made up of individuals whose limitations are definitely related to the standards of the particular culture which surrounds them. In less complex, less intellectually centered societies they would have no trouble in attaining and retaining equality of realizable ambitions. Some might even be capable of gaining superiority by virtue of assets other than those measured by the intelligence tests. . . . They could make successful peasants, hunters, fishermen, tribal dancers. They can, in our own society, achieve success as farm hands, factory workers, miners, waitresses, charwomen. But in our midst their shortcomings, which would remain unrecognized and therefore non-existent in the awareness of a more primitive cultural body, appear

[1] See Blanton (1975) for an historical review.

as soon as scholastic curricula demand competition in spelling, history, geography, long division, and other preparations deemed essential for the tasks of feeding chickens, collecting garbage, and wrapping bundles in a department store. . . . It is preferable to speak of such people as intellectually inadequate rather than mentally deficient (pp. 70–71).[2]

Definition According to Test Score (IQ)

Many writers have attempted to specify quantitative standards for deciding who is to be considered mentally subnormal. The most widely used objective criterion of this sort has been the score obtained on a standardized test of intelligence such as the Stanford-Binet Intelligence Scale or the Wechsler Intelligence Scale for Children (WISC). This approach offers simplicity, ease of communication, and well-defined normative comparison groups, as well as a reasonable degree of validity in predicting behaviors such as school achievement, though much less accuracy with nonschool behaviors.

In 1916, Terman introduced a grouping of ability according to IQs obtained on the 1916 Stanford-Binet. As altered in connection with the 1937 revision of the test, this scheme was widely used and, in fact, became the standard classification system. (See Table 2-1.) Wechsler has suggested that IQ values from his tests be classified in similar fashion. His system and the percentage of his standardization group in each category are also presented in Table 2-1. Both schemes represent descriptions of a continuum of mental ability, not specifications of discrete categories. It should be noted that neither system makes any provision for the fact that IQ scores, like other psychological measures, are subject to errors which are substantial from a practical point of view.

An IQ of 70 has garnered considerable popularity as a cutoff score for the retarded group, although other cutoff scores are also in use. In some school districts IQs of 75 or 80 are used to define eligibility for special class placement, and the definition of the American Association on Mental Deficiency (see below) uses a score of 67 or 69, depending on whether the standard deviation of the test is 16 as in the Stanford-Binet or 15 as in the Wechsler scales and most other tests.

There are a number of difficulties with such arbitrary criteria. Minor confusions arise because of the differing standard deviations. More important, because an IQ is simply a score obtained on the basis of a restricted sample of behavior, there are significant limitations to what can or should be expected of it, even if tests were perfectly reliable and children were always able to put forth their best efforts. Furthermore, no cutoff score will ever be adequate to define mental retardation independent of the setting in which the individual finds himself. Different skills and abilities are required at different ages and in different environments. Retardation must therefore be gauged in large part against current environmental demands.

In a study of parochial schools (McCartin, Dingman, Meyers, & Mercer, 1966), 83 percent of the children with IQs below 85 in middle-class schools were nominated by their teachers as "slow learners," but only 44 percent of equally low scorers in the

---

[2] Kanner also described a third kind of mental retardation, "apparent" feeblemindedness, in which "existing potentialities for the acquisition or reproduction of tested information have not been realized fully because of lack of opportunity, physical handicaps . . . remediable but not as yet remedied specific disabilities, temporary educational blocking, or inadequacies of the person who administers the test" (1948, p. 374).

Table 2-1   Distribution of IQs According to the Stanford-Binet and Wechsler Tests

Terman's Classifications (1937 S-B distribution)*	IQ Range	Wechsler's Classifications (WAIS distribution)†
Very superior (1.33%)	160–169 150–159 140–149	Very superior (2.2%)
Superior (11.3%)	130–139 120–129	Superior (6.7%)
High average (18.1%)	110–119	Bright normal (16.1%)
Normal average (46.5%)	100–109 90–99	Average (50.0%)
Low average (14.5%)	80–89	Dull normal (16.1%)
Borderline defective (7.6%)	70–79 60–69	Borderline (6.7%)
Mentally defective (0.63%)	50–59 40–49 30–39	Defective (2.2%)

* *Source:* Adapted from Terman and Merrill (1973, p. 18). Reproduced by permission of publisher.

† *Source:* Adapted from Wechsler (1955, p. 20). Reproduced by permission. Copyright © 1955, The Psychological Corporation, New York, N.Y. All rights reserved.

schools serving the segregated minority community were so designated. A child considered normal in one of these areas might be deemed handicapped if he were transferred to a school in another. Goodenough (1956, p. 4) pointed out the second psychology in the old saying, "In the company of the blind, the one-eyed man is king." Kanner, too, recognized this factor in his attention to the intellectually inadequate individual who is handicapped in one environment but would not be in another. Cutoff scores applied under all conditions ignore this basic relationship.

Although the IQ-classification approach has had very wide use, often even being written into law, it has been much criticized. Its critics have deplored the facts that IQs are sometimes substantially affected by nonintellectual factors such as language handicaps and motivational barriers and that individual IQs sometimes change markedly over time. They have also cited the frequent misuse of the IQ and the tendency to ignore other sources of information about a child.[3]

Realistically, however, classifications according to IQ, when taken in conjunction with other aspects of behavior, do serve a positive function. Adherence to objective standards can minimize unfairness and capriciousness in many situations. Some decisions must be made consistently, even arbitrarily according to preset standards, as in the determination of eligibility for Social Security allowances. Many others, such as school placement decisions, call for greater flexibility. We must keep always in mind the purposes for which criteria are established and do our best to take as many relevant variables as possible into account in decisions which may deeply affect the lives of individuals and families.

Some Contemporary Definitions

Definition According to a Social System Perspective   As Mercer (1973) has aptly pointed out, most definitions of mental retardation have followed either a *patho-*

[3] The sensible use of intelligence tests will be discussed at length in Chaps. 16 and 17.

logical or a *statistical* model. The pathological model, an outgrowth of a medical orientation, is concerned with physiological malfunction and symptoms of disease or defect. Under this model, normality, the most desirable condition, is the absence of symptoms of pathology. A clinical perspective regards mental retardation as an attribute of the individual, assuming "that the condition exists as an entity regardless of whether the person is aware of its presence or whether others recognize his pathology. . . . a case of mental retardation can exist undiagnosed in much the same sense that a case of rheumatic fever can exist undiagnosed and unrecognized" (p. 7).

In contrast, with a statistical model like that derived from the intelligence-testing movement, mental retardation is defined as a deviant range on a continuum of intellectual ability, normal status then being defined as the average or middle range. Although high intelligence is generally regarded as the most desirable status, it, like low intelligence, is deviant from the average. The AAMD definition to be described below clearly follows a statistical model but also has some characteristics of a pathological model.

Mercer further develops a third mode of definition according to a *social system perspective,* in which "'mental retardate' is an achieved social status and mental retardation is the role associated with that status" (p. 27). From this point of view, an individual is retarded only if he has been so labeled in some social system of which he is a member. The social system which labels most freely is the school, and Mercer's research clearly demonstrates that children regarded as mentally retarded within the schools are often not regarded as such at home, in the neighborhood, or by any social agency. The definition is closely intertwined with the normative standards of each social situation. In a school without special education facilities, for example, "mentally retarded" children may not be found at all. Obvious misfits may have been excluded completely, whereas those who can be accommodated, with whatever degree of difficulty, into the regular classroom will probably not be regarded as mentally retarded, although their teachers and classmates may call them "slow," "dumb," or "lazy." Mental retardation is thus a socially defined role or status, which is different from personal characteristics, such as low IQ, which affect the probability that a particular child will be assigned that status and will play that role.

Definition According to an Experimental Analysis Point of View　Sidney W. Bijou (1966) writing from the theoretical perspective of operant conditioning (see Chapter 15), has suggested that *"a retarded individual is one who has a limited repertory of behavior shaped by events that constitute his history"* (p. 2, italics Bijou's), and that the stimulus-response functions which contribute to retarded behavior should constitute the focus of investigation. Bijou rejects the hypothetical concept of defective intelligence as well as a biological or medical definition and he therefore rejects the notion of mental retardation as a symptom of an underlying condition. He maintains that the coordination of the individual as a total functioning biological system and the environmental events which impinge upon him determine the success or failure of development of serviceable behavioral repertoires. He emphasizes patterns of development in relation to the stimulation and reinforcement afforded the child. Although Bijou's definition has not had a widespread direct impact, his drawing attention to the experiential history of the individual; to the reduction, withholding, or noncontingency of reinforcement; and to the restriction of opportunities for learning, is very much in line with contemporary environmental points of view. The implications of distorted conditions for learning will become clearer in Chapters 7, 8, and 15.

The AAMD Definition

In 1973 the American Association on Mental Deficiency (AAMD) published a revised edition (Grossman, 1973) of a very useful manual on terminology and classification first issued some fourteen years before (Heber, 1959, 1961). This manual, which represents the collaboration of interested workers in many professional areas, presents a succinct definition: *"Mental retardation refers to significantly subaverage general intellectual functioning existing concurrently with deficits in adaptive behavior, and manifested during the developmental period* (p. 11)." As an integral part of the definition, each key term is defined. We quote from the manual:

> MENTAL RETARDATION . . . denotes a level of behavioral performance without reference to etiology. Thus, it does not distinguish between retardation associated with psychosocial or polygenic influences and retardation associated with biological deficit. Mental retardation is descriptive of current behavior and does not imply prognosis. Prognosis is related more to such factors as associated conditions, motivation, treatment and training opportunities than to mental retardation itself.
>
> INTELLECTUAL FUNCTIONING may be assessed by one or more of the standardized tests developed for that purpose; SIGNIFICANTLY SUBAVERAGE refers to performance which is more than two standard deviations from the mean or average of the tests. On the two most frequently used tests of intelligence, Stanford-Binet and Wechsler, this represents I.Q.'s of 67 and 69, respectively. (It is emphasized that despite current practice a finding of low I.Q. is never by itself sufficient to make the diagnosis of mental retardation.)
>
> The upper age limit of the DEVELOPMENTAL PERIOD is placed at *18 years.* . . .
>
> ADAPTIVE BEHAVIOR is defined as the effectiveness or degree with which the individual meets the standards of personal independence and social responsibility expected of his age and cultural group. Since these expectations vary for different age groups, DEFICITS IN ADAPTIVE BEHAVIOR will vary at different ages. . . .
>
> During infancy and early childhood, sensory-motor, communication, self-help and socialization skills ordinarily develop in a sequential pattern reflective of the maturation process. Delays in the acquisition of these skills represent potential deficiencies in adaptive behavior and become the criteria for mental retardation.
>
> The skills required for adaptation during childhood and early adolescence involve more of the learning processes. . . . attention should focus not only on the basic academic skills and their use, but also on skills essential to cope with the environment, including concepts of time and money, self-directed behaviors, social responsiveness, and interactive skills.
>
> In the adult years, vocational performance and social responsibilities assume prime importance assessed in terms of the degree to which the individual is able to maintain himself independently in the community and in gainful employment as well as by his ability to meet and conform to standards set by the community. . . . Only those individuals who demonstrate deficits in both measured intelligence and adaptive behavior are classified as being mentally retarded. . . .
>
> Within the framework of the definition . . . an individual may meet the criteria . . . at one time in his life and not at some other time. A person may change status as a result of changes or alterations in his intellectual functioning, changes in his adap-

tive behaviors, changes in the expectations of the society, or for other known and unknown reasons (pp. 11-14).

The AAMD definition differs in a number of dimensions from the others we have considered:

1 The retarded person is judged in terms of his success with the *developmental* tasks appropriate for his age. During the preschool years, sensorimotor behaviors assume greatest importance; during the school years, academic ability is paramount; and during adulthood, economic independence and the ability to function within the social standards of the society take precedence. The specification that retardation be evident by age eighteen serves the conventional but perhaps dubious purpose of differentiating mental retardation from traumatic or deteriorative disorders originating in adulthood.

2 This definition makes clear that a designation of mental status should be a *description of present behavior* and implicitly disavows the notion of potential intelligence. By separating the processes of description and prognosis, it avoids many difficulties inherent in early formulations. Predicting adult competence during childhood involves some very doubtful assumptions about the reliability of test scores, about the constancy of intellectual, emotional, and social development, and about the abilities necessary for social competence during adulthood. (See Chapter 17.)

3 The AAMD definition is couched in terms of *measurement.* In Chapter 1, intelligence was presented as a hypothetical construct partly to be defined through the operations used to measure it. By relying on tests of general intelligence, the definition implicitly incorporates a g-factor conception of intellectual ability. The importance of an obtained IQ is enhanced by the fact that in practical situations it is the established failure in adaptive behavior which brings an individual to professional attention. Of course, if the test results are used without reference to other information about both intellectual and adaptive function, the test approach is subject to serious error.

4 A further characteristic of the AAMD definition is that it *avoids specific differentiation of mental retardation from other childhood disorders* such as childhood schizophrenia or brain damage. If a child is functioning on a subnormal intellectual level, he may legitimately be called mentally retarded whether this symptom is thought to be primary or secondary to emotional or organic disorders. A number of authors have suggested abandoning altogether such differentiation during childhood.

5 The definition, despite its statistical orientation, also exhibits characteristics of the *pathological model* described by Mercer. The definition is basically oriented toward defects or deficits in the person, rather than toward his social role or status, or toward characteristics of the environment with which he must cope.

6 The most significant change in the 1973 as compared with the 1959 definition is the return to a *more traditional cutoff score,* two standard deviations below the mean. The 1959 definition had defined "borderline retardation" as intelligence only one standard deviation below the mean and thereby had tended to shift the emphasis from the severely retarded to the much larger group with mild and borderline retardation. The 1959 position recognized explicitly that within the highly urbanized, technologically oriented culture of the United States, even minor deficits in intellectual capacity may constitute a substantial handicap. Yet the criterion also led to classifying persons as mentally subnormal who fitted unremarkably into their communities. A change of definition does not change reality, of course, and many persons of borderline intelligence do experience considerable difficulty in mastering the responsibilities demanded of them in a competitive society. It will be unfortunate if the revised definition tends to discourage society from offering supportive services to members of this group.

The AAMD definition has very wide currency in the United States and Canada today and for that reason will be adopted in this book. Its practical utility well outweighs the problems it leaves unsolved, and its emphasis on mental retardation as a symptom which can change from time to time is especially commendable.

The British Definition

In Great Britain, definitions of handicapping conditions are a matter of national legislation, standard throughout the country. Traditionally, emphasis has been placed on the social inadequacy of the mentally retarded individual.

Under the terms of the Mental Health Act of 1959, a general category of *mental disorder* was introduced to cover all forms of mental derangement. One of the main objects of the Act was to remove the rigid distinction which was being drawn between mental illness on the one hand and mental defect on the other. Under the Act, four principal categories of persons are recognized: those suffering from mental illness, from severe subnormality, from subnormality, and from psychopathic disorder. The term *severe subnormality* indicates "a state of arrested or incomplete development of mind which includes subnormality of intelligence and is of such a nature and degree that the patient is incapable of leading an independent life or of guarding himself against serious exploitation, or will be so incapable when of an age to do so" (section 4, paragraph 2). The term *subnormality* refers to a condition "which includes subnormality of intelligence and is of a nature or degree which requires or is susceptible to medical treatment or other special care or training of the patient" (section 4, paragraph 3).

The definitions leave vague the matter of "subnormality of intelligence," but conventionally the severely subnormal are considered those with IQs below about 50, and the subnormal those with IQs roughly from 50 to 70. Both definitions, however, emphasize the services needed for care and training. The severely subnormal person requires protective services and facilities which take into account his inability to maintain himself independently, and the subnormal individual is seen to require medical or other special care and training services.

Until 1971, severely subnormal young people in England and Wales were excluded from schools maintained by local education authorities and given "training" by local health authorities. The Education (Handicapped Children) Act of 1970 brought such children under the purview of the educational system, including some 24,000 children who were in training centers, 8,000 who were in hospitals for the mentally handicapped, 750 who were in special units for mentally handicapped children with serious physical disabilities or behavior disorders, and others who were in private institutions or at home because their handicaps were too severe to allow them to attend school (Great Britain, 1971). In essence, the public facilities are being converted to educational institutions and the qualifications of their educators are being upgraded. There remain a number of unresolved questions about the extent to which these children can or should be integrated with subnormal children, who tend to be in their own special schools, and about how far both groups should be integrated into regular schools. Some writers suggest that the two categories of handicapped children should be given separate classrooms within the same building and that the building should be located on the campus of an ordinary school.

Starting from a somewhat different base than in the United States, then, we see a movement toward extending educational experiences for retarded children, beginning at age five, and toward returning them to a closer proximity to the social mainstream. The British definitions of course differ from the AAMD definition in that two separate categories of mental subnormality are recognized rather than a continuous distribution of intellectual handicap.

CLASSIFICATION SYSTEMS

Retarded children constitute a very heterogeneous group both in their behavior and in the causes of their deficiency. Some children are happy and carefree in their own homes, whereas others are difficult to manage and are impossible to maintain at home. Some have relatively minor handicaps which show up primarily in school achievement, and others are so grossly defective that even in adolescence they have not yet learned to sit, to talk, or to play. Some have maladies which are attributable mainly to the genes they inherited from their parents; others have been injured or diseased; still others suffer mainly the effects of cold or indifferent environments which fail to meet their psychological needs.

Here we shall consider a few of the many ways in which workers have sought order out of this chaos. One source (Gelof, 1963) lists no fewer than twenty-three systems of classification in the English language alone. Most systems have approached the problem from one of three standpoints: severity of the handicap, etiology of the symptoms, and the symptom constellation or syndrome.

Classification According to Severity of the Symptoms

For many years, the terms *idiot, imbecile,* and *moron* were used to denote abilities roughly in the IQ ranges 0 to 30, 30 to 50, and 50 to 70, respectively. In Great Britain, the term *feebleminded* replaced the term moron, and similar terms were used in other countries, but by and large, all these are now quite out of vogue. In 1954, a special subcommittee of the World Health Organization proposed a system of nomenclature based on British, American, French, and German usage in which the terms *mild subnormality, moderate subnormality,* and *severe subnormality* were recommended. These terms do not carry the opprobrious connotations of the older nomenclature, and by their similarity to each other they accentuate the continuous nature of mental ability, but they have not been widely adopted.

The most widely accepted classification system based on the severity of the symptoms (in this instance, IQ) is the one suggested in the 1973 manual of the AAMD which uses four categories of retardation—mild, moderate, severe, and profound (Grossman, 1973). This system is a simple one, based on the standard score obtained by the individual on a reliable test of intelligence. (See Table 2-2.) It is designed to be taken in conjunction with a classification system of adaptive behavior. The system assumes only that intelligence as measured by standardized tests is distributed normally in the general population and that the individual to be classified has been given an appropriate, well-standardized test under conditions which will yield a reliable and valid index of his general intellectual functioning. The more nearly adequate the standardization of the test and the more nearly constant its standard deviation at all ages, the more reliable this classification system can be. (See Chapter 17.)

Table 2-2   AAMD Standard Deviation (SD) Ranges According to Measured Intelligence Levels

Descriptive term	Range in SD Value	Corresponding IQ range for tests with SD	
		15	16
Mild retardation	−3.00 to −2.01	55–69	52–67
Moderate retardation	−4.00 to −3.01	40–54	36–51
Severe retardation	−5.00 to −4.01	25–39	20–35
Profound retardation	Below −5.00	Under 25	Under 20

Source: Adapted from Grossman (1973, p. 18).

We shall adhere to the AAMD classification system throughout the rest of this book, except in Chapter 18, in which it is more reasonable to use accepted educational categories. The AAMD scheme emphasizes the continuous nature of the broad range of mental ability and requires a minimum of assumptions about the stability and implications of deviations in measured intelligence. In addition, this system is popular in the computer-oriented bookkeeping carried on by federal and state agencies throughout the United States and thus has achieved a semiofficial status.

Classification According to Etiology

Since our next chapters will deal so extensively with the many causes of mental retardation, we need introduce this view only briefly here. Many classification systems distinguish between individuals presumed to be simply the representatives of the lower ranges of a normal distribution of intellect and those whose intellectual development has been interfered with by some pathologic condition such as disease, injury, chromosomal abnormality, or a discrete genetic disorder. A number of workers have proposed dichotomous classifications which correspond roughly with these two groups. One such scheme was proposed by E. D. Lewis in 1933, and a similar one by Fraser Roberts in 1952. Lewis had termed the former group *subcultural*. S. B. Sarason (1953) proposed the conceptually similar but rather undignified label of *garden-variety deficiency* for cases in which the evidence points to a common developmental process combining with subaverage potential in the parents and a limited environment. This type today is usually termed *cultural-familial retarded* or *retarded due to psychosocial disadvantage*.

The work of Strauss (see Chapter 11) deserves special mention, although the essential distinctions he drew between *exogenous* and *endogenous* sources of retardation were different only in detail from those mentioned above. Strauss suggested that the exogenous syndrome, said to result from an injury to or an infection of the brain before, during, or after birth, is usually accompanied by a behavioral pattern including perceptual disturbances, thinking disorders, hyperactivity, distractibility, impulsiveness, and aggression. Later research has revealed that many children who have sustained brain injury show quite different behavioral qualities, whereas other children who are hyperactive show no clear evidence of organic damage. Still, something like this syndrome is familiar to teachers and parents, and its elucidation is a focus of current research. (See Chapter 11.)

A system which conceptualizes the field of retardation in terms of etiology has a number of advantages for teaching, research, and prevention, but in many ways it is misleading. A deficit can seldom be diagnosed as due exclusively to biology or to life experience, since the interplay of the two is incessant. The original source of a deficit is very often obscured by subsequent experiences. It is a rare brain-injured child, for example, who does not undergo more than his share of failure, frustration, and rejection. Moreoover, once structural damage has occurred, it makes relatively little practical difference just what caused it, unless there is suspicion of a continuing pathological condition, such as exposure to lead, or genetic causes are questioned with implications for the parents' decision to have additional children. For these reasons an approach based on etiology should be supplemented by other ways of looking at the child, for an assessment of his present capabilities is usually much more important than a search for remote causes.

Classification According to Clinical Variety or Symptom Constellation

The most frequently used syndrome categories are those described by the AAMD (Grossman, 1973), the American Psychiatric Association (1968), and the World Health Organization (1968), all of which bear strong resemblance to one another. A separation of symptom from cause is necessary because only rarely can both be identified. To take but one example, the very striking syndrome of microcephaly, characterized by a small brain and skull, is caused by hereditary factors in some cases and by strictly environmental factors in others. (See Chapter 4.) In many more instances, the causes remain elusive. In any event, the child's degree of intellectual handicap can and should be described independently of any clinical disorder which can be identified.

THE PREVALENCE OF MENTAL RETARDATION[4]

Since mental retardation consists not only of low measured intelligence but also of a failure in adaptive behavior, statistical statements concerning the prevalence of this condition tend to be fraught with error. In the United States, the difficulties in judging both intellectual and adaptive status make large-scale surveys almost impossible, although brief intelligence tests have been included in the National Health Examination Survey of children and youth (Harris & Roberts, 1972; Scanlon, 1973). In any event, estimates have value only if they are directed at questions of consequence. Frequently the issues are locally defined and therefore relevant only to small segments of the population. A school board may want to know how many special classes to plan and where to locate them; preschool compensatory programs may wish to find geographic areas with large proportions of high-risk children; a welfare department may question how many adults on its rolls could be trained for competitive positions and for how many sheltered workshops would be more appropriate, and so on.

Among the published estimates concerning the prevalence of mental retardation, there is much disagreement. Wallin (1958), reviewing sixty studies conducted between 1894 and 1958, found estimates ranging from .05 percent to 13 percent of the population! The generally accepted rule-of-thumb is, however, about 3 percent, roughly corresponding to the percentage of individuals with IQs below 70 (Office of Mental

---

[4] *Prevalence* refers to the number of cases of a condition identified in a population at a given point in time. *Incidence* refers to the number of new cases occurring in a population within a given period, ordinarily a year. For a more extended discussion of the prevalence of mental retardation, see Heber (1970).

Retardation Coordination, 1972b). This figure is in agreement with numerous American and European surveys in recent years which have employed a broad variety of methods and yet consistently yield a modal figure of 2 to 3 percent (Farber, 1968).

Estimates depending primarily on measures of intellectual status fail, of course, to take into account adaptive behavior. Unfortunately, well-standardized measures of adaptive behavior suitable for the general population are simply nonexistent. Practically speaking, professional judgments in individual cases usually depend on informal evidence of poor adaptation. In the clinical situation, this lack is not as critical as it seems, however, since by far the majority of children and adults who are referred for intellectual appraisal on suspicion of mental retardation have already clearly exhibited a serious problem of adaptive behavior such as consistent school failure or inability to maintain competitive employment. Furthermore, IQ and adaptive behavior measures tend to be highly correlated. (See Chapter 17.)

The most thorough epidemiological study of mental retardation in an American metropolitan area was conducted in Riverside, California, by Jane Mercer (1973), who made a direct survey of a sample of the population, and also investigated the number of individuals recognized by various social agencies as mentally retarded as well as those so recognized by their families and neighbors. She found great variation according to the method by which cases were identified, by far the greatest number of mentally retarded persons being identified by the schools. Of particular interest is the comparison she made of individuals scoring below IQ 70 in a direct survey and, of these, the number who also "failed" a measure of adaptive behavior at a similar level. Of the 150 persons in her sample with IQs below 70, only 45 percent also failed the behavioral measure, thus yielding an overall estimate of prevalence of only 1.35 percent. This figure is extremely misleading, however, since none of the Anglo individuals with low IQs "passed" the adaptive measure, whereas 60 percent of the Mexican-American and 91 percent of the black individuals with IQs below 70 "passed" the adaptive-behavior measure. We shall have more to say about the question of racial and ethnic differences later on, but it is clear that simple survey methods which fail to take such variables into account will be of little utility.

Despite the widespread acceptance of the 3 percent prevalence estimate, a number of writers in recent years have defended a lower figure, generally about 1 percent (Mercer, 1973; Tarjan, Wright, Eyman & Keeran, 1973). Indeed, some surveys tend to uphold this lower figure (Birch, Richardson, Baird, Horobin, & Illsley, 1970), though rural, especially Southeastern communities, tend to yield figures higher than 3 percent (Lemkau & Imre, 1969).

Whether one considers a 3 percent estimate high or low depends upon one's frame of reference. As we have seen, the 1959 AAMD definition considered as retarded all children and adults with IQs below 85 whose adaptive behavior was unsuccessful. A full one-sixth of the population would be expected to attain IQs below 85, although of course many of these would exhibit successful levels of adaptive behavior. To include so large a proportion of the population within a definition of mental retardation might be impractical, but it is clear that many persons of borderline intellectual ability suffer because of it a cruel detriment to attaining the "good life."

Prevalence Estimates Compared with a Normal Distribution

When any trait is the result of a large number of factors, some favorable and some unfavorable, most persons fall around the middle of its distribution but some enjoy particularly fortuitous combinations of factors and some suffer equally poor combinations. Because intellectual development is indeed the result of a large number of interacting factors, and also because tests are constructed to yield a normal distribution, a normal (bell-shaped) curve is for the most part an accurate description of the distribution of IQ. On this basis, one would expect approximately 2.5 percent of a population to attain IQs two standard deviations or more below the mean, but almost all these would attain IQs above 50. This prediction is discrepant with the fact that empirical studies find closer to 3 percent of IQs below 70 and the obvious fact that a significant number of individuals attain IQs below 50.

If intelligence in some individuals is overwhelmingly reduced by the action of a single or a small number of highly pathological factors, an excess at the lower end of the distribution would result. This is the most likely explanation of the existing state of affairs. The majority of persons with IQs 50 to 70 come from the lower socioeconomic segments of the population. Below this IQ level, retarded persons come from all segments of the population (though with a higher prevalence in poorer families), suggesting that however favorable their backgrounds, they have suffered damage as the result of overriding interfering factors (Bradway, 1935; Lemkau & Imre, 1969; Peckham, 1974; Sabagh et al., 1959; Tarjan et al., 1973).

Dingman and Tarjan (1960) calculated the number of individuals with low IQs who would be anticipated on the basis of a normal distribution of intelligence, and, in addition, they estimated the actual number of retarded individuals at various IQ levels in the United States. Their estimates, adapted here to a population figure of 210 million, are presented in Table 2-3. Above IQ 50, the two figures show small discrepancies, but there are great excesses in the ranges below IQ 50. The excess group probably consists of individuals suffering from a pronounced pathological process, such as a major genetic abnormality or a brain injury. If the excess group were itself distributed around an average IQ of about 32, with a standard deviation approximating that of the general population, both groups could be accommodated under one curve expressing the total IQ distribution. Such a curve, adapted from Dingman and Tarjan, is reproduced in Figure 2-1.

Some Factors Affecting Estimated Prevalence

A great many environmental factors affect the prevalence of mental retardation. Among the more striking examples are the standards and practices of the community and factors related to age, ethnic group, and geographical residence.

The community　In the developed nations of the world, an individual with a mild intellectual handicap usually must attempt to find a niche in a highly urban,

Table 2-3　Mental Retardation and the Normal Distribution Curve

IQ range	Number calculated from normal curve	Estimated actual prevalence	"Excess"	Percent "excess"
0–20	57	104,935	104,878	185,400
20–50	186,635	420,000	233,365	125
50–70	6,269,106	6,332,106	63,000	1
Total	6,455,798	6,857,041	401,243	6

Source:　Adapted from Dingman and Tarjan (1960) and adjusted to a general population estimate of 210 million.

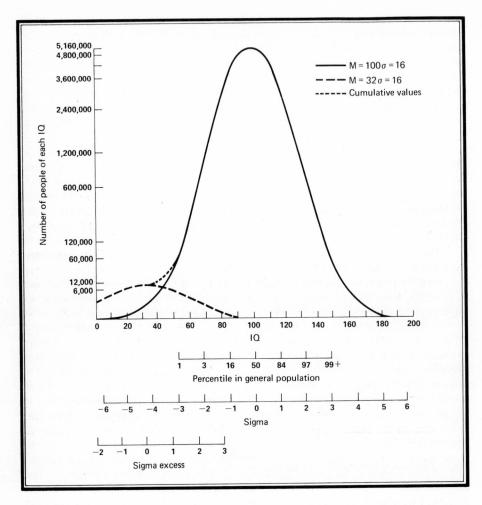

Fig. 2-1 Frequency distribution of intelligence quotients, assuming a total population of 210 million. *(Adapted from Dingman and Tarjan, 1960.)*

industrialized, mobile, and competitive community. The schoolchild must compete with others of his age according to relatively rigid standards of competence, and the adult must usually take responsibility for finding and holding a job in a competitive market and for establishing and maintaining living arrangements. One of the most crucial problems of the retarded adult lies in his or her inability to grasp the complex organization and the integrated network of relationships which constitute the environment (Farber, 1968). In today's society, composed in the main of nuclear families unable to provide the lifelong support of an old-fashioned, extended family, it is inevitable that many mildly retarded individuals will be unable to cope successfully.

Even rural areas no longer tend to provide an easy environment for retarded individuals. The changing architecture of farm homes and the increased mobility of the population make a retarded child more of a family liability than previously, and work on the farm is complicated by the increased use of mechanical equipment and scientific methods. Consolidation of small schools into larger units lacking special education facilities tends to eliminate a number of retarded children from rural schools (Shafter, 1968), although recent legal decisions now require states to provide some form of educational services for all children. Retardation still appears to be suspected and confirmed at a later age in rural areas than in urban areas (Aldrich et al., 1971), but with the increased availability of diagnostic services, the recognition of retardation is on the increase even in rural areas.

Age Prevalence estimates of mental retardation show marked age variation. Surveys consistently show a peak during the school years and particularly during adolescence, with a sharp drop in adulthood (Dingman, 1959; Lemkau & Imre, 1969; Scheerenberger, 1966). Mercer (1973), for example, found the following rates in her case-finding survey: ages zero to four, 0.7 percent; ages five to nine, .54 percent; ages ten to fourteen, 1.15 percent; ages fifteen to nineteen, 1.61 percent; ages twenty to twenty-four, 0.90 percent; and ages above twenty-five, 0.13 percent.

The requirements for school entrance and promotion bring to light handicaps mild enough to have passed unnoticed until then. Before school begins, parents may not sense the backwardness of their children because they do not view them in relation to other children of the same age. Moreover, many mildly retarded children are actually developing according to about the same timetable as the rest of the family. It is principally the moderately, severely, and profoundly retarded who are spotted during infancy or the preschool years. The early school years show a spurt in reported cases of mild retardation. For many children, school is the most difficult and frustrating experience they will ever encounter. To many, school is an alien environment which requires prompt mastery of concepts and skills which tax intellectual abilities and which may be compounded by language handicaps, poor preparation, expectations of failure, and cultural conflicts. The President's Committee on Mental Retardation and Education for the Handicapped (1970b) coined the term "six-hour retarded child" to describe the inner-city or rural child of poverty who is really only retarded in school, since his out-of-school behavior may be considerably more competent. Since adaptation during childhood is judged primarily by school achievement, intellectual and adaptive behavior are almost synonymous during these years; later on, different means of coping may be possible and the two tend to diverge. No one would maintain that children of limited intelligence should not attend school, but it has been convincingly argued that the schooling from which they profit most is more flexible, more concrete, and more concentrated on the child's meaningful real-life experiences and his own motivations than is the traditional classroom (Ginsburg, 1972).

The increase in reported cases during adolescence is probably due to several factors. First, the youngster is rather abruptly faced with more complex and abstract learning tasks in school, as his nonretarded classmates become capable of what Piaget characterizes as the stage of "formal operations" (see Chapter 12). At the same time, he faces more subtle social situations because society begins to expect of him more foresight and more controlled behavior. The adolescent's bodily changes are also upsetting both to him and to adults who may grow unrealistically fearful of possible sexual and aggressive misbehavior. Institutional admissions of mildly retarded children occur primarily during this period.

Once the critical era of adolescence and school attendance is over, however, many of the mildly handicapped are assimilated into society and join the ranks of the

Fig. 2-2 *(J. & M. Menapace)*

dull-normal, living for the most part in marginal socioeconomic circumstances but more or less "making it." (See Chapter 22.) There is also the possibility that many individuals continue to be significantly handicapped but remain unidentified because no appropriate services exist for them, or because their inability to cope with chaotic bureaucratic offices actually prevents their being recognized. Without recognition of their mental retardation, some are also given help for related practical problems such as financial support through the program of Aid to Families with Dependent Children.

Racial and Ethnic Background   In the United States, black children above age two, and children from several ethnic minority groups, on the average perform less well on tests of intelligence than do white children, although the scores of the two groups overlap to a considerable extent (Baughman & Dahlstrom, 1968; Dreger & Miller, 1968; Van De Riet & White, 1963). The psychomotor development of black infants up to about age eighteen months is, if anything, accelerated (Alley & Snider, 1970; Bayley, 1965; Dasen, 1973; Durham Educational Improvement Program 1966-67; King & Seegmiller, 1973). Of course, there is the possibility that hereditary differences are involved to some degree (Jensen, 1969a), but environmental influences are probably capable of producing performance differences of the magnitude used— typically about 15 IQ points—in the verbal and conceptual abilities which begin to emerge in the second year of life. (See Chapters 7 and 8.)

Evidence for environmental handicaps associated with race are plentiful. As a by-product of the massive Collaborative Perinatal Research Project following 50,000 women recruited during their third month of pregnancy, the Stanford-Binet IQs of 12,210 white children and 14,550 black children were found to yield means of 104.5 and 91.3, respectively, a difference consistent with the other studies we have just cited. Further analysis, however, reveals that the black children had a lower birthweight, a smaller placenta, and more instances of failure to breathe spontaneously at birth. They also weighed less at age four months and at age four years and were born into families with lower socioeconomic status to mothers with fewer years of education and lower nonverbal intelligence. The mothers had had a larger number of prior pregnancies including abortion, kept fewer appointments for prenatal care, gained less weight during pregnancy, and had pregnancies of shorter duration (Kennedy, as cited by Matarazzo, 1972).

The overall lower performance of some minority groups on measures of intelligence is reflected, not surprisingly, in increased percentages enrolled in special school classes for the educable mentally retarded. Mercer (1970), for example, found in special classes in the California public schools some two to three times more children of Spanish-surname and black families than were represented in the total population. At the same time, 15.3 percent of the children with Spanish surnames and 12.4 percent of the black children who were in regular classes had IQs below 80, but only 1.2 percent of the English-speaking Caucasian children in regular classes had tested IQs below 80. It is not, then, just a matter of shunting off minority-group children to special classes, although Mercer (1973) believes that this is a factor. Not only IQs but educational achievement measures show discrepancies in the same direction. A national survey of literacy among youths who were from twelve to seventeen years old (Vogt, 1973), for example, found 4.7 percent of white males but 20.5 percent of black males to be illiterate, performing below a beginning fourth-grade reading level. The percentages for females were 1.7 percent and 9.6 percent, respectively. Among some groups, the percentages were even higher and among some, substantially lower. Of youths whose parents had no formal education, one-third of the white boys and nearly half of the black boys could not read, whereas of those whose parents had a college education, only 0.7 percent of the white boys and 3.4 percent of the black boys were illiterate.

Geographic region   Intellectual and scholastic attainment tend to vary to some degree by region. For example, in a sample of children ages six to eleven given parts of the Wechsler Intelligence Scale for Children as part of a National Health Survey (Roberts, 1972), white children in the South scored lower by an average of nearly 6 points than did their counterparts in other regions, and black children in the South scored approximately 4 points lower than black children elsewhere. Similarly, in the literacy study mentioned earlier (Vogt, 1973), illiteracy rates for both white and black youths were more than twice as high in the South as in other regions, and higher in rural than in urban areas. Some of these differences may be tied to selective migration and some probably have to do with the generally lower socioeconomic status of the southeastern region and its comparatively rural nature. Yet children who move from the southeastern states to the North have been shown to increase in IQ over a period of years (Lee, 1951).

Sex   Almost all studies dealing with abnormalities in children report a higher incidence in males than in females. No doubt many factors are involved here, from hereditary mechanisms which make it more likely for the male to manifest recessive characteristics carried by the X chromosome (see Chapter 3) to a social system which requires of males a stricter standard of self-sufficiency. Whatever the causes, the incidences of mental retardation and many other problems among males are considerably higher than among females (Farber, 1968; Singer, Westphal & Niswander, 1967). Mumpower (1970), for example, found a ratio of about seventy males to thirty females over the entire range of retardation. Peckham (1974), however, in an eleven-year-old group she investigated in Britain, found sex differences only among the (educationally) subnormal, not the severely subnormal.

Lest we leap to the conclusion that girls are simply smarter than boys, we should note the existence of highly complex interactions in the determination of intelligence based on biologically based potentials, differential parental relationships with boys and girls, educational practices, and cultural reinforcement of sex-role patterns (Lynn, 1972). Although girls tend to be superior in verbal fluency, accurate language usage and spelling, manual dexterity, clerical skills, and rote memory, boys tend to excel in verbal reasoning, mathematical reasoning, analytic and problem-solving ability, and mechanical aptitude (Davie, Butler, & Goldstein, 1972; Garai & Scheinfeld, 1968). Girls tend to make better grades in school (Maccoby, 1966) but even in some of the subjects in which girls' school marks are better, boys actually score higher on standardized achievement tests (Coleman, 1961; Hanson, 1959).

Further evidence for culturally determined patterns comes from a study in Puerto Rico by Albizu-Miranda and Stanton (1968), who found substantially higher rates of retardation among lower-class women than men, probably on account of the restricted environments of the women. In India, where the birth of a boy in a village is celebrated in anticipation of his economic contribution to the family, but the birth of a girl is mourned as burdensome, mortality rates among village girls are considerably higher than among boys.

ISSUES CONCERNED WITH LABELING

A subject of intense controversy in present-day literature relates to the effects of labeling individual retarded persons. The issue is a very complex one, and it is clouded by its confounding with many other variables such as the effect of placement in special classes (MacMillan, Jones, & Aloia, 1974) and by political and social overtones arising from the disproportionate numbers of poor and ethnic minority children who are labeled mildly retarded. Several other chapters in this book touch on issues concerned with accurate assessment of a child's intellectual ability and social adaptation, so that we may disregard for the moment the effects of *mis*labeling children, surely a practice not to be condoned.

Labeling does not occur in a vacuum, of course. Children ordinarily acquire a label as an entry card to a special program after it has become clear that they are not doing well in an environment which is reasonably supportive to nonretarded children.

Parents who bring their children to diagnostic clinics are usually concerned about slow attainment of motor or language milestones and want professional advice about ways to accelerate the children's lagging development, ways which often involve special services. Much more frequently, labels are assigned by schools in the process of making special class placement (Mercer, 1973). The professionals who determine that children are "retarded" are generally concerned for their welfare and are attempting to open doors to services designed to further their development.

The frequency with which labels are assigned has a great deal to do with the diagnostic and treatment facilities available. Only a few years ago, the label "learning disabled child" did not exist, but with the establishment of educational programs for children of normal intelligence with specific academic problems, we are suddenly in the midst of an epidemic of "learning disability." Similarly, as special programs have multiplied, school personnel are much more frequently willing, even eager, to describe children as mildly retarded in order to place them (and, it might be added, to maintain enrollments and therefore funding of established programs). Especially now that schools must offer services to all children, the designation can no longer serve as an excuse to refuse a child admission to school.

Hypothesized Effects of Labeling

Most effects of labeling have been thought to be highly negative, and the majority of writers, in the best American tradition of identifying with the "underdog," have argued against labels. MacMillan et al. (1974) summarize the hypothesized negative effects as related to (1) the child's self-concept, (2) rejection by his peers, (3) his own level of aspiration, (4) teachers' expectations for his achievement, (5) his chances for a healthy adult adjustment in marriage or employment, and (6) his dislike of bearing the label. Although all these effects are certainly possible, and no doubt each does occur in some cases, MacMillan et al. conclude that unambiguous research evidence is lacking with respect to all but the last of these. Without doubt, children and adults do not like to be called retarded (e.g., Edgerton, 1967; Guskin, Bartel & MacMillan, 1975), and even less do they like any of the more derogatory terms they sometimes hear. It is not at all clear, however, whether the label has changed their concept of themselves and/ or their treatment at the hands of peers, teachers, and employers, or whether in fact they are fastening upon this label, their membership in a special class, or their admission to an institution, as a convenient target on which to blame their feelings of difference and incompetence. A variety of failure experiences antedated and in fact led up to their enrollment or admission. Many retarded persons, though yearning even more than others for acceptance and affection, are inept in their social relationships and tend to drive away the very people whose affection they seek. (See Chapter 9.) Little wonder if they should need an acceptable "reason" for their rejection.

Rather less frequently, positive effects of labeling have been hypothesized. Some, of course, have not to do with the individual but with the workings of a social and educational system which offers services to individuals in terms of the classification of disability they exhibit, a system in which acquisition of a label is the price of admission. (If the services received are ineffective or even oppressive, on the other hand, this admission ticket is valueless or worse.) In terms of peer reactions to retarded children and adults, however, it has been posited by MacMillan et al. (1974), and confirming evidence cited, that a label can help to resolve the dissonance which occurs when a retarded child fails to meet the standards of his peers. If his behavior is seen by them as appropriate for a different group ("Oh, he dropped the ball because he is retarded"), the nonretarded children may find his behavior more acceptable and may not so often reject or ignore him.

Recommendations

Even in the absence of formal data demonstrating unequivocally the deleterious effects of labeling, sufficient anecdotal reports exist to prove to any doubter that at times labels are associated with injustice, with lowered self-aspirations, and with lowered expectations on the part of parents, teachers, and employers. (See Chapters 20, 18, and 15, respectively.) How, then, may we reduce these unwanted consequences of procedures which, for better or worse, are deeply ingrained in our social and educational systems?

Guskin (1974) has suggested that one way to modify labeling effects is to broaden understanding of the label's meaning. If, for example, teachers were made aware of the broad range of children labeled retarded (including some mislabeled) and the variety of their competencies in school and out, and could recognize that most will some day live "normal" adult lives, the grossly oversimplified nature of the label would be reduced.

A second approach has been suggested by the group of experts under Hobbs's leadership (Hobbs, 1975c). They have, with the approval of educational leaders in many states, suggested that governmental funds be appropriated not on the basis of categories of deviant development but rather on the basis of services needed. Under such conditions, schools and other agencies would not have to identify individual children by category to declare them eligible for programs and attendant funding, and services could be rendered on a more flexible and integrated basis. As this group suggests, funds which flow through categorical channels encourage professionals to divide along categorical lines and "thus limit their effectiveness in the service of children, most of whom do not fit into sanctioned categories" (p. 233). The implications of such a change might be striking. Children whose low intelligence or academic ability proves a handicap only in school and not at home or in the community would no longer need be characterized as retarded, but only identified as needing special school services. The "six-hour retarded child" could be explicitly recognized as functioning quite differently in different settings, and the superfluous connotations of his academic disability discarded.

Of equal significance, Hobbs's group also recognized that the available, simplified classification systems "obscure both the uniqueness of individual children and the similarities of children assigned to various categories" (p. 233). They propose that standardized profiling systems be developed to describe individual children, profiles which take into account a broad variety of the child's physical, intellectual, and social characteristics, his relationships with others in particular settings, and specific actions needed in his behalf. They point out that the advent of computer technology frees us from the necessity for single-dimension and therefore inaccurate schemes which ignore individual differences among children, their immediate surroundings, and the society as a working system. Indeed, the beginnings of such profiles have already been developed in some states (Hobbs, 1975c, chap. 4).

In the meantime, it is necessary to proceed with research endeavors, to discover when, where, and to whom labels are beneficial or deleterious, and to be alert in our professional lives to the short-term and long-range implications of the labels we choose to apply or withhold.

THE STATUS OF INTEREST AND ACTIVITY IN THE FIELD OF MENTAL RETARDATION[5]

During most of the first half of the twentieth century, citizens and professionals alike remained indifferent toward the problems of intellectually handicapped children and their families. There was, it is true, a spurt of attention to mental retardation following World War I, when as a result of the first use of standardized testing on a large scale, a great many men had been found unfit for military service by reason of low intelligence. During the 1920s and 1930s, the eugenics movement stirred up fears of a long-range increase in the retarded population. Children were shunted off to understaffed, debilitating rural institutions, and professional interest shifted to the development and application of intelligence tests to identify the retarded. There was resignation to the idea that retardation was incurable, taken to mean that rehabilitative efforts were futile—a self-fulfilling prophecy of the worst order. The pessimism and rejection were compounded by the widespread notion that intelligence developed at a fixed rate, largely dependent on a sort of built-in clock useless to tamper with, and furthermore by an unhealthy belief in the power of the IQ to "tell all" about an individual.

In the 1950s, however, there began a reawakening of interest, largely sparked by parents' groups. In the United States in 1950, representatives from twenty local parent groups formed the National Association of Parents and Friends of Retarded Children, in 1952 renamed the National Association for Retarded Children and, more recently, the National Association for Retarded Citizens (NARC). By 1974, the NARC encompassed 213,000 members, 60 percent of whom were parents and the rest interested professionals and other citizens. Most members of the NARC, like most members of other voluntary groups, are of the middle class, and their children tend to be moderately to severely retarded. Many classes for trainable retarded children were first established privately by local NARC chapters and then taken over by the public schools. Currently, preschools, day-care centers, summer camps, recreational programs, and small residential facilities are typical local projects. The organization has been successful in mobilizing many legislative and administrative bodies at the local, state, and federal levels. On a worldwide basis, in the 1970s parents' groups have shifted from a preoccupation with retarded children to increasing recognition of the needs of retarded adults, and likewise from local self-help projects to national consumer action programs (Dybwad, 1973).

Other events of the 1950s were laying the groundwork for the dramatic shifts of the 1960s. Giant strides were being made in the field of genetics, including the unraveling of the genetic code and new techniques for studying chromosomes, and the precise anomaly causing Down's syndrome was soon identified. These advances created enormous excitement, and several advances in medicine in the same decade seemed to signal that all was not hopeless, even with the genetically "incurable." The discovery of the devastating effects of maternal rubella during the first trimester of pregnancy pointed the way to preventing these tragedies. Equally striking, dietary means were found to prevent brain damage in phenylketonuric (PKU) infants, and simultaneously screening techniques were developed to identify PKU infants before the damage had occurred. Hopes arose that additional means of intervention would quickly follow. (Subsequent progress in prevention has been much slower than progress in identifying new genetic syndromes.) An improved standard of living and spe-

[5] Further historical material will be found in Chaps. 1, 11, 13, 16, 18, and 21.

cific medical techniques also reduced infant mortality. Increasing numbers of infants were saved who previously would have perished, and antibiotics also kept alive many who would have succumbed to infection.

Another development of the 1950s which was to have major repercussions was the 1954 Supreme Court decision which served as the mandate for school integration. It established that educational practices could not be totally controlled by the wit and whimsy of a local populace and that education was a right of all citizens, not a privilege. Not until the 1970s was this decision spelled out in detail for handicapped children. (See Chapter 18.) From 1955 to 1960, there was substantial leadership in Congress for legislative action (Boggs, 1971) which led to the rapid growth of the National Institutes of Health and special appropriations for research in mental retardation. The Office of Education also came forward with additional proposals for educating the retarded.

The developments of the 1950s were followed in the early 1960s by a variety of proposals which culminated in an explosion of concern and action. Alone, none of them could have created a revolution of great magnitude, but in concert they proved irresistible. First, there arose a general concern for the rights of minority-group citizens, a determination to right old civil, social, and economic wrongs extending back to the origins of the nation. Concern was also propelled by the realization that poverty, ignorance, and ill health among the poor were robbing not only them but others of a fully productive society. Aid to the incapable and/or impoverished was seen as not only morally just but imperative for the common good. President Johnson's War on Poverty attempted to maximize the status and competence of adults and to prevent the occurrence of handicaps in children. A great variety of programs—medical, educational, welfare, housing, day care, and community action—all attempted to help the poor; in the process, they of course benefited many of the mildly retarded. The War on Poverty, though far from won, was probably the most relevant war on mental retardation which could have been mounted. An emphasis on education and health services for young children, including Project Head Start, was an important outgrowth of that movement, an attempt to interrupt the intergenerational cycles of poverty, discouragement and low achievement.

Simultaneously, a specific concern for retarded individuals began to emerge in the early 1960s. In part this grew from the scientific advances mentioned previously and in part from educational advances. In that post-sputnik era, the nation had turned to the schools with a renewed emphasis on academic excellence, and the problems of retarded children were thereby highlighted. Another important factor was the concern and commitment of some of the nation's leaders, including President Kennedy and Vice President Humphrey, each of whom had a retarded member in his family. Some of the old taboos fell away and mental retardation became considerably more "respectable."

A broadly representative panel of experts brought together by President Kennedy made extensive recommendations in 1962 for national action to combat mental retardation. Their recommendations included action in research, preventive health measures, strengthened educational programs, more comprehensive and improved clinical and social services, improved methods and facilities for care, new legal and social concepts of the retarded, help to overcome manpower problems in professions concerned with retardation, and programs of education and information to increase public awareness (President's Panel, 1962a, pp. 14–15). To a large extent, the nation took this advice to heart.

Mental retardation has now become a legitimate concern of many professions which previously had ignored it. Close relationships emerged with developmental psychology (Klapper, 1970; Zigler, 1966) and social psychology (Wilson, 1970) and with clinical professions such as dentistry, nursing, nutrition, occupational therapy, pediatrics, physical therapy, psychiatry, clinical and educational psychology, social work, speech and hearing, and vocational rehabilitation (Beck, 1969; Koch & Dobson, 1971; Menolascino, 1970; Wilson, 1970). Personnel in all these areas at professional and at paraprofessional levels have increased manyfold. Research has skyrocketed in volume and to some extent in quality.

One index of activity in the field of mental retardation can be found in the areas of federal involvement. Of course, in many ways it is difficult to gauge how much of the public effort is directed at mental retardation, since many benefits of health, welfare, educational, and social programs are preventive and therefore indirect. A report of the Office of Mental Retardation Coordination (1972a) indicates that in fiscal year 1973, the Department of Health, Education, and Welfare (DHEW) made available $878,951,000 for specific mental retardation program activities, of which nearly $341,000,000 was used for income maintenance of retarded persons. DHEW supported maternity and infant care projects to provide health care to prospective mothers and infants in high-risk populations and supported screening programs for metabolic diseases. It granted funds to state health departments, crippled children's agencies, and state welfare agencies to provide health and welfare services, diagnostic clinics, treatment services for physically handicapped, homemaker services, etc. It provided rehabilitation services including health services, counseling, and assistance in job placement. It helped improve outpatient and inpatient facilities for the retarded supported in the main by state and local bodies. It also granted a large amount of support to local school districts to develop programs for all handicapped children. Training programs formed an integral component of most of the mental retardation programs of DHEW, including research training, clinical preparation of new personnel, inservice training for current personnel, and teacher training. Research support was provided through several DHEW agencies: the National Institutes of Health, the Office of Education, the Social and Rehabilitative Service, the Maternal and Child Health Service, and others. Construction funds for twelve research and training centers and more than thirty university-affiliated diagnostic facilities and for many more community facilities for the retarded were also provided in large part by the federal government. In short, the best thing that happened to mental retardation during the 1960s was an influx of enormous amounts of money, enormous in terms of previous amounts but of course dwarfed in comparison with other national commitments such as military expenditures.

Two developments of the early 1970s are worthy of special note. First, in many states there has been a decided move away from residential institutions as a single solution to the problems of retarded persons and their families and toward a broad array of community services to enable families to keep their retarded members at home or at least close by. The organization of programs has been guided largely by the "principle of normalization" mentioned at the beginning of this chapter. This view implies that retarded children and adults should be integrated as much as possible into the community at large. Many states are actively attempting to reduce the populations of their massive institutions even though increasing lifespans of the severely and profoundly retarded tend to maintain the number and population size of these facilities.

These states are moving toward smaller institutions and small residential facilities such as group homes situated in the communities and depending upon ordinary community services.

Finally, recent court decisions have begun to solidify the rights of the retarded as full-fledged citizens, rights to schooling no matter how profound the handicap, to treatment, and to legal protection in all spheres. The legal position of retarded persons will be discussed in Chapter 22.

The early 1970s have witnessed a distinct slowing in the growth of socially oriented programs of all kinds, with the possible exception of public school provisions for children with developmental disabilities. Perhaps this was inevitable as the first rush of optimism and compassion yielded to the realization that problems of poverty and mental retardation could not be dealt with decisively, once and for all, but represented a long, incremental struggle. The nation's acute economic problems and its shift of concern toward energy conservation and environmental protection have perhaps compounded the issue. But certainly the new plateau—if it is a plateau—is a vast improvement over the old one. Furthermore, the nation has finally acknowledged an inescapable truth: The retarded are *of* us, not *from* us, and they and their families must henceforth be treated accordingly.

PART II
ETIOLOGY, SYMPTOM GROUPINGS, AND PSYCHOLOGICAL DEVELOPMENT

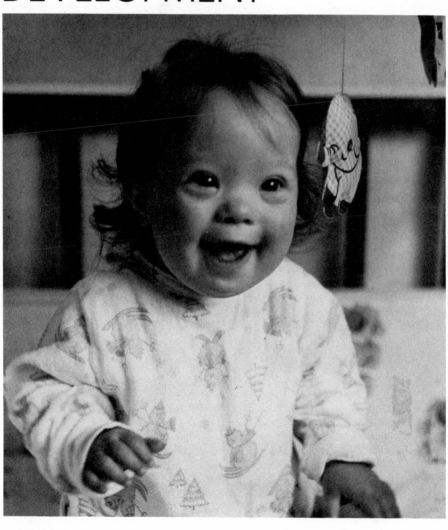

3

Genetic Factors in the Development of Mental Retardation

A single egg from the mother, fertilized by a single sperm from the father and nurtured first within the mother and then within the family and the broader culture, develops during several decades into a mature human being, perhaps a factory worker, a teacher, or even an Einstein. This miracle of development follows a set of specifications and a timetable which are a joint product of the individual's unique biologic inheritance and the unique environment in which he lives. In view of the complexity of the process, it is clear that the possibilities of serious errors during the developmental period are almost infinite. As a matter of fact, many of nature's errors are aborted spontaneously (Carr, 1971). Only a very small percentage are born noticeably defective, and the vast majority of those who are healthy at birth develop relatively normally to maturity.

ETIOLOGIC FACTORS IN MENTAL RETARDATION

In this chapter and in Chapters 5 and 7 we shall consider some of the many causal factors which contribute to mental retardation. In Chapters 4, 6, and 8, we shall discuss some of the more common syndromes of which mental retardation is a symptom. We intend to make it clear that there is rarely a single cause or a simple explanation of any type of intellectual disability. In some cases, the retardation seems to be

This chapter was written with the collaboration of Gilbert S. Omenn.

primarily a function of the hereditary endowment; in others, it seems to be the result of a complex interaction between genetic endowment and a multitude of environmental factors; and in still other cases, the retardation seems to be attributable to factors which are primarily environmental. An etiologic process may affect the child at any stage of the life span. It may occur at the time of conception, at any point *in utero,* during birth, or after birth. One child may suffer the effects of something which happened in a single instant, whereas another's handicap may be caused by a complicated series of interrelated events occurring over several months or years. In one, the defect may be diffused throughout the central nervous system; in another, it may be quite circumscribed.

In the discussion to follow, a rough distinction is made between groups of determinants which are labeled "genetic," "physical-environmental," and "psychosocial." It is, however, much easier to separate these factors in theory than it is to distinguish their disparate effects in an individual child. Their interaction is often so great that placing the primary responsibility on any single factor would be misleading. The responsible agent(s) or mechanism(s) often remain unknown, even after careful history, examination, and testing.

Depending on the sample and the definition or degree of retardation under consideration, various authors give different estimates about the relative importance of the etiological categories. Stern (1973), for example, recognizing that in nearly half of mentally retarded individuals no etiological diagnosis can be assigned, attributes approximately 37 percent of the known sources of retardation to genetic endowment and approximately 20 percent to environmental causes. Other authorities would give somewhat different estimates of the proportion of cases attributable to each category.

Because it is so difficult to specify the cause(s) of mental retardation in a particular child, the diagnostic label he receives may reveal more about the orientation and bias of the diagnostician than about the agents responsible. It is not uncommon for the case history of a child to contain several contradictory diagnoses over a short period of time. Perhaps a look at a typical case will help us to understand this situation.

Annie May J., age seven, is seen by a school psychologist and a pediatrician to determine whether she should be placed in a special class. She is brought in by her father, who is under court order to enter her in school. A truant officer who was looking for one of her older sisters discovered Annie May at home alone, caring for a baby brother.

Annie May is an attractive little girl. The pediatrician finds no striking signs of defect or disease, although she is somewhat undernourished, appears slightly clumsy, and her teeth need attention. She waits patiently while her father talks with the psychologist and enters the office quietly when it is her turn. She tries very hard to do just what the examiner wishes. Still, on the Wechsler Intelligence Scale for Children, she attains an IQ of 63, a mildly retarded level of performance.

Annie May is the sixth oldest of eight children. Her father is a house painter's helper when he can find work. Neither parent completed more than elementary school. Annie May was born at full term and weighed 5 pounds, 4 ounces, at birth. Her mother remembers the birth as easy but says Annie May did not breathe immediately after delivery, although no mention of this can be found in the hospital records. Annie May was frequently ill during infancy, with several episodes of high fever. She has presented no other special problems to this family. Gentle and eager to please, she has spent a good bit of time caring for her younger brother and sister. The older children are often truant from school and few of them do passing work when they do attend. The parents have paid scant attention to the frequent efforts of school officials to remedy this situation or to enroll the younger children in Project Head Start. There is reason to believe that neither parent is of average intelligence, and most of the children appear to be of borderline intellectual development.

The physician and psychologist realize the impossibility of separating possible biological factors from the handicaps imposed by Annie May's indifferent environment. They compromise with the label "psychosocial retardation" but recognize that they still know little about the etiology of this family pattern. (See Chapter 8.)

GENETIC FACTORS IN MENTAL RETARDATION

A sizable proportion of mentally retarded children never had the slightest chance of developing properly. They were destined to be handicapped from the moment of conception, when the particular sperm and the particular ovum united to determine their genetic endowment. Down's syndrome children, for example, inherit an extra chromosome which, so far as we know, inevitably produces some degree of retardation. In other children, however, genetic factors cause damage only in combination with specific environmental factors. A child with galactosemia, for example, will be damaged by toxic metabolic by-products only if he is fed milk, since his hereditary defect is an inability properly to metabolize the galactose contained in milk. Other genetic processes are much subtler than this, but investigators today are approaching the unanswered questions about human heredity with a much broader and more sophisticated perspective than ever before.

Genetic factors deserve considerable emphasis in any serious discussion of mental subnormality. During the past two decades, a much clearer understanding has emerged of the diverse ways in which the genes can affect growth and development. For example, methods have been perfected which allow the geneticist to see and to count accurately the number of chromosomes in a human cell (Tjio & Levan, 1956). As a direct result, a number of disorders resulting in mental retardation have been shown to be caused by errors in cell division which leave the fertilized egg, the zygote, with too many chromosomes (Mittwoch, 1963). (When the zygote has too few chromosomes, it seldom develops into a full-term fetus.) Considerable progress has been made in the exciting exploration of the biochemical composition and properties of the DNA (deoxyribonucleic acid) molecules which carry the genetic codes of all living organisms. Precise knowledge of the translation of these codes into metabolic processes is currently being gained (J. D. Watson, 1970), making it possible to understand just how various gene defects produce syndromes of mental retardation.

Another very important reason for emphasizing genetic factors in a discussion of mental retardation is that during the past several years researchers have come to appreciate more fully the complexity of the possible interactions between hereditary and environmental forces (Ehrman, Omenn, & Caspari, 1972). Certain traits or behavioral patterns in man and in lower animals which are unquestionably determined in part by environmental factors are jointly determined by genetic factors. Several kinds of learning aptitudes have been shown to have important genetic components

(McClearn & DeFries, 1973). Vandenberg (1972; Vandenberg, Stafford & Brown, 1968) analyzed data from longitudinal studies of twins in Louisville, Kentucky. He found marked differences in the heritability, or proportion of variance due to genetic factors, among the subtests of psychological assessment batteries, including tests of motor ability, perceptual speed, language development, reasoning, memory, and numerical ability. As psychologists attempt to unravel the complexities of the intertwining of hereditary and environmental determinants of behavior, they need to be fully conversant with the insights and potential contributions of each of the other professional groups who are working in this broad area.

Fundamental Genetic Processes

During recent years, giant steps have been taken in our understanding of the ways in which the genes direct and control many of the processes of human growth and development. It is now clear that such direction and control are accomplished through complex biochemical processes by which genes determine the structure of proteins and the rate at which they are synthesized. Many proteins act as enzymes, the basic substances which direct and control most of the myriad chemical reactions that take place within a living cell. To summarize very simply the process of genetic control, (1) the living cell is the basic unit of life itself, because it is within the cells that all the new life processes occur; (2) each of the hundreds of different chemical processes that take place within cells is mediated by a particular enzyme; and (3) each of the enzymes (or each protein subunit of an enzyme) is produced according to the specifications of one pair of the thousands of genes distributed in a balanced way among the pairs of chromosomes.

Let us now look briefly at the nature of the living cell, paying special attention to its genetic components. At least an intuitive understanding of what happens at the cellular levels is necessary to comprehend the basic metabolic errors which are responsible for some forms of mental retardation.

Genetic Biology of Living Cells[1]

All living cells contain a dense, somewhat glistening central section called the *nucleus,* which is surrounded by an outer part, the *cytoplasm.* The nuclei of the cells in the same individual vary much less than the cytoplasm, which differs greatly in shape, size, composition, and function from cell to cell. The cytoplasm is in turn encapsulated by the limiting surface of the cell, the *cell membrane.* The nucleus of the cell is of most interest to us, for it is this tiny central part which contains all the genetic material, the *chromatin.* The chromatin consists of DNA and associated proteins (Comings, 1972; Thomas, 1971).

Chromosomes   Microscopic examinations of nuclei have revealed one of the most important organizational principles of cells. At a certain stage of cell development (just before cell division), the chromatin arranges itself into rigidly patterned, threadlike particles that can be deeply stained with certain dyes; these threadlike bodies are called *chromosomes.* Both the number and the kind of chromosomes present in the cells of a given species are almost always invariant. In humans, the body cells contain forty-six chromosomes arranged in twenty-three pairs. The cells responsible

[1] More detailed information can be found in most textbooks on biology and physiology or in texts on genetics, such as Stern (1973) and Thompson and Thompson (1973).

for reproduction (the male sperm cell and the female egg cell), which are called *gametes,* have only twenty-three chromosomes, one member of each pair of the twenty-three pairs in the ordinary body cells.

The chromosomes are not all of the same shape and length. Each member of twenty-two of the pairs, known as *autosomal* chromosomes, does, however, duplicate its partner, or its *homologous* chromosome, as it is more technically known. The twenty-third pair of chromosomes are duplicates in the female (XX) but not in the male (XY), The autosomal chromosomes can be roughly ordered in series by length and are numbered from 1 to 22, from largest to smallest. They can also be described according to their shape and staining properties just before cell division.

Recent technological advances have greatly enhanced the detailed study of chromosomes (Arrighi & Hsu, 1971; Caspersson, Lomakka, & Zech, 1971; Crossen, 1972; Drets & Shaw, 1971; Evans, Buckton & Sumner, 1971). These methods have led to very important discoveries about many syndromes in mental retardation, including the common Down's syndrome. (See Chapter 4.) In these syndromes, there are abnormalities of the chromosomes which are observable in photographs taken with the aid of an ordinary microscope. Sometimes, parts of chromosomes are broken off; there may be extra or missing chromosomes in the body cells. It is not clear as yet exactly how these abnormalities are responsible for producing the syndromes with which they are associated, but there currently is active research in this area.

The chromosomes are not perfectly stable, intact entities. Actually, they wax and wane in a rhythm determined by the rate of cell division. When the cell is not dividing, the chromatin from which they are formed is diffused throughout the nucleus in granules and streaks, but during cell division the chromosomes take shape according to a precise and tremendously complex program.

Genes: Microscopic Units of Heredity Ever since Gregor Mendel's famous experiments with hybrid sweet peas, it has been known that there must be unitary elements within the cells which exert control over inherited characteristics, and for a long time there was considerable speculation about what these were. These elements came to be known as *genes,* and although they were long treated as hypothetical constructs, a great deal of knowledge about them slowly accumulated. It came to be known, for example, that each gene had to be passed along virtually unchanged from generation to generation; that there must be many thousands of these particles in every human cell, distributed unevenly among the twenty-three pairs of chromosomes; that each gene must occupy a very definite place (locus) on its chromosome; and that each pair of homologous chromosomes had to contain homologous assortments of genes, arranged with few exceptions in precisely the same order on each member of the chromosome pairs. New techniques combining linkage analyses, biochemical markers, and interspecies cell fusion have allowed discovery of just which chromosomes carry certain specific genes (McKusick & Chase, 1973). A wonderfully complex and fruitful system has emerged about an aspect of the world which no one has ever directly observed. Let us now turn to some of the newly acquired insights which have greatly expanded the already impressive theory of genetics.

Genes are too small to be seen by any but the most powerful electron microscopes, yet research by geneticists, microbiologists, and biochemists has rapidly advanced information about their constitution and action. The chemical substance of which the genes and thus the chromosomes are made is known to be deoxyribonucleic acid (DNA), a giant molecule containing an advancing double spiral (helical) strand of material which embodies the genetic code (Crick, 1962; J. D. Watson, 1970). Although DNA is capable of transmitting vastly complex "code messages," it is composed of combinations of only four primary chemical subunits, or "code letters." This great insight into the structure and functioning of genetic material, which was first proposed by Watson and Crick in 1953, involves a new description of what genes are like. A gene is simply a specific portion of the double-spiral strand of DNA which consists of a particular combination of the code letters that spell out a particular code word.

Various combinations of the four code letters, forming different code words, provide the biochemical information used in the construction of the proteins in the cell. Many of these proteins act as enzymes. The enzymes as has been pointed out above, are the biological catalysts which direct all the chemical or metabolic reactions that go on in the cells. These metabolic functions are, of course, the basis of all the physical growth and development of any living organism.[2]

The code is embodied in the DNA of the chromosomes, but exactly how does this genetic code determine the production of proteins? The material which mediates this task is ribonucleic acid (RNA), a class of substances chemically very similar to DNA. From the code site on the linear, double-helical DNA molecule (the gene) a messenger RNA (mRNA), specific for that gene, carries the code to the cellular particles out in the cytoplasm of the cell, where proteins are manufactured. This messenger RNA specifies the sequence of amino acid building blocks for the synthesis of a particular protein. Another class of RNA, the transfer RNAs, or tRNAs, collects from within the cytoplasm the raw materials, the amino acids, for protein synthesis. With the coded instructions and the materials, the proteins are formed one step at a time on the cytoplasmic particles called ribosomes. Ribosomes consist of yet another type of RNA (rRNA) plus certain proteins. The proteins whose structures are specified by these "structural genes" function as enzymes, as antibodies, as components of cell structure, as hormones, and as transport or carrier molecules, such as hemoglobin, which carries oxygen in the blood. Other genes are "regulatory" in that their protein products act to determine when structural genes are active in producing their proteins and how much is produced.

Genetic activity thus takes the form of biochemical regulation, through enzymes and other proteins which mediate cellular metabolism. Thus, genetic disorders are primarily metabolic defects, as recognized in a classic book by Garrod (1908) in which he coined the term "inborn errors of metabolism." A defective or changed gene will produce a change in the protein whose structure it specifies. If the only result of such a change is a slight alteration in the function of the protein, there may be little or no observable clinical effect. On the other hand, if the change or defect takes place within the message for an essential part of the protein, the protein may be rendered completely inactive. If this happens, the result can be grave trouble: perhaps death, serious disease, or severe mental retardation due to poisoning of the central nervous system by a metabolite that is toxic to this system. The error in enzyme synthesis may begin to be important early *in utero,* so that the structure of the central nervous system is faulty almost from the beginning of embryonic life, or it may become important much later in the life cycle.

It is quite likely that, in the foreseeable future, many essential biochemical proc-

---

[2] The interested reader should consult J. D. Watson (1970). Articles for nonbiochemists describing progress in this area of molecular biology appear regularly in *Scientific American.*

esses will be understood in terms of the precise genetic codes responsible for them. All the amino acids have already yielded to such analysis; their codes have been identified. With understanding may come control and prevention, such as may be possible by administration of the lacking enzymes, dietary control of substances which the individual is unable to metabolize, or transplantation of normal tissue to the diseased individual to correct a metabolic error (Omenn, 1973a).

Cell Division: Mitosis   With the exception of the cells involved in reproduction (the gametes), new cells are produced by a process of division known as *mitosis.* As the cell prepares to divide, the forty-six chromosomes begin to appear as tiny, stainable threads which gradually shorten and thicken by coiling. By this time, each chromosome has duplicated itself, and the two identical chromosomes lie together, connected in an X or a V shape by a constriction known as a *centromere.* At the midphase of the cell division, known as the *metaphase,* these doubled chromosomes are arranged in a single plane about midway between the two points of a spindle-shaped structure which has formed and now holds them. The metaphase condition is important because it is at this stage that the chromosomes are most easily stained, observed, and counted. The halves of each chromosome then separate from each other and migrate to opposite poles of the spindle. The chromosomes themselves gradually lengthen, uncoil, and become less darkly stainable. The entire cell now divides into two daughter cells, and the chromosomes do not appear distinct again until the cell undergoes another division. The process is illustrated in Figure 3-1.

The frequency with which a cell undergoes mitosis depends upon a number of factors, including the organism's stage in its life cycle, the presence of certain hormones, and the part of the body which is involved. In the neurons of the mature central nervous system, for example, mitosis is quite rare, and cells which are damaged are not replaced. Injury to the central nervous system is thus a more serious matter than a skin or flesh injury, since the cells in these parts of the body replace themselves fairly rapidly. In the bone marrow, blood cells are manufactured by mitosis at the rate of several million per hour. In the uterus, the entire lining is replaced after a menstrual period.

Almost always, the chromosomes which are contained in the nuclei of the two daughter cells are identical. Occasionally, however, the chromosomes do not divide evenly. When this happens, one daughter cell will have too many and one will have too few chromosomes. New lines of cells are thus begun, existing side by side with the original parental line. This phenomenon is known as *mosaicism.* Chromosome counts of the nuclei in metaphase reveal nuclei which contain forty-five, forty-six, or forty-seven chromosomes, or perhaps some other number. Errors in the division of the cells are fortunately rare. Cases of mosaicism in chromosomal anomalies of the types to be

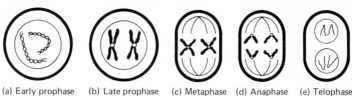

(a) Early prophase   (b) Late prophase   (c) Metaphase   (d) Anaphase   (e) Telophase

Fig. 3-1   Mitosis. Only a single pair of chromosomes is shown. *(From Stanbury, Wyngaarden, & Frederickson, 1960, p. 22)*

discussed in Chapter 4 have, however, been discovered. Depending upon the type and number of the affected cells, some of these cases are on the borderline of normality, whereas others are severely affected.

Cell Division: Meiosis The production of the germ cells or gametes (the ova and the sperm) involves a special sort of cell division known as *meiosis.* In studies of heredity, this process is actually of greater interest than the much more frequent process of mitosis, since it is during meiosis that gametes are formed which determine the precise genetic inheritance to be passed on to the next generation.

A special process is needed to produce gametes which have only twenty-three chromosomes rather than the forty-six contained by the daughter cells resulting from mitosis. During meiosis, first there is duplication of chromosomes, and then these divide. This division is quickly followed by a second one without prior duplication, during which the chromosomes are divided in number to half their original total. Only one member of each pair ends up in the gamete. When the egg and sperm unite, forming the *zygote,* a full complement of chromosomes is reconstituted in a new combination, of which half was contributed by the mother and half by the father. The process of meiosis is shown in Figure 3-2.

The most important feature of meiosis is the fact that in the process of cell division, chromosomes are reshuffled. In forming the germ cells, the chromosomes of each parent line up in pairs; each pair divides in half but hardly ever into the same two separate sets of chromosomes which were received from the grandparents. As a consequence, combinations of chromosomes appear which are not like those in either of the child's parents. During this process, the chromosomes are wound tightly around one another, and at this time equivalent parts sometimes break off and are reattached symmetrically to the homologous chromosome. This means that the new germ cell may receive part of a single chromosome which originated from the grandmother and part of the same chromosome which came from the grandfather. This routinely occurring phenomenon is known as *crossing-over.* The full complement of forty-six chromo-

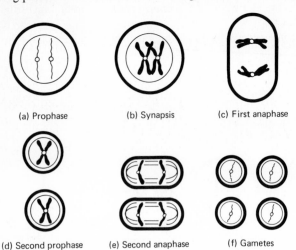

(a) Prophase   (b) Synapsis   (c) First anaphase

(d) Second prophase   (e) Second anaphase   (f) Gametes

Fig. 3-2 Meiosis. Only a single pair of chromosomes is shown. *(From Stanbury, Wyngaarden, & Frederickson, 1960, p. 23)*

somes in the zygote is thus a special mixture which is composed of genetic material contributed from each parent in about equal proportions.

It sometimes happens during meiosis that the chromosomes do not divide into exactly equivalent halves. There are two principal ways in which such an error occurs. First, the replicated chromosomes may not separate as they are supposed to. Remember that each chromosome, prior to the metaphase in the first phase of meiosis, has replicated itself, with the daughter attached to the mother chromosome at the centromere. If, following metaphase, the two for some reason do not separate, they will migrate together to the same pole and thence to the same daughter cell. This phenomenon, known as *nondisjunction,* accounts for most instances of the known chromosomal aberrations, in which extra chromosomes are present in the body cells. Prominent among these syndromes is Down's syndrome, in which there is a trisomy (triplet) of autosomal chromosome number 21. The trisomy usually results from the union of a normal sperm with an egg which bears a double dose of chromosome number 21, although in some instances it may be the sperm which is responsible. The tendency for nondisjunction to occur during meiosis increases markedly in older mothers. (See Chapter 4.)

The second way in which cell division may be unequal is *translocation,* in which one chromosome attaches itself to another. In itself, this fusion does not produce any abnormality, but if the homologous partner of one or the other of the fused chromosomes cannot subsequently align itself correctly during the middle phase of meiosis, it may end up in the wrong daughter cell. If it migrates in error to the same daughter cell as its translocated partner, that cell will have an overdose of one chromosome. This is the case in a much less common form of Down's syndrome, in which chromosome number 21 has become fused, for example, with chromosome number 14. During meiosis, if the free chromosome number 21 migrates in error to the same cell as its fused partner, a double dose of chromosome number 21 occurs, and then trisomy results after a normal fertilization of this abnormal gamete. In most instances, the daughter cell which has too few chromosomes cannot survive. If it is a Y chromosome (male sex chromosome) which is missing, however, Turner's syndrome may result.

Modes of Genetic Transmission

Even before the recent burst of research on cell biochemistry, much was known about the action and transmission of genes from observations of the inheritance patterns of innumerable characteristics. There are a number of rather different ways in which the genes influence behavior. Many specific genes produce distinctive syndromes of mental retardation in which there is an identifiable metabolic defect or a defective structural pattern. Other genes apparently exert only minor effects on intelligence, though these effects may become very significant in combination with many other genes which also affect intelligence, for good or ill. Still other genes influence other aspects of human behavior.[3]

Dominant Genes   A dominant gene determines certain characteristics of the individual no matter what the nature of its homologous gene. It "dominates" its partner. Most of the normal genes involved in patterning the enzymes are dominant. One innocuous dominant gene causes a streak or patch of white hair to occur on the head.

---

[3] For further information about genetics and behavior, the reader may consult Ehrman, Omenn, and Caspari (1972) or McClearn and DeFries (1973).

Dominant genes only rarely cause severe mental retardation. This is true because persons who are severely affected die *in utero* or before they can have children, have impaired fertility, or are too greatly handicapped to marry and have children. Some examples of disorders transmitted by dominant genes are tuberous sclerosis, which may be expressed very slightly in one generation without mental retardation but very severely in another; and Huntington's chorea, which is characterized by progressive mental deterioration but has its onset in middle age after the affected individual may already have had children. Variability in severity of manifestations, delayed age of onset of signs of the disease, and transmission from parent to child are features of autosomal dominant inheritance.

A parent who suffers a defect caused by a dominant gene which is expressed in every affected individual has one chance in two of passing on this characteristic to each of his offspring. A child of such an individual who does not have the defect cannot pass it on since he does not carry the defective dominant gene. It would be possible greatly to reduce the incidence of clear-cut dominant genetic disorders by prohibiting affected individuals from having children. New cases would continue to occur, however, as a result of new mutations in the same gene.

Recessive Genes   Most of the varieties of mental retardation which are attributable to specific hereditary factors belong to the group of conditions caused by recessive genes. A recessive gene is clearly expressed only when there is another recessive gene of its kind at the same locus on the homologous chromosome. Any two genes of precisely the same type at the same locus are said to be a *homozygous pair;* dissimilar matched genes are said to be a *heterozygous pair.*

For purposes of illustration, let us suppose that at a given locus there may appear either a dominant gene *A,* or a recessive gene *a.* When *A* is present in the pair, the possible gene combinations or *genotypes (AA, Aa, aA)* cannot be distinguished, since the characteristic controlled by *a* is not ordinarily detectable. Only when the pair is *aa* will the *a* characteristic be observed. The genotype *Aa* can sometimes be deduced from analysis of the family pedigree, however. If a parent or child of the index case is *aa,* then the index case (having the dominant *A* characteristic or *phenotype*) must be *Aa.* Fortunately, most deleterious genes are recessive. It is entirely possible for individuals in many successive generations of the same family to carry a deleterious recessive gene without showing the characteristics with which it is associated in homozygous form.

The chances of having affected offspring may be calculated in much the same way in which the odds of throwing a given number of heads and tails are calculated if one tosses two coins in the air. All the possible combinations are illustrated in Figure 3-3. It must be emphasized that these chance expectations represent the results of a

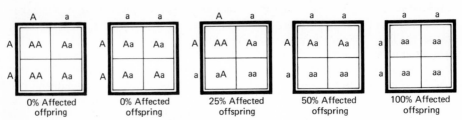

Fig. 3-3   Genotypic combinations possible in offspring of parents with varying combinations of *A* (dominant) and *a* (recessive) genes.

very large number of coin tosses or offspring. Just as it is possible to have two heads turn up several times in a row with still a 75 percent chance of some other combination on the next try, it is possible for a family to have two or three or more children in a row affected with an autosomal recessive disorder, even though the risk on the average is 25 percent for each pregnancy.

Among the thousands of recessive genes, many are innocuous, such as the gene which produces blue eyes and the gene which results in an inability to taste the chemical phenylthiourea, or phenylthiocarbamide (PTC). Among the deleterious recessives are those producing cystic fibrosis and sickle cell anemia, as well as a number to be described in Chapter 4, which produce mental retardation. Practical screening methods are available already to test simultaneously for several genetic disorders essentially all newborns with the few drops of blood obtained in the nursery by heelstick (Guthrie, 1973).

For every person in whom a recessive trait occurs, there are a great many more who carry the gene in a heterozygous pair. For every disorder which occurs with a frequency of about 1 per 1,000 births, there are theoretically about 60 carriers per 1,000 in the nonaffected population; 1 person in 16 is a carrier.[4] For a disorder occurring in 1 child in 10,000, there are theoretically about 200 carriers per 10,000 in the general population; 1 person in 50 carries the gene. For an extremely rare disorder occuring in only 1 in 1 million children, however, there are 2,000 carriers per million population; 1 person in 500 carries the gene (Stern, 1973). Sterilization of affected persons would be only a weak defense against a recessive disorder.

There are, however, a number of deleterious recessives which can be detected in the latent state because the carriers show some slight but recognizable abnormalities in an aspect of body function, body structure, or biochemical response (Raivio & Seegmiller, 1972). For those which can be detected in the carrier (heterozygous) state, premarital examination can be used to discourage the mating of two carriers of the same gene or to prepare for the eventuality of an affected child, as is being done in metropolitan areas for Tay-Sachs disease, which is especially common among Ashkenazic Jewish families (Kaback & O'Brien, 1973). As a greater number of recessives become capable of detection by sophisticated laboratory tests, the process of mate selection would become more complicated for those interested in such information.

Sex-linked Chromosomes   Of the twenty-three pairs of chromosomes in human body cells, twenty-two pairs follow the rules just outlined for the inheritance of dominant and recessive characteristics. These twenty-two pairs are known as *autosomal chromosomes;* their dominant and recessive genes are transmitted to children without regard to the sex of the parent from whom they came.

The twenty-third pair of chromosomes is different. It is this pair which is responsible for the sex of the developing organism. Actually, two types of chromosomes are involved here. One type, which is called the X chromosome, carries a full supply of genes; the other, called the Y chromosome, appears to be almost completely barren of genes but determines whether the child will be male or female. The twenty-third pair of chromosomes in body cells of the human female consists of two X chromosomes (XX); in the male, one of the pair is an X chromosome and the other is a Y chromo-

---

[4] This assumes random mating within the population. Obviously, if there is a tendency for carriers of the same recessive gene to mate, as in consanguineous marriages, these random population frequencies do not apply.

some (XY). Consequently, in the formation of the ova, the mother always contributes an X chromosome to her offspring. Some of the father's sperm, on the other hand, carry an X chromosome and some a Y chromosome. The uniting of the ovum with an X-carrying sperm produces a daughter; the uniting of the ovum with a Y-bearing sperm produces a son.[5]

Because the human female has two X chromosomes, each with a full supply of X-linked genes, inheritance in females follows the rules for dominant and recessive genes previously outlined. In daughters, recessive traits inherited from the mother will be expressed only if the same recessive gene is inherited on the X chromosome contributed by the father. In the body cells of the male, however, there exist genes carried by the X chromosome which have no matching genes in the Y chromosome. In sons, any recessive gene carried by the sex chromosome inherited from the mother will tend to be fully expressed, since there is no counteracting gene on the Y chromosome.

The result of this special situation is that X-linked recessive disorders occur much more often in male children than in female children. Color blindness, hemophilia, and the Duche type of muscular dystrophy are X-linked recessive disorders, and these are many times more frequent in sons than in daughters. For a boy to be color-blind, for example, he need only have inherited one defective gene on the X chromosome he received from his mother. A color-blind girl, however, must have two defective recessive genes, one on each X chromosome. When a mother is color-blind, all her sons will have defective color vision because she has only defective genes to give them; none of her daughters will be color-blind unless her husband is also color-blind. On the other hand, a mother with normal vision may have one defective recessive gene and may pass this gene on to some of her sons. As a result of this genetic "double standard," color-blindness is in fact about sixteen times as frequent in men as in women. (About 8 percent of men are color-blind.) For genes much less common than that for color-blindness, the chance of a female receiving two recessive genes is far smaller and the ratio of affected males to affected females is much larger; essentially all affected persons are males.

There are sex-linked disorders which are due to defective dominant genes carried by the X chromosomes (McKusick, 1971). These are found in both sons and daughters if they are inherited from the mother but only in daughters if they are inherited from the father, since the father does not contribute an X chromosome to his sons. One example is an inherited bone disorder and resulting dwarfism due to resistance to the action of vitamin D.

Polygenic Inheritance   Dominant and recessive genes each can exert major control over the characteristics which depend upon them, such as eye color and the specific genetic syndromes of mental retardation to be discussed in Chapter 4. These are termed single-gene or Mendelian traits, because the pattern of inheritance fits the straightforward rules for transmission of a single dominant or recessive gene from parent to child. (See Figure 3-3.) Although their action may be somewhat modified by other genetic factors or by environmental conditions, these genes may be said to determine either the presence or the absence of characteristics.

Most human traits, however, cannot be characterized as either present or absent. They vary continuously over a range, with a few people on either extreme and the bulk

---

[5] See Chapter 4 for a discussion of abnormalities which result from unusual numbers of X and Y chromosomes.

of the population somewhere in the middle. This is the case, for example, with height, weight, and intelligence. Since it is known that the individual genes themselves do act on a unitary, either-or basis, a genetic theory is needed to take into account the continuous distribution of these human traits and yet retain the unitary action of individual gene pairs. Such a theory is the multiple-factor hypothesis, or the concept of *polygenic inheritance.* According to this theory, the genes are acknowledged to occur in discrete pairs, but combinations of numerous pairs are thought to bear upon the same characteristic. The genes involved in such polygenic combinations are very elusive because their effects are simply small increments which cumulatively influence a trait such as intelligence (Shields, 1973), skin pigmentation (Stern, 1970), or fingerprint patterns (Holt, 1968). The simple formulas for dominant and recessive genes do not apply to this multifactorial type of inheritance, though this does not imply that the biochemical mechanisms mediating polygenic inheritance are different from those involved in single-gene inheritance.

The distribution of traits predicted by the notion of polygenic inheritance coincides with the familiar bell-shaped, normal curve. When a number of discrete units bear upon the same character, the result is a continuous distribution, just as if one were to toss in the air a large number of coins, each of which could have only one of two outcomes. Most of the time, if one tosses coins, an approximately equal distribution of heads and tails will be obtained, but occasionally a predominance of one or the other will occur by chance. If discrete pairs of genes each contribute slightly to the eventual outcome then, like the coins, they will produce a distribution in which most people fall more or less toward the middle, but some by chance fall toward the extremes because of fortunate or unlucky combinations of genes. Similarly, positive and negative environmental influences also contribute to a normal distribution.

Mutation   Every now and then, new forms of specific genes appear in the offspring of creatures of all kinds. The appearance of such new forms (mutants) is the result of a process called *mutation.* Mutation consists in most instances of a very simple change in the genetic code of the DNA molecule of which the gene is constituted. Compared with the complexity of the code for an enzyme, the change is likely to be very small, consisting of the change of one nucleotide base (one code letter) in the double helix. This substitution in the DNA sequence is translated into a substitution in the amino acid sequence of an enzyme protein coded for by that gene. Mutations may result in enzyme changes which range from very minor ones, such as a slight alteration in the immunological reaction of the enzyme, to a complete inactivation of the enzyme and a block in the metabolic process for which that enzyme is responsible.

The difficulties involved in studying mutations in human beings are vast. For that reason, most of what we know about mutation comes from work with plants and lower animals. We know so far that most mutants are recessive. Some of them are harmful to the organism; many others appear to be neutral. Those which have major effects tend to be very rare among the species because they impair the ability of the organism to survive. Occasionally, however, a superior gene arises through mutation. Such mutations, rare as they are, provide one of the most important bases of natural selection and evolution. The rate of spontaneous mutation varies from gene to gene, but has been estimated at approximately one mutation per 100,000 genes per generation (Stern, 1973).

Because of spontaneous mutation, the hope for a population entirely free of harmful genes seems to be nothing but an illusion. On the contrary, there exists the serious possibility that man may increase the rate of mutation quite significantly by the effects of his own technological discoveries. Radiation of the germ plasm in the ovaries or testes of the parents prior to conception is a powerful method of increasing the rate of production of all mutants, yet because most mutants are recessive, their existence will not be apparent until carriers of identical mutants mate with each other. The full effects of the exposure to nuclear fallout, to which living creatures all over the world have already been subjected, will not become apparent for several generations. Even greater concern has been generated from recent findings that many ubiquitous chemicals and food additives in the human environment may be mutagenic (Omenn & Motulsky, 1974a).

Genotype and Phenotype

From the moment of conception, genes are in constant interaction with a multitude of environmental forces. To help us think clearly about this process of interaction, the Danish geneticist W. L. Johansen (1912) proposed that we distinguish between the *genotype* of an organism and its *phenotype*. The genotype is the genetic constitution which the individual receives from his parents. The phenotype is the appearance of the individual at any given time and consists of all his or her characteristics, both gross and microscopic, including size, weight, skin color, sex, chemical composition, and behavior.

Although the phenotype of an individual depends in large part on his or her genotype, it is dependent as well upon his or her particular set of environmental circumstances. For example, a particular genotype probably determines the strength of the tendency toward freckled skin, but exposure to sunlight is likewise required for phenotypic expression of this tendency. There is evidence of an inherited susceptibility to epilepsy, but in many cases brain damage is an additional necessary and precipitating cause of seizures. (See Chapter 6.) An inherited susceptibility to schizophrenia (Kaplan, 1972) may be greatly influenced by qualities in the individual's upbringing, including the stresses to which he is subjected.

The phenotype of an individual changes with time, as can be illustrated by a series of photographs of the same person at different ages. As a matter of fact, because of subtle physiological changes, the phenotype is never exactly the same from one instant to the next. The genotype of an individual, on the other hand, is usually perfectly stable during his or her life span because its constituents, the genes, except for mutations reproduce themselves faithfully throughout life.

Penetrance and Expressivity   Even though defective genes may be dominant or present in homozygous pairs, this does not guarantee that an affected individual will manifest the attendant symptoms. Research as yet has told us little about the factors which determine the degree of *penetrance,* that is, the frequency with which the pathological gene pair produces a clinically recognizable abnormality. The effects of some gene pairs appear in diagnosable form in each affected individual despite differences in environment and despite other genetic factors that may be present. These genes are said to be "clear-cut" or to show "100 percent penetrance." Others appear in almost every individual who carries them; they are said to show "high penetrance." Still others require unusual combinations of genetic and environmental forces before they can occur in recognizable form; such genes are said to show "low penetrance."

Whether a gene is judged to be penetrant depends very much upon the criteria for diagnosis of the inherited condition. As diagnostic tests become more sensitive, a higher percentage of gene carriers is found to have evidence of the condition. In a very few but important instances, the penetrance of a gene has been deliberately reduced by prevention of the environmental conditions necessary for its appearance. The most destructive effects of phenylketonuria have been averted, for example, by feeding children a low-phenylalanine diet, thereby decreasing intake of the substance which cannot be metabolized correctly and whose by-products eventually damage the brain.

Variable expressivity refers to the fact that some genes or gene combinations produce different symptoms and different degrees of defect in different individuals. Thus, the gene responsible for neurofibromatosis is dominant, but in one individual it may be expressed very mildly as a coffee-colored patch of skin, whereas in another it may be expressed strongly with intracranial tumors, severe mental retardation, and seizures. (See Chapter 4.) There are no doubt many reasons for this variability. It is known, however, that the expression of characteristics determined by major (single) gene pairs may also be controlled by the action of other, minor gene pairs. Thus, the ability to taste the substance PTC is determined by a single recessive gene pair, but sensitivity to the substance in various degrees of dilution has been shown to be modified by minor genes (Stern, 1973, p. 382).

The concepts of penetrance and expressivity have sometimes been criticized because they simply name but do not explain the differing symptom pictures observed. In a sense, then, they represent the limitations of our knowledge and the insensitivity of our diagnostic tools.

Genetic Determination of Susceptibility   Genetic endowment may determine merely an individual's susceptibility to a disorder. For example, resistance to some forms of schizophrenia or to seizures may depend partly on hereditary factors, although these disorders may also require certain kinds of adverse environmental events. Some strains of mice are particularly subject to audiogenic seizures, convulsions elicited by such sounds as jingling keys, whistles, or bells. Selective breeding has demonstrated that this susceptibility is clearly determined by genes, and some differences in neurotransmitter metabolism have been described (Schlesinger & Griek, 1970).

Alternate Forms   Some disorders are of genetic origin in some instances but result from environmental forces in others. The hereditary form of such a disorder is sometimes designated the *primary form*, and the nonhereditary form is called a *phenocopy* (Goldschmidt, 1938; Zwilling, 1955). A prominent example of this phenomenon is microcephaly (pathologically small head), which is occasionally of genetic origin but may also result from other causes such as prenatal radiation, maternal alcoholism, or German measles. (See Chapter 5.) The causes can sometimes but not always be distinguished by clinical examination. F. C. Fraser (1956) demonstrated that cleft palate can be produced in rats through the genetic constitution of both parents or of the mother alone, as well as by cortisone or the drainage of amniotic fluid from the pregnant mother. Different forms of the same hereditary disorder may also be produced by different pairs of genes whose net effect is equivalent. An example is nonendemic familial goitrous cretinism, of which there are at least five types, in which different enzymatic failures produce similar symptom pictures (Stanbury, 1972).

Directness of Genetic Influences on Behavior

Let us now examine some ways in which genetic factors influence intellectual behavior. It will become clear that the effects "represent a whole 'continuum of indirectness,' along which are found all degrees of remoteness of causal links" (Anastasi, 1958, p. 199). Along this continuum are causes which range from the direct genetic determination of the structure of the central nervous system to the other extreme, illustrated by the nebulous and variable operation of social stereotypes related to such genetically influenced factors as race, sex, and physiognomy.

The most direct effects of genetic factors upon intellectual function lie in the determination of the actual anatomical substrate of intelligence. The brains of individuals suffering from genetic disorders such as microcephaly and Down's syndrome are small in size and sometimes have structural abnormalities.

At a second step along the "continuum of indirectness," hereditary factors are responsible for biological conditions which affect the functioning of an otherwise adequate central nervous system. Phenylketonuria and galactosemia both are hereditary metabolic disorders in which injurious waste products cause brain damage and intellectual impairment. (See Chapter 4.) If the buildup of toxic substances is avoided, development proceeds normally. Dietary controls, if instituted early enough, can circumvent the damaging metabolic conditions in these two disorders.

A third point on this continuum is illustrated by disorders such as hereditary deafness and blindness. These might cause intellectual retardation by interfering with the individual's full participation in learning situations. Deafness seriously interferes with language development. Special training and the use of mechanical aids, such as special books, hearing aids, and the like, may partly compensate for inherited deficiencies. Thus the degree of actual handicap may depend as much on the technical and medical care available to the child as on the defect itself.

A fourth step on the continuum is provided by instances in which there is a chronic hereditary condition which does not itself have a direct effect on the learning process. Sex is a characteristic determined by the chromosomes, and the long-recognized differences between males and females in some kinds of problem solving have been cited as proof of the inheritability of differential abilities (Hutt, 1972; Ounsted & Taylor, 1972). These differences may or may not be to some extent inherited, but it is clear that not only an individual's sex per se is related to problem-solving ability, but also his or her sex-role identification. Presumably, sex-role identification is primarily dependent upon learning rather than upon biological factors, but it occurs within the context of maleness and femaleness. To cite another example, epilepsy is a chronic illness which is sometimes inherited. (See Chapter 6.) Occasionally, the frequency or severity of attacks requires that a child be sedated or at least be kept under very close observation. In addition to these restrictions, some children subject to seizures may be excluded from regular classes, not for their own benefit but because of the unrealistic fears of the teacher or the parents. In most instances, inappropriate school placement in conjunction with the debilitating effects of a disease itself probably contributes to intellectual handicaps; in others, a child might conceivably turn to intellectual pursuits to compensate for his handicaps in areas requiring physical participation.

Finally, hereditary influences may be mediated through social stereotypes. An individual's intellectual opportunities in most cultures are influenced by such factors as sex, race, and physique. In the United States, for example, the fact of being black constitutes a distinct intellectual handicap because of pervasive social influences. The elusive factor of motivation for achievement must be considered in this respect; many black children have accepted early the dictum that even one's best effort is not likely to be worthwhile. Yet the development of intelligence is related to striving for achievement and to active and passive modes of adjustment (Sontag, Baker, & Nelson, 1955, 1958).

In conclusion, the less direct the hereditary influences, the wider the range of possible results. At each step of indirectness, the causal chain becomes less rigid and more complicated. The more indirect the effects, the greater the opportunity for interaction with other hereditary factors as well as with environmental factors.

Methods of Study in Genetics[6]

In spite of the importance of the study of the interaction between nature and nurture, definitive studies with human subjects are scarce. Most of the questions which have been raised are ultimately susceptible to objective study, but several serious difficulties deter the designing of satisfactory experiments. First, in studies of human beings it is seldom possible to separate the effects of heredity and environment. Second, animal studies, in which more nearly adequate controls are possible, do not necessarily yield results which are applicable to human subjects. Third, all studies of heredity require the measurement of the characteristic under consideration. It is relatively easy to measure aspects of bodily functioning and structure, but the measurement of psychological characteristics is much more difficult. The most practically useful psychological measures have been intelligence tests, and a large proportion of psychological-genetic research consequently has been done in this area.

Animal Studies   Most of the truly experimental studies in genetics have been performed with subhuman species. Many laboratory animals and insects breed rapidly and produce relatively large numbers of offspring. Thus, it is possible in the laboratory to manipulate genetic factors and the environments in which the animals are raised.

There are well-known behavioral differences between breeds of domestic animals, some being more independent than others, some more amenable to teaching, some more excitable, and so on (Fuller & Scott, 1954). In the laboratory, it is possible with careful selection to create and inbreed strains of animals which are contrastingly high or low for a given trait or pattern of behavior. Two strains which are selectively bred become more and more dissimilar over successive generations until each of them is homogeneous for the selected characteristic. Tryon (1940) and Heron (1941) used this method to demonstrate that maze-learning ability in rats is to a large extent determined by the inheritance of a number of characteristics. Tryon's animals which were adept at maze learning tended to utilize spatial cues rather than visual ones (Krechevsky, 1933) and were more emotional than the less adept maze-dull rats, but they were actually inferior to the maze-dull rats in a few other learning tasks (Searle, 1949). The maze-bright animals had a higher level of cholinesterase activity in the brain (Krech, Rosenzweig, & Bennett, 1956). Cholinesterase determines the rate of breakdown of acetylcholine, which is involved in neural transmission. Other early studies of rats found that selective breeding for a very few generations can produce high-activity versus low-activity animals (Rundquist, 1933), emotional versus nonemotional animals (Broadhurst, 1958; Hall, 1938), and aggressive versus nonaggressive animals (Scott,

---

[6] Comprehensive descriptions of methodology in human genetics may be found in Ehrman, Omenn, and Caspari (1972), McClearn and DeFries (1973), Rosenthal (1970), and Vandenberg (1965).

1942).[7] This type of study tends to lend weight to the hypothesis that such psychological variables as learning ability or general intellectual aptitude may be determined in large part by genetic endowment.

Biochemistry and Physiology   A wide variety of techniques for the study of genetics has been developed in the physical and biological sciences (Harris, 1970). Examples of recent developments are mass-screening techniques for testing a large number of biochemical substances with a single analysis, techniques for increasing the rate of mutation, and biochemical tools for the detailed study of metabolism. Carriers of a heterozygous gene pair for some deleterious recessive genes have been detected. With electron microscopes, cell components have been visualized in great detail. Normal human variation for such inherited factors as blood type has been analyzed for correlation with many human diseases (Vogel, 1970a). Further work is being accomplished in the study of the biochemical composition and action of the genes themselves, with exciting implications for prevention and treatment.

Epidemiology   Epidemiology, the study of the distribution of specific traits and disorders in large populations, is an important tool in the identification of inheritable characteristics. Large-scale reliable registers are one way to record data on rather stable populations. Registries in Denmark for mental illness, for example, have provided the material for pioneering studies on schizophrenia in biological and adoptive relatives (Rosenthal & Kety, 1968; Kety, Rosenthal, Wender, & Schulsinger, 1971). A few limited registries exist in the United States, but they are severely hampered by the mobility of the population and by the minimal nature of the requirements for private physicians to report disease and disability.

Studies of communities in which inbreeding is common may bring to light the characteristics of recessive genes which happen to be present in a particular isolated population (Rogers & Merrill, 1919). The fact that such communities also tend to be homogeneous in environment clouds the issue. The mere fact that a disease occurs in isolated clans is not, of course, proof that it is genetic in character.[8] Epidemiological approaches are so far most useful in studying disorders which depend upon a single gene of high penetrance and expressivity. It is expected that as these studies can be enlarged in scope, their sensitivity to more subtle variations will increase.

Analysis of Pedigrees   Instead of utilizing a sample of the general population, it is often informative to start with an affected individual (*proband* or *index case*) and to trace the incidence of the disorder or trait in his ancestors, siblings, and children. Sir Francis Galton (1869) developed pedigree analysis in his studies of the families of very eminent men. (See Chapter 1.) An ambitious study of this type traced the descendents of the grandparents of 289 mentally retarded residents of a state institution, encompassing seven generations and more than 80,000 persons (Reed & Reed, 1965).

---

[7] For reviews of more recent research, see McClearn and DeFries (1973).

[8] Forty years later, a follow-up of all descendents of one of the isolated, intellectually limited families studied by Rogers and Merrill revealed a decided improvement in intellectual and social adequacy. All members of the family had moved away from the miserable, impoverished settlement, and most had integrated into the larger society. A large percentage of their descendents were intellectually normal (Reed & Phillips, 1959).

The chances of delineating hereditary disorders are maximized if the investigation begins with families in which there is more than one defective sibling. Starting with an institutional population of 3,000 cases, one group of investigators found sixty-one families with more than one retarded sibling in the institution. Ten of these families had identifiable hereditary disorders (Wright, Tarjan, & Eyer, 1959). Phenylketonuria was first identified in two affected brothers (Fölling, 1934), and the genetic etiology of Down's syndrome began to be understood when the incidence of families with more than one such child was found slightly to exceed that expected by chance (Penrose, 1954).

This sort of analysis is unfortunately subject to serious limitations. Beyond two or at the most three generations, it is seldom possible to obtain reliable descriptions or diagnoses of family members. In disorders with low penetrance, recognition may be obscured by the fact that the disorder does not appear in every family member with an abnormal genotype. In disorders with variable expressivity, the quite different symptom pictures, some of them very mild, will cause some affected cases to be overlooked. Moreover, disorders resulting from recessive genes may not appear in any relatives of the affected child, especially if he has few siblings or if the disease which he has survived can produce a high proportion of fetal deaths. Even more serious is the fact that, here again, environmental factors tend to go hand in hand with hereditary factors. The child of physically or intellectually disabled parents is much more likely than the child of physically and intellectually superior parents to be raised in an environment characterized by poor care and little motivation for achievement.

Twin Studies   A popular approach is the study of identical (monozygotic) twins, who are a product of the splitting of the same fertilized egg (zygote). Identical twins have usually been compared with fraternal (dizygotic) twins of the same sex. These comparisons are called twin studies; when other family members are included, the more precise term is twin-family studies.

Studies of identical twins take advantage of the unique opportunity of comparing two individuals with known identity of gene potential. The closer resemblance of identical than fraternal twins has been thoroughly established with respect to many traits and factors of intelligence.[9] With simple characteristics such as eye color or blood groups, which are relatively impervious to environmental effects, the twin method is unassailable. For traits determined by a complex of different underlying factors, interpretation is complicated. Kallmann, the researcher perhaps most prominently identified with this method, conducted numerous twin studies of psychoses and mental retardation. For example, Allen and Kallmann (1955) investigated all twins reported as retarded by institutions and clinics under the supervision of the New York State Department of Mental Hygiene from 1937 to 1953. Of the 201 same-sex twin pairs (mixed monozygotic and dizygotic), both members of 96 pairs (48 percent) showed *concordance;* both were institutionalized for mental retardation, almost always in the same diagnostic category. On the other hand, of the 131 pairs of opposite-sex (all dizygotic) twins, only 17 (13 percent) showed concordance.

Significant differences between accurately diagnosed one-egg and two-egg twins in this type of study tend to indicate that genetic factors are operating. A lack of such difference would strongly suggest the absence of such factors. The twin-study method,

---

[9] For a thorough discussion of twin resemblances and differences, see Vandenberg (1965, 1972).

however, is not as straightforward as it would seem on the surface. There are several possible sources of error.

1 Twins differ from the general population in many important dimensions. For example, they are never only children, they have constant companionship, and they are usually somewhat retarded in language presumably because of their preoccupation with each other (Day, 1932; Mittler, 1970a). Twins tend to be born after shorter gestations, to weigh less at birth, and to have older parents (Penrose, 1961). Several studies (e.g., Record, McKeown, & Edwards, 1970) have found lower intelligence-test scores in twins than in the general population.

2 Sampling errors are possible when, for example, the researcher seeks the incidence of twinship in an institutional population. Concordant twins and identical twins are likely more frequently brought to his or her attention than discordant or dissimilar twins. There may also be a tendency to attribute concordance for a given trait more frequently to twins than to unrelated persons because of similarity of appearance and experience.

3 It is unreasonable to attribute the same degree of similarity to the environments of identical and fraternal (even same-sex) twins. The similarity of intrauterine prenatal life is unpredictable for both types of twins, since one or two amniotic sacs and variable circulatory supply may be associated with identical twins. The similarity of the postnatal environment of identical twins is enhanced. Compared with fraternal twins, they spend more time together and tend to share the same friends, to wear the same clothes, and so on (Woodworth, 1941).

4 The psychological relationship between twins operates in complex ways to affect concordance rates. On the one hand, the similarity may be decreased if, in the search for individual identity, one of the twin pair is identified as "weaker" or "more stupid" when actually very little difference exists. On the other hand, identical twins and nonidentical twin sisters frequently share ideas so closely that they hold to the same delusional systems (D. D. Jackson, 1960). The hospitalization of one twin may place undue strain on the other, leading him to adopt the same symptoms in an unconscious attempt to be reunited with his sibling.

We should, however, remind the reader that it would be foolish to "throw the baby out with the bath water." Despite the complexities of environmental influence, the presence of greater concordance for any trait in monozygotic twins should establish that genetic factors are at least predisposing for that trait. If concordance rates in identical twins are no greater than those in fraternal twins, we may discard with relative safety the hypothesis that the traits under examination are inherited.

An important dimension has been added to twin analyses with emphasis on monozygotic twins reared apart (Shields, 1962). As discussed below, this method offers a means of assessing the extent to which environmental separation and environmental differences can introduce discordance between genetically identical twin individuals. Again, objections have been raised that separation did not always occur at birth or that the separate homes were not as different as random homes might be; nevertheless, the fact that identical twins maintain nearly as high concordance rates for indices of certain traits, particularly IQ (see Jensen, 1970b), whether reared together or reared apart, speaks strongly for important genetic factors.

Correlational Studies   Correlational methods have been applied to the analysis of family resemblances since the time of Karl Pearson (1904), who developed the correlation coefficient.[10] Intelligence-test scores have received particular attention. A genetic component in a trait should be revealed by higher correlations between individuals who are more closely related than those who are more distantly related (ignoring for the moment the greater environmental similarity which usually accompanies closer family relationships). Correlations between identical twins should be extremely high, but correlations between fraternal twins should be no higher than those between other siblings in a (hypothetical) perfectly measured inherited trait which is relatively impervious to environmental effects. For such a trait, correlations between adopted children and their adoptive parents should be no higher than between strangers (if brighter children are not placed with brighter parents, etc.), but there should be substantial correlations between the children and their biological parents. This method has been used to assess the inheritance of intelligence in twin studies and in studies of foster children.

The difficulty with this approach, as with the others, of course, is that environmental factors can neither be randomized nor held constant. The environment of twins is more nearly similar than that of their siblings, foster children do tend to be placed according to some notion of their potential development, and so on. Although correlation coefficients in the range of .50 are found routinely between the test scores of parents and children and between those of children and their siblings, this does not necessarily represent the genetic component. Indeed, the correlational method reveals in almost every instance the significant association of environmental forces and intellectual performance.

The Inheritance of Intelligence

Several approaches to the study of genetics have readily yielded circumstantial evidence that intelligence in human beings is at least strongly affected by genetic inheritance. Animal studies, for example, have shown in lower species that special kinds of learning ability depend in part upon genetic factors; in fact, enzymatic differences between "bright" and "dull" animals have been claimed (Krech et al., 1956). Studies of families by means of pedigree analysis and twin-family studies have yielded information which suggests strongly that inheritance may be the single most important factor determining tested intelligence in present Western society.

There are probably few theorists today who would not readily agree with the notion that intelligence (whatever their definition or classification of intelligence) depends at least in part upon genetic inheritance. The only subject of contention among theorists would be the relative weight attributed to genetic factors. Perhaps it would be wise to reiterate at this point the obvious fact that the relative contributions of heredity and environment are intimately related to their relative range of variability. Within a specific strain of laboratory animals which have been inbred over many generations, genetic variations tend to be much less important than in outbred strains. On the other hand, in societies which tend to minimize class differences, in which everyone has, for example, baby vitamins, good public schooling, health care, and television, environmental differences tend to be reduced. Whatever the results of research, therefore, we

---

[10] A correlation coefficient is a statistical term which expresses the degree to which two variables are related to each other.

must be cognizant of the cultural context in which they were gathered.[11] It is our conviction that in present-day America, at least within the middle class, genetic factors are probably the major single source of variation in intelligence. There remain, however, tremendously important variables, especially those related to the social class and ethnic structure of the country, which exert a powerful influence from the moment of conception.

The potent interaction of factors in determining children's intelligence is nowhere better illustrated than in a series of famous studies of adopted children. In 1928, there appeared two studies with somewhat similar findings but with radically different conclusions. One, which concerned mainly pairs of siblings who had been adopted into different homes, was interpreted by its authors (Freeman, Holzinger, & Mitchell, at the University of Chicago) as emphasizing the importance of environmental factors. In contrast, the author of the other study (Burks, at Stanford University) was led to conclude on the basis of studies of adopted children and their adoptive parents versus control children and their own parents: "The total contribution of heredity . . . is probably not far from 75 or 80 per cent" (p. 308).

Other studies of adoptive children have also tended to support an interactive interpretation. Leahy (1935) conducted one of the most carefully controlled of this group of studies. All children had been placed in their adoptive homes at the age of six months or younger, were five to fourteen years old at the time of the study, and met certain other criteria. A control group of children and their own parents was carefully selected to match the adoptive group. Correlations, corrected for attenuation, between the IQs of adopted children and the mean of their adoptive parents' IQs were only .21 (Otis test) and .29 (Stanford-Binet vocabulary). For the control children, on the other hand, comparable correlations were .60 and .56, respectively.

In 1949, Skodak and Skeels published the results of a longitudinal study of 100 adopted children. Although they had originally been greatly impressed with the importance of environmental factors (Skodak, 1939), their conclusions at the close of the study were rather moderate. The research, which began as a service project, was not as rigorously controlled as the authors would have wished. The children were placed before they were six months old and were tested at least four times over a ten-year period. Their mean scores at different testings ranged from 107 to 117. This range was 21 to 31 points higher than that of the sixty-three true mothers of the children, whose average IQ had been 86 when they were tested soon after each had decided to release her baby for adoption. The foster homes were above average for the community, as is typical of such homes, their superiority probably accounting for the high scores of the children in relation to those of their own mothers. It is quite possible that the mothers' IQs were not representative of their usual level of ability, since they were tested during a very stressful interlude, or that at least some of them were brain damaged rather than having genetically conditioned low IQs. The children's scores were negligibly related to their foster parents' education, but as the years went by, they became progressively more closely related to the original test scores of their true mothers. The correlations for the sixty-three mother-child pairs reached a level of .44 by the final testing. Unless there had been much greater selective placement than was apparent from the investigators' report, an environmentalist would find it difficult to explain the

---

[11] R. B. Cattell (1960), among others, has presented correlational formulas which can approximate the relative contributions of heredity and environment under a given set of cultural conditions.

increasing correspondence between the scores of the children and their true mothers, whom they had not seen since the early weeks of life.

Twin studies have also yielded convincing evidence of the importance of the genetic component in intelligence. Identical twins reared together consistently obtain IQ correlations approaching or exceeding .90, whereas those of fraternal twins tend to be between .50 and .60. Four studies which have compared the IQs of identical twins separated early in life and reared in separate homes reveal considerably greater similarity in IQ than that shown by fraternal twins reared together. Correlations for the identical twins reared apart ranged from .77 to .87, while those of the fraternal twins reared together varied from .51 to .63 (Jensen, 1970b; Shields, 1973).

An elegant mathematical-biometrical analysis of investigations related to intelligence has been performed by Jinks and Fulker (1970). Intelligence is surely not an entirely unitary trait (Vandenberg, 1968; see also Chapter 1). A twin who is more intelligent than his co-twin as judged by total IQ score does not necessarily do better on all subtests, and this variation is more the case with dizygotic than monozygotic pairs. The Jinks and Fulker analysis, applied to several sets of data, provides estimates of heritability between 71 percent and 86 percent; i.e., 71 to 86 percent of the observed variance in IQ was attributed to genetic factors in the samples studied. Sir Cyril Burt (1958), analyzing his own data with simpler methods, estimated that the variance was distributed as 70 percent polygenic and dominance genetic components, 18 percent for assortative mating (also a genetic effect), 7 percent for environmental variation, and 5 percent for unreliability of measurement.[12]

In summary, the literature of the past fifty years reveals considerable consistency in the accumulated data relating intelligence to the degree of genetic relationship. The closer the blood relationship, the closer the correspondence in mental functioning. One oft-cited review of fifty-two genetic studies from eight countries (Erlenmeyer-Kimling & Jarvik, 1963) yielded the median correlations listed in Table 3-1. These correspond to differing degrees of relationship and differing similarities in environment. Although the studies varied considerably in results, rigorousness of scientific methodology, and bias of the investigators, a comparison of all the available studies lends considerable weight to the notion that genetic factors play an important role in the determination of intelligence.

In the late 1960s and early 1970s, the issue of the genetic component in the variance of IQ became deeply embroiled in the racial turmoil of the times. Jensen (1969a) published, in the *Harvard Educational Review,* a lengthy paper dealing with the broad area of compensatory education and the heritability of IQ. Vitriolic rebuttals (e.g., Lewontin, 1970) soon appeared, charging that Jensen's claim of high heritability for IQ was excessive and that the difference between measured IQ distributions for whites and for blacks must be due to social-racial factors, not genetic factors. Two respected geneticists (Bodmer & Cavalli-Sforza, 1970) argued that research on this topic should not be performed, because of the overwhelming difficulties in separating environmental and inherited factors and because of the inflammatory nature of the studies.

It must be admitted that, on the tests administered, blacks (with up to 30 percent admixture of genes from white intermarriage) give a distribution of IQ scores about

---

[12] One should note that several major studies of the heritability of IQ, the Burt studies in particular, have been severely criticized by Kamin (1974).

Table 3-1   Median Correlation Coefficients for Intelligence-Test Scores

Category	Median coefficient	Number of groups studied
One-egg twins:		
Reared together	.87	14
Reared apart	.75	4
Two-egg twins:		
Like sex	.53	11
Opposite sex	.53	9
Siblings:		
Reared together	.49	35
Reared apart	.40	2
Parent-child	.50	12
Fosterparent-child	.20	3
Unrelated persons:		
Reared together	.23	5
Reared apart	-.01	4

Source: Compiled from Erlenmeyer-Kimling and Jarvik (1963, p. 1478). More than two-thirds of the coefficients were derived from IQs; the rest, from special tests.

one standard deviation, or 15 IQ points, lower than the distribution of scores for whites in the same region of the country. In both groups, IQs vary with socioeconomic status, age, and geographical location. Head Start programs and other types of compensatory educational opportunities have failed to produce very startling or sustained enhancement of IQ in disadvantaged groups, despite earlier high hopes for the programs (Bronfenbrenner, 1974). Yet it should be noted that the gains of white and black children in these programs have not been discriminably different.

None of the analyses of factors possibly contributing to the differences between racial groups has been able to account sufficiently for these persistent discrepancies. Among the factors studied have been the effects of language deprivation, malnutrition, prenatal and perinatal disadvantages, poor motivation, and so on. Yet it must be emphasized that the position of blacks in American society is peculiarly beset with social complications. The cumulative effects of discrimination in addition to problems in the areas of employment, education, health, cultural and social differences, no doubt combine to produce qualitative differences among groups which cannot be statistically estimated.

Jensen (1970c) has argued that the difference between IQ scores of whites and blacks must be due to genetic differences, since such a substantial portion of the variance within the white groups and probably within the black groups tested can be attributed to genetic factors. However, a careful mathematical analysis of this issue by DeFries (1972) demonstrates that *between-group* heritability simply cannot be derived unambiguously from *within-group* heritabilities; on this theoretical basis, Jensen's claim cannot be proved or rejected. One attempt to assess the between-group effects was a report by Willerman, Naylor, and Myrianthopoulos (1970) examining IQs of the offspring of interracial matings, but the data were too scanty to generate useful conclusions.

More general, and basically more important, than the interracial issues are the differences which occur as a function of socioeconomic status. (See Scarr-Salapatek, 1971, and Chapters 7 and 8.) Herrnstein (1971, 1973) popularized a widely articulated view that in a society with increasing evidence of a meritocracy, those with greater ability will achieve more and those with lesser ability may decline from their inherited status. His simple syllogism went as follows: *If* IQ is influenced to a significant extent by genetic factors, and *if* scholastic achievement is correlated significantly with IQ, and *if* later financial and social status is correlated with scholastic achievement, *then,* in an open society, individuals of higher IQ should do increasingly well and those of lower IQ, increasingly badly. Assortative mating accentuates such trends. To the extent that such considerations may reflect social reality, our society must become more generous and humane in recognizing all sorts of human abilities and rewarding people for a broad range of contributions to the common good.

Summary

To summarize this chapter briefly, we have reviewed the mechanisms by which deleterious genetic inheritance may be implicated in the etiology of mental retardation, both directly and indirectly, and we have discussed a number of ways in which the inheritance of intelligence has been investigated. There is powerful evidence that, indeed, mental retardation does result both from polygenic factors and from single-gene or single-chromosome sources. At the same time, a genuinely interactionist view is dictated by our increasing understanding of this area. The greater our knowledge of genetic structure and function, the more sensitive we become to the effects of environmental factors in causing genetic errors (e.g., radiation, chemical mutagens, maternal aging) and in affecting the expression of genetically determined biochemical functions (e.g., dietary control). We become more cognizant, at the same time, of the more nebulous but no less powerful effects of psychosocial, economic, educational, and health experiences which determine the eventual intellectual competence of the individual. Thus, the greater our understanding of the precise nature of genetic heritage, the greater our opportunities for intervention and thereby for prevention of intellectual handicap.

4
Genetic Syndromes in Mental Retardation

We have called attention in Chapter 3 to a consensus among geneticists that intelligence as a trait or complex of traits depends for the most part upon polygenic modes of inheritance in constant interaction with a multiplicity of environmental factors. Within the normal population, no single gene pair or chromosomal pattern can be said to determine intelligence, since it is only the joint influence of many genes, some positive and some negative in their effects, which constitutes the contribution of genetic factors to the nature-nurture interaction.

As the reader will recall from Chapter 2, polygenic modes of inheritance are fully consistent with a normal distribution of intelligence, and most cases of mild mental retardation can be accommodated within that normal distribution. The number of individuals with more marked intellectual handicap, however, far exceeds the number predicted on a statistical basis. Of the excess cases, one of the most important causes is a striking genetic defect. The presence or absence of a single chromosome, the loss or gain of part of a chromosome, or a defect in a single gene or gene pair makes it virtually impossible for the affected individual to develop normally. Most of these abnormalities are individually rare, but, when they occur, their effects are often severe. Researchers are rapidly discovering new genetic syndromes (clusters of symptoms due to a given genetically determined etiologic condition). It is unlikely that the total of identifiable syndromes will ever account for a major proportion of the mildly retarded

This chapter was written with the collaboration of Gilbert S. Omenn.

population, but their relative frequency among the severely and profoundly retarded is much higher. By far the majority of profoundly retarded children are impaired not because of their polygenic inheritance and psychosocial environment but because of overriding damage by some single catastrophe in their genetic makeup or in their environment.

Several of these syndromes, including Down's syndrome and a number of other chromosomal anomalies, are associated with malfunctions in very early prenatal growth and morphogenesis (organ differentiation) which adversely affect the development of the central nervous system, the skeleton, the heart, the skin, and other organs of the body. In other genetic disorders such as phenylketonuria, the central nervous system is damaged as a result of improper metabolism of particular chemicals after birth, when the infant must function without the aid of the mother's metabolic, excretory, and hormonal systems. In still other instances, there appears to be no simple one-to-one correspondence, genetic factors instead making the individual more vulnerable to certain kinds of dangers in the environment. Such, for example, seems to be the case in some convulsive disorders, in which hereditary factors seem to make affected individuals especially likely to respond to trauma or stress with seizures. (See Chapter 6.)

With the advent of amniocentesis and prenatal genetic diagnosis, the recognition of specific entities for which chromosomal or biochemical abnormalities can be tested during pregnancy has acquired great importance (Bergsma & Motulsky, 1971; Epstein, Schneider, Conte, & Friedman, 1972; Nadler & Gerbie, 1970; Omenn & Motulsky, 1974b). The technique of amniocentesis will be described in connection with Down's syndrome.

SYNDROMES DUE TO CHROMOSOMAL ABERRATIONS

Down's Syndrome (Trisomy 21)[1]

By far the single most common chromosomal cause of moderate to severe mental retardation is Down's syndrome, formerly often called "mongolism." At least 10 percent of children with this degree of retardation exhibit Down's syndrome, now known to result from an extra copy of the number 21 chromosome, hence "trisomy 21." One in every 660 births in the general population is an affected child, although the risk is considerably higher if the couple already has had an affected child, or if the mother is thirty-five or older.

As early as 1866, this syndrome was distinguished by the English physician Langdon Down, who drew attention to the physical features shared by these retarded children. Too much has been made of the epicanthal folds at the corners of the eyes and of the supposed "slanting eyes" associated with the term "mongoloid child." Even among Chinese children, the characteristics of Down's syndrome are not masked by the racial featues (Tsuang & Lin, 1964). Because resemblance to Mongoloid peoples is slight and because the term carries negative connotations to many people, the older term has generally been discarded in favor of the term "Down's syndrome."

The Chromosomal Abnormality Down's syndrome is caused by a genetic imbalance, the presence of an extra set of genes of the number 21 chromosome. The

---

[1] An excellent summary of the chromosomal makeup, physical findings, and behavioral development of these individuals is available in a sympathetic presentation for parents and others concerned with the education and care of children with Down's syndrome (Smith & Wilson, 1973).

finding that Down's syndrome was associated with an extra chromosome opened a vast area of cytogenetic research. Until 1956, the number of chromosomes in normal human cells was thought to be forty-eight; in that year, Tjio and Levan applied new techniques that separated the chromosomes sufficiently to count them precisely and to show that the normal number is forty-six. Shortly after, several groups, led by Lejeune in Paris, discovered the characteristic aberration of trisomy 21 in Down's syndrome children (Lejeune, Gautier, & Turpin, 1959).

Normally, of course, the autosomal chromosomes occur in pairs, one each from the mother and from the father. In Down's syndrome, there is a third 21 chromosome. In 90 percent of cases, this occurs as a result of faulty chromosomal distribution in the formation of the egg or sperm (meiosis). This failure of separation of the pair of twenty-one chromosomes in the formation of the egg or sperm occurs before fertilization. The karyotype of chromosomes in this type of Down's syndrome, called trisomy 21, is shown in Figure 4-1. The process of nondisjunction for the 21 chromosome is diagramed schematically in Figure 4-2. The probability of nondisjunction rises markedly with the age of the mother. Mikkelsen and Stene (1970) show the risk of Down's syndrome rising from one in 1,500 under age thirty years to one in 65 above age forty-five. After age thirty, the likelihood approximately doubles for each successive five-year period. (See Figure 4-3.) Higher estimates come from data of Lindsjö (1974) in

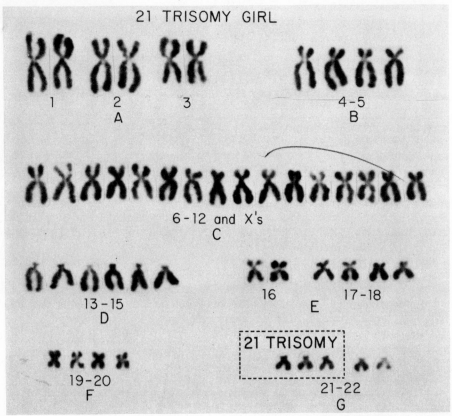

Fig. 4-1 Chromosomes of a girl with Down's syndrome, trisomy 21. *(From Smith & Wilson, 1973, p. 6)*

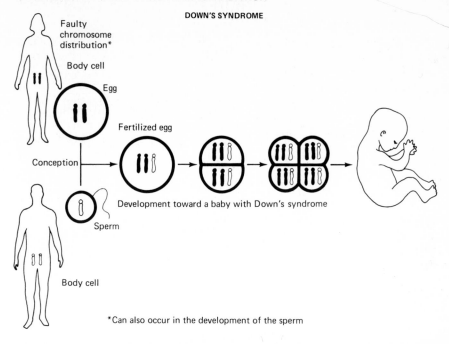

Fig. 4-2 Faulty chromosome distribution to the egg or sperm can lead to trisomy 21 in the fertilized egg. *(From Smith & Wilson, 1973, p. 9)*

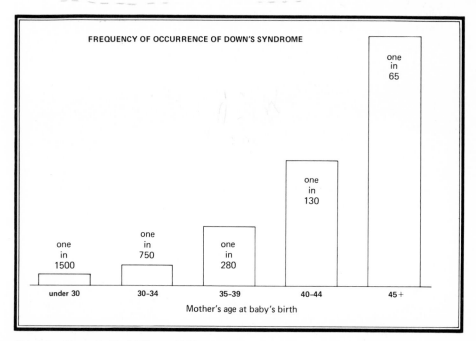

Fig. 4-3 *(From Smith & Wilson, 1973, p. 17)*

Sweden, who found an overall incidence of one in 755, with 1/1133 for ages twenty-five to twenty-nine, 1/687 for ages thirty to thirty-four, 1/267 for thirty-five to thirty-nine, 1/67 for forty to forty-four, and 1/16 for women over forty-five. Approximately half of all children born with Down's syndrome are born to mothers thirty-five years of age or older. As fewer women now have children after the age of thirty-five, the incidence of Down's syndrome has begun to decline (Penrose, 1967; Richards, 1967).

One factor which has been identified as predisposing to maternal nondisjunction in the formation of the egg is autoimmunity (Fialkow, 1967). Younger mothers, particularly, have a higher incidence of antibodies against their own tissue (thyroid tissue in the test system) if they have borne children with Down's syndrome, compared with mothers of control children. It is possible that antibodies directed against the spindle apparatus for meiotic separation of chromosomes also occur in these women (Fialkow, 1969).

It is important to note that faults in chromosome distribution are not rare. At least 4 or 5 percent of recognizable pregnancies (surely a higher percentage of conceptions) begin with an unbalanced chromosome set. The vast majority of these pregnancies end in miscarriages, because most genetic imbalances do not allow for the continued development of the growing embryo. For every case in which the egg or sperm receives two of a chromosome pair during meiosis, the counterpart cell receives none of that pair, producing monosomy (single chromosome) should that egg or sperm be normally fertilized. Essentially no cases of well-documented monosomy for any of the twenty-two autosomes have survived to birth; in fact, monosomies produce lethality so early that they are rarely encountered even in early spontaneous miscarriages. On the other hand, one-half of all embryos lost by spontaneous miscarriage have an excessive number of chromosomes, usually trisomy for an autosomal chromosome or sometimes *triploidy,* or three of each set, totaling sixty-nine chromosomes. The bigger the chromosome, the bigger the imbalance, and the earlier the miscarriage. Trisomy 21, in fact, involves the smallest autosome.

Two other less frequent types of chromosomal abnormality each contribute at most 4 or 5 percent of Down's syndrome cases: *mosaicism* and *translocation.* Mosaicism results when faulty chromosomal distribution occurs after fertilization in the second (or third) division of the newly developing embryo. When the very first cell division includes nondisjunction of chromosome 21, one new cell receives 21 trisomy and the other receives 21 monosomy. The cell with 21 monosomy dies out, leaving the embryo to develop from the 21 trisomy cell, just as though the error had occurred in the ovum or sperm. When nondisjunction occurs at the second division, however, two of the cells have forty-six chromosomes and are normal, but one has forty-seven and the other forty-five. After the monosomic cell dies out, the embryo has a mixture of normal and trisomy 21 cells. These mosaic individuals tend to have less striking physical signs and less severe mental retardation. The degree of mixture of normal cells detected by testing the skin or blood may not, however, be a reliable indication of the proportion of normal and trisomic cells in the brain, gonads, or other tissues.

The other infrequent type of Down's syndrome, the translocation type, is very important, because it carries a potential for a much higher risk of recurrence in future siblings of the affected child. A translocation means that all or part of one chromosome has become attached to all or part of another chromosome. Often the chromosomes involved are the 13–15 group and the 21–22 group, chromosomes which are termed acrocentric, since their centromeric constriction is near the end of the chromosome rather than near the middle. This process is diagramed in Figure 4-4. Such a

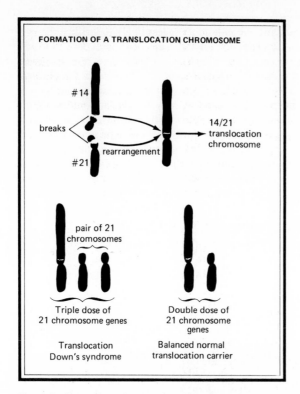

FORMATION OF A TRANSLOCATION CHROMOSOME

#14

breaks

rearrangement

#21

14/21
translocation
chromosome

pair of 21
chromosomes

Triple dose of
21 chromosome genes

Translocation
Down's syndrome

Double dose of
21 chromosome
genes

Balanced normal
translocation carrier

Fig. 4-4 Formation of a translocation chromosome by breakage and rejoining of the major parts of two chromosomes into a single "translocation" chromosome (with the loss of the tiny broken pieces). *(From Smith & Wilson, 1973, p. 14)*

translocation chromosome may be composed of a number 14 plus a number 21 chromosome. With a pair of normal 21 chromosomes and the translocation chromosome, the individual carries three full sets of the 21 chromosome and has typical Down's syndrome. This type of Down's syndrome can be identified only by chromosomal studies. Its importance lies in the fact that, in about a third of translocation cases, one of the parents is a genetically balanced carrier of the same translocation chromosome.[2] The parent is normal physically and mentally but has only forty-five chromosomes, since the translocation chromosome is the equivalent of two normal chromosomes. In the development of an egg or sperm during meiosis in the translocation carrier parent, the translocation chromosome may be distributed to a cell along with the normal number 21 chromosome, so that the resulting egg or sperm has two sets of number 21 chromosome genes. After fertilization, the embryo will then have three sets of the number 21 chromosome genes, but a total of only forty-six chromosomes. The risk of a balanced carrier parent having a child with Down's syndrome varies with the type of translocation. In the more common type, exemplified by the 14/21 combination, Down's syndrome children will result in about 15 percent of pregnancies when the mother is the carrier, but only about 5 percent of pregnancies when the father is the

[2] In the remainder of translocation cases, the error occurs in the formation of the egg or sperm or in the first cell division after conception, as a fresh occurrence.

carrier. Presumably, the sperm carrying the imbalance is less likely to fertilize the egg. Although the theoretical risk for transmission of the translocation type of Down's syndrome is 33 percent, actual observations of at-risk families have revealed these much lower figures. There is a rare type of translocation involving both the 21 chromosomes (21/21) in which all viable offspring will have Down's syndrome.

Many physicians have felt that a chromosome study was necessary only when the diagnosis was in doubt, or for younger parents. Now that chromosomal analysis is readily available to most hospitals, chromosome analysis should be encouraged for genetic counseling in all cases of Down's syndrome, especially when additional children are planned. Phenotypically normal siblings of children with Down's syndrome need worry about their own children only in the case of an inherited translocation type in the affected sibling; otherwise the risks are the same as for the general population.

Prenatal Detection   It is now possible to obtain amniotic fluid from the sac surrounding the fetus at fourteen to fifteen weeks of pregnancy and to perform certain tests on the cells present in the fluid. The cells are of fetal origin, sloughed from the skin or the respiratory or urinary tracts. In this technique, known as *amniocentesis,* the fluid is obtained by inserting a needle through the pregnant woman's abdominal and uterine walls into the amniotic fluid sac, and a cell culture is grown in the laboratory. In the case of Down's syndrome, such a chromosomal analysis can provide certain information as to whether the fetus has trisomy 21 (or translocation type of Down's syndrome). The laboratory studies require about three weeks, so that the couple must wait until seventeen or eighteen weeks of pregnancy for the results. Should the analysis indicate Down's syndrome, the parents may then choose to terminate the pregnancy. There is no way, of course, that one or a few specific tests can rule out all the myriad errors possible in the amazingly complex process of human development. Thus, it is not possible by this means to reassure the parents that the baby will be "normal," but only that it will not have Down's syndrome or another disease for which a specific test was performed.

To prevent all cases of Down's syndrome, it would be necessary to perform amniocentesis and chromosome studies in all pregnancies. At the present time, however, the possible risks to the mother and to the fetus have not been clarified sufficiently to warrant amniocentesis as a routine procedure, nor are there sufficient facilities. Therefore, the procedure is now recommended for pregnancies in which a parent is known to be a blanced translocation carrier for the 21 chromosome, in which the couple has had one or more children with Down's syndrome, or in which the mother is over forty or perhaps thirty-eight years of age.

Physical Features   Trisomy 21 affects many aspects of physical development, with both serious and trivial consequences. An experienced physician or nurse can usually recognize the features of Down's syndrome in the newborn, even though the baby's appearance may not seem unusual to the parents. The number of diagnostic signs varies from one case to another and as a function of age, but the overall physical appearance is strikingly similar (Penrose, 1934; Smith & Wilson, 1973).[3] Neither the number nor type of physical stigmata is apparently related to IQ (Domino & New-

---

[3] Smith and Wilson (1973) have provided an excellent set of photographs of persons with Down's syndrome, some of which are reprinted as Figs. 4-5, 4-6, 18-1, and 20-1.

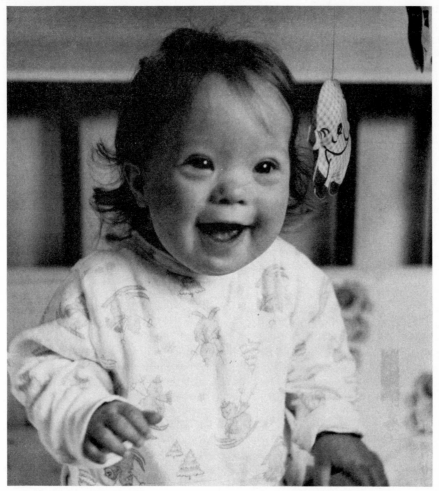

Fig. 4-5 This pretty baby has the small nose, the folds in the corners of the eyes, and the flat profile typical of Down's syndrome. *(From Smith & Wilson, 1973, p. 51)*

man, 1965). Thus, it is impossible to estimate, by examining a baby, the degree of intellectual deficit he is likely to show later.

Fortunately, many of the typical physical abnormalities do not affect the child's health in any major way and are of importance primarily as aids in diagnosis. Some of them have more serious consequences, however. The most serious effect is the diminished brain development in every child. In perhaps 40 percent of the children, there is also an important defect in the development of the heart. In a few children, there is blockage of the upper intestinal tract or gross malfunctioning of the lower large bowel. Approximately 1 percent of Down's syndrome children develop leukemia. The following is a list of other physical abnormalities associated with this syndrome.

1 Muscle tone: Hypotonicity, which improves with age, makes the babies "floppy" and loose-jointed, with prominent abdomens.

2 Skull: The back of the head (occiput) is flat, and soft spots (fontanels) may be large, closing later than usual. Head circumference or skull size is small, and sinuses are underdeveloped.

3 Nose: The nose is small and the bridge somewhat low on account of under-development of the nasal bones of the skull. From a profile angle, the face appears flat.

4 Eyes: Eyes tend to slant upward (slanting palpebral fissures), with small folds of skin at the inside corners (inner epicanthal folds). These folds, which occur also among normal babies, tend to become less prominent later in childhood, often disappearing by age ten or twelve. The outer border of the iris may be speckled with lightly colored spots ("Brushfield spots"), which are especially noticeable in blue-eyed babies. Fine opacities of the lens, refractive errors, and crossed eyes (strabismus) are common.

5 Ears: Ears are usually small, especially the lobes. The top rim of the ear lobe (the helix) may be folded over slightly.

6 Mouth: Although the tongue is of normal size, the mouth may be relatively small and the roof short. Together with poor muscle tone, this situation makes the baby's tongue protrude intermittently. In older children, a furrowed tongue develops. Mouth breathing, chapped lips, and increased susceptibility to upper respiratory infections result.

7 Teeth: Eruption of the teeth is delayed, and the teeth may be small, abnormally shaped, and abnormally positioned. One or more may be missing. Even with good dental hygiene, these children suffer inflammation and recession of the gums, with later loss of teeth.

8 Voice and speech: Voice may have a deep quality; onset of speech is delayed; learning to talk articulately is difficult.

9 Neck: The neck is short and broad, with loose skin at the sides and in the back. The loose folds become less prominent with time.

10 Hands: Hands are often small and square, with relatively short fingers. The fifth finger is especially short and tends to curve inward and to have only one crease instead of the usual two. There may be only a single crease across the palm instead of two. Fingerprints are characterized by ulnar loops rather than the usual whorls and by a displaced axial triradius configuration.

11 Feet: There is increased space between the first and second toes, with a short crease running up between them on the sole of the foot.

12 Skin: The skin may have a mottled appearance and dryness, with a tendency to chap.

13 Hair: Hair is usually sparse, fine, and straight, including the pubic hair.

14 Height: The individual is somewhat shorter than average and is stocky in build because arms and legs are short in relation to the trunk. Birthlength is usually within the normal range, and growth to age four is only slightly behind the average. After this, the rate of growth tends to fall farther below the normal range with each successive year. Average final height for men is about five feet and for women, about four feet seven inches. Today children with Down's syndrome grow larger than in the past, presumably because of better nutrition and fewer serious infections.

15 Weight: Birthweight is usually within the normal range but low. Mild to moderate obesity often develops in late childhood or adulthood, requiring some supervision of eating habits.

16 General health: About 20 to 30 percent of babies do not survive the first few years. However, if the child survives without serious complications affecting the heart or intestine, or producing leukemia or infections, the prospect for survival to middle age is quite good.

17 Adolescent and sexual development: Sexual development may be delayed or incomplete or both. Genitalia and secondary sex characteristics are underdeveloped in most cases. There is a spurt in height at adolescence, however, and menstruation usually begins at the average age and follows a normal course. Affected persons rarely marry and their libido is said to be diminished. Only a few affected women have reproduced; as expected, about half their offspring have had Down's syndrome. Males are apparently infertile.

18 Aging: The aging process tends to occur early, including dryness and coarsening of the skin and recession of the gums with loss of teeth. As in other individuals of the same IQ level, the relative mortality is high after age forty, but the causes of death tend to be the same as those which affect the normal aging population. An interesting histopathological sign of early aging has been noted in the brains of adults with Down's syndrome. The typical changes associated with Alzheimer's disease or presenile dementia—senile plaques, neurofibrillary tangles, and granulovacuolar changes in cortical and other brain cells—have been present in all brains so examined from patients over age thirty-five (Olson & Shaw, 1969; Solitaire & Lamarche, 1966; Struwe, 1929). Patients with other types of mental retardation lack similar early changes in the brain.

Intellectual and Social Characteristics Down's syndrome children do not usually appear very abnormal at first in mental (sensorimotor) development, although they may appear "floppy" and the physical stigmata are recognizable at birth. The typical developmental course of such children exhibits a relative decline during the first year or two of life, followed by a slower decline in developmental quotient to age three or four, and then a relative leveling off (Cowie, 1970; Cornwell & Birch, 1969; Dicks-Mireaux, 1972; Lodge & Kleinfeld, 1973; Zeaman & House, 1962). The modal IQs of school-age Down's syndrome children living at home are in the moderately retarded range (40–54), with a few in the mildly retarded range and a few severely retarded. Of children living in an institution, the majority tend to have IQs below 35 (Lodge & Kleinfeld, 1973). The brains and therefore the skulls of Down's syndrome children are abnormally small; because of their shorter stature, this fact may not be immediately apparent to the casual observer. At age fifteen, Down's syndrome children have, on the average, a head size of a normal child of only age two and one-half. No specific structural brain abnormalities have been identified (Olson & Shaw, 1969; Solitare & Lamarche, 1966, 1967).

Aside from overall deficits in intellectual competence, there is often evidence in Down's syndrome children of limitations in higher-level integrative abilities, such as concept formation, abstraction, and expressive language (Cornwell, 1974). Abstract and complex uses of language are particularly likely to be deficient (Lyle, 1960). Miranda and Fantz (1973) were able to demonstrate an immaturity in visual-attentional responses in affected infants as early as age eight months. Among the perceptual channels, Belmont (1971) concludes that tactile perception is particularly weak in these children, although auditory perception and auditory-vocal integration are also

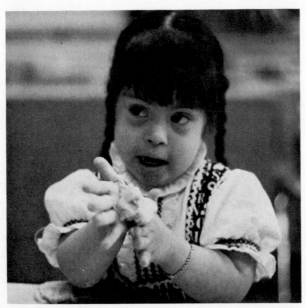

Fig. 4-6 This Down's syndrome preschooler is making cookies. *(From Smith & Wilson, 1973, p. 61)*

areas of relative weakness. Even taking into account the low mental ages of Down's syndrome children, one finds that they are particularly deficient (as a group) at abstract and conceptual processes, perhaps related in part to faulty perceptual input. As we shall see in Chapter 11, perceptual difficulties in brain-damaged children have been indicted (though not unequivocally demonstrated) as a central aspect of conceptual and learning disabilities.

When one examines less complex types of learning, such as rote skills (Cornwell, 1974), concrete language usage (Lenneberg, Nichols, & Rosenberger, 1962; Lyle, 1960), and visual-motor behaviors (Belmont, 1971), the discrepancies with other children of the same mental level are not marked. Because one's social development at this competence level depends less upon abstract or integrative abilities and more on the acquisition of practical, everyday skills, the social adaptation of Down's syndrome children tends to be somewhat less retarded than their cognitive development would lead one to expect (Centerwall & Centerwall, 1960; Cornwell & Birch, 1969; Johnson & Abelson, 1969). Indeed, the adult with Down's syndrome, given supervision, practice, and encouragement, may well be capable of valued and productive work such as running a tractor, doing housework, or performing simple carpentry.

It would, however, be a serious error to conclude that Down's syndrome children show little variability among themselves. Quite the opposite is the case. Their IQs vary widely, from profound to mild levels of retardation, and there is considerable variation in the ages at which they attain developmental milestones. In keeping with the decline in IQ during the early years, one finds that retardation in tasks usually achieved very early is less than in those normally attained later, but there is a much wider range than in any group of normal children. Figure 4-7 illustrates the dramatic spread in some

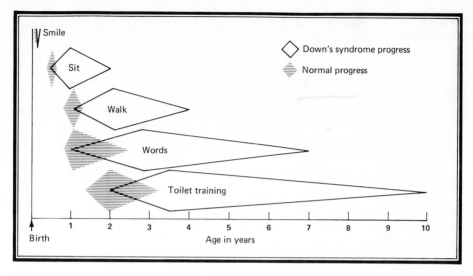

Fig. 4-7 Early development of Down's syndrome children living at home compared to that of normal children. The widest point in each diamond represents the average age of attainment and the spread of the diamonds represents the range. *(From Smith & Wilson, 1973, p. 37)*

attainments. It is clear that the mere diagnosis of Down's syndrome says little about the rate of development of a particular child.

Personality Characteristics   Many Down's syndrome children have a special reputation for being happier, more friendly, and more easily managed than other retarded children, although they are also reputed to be capable of unusual stubbornness. Consider, for example, this description: "Mongoloid children, if treated well, are lovable little creatures full of affection and tenderness. . . . They come up and put their arms around the stranger as confidently as a puppy jumping up on a visitor, and though not understanding a word said to them, good-naturedly answer yes to any question, hoping that will please (Benda, 1946, p. 61).[4]

Reviewing the empirical evidence bearing on this stereotype, Belmont (1971) concluded that as a group, Down's syndrome individuals do show fewer instances of severe disturbance and that they "seem to find themselves in a somewhat more pleasant or promising condition than do other retarded children" (p. 45). As he is careful to point out, however, this finding does not necessarily support Benda's "happy puppy" stereotype or what Menolascino (1965b) has referred to as the "Prince Charming" stereotype. Belmont's review cites both confirmatory and contradictory evidence. There is far from a uniformity of personality among these individuals, and even in studies such as one by Domino, Goldschmid, and Kaplan (1964) which found many Down's syndrome children in an institution to be affectionate, content, friendly, and relaxed individuals, the various retarded groups they studied overlapped to a considerable extent.

Environmental Effects   Because Down's syndrome can be diagnosed at birth, professionals (especially physicians) once thought it kinder for parents and children if

[4] By permission from Benda, C. E. *Mongolism and cretinism.* New York: Grune & Stratton, 1946.

the child was institutionalized without ever becoming a true member of a family. The expectation that the child would be severely or profoundly retarded thus became a self-fulfilling prophecy. It was not until the 1960s that it was realized how handicapping the experience of growing up in an institution had proved to be for these children. (See Chaps. 20 and 21.)

The quality of parenting in the home is also apparently related to developmental competence. Gibson (1967) found that after eleven years or more of home care prior to institutionalization, there was a substantial relationship between parental education and child's IQ. To what degree this finding expresses "nature," "nurture," or their interaction is, of course, unknown. Two rather remarkable diaries (Hunt, 1967; Seagoe, 1964) of young men with Down's syndrome who had been brought up in devoted, stimulating families also suggest that superb parenting may produce unusual results, although it cannot eradicate the mental handicap entirely.

Witnessing the substantial decline in the rate of intellectual development in very young Down's syndrome children, a number of investigators have attempted to prevent this deterioration. Biochemical and dietary manipulation to correct for a low level of serotonin, a neurotransmitter found in tests of blood platelets, has not been successful in improving behavioral indices (Coleman, 1973; Weise, Koch, Shaw, & Rosenfeld, 1974). A number of stimulation efforts with Down's syndrome children living at home have been inaugurated, but thus far, firm results are lacking as to their effectiveness. A program of sensorimotor stimulation by parents (Zausmer, Pueschel, & Shea, 1972; Zausmer, personal communication) and a long-term group infant stimulation and preschool program (Hayden & Dmitriev, 1974) both report informal evidence of some modification of the typical early downward course of developmental rate, but as yet it is impossible to evaluate the degree to which they have been successful. With a group of Down's syndrome children placed before age four and one-half months in an above-average institutional setting, a preschool program and intensive verbal stimulation were shown by Bayley, Rhodes, Gooch, and Marcus (1971) to produce development at age eight equivalent to that of a preschool group living at home (IQs of both groups approximately 40), although earlier the children in the institution had fallen behind the controls.

It is clear that Down's syndrome children, like other children, within the limits set by their biological potential are responsive to opportunities for intellectual development, social competence, and healthy personality growth. Although the limitations are real, their extent has not been sufficiently tested. Intensive stimulation, beginning very early and continuing throughout the growing years, appears at this point to be the most promising line of attack. Nevertheless, expectations that such efforts can fully overcome the effects of the chromosomal aberration are unrealistic.

Other Aberrations of Autosomal Chromosomes[5]

Developmental abnormalities usually, if not always, result from the addition of part or all of an autosome to the normal karyotype. Trisomies of the larger chromosomes are unusual at birth, although they are frequently found in spontaneous miscarriages. Individuals may, however, carry extra chromosomal material other than full trisomies.

---

[5] Descriptions of chromosome aberrations associated with mental retardation with excellent photographs of the somatic abnormalities may be found in Bergsma (1973), Gellis and Feingold (1969), and Smith (1970). Pediatric and genetic journals currently carry numerous reports of discoveries of rare syndromes resulting from abnormalities of chromosomes and genes.

Occasionally, for example, children are found to be mosaic for cells with the normal forty-six chromosomes and for cells with trisomy, particularly of number 8, for which a characteristic clinical syndrome has recently been delineated (Bijlsma, Wijffels, & Tegelaers, 1972; Sanchez & Junis, 1974). Autosomal aberrations need not, on the other hand, involve a full chromosome. There may be translocation of part of one chromosome onto another in unaffected parents or in a newly fertilized egg producing a partial trisomy. Now that chromosome-banding techniques permit differentiation of each chromosome, one can expect a series of publications of mosaic and partial trisomy cases. The severity of defect in mosaic cases is related to the proportion of cells bearing the abnormal karyotype, whereas in partial trisomies it is roughly related to the amount of extra chromatin.

In addition to trisomy 21, there are two other commonly encountered trisomies of autosomal chromosomes, trisomy 18 and trisomy 13. Discovery of these disorders followed promptly the recognition of trisomy 21 in children with Down's syndrome, as researchers grasped the possibility that chromosomal aberrations might be associated with distinctive syndromes.

Trisomy 18   The trisomy 18 syndrome (Edwards, Harndon, Cameron, Cross, & Wolff, 1960; Smith, Patau, Therman, & Inhorn, 1962) is the second most common multiple malformation syndrome, with an incidence of 1 per 3,000 newborns. The true frequency of this syndrome is higher, since most trisomy 18 fetuses die before birth. The newborns are usually feeble and may require resuscitation. Even with optimal management, they fail to thrive and only 10 percent survive a full year; the survivors are severely mentally retarded (Weber, 1967). More than 130 different abnormalities have been reported in these children, the most common being feeble fetal activity, low birthweight, weak cry, diminished response to sound, incomplete development of skeletal muscle, abnormally shaped head with malformed and low-set earlobes, small jaw, clenched hand with overlapping fingers, hernias of the abdominal wall, undescended testes in males, and cardiac defects (Smith, 1970; Warkany, Passarge, & Smith, 1966). The parents face an increased risk that any trisomy (especially Down's syndrome) will occur in future pregnancies, with a risk rate similar to that following birth of a child with trisomy 21 (Hecht, Bryant, Gruber, & Townes, 1964).

Trisomy 13   The trisomy 13 syndrome (Patau, Smith, Therman, Inhorn, & Wagner, 1960) occurs in 1 per 5,000 births and includes defects of the eyes, nose, lip, scalp, and forebrain as well as extra fingers (polydactyly), narrow curved fingernails, cardiac defects, and a single umbilical artery (Patau et al., 1960; Smith, 1964; Warkany et al., 1966). The 18 percent who survive the first year exhibit severe mental retardation, seizures, and poor growth (Smith, 1970). Only one adult, age thirty-three, has been reported. A likely case was described as long ago as 1657 (Warburg & Mikkelsen, 1963). As with trisomy 21 and trisomy 18, the parents face a somewhat increased recurrence risk for nondisjunction and future trisomies. The child's karyotype should be examined to rule out the possibility of a translocation pattern which, if inherited from a parent, would carry a much higher risk of recurrence than the straightforward trisomy.

Partial Deletions   Deletion of chromosomal material other than the Y chromosome has even more serious consequences than does the presence of additional chromatin, with the result that deletion of only a chromosomal segment is apparently compatible with life. A number of such syndromes have been recognized in recent years.

Partial deletion of the *long arm of chromosome 18,* for example, is associated with moderate to severe mental retardation, microcephaly, low birthweight, retraction or depression of the mid-facial structures, low-set earlobes with unusually prominent abnormal ridges, unopened ear canals and deafness, cleft lip and palate, and various defects of the heart, urinary tract, and fingerprint pattern (deGrouchy, Royer, Salmon, & Lamy, 1964; Insley, 1967; Lejeune, Berger, Lafourcade, & Réthorné, 1966). Usually these individuals are severely handicapped, with visual and hearing defects as well as mild mental retardation, although one ten-year-old child has been reported who was not severely affected (Wertelecki, Schindler, & Gerald, 1966).

Partial deletion of the *short arm of chromosome 5,* or "cri-du-chat" syndrome, is distinguished by a characteristic high-pitched, catlike cry immediately after birth and during infancy, microcephaly, epicanthal folds and downward slant of the palpebral fissures of the eye, a broad-based widely spread nose, and poor growth (Lejeune, Lafourcade, Berger, Vialatte, Boeswillwald, Seringe, & Turpin, 1963). Mental retardation is severe. The mewing cry, ascribed to abnormal development of the larynx, later vanishes, making the diagnosis very difficult in older patients without chromosomal studies. This deletion appears as a fresh phenomenon in the vast majority of cases, but it may be due to an inherited translocation in a parent with a balanced carrier status (Laurent & Robert, 1966; Lejeune et al., 1963). The extent of abnormality is probably correlated with the extent of deletion, although bands 14 and 15 of the short arm of chromosome 5 are typically deleted (Berger, Touati, Derre, Ortiz, & Martinetti, 1974; Niebuhr, 1972).

Syndromes Due to Aberrations in Sex Chromosomes

In contrast with the severe defects associated with aberrations of the autosomal chromosomes, there is considerably greater flexibility in the complement of sex chromosomes compatible with survival and, indeed, with relatively unaffected mental development. There are no known cases surviving in the absence of any X chromosome, but many persons have been discovered with additional X or Y chromosomes. Variations in the number of X chromosomes were investigated relatively early because of the availability of simple counting techniques. The nuclei of most cells of a normal female contain, at the periphery of the nucleus, a darkly stainable concentration of chromatin (Barr & Bertram, 1949). The cells are said to be chromatin-positive; normal male cells, which have no such concentration, are chromatin-negative. The stained chromatin is called a *Barr body* after its discoverer. The number of Barr bodies in the nucleus is usually one less than the number of X chromosomes. This approach did not identify the number of Y chromosomes, of course. These should still be counted by complete karyotype analyses, even though a screening method for the number of Y chromosomes has been developed. Fluorescent staining of Y chromosome is present, the individual will almost invariably be a male, and without any, the individual will almost invariably be a female (Mittwoch, 1963).

Turner's Syndrome (Gonadal Dysgenesis)   The girl with this syndrome has only one X chromosome and of course no Y chromosome. The cardinal features are short stature (less than five feet in the 45,XO full-blown case),[6] a mere streak of fibrous gonadal tissue in place of each ovary, lack of sexual development, and a variety of anomalies of somatic tissues (Ferguson-Smith, 1965). The full syndrome was described by Turner (1938), though the association between short stature and defective ovarian development had been noted earlier (Rössle, 1922). If problems are first noted in adolescence, the complaint will be lack of sexual development and shortness; if diagnosed at birth, the key findings may include webbing of the neck, swelling of the hands and feet, a broad chest with widely spaced nipples, prominent earlobes, anomalies of the knee and elbow, horseshoe kidney or other renal anomaly, and coarctation of the thoracic aorta. A great range of severity is associated with this chromosomal aberration. In fact, some 95 to 98 percent of 45,XO fetuses fail to survive to birth (Hecht & MacFarlane, 1969), and XO fetuses are one of the most common types of chromosomally abnormal spontaneous abortions, although the lethal mechanism has not been elucidated. Even so, the frequency of XO individuals at birth is 1 in 2,500 females. Occurrence of the syndrome is sporadic in families. The XO karyotype may result from loss of the second sex chromosome at the first mitotic division of the fertilized egg[7] or in the first meiotic division in either parent. The missing chromosome is usually that derived from the father, according to analyses of X chromosomes carrying marker genes (Lindsten, 1963). Thyroid autoimmunity and thyroiditis occur in increased frequency in these patients and in their mothers, as do diabetes mellitus and abnormal glucose tolerance (Forbes & Engel, 1963; Hamilton, Moldawer, & Rosenberg, 1968). There is evidence here, as in Down's syndrome for a relationship between autoimmunity and chromosomal nondisjunction (Fialkow, 1969). Cyclic therapy with female hormones can remedy the lack of sexual development but these women are of course sterile.

Turner's syndrome sheds important light upon the hypothesis that the Barr body represents an inactivated X chromosome (Lyon, 1962). If the second X chromosome were not necessary for normal cell function, women with one X chromosome should be equivalent to women with two. Clearly they are not. Presumably, the second X chromosome is important in many tissues for the first few divisions of the cells until X-inactivation occurs, and in the normal ovary, both X chromosomes remain active (Gartler, Liskay, Campbell, Sparkes, & Gant, 1972; Gartler, Liskay, & Gant, 1973).

Mental retardation is *not* a frequent feature of Turner's syndrome, though some cases are mildly retarded (Haddad & Wilkins, 1959). There are, however, striking cognitive defects in space-form perception, producing a discrepancy between verbal and performance IQs. In a sample of eighteen patients, Alexander, Ehrhardt, & Money (1966) obtained a mean WAIS Verbal IQ of 112, a mean Performance IQ of 88, and a mean Full Scale IQ of 101. The space-form difficulty can be demonstrated in drawings of a human figure and reproductions of geometric designs. The defect involves visuo-constructional recognition and performance rather than visual memory (Alexander et al., 1966). These patients also have trouble mastering maps (Alexander & Money, 1964) and, at a rather practical level, in finding their way into and out of the

---

[6] Genetic background influences height; the tallest XO children have the tallest parents (Lemli & Smith, 1963).

[7] A substantial proportion of girls with Turner's syndrome have either a structurally abnormal second X chromosome or a mosaic combination of XO with XX or XY or even both XX and XXX. The somatic and gonadal abnormalities are usually less severe in the mosaic cases (Ferguson-Smith, 1965).

typical maze of an outpatient department. This fascinating and localized cognitive defect in XO women has stimulated studies of the possibility that X-chromosome genes might be involved in various visual-spatial abilities (Bock & Kolakowski, 1973), but no detailed mechanisms have been discovered.

Klinefelter's Syndrome   In 1942, Klinefelter, Reifenstein, and Albright described a specific form of male hypogonadism with excessive development of the mammary glands. Several investigators in 1956 demonstrated independently that an extra X chromosome is present in this anomaly. True Klinefelter's syndrome cannot be diagnosed symptomatically on the basis of retardation of growth and sexual development, because some 20 to 60 percent of hypogonadal males are chromatin-negative (Rimoin & Schimke, 1971). The chromatin-positive men most commonly are 47,XXY, appearing with a frequency of 1 per 450 male births (Jacobs & Strong, 1959), although in some cases even more X chromosomes, up to XXXXXY, are present.

Subnormal IQs have been reported in 25 to 50 percent of the patients, but severe mental retardation is not a characteristic of this syndrome. Males with more than two X chromosomes have a much higher risk of significant mental retardation than those with only two. No specific cognitive defect has been noted. As preadolescents, these XXY males often are socially inept and are apt to drop out of school and of other activities (Nielsen, 1969; Nielsen, Sørensen, Theilgard, Frøland, & Johnsen, 1969). Nielsen (1970) found that 56 percent of his sixty-one XXY males had a criminal record, particularly involving sexual offenses and arson, although these features probably should be viewed as secondary to the patients' immaturity and lack of sexual development. Nielsen (1969) discovered significantly more insecurity, immaturity, and psychopathology in XXY males than in similarly hypogonadal XY males attending the same infertility clinic in Denmark. The mean IQ for the XXY patients with criminal records (IQ 89.3) was not different from that in XXY patients without such records (IQ 90.9) (Nielsen, 1970). Replacement therapy with testosterone (male sex hormone) produces desirable development of secondary sex characteristics, including greater hair growth, penis enlargement, and deeper voice.

XYY Males   No distinctive syndrome can be attributed to XYY males in the general population. They do, however, tend to be tall and to have a tendency toward severe nodulocystic acne, and many show prolonged P-R intervals and conduction abnormalities on an electrocardiogram. This syndrome has received a great deal of publicity and has been the subject of intense controversy.

At a time when the XYY karyotype was thought to be quite rare (Sandberg, Koepf, Ishihara & Hauschka, 1961), a stunning report cited its presence in 2 percent or more of tall inmates in maximum-security prisons in Scotland (Jacobs, Brunton, Melville, Brittain, & McClement, 1965). Population surveys using the techniques now available for complete karyotype analysis currently indicate an approximate frequency of XYY of 1 in 800 males, and the best estimates suggest that the risk of criminal behavior is elevated only two- to fivefold (Hook, 1973). On the basis of numerous studies, one must now conclude that although both XYY and XXY males are found in enhanced frequencies among imprisoned or retarded populations, fewer than 1 percent of XYY males are to be found in prisons. The vast majority must be among the "normal" population. In the XXY and XYY groups IQs probably average some 10 points below the population mean, even after biases of ascertainment are removed (Baker, Telfer, Richardson, & Clark, 1970; Hook, 1973; Nielsen, 1970).

An influential early paper which furthered the controversy about "criminal tendencies" in XYY males claimed that its nine XYY criminal subjects could be distinguished from eighteen XY counterpart prisoners by lack of broken families and lack of criminal records among their siblings, as well as a tendency to get into trouble earlier and to be less concerned about their criminal behavior. In other words, such individuals appeared to represent chromosomal accidents that made them "black sheep" in otherwise upstanding families. At least four subsequent studies of this sort have *failed* to confirm these findings. The pooled data suggest that XYY males in prisons have family situations similar to those of XY males.

A distinctive personality pattern may, however, tend to characterize XYY individuals. Money (1970) drew a composite image of the first thirty-five reported cases (including thirty in prisons), which stressed a history of being a difficult child of a broken family, with school misbehavior and underachievement despite average intelligence. Money's subjects seemed to be daydreamers, loners, and occupational drifters, with a tendency to impulsive aggression and/or violence but not an aggressive personality. Bisexual or homosexual, they were impulsive in sexual expression without depth or continuance of affection. The validity of this composite portrait is yet to be fully tested; surveys are needed of XYY individuals in the normal population.

A final note about this syndrome involves a French report (Noël, Duport, Revil, Dussuyer, & Quack, 1974) indicating that a double-blind psychological evaluation correctly identified the seven XYY males among thirty-five subjects matched for age, height, socioeconomic status, and education. None of the XYY males had a criminal record; all were discovered in the course of screening conscripts and blood donors. The XYY males appeared to have a lower threshold for expression of aggression in frustrating or provocative situations.

Prospective studies of the effects of sex chromosomal aberrations have been instituted as the result of large-scale surveys of newborns.[8] Of 4,400 consecutive newborns screened in one series, eleven had abnormalities of sex chromosomes, including three XXX, one XO, four XXY, and three XYY (Leonard, Landy, Ruddle, & Lubs, 1974). At ages one to two and one-half years, no clinical features characteristically associated with any of these karyotypes could be detected. The three XYYs, in particular, showed no indications of excessive size or of difficult or aggressive behavior. Compared with a matched group of newborns with normal karyotype, however, these eleven young children had an increasing delay in language development. Using the Revised Yale Developmental Evaluation, their language quotient by age two was only 82 compared with 111 for the controls, whereas the developmental quotients of the two groups were 93 and 106, respectively. The heterogeneity of disorders in even this large prospective study signals the need for collaborative studies using common testing tools.

DISORDERS DUE TO SPECIFIC DOMINANT GENES

Many syndromes, most of them rare and isolated, are inherited in simple Mendelian fashion within families. As we noted in Chapter 3, genes determine body growth and

---

[8] The ethical issues surrounding ascertainment and follow-up of these cases, with or without notification of the parents, have generated a considerable controversy (Culliton, 1974).

function by furnishing the structures of enzymes. In this sense, all genetically deter-mined disorders are metabolic, although in some cases a faulty growth pattern with tumor formation is the primary manifestation.

Autosomal dominant disorders are characterized by vertical transmission from parent to child, by variable expression in different gene carriers, by late onset of symptoms in many cases, and thus far by lack of good evidence of the precise bio-chemical lesions. Often the first case recognized in a family represents a fresh (new) mutation of that gene, rather than transmission from a parent. New mutations are more frequent as the age of the father rises. The number of known dominant disorders associated with mental retardation is much smaller than the number of known reces-sive disorders. A few examples will be described.

Tuberous Sclerosis

In its classic form, this disease is manifested by severe mental retardation, seizures, and a peculiar facial skin condition known as adenoma sebaceum, which is a butterfly-shaped collection of reddish yellow, circumscribed, solid elevations usually on the cheeks alongside the nose. The skin lesion is actually due to small fibrous tumors, and nonmalignant tumors occur in the kidney, retina, and heart as well. Malignant tumors (gliomas) may occur in the supportive tissues of the brain (Lagos & Gomez, 1967). There may be other distinctive abnormalities of the skin, including small patches of coffee-color, underpigmentation, and leathery surface. Diagnosis without a family his-tory can be difficult because mental retardation may be the first abnormality noted, the seizures often not appearing until age three and the facial skin tumors not until age

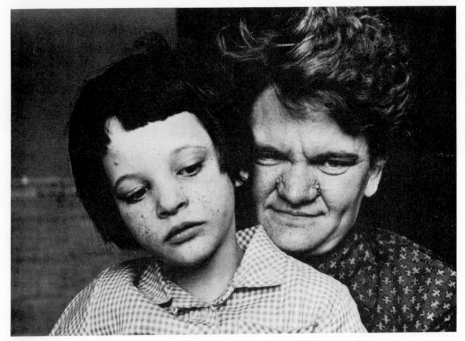

Fig. 4-8 Two unrelated cases of tuberous sclerosis. *(J. & M. Menapace)*

five. As in other dominantly inherited disorders, some family members may be very mildly affected, without any mental retardation. In fact, tuberous sclerosis may be first discovered in adulthood in conjunction with involvement of kidneys, lung, or other internal organs.

Neurofibromatosis

This condition is characterized by light-brown patches on the skin, the color of milky coffee (café-au-lait spots), and by tumors on the nerves and in the skin. These tumors vary from small dots to grotesque overgrowths. The presence of at least six spots, each more than 1.5 centimeters in diameter, is usually necessary for the diagnosis, since some normal people have one or a few spots. Freckling in the armpits is also highly suggestive of neurofibromatosis (Crowe, 1964). Mental retardation and epilepsy occur in approximately 10 percent of cases, possibly because of tumors within the brain. The diagnostic criteria and variation in manifestations have been described by Crowe, Schull, and Neel (1956). The disorder occurs in one in 3,000 people.

Sturge-Weber Syndrome (Cerebral Angiomatosis)

Affected children have a port-wine colored growth (nevus) formed of blood vessels on the face, usually in the area of distribution of the trigeminal nerve on the cheek or forehead. Similar vascular malformations within the meninges covering the brain can give rise to the mental retardation and seizures. After age two, intracranial calcifications can be demonstrated by skull x-rays. No definite pattern of inheritance is known, though this disorder is classified clinically together with tuberous sclerosis and neurofibromatosis.

Myotonic Dystrophy

This remarkable autosomal dominant disorder of muscle and many other tissues is clearly systemic. It is manifested by cataracts, testicular atrophy, frontal baldness, exaggerated insulin responses to carbohydrates, enhanced degradation of antibodies, myotonia (tonic muscle spasms), and muscle wasting (Bundey, Carter, & Soothill, 1970). There is often considerable behavioral abnormality in adults, and a small proportion are mentally retarded. A number of young affected children have recently been recognized as neonates or before age five, with hypotonicity, breathing difficulties, and failure to thrive. In nearly every case, the young child had received the dominant gene for this disorder from an affected mother, suggesting that the combination of the abnormal gene and the abnormal prenatal environment provided by the mother is necessary for very early onset (Harper & Dyken, 1972). Prenatal prediction of the presence of this disease is feasible (Schrott, Karp, & Omenn, 1973).

Familial Cranial Anomalies: Apert's Syndrome

This condition is characterized by acrocephaly, which consists of a tower- or steeple-shaped skull with a high, narrow forehead and a dome-shaped vertex. The eyes are prominent, widely set in shallow orbits, and slanting downward toward the outside, with a small nose, webbing or union of fingers or toes, and sometimes other skeletal deformities. Early closure of the coronal and other sutures of the skull can lead to increased intracranial pressure and possible damage to the growing brain. Intellectual functioning ranges from normal in some cases to severe mental retardation (Blank,

1960; Smith, 1970). An autosomal dominant gene is responsible, but the first case in a family is almost always due to a new mutation. Average paternal age is thirty-seven years, consistent with the finding that advanced paternal age is associated with higher risk of new mutations (Smith, 1970).

Pseudohypoparathyroidism (Albright's Hereditary Osteodystrophy)

Defects in parathyroid hormone function, whatever the cause, can result in lesions in both the central and peripheral nervous systems. The most common symptoms are short stature, round facial appearance, stubby hands, tetany and convulsions from hypocalcemia, cerebral calcification, cataracts, cerebral accumulation of fluid, psychotic behavior, and mental retardation. Hypoparathyroidism due to defective production or secretion of parathyroid hormone is usually not genetic in origin, but pseudohypoparathyroidism is the result of a rare X-linked dominant genetic defect which makes kidneys and bone relatively insensitive to the action of the parathyroid hormone (Mann, Alterman, & Hills, 1962; Potts, 1972). This disorder can appear as "pseudo-pseudohypoparathyroidism" in relatives or in the same patient at a different time, with similar symptoms but with normal calcium and phosphate levels in the blood.

DISORDERS DUE TO SPECIFIC RECESSIVE GENES

Autosomal recessive disorders often occur within sibships, affecting an average of one in four of the children. The parents, heterozygous carriers of the deficient gene, are phenotypically normal but produce only half the normal level of the relevant enzyme. (See Chapter 3.) The number of specific metabolic disorders for which biochemical lesions have been identified continues to multiply, and many of these are now detectable in amniotic fluid cells, permitting monitoring of pregnancies known to be at high risk. Many of the children are undamaged during gestation, since their mothers have the necessary enzymes. Prompt intervention is therefore potentially possible in some of these diseases, provided that the condition can be readily identified and that preventive means are available.

Disorders of Carbohydrate Metabolism

Galactosemia   Galactose is formed when lactose, the primary sugar in milk, is cleaved into its two constituents, galactose and glucose. Galactose must be converted to glucose-1-phosphate in order to enter the energy-generating pathways of the cell. The newborn infant who cannot properly metabolize galactose rapidly develops life-threatening symptoms on a milk diet, with jaundice, vomiting, cataracts, malnutrition, and potentially fatal susceptibility to infection. The damage in this disease results from the toxicity of galactose and its alcohol derivative, galactitol, on the lens, brain, liver, and other tissues (Kalckar, Kinoshita, & Donnell, 1973). Early removal of milk from the diet has been known for a long time to result in the disappearance of symptoms (Mason & Turner, 1935). Elimination of lactose-containing foods must be fastidious. How long such dietary restriction is essential is unknown, though by school age all but obvious milk products may be allowed.

Long-term evaluation of the treatment approach is rather difficult, given the rarity of the disease. Kalckar et al. (1973) have summarized the results from three major centers, Chicago, Los Angeles, and Manchester (England). The general health of treated children has been good, but approximately 30 percent have been below the tenth percentile for height and weight. Intellectual development of these children also appears to be good, but somewhat lower than their unaffected siblings. In the Los Angeles data, thirty-nine treated children had IQs of 43 to 147, with a mean of 94. The mean IQ of their parents was 109 and that of their carrier and normal siblings, 101. The Chicago group obtained a mean IQ of 91 for affected children and 110 for unaffected siblings (Nadler, Inouye, & Hsia, 1969). To demonstrate the importance of immediate treatment, the Los Angeles group (Kalckar et al., 1973) compared the ten pairs of galactosemic siblings they encountered. The mean IQ for the older siblings (who had been identified after the appearance of symptoms) was 91, whereas the younger siblings, who had been identified promptly, had a mean of 102. Unfortunately, the school achievement of these treated children has not been as good as might be expected from the test results. Of the twenty-eight school-age patients in the Los Angeles group, seven were in special education classes. Of the twenty-one children in regular classes, ten were in the proper grade, ten were one class behind, and one was three years behind. The placement of the children in special classes can be accounted for by their IQs (40–74), but no similar relationship with IQ exists for the other children. Perhaps cataracts provide an additional handicap; fourteen had slight opacities in the lens. Of the patients 65 percent had demonstrable visual-motor difficulties even though none had detectable impairment of vision.

Hereditary Fructose Intolerance   One-sixth to one-third of normal carbohydrate intake is furnished by fructose, which occurs free in fruits and vegetables and constitutes half of ordinary kitchen sugar. This rare disorder is characterized by severe hypoglycemia and vomiting shortly after ingestion of fructose. Prolonged periods of fructose ingestion in children lead to failure to thrive, jaundice, enlarged liver, loss of albumin and amino acids in the urine, and a wasting death (Froesch, 1972). Patients develop a strong distaste for sweets and fruit. Liver fructose-1-phosphate aldolase is the missing enzyme, and fructose-1-phosphate accumulates in the cells. These children will be well on a diet that omits fruits, vegetables, sucrose, and if necessary, potatoes.

Disorders of Protein and Amino Acid Metabolism

Control of the disorders of protein and amino acid metabolism is more complicated than control of the carbohydrate disorders, since many of the amino acids of which proteins are composed are essential for normal development.

Phenylketonuria (PKU).   In 1934, Følling described ten mentally retarded patients, several of them siblings, who excreted phenylpyruvic acid in urine. Jervis (1939, 1947) proved the inheritance of this disorder as an autosomal recessive trait, demonstrated the accumulation of phenylalanine, and localized the metabolic error to the inability to oxidize phenylalanine to tyrosine. Later it was shown that the phenylalanine hydroxylase enzyme in liver was inactive, and a rational therapy was devised, a preventive dietary regimen restricting phenylalanine intake. Tests for identifying the heterozygote carrier and screening methods applicable to all newborns were developed as well (Guthrie & Susi, 1963).

The effect of untreated PKU on mental performance is severe; very few persons achieve an IQ above 50 and many are well below that figure (Knox, 1972). About one-

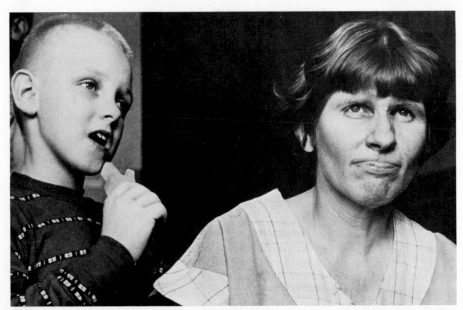

Fig. 4-9 Two unrelated cases of PKU. The boy received partial dietary treatment and is less severely retarded than the woman, who received no treatment. *(J. & M. Menapace)*

third cannot walk or control excretion, and about two-thirds cannot talk. Furthermore, they are distinguishable by their unpleasant behavior from others at the same mental level. According to Wright and Tarjan (1957), "None could be described as friendly, placid, or happy." Apart from completely helpless, bedridden cases, PKU persons are restless, jerky, and fearful. Their behavior ranges from that of the shy, anxious, and restless moderately retarded patient who may be subject to night terrors, to the destructive and noisy psychotic episodes sometimes seen in the more severely affected. Hyperactivity, irritability, and uncontrollable temper tantrums are the reasons usually given for admitting these patients to institutions.

Despite numerous claims of biochemical abnormalities, the precise mechanisms by which phenylalanine and phenylketones damage the nervous system are unknown. The basic lesion is in the liver, where the enzyme deficiency occurs, so from the point of view of the brain, the overall effect is a toxic mechanism such like any other poisoning. The most dramatic proof of the toxic nature of PKU comes from observations of offspring of PKU women. Their mothers provide a prenatal environment containing high amounts of phenylalanine and ketones, with resulting severe and early mental retardation. In contrast, PKU children born to heterozygous carrier mothers are damaged *after* birth. Apart from damage to the central nervous system, the primary abnormalities reported have been eczema of the skin and defects of teeth and bones, with microcephaly in half the cases. Since tyrosine is important to formation of melanin for skin pigment, it is not surprising that deficient pigmentation with blond hair and blue eyes is frequent in children with PKU; these are especially striking in children of dark-skinned parents. Underdevelopment of the dental enamel is another sign of this disorder.

Since most of these changes can be prevented with a diet restrictive for phenylalanine, prompt diagnosis is essential. About half of the patients are younger siblings of an older PKU child (though this figure may decrease with today's smaller families). With forewarning, they can be identified within a few days after birth. To detect the other half of affected children, a different dimension of effort is required; many thousands of newborns must be screened to find each additional case. (Total incidence in the population is 1 in 13,000 to 20,000 births.)

The development of rapid screening methods based upon the blood plasma concentration of phenylalanine, instead of the tedious measurement of phenylpyruvic acid in urine, brought unsuspected complications. Newborns may have moderately elevated or transiently elevated plasma phenylalanine concentrations for a variety of reasons which may be misdiagnosed as PKU unless careful follow-up evaluation is performed. The failure to recognize these false positives had tragic consequences for a few high-phenylalanine children who were not PKU. They became impaired by the very restrictive diet when they would have been all right without such intervention. When phenylalanine intake is overly restricted, results include dietary insufficiency with loss of body protein and cessation of growth. Frank phenylalanine deficiency and metabolic starvation occurred also in a few early PKU patients before principles of dietary control and optimal phenylalanine levels were worked out. Adequate control involves meeting but not exceeding phenylalanine requirements for growth, as well as providing caloric and other nutrient requirements (Report to Medical Research Council, 1963).

All the major biochemical abnormalities of PKU are reversed by the controlled phenylalanine diet (Knox, 1972). Structural defects and severe brain damage, however, cannot be reversed, but eczema usually clears promptly, pigmentation increases, and seizures lessen or disappear. Even in the most severely affected patients, the diet may permit conventional antiseizure medications to become effective. A prompt improvement in social and motor behavior is commonly observed. Anderson, Siegel, Tellegen, and Fisch (1968), for example, found that a group of twelve treated PKU children did not differ from twelve matched controls or a normative group of seventy-two elementary schoolchildren on motor tasks involving speed and manual dexterity, though PKU subjects off their diet did perform more poorly than controls.

Among the numerous studies which demonstrate that most PKU children begun early on phenylalanine-restricted diets achieve IQs within the normal range, two are particularly worthy of note. Berman and Ford (1970) administered intelligence tests to a mixed group of sixty-four high-phenylalanine children and to the siblings and parents in their forty-eight families. Thirty-three promptly treated children from twenty-seven families had classical PKU with blood phenylalanine greater than 20 milligrams percent (20 milligrams per hundred cubic centimeters); twenty-four children from sixteen families were categorized as having a hyperphenylalaninemic variant state with blood levels of 6.0 to 9.9 milligrams percent; the remaining seven children from five families had high levels when tested as newborns but later exhibited blood levels less than 4 milligrams percent and were classified as transient variants. The mean IQs of these groups were 96 for the PKU children, 111 for those with a variant state, and 102 for those with transient conditions. There was no IQ loss estimated on the basis of the family data for the variant or transient groups, but there was a deficit of 11.5 IQ points for the PKU group. These data indicated that the successfully treated PKU child tends to perform within the average range of intelligence but somewhat below the intellectual level of his family. From a practical viewpoint, six of the PKU children but none of the others needed educational programs designed for mentally handicapped children.

The Collaborative Study of Children Treated for Phenylketonuria (1975) is currently following a group of more than 150 true PKU cases for whom treatment was initiated before age four months (mean age: nineteen days). Different levels of phenylalanine are being maintained in the blood sera of two subgroups of these patients, neither level as low as that which originally was shown to be damaging (Fuller & Shuman, 1971). Preliminary analysis suggests that the two levels do not produce significantly different effects. The results of this study are similar to those of Berman and Ford (1970). Neurological examinations at ages two to four reveal essentially normal status in 95 to 98 percent of the subjects. Stanford-Binet IQs (1972 norms) obtained for 110 subjects at age three and for 85 subjects at age four were 91 and 92 respectively, whereas 43 four-year-old unaffected siblings attained a mean IQ of 97. Considering only those thirty-six cases who could be compared with their own siblings at comparable ages, a significant 5-point IQ difference was demonstrated on the Stanford-Binet.

The widely implemented newborn-screening program for PKU (Guthrie & Susi, 1963) has permitted the parallel analysis of several other amino acid disorders. The extensive data gathered from screening many thousands of subjects provides a far broader view of the effects of the metabolic disorder than was gained at first by screening children in institutions for the mentally retarded. In the case of PKU, the screening programs have identified multiple causes for high phenylalanine with normal tyrosine levels (Berman et al., 1969). The reader should be aware that diagnosis of the precise metabolic disorder in these children requires a sophisticated back-up laboratory with experienced medical and biochemical personnel.

Maple Syrup Urine Disease   In 1954, Menkes, Hurst, and Craig described a family in which four of six infants died during the first weeks of life with vomiting, muscular hypertonicity, and a maple syrup odor to the urine. Soon after, a similar infant was found to have increased levels of the branched-chain amino acids (leucine, isoleucine, and valine) in the blood and urine (Westall, Dancis, & Miller, 1957) and a deficiency of the decarboxylase enzyme involved in the metabolism of these amino acids. Diets low in branched-chain amino acids relieve and prevent such symptoms as ataxia, convulsions, and coma. Leucine appears to be the main culprit (Silberberg, 1964; Snyderman, Norton, Roitman, & Holt, 1964). The untreated disease is far more lethal than PKU, with survival rare beyond the second year. Dietary control is complicated by the three different amino acids to be monitored, by the likelihood that even

Table 4-1   IQs of Treated PKU Subjects and Family Members

Group	N	Test	Mean IQ
PKU subjects, age three	110	1972 Stanford-Binet	91
PKU subjects, age four	85	1972 Stanford-Binet	92
Non-PKU sibs, ages three to six	90	1972 Stanford-Binet	97
Mothers	144	WAIS Full Scale	105
Fathers	131	WAIS Full Scale	110

Source: Collaborative Study of Children Treated for Phenylketonuria (1975).

minor infections will upset the balance, and by the probability that dietary restrictions may not be eased even after school age.

A less severe deficiency of the same enzyme system has been described in two families, with instructive clinical effects (Dancis & Levitz, 1972). These children showed normal mental and physical development, but suffered episodes of ataxia, irritability, vomiting, and lethargy, with maple syrup odor and elevated blood and urine levels of the branched-chain amino acids. Excessive protein intake triggered these attacks, which proved fatal to one child in each family. This example illustrates the way in which knowledge of the biochemistry of a severe, lethal illness may allow elucidation and prevention of abnormal episodes in otherwise normal individuals. There is little or no information about the susceptibility of heterozygous (half-deficient) parents or siblings to neurological or behavioral impairment after high-protein loads.

Histidinemia   Elevated levels of histidine in blood and urine, due to a block in the metabolism of histidine, have been found in a few dozen children. Most histidinemic patients with mental retardation have also shown abnormal speech patterns or retardation in language development, but several have had speech defects without mental retardation. Deficient short-term auditory memory has been proposed as the causative factor (Bruckman, Berry, & Dasenbrock, 1970; Witkop & Henry, 1963). Under normal diet conditions, histidine accumulates in blood, urine, and cerebrospinal fluid; a low-histidine diet has been devised and administered to histidinemic infants (Thalhammer, Scheibenreiter, & Pantlitschko, 1971).

Despite the interesting speech defects and the availability of a special diet, serious doubt remains that histidinemia is causally related to these defects or requires any therapy. Impressive data in favor of the view that histidinemia is a benign metabolic disorder come from routine chromatographic screening of neonatal urines, as part of the Massachusetts Metabolic Disorders Screening Program (Levy, Madigan, & Shih, 1972). Of 400,000 infants tested by May, 1974, twenty were diagnosed as having histidinemia, an incidence of 1 per 20,000, similar to the incidence of 1 per 15,000 they obtained for PKU.[8] These twenty infants and an additional six histidinemic siblings were studied prospectively (Levy, Shih, & Madigan, 1974). None received any form of treatment for the disorder. Their biochemical abnormalities were similar to cases in the literature (LaDu, 1972), but there were no clinical abnormalities at all. The mean IQ of the twelve children over 3.5 years of age was within one point of the mean IQ of their nonhistidinemic siblings. The only affected child with speech difficulties had an unaffected sibling with even more serious speech problems. None had deficient short-term auditory memory. An unusual opportunity to compare siblings was presented by one of the families in which there were two sets of dizygotic twins, one of each set being histidinemic. In each pair, the affected twin had the higher IQ.

Of the twenty-five histidinemic children previously reported to have IQs below 85, nineteen were tested because of already recognized mental subnormality, three because of speech problems which could have reflected mental subnormality, and only three as a result of routine family screening. Conversely, of thirty-three histidinemic

---

[8] Together with cystinuria, Hartnup disease, and iminoglycinuria, which will not be discussed here, PKU and histidinemia constitute the most common errors of metabolism diagnosed in the screening program, all having incidences of approximately 1 per 20,000 birth.

children identified as the result of family screening or because of a medical problem unrelated to mentality or speech, only the three already mentioned were mentally retarded, and only three with speech problems were found in routine screening. Given the likelihood that histidinemia is benign and given the difficulties involved in maintaining the child on a restricted diet (Steisel, Katz, & Harris, 1973), Levy and his colleagues (1974) recommend that no treatment be administered for this disorder. As in all branches of medicine and psychology, good judgment in omitting therapy may be just as important as good judgment in instituting it.

Homocystinuria   This fascinating metabolic disorder illustrates the importance of genetic heterogeneity and provides some clues to brain metabolism. In a survey of institutionalized mentally retarded persons in Northern Ireland, Carson and Neill (1962) detected several cases with homocystine in the urine. These patients were distinguished clinically by displaced lenses in the eyes and by long, gangling skeletal features similar to Marfan's syndrome, which is an autosomal dominant disorder. The genetic pattern of inheritance plus the homocystinuria indicates that a similar phenotype is caused by at least these two different disorders. The homocystinuric patients, unlike those with Marfan's syndrome, have high risks of arterial and venous clotting (thromboses). Further screening showed that only about half the patients with homocystinuria are mentally retarded, and some have had superior IQs (McKusick, Hall, & Char, 1971). The enzyme cystathionine synthetase is deficient in these persons, both in liver and in brain, where the enzyme normally produces large amounts of the complex amino acid, cystathionine. The role of this amino acid is unknown, but it may possibly serve as a neurotransmitter. Cystathionine is found at highest concentrations in the brain, and its concentration in the brains of man and monkeys is far higher than in brains of lower mammals (Tallan, Moore, & Stein, 1958).

The present estimate for the frequency of homocystinuria is roughly 1 in 45,000 births (McKusick, 1972), with a corresponding frequency of heterozygous carriers of 1 percent. At least two forms of homocystinuria can be inferred from the response of patients to administration of vitamin B6, pyridoxine. Most patients of normal intelligence do respond metabolically to vitamin B6, but the response is not predictable in the retarded patients. The two forms do not, however, correspond directly with level of intelligence (McKusick, 1972). Administration of B6 may prevent or even reverse behavioral abnormalities. Since pyridoxine is a vitamin, it serves as an example for those who would hope to improve mental performance by ingestion of huge amounts of vitamins. In this case, however, a specific mechanism is clear, with pyridoxine acting as a cofactor for the function of the enzyme cystathionine synthetase.

An entirely different disorder, also involving cystathionine, is cystathioninuria, which results from deficiency of the cystathionine-cleaving enzyme. The biochemical abnormality is readily reversed by administration of pyridoxine, since B6 is cofactor for this enzyme as well. Some patients have shown developmental defects or mental retardation, but others have been clinically normal (Frimpter, 1972).

Disorders in the Synthesis of Thyroid Hormone

Thyroid hormone, which consists of iodinated derivatives of the amino acid tyrosine, is essential for the normal development of the central nervous system and speeds cellular processes throughout the body. It is produced by a gland at the base of the neck just above the vocal cords. The most common cause of congenital hypothyroidism now is lack of development of the thyroid gland, so-called athyreotic hypothyroidism. In addition, there are several types of genetic defects in thyroid hormone biosynthesis which result in goitrous hypothyroidism. The goiter, a visible enlargement of the thyroid gland, is due to continued stimulation of the thyroid by the pituitary. Defects have been identified which affect each of the five steps in thyroid hormone synthesis (Stanbury, 1972). Exhaustive biochemical investigation of these rare inherited defects has revealed much about the normal synthesis of thyroid hormone. Administration of the hormone to these children will cause the goiter to shrink and will correct the abnormalities, if irreversible changes in the brain have not yet occurred. In some cases, however, damage may occur *in utero* even if the mother's own thyroid function is normal, so that no amount of replacement therapy will prevent mental retardation.

Endemic hypothyroidism is an environmentally related form of congenital hypothyroidism. It occurs in geographic regions of severe endemic goiter due to iodine deficiency. In the United States, goiter was once very common in the Great Lakes region. The incidence has been drastically reduced by the simple expedient of adding iodine to table salt.

Deficiency beginning in fetal life or at birth results in retention of the infantile characteristics of the brain, underdevelopment of cortical neurons and their cellular processes, retarded myelination, and reduced vascularity (Eayrs, 1966). The age at which symptoms appear depends upon the degree of impairment of thyroid hormone production. Retardation of mental development and growth is the postnatal hallmark of congenital hypothyroidism. An early clue is an abnormally long persistence of physiological jaundice in the newborn (Ingbar & Woeber, 1974). During the first few months of life, symptoms include feeding problems, failure to thrive, constipation, hoarse cry, and lethargy. Then protuberance of the abdomen, dry skin, poor growth of hair and nails, and delayed tooth eruption are noted, together with delay in reaching the normal milestones of development. Postnatal linear growth is severely impaired, and closure of the fontanelles is delayed.

Although prompt treatment with thyroid hormone in early infancy is often successful, management of the patient with fully developed hypothyroidism and permanent retardation is often unsatisfactory. Little is accomplished by replacement therapy in the adult, and unacceptable aggressiveness or other undesirable behaviors may result. Dosage is best adjusted to that which keeps the patient active and comfortable without arousing unwanted side effects.

Mucopolysaccharide Storage Diseases

A whole category of disorders results from various blocks in the degradation of complex carbohydrate substances and the resultant storage of these mucopolysaccharides. By means of elegant biochemical studies on cells from skin biopsies grown *in vitro*, six types of disorders have been distinguished, several of these with subtypes as well (Neufeld & Barton, 1973; Neufeld & Fratantoni, 1970). The culture medium, containing lysosomal enzymes leaked out from the cells of patients with one type of disorder, can be used to correct the defect of cultured cells of another of the six types, but not cells from another patient with the same type of mucopolysaccharidosis. These enzymes are now being prepared from blood plasma and from urine to be administered as replacement therapy for newly diagnosed cases.

Hurler Syndrome
Hurler syndrome children are dwarfed, with deafness, clouded cornea, widely spaced teeth, short neck, protuberant abdomen due to en-

larged liver and spleen, inguinal hernias, broad, stiff hands, noisy respiration, and a large and bulging head. Their appearance long ago drew the descriptive term "gargoylism." In the first year of life, these children are often unusually large, before deterioration of their mental and physical development occurs (McKusick, 1972). Hydrocephalus, due to deposition of mucopolysaccharide within the meningeal lining, is often found at autopsy and may contribute significantly to the cerebral impairment.

Hunter Syndrome   The Hunter syndrome was recognized early to be different in severity and in pattern of inheritance. It is an X-linked recessive trait, unlike the autosomal recessive Hurler syndrome. In all respects, this condition is less severe, though the typical features include gargoyle facies, stiff joints, dwarfing, and enlarged liver and spleen. Mental deterioration progresses more slowly, however, and neither lumbar gibbus nor clouding of the cornea occurs. The biochemical findings are very similar, but the precise lesion is known to involve a related but different enzyme.

One of the most fascinating differences between the Hurler and Hunter children involves their temperaments. Hurler children tend to be friendly and affectionate, sometimes placid or apathetic. Hunter children are characteristically hyperactive and hard to manage. Both the amount and the rate of accumulation of mucopolysaccharide and related substances are lower in Hunter children, possibly implying that the developing brain is affected at a relatively less susceptible or different stage of development. Just which portions of the brain are more vulnerable has not been elucidated. Since the children are normal or nearly normal at birth, early diagnosis and administration of the deficient enzyme could be effective.

Lipid Storage Disorders: Tay-Sachs Disease

Very rapid advances in the analysis of complex lipids (fats) and the assay of the relevant enzymes have revealed a series of inborn metabolic disorders in each of which one of the nine successive steps of sphingolipid degradation is deficient. These patients accumulate abnormal amounts of the uncleaved lipids (Brady, 1972). With the notable exception of the X-linked Fabry's disease, those of the disorders with onset during infancy are associated with profound mental retardation or mental deterioration.

The most commonly encountered of these disorders is Tay-Sachs disease (Sloan & Fredrickson, 1972). Some fifty or sixty new cases a year are discovered in the United States. Tay, a British ophthalmologist, in 1881 described an infant with a cherry-red macular degeneration of the retina and with marked weakness of the trunk and limbs. Later he described the same syndrome in two siblings. Sachs, an American neurologist, in 1887 reported clinical and pathological observations of an infant with blindness and profound retardation; he called the condition "amaurotic family idiocy."

The largest series of cases with this disease is that of Aronson and Volk (1962) at the Jewish Chronic Disease Hospital in Brooklyn, New York, comprising both Jewish and non-Jewish infants. The disease is inherited as an autosomal recessive. The abnormal gene is peculiarly frequent among Ashkenazic Jews of whom 1 in 30 is a carrier, as opposed to 1 in 300 in other groups. The responsible enzyme is N-acetyl hexosaminidase (Okada & O'Brien, 1969), and its deficiency can be detected not only in cells of brain, retina, liver, skin fibroblast, and amniotic fluid, but also in blood serum samples. Major screening programs using blood tests have been initiated in the large metropolitan centers of the United States (Kaback & O'Brien, 1973). More than fifty pregnancies of two carrier parents have been monitored with amniocentesis, and the expected one-fourth of fetuses have been found to be affected.

Clinically, the disease usually begins insidiously by age six months with listlessness, weakness, feeding difficulty, hypotonia, spasticity, a characteristic hypersensitivity to sounds (startle reaction), and visual difficulties due to the depositions of lipid material in the light-sensitive macula of the eye. Blindness occurs by age twelve to eighteen months. If the child learns to sit, he loses that ability; by two years of age, he is unable to initiate any spontaneous motor activity. Death ensues by age three years or so from intercurrent infections. A partial deficiency of the same enzyme has been reported in several families in association with a less severe accumulation of GM2 gangliosides and with onset of progressive psychomotor deterioration between ages two and five years, with death between ages five and fifteen (Sloan & Fredrickson, 1972).

X-Linked Recessive Disorder of Nucleic Acid Metabolism: Lesch-Nyhan Syndrome

X-linked recessive traits transmitted by heterozygous carrier mothers almost exclusively affect boys. An important example is the Lesch-Nyhan syndrome, characterized by moderate to severe mental retardation, spastic cerebral palsy, choreoathetosis, and a dramatic self-mutilating behavior (Lesch & Nyhan, 1964). These boys have hyperuricemia (high uric acid in the blood) and associated severe gout, with nodules of uric crystals, kidney stones, and arthritis. All these findings are due to a deficiency of an enzyme in nucleic acid (purine) metabolism (Kelley & Wyngaarden, 1972).

The affected boys are apparently normal at birth and often for a few months afterward. The earliest consistent abnormality is a delay in motor development, beginning at three to four months of age, followed by involuntary, abnormal movements and loss of the motor control required to sit and hold up the head. The motor defect is of much greater severity than the defect in intelligence, although all reported cases have been mentally retarded, none toilet trained, and most with IQs below 50 (Nyhan, 1973). The athetoid dysarthria and dysphagia (difficulty in speaking and swallowing) are serious and frustrating problems. The most remarkable manifestation, however, is the aggressive, self-mutilating behavior. Self-mutilation is not uncommon in institutions for the mentally retarded, but the extent and ferocity of the phenomenon here is altogether remarkable. These children do not have a sensory defect. They scream in pain while they bite themselves, and they are really happy only when securely protected from themselves by physical restraint. Sometimes they are unusually engaging children when restrained. According to Nyhan (1973), each has had a good sense of humor, and given their motor limitations, they probably have higher mental ability than test scores indicate. When restraints are removed, however, their personality changes abruptly. They appear terrified. As they grow older, they learn to call for help. If capable of the motor behavior, they do constitute a risk to others, including their favorite ward personnel, and they may become verbally aggressive, with gross language peppering their jokes. Although there is good treatment for the hyperuricemia and gout, there is no effective therapy for this striking behavioral complex.

Microcephaly

Microcephaly refers to a reduced circumference of the skull (i.e., small head). The primary form of microcephaly, which occurs without environmental cause, is transmitted as an autosomal recessive disorder (Komai, Kishimoto, & Ozaki, 1955) and invariably is accompanied by severe mental subnormality (Brandon, Kirman, & Williams, 1959). A prenatal test for microcephaly in a family with two previously affected cases was possible by use of ultrasound (Karp, Smith, Omenn, Johnson, & Jones, 1975). Microcephaly is more frequently the result of environmental factors, including many of the agents discussed in Chapter 5.

DISORDERS ASSOCIATED WITH HIGHER THAN NORMAL IQ

Understanding of the development of human intellectual functions may come from investigations of exceptionally able, as well as retarded, children. Very little is known of underlying genetic mechanisms, and investigations of carriers of specific inherited disorders have yet to provide dramatic associations with high IQ. Three disorders for which extensive family data have been published are torsion dystonia (Eldridge, 1970), adrenogenital syndrome (Money & Lewis, 1966; McGuire & Omenn, 1975) and retinoblastoma (Eldridge, O'Meara, & Kitchin, 1972; Levitt, Rosenbaum, Willerman, & Levitt, 1972). In all three cases, the affected children have rather high IQs but are drawn from families with higher-than-average IQ. Only the gene for torsion dystonia may be suspected of having an additional enhancing effect on IQ.

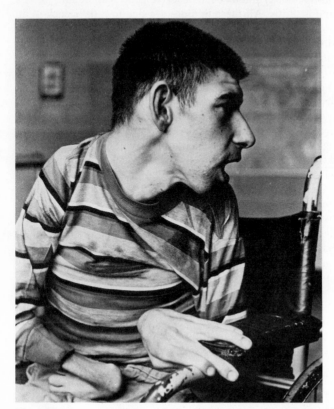

Fig. 4-10   A case of primary microcephaly with furrowed scalp. *(J. & M. Menapace)*

SUMMARY

In this chapter have been described in some detail a sampling of the genetic syndromes about which knowledge is accumulating. The reader cannot be expected to remember many of the details presented here. We have described the syndromes rather carefully, however, in order that the reader may grasp the depth and breadth of understanding which have emerged at an accelerating rate in the past few decades. One should sense the excitement and the triumph which have accompanied discoveries not only of the mechanisms by which genetic disorders are transmitted and the precise deficiencies which account for the metabolic errors but, in many instances, of new capabilities for prediction and detection of affected fetuses and for treatment of affected infants and children. Many syndromes remain to be identified and explained. New and more efficient means of prevention and treatment are yet to be devised. There is work to be done, but there is also a heady sense of progress and of optimism.

At the same time, the reader should perhaps be reminded that only a small proportion of all mentally retarded children suffer deficits stemming from single-chromosome or single-gene disorders. By far the most frequent such condition which is accompanied by mental retardation is Down's syndrome, which is familiar to anyone working in the field of mental retardation. Most of the other syndromes are rare enough that they are seldom encountered outside of specialized diagnostic settings, with the result that many nonmedical specialists in the area of mental retardation are unaware of the sophistication and vitality of genetic research and clinical progress.

5

The Physical Environment as a Factor in Mental Retardation

In the previous two chapters, we considered the role of genetic constitution as an etiologic factor in mental retardation. Now we shall deal with various environmental misfortunes which may do injury to the central nervous system (CNS) of the individual during his life cycle. Some of these factors come into play even before conception, resulting in injury to the egg or sperm (as in nondisjunctive Down's syndrome) or impairment of the mother's ability to bear a normal child. The processes by which the physical environment affects intellectual functioning are at times exceedingly complex and as yet little understood. Information is available concerning numerous agents which may cause damage, but in a great many instances we are unable to predict with any accuracy the consequences of the damage or to differentiate the effects of one sort of trauma from another. The most essential factors appear to be the timing of the injury, the organism's state of development before the assault, and the capacities remaining intact which may compensate for the loss or delay in development. The location, extent, and diffuseness of the injury are of course important as well. (See Chapter 11.)

Each part of the organism is more vulnerable at some stages of development than at others. The overall danger is greatest during the first trimester of pregnancy, when specific structures or functions are beginning to emerge and cell proliferation is most rapid. The specific structures which are in their most critical period vary, however, from week to week and from day to day during these three months.

Because there is no practical limit to the number of agents and imbalances which

This chapter was written with the collaboration of Gilbert S. Omenn.

may cause a growth pattern to go awry, observations of accidents to human beings is of limited help. On the other hand, though much of our knowledge comes from studies in which normal processes in experimental animals have been deliberately interfered with, these findings cannot with any certainty be extrapolated to human beings. Questions concerning prenatal damage are technically much more difficult to handle than questions concerning perinatal and postnatal damage, since the immediate effects cannot be observed and since the symbiotic relationship of mother and fetus is so complex.[1] They are of great significance, however, because so large a proportion of mentally retarded children is damaged before birth.

DEVELOPMENT OF THE CENTRAL NERVOUS SYSTEM[2]

Prenatal Growth: Developmental Sequence in the Embryo

Between the moment of fertilization and the moment of birth, the human organism undergoes a developmental process unparalleled in its speed and intricacy. Although continued maturation takes place after birth, the basic structures of the central nervous system are laid down during fetal life, and many are complete by the time the infant is born. As a matter of fact, cell division in the CNS slows down dramatically by six months of postnatal life and ceases completely when the child is one or two years old. All the cells of the adult are present at this time, although many of them must continue to grow and mature. The maturation process includes formation of extensive networks of cell-to-cell connections from the axon of one cell to dendrites of others, as well as the laying down of the myelin sheath around the axons.

As a result of the halt in cell division, CNS cells, unlike most of those in other parts of the body, are not replaced if they are injured or destroyed. Cell death cannot be overcome by regrowth in the brain, although the particular functions of the missing cells can sometimes be assumed by other regions of the brain. Thus, cell destruction in the CNS often produces an irreparable handicap, particularly if it occurs early in development, when its effects are likely to be more widespread.

Embryologists have gradually acquired detailed information about the stages through which embryonic human beings pass in the course of their development. Their studies have been aided greatly by experimental work with lower animals, since it is possible to discover embryos of man, pig, reptile, and bird which strikingly resemble one another, although each will develop eventually into quite a different sort of creature (Patten, 1968).

During embryonic development, growth and differentiation follow metabolic and physiological gradients, which means that some parts of the organism develop significantly faster than others. One of the most important of these gradients is the *cephalocaudal gradient,* which refers to the fact that growth is earlier and more rapid in the region of the head than in lower regions of the body. This difference provides for more rapid growth of the brain than of the lower spinal cord. After birth, it is easily discernible in the fact that the infant establishes voluntary control over his head movements earlier than over his arms and that he may begin reaching for objects with his arms while his legs are still making only involuntary, random movements. A second growth gradient which operates before and after birth is the *proximodistal* (or *axial*) *gradient,*

---

[1] It is worth noting that some basic researchers are studying the mechanisms for maternal tolerance of the fetus (i.e., not rejecting the fetus as a foreign organ transplant) in order to understand why cancer cells are not rejected and why organ transplants are rejected.

[2] The student who is seriously interested in this area will want to consult specialized texts such as Langman (1969), Patten (1968), and Schmitt (1970).

which refers to the fact that sensorimotor development tends to be more rapid in the center than at the periphery of the body. Thus the high level of growth and differentiation of the spinal column and brain is associated with their central position in the body. After birth, this gradient may be observed in the child's early reaching for objects by using gross movements of his arms without aid from his hands.

Within two weeks after fertilization, cell multiplication and differentiation in the human embryo have reached the point at which three layers of cells are discernible: the *ectoderm,* from which the skin and nervous system are later derived; the *endoderm,* from which come the digestive and respiratory tracts and their accompanying glands; and the *mesoderm,* from which derive the skeleton, muscles, connective tissue, heart, and blood vessels. In the ectoderm, which lies along the back portion of the embryo, can soon be seen a thickened plate which extends from head to tail. This plate rapidly develops into a *neural groove,* which eventually deepens and separates from the overlying layer in the form of a *neural tube,* the forerunner of the spinal cord and brain. The portion of the tube within the skull eventually becomes the brain; that within the canal formed by the vertebrae becomes the spinal cord. The cells of the neural tube and those lying directly over it form the basis for the growth of the entire nervous system. Even in the adult, the nervous system retains its essentially tubular structure.

Very quickly, three separate sections of the cranial portion of the neural tube become apparent: the *forebrain,* the *midbrain,* and the *hindbrain.* Soon five subdivisions are observable: the forebrain divides into the *telencephalon,* the largest part of which develops into the cerebral cortex; and the *diencephalon,* which contains the beginnings of the thalamus and hypothalamus. The midbrain (called the *mesencephalon*) contains connecting parts of the brain. The hindbrain divides into the *metencephalon,* which comprises the pons and cerebellum; and the *myelencephalon,* from which the medulla oblongata is derived.

The cells in the growing neural tube follow one of two types of development. They may either develop into nerve cells *(neurons),* the working portions of the CNS, or they may become cells *(neuroglia,* or *glial cells)* which take on the specialized role of a supportive framework in the CNS. Each of the nerve cells sends out an outgrowth, or *axon,* which extends toward other cells and forms the basis for the transmission of impulses from one nerve cell to another. Axons release chemical transmitters of the neuronal electrical impulse across a fine physical space known as the *synapse* to interact with *receptors* on the surface of the many *dendrites* (*dendritic* processes) of another neuronal cell body.

In the spinal cord and brain, the axons eventually become enclosed in a fatty sheath rich in *myelin,* which gives them a white color. These are known as the *white matter* of the spinal cord and the brain, as distinguished from the *gray matter,* which is the natural coloration of the nuclei of the nerve cells. Anything which attacks the protective myelin sheaths may lead to irreparable damage of the underlying neurons. The nervous system is extremely vulnerable until myelinization is complete in early childhood.

GROWTH AND DIFFERENTIATION AFTER BIRTH: OLD BRAIN VERSUS NEW BRAIN

The midbrain and hindbrain compose what is known as the *old brain,* since these portions constitute the largest part of the brain in lower animals and are thus older in the phylogenetic sense than the forebrain, or *new brain.* The old brain is responsible for many important functions. For example, the *cerebellum* is particularly important in maintaining motor coordination and postural control and the *medulla oblongata* contains nerve centers that control swallowing, breathing, the heartbeat, the blood flow, muscle tone and posture, and the movement of the stomach and intestines. It also has centers which are connected with the organs of balance in the ears. Even more important, however, is the network of nerve cells which lies between the nerve centers of the medulla. This system, known as the *reticular formation*, extends upward into higher levels of the brain stem but has its major base in the medulla. The reticular formation helps to keep the brain alert, attentive, and aroused and regulates and coordinates many of its functions. Fibers from the reticular formation extend to almost all parts of the brain. The midbrain, the other principal part of the old brain, primarily contains nerve tracts for carrying impulses up and down the central nervous system. It also has centers which are parts of visual and auditory pathways.

The important relay centers for sending nervous impulses to the new brain provide for the old brain's continuous involvement in both the involuntary and the higher thought processes of the organism. Injury to the old brain may result in relatively clear-cut neurological disorders as well as in more pervasive emotional and cognitive handicaps.

The new brain, or forebrain, constitutes the major part of the brain in human beings. Its diencephalon contains three parts: the *hypothalamus*, the *subthalamus*, and the *thalamus*. The hypothalamus controls such bodily functions as temperature, hunger, and thirst. It also controls (but does not contain) the nearby pituitary gland, which is involved in most growth functions of the body. The hypothalamus is thought to contain centers important in the expression of the emotions; with other cortical centers (in the *limbic system*), it is responsible for smiling, crying, fear, anger, aggression, and withdrawal. In addition, it is involved with the reticular formation. The subthalamus acts as a crossroads which plays an important role in coordinating movements. The

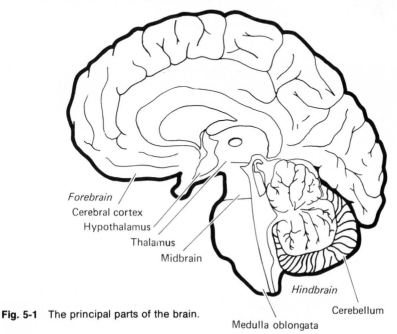

Forebrain
Cerebral cortex
Hypothalamus
Thalamus
Midbrain

Hindbrain

Cerebellum

Medulla oblongata

Fig. 5-1 The principal parts of the brain.

thalamus mainly relays sensory impulses to the surface of the cerebrum and from one part of the brain to another. It, too, is involved with the reticular formation and helps coordinate sensory messages and regulate the activity within the brain.

It is, however, the cerebral hemispheres, by far the largest portion of the new brain, which make up the most complex and the least understood region of all. The cerebral hemispheres, which appear to be mirror images of each other, are divided into four *lobes,* or portions, which are separated by deep grooves in the cortex. The *frontal, temporal, parietal,* and *occipital* lobes are named for the corresponding bones of the skull which cover them. The occipital cortex is the most specialized, dealing almost exclusively with vision. The hemispheres are connected by a large bundle of fibers called the *corpus callosum,* and each is also connected with lower portions of the brain. The left hemisphere of the cerebrum dominates the right side of the body and vice versa; the sensorimotor pathways cross over in the spinal cord and in parts of the brain stem. The cortical centers responsible for language, however, are usually in the left hemisphere only.

The cerebral hemispheres consist of the external mantle (the *cerebral cortex*) and, below it, a complex of varied centers and nuclei. The cerebral cortex is a carpet of nerve cells (gray matter) which covers the cerebrum. It is folded in upon itself forming many grooves, or *fissures,* and thus containing a very large surface of nerve cells within the confines of the skull. Beneath it is the white matter, with nerve fibers connecting the cortex with the other regions of the brain. Far from being a simple covering, the cerebral cortex is responsible for most of man's higher thought processes and for many of his learned behaviors, and it probably plays a major role in many cases of mental retardation. It is involved with integrated motor and sensory behaviors such as speech and writing and is primarily responsible for associative learning.

Deep within the cortex are gray-matter structures which are interconnected in what is known as the *limbic system.* These structures include parts of the temporal lobe (amygdala, hippocampus, uncus), regions outside the temporal lobe (mammilary bodies, parts of the thalamus, other nuclei), and the fiber tracts connecting them. At the time Papez (1937) first described the limbic system, Freudian theory was in wide vogue, leading theorists to be highly receptive to the idea of a phylogenetically ancient, deep, central portion of the CNS which influenced emotional behavior and thought without conscious, neocortical control. Although the functions of the limbic system are

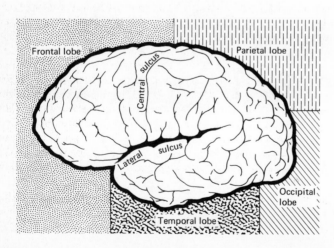

Frontal lobe

Central sulcus

Parietal lobe

Lateral sulcus

Occipital lobe

Temporal lobe

Fig. 5-2 The four lobes of the cerebral cortex.

no longer described so simplistically, disturbances in this system are thought to disrupt visceral responses, memory, and emotions (Pincus & Tucker, 1974).

Of particular importance in the growth and socialization of the human child is the softening and inhibiting power which the cerebral cortex develops. Without this part of the brain, the human being would be subject to uncontrollable and violent expressions of emotion, sudden outbursts of laughter or crying, restlessness, aggression, and withdrawal. The new brain provides a balancing power, the basis for self-control and emotional consistency, which is necessary for harmonious relationships as well as for ordinary learning. Injury which affects only the new brain, leaving the old brain untouched, is more likely to occur after birth, since it is not until after this time that the new brain achieves independent, mature development. Both parts of the brain are vulnerable to prenatal injury.

The question of whether all the geographic areas in the cortex are specialized or whether they have general functions which cannot be precisely located in the anatomy of the brain has resulted in a long-standing controversy which need not particularly concern us here. Some portions are known to be intimately connected with certain sensorimotor activities. It appears likely that some areas become specialized for particular neurological and psychological functions, whereas others lack such specialization.

Despite the fact that a given structure of the brain may ordinarily be involved in a particular response, the ability to make the response may sometimes be regained even if the structure is lost. This compensation is possible partly because the process of evolution has provided redundant centers which are simultaneously capable of the same response and partly because functions in the brain are incompletely localized. In addition, the injured individual can sometimes be trained to circumvent a missing ability by using another, much as the blind can learn to use their fingertips to read. For this reason, such a generalized assault on the brain as an infection or a high fever is a more dangerous threat to mental growth than an injury to a specific, localized area. Many developmental anomalies and minor brain injuries may pass quite unnoticed. Many normally functioning adult brains, as a matter of fact, have some minor abnormalities.

Biochemical features of brain development have been investigated quite extensively, expecially in efforts to define the effects of nutritional deficiency (Winick & Rosso, 1973). Growth of any organ, including the brain, is accompanied by an increase in the number of cells and often an increase in the average size of cells. Since the chromosome content of all somatic cells within a species is the same (see Chapter 3), measurements of total DNA provide a good estimate of the total number of cells. Once the number of cells has been determined, one can also determine the average weight per cell, protein and lipid (fat) content per cell, and RNA content per cell, by analyzing for the total amount of each of these components in the whole brain or in specific regions at given times in development and dividing by the number of cells. Of course, total DNA content does not differentiate between different types of cells.

The rat brain is relatively less mature than the human brain at birth, with approximately 17 percent of its adult cells present, whereas the guinea pig brain is more mature, having all its adult cells by birth. The human brain accumulates approximately 40 to 50 percent of its adult cells by birth, though only 25 percent of its adult weight; by age one year the brain has 75 percent of its adult weight (Chase, 1973). In human beings, most of the nerve cells of the CNS are formed prior to birth, essentially all by six months postnatally; so *glial* (supportive) cells form the bulk of the postnatal increase together with an increase in size and morphological complexity of the neuronal cells. There are marked differences by brain region. The human cortex and brain stem are roughly twice as advanced at birth as the cerebellum, the part of the brain concerned with coordination; so early postnatal metabolic or physical trauma will find the cerebellum more vulnerable (Chase, 1973).

Problems in Studying Prenatal Factors in Mental Retardation

Factors operating during the prenatal period can have dramatic effects on the subsequent well-being of a child, but attempts to find specific causes for mental retardation have been arduous. The barriers to this search for cause-and-effect sequences are many.

First, there are so many different agents that enormous groups of mother-child pairs must be studied. The proportion of mentally retarded children whose handicaps stem from a particular source is no doubt small. Second, the problem of identifying prenatal agents is complicated by the fact that the results are usually not evident until long after the critical period. This is especially true when the degree of handicap is not profound. Third, certain causes of mental retardation may have developed in the mother long before the pregnancy, such as poor nutrition during her childhood or irradiation of her gonadal tissues. Fourth, many pertinent data are lost because their relevance was not recognized. Many cases of rubella (German measles) during early pregnancy went unrecorded, for example, before the danger of this disease was known. Fifth, seemingly identical results can have quite different causes. Microcephaly (small brain), for example, can result from genetic factors or from any of several prenatal environmental causes. Sixth is the difficulty in distinguishing cause from effect. Perinatal complications such as low birthweight and failure to breathe may be especially confusing. Each of these is usually the result of prenatal developmental difficulties, but each may in turn be the cause of additional postnatal problems. The neonate who has not developed well may be especially vulnerable to conditions which a stronger neonate would weather successfully.

A seventh problem of special pertinence to the psychologist who deals with parents is that, as a group, they are notoriously poor informants. Mothers and fathers of normal children remember poorly the details of pregnancy and delivery, overlook mild diseases, mistake one illness for another, and confuse the health history of one of their children with another. It is not at all surprising that parents who feel distressed and guilty about the handicap of their child should be biased in what they report. In some instances, a particular fall or fright which is probably irrelevant becomes the family's focus of concern. In others, the true causal agent may unconsciously be denied by parents who fear that they have been responsible for their child's tragedy. The investigator who works with parents requires special tact and objectivity.

In spite of all these handicaps, however, many cause-and-effect sequences have been established, and many more are suspected. Let us examine some of the factors which are thought to be important in mental retardation.

SOME ENVIRONMENTAL CAUSES OF MENTAL SUBNORMALITY

Sociocultural Factors

Although the tiny fetus seems to be protected and remote from the society into which he will be born, his mother is by no means impervious to her social surroundings, and her baby cannot be impervious either. Sociocultural factors can influence the development of the fetus in many indirect ways. Mothers from more favorable backgrounds tend to make better use of reliable sources of obstetrical information and care, to have better diets and a better general state of health, to have their babies at more favorable ages, and so on. All these factors are related to the incidences of complications during pregnancy, prematurity, congenital malformations, and brain damage.

The possibility exists that factors operating long before the pregnancy, such as the early childhood nutrition of the mother, may affect her reproductive efficiency. Baird and Scott (1953), for example, found a significant positive relationship between the social class of the mother's family and both her height and the adequacy of her pelvic shape and size, which were determined during her growing years.

To illustrate the interlocking roles of a number of social factors, let us examine some data from a detailed analysis of all births and subsequent infant deaths occurring in New York City in 1968 (Institute of Medicine, 1973). The investigators looked at adequacy of medical care and various social and medical risk factors. Social factors included mother's education, age, parity, and medical status, and medical factors included specific medical and obstetrical handicaps known to influence the outcomes of pregnancies. A sampling of the data from this investigation is presented in Table 5-1. It is clear that maternal social and medical characteristics have an important bearing on the outcome of pregnancy. Interpretation of the adequacy-of-care factor is perhaps not so straightforward. Emanuel (in press) has suggested that this factor may be more reflective of characteristics of the mothers, such as socioeconomic status and

Table 5-1 Infant Mortality Rates by Maternal Characteristics and Adequacy of Health Care

	Total population	White native-born	Puerto Rican	Black native-born
	Deaths per 1,000 live births			
Total	21.9	15.2	25.4	35.7
No risk				
Adequate care	8.7	8.6	12.2	13.1
Inadequate care	21.0	16.1	21.0	30.2
Social risk				
Adequate care	12.3	9.7	14.1	30.8
Inadequate care	34.7	25.3	28.6	43.1
Medical risk				
Adequate care	22.6	23.2	19.0	18.5
Inadequate care	46.4	40.6	48.2	67.8
Social and medical risk				
Adequate care	29.9	24.6	53.1	51.3
Inadequate care	55.1	50.8	45.7	68.1
Education of mother				
Elementary school	27.7	32.8	26.0	50.7
High school (1–3 years)	28.5	21.8	25.4	37.4
High school (4 years)	19.4	14.7	19.4	31.9
College	12.9	10.3	15.1	25.3

Source: Institute of Medicine (1973, pp. 23, 44).

care-seeking behavior, than of the care available, and that quality of care itself probably accounts for a rather minor part of the relationship observed.

Prenatal Hazards

Maternal Undernutrition during Pregnancy   Dietary manipulation of pregnant
laboratory animals has demonstrated clearly that undernutrition *can* produce profound impairment of health and brain function in offspring, but the evidence in human beings is much less definitive. Human beings seldom experience the marked
degrees of nutritional deprivation typical of these experiments and, furthermore, the
human newborn represents only 5 percent of the mother's body weight in contrast, for
example, with the laboratory rat in which a litter represents about 25 percent of the
mother's weight.

Protein restriction in pregnant rats can retard both placental and fetal growth,
with as much as a 15 percent reduction in the number of brain cells in the offspring
(Winick & Rosso, 1973; Zamenhof, Van Marthens, & Margolis, 1968). Fetal inanition
(exhaustion from starvation) in the rat has been linked with reduced placental size as
well. Similarly, in newborn guinea pig brains after maternal malnutrition, total DNA
and protein contents are diminished. The effects are especially marked in the cerebellum, which normally undergoes more rapid development late in pregnancy, and in the
lipid content of the brain myelin, which also develops late in the gestational schedule
(Chase, Dabiere, Welch, & O'Brien, 1971).

In human beings, severe maternal undernutrition during pregnancy does result in
lower birthweights, but the reduction is slight. Even in the well-studied cases of the
Leningrad siege of 1942 (Anatov, 1947) and the Nazi blockade of food supply to the
Netherlands in 1944 (Smith, 1947), apparently few babies were badly damaged, even
when studied later at age nineteen (Stein, Susser, Saenger, & Marolla, 1972). The
mothers did, however, have increased incidences of abortions, premature births, and
infertility, presumably related to the effects of poor nutrition on the placenta and other
essential maternal organs.

Prenatal undernutrition is known to reduce the number of cells in human placenta, as it does in rats. Such results have been demonstrated in malnourished indigent
populations in Chile and Guatemala, for example, and in a severely emaciated mother
with the condition known as anorexia nervosa. Infants nourished by inadequate pla-
centas may show intrauterine growth deficiency, so that even after a gestation of
normal length they are of low birthweight (Winick, 1970; Winick & Rosso, 1973). A
fairly sensitive index of fetal-placental function is the maternal urinary excretion of the
estrogen hormone, estriol. Low maternal excretion of estriol in the last trimester of
pregnancy has been associated with respiratory difficulty, jaundice, and cyanosis at
birth, with low birthweight, and with later neurological and psychological impairment
(Wallace & Michie, 1966).

Acute Maternal Infections   The placental barrier serves in the main as a shield
against many infections of the fetus by diseases of the mother. Acute bacterial and
viral diseases which attack the mother often do not harm the fetus. Yet there are
enough exceptions to this rule to account for a considerable number of handicapped
children. Mothers who suffer febrile infections during the first trimester bear an increased risk of abortion or serious defects in their babies. Research in this area is
complicated by the fact that certain viruses which produce no recognizable clinical
condition in the mother, or at most very mild symptoms, may profoundly affect the

fetus. In view of the large number of viruses which are encountered in the average community each year, the importance of this factor in mental retardation is worrisome and yet the problem of identifying a responsible virus can be very difficult.

About 5 percent of pregnancies are complicated by clinically apparent viral infections according to the Collaborative Perinatal Study (Hellman & Pritchard, 1971, p. 808). Viruses which are known to reach the fetus include those causing measles (rubeola), chickenpox (varicella), smallpox (variola), vaccinia, poliomyelitis, hepatitis, Western equine encephalitis, mumps, and the Coxsackie B group, but only rubella (German measles) virus, cytomegalovirus, and herpes virus hominis (herpes simplex) have proved to cause defects in the fetus. Of these three dangerous agents, only rubella is an acute condition commonly acquired during the pregnancy, the other two being chronic infections to be discussed in the next section. The distinction between these three viral conditions and the other viral diseases reaching the fetus is that these three can cause congenital malformations, whereas the others generally cause more transient symptoms of illness, although abortions and stillbirths may also result (Sever, 1970).

Gregg (1941) first called attention to the permanent damage which may result from fetal *rubella* infection, although his observations were restricted to the appearance of cataracts in infants whose mothers contracted the disease in early pregnancy. Since his discovery, a great deal more has become known about the insidious and often devastating effects of this virus. Approximately half of the fetuses whose mothers contract rubella during the first trimester are infected (Cooper & Krugman, 1966), though there is some risk even when the mother contracts the disease later in the pregnancy (Hardy, McCracken, Gilkeson, & Sever, 1969). The disease is chronic, and the virus may be cultured from the infant's cells for a protracted period after birth, even though the baby develops antibodies against it. The virus destroys some cells and changes the rate of growth in others and also may interfere with the blood supply to developing fetal tissues, producing permanent growth deficiency, heart disease, microcephaly, deafness, and cataracts, glaucoma, and other eye problems. More transient symptoms include low platelets and anemia, enlargement of liver and spleen, bone lesions, and viral pneumonia. Of all the symptoms, deafness is the most frequent. In the most recent rubella epidemic which occurred in 1964, mental retardation was more common than in previous epidemics. Chess, Korn, and Fernandez (1971) found mild to profound mental retardation in one-fourth of a group of 153 affected children studied prospectively, and dull-normal intelligence or borderline mental retardation in another one-fourth. (A more detailed description of the handicapping conditions in this sample may be found in Table 10-1.)

Since that epidemic, a vaccine to prevent rubella infection has been developed, and its widespread administration constitutes the ideal means of combating this disorder. Precautions are advised to avoid accidentally vaccinating a woman who is already pregnant but as yet unaware of the fact. There is some uncertainty whether vaccinations of young girls will generate sufficiently long-lasting antibody responses to protect them through the childbearing period. Vaccination of all children and, if necessary, adult males will greatly reduce the likelihood that a pregnant woman will be exposed to the infection. A woman's ability to fight off rubella infection may be impaired during pregnancy (Thong, Steele, Vincent, Hensen, & Bellanti, 1973). Hopefully, rubella epidemics are a thing of the past.

Chronic Maternal Infections Some chronic infections, both viral and bacterial, may also be transmitted to the fetus, causing developmental damage before as well as

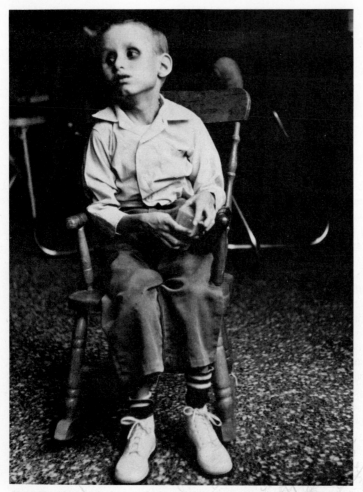

Fig. 5-3 A case of microcephaly and blindness following prenatal rubella. *(J. & M. Menapace)*

after birth. These conditions can be diagnosed accurately (as can rubella infection) since the baby retains symptoms after birth.

The virus responsible for *cytomegalic inclusion disease* may be harbored by a healthy mother and then transmitted to the fetus, occasionally causing mental retardation, hydrocephaly, microcephaly, microphthalmia (abnormally small eyes), seizures, encephalitis, blindness, enlarged liver and spleen, and blood changes with low platelets and destruction of red blood cells. The virus is readily isolated from many of the affected tissues. About 3 percent of women asymptomatically excrete this virus in the urine during pregnancy, but few of the offspring are afflicted, so that it is rare that a second child be affected in the same sibship. There is no effective therapy for mother or infant, and the infection may persist in the infant for months or years.

Herpes virus hominis (Type II) infection in adults and older children is quite mild, with only local manifestations such as cold sores or fever blisters or occasionally vaginal inflammation. Nonetheless, the virus may be lethal to the fetus or newborn infant, with disseminated infection including the brain. The antimetabolite drug idoxuridine has been a successful therapy in a few cases. Although the herpes virus can be transmitted through the placenta, the mode of spread is usually by direct contact in the genital tract during labor and delivery. Therefore, to avoid neonatal infection, cesarean section is recommended whenever the mother has had a herpetic infection involving the genitalia within three weeks of rupture of the membranes or labor.

Toxoplasmosis is a protozoan infection which in adults may be no more serious than the common cold. The fetus is especially susceptible to this disease, which is manifested by inflammation of the choroid coat of the eye and the retina, cerebral calcification, hydrocephaly, microcephaly, psychomotor disturbances, seizures, feeding difficulties, sudden rises in temperature, and increased muscle tone. The prognosis in congenital toxoplasmosis is extremely poor. Approximately 85 percent of the survivors are mentally retarded and many have other very serious sequelae (Sever, 1970).

In the recent past, *syphilis* was an important cause of fetal deaths and of mental retardation. Although its incidence has been reduced by medical advances in treatment of the disease in the parents and by compulsory blood tests of pregnant women seen in prenatal clinics, new cases do occur and the frequency is on the rise. The spirochete organism *(Treponema pallidum)* exacts a severe prenatal toll in miscarriages, stillbirths, mental retardation, blindness, deafness, and inflammation in the bones and

Fig. 5-4 A case of congenital syphilis. Note especially the characteristic saddle-shaped bridge of the nose. *(J. & M. Menapace)*

internal organs. In the milder cases, symptoms of the disease may not appear in the baby until several weeks after birth or rarely not for a year or two. It is firmly established that adequate treatment of the mother before the eighteenth week of pregnancy prevents infection of the fetus. Because penicillin crosses the placenta, treatment of the mother later in pregnancy will also successfully treat the infected fetus. Vigorous antibiotic treatment must therefore be instituted as soon as the presence of the disease is discovered in the mother.

Maternal Sensitization   In some instances, the mother may actually develop an antibody response against biochemical substances in her fetus, and these antibodies may damage fetal tissues. A large variety of blood-type and other biochemical differences between mother and fetus have been discovered, but only a few have strong antigenic effects in human beings.

About 15 percent of the Caucasian population has the Rh-negative (Rh-) blood type,[3] i.e., a homozygous condition for the recessive gene producing the Rh-blood type, the Rh-positive type being dominant. There is, then, an 85 percent chance that the father will be Rh-positive, though he may carry a recessive Rh-negative gene, and about a 60 percent chance that a baby of an Rh-negative mother will be Rh-positive. The mother may become sensitized against Rh-positive blood cells by an Rh-positive blood transfusion or if the Rh-positive fetal blood cells reach her circulatory system, as often happens during labor and delivery. If a sufficient immune response is engendered, the mother will thereafter carry antibodies against Rh-positive blood cells. Such sensitization actually used to occur in about 1 in 200 pregnancies, making Rh incompatibility a common major threat in pregnancy (Clarke, 1973). The first baby is not at risk unless the mother has previously been sensitized, but if there is any leakage of blood cells of subsequent babies, the cells may further sensitize the mother and the babies may be attacked late in pregnancy by maternal antibodies which tend to destroy the "foreign" fetal Rh-positive red blood cells. Such a phenomenon causes not only life-threatening anemia (erythroblastosis fetalis) by loss of the red blood cells, but also hyperbilirubinemia (a form of jaundice caused by high bilirubin in the blood) by accumulation of bilirubin from the hemoglobin in the red blood cells. The bilirubin cannot be metabolized by the immature fetal liver and may reach toxic concentrations that produce damage to the brain known as kernicterus.

Because of the frequency and severe consequences of this condition, it is gratifying that excellent progress has been made in treating and preventing Rh incompatibility. The first techniques to be developed involved treatment at birth or even *in utero* by exchange transfusion. Most babies were saved, though some had residual brain damage. Now, however, sensitization in the mother can be avoided by administering antibodies against the Rh factor to an Rh-negative mother who has just given birth to an Rh-positive infant, thereby creating "passive immunization" and destroying the Rh-positive fetal cells in the mother's circulatory system before her immune system has been stimulated to produce its own antibodies. At first the anti-Rh antibodies were obtained from blood donations by previously sensitized women, but now that few women become sensitized, the substance (commercially known as "Rhogam") is produced by injecting Rh-positive cells into Rh-negative volunteers (usually paid or otherwise cooperative male prisoners).

The Rh factor is not the only blood factor for which the mother and fetus may be

---

[3] Rh stands for *rh*esus monkeys, in which the Rh factor was first detected (Landsteiner & Wiener, 1940).

incompatible. Indeed, ABO blood group incompatibility is twice as common as Rh incompatibility. Because the anti-A and anti-B antibodies carried by mothers are larger molecules, they do not readily pass the placenta into the fetal circulation. Those that do tend to attack the free A or B blood group substances secreted into the fetal blood plasma, with the result that the A or B substances present on the surface of the red blood cells are left undamaged. Although cases of damage from ABO incompatibility are not unknown, they are relatively rare and the complications are less severe (Hsia & Gelles, 1954).

Maternal Dysfunction   Noninfectious medical conditions in the mother may seriously affect the development of the fetus. These include anemia, symptomatic heart disease, impairment of liver and kidney function, and various disorders of the endocrine glands. The two most common and important maternal disorders are hypertension (high blood pressure) and diabetes mellitus.

Hypertensive disorders occur in the third trimester in 6 to 7 percent of all pregnancies and account for 20 percent of maternal deaths in the United States. Together with hemorrhage and sepsis (overwhelming blood infection), it accounts for more than half of the maternal deaths. Fetal loss is very frequent. Chesley and Annetto (1947) reported the rate of fetal loss in hypertensive mothers to be 38 percent, and Hellman and Pritchard (1971, p. 685) estimate that at least 25,000 stillbirths and neonatal deaths in the United States each year result from maternal hypertensive disorders. This loss is particularly lamentable because it is largely preventable through good prenatal supervision. Life-threatening hypertensive complications (eclampsia) occur most often in first pregnancies at both extremes of the spectrum of maternal age. Among teen-agers this problem is on the rise. The contribution of hypertensive disorders to mental retardation in surviving infants is not known.

Before the advent of insulin in 1921, women with *diabetes* were usually too ill to conceive, and in the few cases of pregnancy, deaths occurred in about one-fourth of the mothers and about half of their fetuses and infants (Hellman & Pritchard, 1971, p. 788). Even with modern management of diabetes, pregnancy carries enhanced risks for the mother and especially for the baby. The likelihood of severe hypertensive disorders is increased fourfold; infections are more common and more severe; the fetus is often much larger, making delivery difficult and often necessitating cesarean section; postpartum hemorrhage is more common.

In the offspring, the perinatal death rate is elevated several times, and the frequency of abortion may be significantly increased. Respiratory distress is more frequent; malformations of many types are doubled in frequency; and the risk of diabetes in the child before age twenty is increased from 0.2 percent to 4 percent (Simpson, 1968). Finally, neurologic and intellectual deficits are more frequent. In one study, children whose diabetic mothers had developed ketosis during pregnancy had a mean IQ of only 93 at age four years, compared with a mean IQ of 102 in the offspring of mothers whose diabetes was well controlled or in the offspring of nondiabetic mothers (Churchill, Berendes, & Nemore, 1969). A test for glucose in the urine as a sign of diabetes is now part of routine prenatal care, since good management of the diabetic woman greatly improves the prospects both for her and for her child.

Parental Age   As noted in Chapter 4, chromosomal nondisjunction increases markedly with the age of the mother and other complications of pregnancy also become somewhat more frequent with age. New mutations, most readily recognized as first occurrences of autosomal dominant inherited disorders, occur more frequently as the father's age rises, presumably reflecting some cumulative damage on the stem cells for sperm formation.

Age of the parents often interacts with such other factors as parity (number of previous pregnancies), family size, birth order, and socioeconomic status. In an oft-quoted study by Lilienfeld and Pasamanick (1956) of 1,107 mentally retarded children and an equal number of matched control children, risks of mental retardation were highest in those born to young mothers who had had three children before age twenty and in older mothers who were bearing their first child after age thirty-five.

Particular attention has been turned in recent years to the plight of unwed teen-age mothers, who run an alarmingly high risk of prenatal complications and prematurity. Aside from their reproductive immaturity and the demands made by their own growing bodies, these young women are often seriously disadvantaged nutritionally, socially. and psychologically. Many of them seek health care services only late in pregnancy. In an attempt to meet their needs, a number of programs have been undertaken in the United States under the auspices of the Children's Bureau to enable these young women to continue their education and at the same time to receive nutritional, medical, and counseling services.

Radiation   Exposure to massive radiation within the first few months of pregnancy often causes termination of the pregnancy or other serious complications, though no serious problems have been clearly linked to the lower levels associated with diagnostic x-ray examinations. In one early series of seventy-four mothers treated for cancer with massive doses of x-rays during pregnancy, only thirty-six bore healthy children (Murphy, 1928). In studies of the effects of the atomic bomb explosions in Hiroshima and Nagasaki, high frequencies of mental retardation and/or microcephaly were found in those individuals whose mothers had been within 1,200 to 1,500 meters of the epicenter and who had been between seven and fifteen weeks gestation (Wood, Johnson, & Omori, 1967). In contrast, follow-up of some 71,000 children conceived after the explosions has failed to reveal any unequivocal effects of radiation (Miller, 1969).

Drugs   Ingestion of chemical substances in the form of medications, food additives, and various forms of pollution is epidemic in Western societies. As Barnes (1968) has put it, "most people in our contemporary society (as well as their physicians) seem to regard life as a drug-deficient disease, to be cured or even endured only with the aid of innumerable medications" (p. 370). Barnes cites figures from the Collaborative Perinatal Research Study which show that pregnant women could recall the consumption of an average of four medications, the most popular being aspirin, antihistamines, tranquilizers, antiemetics, laxatives, and nasal decongestants. Apgar (1965) estimated that 92 percent of all women use at least one drug during any pregnancy and that 4 percent use ten or more drugs. In addition to this voluntary behavior, the involuntary ingestion of chemical substances in foods, air, and water is quite staggering. Because of differential maternal susceptibility and the likelihood that many teratogens have weak effects which cause malformations in only some fetuses, it is extremely difficult to determine with any certainty what the effects of each drug on human fetuses might be. Thus far, of the more than six hundred drugs known to produce congenital anomalies in experimental animals, fewer than twenty are definitely known to cause defects in the human fetus (Shepard, 1974; Wilson, 1973). Yet, one need only mention the dramatic case of the mild tranquilizer and sedative, thalidomide, to remind every layman of the potential dangers of presumably innocuous drugs. Some 20 percent of children whose mothers took this drug during the sensitive developmental period suffered damage to limbs and other body parts, though fortunately they did not sustain CNS damage.

Drugs taken by the mother can be transmitted through the placenta to the fetus. Quinine, for example, can cause deafness, and withdrawal symptoms can be dramatic in newborns whose mothers had taken significant amounts of morphine, heroin, methadone, or other addicting agents during pregnancy (Blatman, 1974). Heavy sedation of the mother and use of general anesthetics have been avoided during labor and delivery since it was discovered that these drugs depress respiratory and neurological function in the newborn (Schreiber, 1940).

Among children born to mothers who are *chronic alcoholics,* a malformation syndrome has recently been recognized (Jones, Smith, Ulleland, & Streissguth, 1973). These children exhibit retarded intrauterine and postnatal physical and mental development, microcephaly, short eye slits, and variable limb and cardiac malformations. The degree of linear growth deficiency is more severe than the weight deficit at birth, a quite uncommon finding. The mechanism of toxicity and the issue of genetic variation in susceptibility are not yet resolved.

Jones and Smith (1973) have presented autopsy findings in one case, distinguished by aberrant neuronal migration in the brain. They also described one family with two affected children and another family in which a woman had seven normal children before she became alcoholic and then had three spontaneous abortions and an affected child after she became alcoholic. Likely occurrences of this syndrome were identified in British reports of a century ago. Jones, Smith, Streissguth, and Myrianthopoulos (1974) have also reviewed the data of the large Collaborative Perinatal Research Study in a search for additional cases. Alcoholism was generally not recorded in that massive prospective study, but among the offspring of twenty-three women who were identified as chronic alcoholics, four died in the perinatal period, six had the features of this fetal alcohol syndrome, and others had less severe growth retardation and intellectual impairment at age seven. On the WISC, at age seven the mean Full Scale IQs were 80.7 for sixteen children of alcoholic mothers and 94.9 for thirty-two matched controls (Streissguth & Rohsenow, personal communication). Whereas behavioral profiles did not distinguish the groups at ages eight months and four years, at age seven the children of alcoholic mothers appeared more fearless, less goal-oriented, more assertive, and less controllable, and they exhibited briefer attention spans and more irrelevant verbalization. It may be noted as well that children who are spared such damage apparently have a genetic predisposition to becoming alcoholic themselves later in life (Omenn, 1974), even if raised in adoptive families where there is no alcoholism (Goodwin, Schulsinger, Hermansen, Guze, & Winokur, 1973).

Even very commonly used, presumably minimally toxic drugs such as meprobamate and chlordiazepoxide (Librium), used to control anxiety, may be dangerous. A statistically significant increase has been noted in the incidence of serious malformations, some associated with mental retardation, among the offspring of women at the Kaiser Permanente Clinics who received either of these two drugs, compared with offspring of women who received no drugs but also were anxious (Milkovich & Van den Berg, 1974). Even in that large prospective study, the numbers of cases of particular anomalies were extremely small.

In general, any drug should be avoided, if possible, because of its potential teratogenic effects on the development of the fetus. The first few weeks of embryonic development are most crucial for the proper formation of the internal organs, a time largely past before most women realize that they are pregnant. This fact suggests that use of drugs in all potentially childbearing women should be restricted to those for which the clinical indications are strong.

Maternal Emotions Speculations and fears about the possible effects of maternal emotions and anxieties on the fetus have been the subject of much folklore and astrology (Warkany, 1971, pp. 12-15). The theories of maternal impression have reappeared in modern scientific garb, according to Warkany, with the recognition that anxiety is expressed physiologically with release of adrenal corticosteroid hormones and changes in the autonomic nervous system. Animal experiments indicate that anxiety-producing experiences during pregnancy may affect activity level, heart rate, birthweight, and motor development of the fetuses (Sontag, 1960).

The amount of stress experienced by the mother and, perhaps more important, the personal support she receives while she is pregnant, are related to the number of complications during pregnancy and delivery (Nuckolls, Cassel, & Kaplan, 1972) and the birthweight of the infant (Mitchell, 1974). Stott (1973) found no significant effects of situational or transient stress, but stresses involving severe, continuing personal tensions such as marital discord during the pregnancy were associated in a group of 153 mothers with increased child morbidity in the form of ill health, neurological dysfunction, delayed language development, and behavioral disturbances. This area may be ripe for further research.

Hazards at Birth

The process of labor and delivery of a newborn child is a stirring biological event. Some observers marvel at the resiliency of the child and his ability to recover from stressful perinatal events and to develop normally. Others psychodynamically interpret the process of birth as the prototype of all psychic injury and trauma. Realistically, the birth process should be regarded as an essentially normal occurrence which is weathered successfully by most infants but not by all. The significance of minor birth injuries or difficulties is often hard to evaluate, particularly in view of the fact that infants who have developed poorly during gestation are unusually likely to have problems during the perinatal period, but such events probably contribute to some cases of mild retardation and to learning disorders with hyperactivity (Sechzer, Faro, & Windle, 1973). Among the potential hazards at this time are prematurity, anoxia, and kernicterus.

Prematurity Infants who are of low weight at birth (conventionally meaning under 2,500 grams or 5½ pounds) actually constitute two general groups: those who apparently have been developing rather normally but are delivered prior to full term, and those who are delivered at or close to term but whose growth has been deficient during gestation. Unfortunately, only a few studies thus far have separated these two groups, and almost all the long-term studies of "premature" children have used birthweight as the sole criterion for selection.

For some groups of mothers, the frequency of low birthweight in their offspring is alarmingly high. In the Collaborative Perinatal Research Study (Niswander & Gordon, 1972), for example, the frequency was 7.1 percent among white but 13.4 percent among black, single-born infants. In the New York City survey cited previously (Institute of Medicine, 1973), rates ranged from 6.4 percent of the infants born of white, native-born mothers without special risks, to 21.5 percent for black native-born mothers with both social and medical risks.

A strong association of prematurity with low social class has been well identified (e.g., Drillien, 1970; Robinson & Robinson, 1965). Mothers from lower socioeconomic classes not only tend to have a greater proportion of low birthweight infants but are apparently less able to compensate for this developmental disadvantage as the child is growing up. (See Chapter 8.) Other specific factors known to predispose to low-birth-weight infants are extremes of maternal age, short stature, heavy cigarette smoking, the presence of certain pathological states in the mother, and low maternal weight gain (poor nutrition). These factors were confirmed in large surveys in both Great Britain (Butler & Alberman, 1969) and the United States (Niswander & Gordon, 1972). One very important factor was the mother's weight gain during pregnancy, with optimal gain of 11 to 14 kilograms (24 to 31 pounds) being associated with the lowest rates of perinatal mortality and of low-birthweight infants (Weiss & Jackson, 1969). This finding came as a distinct surprise to American physicians, who had typically counseled mothers to restrict their gain to perhaps half that amount. Excessive maternal weight gain may, however, be harmful, especially if it is due to toxemia of pregnancy or diabetes. Excessive fetal weight at birth (over 4,500 grams or 10 pounds) may be detrimental because of association with maternal diabetes and with difficulties during labor and delivery.

The relation between low birthweight and increased risk of adverse outcome has been well established, beginning with Little's (1862) report linking prematurity and cerebral palsy. Infants of low birthweight contribute a disproportionate share to those dying in the neonatal period and those exhibiting later neurological abnormalities. The perinatal mortality rate in the Collaborative Perinatal Study (Niswander & Gordon, 1972) was twenty-five times higher for low-birthweight white infants than for larger white infants and constituted 70 percent of the infants dying in the perinatal period. Similar results were obtained for the black infants. At age one year, the rates of definite neurologic abnormality were more than three times higher for the low-birthweight infants than for the larger infants. One follow-up study (Wiener, Rider, Oppel, Fischer, & Harper, 1965) examined a group of low-birthweight infants and a control group when the subjects were six to seven years old. Subjects were excluded who showed gross sensory or motor handicaps, severe emotional problems, and IQs below 60; race, maternal attitudes and practices, and socioeconomic factors were controlled for. Even so, low-birthweight children exhibited increased incidences of perceptual motor disturbances, flaws in comprehension and abstract reasoning, gross motor deficits, immature speech, and impaired IQ.

The weight of an infant at birth is an important developmental milestone which, in conjunction with gestational age, provides a useful index of intrauterine growth (Gruenwald, 1966; Lubchenco, Hansman, & Dressler, 1963; Penchaszadeh, Hardy, & Mellits, 1972). Some low birthweight children, as we have indicated, seem to have been developing rather normally prior to premature delivery, and their size is about what would be expected in terms of their gestational age. In others, low birthweight is a sign that development has not proceeded normally. In many respects, the latter group, termed "small for date" (SFD), are at greater risk because of prenatal developmental difficulties. McDonald (1967), for example, surveyed more than 1,000 infants with birthweights below 4 pounds who had been born in a number of British hospitals. With the exception of spastic diplegia, one form of cerebral palsy, which was more frequent in the very early-born children (twenty-seven to thirty-four weeks of gestational age) and probably reflected postnatal difficulties, a variety of developmental problems seemed to be more frequent in the infants born at thirty-five weeks of gestation or more (SFDs). Although SFD infants apparently show fewer neonatal complications and deaths than weight-matched preterm infants (Cushner & Mellits, 1971; North, 1966), their developmental disadvantage later becomes increasingly evident (Eaves, Nuttall, Klonoff, & Dunn, 1970).

With improvement in the techniques of postnatal care for extremely small prematures (birthweight 1,500 grams or less), many more of these fragile infants are now surviving than ever before. Heroic nursery care is usually required even for survival, and many subtle factors in their care and feeding, such as the level of protein intake, must be adjusted carefully (Goldman, Goldman, Kaufman, & Liebman, 1974). The incidence of major defects in this group is much higher than among larger infants. Drillien (1967) followed fifty children with birthweights of 3 pounds (1,360 grams) or less and found that at age five, fifty-eight percent had IQs of 80 or lower and only 30 percent were able to attend regular school without special attention because of educational retardation.

A genetically controlled study of the effects of low birthweight is provided by analyses of identical twins differing in birthweight. These children share the same genes, the same maternal environment, the same socioeconomic and temporal status, the same gestational age, and much of the same postnatal environment, but for unknown reasons (possibly circulatory asymmetry in the placental blood flow), one has gained an advantage over the other. In a study of nine pairs of identical twins who differed by an average of 36 percent in birthweight (Babson & Phillips, 1973), the undersized member continued to be inferior in both physical growth and intelligence into adult life. Similar results have been obtained in other comparisons of identical twins, but not fraternal twins (Kaelber & Pugh, 1969; Scarr, 1969; Willerman & Churchill, 1967). It should be noted that a large weight difference (300 grams) is usually required before an IQ difference of as much as 5 points occurs between groups of larger and smaller twins.

Several studies have assessed the effects of extra stimulation of premature infants, recognizing the deprivation of sensory input which occurs in an incubator as opposed to either the womb or to normal postnatal care. In some cases, hospital staff have provided the extra stimulation and in others the mothers have been involved in order to stimulate emotional ties with the baby (e.g., Powell, 1974; Scarr-Salapatek & Williams, 1973). Although better initial development is often demonstrable, the effects in most studies are soon dissipated. Also, there is no convincing evidence that the mothers' subsequent behavior at home is influenced by a greater opportunity to hold and cuddle the premature in the nursery.

Postmaturity   Correcting for probable errors in the date of the last menstrual period, approximately 4 percent of pregnancies exceed the full term of forty weeks by fourteen days or more. The effects of prolonged pregnancy are quite variable. Sometimes the fetus continues to grow and gain weight and seems to suffer no harm at all. In other instances, the fetus fails to gain and is starved *in utero* to the extent that it loses weight. Whereas British obstetricians usually induce labor when full term is exceeded, most obstetricians in the United States prefer to let nature take its course until at least three weeks beyond the expected date (Hellman & Pritchard, 1971, p. 1057), meanwhile testing for placental dysfunction by studies of urinary estriol, by ultrasound, and by amniotic fluid sampling.

Perinatal Asphyxia   The view that a baby will be permanently damaged by oxygen deprivation during or immediately after birth is also somewhat controversial. Deprivation may occur through blockage of placental blood supply or lack of spontaneous breathing, often seen in fetuses who were abnormal prior to birth. It is common for couples to recall that "the cord was wrapped around the baby's neck" in cases of retardation or malformations, but such positioning of the cord is not unusual, without any untoward consequences. Nevertheless, there is no doubt from animal studies that anoxia at birth *can* cause persistent impairment (Bailey & Windle, 1959). Sechzer, Faro, and Windle (1973) deprived rhesus monkeys of oxygen at birth. The fetuses withstood nearly seven minutes of asphyxia without any detectable signs of brain damage, but when asphyxia lasted 8 to $11\frac{1}{2}$ minutes, permanent brain damage was observed, with lesions most common in centers of the brain stem and diencephalon concerned with sensory input. Surprisingly, however, the latter monkeys showed only transient neurologic abnormalities such as poor sucking, poor coordination, and reduced reactivity, all of which soon disappeared. A more marked effect was observed with asphyxiation for twelve to seventeen minutes, with more extensive brain lesions and functional deficits which persisted for some time. Nevertheless, compensation occurred and casual inspection revealed little or nothing abnormal. Since the brain lesions involved centers that integrate sensory information, these workers were able to show that certain adaptive behaviors were impaired and proposed that similar difficulties might underlie some of the problems of children with minimal brain damage or hyperactivity syndrome. (See Chapter 11.)

One major study with human beings involved 355 preschool children (Graham, Ernhart, Craft, & Berman, 1963). Of the total, 159 had been born normally at full term, 116 had been full term but hypoxic, and 80 had suffered miscellaneous other complications of birth. The hypoxic subjects were significantly poorer than the controls on all tests of cognitive and perceptual function and exhibited more neurological abnormalities. Although they received lower ratings on several personality measures, the syndrome of hyperactivity, impulsivity, and distractibility long considered a hallmark of brain damage in young children characterized only a few of them.

As with many other matters, too much of a good thing may be dangerous. Premature babies are extremely sensitive to concentrations of oxygen greater than 40 percent in the air they breathe. Before this fact was discovered, many premature babies were unfortunately blinded from a condition known as retrolental fibroplasia, which can result when high concentrations of oxygen are utilized for a prolonged time, and many of these children have become retarded as well (Bender & Andermann, 1965).

Neurotoxicity from Hexachlorophene   The 3 percent hexachlorophene soap (called pHisoHex[R]) which was widely used for bathing newborn infants has been indicted rather dramatically as a cause of brain damage. Hexachlorophene was known by 1971 to produce extensive vacuolation (cavities) of myelin in the CNS of animals and similar changes, sometimes fatal, in rare cases when human beings were exposed through abnormal skin or through the gastrointestinal tract or vagina. In late 1971, the

Food and Drug Administration issued a warning about this toxic effect and sought further information. Shuman, Leech, and Alvord (1974) found the prevalence of the pathological evidence of brain damage in 248 children coming to autopsy to be related to the number of exposures and the concentration of hexachlorophene, the birthweight (gestational age), the length of survival, and the thoroughness of rinsing. The investigators concluded that hexachlorophene should not be used at all on neonates under 1,400 grams birthweight and should in general be used sparingly and in lower concentration. In a subsequent report (Shuman et al., 1975) of forty-six infants who survived at least four days after a birthweight under 1,400 grams, autopsies revealed two ameliorating factors: the use of phototherapy in the newborn nursery to induce liver enzymes that metabolize both bilirubin (see below) and hexachlorophene, and much more thorough rinsing. The drug has now been removed from over-the-counter sales. The clinical effects of this agent include impairment of muscle tone, gastric motility, bladder function, cardiovascular tone, and finally respiratory drive, so that death is often mistakenly attributed to apnea. The long-term CNS residuals in survivors exposed to hexachlorophene are as yet unknown.

Kernicterus Bilirubin is the breakdown product of hemoglobin, the oxygen-carrying protein of red blood cells. High circulating levels of bilirubin occur when the red blood cells are being destroyed too fast for the liver to metabolize the bilirubin. Thus, Rh incompatibility and certain red blood cell inherited enzyme deficiencies stress the capacity of the liver, which is especially limited in premature or low birthweight infants. In addition, there are disorders of the liver which further impair the metabolism or excretion of bilirubin. The presence of excessive concentrations of bilirubin in the bloodstream leads to jaundice (yellowish coloration) of the skin and of the sclerae of the eyes and can result in deposition of bilirubin in the brain. At very high levels, the toxicity to brain cells results in the features of rigidity and spasticity. If untreated, hyperbilirubinemia and kernicterus may cause death or, in the survivors, mental retardation, cerebral palsy, seizures, speech difficulties, or deafness. If the serum bilirubin concentration is kept below 20 milligrams per 100 cubic centimeters of blood (by phototherapy or by transfusion, if necessary), all of these complications can be avoided. Bilirubin levels in newborns are evaluated at the first signs of jaundice nowadays, though it should be noted that many newborns show transient mild jaundice without complications.

Direct Injury to the Head and Brain Delivery of the baby through the birth canal can be a difficult and traumatic process, especially if the baby or the baby's head is relatively large for the dimensions of the mother's pelvis. Usually, however, even the strong muscular contractions of the uterus during labor represent little hazard if the baby presents head first, if there is sufficient time for the head to be gently molded rather than thrust precipitously through a small cervical opening, and if during this time the placenta continues to supply oxygen and other nutrients. In case of hemorrhage, separation of the placenta, or precipitous delivery, the baby may be damaged. It is hard to be quantitative about the degree of trauma suffered. In case of a breech birth (buttocks first) or transverse presentation (fetus crosswise in the uterus), the risk of injury or suffocation is increased, though the physician often can turn the fetus to a head-first position. Studies of intellectual function related to fetal head position during delivery have found some differences in IQ and in postural control (Rosenbaum, 1970; Willerman, 1970a).

Although mechanical and physiological factors are responsible for actual injuries, psychological factors may contribute even here. It has been suggested, for example, that poorly adjusted mothers tend to have more difficult, prolonged labor and delivery with more complications (Davids, Spencer, & Talmadge, 1961).

In fact, mechanical injuries during the birth process appear to be much less often a source of neurological deficit than a number of other factors we have considered, particularly those occurring before birth begins. Yet, because the birth process is higly dramatic and often a time of stress for the mother, it tends to figure large in parental explanations of their children's problems.

Postnatal Hazards

Injury to the CNS may occur after birth in many ways, including severe blows to the head from accidents or child abuse, asphyxiation, toxins, tumors, infectious diseases, and metabolic derangements. The complexity of factors noted with respect to hazards occurring before or during birth applies also to postnatal hazards. In general, injury to the brain from infection has more widespread consequences than injury from single episodes of trauma. Furthermore, injuries to children who have already begun to walk, speak, and develop satisfying personal relationships usually result in different developmental problems than the generalized effects of earlier damage. (See Chapter 11.) The proportion of cases of mental retardation accounted for by all sorts of postnatal factors may be rather small. For example, Yannet (1950) attributed mental retardation in only 6 of 1,729 patients in one training school to postnatal physical causes. The role of these factors may be much higher among mildly retarded children or children with other behavioral problems who are not institutionalized.

Head Injury   It is a poignant commentary on present-day society that the two most common causes of severe head injury in young children are automobile accidents and child abuse. Except for these occurrences, head injury is probably a rare cause of mental retardation, though parents of a defective child may often date the onset of his difficulties from a fall or a blow on the head. On the other hand, abusive parents are likely to blame accidental injury for distinctive patterns of fractures and bruises which they have caused themselves. (See Chapter 7.)

Kanner (1957) classified the possible serious consequences of head injury in children as follows: (1) acute psychosis immediately after regaining consciousness, with recovery within a month; (2) chronic behavioral disorders, characterized by irritability, emotional instability, antisocial behavior, and, less commonly, sexual maladjustment, destructiveness, lying, disobedience, depression, vasomotor instability, fatigability, bed wetting, and grimacing; (3) seizures with or without secondary mental deterioration; and (4) cerebral deficits, including aphasia, memory defects, and intellectual deterioration. Fortunately, there is some evidence to support the hypothesis that the effects of trauma may be compensated better in younger children than in adults or older children, on the basis that the organization of certain functions is more plastic at an early age (Teuber, 1970).

Brain Tumors   The symptoms and signs of brain tumors vary according to the precise site of the tumor within the brain and the rapidity with which intracranial pressure rises to dangerous levels within the fixed volume of the skull. Seizures, staggering gait, loss of vision, and other specific changes may indicate the presence and growth of a tumor. In children under age two years, sensory and motor disturbances may be attributed to developmental delay, obscuring proper diagnosis and treatment (Fessard, 1968). The symptoms of increased intracranial pressure include headache, dizziness, projectile vomiting, slow pulse, stupor, and convulsion. Diagnosis depends upon careful physical examination and, if indicated, spinal fluid examination. Subsequent brain scan, arteriographic x-rays, or psychological testing (in older children) may localize the tumor.

Infections: Meningitis and Encephalitis   Inflammation of the brain (encephalitis) or its lining membrane (meningitis) due to infections by bacteria, viruses, or tuberculosis organisms account for some cases of mental subnormality attributable to postnatal physical causes, but mainly in children infected during infancy. Occasionally the inflammation results in lesions which obstruct circulation of cerebrospinal fluid, causing hydrocephalus. (See Chapter 6.) Even though mental retardation may not occur, personality changes are quite common and sometimes persist (Matejcek, Doutlik, & Janda, 1964).

Meningitis is recognized as a life-threatening but treatable infection of early childhood. With appropriate antibiotic and supportive care, preservation of brain function is usually excellent. For example, Lawson, Metcalfe, and Pampiglione (1965) assessed clinical, psychological, and scholastic status of eighty-six children who had had meningitis an average of four years earlier. There was no indication of depressed IQ (mean 105, without matched controls), nor did there appear more instances of personality or behavioral disorders than were expected even though abnormal EEGs were common. Among children who had had meningitis before age one year, however, there was an excess of cases with IQs below 90.

Encephalitis is usually caused by viruses, including measles, chickenpox, whooping cough, influenza, and vaccinia, and is therefore impervious to treatment with antibiotics. Although its occurrence was not new, the syndrome of epidemic encephalitis (sleeping sickness) became widely known to modern medicine in 1917-1918, during a worldwide epidemic.

The disease may occur at any age, and is extremely varied in form. Cases, subsequently proving to be encephalitis, had presented the clinical signs of, and had been first diagnosed as, such widely different conditions as influenza, cerebral tumor, cerebral haemorrhage, chorea, epilepsy, hysteria, neurasthenia, melancholia, confusional insanity, sunstroke, infantile paralysis, myasthenia gravis, trigeminal neuralgia, multiple neuritis, and appendicitis. With regard to severity, some patients have been stricken with such suddenness and violence as to be brought within sight of death in a few hours. Others have had the disease in such a mild form that they have not even discontinued work or sought medical advice. There is not the slightest doubt . . . that encephalitis may exist without any acute onset at all, and in many cases the initial symptoms have been merely those of a common cold or a mild attack of influenza. The results are similarly very varied. In about a third of the recognized cases the patient dies. In about another third or less he appears to make a complete recovery, although serious changes subsequently appear in many of these. In approximately another third there is no recovery, and the patient passes directly into a state of physical or mental infirmity. (Tredgold & Soddy, 1956, pp. 341-342)

The chronic stage of encephalitis is of great importance, since permanent patterns of psychological disturbance may follow the infection and recovery and since changes may be quite delayed. The most dramatic sequelae of the 1918 influenza epidemic are the new cases still occurring of Parkinson's disease (characterized by uncontrollable tremors).

Hunger and Malnutrition   With starvation a horrifying reality in much of the less developed world, compelling questions are being asked about the effects of various degrees and kinds of poor nutrition during the developmental years. Closer to home, there is concern in the developed nations about the effects of hunger and undernutrition of a milder sort on the development and functioning of infants and children (Birch & Gussow, 1970; Gussow, 1973). Indeed, of all the factors possibly contributing to mental subnormality, malnutrition and hunger are the most politically charged.

Malnutrition seldom appears in isolation, of course. Social status, educational level, incidence of infectious and other diseases, and various prenatal and perinatal hazards are compounded in human populations and deter efforts to assess the impact of poor nutrition on development. In preindustrialized societies, severe malnutrition and starvation are chronically of epidemic proportions. Severe protein-calorie undernutrition clearly can cause infantile marasmus (wasting) and kwashiorkor. The term "kwashiorkor," meaning "deposed child" (deposed from the mother's breast by a newborn sibling) in one African dialect and "red boy" in another (from the reddish orange color of the hair found in affected black infants), denotes a syndrome of dry skin and rash, potbelly and edema, weakness and irritability, and digestive disturbances. Although marasmus occurs among babies weaned early without receiving suitable substitutes for human milk, kwashiorkor is encountered in children not weaned until the second or third year of life and therefore deprived of sufficient protein. Even the effects of these diseases are difficult to ferret out, however, for the parents almost always are economically, educationally, and intellectually depressed and the children themselves are extremely vulnerable to infection, with a vicious cycle of chronic diarrhea, increased metabolic demands, decreased food intake and poor absorption, further infection, and inevitable deterioration. Data from Mexico, Guatemala, Peru, Yugoslavia, Uganda, South Africa, Jamaica, and the United States all suggest that children with poor early nitrition attain shorter physical height and do less well on various cognitive measures (e.g., Birch & Cravioto, 1968; Stoch & Smythe, 1963). Aggressive efforts to feed a nutritious diet seem to produce substantial improvement (Chase & Martin, 1970).

Numerous observations in animals indicate that early malnutrition can retard physical growth even when the diet is supplemented later on (Eichenwald & Fry, 1969). There is some evidence that CNS damage may be reduced by protective mechanisms in the brain, however. Dallman & Spirito (1972), for example, found in rats that brain protein was conserved by utilizing amino acids released by other tissues such as skeletal muscle and liver which were losing mass under the depriving diet. Other studies, however, show lower brain weight, reduction in brain lipids and DNA in rats underfed during the weaning period (Chase, 1973), and these effects are much greater if maternal malnutrition occurred during gestation (Winick & Rosso, 1973). In rats and swine, simple caloric deprivation during the nursing period results in behavioral changes without impaired problem solving, but protein deprivation in early life does reduce the capacity to learn at a later age (see Eichenwald & Fry, 1969).

Some particularly interesting data have been obtained in the United States with children suffering cystic fibrosis (pancreatic insufficiency plus chronic respiratory tract disease). Such children were chosen as models to observe the effects of malnutrition without the confounding complications of socioeconomic deprivation (Lloyd-Still, Hurwitz, Wolff, & Shwachman, 1974). Up to the age of five, a subgroup of these patients performed less well than their unaffected siblings on the Merrill-Palmer scale, but after age five, the groups fared equally well on appropriate Wechsler tests (IQ 102 versus 104). Similarly, there were no differences on the Lincoln-Oseretsky test of motor development or the Vineland Scale of Social Maturity. The poorer performance of the young children appeared to be reversed as their families, most of them middle class, adjusted to the emotional trauma of the child's chronic disease and its unfortunate prognosis.

Within the range of nutritional deprivation likely to be encountered in the developed nations, then, diet apparently plays a minor role in producing irreversible CNS changes and consequent mental retardation. On the other hand, hunger itself probably has a depressing effect on the alertness, vitality, curiosity, and attention of children (Birch & Gussow, 1970). There is little excuse for tolerating children's hunger in food-rich nations which number overconsumption and obesity among their primary health problems.

Food Additives   The environment of every child contains numerous toxic substances which are potentially dangerous. In Chapter 6 we will consider the clinical disorders which arise from ingestion of lead and mercury. A more controversial issue is the addition of chemical substances to food. About 3,000 different substances are added intentionally to foods during their growth, processing, or packaging (Sanders, 1966). Additives aid preservation, enhance flavor or color, improve texture, or increase yields in the production phase (Kermode, 1972). Although food additives are regulated by the Food and Drug Administration, deleterious effects may go unrecognized for a long time, as in the celebrated cases of cyclamates and monosodium glutamate (MSG). Since MSG produces brain lesions in very young mice and monkeys, it has been banned from foods prepared for infants. Cyclamates have likewise been banned after being shown to be carcinogenic in large doses in some lower species of animals. Antibiotics and hormones added to poultry and beef feed grains are another source of controversy.

CONCLUSION

In this chapter, we have considered in detail a number of the factors in the child's experience with the physical environment which can damage his central nervous system and thus limit his intellectual growth. Others leading to specific syndromes will be discussed in Chapter 6. Many or all of these factors are interrelated and probably additive in their effects. Obviously, there is a broad continuum of degree of severity with which the environment threatens the integrity of the developing individual, a continuum bounded on the one end by early spontaneous abortion, stillbirth, and neonatal death from severe congenital anomalies and on the other end by healthy development nearly indistinguishable from that of normal children.

In general, we can be optimistic about research into the effects of the physical environment on mental development, because identification of dangerous physical agents can eventually lead to programs of action. Much of the environment is under human control, and conscious efforts can usually lead to its modification. We have already witnessed encouraging progress in this direction. Minimization of the use of general anesthetics at delivery, removal of lead from indoor paints and the use of unleaded gasoline in newer-model automobiles, creation of vaccines against rubella and rubeola, prevention of maternal Rh-antibody formation, and administration of effective antibiotics in cases of meningitis are examples of such actions which have saved a great many children from life-long mental subnormality. As we have seen, however, there is much work left, but the state of our technology promises handsome returns for our efforts.

6

Common Clinical Disorders Associated with Mental Retardation

In Chapter 5, we discussed a large number of factors in the physical environment which may damage a growing child. Despite the many potential dangers that have been identified and despite the wide variety of symptoms and handicaps which brain-damaged children sustain, there are relatively few specific clinical patterns of CNS damage which can be clearly delineated among retarded children. This chapter will be devoted to some of the specific patterns of clinical problems which appear in populations of brain-damaged children. Five groups of disorders will be described: cerebral palsy, seizure disorders, neural tube closure defects, congenital hypothyroidism, and lead and mercury poisoning. "Hyperactivity syndrome" of brain-damaged children will be covered in Chapter 11.

CEREBRAL PALSY (NEUROLOGICAL MOTOR DYSFUNCTION)

Cerebral palsy is a category, not a diagnosis. The term refers to a heterogeneous group of disorders characterized by a disorganization of motor control which results from damage to the brain at birth or in early childhood. There are numerous ways in which these brain abnormalities arise, including malformations, rare hereditary degenerative CNS diseases, acquired postnatal abnormalities of a traumatic or infectious nature,

This chapter was written with the collaboration of Gilbert S. Omenn.

and brain injury during the birth process. There is some indication that oxygen deprivation before and during birth plays a more important role than does mechanical injury (Lilienfeld & Parkhurst, 1951).

Symptoms

Although the neurological lesions are generally not progressive, the manifestations depend upon maturational stage and thus expression of the disorder changes during infancy. During early infancy, when behavior is dominated by the lower CNS structures, symptoms may not be apparent, though the very young baby may be delayed in motor development and may lack muscle tone. As the higher centers are activated, however, CNS disorganization becomes more apparent and the baby develops increased muscle tone in the form of spasticity, rigidity, or involuntary movements. The transient reflexes which are normal in the young baby persist in the older child. The lack of integration of reflexive behavior resulting in abnormal postural responses, abnormal sensory input, faulty feedback from the body, and purposeless motor output, form a vicious repetitive cycle interfering with normal motor development.

About 65 percent of children with cerebral palsy have one or more limbs which are rigidly immobilized by constant muscular contractions. This *spastic* group is usually classified according to the number of limbs involved. *Monoplegia,* involvement of a single limb, is unusual. *Hemiplegia* refers to the involvement of two limbs on one side of the body, and *paraplegia* refers to involvement of the two lower limbs. *Triplegia,* which is also unusual, involves one arm and both legs; in *quadriplegia,* all four limbs are affected. In *diplegia,* all four limbs are involved, but the legs are more severely affected.

Another major group, accounting for about 30 percent of the cases, is afflicted with *dyskinesia,* which refers to abnormalities in the amount and type of motor activities. Included here are *chorea* (rapid, jerky, involuntary movements) and *athetosis* (slow, wormlike, purposeless movements exaggerated by voluntary action). Less common dyskinetic muscular disorders are *dystonia* (muscle tonus above normal), *tremors,* and *rigidity.*

Ataxia (impairment of postural activity and walking) is the third major group of disorders, accounting for approximately 5 percent of the cases of cerebral palsy.

The signs and symptoms of disruption in motor function depend upon the site and extent of the damage. Spastic symptoms are common when there are lesions in the pyramidal tract of the brain and spinal column, causing unceasing contraction of the muscles. Athetosis is more likely to result from lesions occurring in the extrapyramidal system, whose effects are normally inhibitory. There is some indication that athetoid symptoms tend to follow anoxia, whereas cerebral hemorrhage tends to cause spasticity (Perlstein, 1955). Asymmetric and athetoid (limb-waving) palsies are apparently caused more often by birth and postnatal injuries or jaundice (kernicterus); the symmetric symptoms, such as spastic involvement of both arms, are probably more often the sequels of developmental anomalies (Asher & Schonell, 1950).

Intelligence and Cerebral Palsy

The classic paper on cerebral palsy was written by Little (1862), who recognized the importance of prematurity, mechanical birth trauma, and poor condition at birth of these children. He also noted that they might prove intellectually very able despite their handicap. Little quoted Shakespeare's description of Richard III:

I, that am curtail'd of this fair proportion,
Cheated of feature by dissembling nature,
Deform'd, unfinish'd, sent before my time
Into this breathing world scarce half made up,
And that so lamely and unfashionable
That dogs bark at me as I halt by them. (Act I, scene 1)

The frequency and extent of intellectual deficiency in children with cerebral palsy has been a matter of debate for some time, largely because of problems in appraising the capacities of children who are severely handicapped in motor activity and communication. Some authors have tended to take the results of ordinary intelligence tests at face value and to estimate the frequency of mental retardation as very high; others have tended to give palsied children the benefit of every doubt and to estimate the frequency as quite low. The best estimates appear to be that about 50 percent of cerebral palsied children have IQs below 70, about 25 percent attain IQs in the borderline range (70 to 90), and the remainder attain scores in the normal range or above (Perlstein, 1955). Mental retardation is apparently more common when injury has been sustained by the dominant cerebral hemisphere (ordinarily, the left hemisphere) than by the nondominant one. Even when the individual is not retarded, however, the physical handicaps are often so crippling that achievement of economic and social independence is almost impossible. In addition, many cerebral palsied individuals have associated handicaps affecting vision, hearing, speech, and proprioception. Seizures and emotional and behavioral disturbances are also not infrequent.

The special disabilities of the cerebral palsied child add immeasurably to the severity of whatever intellectual deficit he may have sustained. Often he has such speech and motor difficulties that he cannot make his wants known, is unable to achieve a sense of independent accomplishment, and remains as helpless and dependent as if he were still an infant.

Treatment

Cerebral palsy is a common clinical problem in institutions for retarded children. A number of states of the United States provide special facilities for the education of cerebral palsied children, but too often the retarded child with cerebral palsy is excluded from such facilities. In the national population as a whole, the incidence is staggering. Several sources quoted by Warkany (1971) estimate the number to be in the hundreds of thousands; some think that there may be as many as half a million, with as many as ten thousand new cases born every year.

Early identification and prompt institution of physical therapy during infancy are important aspects of care. The physical therapist is often the primary professional involved in treatment of the child (Wolf, 1969). There are indications that very early physical therapy, instituted by age six months in severe cases and by age one year in milder cases, can be effective in minimizing the handicap (Köng, 1969), but treatment instituted after that age is much less effective (Wright & Nicholson, 1973), though probably not without its value (Beals, 1966).

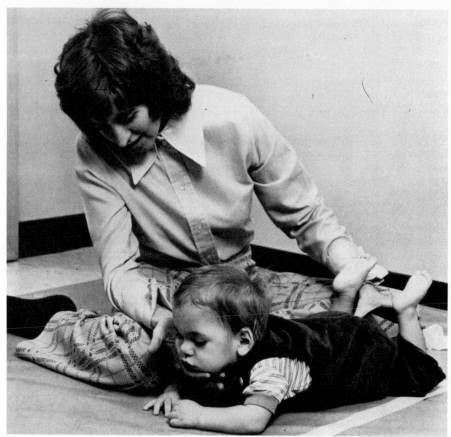

Fig. 6-1 Early treatment of cerebral palsy. *(University of Washington Child Development and Mental Retardation Center)*

SEIZURE DISORDERS (EPILEPSY)

A seizure may be defined as a paroxysmal and transitory disturbance of the function of the brain which develops suddenly, ceases spontaneously, and exhibits a conspicuous tendency to recur (Slater & Cowie, 1971, p. 160). Spontaneous neuronal excitation starts at a focus in the brain. It may remain localized or may spread from that focus, and consequently the observable phenomena and subjective experiences may remain localized or become general, as in a major convulsion. About 1 person in 20 has a seizure at some time in his life, and about 1 in 160 develops chronic seizures, often referred to as *epilepsy*. The patient's age at the onset of seizures gives an important clue to etiology. (Pincus & Tucker, 1974). Seizures beginning before age six months usually reflect CNS malformation, birth injury, metabolic error, or infection. Seizures beginning between ages two and twenty years may be related to genetic factors and are termed *idiopathic* when they lack any identifiable precipitating cause. When seizures first occur after age thirty-five, vascular insufficiency or brain tumor must be suspected. Seizures seldom begin between ages twenty and thirty-five except as the result of trauma, drug abuse (particularly alcohol), or infection.

Many extensive studies have demonstrated the importance of genetic factors in epilepsy as well as precipitating physical factors. Among first-degree relatives (parents, siblings, and children) of individuals with idiopathic epilepsy, the risk of chronic seizure disorder is elevated about sevenfold over the general population. The risk is elevated almost as much (perhaps fivefold) among such relatives of individuals with what is termed "symptomatic epilepsy," i.e., epilepsy following an obvious precipitating event. The latter figure surely means that among the many children who endure traumatic events such as birth injury, childhood fever, or head trauma, the much smaller number who develop a chronic seizure disorder must be genetically predisposed to do so. As in so many common conditions, an interaction between genetic predisposing factors and external factors is required for manifestation of the signs of the disorder. Far more relatives of epileptics have abnormal EEGs than have seizures, and in fact the underlying EEG pattern is very much under genetic control. In addition, seemingly quite normal individuals may have one of several variant patterns of voltage or frequency in the EEG because of the inheritance of one of several autosomal dominant genes (Vogel, 1970b). EEGs are one of the most discriminating tests to distinguish identical from fraternal twins, since identical twins have truly identical EEGs, whereas fraternal twins who, like siblings, share about half the genes, show considerable EEG differences.

Petit Mal Seizures

The deep central masses of gray matter in the brain, the centrencephalic region, have retained a much greater capacity than the cortex to go into excitation autonomously or under relatively slight stimulation. When this excitation occurs but remains localized, a petit mal seizure results. Such seizures are characterized clinically by "absences," a loss of awareness during which there is no motor activity other than blinking or rolling up of the eyes. The episodes are brief, usually lasting less than ten seconds, and may not be noticed by the casual observer nor even by the child himself. Patients do not fall to the ground, nor is there a postictal (postseizure) depression. The child may, however, lose track of what he is doing because of the interruption and may therefore seem in school to be inattentive. The seizures rarely occur in anyone over fifteen years of age, and most patients (50 to 75 percent) with petit mal epilepsy have no other types of seizures and are not mentally retarded.

Petit mal epilepsy is distinguishable in EEG records by bursts of three cycles-per-second spike-and-wave complexes. Metrakos and Metrakos (1969) have demonstrated that the childhood petit mal epilepsy of subcortical (centrencephalic) origin appears to be transmitted as an autosomal dominant trait, with 50 percent risk of typical EEG patterns among first-degree relatives, but a much lower risk of clinical epilepsy. The manifestation of both the EEG abnormality and the clinical epilepsy is strikingly related to age, almost all those affected manifesting EEG abnormalities only between ages four and forty years. The highest frequencies occur between five and sixteen years. Among those with clinical evidence of the disorder, 85 percent show the spike-and-wave complex trait in the simple resting EEG, whereas the remainder require extra stimulation in the form of hyperventilation or photic stimulation. Among the asymptomatic siblings, however, a higher percentage require stimulation beyond the resting EEG.

Grand Mal Seizures

Grand mal seizures, in contrast with petit mal seizures, are characterized by total loss of consciousness and stereotyped motor activity. During the initial tonic stage, the body stiffens and breathing often stops. The subsequent clonic phase consists of rhythmic shaking of the extremities and the trunk. This sequence may last for a minute or two and sometimes repeats. After the convulsion stops, there is a postictal depression of consciousness including drowsiness, confusion, headache, and somnolence which may last from a few minutes up to a day or two. About 50 percent of patients experience some sort of aura preceding the attack. The aura is an integral part of the seizure and usually consists of an ill-defined sensation of not feeling well or sometimes a psychomotor seizure. Patients with focal lesions in the cortex are apt to have an aura which can be related to the damaged area. During the seizure there are characteristic EEG changes in the tonic and clonic phases and immediately afterwards, but in half the cases the resting EEG between seizures is normal. Only a quarter of cases remain normal if the EEG is taken during sleep.

Focal Seizures

Focal seizures may be motor or sensory or both, coinciding with focal disease in the side of the brain opposite the affected side of the body. After the seizure, there is often a "Todd's paralysis" of the affected area. Especially in young children, certain metabolic disturbances such as hypoglycemia and hypocalcemia may produce focal seizures in the absence of any local structural abnormality in the brain.

Minor Motor Seizures

Infantile Spasms   Infantile spasms consist of a sudden flexion or extension of the body after a cry and usually appear between three and seven months of age. They are associated with an EEG pattern known as hypsarrhythmia. Nine of every ten children with infantile spasms are also seriously retarded (Pincus & Tucker, 1974). These infantile spasms may be considered the response of an immature nervous system to such serious insults as phenylketonuria, hypoglycemia, subdural effusions, encephalitis, and malformations of the brain itself.

Akinetic Seizures   Akinetic seizures, or myoclonic spells, last only a few seconds during which the child falls passively without warning. The fall starts with an active flexion of the neck and hips, and the child is very likely to injure his head and face unless he is wearing a protective helmet. Although the seizures are often controllable by appropriate medication, most cases are associated with brain damage and have a poor prognosis for intellectual development. They may be considered the counterpart during ages one to seven of the infantile spasms. The usual EEG pattern is an "atypical" spike-and-wave complex which is different from the petit mal type.

Myoclonic Jerks   This benign disorder involves smaller muscle groups and may occur alone or as a prodrome to grand mal seizures. Myoclonic jerks occur occasionally in healthy individuals as they are falling asleep. In some cases, however, serious underlying disease is present (Pincus & Tucker, 1974).

Psychomotor Seizures

Psychomotor seizures are usually, but not always, due to spiking discharges in the temporal lobes. Part of the temporal lobe, the hippocampus, is especially susceptible to reduction of energy production by such conditions as anoxia, carbon monoxide poisoning, respiratory failure, or hypoglycemia (Green, 1964). The hippocampus has the lowest seizure threshold of all cortical regions. A loss of neurons in this region is often seen in individuals with psychomotor seizures. Lesions of the hippocampus may give rise to seizures of the psychomotor type, in association with deterioration of intellect and personality. Psychomotor seizures fall into three clinical categories.

Subjective Feelings One group of disorders includes a variety of subjective feelings including forced, repetitive, and disturbing thoughts, alterations of mood, sensations of impending disaster and anxiety, and inappropriate sensations of familiarity or unfamiliarity *(déjà vu, jamais vu).* Some patients have episodes of depersonalization, dreamlike states, or sensations like those of alcoholic intoxication, including hallucinations and acute abdominal pains.

Automatisms Subtle and inappropriate repetitive movements such as lip-smacking, chewing, gagging, retching, or swallowing, may be blended into normal activities. More extreme manifestations are repetition of a phrase over and over or buttoning and unbuttoning clothing. In rare instances, these patients have outbursts of directed, aggressive behavior.

Bizarre Postures The individual may assume an unusual posture for variable periods of time, much like the postures observed in catatonic schizophrenics, and is unlikely to be aware of or to remember the episode.

Therapy for Epilepsy

Several different types of drugs are used for the various seizure disorders. Although it is certainly not the intention to discuss the pharmacology of seizure disorders here, readers may benefit from some familiarization with the names and primary indications for the more commonly used agents, since their patients or subjects may be taking these drugs.

Phenobarbital is the most commonly used. It may be effective in all types of seizure disorders, including petit mal. *Diphenylhydantoin* (Dilantin) is used particularly in adults, but also in children for control of grand mal, focal, and psychomotor seizures. It is ineffective in petit mal and myoclonic seizures. *Primidone* (Mysoline) is a barbituratelike compound which is most useful in psychomotor seizures. *Ethosuccimide* (Zarontin) is the drug of choice in petit mal, but of essentially no value for other seizure disorders. *Acetazolamide* (Diamox) may be effective in all types of seizures, especially in minor motor and petit mal seizures. *Diazepam* (Valium) is useful in minor motor seizures, but used primarily for intravenous injection in status epilepticus (long-lasting seizure). *ACTH* is useful in infantile spasms and juvenile minor motor seizures but can cause seizures in other types. Manipulation of diet *(ketogenic diet)* is claimed to be helpful only with minor motor seizures. Sometimes a *combination* of medications is better than any one agent alone.

"Epileptoid Personality" and "Epileptic Psychoses"

Considerable dispute surrounds the existence, nature, and frequency of the so-called epileptoid personality and epileptic psychoses. The postulated personality pattern consists of a liability to sudden unmotivated or lightly triggered mood changes, especially in the direction of irritability, anger, aggression, or severe depression. Panic, impulsive actions, "short-circuit" reactions, or fugue states may also be involved. At least one substantial study indicates a relationship between psychomotor epilepsy and a form of schizophrenia. Slater, Beard, and Glithero (1963) described sixty-nine patients with a mean age of onset of the psychosis at thirty years, following a history of epilepsy lasting, on the average, for fourteen years. Evidence of temporal lobe dysfunction was found in 80 percent. Frequency of seizures varied markedly, but all had incomplete control of the seizures at the time they became psychotic. The most convincing element of these histories was the low incidence of schizophrenia in the first-degree relatives, suggesting that the patients were experiencing something different from other types of schizophrenia. They showed all the cardinal features of schizophrenia but affective responsiveness was preserved very well and later deterioration of personality seemed not to occur. There is no evidence that individuals with grand mal or petit mal seizures have any such propensity to personality changes or psychotic disorders (Pincus & Tucker, 1974). Many authors have long maintained that schizophrenia actually constitutes a heterogeneous group of disorders, and the existence of this distinguishable disorder, like the earlier discovery of paresis (tertiary syphilis) with its schizophreniclike symptoms, would tend to substantiate that view.

Relationship of Seizures to Intellectual Capacity

The whole question about the causal role of seizures in mental subnormality remains somewhat unsettled. The bulk of the evidence supports the view that seizures per se are not a major contributor to mental retardation. When a severe degree of mental handicap is combined with epileptic fits, one can be sure that there is underlying gross brain pathology, the common cause of both manifestations. Investigations of this relationship are enormously complicated. To perform a definitive study, investigators would have to distinguish the several classes of seizure disorders outlined above, control for the age of the patient at onset of seizures, the presence or absence of brain damage and other diseases, the duration of the seizure disorder, the number and severity of seizures, the social class and intelligence of the patient prior to onset, the medications used and their dosage and blood level, and the length of time since the last seizure. It is little wonder that this issue remains in doubt.

As already mentioned, infantile spasms and akinetic minor motor seizures are commonly associated with severe underlying disease and very poor prognosis. Focal seizures usually indicate local pathology in the brain. There is a high incidence of epilepsy in individuals with profound and severe mental retardation with perhaps 25 to 30 percent of those in institutions having seizure disorders (Jasper, Ward, & Pope, 1969). Reviewing studies of the large number of children with petit mal or centrencephalic epilepsy, however, Slater and Cowie (1971) conclude that there is no reliable evidence that the mean IQ in such patients is lower than the population average, nor that borderline or mildly retarded individuals are more subject to seizures than the general population.

We should note that individuals with seizures have been treated severely for decades at least. Until recent years, involuntary sterilization was the law (usually unenforced) in several countries including Sweden and Denmark and in several states of the United States. Fortunately, attitudes in contemporary society are becoming much more realistic and, with the successful control by medication of most seizure states, the plight of the individual with seizures is no longer so difficult and lonely.

NEURAL TUBE CLOSURE DEFECTS: ANENCEPHALY
AND MENINGOMYELOCELE

A broad spectrum of related embryological defects involving the nervous system can be designated neural tube closure defects. The spinal cord and brain are derived from a thickened area of the ectoderm located along the mid-dorsal line of the embryo, the neural plate. In embryos seventeen and eighteen days of age, a central groove can be recognized. Soon, the groove deepens and its elevated lateral folds approach one another in the midline, forming the neural tube. Closure begins at the cervical border (neck level) of the spinal cord and brain and progresses in both directions. In normal human embryos, closure is completed at the head at gestational age twenty-three days and at the "tail" end by twenty-five to twenty-eight days of gestation, establishing the primitive central nervous system. (See Chapter 4.)

Clinical Defects

Anencephaly represents a defect in closure at the anterior or head portion of the neural groove. As a result, the unfused forebrain develops only partially and then degenerates. The skull cannot complete its development, and the facial features and external ear may also be secondarily altered. Affected individuals seldom survive more than a few hours or days after birth.

Less extensive but viable defects can occur farther down the neural groove. Failure to close the lumbar or thoracic spine will allow the spinal cord and meninges to bulge out as a *meningomyelocele*, subject to infection, mechanical trauma, and distortion of nerve trunks because of exposure and bulging. Paralysis below the level of the bulge is the rule, with lack of bladder and bowel control, and infections through the spinal canal to the upper cord and brain are common complications, though the precise complications depend on the exact site of the defect (Smith, 1965). The brain may be unaffected, but even with extensive surgery there is usually moderate to severe disability.

Hydrocephalus refers to increased volume of cerebrospinal fluid within the skull, from any cause. Hydrocephalus can be secondary to the neural tube closure defects, if the lower spinal cord becomes attached to surrounding tissue and cannot move upward inside the cavity of the spinal column as the child grows. The brain is thus pulled downward into the spinal column. In Lorber and Bassi's (1968) series, 478 of 588 cases of hydrocephalus in infants were associated with spina bifida (gaps in the spine).

Other causes of hydrocephalus are not related to neural tube closure defects. Sometimes there is an inability to manage a fluid overload in the brain, on account of either overproduction or underabsorption of the cerebrospinal fluid. In other cases, blockage occurs in the usual circulation of the spinal fluid, often at the narrowest point, the aqueduct of Sylvius. In such cases, the fluid produced in the lining of the ventricles causes the brain to be thinned and the skull to expand. If the suture lines of the skull are already closed, however, the skull cannot expand and the increased fluid compresses the brain.

As fluid accumulates in the infant brain (though, as explained above, not in that of the older child), the sutures of the skull begin to spread and the cerebral cortex may appear paper thin because of its expansion from within. The cranium expands in a globular shape. The upper part of the face is also affected, so that the eyes become more widely spaced, the bridge of the nose is flattened, and visual impairment ensues. The severity of symptoms varies widely. Some cases die, some are bedridden and

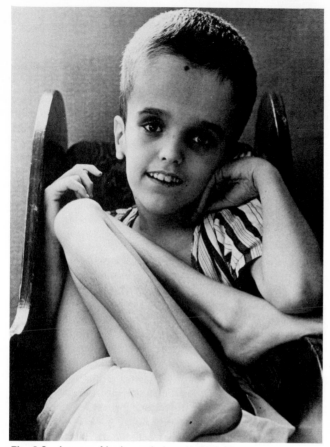

Fig. 6-2 A case of hydrocephalus. *(J. & M. Menapace)*

helpless, some have spastic paralysis of the lower limbs and seizures, whereas others continue to participate in normal activities and sustain only relatively mild intellectual handicaps. Prompt action when the problem is first noted often can prevent the development of a full-blown disorder. Operations that place a tube from the ventricles of the brain to the heart drain off the excess of blocked fluid and can prevent the complications due to continued pressure on the brain. Exquisite care to prevent infection of the ventriculo-atrial shunt is essential.

Etiology

The causes of neural tube closure defects are unknown. Future children of a couple who have had one such child have a risk of about 5 percent, compared with a general population incidence of 0.1 to 0.2 percent. There are equal chances of having a child with anencephaly or meningomyelocele, and some cases also have hydrocephalus. It is generally thought that multiple genetic factors and possibly some unspecified environmental or intrauterine maternal factors interact to interfere with the closely timed schedule for neural tube closure.

As in cases of low birthweight and fetal mortality, the frequencies of anencephaly and meningomyelocele around the world vary with social class, maternal age, parity, ethnic group, geography, time, and even season (Emanuel, 1972). Since frequencies of these conditions are related also to social status of the baby's father and maternal grandfather, Emanuel and Sever (1973) propose that the conditions of the mother's childhood, as well as of the pregnancy itself, influence reproductive results.

Whatever the complex interplay of factors involved in disturbing the neural tube closure process, a dramatic new test now allows the detection of pregnancies with neural tube defects. Amniotic fluid is obtained about the sixteenth week of pregnancy and is tested for the presence of a fetal circulating serum protein (alpha-feto-protein), which seems to escape in significant amounts into the amniotic fluid only in the presence of a neural tube closure defect (Allan, Ferguson-Smith, Donald, Sweet, & Gibson, 1973).

LEAD AND MERCURY POISONING

Lead Poisoning

Lead poisoning was once considered solely an occupational disease of painters and industrial workers until poisoning of urban children was revealed over fifty years ago (Griggs, Sunshine, Newhill, Newton, Buchanan, & Rasch, 1964). In eastern and midwestern cities in the United States, up to 50 percent by weight of paints and plaster in slum dwellings was found to be lead. As housing fell into disrepair, crumbling plaster and flaking paint found their way into the respiratory and digestive tracts of infants and young children growing up there. The disease was thus largely restricted to the slums. By the 1960s, this housing problem had become a national scandal (Oberle, 1969), and legislation was passed to prohibit the use of indoor lead-based paints.

Large-scale screening in New York City, Chicago, and smaller cities has revealed that about 10 percent of all children had lead levels in the range where toxicity may be detected clinically. Most of these children lived in good housing. With lead paints largely a product of the past, lead poisoning is now coming from polluted air, more than 98 percent of the lead being derived from automobile exhausts (Chow & Earl, 1970.) Tetraethyl and other alkyl leads are added to fuels in order to permit high compression without knocking and without additional refining. Exhaustive studies have demonstrated that urban air over a wide area is contaminated with lead in proportion to the density of automobile traffic. Particulate matter falls out and contaminates ordinary dust and soil in which children are commonly playing. For these obvious reasons, automobiles manufactured in the United States are now required to use lead-free gasoline.

In severe lead poisoning, mortality rates are high and permanent damage is frequent. In adults, anemia, intestinal colic, and peripheral neuropathy are observed. In children, encephalopathy can occur, with mental retardation, recurrent seizures, and cerebral palsy (Perlstein & Attala, 1966). The younger the fetus or child, the greater the susceptibility of the nervous system to permanent damage. Furthermore, a single episode of acute toxicity involving the nervous system may cause permanent derangement, even though the toxic agent is rapidly removed. This danger applies to chlorinated hydrocarbon pesticides (Angle, McIntire, & Meile, 1968) as well as lead, mercury, and other metals (Snyder, 1971).

It is simply not known how many cases of mental retardation and other neurologic problems of undiagnosed etiology are due to childhood poisoning. Mass epidemics are readily investigated but poisoning that goes on year after year tends to escape notice, partly because the connection may be inapparent and partly because the underprivileged population subgroups which live in poor housing and in central areas with high traffic density do not find adequate medical care. Lead poisoning is, however, highly suited to aggressive case finding, because simple tests can demonstrate and quantitate the presence of the metal in body fluids and tissues, including bone, teeth, and gums (Needleman, Tuncay, & Shapiro, 1972). There is growing evidence that elevated blood and tooth levels of lead below those which are associated with encephalopathy and mental retardation may be associated with minimal brain dysfunction or hyperactivity syndrome (David, 1974; Needleman, Davidson, Sewall, & Shapiro, 1974). Lead is probably one of several environmental agents (food additives have been mentioned as another) which trigger the behavioral and learning abnormalities of the hyperactivity disorder in children who are genetically susceptible (Omenn, 1973).

Mercury Poisoning

As in the case of lead poisoning, mercury poisoning, which used to be considered a rare occupational hazard, has today been recognized as a potential problem for whole populations (Miller, 1967; Wallace, Fulkerson, Shults, & Lyon, 1971). Metallic mercury vapor was responsible for poisoning of miners and hat-felt workers ("mad as a hatter") with kidney and brain damage. Use of mercury compounds in certain industrial processes led to an extraordinary outbreak in Japan of Minamata Disease (Kurland, Faro, & Siedler, 1960; Tsuchiya, 1969). In 1956, a new factory on the shores of Minamata Bay began producing vinyl chloride and acetaldehyde, and its wastes containing methyl mercury were dumped into a nearby creek. Within a year, in families of fishermen there appeared a strange illness, with memory loss, paresthesia, imbalance of gait, narrowing of visual field, and emotional instability. Small children and infants were affected with cerebral palsy and impaired intelligence (Miller, 1967). The methyl mercury was concentrated through the food chain, eaten by shellfish, and these in turn finally by cats and people. Methyl mercury passes the blood-brain barrier readily, producing an especially high toxicity to the brain. Another kind of mini-epidemic occurred in a New Mexico family who ate meat from hogs which had been fed grain containing a mercury compound intended for seed purposes only. The extent of mercury-induced damage is unknown worldwide, but it is known that fish in Lake Michigan, in Swedish coastal waters, and elsewhere contain more than the amount of mercury known to be toxic with long-term exposure (Eyl, Wilcox, & Reizen, 1970). As a result, dumping of mercury-laden wastes into sewage effluents has been prohibited, and mercury-based fungicides have been phased out. Risks from atmospheric mercury content are only now, however, being investigated.

CONCLUSION

The best medical practice cannot undo damage already done to the sensitive and vulnerable fetus and young child, and it is therefore encouraging to survey the progress which has been made in preventing or circumventing assaults on the nervous system. Prompt diagnosis and effective personal medical care can block many of the deteriorative effects of congenital hypothyroidism, seizure disorders, hydrocephalus, and early toxic states. For disorders such as the neural tube closure defects the basic etiology remains unexplained and yet early amniocentesis can detect affected fetuses and allow for early termination of these pregnancies. Public health measures fortified by legislation can be potentially even more effective in preventing damage before it occurs as, for example, by prohibiting the use of lead in indoor paints and gasoline and halting the dumping of harmful effluents into water, soil, and air. Still, as we saw in Chapter 5, the threats posed by many agents in the physical environment are still uncontrolled and in many ways our work has just begun.

7
Psychological Factors in Mental Retardation

For all children, retarded and nonretarded, countless environmental factors affect intellectual functioning and success of adjustment. Furthermore, all children, even the most grossly handicapped, are exquisitely tuned to their environments (Hereford, Cleland, & Fellner, 1973). Unfortunately, most of the evidence concerning the psychological factors contributing to mental retardation is fragmentary, speculative, and difficult to interpret. Much of it is exceptionally controversial. Some children weather successfully much the same conditions which seem to produce retardation in others. Family conditions which may lead to acceleration during one period of development may lead to deceleration in another. The complexities of life make it very difficult to ferret out the exact element in a given instance which should receive the highest priority or to assess the interplay of the many components which constitute the real-life environment. In the present chapter, we will discuss some factors which bear in a general way on the development of all children.

GENERAL PRINCIPLES OF PSYCHOLOGICAL DEVELOPMENT

Sociocultural Determination

People's distinctive characteristics, even their most basically human attributes, are to a large extent the product of their experiences with other human beings. As children grow, they interact with many persons in a wide variety of situations. Some aspects of their development are determined by broad cultural variables, the heritage of many generations. The resulting customs, attitudes, and habits affect the most basic behaviors, the expressions of anger, love, and fear, as well as the values accorded to intellectual, aesthetic, and athletic competencies. As children are members of large cultural groups, they are simultaneously members of various influential subcultures. Their social class, religion, sex, race, age, school, parents' occupations, and neighborhood all help to define the subgroups to which they owe allegiance. Finally, it is within the family that children are nurtured, and through the family that the effects of the larger units are filtered. The importance of the parents, the first and most important socializing agents, is heightened for retarded children who may be dependent upon them long past the usual ages of emancipation.

The Dynamic Approach to Psychological Development

Most theorists today emphasize a holistic approach to understanding the development and functioning of the organism. Genetic, biologic, and environmental processes are seen as interacting at every stage of development and in every behavioral sequence. No aspect of adjustment can function independently of another. Although psychological theorists differ in the variables they emphasize and the explanatory principles they propose, nearly all accept what is known as a dynamic point of view. Dynamic theories assert that personality cannot be understood in terms of simple traits or elements which exist in rigid relationships to each other. Instead, there is constant change, assimilation, and accommodation within the personality system.

The dynamic approach is similar in some ways to the formulation of the laws which govern the motion of bodies, physical force, and energy, with an emphasis on movement, on reaction and counterreaction. The dynamic view implies that anything which interferes with normal personality growth or with emotional or physical well-being is likely to interfere with intellectual functioning. It is from this point of view not surprising to find that children who are emotionally disturbed are also often retarded. Likewise, children retarded in mental ability are likely to be retarded in social maturity and often exhibit serious problem behaviors. Children with limited ability to cope with the demands of their environment experience repeated failure in their attempts to control their own behavior and events in the world around them.

Certainly the best-known dynamic theory of personality development is the one formulated by Sigmund Freud (1949). An hypothesis which typifies his dynamic orientation is that at any time in life a person has only a limited quantity of psychophysiological energy. A retarded child for whom the simplest everyday activities require great intellectual effort may have only a small amount of psychic energy to deal with anything else.

A similar idea underlies the general-adaptation syndrome described by the endocrinologist Hans Selye (1950, 1956). After an initial alarm reaction, the organism achieves an adaptation to the source of stress and resumes apparently normal functioning, but loses some of its ability to handle additional stresses. A retarded child who has recently made an apparently smooth transition from home to an institution might, for example, be unable to cope with a minor change of routine, with the transfer of a favorite ward attendant, or with discipline imposed for breaking rules.

The case of Paul, an abandoned baby described by Gelinier-Ortigues and Aubry (1955), illustrates a severe withdrawal reaction accompanied by mental retardation and psychogenic deafness. The primary source of difficulty was probably the failure to establish any important human relationships, yet Paul did not develop normally in any respect. His intelligence, physical growth, motor skills, and interpersonal reactions all remained those of a small infant.

Paul was eighteen months old when he entered a reception center for very young children under the care of the public welfare department in the Seine District in Paris. He had been abandoned by his mother when he was two months old and had been moved fourteen times during the next sixteen months. He was very thin and weak and seemed almost totally deaf. His face was quite inert and expressionless except for his eyes, which watched everything that went on and closely examined objects but avoided looking directly at people. Even at eighteen months, he was unable to sit without support. He seldom cried and never laughed. Evaluations at ages twenty-four and thirty months yielded developmental quotients[1] of 38 and 37, respectively, indicating unmistakable retardation.

In the institution, Paul became a little less wretched during the next year. He cared for him. They were convinced that he was not deaf, since he sometimes turned toward them when they called him and because they heard him begin to vocalize, but he was totally unresponsive in the presence of other people. When he was 2½ years old, a specialized form of psychotherapy was instituted which involved as much close physical contact as Paul could tolerate. His relationship with his therapist crystallized rapidly, and he soon began to seek contact with the nurses and other children. He looked more alert and began to speak a few syllables.

Paul's retardation and his refusal to react to sounds expressed his lack of attachment to a world of people and possibly his self-protection against further rejection. A vicious circle was established in which even the best-intentioned of his fourteen foster mothers probably grew indifferent to him as he became more and more unresponsive. When, through skillful therapeutic mothering, he was able to build a warm and trusting relationship, his rapid development was dramatic.

Differentiation, Growth, and Organization

Thompson and Grusec (1970) have suggested that it is possible to derive most principles of development from three components: differentiation, growth, and organization. By differentiation, they refer to "the transition from a relatively unitary system to one with independent parts" (p. 571). This progressive differentiation can be viewed during embryological development and continues throughout the developmental periods. The entire body responds in a newborn's startle reflex. At a later stage, an infant will withdraw with precision the tickled foot or the stimulated hand. The tiny baby who is hungry is unable to respond to anything in his environment but a source of food. Subsequently his overall integrity will not be so threatened by hunger, and he will be able to be cajoled into waiting a while, even to the point of attending persistently to stimuli quite irrelevant to feeding. As an adult, he will be able to tolerate even severe hunger without significant intellectual impairment.

---

[1] A developmental quotient is similar to an intelligence quotient (IQ) except that it is concerned with overall sensorimotor and mental development.

The second element of Thompson's and Grusec's formulation, growth, "refers basically to the increments in size or in numbers of elements that occur in living systems as they change with age" (p. 572). The baby grows as cells proliferate, and the brain becomes heavier, although neuronal cells have done most of the multiplying prior to birth. As growth continues, various functions are replicated through different pathways, providing some built-in protection against gross impairment which is lacking in the very young organism.

The third element, which is the least well understood, has to do with the developing hierarchical organization of functions in the central nervous system. One theory related to brain organization is that of D. O. Hebb (1949). This theory concerns the transmission of electrical impulses from one part of the nervous system to another over pathways which become increasingly integrated as they are used over and over in an orderly fashion. Another theorist, Piaget, proposes the development of different cognitive organizations which are sequentially ordered and result from complex interactions between the individual and environment. (See Chapter 12.)

Maturation and Learning

Behavioral changes during the growing-up process depend upon two different but inseparable aspects of development: *maturation* and *learning.* Maturation refers to biological growth processes that result in orderly changes in behavior, relatively independent of exercise or experience, the blooming of the physiological organism according to inborn timing mechanisms. Learning refers to behavioral changes which depend upon training, experience, and practice. Few items in the repertoire of the child depend exclusively on one or the other of these aspects of growth. Locomotor activity, smiling, and other behaviors may make a first appearance quite independent of practice, but they will not persist unless they are reinforced by appropriate experiences. On the other hand, learning cannot occur until the organism is sufficiently mature. Most little children learn to speak, and the age at which words first appear is relatively constant from culture to culture, though of course the words themselves are not. It is, however, quite foolish to try to teach most six-month-old babies to speak. Their biological equipment will not permit it, no matter how patient the teacher may be.

Mentally retarded children are slow to mature in many aspects of development. The ages of sitting, walking, and especially talking are likely to be delayed. Retarded children are not likely to be ready to learn to read when they are six. They may never grasp historical concepts. Yet their bodies continue to grow, and in appearance they may seem at first no different from other boys and girls their age. This disparity between size and appearance, on the one hand, and immature capabilities, on the other, can lead to particularly unhappy experiences. Although almost all children learn to use the toilet by the age of three, the markedly retarded child may continue to use diapers for several additional years. Neighbors will look askance, and the mother may persist fruitlessly with training until she and the child are both miserable.

The problem here is essentially what Hunt (1961) has termed "the problem of the match." Fostering development depends upon presenting tasks to children that elicit their interest and call upon the skills and abilities they possess to help them "stretch" a little to achieve success. Giving them tasks that are too easy will bore them, but giving them those too difficult will create frustration, distress, withdrawal, and a sense of failure. Children often develop unevenly from one sphere to another. One retarded child may be agile and graceful but unable to use language. Another may be clumsy but able to remember names and pictures at a nearly normal level. The clever parent or teacher will arrange the child's experiences in a continual succession of appropriate "matches."

Age and Vulnerability

In Chapter 5 it was pointed out that the child's response to physical trauma is related to the stage of growth and that, to some extent, age is more important than the kind of trauma. In the same way, responses to the psychological environment depend in part upon the stage of development. At the time when a particular behavior or skill is beginning to emerge, usually its period of fastest growth, the fate of that behavior is most precarious (Scott & Marston, 1950).

Critical Periods Many authors maintain that there are critical periods in development, specific times during which normal growth patterns may be irrevocably interrupted. Harlow (1961, 1963) has developed this theme in discussing some aspects of the development of affectional patterns in infant monkeys. Adequate maternal-infant and infant-maternal affection is prerequisite to satisfactory interchange with peers. There is an appropriate time for the mother to begin to push the infant away and to loosen maternal ties. Otherwise, the young monkey is unable to engage in normal play relationships with peers and later fails to adopt normal adult patterns, including mating and the rearing of young.

Several theorists have incorporated some notion of critical periods into their schemes of personality development. J. Bowlby (1969, 1973) has postulated critical phases of development in the child's capacity for human relationships. He considers the second half of the first year of life as crucial for the establishment of the child's attachment to the mother and the entire first two or three years as a period of intense interaction between mother and child.[2] It is for this reason that psychoanalysts and others of similar persuasion so staunchly oppose the substitution of group care for maternal care of young children.

H. T. Epstein (1974a, 1974b), a psychobiologist, has assembled data indicating that there are spurts of cerebral growth which alternate with spurts of somatic growth. Beyond infancy, he maintains that there are cerebral-growth "spurt" ages at seven, eleven, and fifteen which are associated with rapid mental development and that environmental supports are particularly crucial at these ages.

Environmental changes related to normal tempos of development can also critically affect adjustment patterns. A retarded child beginning to read in the third or fourth grade is out of phase. Materials at his grade level are beyond his emerging abilities, but he has little interest in "baby" primers. This common problem has prompted the publication of specially designed materials, yet retarded children in regular classes often still experience the discrepancy between their relatively mature interests and their lagging skills.

Imprinting The notion of critical periods received considerable impetus from the work of Konrad Lorenz, an European ethologist, and his followers. Lorenz (1937) developed the concept of *imprinting* to explain the unusual behavior of birds which

---

[2] See also the work of Shaffer, discussed later in this chapter.

during the first hours of life were exposed to members of a different species including the human being. These birds have a tendency to follow a moving object as soon as they acquire locomotion. This object is usually the mother bird and the appropriate responses in the chick are directed toward one of its own species. When the chick is exposed first to a member of another species, however, it becomes attached to that species and in later life it will usually attempt to mate only with its adopted group. Once an animal has been imprinted, it will be relatively impervious to other attractions. It is doubtful that the condition is completely irreversible, but imprinted reactions unquestionably tend to be strong and persistent. Their strength ordinarily is maintained by repeated reinforcement and by the young organism's natural avoidance of very novel stimuli (Gewirtz, 1961). Establishment of imprinting is confined to a definite period of time, usually quite brief. In fact, it may be possible to explain the entire phenomenon by the timing of its components: the development of locomotion, the desire to remain near a familiar figure (the following response), and the parallel development of fear of the unfamiliar. Only during the short period when maternally oriented locomotion is established, but fear is not yet too strong, can the chick be imprinted (Hess, 1959). Sensory deprivation can retard the period in which imprinting occurs, and enhanced environmental complexity can both advance the period and strengthen the behavior (Haywood & Tapp, 1966). Apparently, enrichment stimulates the general responsive capacity of the organism.

SPECIFIC PSYCHOSOCIAL FACTORS IN THE ETIOLOGY OF MENTAL RETARDATION

In the remainder of this chapter, we shall consider a few of the many social factors which seem to be involved in the etiology of mental subnormality. Although almost any factor which interferes with emotional or physical well-being may also interfere with intellectual growth, the list of variables which have been empirically tied to mental subnormality is surprisingly short.

The major difficulty in research lies in isolating the precise variables which may be responsible for increments or deficits in intelligence. If we want to study the possible effect of nursery school experiences upon the subsequent intelligence of retarded children, how can we specify which of the school experiences are important determinants of intellectual growth or separate these experiences from a host of correlated factors? Which parents send their children to such nursery schools or permit them to be members of an experimental group? Perhaps these include brighter or duller, richer or poorer, more permissive or more overprotective parents than are average for the community. Perhaps they send some of their children and keep others at home. Presumably, these parents provide other stimulating activities for their children as well. To examine a number of these factors more closely, some investigators have sought to follow the same subjects over a period of years. These longitudinal studies are, of course, difficult and expensive. The fact that their samples are ordinarily rather small makes it unlikely that the effects of any single factor can be conclusively determined.

Research investigators have an obligation to protect the well-being of their subjects. They may subject subhuman animals to adverse conditions if there is likely to be important scientific gain, but it is doubtful whether the subtleties of the human social milieu can ever be approximated in the animal laboratory. The psychologist who wants to introduce experimental variables in his work with children does, however, have one important method at his disposal. He can change the environment in a way which is expected to favor the children's welfare. Thus, Rheingold (1956; Rheingold & Bayley, 1959) gave added care and affection to infants in an institutional nursery. This treatment temporarily accelerated their social responsiveness, and both the experimenter and the babies enjoyed themselves thoroughly.

Social Factors

Before we discuss some facets of the environment which impinge directly on children, perhaps it would be well to take a more macrocosmic view of the society and its customs, with their more indirect effects.

Socioeconomic Class[3]   Social class represents a matrix of interrelated variables, both genetic and acquired. Among the distinguishing features of social classes are parental education and occupation, parental IQ and verbal behavior, family income, health status, childrearing practices, neighborhood and housing conditions, a variety of attitudes toward education, achievement, and the possibility of controlling one's destiny, and so on. The effects of a variety of socioeconomic factors are important in the etiology of retardation due to psychosocial disadvantage (cultural-familial retardation). We shall, therefore, treat the effects of specific aspects of a poverty-level existence in a separate chapter following this one.

It has long been recognized that *children's IQs tend to vary with the status of their families.* Numerous investigators have found that children's scores on conventional intelligence tests are substantially correlated with the father's occupation, the parents' education, and family income (Matarazzo, 1972; Roberts & Engel, 1974; Willerman, 1972). In the course of standardizing the 1937 revision of the Stanford-Binet, it was found that children whose fathers were professional workers averaged about 20 IQ points higher than children whose fathers were farmers, slightly skilled workers, or day laborers (McNemar, 1942; Terman & Merrill, 1973). In a follow-up in 1965 of all children born in Great Britain in one week in March, 1958, Davie, Butler, and Goldstein (1972) similarly found very strong class effects in almost all areas of ability, achievement, and adjustment, children from the upper classes invariably being favored. Jencks (1972) estimates a difference of 13 to 15 IQ points between the top and bottom fifths of the population according to occupation or education.

Studies of foster children have tended to demonstrate a substantial correlation between children's IQs and the intelligence level of their own mothers, from whom they have been long separated, but at the same time, their general development is apparently accelerated by growing up in a middle-class home (Horn, Loehlin, & Willerman, 1974; Skodak & Skeels, 1949). The social environment in which a mother spent *her* childhood is related to her children's birthweight (Drillien, 1957), presumably through its influence on her health and/or reproductive capacity, especially her pelvic dimensions (Willerman, 1970).

Most researchers have reported that positive and negative *effects associated with social status probably manifest themselves progressively* as children grow older. An oft-quoted study by Sherman and Key (1932) in the sheltered hollows of the Blue Ridge Mountains found not only that the average child had an IQ of only 62, but that older children attained lower IQs than did younger ones. Brown and Halpern (1971) found that the developmental quotients of a group of rural black infants declined from 117 in the first three months to 86 at age three.[4] M. Deutsch (1954, 1969), too, found social

---

[3] See C. P. Deutsch (1973) for a review of social class influences on development.

[4] It must be kept in mind that somewhat different abilities are assessed in infancy than during early childhood.

class differences significantly more pronounced in fifth-grade than in first-grade children in New York City. The differences were greater on syntactical and categorizing measures than they were on measures tapping vocabulary or simple content.

Projects which have followed the same subjects throughout childhood have found increasing correlations between intelligence and various economic and cultural home indices, but mainly up to middle childhood (Bayley, 1940; Honzik, 1940). Bradway (1945) found with children tested first when they were ages 2½ to five and again when they were in junior high school that IQ changes tended to be in the direction predicted by an estimate of parents' and grandfathers' occupations and intelligence. When these subjects were tested again as young adults, however, the IQ changes were unrelated to the familial index (Bradway & Robinson, 1961).

A review of data bearing on the possibility of a progressive decline in mental ability among disadvantaged groups has been presented by Jensen (1974). Unlike the majority of investigators, he maintains that there is no methodologically sound evidence for a progressive decrement in mental ability. He administered the Lorge Thorndike group intelligence test to all elementary school children in Berkeley, California, and found only a small age decrement in verbal ability among black (disadvantaged) children, a decrement he attributed to reading problems. Indeed, reading skills frequently fall victim to factors associated with lower-class status. A report from a Harlem school project indicated that in its target area 30 percent of third-grade students were reading below grade level, but by sixth grade 81 percent had fallen behind (Harlem Youth Opportunities Unlimited, 1964).

Jensen's argument is certainly not without support. Hertzig and Birch (1971) found a slight rise in IQ from ages three to six for a group of Puerto-Rican working-class children in New York City, though they noted a larger rise for a white middle-class group of the same ages. Milgram (1971) found no decline between ages three and eight for a group of disadvantaged Negro children. Kennedy (1968), retesting after several years a group of disadvantaged children, similarly found no decline in IQ, although he did find progressive retardation in school achievement. Heber, Dever, and Conry (1968) reported a particularly interesting finding that, among impoverished families, older children of mentally retarded mothers attained lower IQs than their younger siblings. No such difference was found between older and younger siblings of nonretarded mothers from the same neighborhood. At a minimum, then, one must conclude that many questions remain unanswered relating to the possibility of cumulative deficits in mental abilities among culturally disadvantaged social groups.

Distribution of Resources   The manner in which a society distributes its resources and services determines to some extent the adequacy of families in caring for their young children. A country in which some are very rich and others very poor obviously creates acute problems for the poor families in meeting the needs of their children. Some societies distribute services evenhandedly and guarantee minimum incomes to all sectors, whereas others grant public funds and services mainly to the poorest families. In the United States, health care is, for example, often available to the poor free of charge under federally funded programs, but it may be prohibitively expensive to families on the next higher rung of the economic ladder. Proposed national health insurance programs are designed to remedy that situation. In many other developed countries, health care is already available to all at little or no cost, especially prenatal care and health maintenance of young children.

Institutional Supports   Services of various kinds can be undertaken by a society which takes seriously its responsibilities to children. Although there are no empirical studies to substantiate the effects on infant development of maternity leaves for employed women, or restricted working schedules and paid leaves for mothers of very young children, these practices probably offer support at a critical time and contribute to the well-being of both the mothers and their offspring. Family allowances, layettes, and dietary supplements are made available in many other countries, sometimes contingent on the parents' fulfilling certain obligations such as the children's regular health checkups.[5]

A prevalent practice in other countries but almost unknown in the United States, except for some of the poorest families, is regular home visitation by a nurse. Ordinarily, these visits occur both before and after the birth of the child to make sure that the young parents have someone to turn to as needed and that they have the means and the skills to care for the baby. When such visits are made to all families, not only to those identified as having special needs, they tend to be welcomed. Such services offer a vital opportunity for preventive intervention in problem cases and can support effective childrearing even in strong families with a normal share of the tribulations of young parenthood.

Reproductive Customs   Mating patterns and reproductivity obviously have both genetic and environmental consequences. Selective mating tendencies are strong. Heber, Dever, and Conry (1968) administered the Peabody Picture Vocabulary Test to families in a very impoverished neighborhood. They found that 62 percent of the mothers with IQs below 70 had husbands whose IQs were also below 70, and only 12 percent had husbands with IQs above 100; 59 percent of mothers with IQs over 100 had married men with IQs over 100, whereas none of their husbands had IQs below 80. Whatever the genetic outcomes of such matings, the consequences of a child's growing up with neither parent functioning at an intellectual level above IQ 70 must be severe. (See Chapter 22.) Indeed, the IQs of children with low-IQ mothers were lower than would be expected on a purely statistical basis.

Mating sometimes occurs within families through incest; because of preferential practice, as it was in some groups in Japan until rather recently; or as the result of geographic isolation, as in Appalachian communities not reached by highways. In any event, recessive genetic disorders are usually increased because of the greater probability of the mating of two carriers of the same deleterious gene. The incidence of mental retardation is, thus, likely to be higher in groups in which inbreeding is prevalent.

The reduction in the birthrate which has occurred very rapidly in developed countries in recent years must have significant consequences for the proportion of mentally retarded children in the population. Birthrates in low-income families, which previously had been much higher than in nonpoor families, are dropping rapidly. This should have beneficial effects, for as we shall see, growing up in a large family, especially a large family with a low income, is not conducive to optimal development. To

[5] For descriptions of child care in other countries, see Berfenstam & William-Olsson, 1973 (Sweden); Hermann & Komlósi, 1972 (Hungary); David & Lézine, 1974 (France); Lüscher, Gross, & Ritter, 1973 (Switzerland); and Pringle & Naidoo, 1974 (Great Britain).

reduce unwanted births, contraceptives and abortions are increasingly used by members of a number of high-risk groups, including the unmarried of all ages, adolescent girls and women "past their prime," women with chronic health disorders or histories of poor reproductive outcomes, and couples known to be carriers of genetic disorders. The average interval between births is also being extended. As never before, parents are able to plan for their children, to have offspring they welcome and are adequately prepared to care for. These changes cannot help but have beneficial outcomes for families in general and families of high-risk groups in particular. Some positive results have already been documented. The relative incidence of Down's syndrome has been reduced (Collmann & Stoller, 1969) because older mothers are having fewer children, and the overall reduction in perinatal mortality seems to be related in part to the prevention of high-risk pregnancies (Matsunaga, 1966).

Family Structure   Parents and children in a family unit have considerable impact on one another. The rapid pace of urbanization and the mobility of families have broken extended families into nuclear units, perhaps in touch by letters, telephone, and visits, but not in everyday contact. Fifty years ago, about half of all households included at least one other adult besides the parents; today that figure is below 5 percent. The "ideal" nuclear family, mother, father, and their own two children, is also much less common than we tend to think.

When there is a low ratio of adults to children, as in single-parent families or families with many children, there seldom will be sufficient time and energy for the adults to attend to the children's needs, either physical or psychological. Parents may be unable to observe their children's efforts at mastery, to reinforce their progress, to avert crippling frustration by giving help over the rough spots, to make available interesting objects and opportunities, to talk with the child, or to respond to the child's communications. When there are not at least two adults in the household, the child seldom has the opportunity to observe mature forms of interaction and role differentiation or to hear adults conversing with one another.

Equally important may be the affectional support which the mother receives from the presence and help of another adult. The extent of psychosocial support a mother receives while she is pregnant has been shown to be related to the number of complications during pregnancy and delivery (Nuckolls, Cassel, & Kaplan, 1972) and the birthweight of the infant (Mitchell, 1974). There are special stresses for the single mother, the very young mother, and the mother with too many children too close together. All these groups have high reproductive casualty rates.

Family Size   It is now well established that children from larger families are at a disadvantage in intellectual development (Clausen & Clausen, 1973; Davie, Butler, & Goldstein, 1972; Nisbet & Entwistle, 1967). Because the birthrate has been higher in lower-class families and in rural areas, it is important to hold these factors constant when examining the influence of family size, but even in societies such as Ireland where family size does not vary greatly by social class, the effects of class and size of family have been documented (Kellaghan & Macnamara, 1972).

In larger families the well-being of the children may be compromised simply by the fact that the available resources must be divided into smaller shares. Especially in the lower socioeconomic groups, adverse physical conditions may be intensified when many family members must share a meager subsistence. Although the camaraderie and flexibility of a larger family may be an advantage, often young children receive less attention from the parents and obtain many of their lessons about life from sisters and brothers who are only a little older and wiser. When the spacing between children is increased, however, the usual IQ decrement is reduced (Rosenberg & Sutton-Smith, 1969). Davie et al. (1972) suggest also that

> The parents who *opt* for a large family will have a different set of priorities. . . . Amongst larger families which are not planned in size, apart from those where religious considerations predominate, there is likely to be a higher proportion of parents whose attitude is rather feckless and irresponsible, those who in general do not manage their affairs very successfully and those who tend to live for the present. . . . The parents and children will tend to have a scale of values which contrasts quite sharply with what has been described as "the middle-class ethic of postponed gratification." In Biblical terms they are remembering the "lilies of the field" whilst the remainder proceeds on the basis that "God helps him who helps himself"! (p. 54)

The Early Environment: Deprivation

Four aspects of the environment of the very young have received particular attention of late: depriving circumstances, enrichment, verbal stimulation, and the parent-child interaction. Each of these is thought to be highly relevant to intellectual development. Extensive experimental studies with mammals and observational studies of human beings attest to the importance of very early experiences in determining later behavioral patterns, even though the mechanisms by which this influence is established are not well understood.[6]

Deprivation of stimulation can have devastating effects on the young organism. Some theorists have developed a model which explains mental retardation primarily as a function of the deficits in attention, activity, language, and motivation which are known to follow early human deprivation (Yarrow, 1970).

Animal Studies

Animals reared with very restricted stimulation tend to show cognitive deficits on complex tasks (Davenport, Rogers, & Rumbaugh, 1973) although not necessarily on simple ones (Harlow & Griffin, 1965). They are also timid, dull, and stereotyped in their behavior (Menzel, Davenport, & Rogers, 1963) and apathetic even to pain (Melzack & Scott, 1957). They apparently fail to learn to filter stimulation or to organize their perceptions, so that when removed from restricted conditions they are bombarded by stimulus overload, excessively aroused by novel stimuli, and unable to select the cues for adaptive responses (Melzack, 1968). If there is prolonged visual deprivation, the normal organization of visual connections present at birth may deteriorate, and this condition may eventually become irreversible (Hubel, 1967; Riesen, 1965). Considerably lesser amounts of impoverishment can be detected in brain chemistry and anatomy (Rosenzweig, Krech, Bennett, & Diamond, 1968).

By far the greatest amount of work on the effects of deprivation has been done with animals, particularly rats, dogs, and subhuman primates. Some of the best-known work in this area is that conducted with young rhesus monkeys in the psychological laboratories of the University of Wisconsin (Harlow, 1961, 1963; Harlow & Griffin,

---

[6] See Haywood and Tapp (1966), Hunt (1961), Sluckin (1971), and Thompson and Grusec (1970).

1965; Sackett, 1967). Social isolation in the first six months of a monkey's life can have very detrimental effects on later age-mate interaction, but peer relationships can make up in part for very early separation from the mother. Isolated females tend to become very inadequate mothers. They are disturbed in their mating behavior and indifferent and brutal toward their young. '

Children in Institutions   Much of the evidence about human deprivation comes from studies of infants who have been placed in institutions rendering only custodial care. In some countries in North Africa, Eastern Europe, and elsewhere, family care has not been widely substituted for the hospital or orphanage. Even in the United States, where resistance to institutional care for young children is very strong, in 1970, public institutions cared for better than 7,000 retarded infants and children under age five.

By and large, group care for infants and young children is improving rapidly. Typically, residential facilities in the past were understaffed and even the best-intentioned nurses were able to do little for their charges beyond keeping them fed, changed, and bathed. A baby or a nonambulatory retarded child might well have spent his entire day in an antiseptic crib or cubicle without hearing, seeing, feeling, or smelling any moving, living, changing stimulus except for the briefest and most perfunctory intervals. If he rolled over, babbled, or sat up, there was no one to take notice or encourage him to do it again. He might, in fact, stay so long in the same position that the crib mattress would contour to his body, making efforts to move more difficult. Studies of institutionalized infants therefore have tended to be studies not only of babies deprived of parental affection and attention, but of babies deprived of normal activity, of sensory stimulation, of exploratory ventures, and of any reinforcement of their responses. Residential institutions for severely and profoundly retarded children and adults still, far too often, resemble these horrors of the past with the barest minima of stimulation, diversion, physical freedom, or meaningful human contact.[7]

Maternal Deprivation   Institutions are not, of course, the only settings in which babies may receive impersonal care. An unstable or indifferent mother, one who is overburdened with the care of many children, or antagonistic toward her baby or her role as a mother, may provide minimal care unembellished by warmth or by variety, stimulation, and responsiveness (Prugh & Harlow, 1962). Under such conditions, disturbances in intellectual, motor, and emotional development may result (Hannaway, 1970).[8] Even with good food intake, growth may be stunted, possibly as the result of sleep disturbances which inhibit the secretion of pituitary hormones including growth hormone (Gardner, 1972). Improvement of the environment often produces striking initial improvements in development, but the children usually remain below average in growth and IQ (Patton & Gardner, 1969).

It was hypothesized by many earlier investigators that the essential ingredient missing in institutions and in disturbed mother-child pairs was an adequate relationship between the infants and their *own* mothers. Although much of the research data has been reinterpreted in recognition of the necessity for adequate sensory and cogni-

---

[7] Because studies of the effects of institutional deprivation are discussed at length in Chapter 21, they are omitted here.

[8] Deafness in an infant may create a deprivationlike environment and may, in addition, interfere with the mother-child relationship (Luszki, 1964).

tive stimulation (Casler, 1961, 1968; Yarrow, 1961), the controversy concerning "maternal deprivation" and "attachment" continues. Questions center on whether children's need for the attention and affection of a mother is inborn or learned through an association of the mother with satisfaction of physical needs and on the effects of "multiple mothering" (Caldwell, Wright, Honig, & Tannenbaum, 1970).

In this respect, some theorists have been particularly interested in the critical-periods hypothesis discussed earlier (C. F. Bowlby, 1969, 1973). Surveying the evidence, they have concluded that the child's requirements for maternal care differ with his stage of development. Schaffer (1963), for example, has suggested a three-stage progression. He postulates that at first children need sensory stimulation, simply by movement, change, and novelty in what they see, hear, feel, smell, and taste.[9] This requirement is supplemented in the second stage of development by the necessity for human stimulation, whether the need is inborn or learned. The human beings caring for the baby may be one or many. It is not until the third stage, which begins sometime during the second half of the first year, that children begin to develop a specific attachment to a single person or a few persons. At this stage, they need to be cared for by at most a few stable figures. Changes at this stage can severely disrupt their ability to relate to others.

This progression argues against breaking up an established mother-child relationship during the second half of the first year. Separation during the first six months apparently need have no ill effects if the child is given adequate care and stimulation. When separation is delayed until the infant has established a stable attachment and has achieved a rudimentary use of language, he can probably survive the shift with greater equanimity, his basic cognitive processes no longer so dependent upon the maternal relationship. Moreover, the child's greater mobility when he is two or three years old enables him to discover at least a minimum of stimulation. This tentative three-stage interpretation makes it clear that developmental changes must be taken into account in one way or another.

Reversibility   Some research has raised serious doubts as to the permanence and irreversibility of the effects of the various types of deprivation. In many animal studies of incomplete sensory deprivation, improvement has been fairly rapid after the depriving condition is alleviated. For example, though rhesus monkeys deprived of pattern vision for as much as two months acted in many ways like newborns when first exposed to patterns, the savings in time required to achieve normal visual behavior showed that both maturation and experience contribute to visual competence (Wilson & Riesen, 1966).

Dennis and Najarian (1957) studied children in a Lebanese institution who had had very little care. As babies, they showed extreme retardation. The older children who had undergone the same sorts of experiences as babies, however, did not appear retarded. On a number of nonverbal measures, their scores were well within the normal range. The data suggest that the older children were able to catch up once they became mobile and could seek stimulation themselves.

The most dramatic evidence of recovery after early deprivation comes from a

---

[9] On the basis of his review of institutionalized babies under six months of age, Casler (1961) came to the same conclusion. Further evidence from the work of Yarrow, Rubenstein, & Pedersen (1971) clarifies that not only the amount but the variety of stimulation is important for early development and active curiosity.

follow-up study by Skeels (1966) of twenty-five children investigated a quarter-century earlier (Skeels & Dye, 1939). In the 1939 study, thirteen very young children had been removed from an understaffed orphanage and placed on female wards of a residential institution for retarded individuals. Eventually they were moved to adoptive or foster homes. Another dozen children had remained in the orphanage. Although they were also eligible for adoption, many remained permanently institutionalized. At the time of follow-up, the median subject in the transferred group had completed twelfth grade, a third of the group had attended college, and all were leading apparently normal lives. In stark contrast, the children remaining in the unstimulating environment had, on the average, completed only third grade. Half of them were unemployed, and with one exception the workers were unskilled laborers.

The Early Environment: Verbal Stimulation

There is remarkable agreement among investigation of social class, family size, and institutional upbringing, that verbal behaviors are especially vulnerable to depriving experiences. Social class differences are regularly greatest on tests tapping verbal ability and general information and less on items of reading and mathematical skills, nonverbal ability, and spelling (Davie et al. 1972; Jencks, 1972; Mittler, 1970; Rykman, 1967). Better educated, more highly verbal parents probably are able to provide richer verbal environments for their young children, but it is not yet possible to pin down precise correspondences between well-defined characteristics of the environment and the development of specific abilities (Uzgiris, 1970).

Family size is also associated with verbal abilities more closely than with other abilities. In a large-scale British study mentioned previously (Davie et al., 1972), seven-year-old children in one- or two-child families on reading tests scored some twelve months ahead of children in families with five or more children, even when social class, place of residence, and sex were equated. The average difference in arithmetic test scores, however, was only about three months.

A number of investigators have recognized that early deprivation may have its greatest consequences on verbal processing (Fowler, 1970; Pringle & Bossio, 1958; Tizard & Tizard, 1971). Language does not develop in a vacuum. Children need competent models after which to copy their speech and from which to extract the rules of language. They need listeners who are responsive to their successive products. They must find speech essential to their everyday transactions and must be called upon to use increasingly complex constructions if their language development is to proceed effectively. Institutions and large families are alike in their failure to provide these conditions. In an institution, typically segregated into narrow age ranges, young children may be even more deprived than in a large family, where at least there are likely to be older siblings. In the view of many theorists for whom language plays a central role in the development of intelligence, these are matters of utmost importance. Early verbal stimulation is highly related to later intelligence (Moore, 1968), and early language scores are the best predictors we have of later IQs (Schaefer, 1970). In school and out, effective human interactions depend extensively on facility with language, both spoken and written. Language deficits must in any theory of mental retardation be construed as crucial.

The Early Environment: Parent-Child Relationships

The family environment constitutes a powerful influence against which all other environmental influences on the child's development tend to seem rather puny. Werner,

Bierman, and French (1971), for example, studied the effects of perinatal complications as related to social class, educational stimulation, and emotional support within the home. They found that the relationship between perinatal stress and the child's competence decreased over time but that influences of the family became increasingly apparent. At age twenty months, an IQ difference of only 4 points separated children from the least and most favored environments, but by age ten, the difference was 20 points. In the same vein, a national survey of school achievement in the United States (Coleman et al., 1966) and a detailed review of all the available evidence (Jencks, 1972) both emphasize that home influences far outweigh the contribution made by the schools to variations in children's school achievement.

Social Class Variables In any study of parent-child relationships, social class must be taken into account. Studies of childrearing practices invariably find marked differences related to social status (Bronfenbrenner, 1958; C. P. Deutsch, 1973; Hess, 1970). The specific cause-effect sequences, however, can only be surmised. Perhaps it should be reiterated that *group* differences are being described and that substantial overlap characterizes any comparison between lower- and middle-class samples.

Although they are more tolerant in most respects, middle-class parents set higher standards for children than do lower-class parents.

> The middle-class youngster is expected to learn to take care of himself earlier, to accept more responsibilities about the home, and above all—to progress further in school. . . . [In matters of discipline] middle-class families rely more on reasoning, isolation, appeals to guilt, and other methods involving the threat of loss of love (Bronfenbrenner, 1958, pp. 424-425).

Physical punishment, by contrast, is more frequently employed by lower-class parents. They also lean toward the simple explanation of their own and their children's behavior in preference to the complex, and they more often require immediate obedience and acknowledgement of power rather than a reasoned solution or a possible compromise. Life in a middle-class family is likely to be verbally richer, cognitively more complex, and emotionally more supportive.

A number of recent investigators (e.g., Hess & Shipman, 1965; Streissguth & Bee, 1972) have observed mothers in the process of teaching their children. In one protypical experiment (Bee, Van Egeren, Streissguth, Nyman, & Leckie, 1969) middle- and lower-class mothers and their four- and five-year-old children were the subjects. In the waiting room, the lower-class mothers were more disapproving and controlling and probably more tense. Later, when teaching their children, they were more likely to give concrete suggestions, to intrude physically into the child's problem solving, and to give negative rather than positive feedback.

Working from similar data, the British psycholinguist, Bernstein (1962) characterized the speech of lower-class mothers as based on "restricted" rather than "elaborated" codes. By a restricted code, Bernstein referred to a sort of telegraphic and stereotyped language which is simplified, reduced to its structural elements, and lacking in details and exactness. The use of restricted codes is apparently less effective in promoting active, differentiated cognitive processes, and lends itself to concrete commands, authoritarian relationships, and inhibition of curiosity. Elaborated codes provide for highly individualized communications since they are rich in details and nuances and generally more complex in form. Again, it must be remembered that individual differences in this area are only partly related to social class (Holzman, 1974).

Quality of Stimulation   A number of longitudinal studies (Bayley & Schaefer, 1964; Hess, Shipman, Brophy, & Bear, 1969; Honzik, 1967) point to the importance of able, concerned parents and particularly of activating mothers in stimulating cognitive development. The level of stimulation, which depends upon the parents' interest and ability to engineer the environment in their children's behalf, is a powerful predictor of later IQ changes (Caldwell & Richmond, 1967; Moore, 1968). White and Watts (1973), on the basis of extensive observations, described mothers who seemed to be raising especially able preschool children.

> Our A mothers talk a great deal to their children, and usually at a level the child can handle. They make them feel as though whatever they are doing is usually interesting. They provide access to many objects and diverse situations. They lead the child to believe that he can expect help and encouragement most, but *not all* the time. They demonstrate and explain things to the child, but mostly on the child's instigation rather than their own. They prohibit certain activities, and they do so consistently and firmly. . . . They are imaginative. . . . They very skillfully and naturally strengthen the child's intrinsic motivation to learn. They also give him a sense of task orientation, a notion that it is desirable to do things well and completely. They make the child feel secure (pp. 242–243).

Over a nine-month period, Clarke-Stewart (1973) observed the interactions of thirty-six mothers with their first-born infants, ages nine to eighteen months. She derived one major complex maternal variable, which included expression of affection, provision of social stimulation, contingent responsiveness to and acceptance of the child's behavior, effectiveness in using materials to stimulate the child's play, and appropriateness of the mother's behavior for the child's age and ability. She discovered a highly significant relationship between the children's overall competence and the quality of the mothers' care. Several specific relationships between aspects of the mothers' behavior and aspects of the children's development were also delineated. Language development was related to the mothers' verbal stimulation, for example, as was children's skill with objects related to the mothers' presentation of play materials. Similarly, Beckwith (1971), who studied twenty-four middle-class mothers and their adoptive infants, found that the children's developmental progress was related to the amount of material physical and verbal contact, opportunity for the children to explore the home, and the amount of experience they had with other people.

Relatively "pushy" mothers of infants tend to accelerate cognitive development, especially in boys, although this effect may not be apparent until years later (Kagan & Moss, 1962). Bayley and Schaefer (1964) found that boy babies of happy, loving mothers had relatively low IQs during the first year of life and those with hostile mothers had relatively high scores, but that by age five these patterns had reversed and remained stable thereafter. Paradoxically, girls' infant scores were related to ratings of their mothers' current behavior but later on were almost completely independent of these early ratings.

Some authors have sounded a warning that American parents are tending to drift away from their children, to let them be socialized by their peers and the omnipresent television (e.g., Bronfenbrenner, 1973). A number of programs have recently been undertaken in an effort to enhance parents' interest and skills in serving as educators for their children. Some of these will be described in Chapter 19.

Neglect and Child Abuse   Some parents are frankly ill-suited for their roles and responsibilities. Some are simply too young, being teen-agers themselves (Oppel & Royston, 1971). Some are handicapped by mental retardation and the burdens of poverty. Some suffer severe psychopathology, a limited capacity for planning, and a tendency to act out their conflicts (Fischhoff, Whitten, & Pettit, 1971). Sometimes adults who probably could have reared "easy" children with equanimity are unable to handle "difficult" ones with the sensitivity, flexibility, and evenhanded firmness required.

Some ill-suited parents respond with such indifference and neglect that their children exhibit severe growth failure. Others are affected to lesser degrees, but neglect severe enough to reach the attention of a court is apparently often associated with intellectual deficit (Sandgrund, Gaines, & Green, 1974).

Physical injury and even death are real possibilities at the hands of some parents. One author (Elmer, 1967) located fifty families in which a child had been admitted to a hospital because of multiple bone injuries which were judged to be the result of abuse. By the time of a follow-up study, eight children had died from intracranial trauma, malnutrition, deliberate murder by the mother, or unknown causes, and five were in institutions for the retarded. Over half of the children were mentally retarded.[10]

In another group of physically abused children, from which those with major head injuries were excluded, 25 percent achieved IQs below 70, compared with 3 percent in a control group of similar economic background (Sandgrund et al., 1974). In many cases there is a clear intergenerational pattern, the parents having been abused by the grandparents and in turn experiencing stressful marriages accentuated by pregnancy and childrearing. Child abuse is a widespread phenomenon (Gil, 1971) and perhaps a major cause of retardation.

The Child's Contribution   Care must be taken not to imply that parent-child interactions are a one-way street, the parents always being the free agent and the child always the responder. On the contrary, the interaction is thoroughly reciprocal. Children exhibit significant individual differences from the moment of birth and are powerful modifying agents themselves (Bell, 1968; Lewis, 1974). It is often difficult to sort out cause from effect. Osofsky and Danzger (1974), for example, looked at fifty-one pairs of mothers and their newborns, still in the hospital. They found that the sensitive, attentive mothers tended to have responsive babies, and the insensitive, disengaged mothers to have unresponsive babies. Who was responding to whom, or were they responding to each other?

Mothers and babies must adapt as pairs. The specific sensitivities of the infant probably require considerable modulation on the part of the effective mother. She must serve as a filter between baby and larger world, protecting the jumpy baby from too much exposure, increasing stimulation for the placid one (Korner, 1973). The match is not always perfect. A mother who wants a cuddly baby may be off to a bad start if she happens to have an active one who resists being held (Schaffer & Emerson,

---

[10] It is possible, of course, that in some cases the child's retardation preceded the abuse and added to the pressures experienced by the parent.

1964). Infants who are irregular sleepers and eaters, who adapt slowly to novel experiences and tend to react intensely to negative situations, are likely to make life difficult for their parents (Thomas, Chess, Birch, Hertzig, & Korn, 1963), and later are prone to exhibit behavior disorders (Thomas, Chess, & Birch, 1968). The effects of the interaction of child patterns with parental behaviors are discernible, but in large part the parents can be seen to be reacting to the children. Let us no more consider newborn infants as totally malleable creatures to be shaped by adults. They are individuals with their own inborn tempos, constitutions, and a complex variety of other attributes.

In summary, we have examined in this chapter some of the many kinds of psychosocial influences impinging on the developing child. Whether or not a child begins life with intact metabolic and central nervous systems, his parents and his society contribute immensely to the degree of competence he achieves. Social change is difficult to bring about and there is no easy way to improve childrearing practices in a society as complex and fiercely individualistic as ours. Yet it is clear that even now, in our imperfect state of knowledge, we do know ways in which childrearing might be improved and by which children's potentials might better be realized. There is extensive work to be done and concerned professionals and other citizens must join forces to achieve the best that is possible for future generations.

8

Mental Retardation Due to Psychosocial Disadvantage

The disorders described in Chapters 4 and 6 comprise rather discrete clinical entities associated with intellectual deficit. Among the millions of individuals who are retarded, however, those suffering from syndromes in which precise biological causal sequences have been established constitute a minority. In this chapter and in Chapters 10 and 11, we will consider three more-or-less distinguishable clusters of characteristics which are by no means as specific as those discussed before. These clusters correspond roughly to three underlying causes of retardation: psychosocial disadvantage, emotional disturbance, and brain damage. Some children seem clearly to belong to one of these groups, but others reflect a combination of two or all three of these etiological categories. Moreover, each group contains such a widely heterogeneous assortment of children that the individual differences within a given group are much more impressive than the differences which can be detected between the groups taken separately.

The three clusters should be viewed as resembling statistical factors which have been drawn from masses of data rather than as neat diagnostic syndromes. They have proven to be convenient descriptive categories because certain phenomena which are associated with mental retardation tend to cluster together. Indeed, some researchers who have used factor analytic techniques have obtained clusters which closely resemble them (Dingman, 1959).

Children who come from substandard homes and who have parents, sisters, and brothers who are also retarded tend to exhibit a rather uncomplicated picture of mild mental retardation. They are ordinarily institutionalized only if as adolescents they have difficulties with the law or if their families disintegrate. As adults they tend to blend into the lower socioeconomic segments of the general population. It is, however, entirely possible for a child from a substandard family to suffer brain damage and subsequently to become severely disturbed and unhappy, for a psychotic child to come from a substandard home in which his parents and siblings are mildly retarded, or for some other combination of causes to occur. One such complicated case, for example, was Yolanda.

> Yolanda had suffered from congenital syphilis, having the spirochetes in her blood stream and also in her spinal fluid. Although Yolanda's two brothers and one sister showed no indication of having had syphilis, they had always been retarded in school and had been placed in ungraded classes. The parents had not been given psychometric tests, but it was apparent that they were of fairly low intelligence. The father worked as a laborer, doing only rough, unskilled jobs. Neither he nor the mother could read or write. They were eager to have Yolanda learn to sew quickly so that she could earn money for the family and resented having her sent to a clinic for treatments, since this took her away from school. They even blamed her poor physical condition on the fact that a social worker had insisted that they buy Grade A rather than Grade B milk for Yolanda. The father said "Grade A milk costs more but they put something in it to make it look rich and that something is no good." It is evident that endogenic factors were also operative in causing Yolanda's subnormality. (Abel & Kinder, 1942, p. 176)

By far the majority of retarded children living in the community belong to the psychosocial cluster. Lacking the gross physical handicaps or dramatic symptoms of the pathologic disorders discussed in Chapters 4 and 6, they often seem to be developing in a rather normal intellectual pattern which is remarkable primarily for its slowness. Most of these children could pass cursory inspection without seeming to differ blatantly from their nonretarded age mates. As a group, they do tend to be a little clumsier and not quite so tall or healthy as their peers, but on the average these differences are small. Just as with any group of normal children, great variation is found from one child to another within this retarded group.

DIAGNOSTIC CRITERIA FOR RETARDATION DUE TO PSYCHOSOCIAL DISADVANTAGE

There are four criteria by which a child is judged to exhibit retardation in this category (Grossman, 1973). First, of course, he must function at a retarded intellectual and adaptive level. Second, there must be evidence of retarded intellectual functioning within his immediate family, and usually there will also be evidence of low intelligence in members of the larger family circle. Third, there must be no clear indication of a cerebral pathologic condition, although it is perfectly possible that a child who would otherwise meet the criteria has also sustained brain damage. Finally, the background will usually be impoverished, with consequent poor housing, undernutrition, and inadequate medical care. There may also be a history of prematurity, frequent infectious diseases and accidents, but none severe enough to account alone for the slow development. Thus, a diagnosis of retardation due to psychosocial disadvantage rests chiefly on the absence of neurologic symptoms and on family background. It is a presumptive rather than a positive diagnosis.

Retardation of this kind is very likely not to show up until school entry, unless a deliberate case-finding effort is made. For good reason, parents may not note that anything about their child's development is very different from that of other children. The slowness of intellectual development rarely constitutes a problem until such children reach school and are asked to master the same tasks as their nonretarded age mates. Indeed, it is not uncommon to find that one child in such families has been identified as retarded while another one has been missed (Wortis, Jedrysek, & Wortis, 1967).

This general syndrome is about the same as that which has been recognized over the years under many different names, including "simple amentia" (Tredgold & Soddy, 1956), "subcultural mental deficiency" (E. D. Lewis, 1933), "garden-variety mental deficiency" (S. B. Sarason, 1953), "endogenous mental deficiency" (Strauss & Lehtinen, 1947), and "familial mental deficiency" (G. Allen, 1958). The current most popular designation for this syndrome is "cultural-familial mental retardation," the term used in the 1959 edition of the AAMD manual on terminology (Heber, 1959). The new term "retardation due to psychosocial disadvantage," adopted in the 1973 revision of the AAMD manual (Grossman, 1973), will probably become the standard diagnostic label.[1]

In the fourteen-year span between the two editions, some slight but very important changes were made in the diagnostic criteria and in the classification system. They should not be overlooked.

The earlier definition stated, "Cultural-familial mental retardates invariably exhibit a mild degree of retardation in measured intelligence and adaptive behavior" (Heber, 1959, p. 40), although the 1973 standards do not specify a degree of retardation. The former definition was based on the practical observation that a very large population of children with IQs below about 55 exhibit evidence of physiological pathology inconsistent with the diagnosis. It also reflected the notion that "the familial mental retardate is not defective or pathological but is essentially a normal individual of low intelligence" (Zigler, 1967, p. 294). Based on normal distribution of IQ, a few individuals meeting all the criteria for a diagnosis of mental retardation due to psychosocial disadvantage would be expected to attain IQs below 55. For this reason, it is probably helpful to drop the restriction concerning degree of handicap, but this does not change the reality that most children so diagnosed will still be mildly retarded.

Johnny was a 6½-year-old blond, blue-eyed youngster who was spending his second year in the kindergarten of a school in a predominantly middle-class neighborhood. He was the fifth of eight children of a rather pleasant, quiet mother who had seemed not at all upset when the teacher informed her that Johnny would not be promoted. His father, a cloth man in a textile mill, provided the family living by loading finished bolts of material from weaving machines onto carts to be taken elsewhere in the mill. Johnny's mother occasionally worked in the mill while the grandmother took care of the younger children. Three of Johnny's four older brothers and sisters were in the slowest groups in their schoolrooms.

Johnny was not able to master the reading-readiness materials of the kindergarten. He had difficulty in wielding a pencil, folding paper, coloring within lines, and differentiating one symbol from another. He usually had a pleasant smile and often seemed to be listening carefully to what the teacher told him, but half the

---

[1] In other chapters of this book, the two terms are used interchangeably.

time he was unable to repeat her instructions. His attention span was considerably shorter than that of his classmates. Johnny liked the other children, but they paid him little attention and usually left him out of their play at recess. At best, he was allowed to be one of the firemen who held the ladder while the others put out the fire.

The school psychologist administered a Stanford-Binet to Johnny, who gave a rather even, cooperative performance and attained an IQ of 67 (a mental age of 4 years, 9 months). On the Goodenough Draw-a-Man Test, his drawing, a large head with arms and legs extending from it, earned an IQ of 73.

Johnny's parents, their children, and the maternal grandmother lived in a four-room house situated on the edge of town, near a middle-class apartment development. The family kept a cow and several chickens. Johnny shared a bed with three older brothers; three sisters were in another bed. The house was untidy and run-down. Meals were cooked somewhat erratically, and the children often ate their meals cold while walking about the house.

His mother reported that Johnny was a very good child who played outdoors much of the day and seldom cried. His health was mediocre; he usually had a runny nose and cough throughout the winter. She was somewhat surprised by the teacher's interest in Johnny's "special" problem, since he seemed so much like her other children and had never given her any trouble.

ETIOLOGY

The second change in the AAMD specifications represents a significant shift in assumptions about etiology. The 1973 version reflects a totally environmentalist position, ignoring the possibility of genetic disadvantage. The 1959 diagnostic manual specifically disclaimed

> . . . intent . . . to specify either the independent action of, or the relationship between, genetic and cultural factors in the etiology of cultural-familial mental retardation. The exact role of genetic factors cannot be specified since the nature and mode of transmission of genetic aspects of intelligence is not yet understood. Similarly, there is no clear understanding of the specific manner in which environmental factors operate to modify intellectual functioning. (p. 40)

The 1973 specifications do not appear to be justified. Although there are plenty of environmental factors on which to pin much of the blame for cultural-familial retardation, it does not follow that deleterious genetic factors may not also be responsible, perhaps more significantly in some cases than in other ones. The 1973 position represents another swing of the pendulum in what seems to be an everlasting controversy about the contributions of heredity and environment to human capacities. Some of the most respected studies, which for a long time have seemed strongly to support the heritability of intelligence, may not perhaps be as trustworthy as psychologists have been led to believe (Kamin, 1974). Still, there is ample evidence of the importance of hereditary factors in the determination of mental abilities (see Hernnstein, 1971, 1973; Jensen, 1969a, 1970b).

The history of attention to the familial aspects of mental retardation illustrates the disagreement which has characterized the field. The reader is probably familiar with Dugdale's (1877) genealogical survey of the notorious family to which he gave the pseudonym Jukes. Dugdale found a striking incidence of criminality, immorality, pauperism, and mental retardation in this family. He estimated that over a seventy-five-year period the family had cost the state more than a million dollars in welfare support, institutional care, and the like. Following up this family about forty years later, Estabrook (1916) located some 1,258 living members. Half of them he found to be feebleminded, "mentally incapable of responding normally to the expectations of society, brought up under faulty environmental conditions which they consider normal, satisfied with the fulfillment of natural passions and desires, and with no ambition or ideals of life" (p. 85).

Whether the remaining nonretarded members had become socially adequate or inadequate depended, it seemed to Estabrook, upon how favorable their environments had been. Both Dugdale and Estabrook drew rather conservative conclusions from their studies. Both heredity and environment were implicated in the sordid picture as they saw it.

Equally famous is Goddard's (1912) study of the family to whom he gave the name Kallikak. He traced two lines of descent from Martin Kallikak, a soldier in the Revolutionary War. Through an illicit affair with a retarded girl whom he met at a tavern, Martin Kallikak began one line which by the time of Goddard's study numbered 480 and much resembled the Jukes family. By Kallikak's marriage with a girl of "good family," another branch was established, almost all the descendents of which were normal and sometimes even outstanding members of society. Goddard did not take a conservative stance. He interpreted his findings as evidence of the overwhelming contribution of inheritance to intelligence and social adequacy.

A modern-day study by Reed and Reed (1966) traced the families of 289 mentally retarded persons who had been in state institutions in 1911–1918. Practically all the descendents of the grandparents of these persons, some 82,217 relatives, were traced. They found that nearly half the children whose parents were both retarded were also retarded, although only 0.5 percent of the children who had normal parents and siblings were retarded. Reed and Reed, whose position is heavily weighted on the side of hereditary influence, concluded that 1 to 2 percent of the population is composed of fertile retarded individuals who will produce a third of the retarded population of the next generation.

These studies and others similar in design have been cited as substantiating evidence by proponents both of nature and of nurture. Hereditarians emphasize the genetic lineage of the families. Environmentalists point to the very poor conditions under which the children were reared, with parents who were ignorant, amoral, and unable adequately to support themselves or their offspring. Yet it is clear that, no matter how sophisticated the investigation of retarded families in their natural setting, it cannot furnish proof for either environmentalists or hereditarians. It is wisest to assume that both factors are involved in an interactive relationship which has not been untangled.

The assumption that children with cultural-familial retardation are a part of the normal population requires no commitment concerning etiology. A normal distribution is expected when a large number of factors, operating somewhat fortuitously, are involved in the trait being studied. The factors responsible for cultural-familial mental retardation may well include a large number of independent gene pairs whose cumulative effects are expressed in the adequacy of the structure and function of the central nervous system. Other factors probably include inadequacy of nutrition, emotional instability of the parents, low achievement motivation, racial discrimination, low economic status, parental disharmony, family size, inappropriate school instruction, poor medical care, and so on. Some factors no doubt play more important roles than others. The main point is that the number of influences is large, that they function somewhat independently of each other, and that they are genetically and environmentally determined.

HOW DOES THE RETARDED CHILD DIFFER FROM THE NORMAL CHILD?

Let us take a hypothetical child in an urban school who fits the diagnostic criteria we have described. This ten-year-old boy has an IQ of 65, his mental age resembling that of a first-grader. Is there something special, some defect, in his makeup which makes his cognitive functioning different from that of a nonretarded first-grader? A number of theorists have maintained that this is the case, that a crucial handicap underlies the cognitive deficiencies of those diagnosed as culturally-familially retarded. The problem is that the theorists disagree about what that defect must be. Most of them assume that some sort of biological defect underlies the cognitive defect, and by implication, at least, they tend to reject the idea that this group represents simply the lower end of the normal distribution of intelligence. They maintain, that is, that there are qualitative differences which set this group apart, even though the differences may be subtle.

A number of these theoretical ideas will be discussed in Chapters 13 and 14.[2] Some of them are very convincing and are apparently backed by strong experimental evidence. Few can be rejected out of hand, though the very diversity of opinions among the theorists gives one pause. A representative list of proposed cognitive defects would include the following:

Relative impermeability of the boundaries between regions of the cognitive structures (Kounin, 1943; Lewin, 1935)

Primary and secondary rigidity caused by subcortical and cortical malformations, respectively (Goldstein, 1942–43)

Inadequate neural satiation related to brain modifiability or cortical conductivity (Spitz, 1963)

Malfunctioning disinhibitory mechanisms (Siegel & Foshee, 1960)

Improper development of the verbal system, resulting in a dissociation between verbal and motor systems (Luria, 1963; O'Connor & Hermelin, 1959)

Impaired short-term memory (Ellis, 1963, 1970)

Impaired attention-directing mechanisms (Zeaman & House, 1963)

Failure to employ active strategies to aid learning and memory (Brown, 1974)

Impaired cognitive (abstract, as opposed to associative) learning processes (Jensen, 1970a)

Lack of the capacity for reasoning according to formal operations (Inhelder, 1968)

Impaired development due to failures of coordination of stimulus-response functions which make up behavior repertoires (Bijou, 1966)

---

[2] See Zigler (1967) for a succinct review of several such theories.

It is quite possible that some of these defect theories, postulating an inherent qualitative distinction between retarded and normal groups, may prove valid (see Zigler & Balla, 1971). It is also possible that there are qualitative differences which do separate this retarded population from normal populations but that these differences were not originally part of the handicap, having resulted instead from the children's experiences. The cumulative effects of limited intelligence, a life of poverty, a continually lengthening history of school failure as well as failure in other life tasks, can eventually produce a pattern of behavior and motivation quite different from the norm (see Chapter 9).

Furthermore, it is only with certain types of tasks that we might expect a retarded child to act precisely like a normal or a bright child of the same mental age. Their experiences have been very different and their capabilities are different because of their age and maturity. They have lived longer, are larger and stronger, and are often emotionally more mature. Their scores on general tests of intelligence such as the Stanford-Binet are likely to be based on somewhat different patterns of success and failure than those of younger persons (Achenbach, 1970), and they more often demonstrate a lack of verbal facility (Belmont, Birch, & Belmont, 1967).

POVERTY AND RETARDATION

In the 1950s and 1960s, there emerged a heightened public concern and sensitivity to the problems of the mentally retarded. (See Chapter 2.) The association between poverty and limited achievement in school and in work was recognized. Compensatory programs were undertaken. Fitting the climate of the times, a post-Sputnik era in which Americans were assigning increasing importance to school success, both for the individual and for the nation, intellectual handicap of even borderline degree was recognized as a substantial barrier to a fulfilling life.

The connection between poverty and cultural-familial mental retardation is not difficult to establish. Among youths in families with incomes under $3,000 per year, illiteracy rates are three times the average for the country, and in families with incomes between $3,000 and $5,000 they are twice the national average (Vogt, 1973). In 1963, one out of six eighteen-year-olds evaluated for military service was rejected because he failed the Armed Forces Qualification Test. Fully half of these came from families earning less than $4,000, and 70 percent came from homes with more than four children (President's Task Force on Manpower Conservation, 1964). The incidence of mental retardation, and, in fact, of most health and social problems as well, is consistently found to be higher in poorer urban areas characterized by overcrowding, increased maternal and infant mortality rates, poor infant care, high birthrate, social disorganization, delinquency, and frequent illegitimacy (Cassel, 1973; Jackson, 1968). One careful epidemiological study of mental retardation in a single community in Scotland (Birch, Richardson, Baird, Horobin, & Illsley, 1970) found an association between mild mental retardation and the joint occurrence of five or more children in a family; residence in older, crowded housing; and mothers who had been engaged in semiskilled or unskilled occupations prior to marriage. That only a small percentage of the parents of the retarded children had themselves been reared in the lowest social class suggests perhaps a "downward social movement . . . of some men and women who may provide either a poor endowment or an inadequate environment for the development of their children" (p. 74). Clearly, we must look to intergenerational cycles for a full understanding of the problem.

There are those professionals (e.g., Baratz & Baratz, 1970) who maintain that it is only middle-class bias to characterize the poverty culture as defective or pathological as a childrearing environment. They maintain that from our own narrow, middle-class perspective, we are blinded to capabilities of children in this environment and to the richness of the dialects they speak. One may be too quick to see pathology in difference, but it is impossible, on the basis of what is known about child development, to find more than a few ways in which poor families *as a group* provide equivalent or better conditions for growth compared with families higher on the socioeconomic ladder. In a highly technological culture like our own, a high level of skill and adaptability will inevitably be demanded. By and large, the poor are less competent and less successful than they are asked to be. In this sense, the poverty environment is indeed pathological (Hunt & Kirk, 1971).

Not only do difficulties arise more frequently in this group, but the families are on the average less competent to cope with them. Of infants scoring in the lowest quartile on a developmental examination at age eight months, those from the lower socioeconomic classes were seven times more likely than those from higher classes to obtain IQs below 80 when retested at age four (Willerman, Broman, & Fiedler, 1970). Presumably the middle-class families were better able to meet the needs of the slow developers. Other studies (Davis, 1970; Drage, Berendes, & Fisher, 1969; Drillien, 1964; Werner, Simonian, Bierman, & French, 1967) in Scotland, Hawaii, and the continental United States have shown that severe perinatal stress and prematurity can be compensated for in a superior home but that in a poor home even moderate stress or prematurity can become handicapping.

What is there about the conditions of poverty which so powerfully predisposes toward mental retardation?[3] The answer is not simple, and for that reason solutions are not simple. Poverty consists of much more than a mere lack of money. The War on Poverty was able to make only limited progress, perhaps in part because it was not sufficiently funded, but mainly because the problems are so complex and interwoven that they have consistently defied solution. For heuristic purposes, we shall divide the major relevant dimensions of poverty into five areas—problems of physical health, home and living conditions, practical difficulties, family structure, and patterns of childrearing.

Physical Health

Children born to poorer families are exposed from the moment of conception to a greater risk of damage to their physical integrity. All the hazards examined in Chapter 5 are more frequent among the poor—inadequate nutrition, bacterial and viral infections, chronic dysfunctions in the mother, exposure to toxic substances, and, frequently, closely spaced and complicated pregnancies. Prematurity is considerably more common and postnatal mortality is much higher in poverty families than in others (Bauer, 1972; Fomon & Anderson, 1972; Hood, 1971). It has been suggested (Knobloch & Pasamanick, 1960) that a very large part of what we know as psychosocial retardation is actually the result of damage to the central nervous system. In fact, one study (Kugel & Parsons, 1969) of young, lower-class children with at least one retarded parent discovered evidence of minor neurological dysfunction in a great

---

[3] The interested reader is directed to Graves, Freeman, and Thompson (1970), H. Wortis (1970), and J. Wortis (1970), but especially to Birch and Gussow (1970), a masterly and compassionate account of the interplay of biological and social factors in poor families.

many of the children and abnormal EEG's in almost half. Such physical disabilities take a heavy toll, not only directly on the structure of the central nervous system, but indirectly as well.

> The child who is apathetic because of malnutrition, whose sequence of prior experiences may have been modified by acute or chronic illness, whose selectivity as a perceiver and whose organizing ability as a learner may have been affected by previous exposure to risks of damage to the central nervous system, cannot be expected to respond to opportunities for learning in the same way as does a child who has not been exposed to such conditions; for the effective environment of any organism is never merely the objective situation in which he finds himself, but is rather the product of an interaction between his unique organismic characteristics and whatever opportunities for experience his objective surroundings may provide. Thus there is no reason to think that we can fully compensate the child handicapped by an existing biologic disadvantage merely by increasing his objective opportunities for learning in school settings. (Birch & Gussow, 1970. p. 7)

Documentation of these hazards is abundant. Congenital pneumonia or widespread infection, or both, in perinatal deaths is about twice as common in the poorest families as the most prosperous (Naeye & Blanc, 1970). Taking race as an index of differing socioeconomic status, the percentage of birthweights under 2,500 grams in 1967 was nearly double in nonwhites (13.6 percent) the rate for white births (7.1 percent). Although the white rate had remained constant, the nonwhite rate had climbed alarmingly from the 1951 level of 10.8 percent (Birch & Gussow, 1970). Similarly, infant deathrates are highly correlated with income, race, and a host of other social variables (Bedger, Gelperin, & Jacobs, 1966), particularly in that small number of infants who die after the immediate newborn period, from causes which are essentially preventable. Infant deaths are, of course, but the tip of the iceberg. Many more infants survive the same kinds of hazards but are doomed to carry forever the aftermaths.

Not only are poor children exposed to greater health risks, but their health care is grossly inferior to that of children in more affluent families. Of poor children examined in over 2,000 communities operating Head Start programs in the summer of 1966, 40-90 percent had iron deficiency anemia, 34 percent had not been seen by a physician for two years, 75 percent had never seen a dentist, 50 percent had not been immunized for DPT, polio, and smallpox, 88 percent had not received measles vaccine, 88 percent had not received a tuberculin test, and 14 percent had not been born in a hospital (North, 1967). A major contribution of Project Head Start has been the provision of medical examinations and referrals for treatment. There has, in fact, been considerable governmental effort of late to provide better medical care for the poor, but the needs are enormous.

The Home Environment

The poor home harbors many hazards for the developing child. A variety of substandard living conditions have been shown to contribute to poor physical status, including overcrowding, lack of hot water, poor temperature control, infestations of rodents, flaking lead-based paint, unprotected stairs, open heaters, and lack of safe outdoor play space. Poor homes lack many features which are standard in more affluent homes, such as toys, crayons, books, and paper to be squandered; a place in which a child can engage in a sustained project too difficult for a single sitting; one's own bed; a place to be noisy, expansive, messy, or carefree. Aside from the physical effects on health, the living conditions of the poor have a number of other consequences for childrearing, nearly all of them detrimental to what we know as optimal child development.

First, *the passive and conforming child is valued* (Hood, 1971). The child who stays out from underfoot, who obeys and asks few questions, who perhaps watches television day in and day out, and who goes outside to play is the good child. Until children are old enough to do these things, they are likely to be confined in a play pen or high chair much of the day for their own safety. Crowding requires that, if many people are going to live together tolerably, they must devise means to stay out of one another's way. Children who are unconforming, irritable, or difficult to manage may suffer physical abuse at the hands of parents pushed beyond endurance (Gregg & Elmer, 1969). There is some evidence, too, that passive children tend to decline in intelligence as they grow older (Sontag, Baker, & Nelson, 1955, 1958).

Second, *home becomes a place from which to escape.* Many more teen-agers of poor families leave home than do teen-agers of nonpoor families (Orshansky, 1965). Prematurely leaving home often leads to inadequate preparation for employment, early establishment of one's own family, and a desperate repetition of the poverty cycle. Of the million young people who drop out of American secondary schools each year, 65 percent come from families earning under $5,000.

Third, *poor children have little exposure to the kinds of materials they will use in school* and little practice with "readiness" games which middle-class children play spontaneously. They may not even know how to use indoor plumbing. Once in school, they will have little opportunity at home to read quietly, to do their homework in an appropriate place, or to consult reference books of the type usually found in middle-class homes.

Fourth, and possibly most important of all, *home is likely to be disorganized and chaotic,* a noisy bedlam to be tuned out for sanity's sake. The constant coming and going, the TV blaring, the baby's place in the center of action, may not be a very detrimental environment for the first year of life. This may in part explain why, on the average, gross social class differences do not show up until well into the second or even the third year (Golden & Birns, 1968; Golden, Birns, Bridger, & Moss, 1971; Palmer, 1970) and why black babies in lower- but not middle-class homes are likely to be accelerated in gross motor development during infancy (Williams & Scott, 1953). Even during the first year, however, there may be subtle effects of overstimulation. White and Held (1966), for example, found that a very high degree of visual stimulation in young infants' cribs actually hampered the development of visual attention, reaching, and handwatching, and led to more crying than in a group given a moderate amount of stimulation.

Compelling evidence of the deleterious effects of overstimulation comes from a study by Wachs, Uzgiris, and Hunt (1971), in which infants' performance on several Piagetian tasks was correlated with a number of background variables. They found that "high intensity stimulation from which the infant cannot escape and involuntary exposure to an excessive variety of circumstances are negatively correlated with several aspects of psychological development" (p. 309). The negative background characteristics included such observations as, "House is both noisy and small," "Television on most of the time when observer there," and "Mother and child visit neighbors almost every day." Evidence was obtained of the negative effects of poverty on the performance of infants as young as seven months.

In older children, several investigators have corroborated the hampering effects of confusion and overstimulation in the home (e.g., C. P. Deutsch, 1964; Klaus & Gray, 1968). Clark and Richards (1966), using a test of auditory discrimination with preschool children, found a significant deficiency in the disadvantaged group. People talking to one another and the incessant television simply have to be tuned out. Children do not learn to expect the adults' speech to be responsive to their own vocalizing (Lewis, 1971b) or anything else they do, so long as they do not misbehave. As a consequence, children become inattentive and actually less able to discriminate sounds, one of the prerequisites for language and reading development. Describing a group of twenty-one children from multiproblem families, one investigator observed,

> When the children first came to nursery school they lacked interest in learning the names and properties of objects. Colors, numbers, shapes, locations, all seemed interchangeable. Nothing in the room seemed to have meaning for the child apart from the fact that another child had approached or handled it or that the teacher's attention was turned toward it. Even brief play depended on the teacher's involvement and support. (Malone, 1966, p. 5)

This lack of structure in the home environment, and children's having "tuned out," may explain the fact that structured preschool programs, which elicit attention and provide a predictable routine and organization, have been somewhat more successful with disadvantaged preschool children than have unstructured programs (Datta, Mitchell, & McHale, 1972). It is clearly a semantic mistake to characterize the poverty home as "deprived" in the meaning of "stimulus deprivation," though there does appear to exist "deprivation" of a different sort.

Practical Difficulties

Life presents a seemingly endless series of nagging problems to most families with limited resources. The need to replace a tire for the family car so that father can get to work may mean that there is no food for some days. The only available medical care may be in inaccessible clinics, requiring the working parent to take off time he can ill afford. Decent housing may be unavailable for a price the family can pay. Moves are frequent. A layoff for the wage earner, inflationary prices, a fast-growing child who needs too many pairs of shoes, an unwanted pregnancy, or a transient illness which excludes a child from a day care center are all problems which loom very large for the family which has insufficient funds. When one adds to this picture the chaotic patchwork of the social and health services which make it difficult for many poor families even to realize that appropriate services exist for their children (Feldman, 1969), it is easy to see that an individual of less-than-average intellectual ability may have a very difficult time coping with everyday affairs.

Little wonder, then, that parents become depressed, discouraged, and alienated, that at some point they give up their dreams of "getting ahead" and settle for "getting by." They become fatalistic because, in fact, much of their future does depend on luck and not on hard work. They have neither the funds nor the competence to break out of a marginal existence. Disaster is always just around the corner. A sense of powerlessness and helplessness pervades parents' attitudes toward their children's development.

Wortis and her colleagues followed the development of 250 babies who had been born prematurely, but it soon became obvious that the prematurity itself was a minor element.

The inadequate incomes, crowded homes, lack of consistent family ties, the mother's depression and helplessness in her own situation, were as important as her child-rearing practices in influencing the child's development and preparing him for an adult role. It was for us a sobering experience to watch a large group of newborn infants, plastic human beings of unknown potential, and observe over a five-year period their social preparation to enter the class of the least skilled, least educated, and most rejected in our society. (H. Wortis, Bardach, Cutler, Rue, & Freedman, 1963, p. 307)

Family Structure

Poor families have more children and fewer adults, and the adult who is head of the family is more likely to be a woman, than is the case with nonpoor families. The negative relationship between intelligence and family size was reviewed in Chapter 7. It is unfortunate in light of this evidence that of 15 million children being reared in poverty in the United States in 1964, 43 percent were growing up in a home with at least four others under age eighteen. On the average, there were more children than adults in poor families (Orshansky, 1965). The typical poor family is burdened by the care of several children, and the mother's health may be further depleted by the frequency and the close spacing of the births. The effects of family size on intelligence are accordingly more pronounced in lower-class families than in others (Clausen & Clausen, 1973).

Although most poor families have male heads, in 1970, 31 percent of black families having children under the age of eighteen were headed by a woman, whereas 8 percent of such white families had female heads.[4] Among poor families, even when the father is present, he is likely not to be held up to his children as a very strong figure. By definition he has been unable to provide sufficiently to meet the basic needs of his family, whether by lack of needed skills, lack of acumen to cope with the business world, or physical disability. Consequently, a large proportion of the mothers work outside the home. In families where the husband's income is less than $3,000, the mother is more likely to be in paid employment. In 1974, this was true of 55 percent of such low-income mothers with children from six to seventeen years of age only, and of 37 percent of those with children under six years. When the husband's income was $10,000 or over, the proportions were 49 percent and 30 percent, respectively. Of women who were heads of families, 54 percent worked outside the home (U.S. Dept. of Labor, 1975). Few of the poorer mothers were employed in positions which were personally or economically very rewarding. Most viewed the necessity of holding a job as simply an added burden in an otherwise already burdened existence. When mothers work, the care of the child is likely to be turned over to a babysitter (often a neighbor who is incapable herself of gainful employment outside the home), an older sibling, or an elderly family member. Even when the mother is at home, she is often distracted by household chores which must be crowded into a few hours. Children are likely to be "looked after" rather than "cared for," and the endless little interchanges which characterize successful parent-child relationships (White & Watts, 1973) are likely to be missing.

Fathers in this group are apt to spend little of their leisure time at home and to assume a minor role with their children. They also tend to drift out of touch with their own families more than do fathers of middle-class homes. Wives, on the other hand, are likely to remain close to their own families, and thus the extended family circle is

---

[4] Black-white differences are here taken as indices of socioeconomic differences.

frequently on the mothers' side (Chilman, 1965). All these factors often add up to a matriarchal pattern in which the mother has an inordinate share of responsibility for the children, with only minimal kinds of support. As was pointed out in Chapter 7, the amount of psychosocial support a woman can call upon in times of stress can be directly related to the outcome of her pregnancy. There is every reason to suspect that her ability to care for her children after they are born is likewise related to the amount of support she receives. When there is no father, especially if the mother is the only adult in the family, stresses are likely to mount unbearably.

Childrearing Patterns

Childrearing in poverty families, as we have seen, operates under a number of difficulties. Parents are hard-pressed by the problems of daily living and are often lonely and discouraged. They feel helpless to affect the course of their children's development, and they prefer the passive, even apathetic, child because he is easier to live with.

In Chapter 7, some other aspects of childrearing practices among lower-class families were mentioned, but they deserve repetition here. A reliance on authoritarian methods was discussed, as well as a status-oriented approach which tends to be inflexible and to discourage a reasoned discourse. It was also mentioned that lower-class families tend to rely on punishment, especially physical punishment, more than do middle-class families. They use, then, a relatively ineffective teaching technique, at the same time tending to establish externalized rather than internalized controls for the children. They also provide an aggressive model which is sure to make its own impact.

Training children for independence is another example of a childrearing practice which takes a somewhat different form in many poverty families than in middle-class families. Teaching in poor families tends to be delayed until children can learn rapidly to perform a task, and then they may be given considerable responsibility for carrying it out on a routine basis. Harried mothers will not give their babies a spoon or cup to feed themselves until perhaps age eighteen months old or more when they are ready to use it neatly, without spilling. Children's inevitable spills are not taken lightly, for food is a precious commodity. Children may not be allowed to "help" in the kitchen at all until age nine or ten, at which time they may be taught a few simple recipes and then be expected to get supper ready before mother comes home from work. The in-between steps are missing, the valuable lessons of how to make mistakes and to fail without disgrace. As a consequence, failures tend to be very threatening, a tragic affair for children who in school meet failure as a constant companion.

Some of the consequences are not surprising. Comparing white middle-class preschoolers and Puerto Rican working-class preschoolers, for example, Hertzig, Birch, Thomas, and Mendez (1968) found that the former group made many more work responses and the latter group made more failure-avoidant responses on an intelligence test. The working-class children were more often passive and silently unresponsive, or made irrelevant substitutions, especially to verbal items. Although these responses were understandable, they are not designed to serve the children well in constructive pursuits.

There is some evidence that retarded children from lower socioeconomic groups have untapped potentials for success, possibly because they have tended to retreat from situations threatening failure. Both Jensen (1969b) and Rapier (1968) compared retarded children of the same IQ from two social classes and found that on some items, at least, the lower-status children actually did better. Jensen (1970a), it should be noted, attributes the differences to a relative lack of impairment of associative functions in the lower-class children. (See Chapter 1.)

The role of subcultural attitudes and expectations, and dialectical forms of the English language, are controversial issues. The use of standard English is significantly poorer in lower-class black and white children than in their middle-class counterparts, and the extent of the differences increases with age (M. Deutsch, 1969). It is easy to overlook the positive qualities in an ethnic, racial, or poor minority which deviate from the middle-class norms of the dominant group. The argument between "deficit" and "difference" positions has been epitomized among investigators studying language in poverty groups (Williams, 1970), but it holds for other aspects of interaction as well. One example is the way in which parents view the school experience and their preparation of the child for school. Even though most parents share a common desire to see their children succeed in school, there are sharp differences in specific goals and expectations. Hess (1964) asked a group of black mothers from four different social classes, "Imagine your child is old enough to go to public school for the first time. How would you prepare him? What would you tell him?" One middle-class mother said,

> First of all, I would remind Portia that she was going to school to learn, that her teacher would take my place, and that she would be expected to follow instructions. Also that her time was to be spent mostly in the classroom with other children, and that any questions or any problems that she might have she should consult with her teacher for assistance.

In contrast, a lower-class mother replied,

> Well, John, it's time to go to school now. You must know how to behave. The first day at school you should be a good boy and should do just what the teacher tells you to do.

It is a fact of life that most schools do reflect the dominant, middle-class orientation of the society and, furthermore, that a very large part of one's success both in school and out of it, during childhood and during adulthood, depends precisely upon one's ability to cope in terms of these dominant norms. Modern societies cannot function as conglomerates of totally segregated enclaves, although to some extent those enclaves exist and are welcome. Children whose families function within a distinct subcultural group have a double burden, for they must learn to function in at least two worlds.

The foregoing discussion barely skims the surface of the matrix of problems which constitute real poverty. The picture is perhaps not quite so one-sided as it has been painted. There are ways in which the poor learn to survive and to cope which differ from the middle-class patterns. There can be no doubt, however, that a realistic portrayal of poverty must be a bleak one. Efforts to improve the life situations of the poor may be the single most important step toward preventing mental handicap.

9

Deviant Personality Development as the Result of Mental Retardation and Its Social Consequences [1]

Mental handicap bestows no blessing so far as emotional comfort, social conduct, or general mental health are concerned. The romantic and appealing notion of the retarded child growing like a garden flower in innocence, contentment, and trust, which is sometimes promulgated by well-meaning but misinformed novelists and fund raisers, simply is not supported by the facts. Many retarded children, especially those of preschool age, do seem to feel contented, fulfilled, and secure, but many others experience crippling unhappiness, anxiety, hostility, rejection, and feelings of unworthiness. They use a variety of self-defeating techniques to handle these feelings and their confusion about the world around them.

The present chapter deals with some aspects of personality, motivation, and self-perception of mentally retarded children—primarily the mildly retarded—which tend to represent the means by which the child deals with his handicap and with the social situations which arise as a consequence of it. The next chapter deals with more severely crippling and intractable emotional conditions, the childhood psychoses, which are exhibited by a small minority of children at all levels of retardation and which present baffling diagnostic problems.

[1] See also review articles by Bialer (1970a, 1970b), Gardner (1966), Heber (1964), Sternlicht & Deutsch (1972), Tymchuck (1974), and Zigler (1966).

AN OVERALL LOOK AT PERSONALITY DEVIANCE IN THE RETARDED

Retarded children come in all sizes, shapes, sexes, and colors, and they probably vary as widely in personality and adjustment as do normal groups. Although there may be some forms of malfunction of the central nervous system which result more or less directly in deviant behavioral patterns, for the vast majority of mildly retarded children there is no evidence of any such direct relationship. Nevertheless, every retarded child has to live with his deficit. This fact, together with its social consequences, leads to problems which are further magnified by the child's simplified understandings and his narrow repertoire of coping behaviors.

To gain an inkling of the difficult life situation with which retarded children must cope, our readers are asked to consider the plight of the individual who visits a foreign country whose language he speaks poorly. The authors spent just such a year in Paris, contending with a severe language handicap. In many ways we felt and acted like retarded individuals in handling our everyday affairs. We were reduced to the most concrete communications, we watched carefully for cues from our interlocutors about the right thing to say or do, we tended to nod in agreement when we did not agree, and we depended heavily on benefactors for guidance and for intercession in more complicated matters. We came to avoid situations such as telephone conversations in which we had learned to expect failure. We became much more dependent upon our family life than we had previously been. Because we were blessed with many assets that retarded persons do not have, we soon learned to regulate our adventures in the French language to a level we could handle, but we used extensive defense techniques and means of subterfuge for which, in the United States, we have no need. The retarded individual, even in his own land, has just such needs.

Personality as a Function of Mental Age

To some extent, of course, we can look at personality deviance in retarded children as a manifestation of generalized developmental retardation. When examining a difference between a retarded and a normal group, one must ask whether the former are simply exhibiting behavior appropriate for children of equivalent mental age, or whether there are qualitative differences resulting from the mixture of intellectual disability and learned maladaptive behaviors. Kessler, Ablon, and Smith (1969) noted rather surprising separation reactions in mildly retarded children, three to five years old, enrolled in a playgroup. Actually, these reactions would have been considered normal in toddlers of equivalent mental age. We shall see a similar MA-equivalence with respect to locus-of-control studies to be reported later.

In much of the psychiatric literature, deviant behavior of the retarded child tends to be attributed to retardation of ego development (e.g., Webster, 1970). This theoretical viewpoint suggests that some difficulties with both the executive function of the personality (the ego) and the conscience (the superego) are inevitable consequences of mental retardation.

Yet, the matter is not that simple. Because of social demands calibrated with their chronological age, retarded individuals are exposed to situations and are taught rules to which younger children are not exposed. Development in the area of moral judgment in retarded children is somewhat slower than in normal children (Witkowski, 1967), but by the time they reach adolescence, mildly retarded children have received many lessons in this area which enable them to exceed the level that might be expected on the basis of intellectual capacity alone. We must, then, look not only at the mental age of retarded children, but at the effects of their experience—both positive and negative—which determine their patterns of adjustment.

The Development of Competence

Robert W. White, a psychologist, in papers published in 1959 and 1960 focused attention on the development of competence, an aspect of motivation which had until then received little systematic attention. White defined *competence* in its broad, biological sense as "fitness or ability" (1960, p. 100). Competence, the organism's effectiveness in its interaction with its environment, is not a characteristic that the human being at first acquires rapidly, although ultimately he can reach a level of effectiveness which far surpasses that of any other living creature.

Humans have been able to survive over the centuries and to subjugate the environment to their will, White suggests, only because they are constantly engaged in increasing and sharpening their abilities to deal with the world. This is particularly true in childhood. Not only in times when children are driven to interact with their environment by strong biologic motives but also in moments of leisure, children are constantly investigating, exploring, trying out, changing, and controlling the world about them. Underlying children's sparetime activity, their exploration, and their manipulation, is a motive which White calls *effectance.* The behaviors which it motivates are characterized by rapt attention and experimentation. Effectance is most easily observed in play behavior, which occurs when children's physiological needs are reasonably well satisfied. Children manufacture little games and develop and perfect new skills until, these mastered, they go on to more complex affairs.

The result of the behaviors motivated by effectance is ever-increasing competence. At the same time, children are developing a subjective sense of competence. This feeling is derived not only from their playful manipulation of the environment, but also from the satisfactions they have obtained from fulfillment of their physiological needs and, indeed, from their entire history of successes and failures in many realms.

The concept of something like effectance motivation is, of course, not unique to White. It has been noted by other theorists, including Erikson (1950), Hunt (1965), and Piaget (1952). Harter and Zigler (1974), reviewing the available body of research, point out that mastery clearly produces pleasure and that "the greatest pleasure is derived when a task is optimally challenging" (p. 169).

The implications for retarded children of a theory which stresses the development of competence are self-evident. White's theory implies that if children live in an accepting environment in which they are not forced to attempt tasks for which they are unready, their sense of competence need not suffer during early childhood. Walking may be delayed and weaning may be late, but each of these achievements may be challenging and successful experiences. When young retarded children develop strong feelings of inferiority, the environment may not be suitably simplified or there may be difficulties in the children's relationships with family members.

The theory would imply, however, that despite the most propitious family environment, school-age retarded children will almost inevitably suffer a painful shock to their sense of competence when they begin to widen their horizons. Except for the most severely retarded children, adventures and training outside the home are needed

Fig. 9-1 Effectance motivation at work. *(University of Washington Child Development and Mental Retardation Center)*

for the healthy expression of behaviors motivated by effectance, but in the process the children are likely to meet failure and rebuff which are painful and crippling. As they begin to be more aware of the world outside the home, they will fare badly in competition with age mates in the schoolroom and on the playground despite their ardent yearning for their respect.

Retarded children typically encounter tasks which are so difficult for them that there can be little pleasure in accomplishment. White's theory holds that there is less intrinsic reward in doing things which come very hard. For many retarded children, school presents tasks so difficult that the prevailing feeling is of pure laboriousness and frustration. This situation is especially likely to occur in the regular classroom, yet if the children attend a special class or special school, at some point they are likely to consider this to be further evidence of their inferiority.

Harter and Zigler (1974) devised four measures of effectance motivation: tasks which assessed a tendency to seek variety, curiosity, mastery for the sake of competence, and preference for challenging tasks. They administered the measures to groups of nonretarded children and to cultural-familial retarded children in an institution and in the community. For each measure, they found that the nonretarded children demonstrated the highest degree of effectance motivation, followed by the noninstitutionalized retarded children and then those in the institution.[2] Apparently, retarded children have had the "wind knocked out of their sails" by a long succession of defeats and perhaps the same kind of passive orientation that we shall note in studies of learning and memory. (See Chapters 13 and 14.) Institutionalization, with its pressures for conformity and passivity, may extend the process.

The picture is not necessarily quite this unfavorable. Many retarded children have special areas of competence in music, art, or physical prowess which give them satisfaction. To the extent that the subnormal boy or girl has an important place in the family, with as much responsibility and independence as he or she can handle, there need not be discouragement on all fronts. The tasks of the school years are, however, difficult for the subnormal boy or girl.

The fact that many retarded adults are assimilated into the normal population can be interpreted to mean that the tasks of adulthood, particularly the necessity for perseverance at work, can be mastered by many retarded individuals. Reliability, efficiency, and conformity in carrying out tasks within their levels of ability may compensate for difficult trials in previous years. White's point of view argues for training even severely retarded children in self-help and in useful tasks. If they can help to feed a younger child or mop a floor clean, they may gain a measure of worth which can become the focus of their sense of competence for, like everyone else, they seek to be the master of their environment.

Status of Personality Research with the Retarded

There are marked trends and fads in personality research which result largely from the difficulty in finding instruments to assess important personality variables, a problem which is compounded with retarded children because of their difficulties in communication and abstraction and probably some limitations in self-awareness. When a pioneer researcher develops a technique suitable for retarded subjects, his or her work is followed by a deluge of studies employing the same technique, as researchers grasp for ways to unlock this tremendously complicated area. The areas about which something is known with respect to the personalities of retarded individuals are, as a result, both rather modest and rather circumscribed.

For two very practical reasons, nearly all the personality research with retarded subjects has involved school-age children, primarily those who are mildly retarded and adolescent, in special classes in public schools and in institutions. First, school-age children and institutional populations are easily accessible, whereas once they leave the school or institution they scatter and tend to disappear from professional contact. (See Chapter 22.) Although the public school children are not fully representative of the retarded population, excluding as they do children not in school or not identified

---

[2] Intercorrelations among the measures were weak, however, suggesting that somewhat independent components are involved in Harter and Zigler's concept of effectance motivation.

there as retarded, they are certainly more representative than are groups available through any other avenue. Second, mildly retarded, adolescent subjects tend to be more verbally adept than younger retarded children or than more severely retarded individuals. The latter group often exhibits gross sensory and neurological disabilities which may produce special problems quite independent of the effects of limited intelligence.

Concomitance of Problem Behaviors and Mental Retardation

In view of all the difficulties which retarded individuals face, it is not at all surprising that they exhibit behavior problems more frequently than do normal populations (Brown & Jones, 1970; Garfield, 1963; Kirkendall & Ismail, 1970). Dewan (1948) examined the records of more than 3,000 army recruits who had been inducted in Canada during a fifteen-month period.[3] He found "emotional instability" much more frequent among the retarded recruits (48 percent) than among the nonretarded recruits (20 percent).

A detailed study of all the children nine to eleven years old, living on the Isle of Wight, also shed light on this relationship (Rutter, 1971; Rutter, Tizard, & Whitmore, 1970). These children were all given group tests of nonverbal intelligence and reading, and behavioral questionnaires were completed by the teachers and by the parents. Children scoring two standard deviations below the mean on any of the tests, together with a random group of the rest, were seen individually for psychiatric assessment and were given a brief version of the Wechsler Intelligence Scale for Children as well as a reading test. On the basis of their parents' responses to the questionnaire, approximately 30 percent of the retarded children appeared to exhibit psychiatric disorders, approximately four times the percentage in the control group. Similarly, teachers judged 42 percent of the retarded children to be disturbed versus 9.5 percent of the controls. Even larger differences were indicated on the basis of the psychiatric examination (50 percent versus 6.6 percent). The intellectually retarded children were more often rated deviant on all categories of behavior, but most striking was the poor concentration which was noted by both teachers and parents. In both the Dewan and Isle of Wight studies, however, deviant behavior was by no means restricted to the retarded group. (See Table 9-1.)

Personality Adjustment and School Achievement

While attempting to avoid a chicken-and-egg dispute, we should take note of the fact that researchers in many settings have substantiated a relationship between emotional disturbance and poor school achievement, independent of IQ. Chazan (1964), in a study of retarded children in special schools in Wales, noted increased evidence of maladjustment in those with poor achievement in reading and arithmetic. Snyder (1966), who studied 170 mildly retarded adolescents in the United States, observed that high achievers obtained more favorable scores than low achievers on a standard personality test, a test of self-concept, and a measure of manifest anxiety. Snyder, Jefferson, and Strauss (1965) compared two groups of black retarded junior high school students who were matched for IQ but differed in reading ability. On the California Test of Personality, the better readers showed more positive self-concepts and more adequate social and personal adjustment. In a similar design, Reger (1964)

---

[3] Bear in mind that many young people are rejected for military service *before* induction for reasons of low mentality and/or emotional problems.

Table 9-1   Percentages of Boys Rated by Teachers as Exhibiting Deviant Behavior

	IQ			
	120+	100–119	80–99	<80
Poor concentration	10.6	28.9	49.5	76.0
Fights	4.5	10.6	16.8	25.7
Irritable	7.6	10.4	12.7	21.1
Not liked	12.1	13.9	17.4	25.1
Fearful	6.1	13.9	22.9	40.9
Miserable	3.0	6.0	11.2	19.9
Fidgety	9.1	19.6	28.0	35.1
Number of boys	66	894	529	171

Source: Adapted from Rutter and Hemming (1970, p. 229).

found that a high reading group obtained significantly more positive scores on the Children's Manifest Anxiety Scale.

Chess and Korn (1970) conducted a six-year study of fifty-two mildly retarded children, thirty-five of whom attended special classes and seventeen of whom attended a special day school for mentally retarded and emotionally disturbed children. They found that comparatively high academic achievement tended to be related to high activity, regularity, adaptability, approaching behavior, a positive mood, persistence, and nondistractibility. There were significant relationships between high achievement and possession of five or more of these traits and between low achievement and possession of four or fewer. They concluded that "difficult" young children may be expected to achieve more poorly in school than would be predicted by their mental development.

SOME ASPECTS OF PERSONALITY IN RETARDED INDIVIDUALS

As we indicated earlier, personality research with retarded subjects has tended to be somewhat serendipitous, emanating from the disparate theoretical views of the researchers regarding personality development and from their success in devising appropriate research measures. The remainder of the chapter will be devoted to a discussion of several lines of research which have been refined at least to the point at which some reasonable conclusions may be drawn.

Anxiety

The feeling of anxiety is a universal human experience. It is generally considered to be a state of arousal in which the individual senses a vague danger signal but does not identify it with a specific stimulus, as he would localize a fear. A great many writers have attempted to define the anxiety concept, and their marked disagreement is evidence of the imprecision with which the concept has been viewed since the time of Freud, who gave it prominence (Ullmann & Krasner, 1969). Despite its acceptance in the common vernacular and its central role in numerous psychological theories, anxiety is an extremely difficult, if not impossible, concept to define or to differentiate operationally from any other high state of arousal. The task is complicated by the fact that anxiety is not a constant state but rather arises in response to specific situations.

Various investigators have attempted to describe anxiety from an observational or a physiological point of view, but there is far from a perfect correspondence in the measures they have employed. Most psychologists have resorted, finally, to an operational definition based on questionnaires in which the subject is asked to report his typical responses in various situations. Some questionnaires are oriented toward assessing an overall tendency to respond to a threat with anxiety (Castaneda, McCandless, & Palermo, 1956), whereas others are directed to specific situation, the most frequent being anxiety while taking a test (Sarason, Davidson, Lighthall, Waite, & Ruebush, 1960). Children's responses to pictures have also been used (Huber, 1965).

S. B. Sarason and others at Yale University conducted a protracted program of research to investigate several correlates of anxiety in school children (Sarason et al., 1960). They found, with 2,211 pupils in grades two to five, that test-anxiety and general-anxiety scores, as well as teachers' ratings of anxiety, were consistently and negatively related to children's scores on group intelligence tests and on group achievement tests. Mentally retarded children, adolescents, and young adults consistently have usually shown higher levels of anxiety than have nonretarded persons of the same age or younger (Cochran & Cleland, 1963; Malpass, Mark, & Palermo, 1960; Silverstein, 1970). This is fully to be expected in view of the reality problems which retarded individuals face.

According to traditional theories of learning, anxiety is additive with other existing drives, in either a positive or a negative manner. In simple situations, where the desired response is readily available, the presence of anxiety should facilitate performance; where the task is complex and the desired response is not so easily produced, anxiety would be expected to have a debilitating effect. This, in fact, is what the bulk of the research on this topic tends to confirm. In simple arithmetic computation tasks presented to retarded subjects, anxiety scores tend, as expected, to be positively correlated with achievement (Feldhusen & Klausmeier, 1962), whereas in concept-formation tasks, high anxiety tends to produce a poorer performance (Lipman & Griffith, 1960). Since achievement on standardized scholastic assessment instruments tends to require relatively more complex problem solving, it is not surprising that it is negatively related to measures of test anxiety (Wiener, Crawford, & Snyder, 1960). In retarded children, as in other children, *test* anxiety scores tend to be negatively related to performance on intelligence tests (Mandler & Sarason, 1952; Wrightsman, 1962), on tests of reading ability (Reger, 1964), and on human-figure drawings (Silverstein, 1966). Although *generalized* anxiety tendencies in retarded children may not be correlated consistently with test scores, they do seem to be related to poor self-concepts (Cowen, Zax, Klein, Izzo, & Trost, 1965; Katz, 1970), with teachers' ratings of maladjustment (Cowen et al., 1965) and with unpopularity with peers (Lunneborg, 1964).

Extremely high levels of anxiety even in a simple learning situation may be debilitating, reaching a level at which a child simply cannot function at all. The research suggests, then, that the wise course of action with retarded children may not be to attempt to protect them altogether from anxiety-provoking situations, but to regulate their experiences so that they learn to handle them without becoming paralyzed. Fortifying them with coping skills, with a feeling of competence, and with a history of mastering more and more difficult problems with success, may be much more effective at reducing anxiety than is overprotecting them, although of course repeated defeat experiences can be themselves quite damaging.

Positive and Negative Reaction Tendencies

Interwoven with studies of the effects of social deprivation in institutions (see Chapter 21), Zigler (1966, 1971, 1973) has elaborated a theory of competing tendencies in retarded children's responses to adults. On the one hand, he maintains, they possess positive reaction tendencies (e.g., an eagerness to interact), tendencies which are increased in children deprived of warm adult contacts; on the other hand, they also possess negative reaction tendencies (i.e., reluctance and wariness about the interaction) because of past punishing or disappointing experiences. Although this generalization rests on work done for the most part with institutionalized children, in whom both tendencies should be strong (Gayton & Bassett, 1972; Zigler, Balla, & Butterfield, 1968), it has also been confirmed in studies of retarded children outside of institutions (Harter, 1967; Weaver, 1966).

The major kind of task employed in these studies has been the comparison of voluntary persistence on the first and second parts of a boring two-part task. In most of the studies, during the first part of the task, the experimenter is warmly socially reinforcing toward some subjects and neutral toward others. If children begin the task with both high-positive and high-negative reaction tendencies, then the warm condition more than the neutral condition should reduce the negative tendency and strengthen the positive one, with the result that the child will persist longer at the second part of the task, in order to prolong the interaction, than he did on the first. This is, indeed, what seems to happen with socially deprived youngsters, particularly those in institutions. They are especially likely to persist longer during the second part. In a different approach, Weaver (1966) required the child to place a series of cutout shapes on a long felt board, the adult sitting at one end of the board. The measure of the child's approach or avoidance tendencies was taken as the distance from the experimenter at which the child placed the shapes. With noninstitutionalized retarded children, Weaver found that those who were positively reinforced placed the shapes closer to the experimenter but that those who were critized moved away from him. The results of such manipulations of the experimental situation have been confirmed in a number of studies with nonretarded children. (See Zigler, 1966.)

It is clear, then, that both the children's past history of interactions with adults and the conditions under which the experiment is conducted influence the conflicting tendencies with which they approach an adult. When positive reaction tendencies are strong, the children may be willing to persist at an inherently boring task for an amazingly long time, if by so doing they can gain the support and attention of the adult. Under some circumstances, this tendency may actually interfere with the competence of their performance. Harter (1967), for example, used a learning-set discrimination task[4] and found that the institutionalized retarded subjects in a positive social condition were so highly motivated to interact with the experimenter that they reduced their attentiveness to the task at hand and, therefore, their success.

Expectancy of Failure

Children exposed to a predominant pattern of successes in coping with demands are typically able to learn to respond gracefully to their occasional failures—to "pick up the pieces," figure out what they have done wrong, and try to do better next time. Children much more experienced with failure, paradoxically, usually learn less effec-

[4] See Chap. 13.

tive ways of handling it. They may adopt any of a variety of ways to soften the blows of what Noonan and Barry (1967) refer to as "success deprivation." They may simply learn to expect failure and to react impassively when it occurs; they may make stereo-typed responses which reflect a lack of active effort and involvement; they may avoid situations which threaten further failure; they may develop unrealistic excuses and defenses to explain their defects; or they may become willing to deem as satisfactory low rates of successes which other children would not accept. Except for their self-protective features, none of these reactions is very constructive. None is likely to lead to future successes or even the willingness to try. Although the research literature is not entirely consistent (Zigler, 1966), all these modes of responding have been docu-mented in studies with retarded children.

Much of the work in this area has stemmed from the social learning theory of Julian Rotter (1954), who called attention to the power of the expectancy of success or failure in determining an individual's behavior. Moss (1958) suggested that this idea had particular potency for explaining the behavior of retarded children, because of their long-term and intimate experiences with failure. Although some studies have documented that, even among retarded children, one may identify "success strivers" and "failure avoiders" (Bialer & Cromwell, 1965; McManis, Bell, & Pike, 1969), the great weight of the evidence has supported Moss's hypothesis (Bialer & Cromwell, 1960; Goulet & Barclay, 1967; Gruen & Zigler, 1968; MacMillan & Keogh, 1971; Schwarz & Jens, 1969).[5] A variety of situations have been used in these experiments. Under failure conditions, even perceptual distortions may be induced in retarded subjects to greater extent than in normal subjects (Wachs & Cromwell, 1966). One investigation (Zeaman & House, 1963) which subjected retarded subjects to a long string of failures found that eventually they were so beaten by the experience that they were unable to solve even simple types of discrimination problems which they had previously been able to solve with ease.

The reduced aspirations which retarded children may develop are illustrated in a finding by Osler (reported by MacMillan, 1974). She gave a simple two-choice dis-crimination problem and rewarded each correct choice with a piece of candy. In 150 to 200 trials, the retarded children still had failed to solve the problem, apparently being content to settle for a 50 percent (random) level of success. After she then told the children that they would have to give back a piece of candy for each wrong response, they learned very quickly, in two or three more trials!

The implications of this powerful expectancy for failure in retarded children has obvious implications for teachers (MacMillan, 1974), since continual presentation of tasks beyond a child's capacity is likely to have devastating effects on school learning. S. A. Ross (1969) has pointed out the efficacy of using familiar events and attractive objects to gain the attention and confidence of retarded children because of their tendency toward passive avoidance when confronted with new learning tasks, a passiv-ity which has been reinforced by adult attention and even overprotection. For children transferring from school placements in which they have been spectacular failures, the teacher may do well to arrange matters so that initially they experience a barrage of

---

[5] The few inconsistencies, including some studies in which retarded and normal groups have not differed (Blackman, 1965; Schuster & Gruen, 1971), may be explainable by individual differences in responsiveness to social reinforcement (Butterfield & Zigler, 1965b) and/or by the fact that the experi-ments have been too brief to serve as analogues for the long histories of failure which retarded children have experienced.

successes to counteract their view of themselves as incapable of doing anything right. Success sometimes contrasts so dramatically with the expectancies of retarded children that it spurs them onward more than it does children for whom success is common. Yet, they must learn to cope with the bitter and the sweet, and a good teacher will help in this process.

Internal-External Dimensions

Several independent lines of investigation have drawn a distinction between the internal and external aspects of motivation. An important question in some learning theories has been the extent to which individuals are affected by stimuli which come from within, including their own drive states and their interpretations of the tasks with which they are confronted, as opposed to the external variables inherent in the environment. Such a conception is generally not considered relevant by operant behavior theorists who maintain the supremacy of reinforcement contingencies in affecting behavior (see Chapter 15), but other investigators have uncovered interesting differences among retarded subjects and ways in which they tend to differ from nonretarded individuals.

Motivation-hygiene Concept   One variable stressed by H. Carl Haywood (1968) and his students is referred to as the motivation-hygiene dimension. The hygiene-oriented (HO) individual is motivated by extrinsic factors and seeks to avoid dissatisfaction by concentrating on aspects of the environment which are independent of the task itself, such as the ease, comfort, or safety of a situation. According to Haywood, this is a particularly frequent orientation of culturally disadvantaged groups. Middle-class children, on the other hand, are more likely to be motivation-oriented (MO), responsive to intrinsic, self-actualizing aspects of the task, such as fulfillment of a need for achievement or responsibility. In a typical experimental situation (Haywood, 1967), retarded MO subjects performed better on a hole-punching task when the incentive was simply the opportunity to do another task. Conversely, retarded HO subjects worked harder for a monetary reward. MO individuals tend to be more persistent on tasks (Haywood & Weaver, 1967), to perform better on standardized achievement tests (Haywood, 1968), and to be found much less often in institutions than in the community (Haywood & Weaver, 1967).

Locus of Control   The conceptualization of success and failure as the outcome of one's own efforts is a developmental phenomenon (Bialer, 1961). Rewards and punishment administered by others are not necessarily congruent with acquired notions of success and failure, which may cause a child to prefer to undergo considerable discomfort for a goal which spells "success" rather than to choose an easier and more comfortable route. The belief that one is responsible for one's own successes and failures depends upon growing intellectual and physical maturity, but apparently is well developed in nonretarded children early in the elementary school years (Crandall, Katkovsky, & Crandall, 1965).

Bialer and Cromwell (1960) allowed retarded children to complete one puzzle but interrupted them before they had finished a second one. They found that the younger and duller children were more likely to return to the puzzle they had completed (seemingly seeking reward), whereas the older and brighter ones tended to return to the interrupted puzzle (apparently seeking success). Bialer (1961) followed this study with a more complex one using both normal and retarded subjects. Besides the two puzzles, he used a questionnaire designed to tap the children's ability to see the outcome of events as being under their own control and measures of their tendency to postpone immediate gratification in order to receive a greater reward at a later time. As Bialer had predicted, with increasing age there was a significant tendency for the subjects, whether normal or retarded, to perceive the locus of control as lying within themselves, to respond to success-failure cues rather than to pleasantness-unpleasantness ones, and to delay gratification. Mental age was more relevant to the development of these characteristics than chronological age. Bialer concluded that, on these dimensions, the retarded children followed the same developmental pattern as did normal children, but that they did so at a slower pace. Subsequent research has almost without exception validated that conclusion (Bialer, 1970).

Reasoning from the same theory and extending it, M. B. Miller (1961) compared subjects with an internalized locus of control to those with an externalized locus, as indicated by responses to a questionnaire. He found that under success-reward conditions, both groups performed equally well. When the external conditions were not rewarding, however, the subjects with an internalized locus of control were much better able to withstand failure or a lack of reinforcement. As expected, the externalized-locus subjects improved dramatically when shifted from failure to success.

Cromwell (1967a) has reviewed the pitfalls of both the less mature external locus-of-control orientation (which he terms "the intact hedonist") and the internalized orientation (termed "the conceptual motivational system"). The child in the hedonist stage may, for example, be impulsive and dependent on external coercion for control. When subjected to high performance standards or other forms of pressure, he may decrease his effort or try to withdraw. He places little value on the products of his efforts, and he may seem hyperkinetic because he shifts his behavior and "gets into everything," seeking enjoyment rather than success.

Children who have developed the conceptual motivational system have proceeded along the road to maturity, and they will generally put more effort into learning tasks (Northcutt, 1963; Shipe, 1971). Cromwell points out that they may pursue their own goals and may strive less hard than hedonist children to please adults. Conceptually motivated children may have so much invested in their performance that they seek an "out," perhaps indicating that their failure was all a matter of luck or blaming someone else (Chance, 1965; Wright, 1964). Such children may develop feelings of inadequacy or even depression because they see their successes or failures as of their own making but realize that they are doing a poor job of managing their affairs.

Studies of differences among groups in locus of control have by no means been limited to retarded populations. Several studies (Coleman et al., 1966; Friend & Neale, 1972), for example, have confirmed the effect of social class membership and, more strikingly, minority-group status in relation to locus of control or to a fatalistic versus self-determined conception of the world. Epstein and Komorita (1971) found that black boys with high self-esteem gave more internalized responses than those with low or moderate self-esteem, suggesting that a positive self-concept may counteract the belief in or fear of one's powerlessness which often arises from membership in a minority group.

Outer-directedness When children frequently meet failure or encounter tasks beyond their ability, it is natural that they come to distrust their own resources and look elsewhere for cues as to how to proceed. The established tendency of retarded individuals to depend upon external guides to action has been termed by Zigler (e.g., 1966) and his associates "outer-directedness." In some of Zigler's earlier experiments (Green & Zigler, 1962; Zigler, Hodgden, & Stevenson, 1958), it was noted that retarded subjects tended to cut short their performance on games following a suggestion that they might do so, whereas normal children tended to stop when they themselves chose. It was from findings such as these, and from later experiments with much more diverse methodologies, that the concept of outer-directedness was formulated. It was postulated that not only low mental age but a history of failure would contribute to a tendency for the retarded child to rely on external cues, and such seems to be the case. Even normal children who have been subjected to a series of failures tend to place increasing reliance on external cues (Turnure & Zigler, 1964). Furthermore, in experimental situations, the retarded children most deficient in the concepts demanded tend to function in the most outer-directed fashion (Balla, Styfco, & Zigler, 1971; Yando & Zigler, 1971).

The relationship of outer-directedness to segregated placements such as institutions and special classes is of interest, since this appears to be an instance in which such placement may have a positive effect. Institutionalized residents, probably because they live in an environment which is modified to suit their developmental level, apparently rely less on external cues than do equally retarded children living in the community (Green & Zigler, 1962; Noonan & Barry, 1967). McConnell (1965) found that during the first few months of residential placement, when newly admitted children are striving to establish relationships with adults and peers, they are very suggestible and imitative and rely greatly on peer approval. Later, however, when relationships and status have stabilized, this outer-directedness is often reduced. Trippi (1973) found that retarded students in special classes were less suggestible than retarded students in regular classes, which typically present challenges beyond their ability to handle.

For the most part, retarded children's tendency to look for external cues is probably reinforced, for others can indeed help them to solve problems. Cues are most useful to them if present at the time when they are endeavoring to solve the problem (Drotar, 1972). As Sternlicht and Deutsch (1972) point out, however, this orientation may lead to an oversensitivity to external models, with a consequent reduction in spontaneity and creativity. It may also be one factor leading to the distractibility or lack of concentration which has been so often noted in retarded children. To some degree, what is seen as distractibility may in fact be a heightened sensitivity to outward cues (Turnure, 1973). Goldstein (1942–43), for example, noted that retarded children were often attracted by stimuli in a picture which other people did not even notice. As we shall see in Chapter 11, there are other explanations for distractibility which are equally attractive. Nevertheless, the adaptive functions of an outer-directed orientation should not be underestimated. Indeed, they can be capitalized on by a clever teacher who furnishes cues for correct responses and then gradually fades them until the child can function independently (MacMillan, 1974). (See Chapter 15 for a discussion of modeling and imitation.)

Conformity, Cooperation, and Helpfulness

Cooperation, helpfulness, and conformity are generally valued as highly positive traits. Simultaneously, though, a high premium is placed in our society on individuality and competitiveness, one's efforts "to get ahead" and "not to give in." As a group, mentally retarded individuals seem to have been better socialized to the former group of values than the latter.

Lacking confidence in their own ability to compete and unable to make fine distinctions and judgments based on experience (Wooster, 1970), retarded children are at a disadvantage in social situations. Further handicapped by their relative inability to discover alternative or divergent modes of arriving at their goals (Klausmeier & Wiersma, 1965; Smith, 1967), they tend to rely on the explicit rules of conforming behavior they have been taught. No doubt, their "outer-directedness" is involved as well. The result is that many retarded adults have a rather childlike and passive orientation, feeling that they must be good to be loved and that they must not express hostility or aggression (Sternlicht, 1967).

Retarded individuals not only value conformity in their own behavior, but also value it in others, as shown by sociometric measures given to children and adolescents in institutions (Pandey, 1971) and special classes (Lucito, 1964). Retarded children tend to reject others who show emotional lability, impulsivity, and hyperkinesis—all traits associated with brain damage—which tend to make behavior less predictable and less conforming (Jacobs & Pierce, 1968).

A revealing study by Dentler and Mackler (1964) followed the course of adaptation of a group of relatively bright retarded boys admitted to an institution. At first, these boys were popular, but within a month their popularity showed a marked decline. They had initially engaged in a high level of attempted contacts with their peers and had had to be restricted by aides for breaches of the rules more often than duller new boys. They began to drop in status and then intensified their efforts at dominance and contact, which resulted in increasing restriction and further avoidance by their peers. The more retarded new boys became withdrawn and passive, avoiding disciplinary measures, and they were increasingly preferred by the other residents. One is compelled to wonder which of the two patterns of behavior is, in the long run, more adjustive.

Two studies of noninstitutionalized preadolescent normal and retarded children focused on cooperation and competition. Madsen and Connor (1973) engaged six- to seven-year-olds and eleven- to twelve-year-olds in a string-pulling game in which cooperative interactions gained more rewards (marbles) than did competition. True to form, the older children, both retarded and nonretarded, made fewer cooperative responses than did the younger ones in their own IQ group, but the retarded subjects of both ages exhibited more cooperation than did the nonretarded children. Furthermore, the older retarded children tended to increase their cooperativeness over trials, whereas both the nonretarded groups and the younger retarded children did not, although in this situation it would have been "smarter" to do so. These results probably reveal a greater effort on the part of the retarded children to conform to what they saw as the wishes of the experimenter.

In the second study, which investigated helpfulness in retarded and normal children ages three to five and eight to ten (Severy & Davis, 1971), younger normal and older retarded subjects were more helpful than the older normal and younger retarded ones. Helpfulness requires not only concern for the other, but an ability to discern what would be of aid. The tentative explanation for the failure of the older nonretarded children to be more helpful is that, although they have developed greater capacities to help and to recognize the need for help, they have also accepted conflicting and ‌‌‌‌‌‌‌‌‌ting norms of achievement, independence, and competitiveness. Older mentally retarded children, on the other hand, with their conforming orientation, are both competent and motivated to be helpful.

Self-concepts of Retarded versus Normal Children

Since the mid-1960s, investigators have attempted to describe the self-concepts of mentally retarded children and adolescents. Many see this effort as a critical crossroad reflecting both internal and external variables in the life of retarded persons. It is generally agreed that a realistic self-appraisal is desirable, but that even individuals who accurately perceive themselves to be of low competence in many situations should at the same time feel themselves worthy as persons in their own right. "Here is a case in which the goal is not necessarily to develop higher and higher feelings of worth but rather to avoid any instances of extremely negative self-deprecation" (Anderson & Messick, 1974, p. 289).

It is unfortunate that investigations thus far have not shed more light on this important topic. Even on the major question of whether retarded children actually see themselves in a more negative light than do normal children, there is conflicting evidence, although the weight of the data indicates a more negative self-image in mentally retarded children (Collins, Burger, & Koherty, 1970; Harrison & Budoff, 1972; Piers & Harris, 1964).

Self-concept and School Performance One area in which there does seem to be considerable agreement is the finding of a substantial interlocking correspondence between positiveness of self-concept, school grades, academic achievement, and intelligence (Brookover, Erickson, & Joiner, 1967; Gorlow, Butler, & Guthrie, 1963; Snyder, 1966). Two studies illustrate the concomitance of higher self-concept and enhanced learning ability. Both employed the usual approach to measurement in this area, a questionnaire designed to assess self-concept. Hardy (1967), with special-class early adolescents, demonstrated that those with higher self-concepts learned a paired-associates task more efficiently, although they were equivalent in age and IQ to the low self-concept group. Wink (1963), studying institutionalized late adolescent girls, found that the high self-concept group learned more effectively to begin with and withstood much better the effects of negative reinforcement conditions.

School Placement Numerous studies attempted to compare the self-concepts of retarded students in regular classes with those placed in classes where their classmates are of low academic ability like themselves. The evidence is, to say the least, equivocal. One investigator (Borg, 1966) observed that students in special classes had lower self-concepts; some investigators showed no differences (Bacher, 1965; Knight, 1967; Mayer, 1966); and some demonstrated higher self-concepts in special-class students (Carroll, 1967; Drews, 1962; Towne, Joiner, & Schurr, 1967).

Perhaps the clearest evidence available of the effects of special-class placement, at least in preadolescent children, comes from the study of Towne et al. (1967). They repeatedly tested sixty-two mentally retarded students during a period beginning prior to the special-class placement and extending through the first year in the class. They found a steady rise in positive self-concept responses through March and then a slight fall to year's end. In a follow-up of fifty-one of the original subjects and fourteen newly placed students, Schurr and Brookover (1967) discovered a steadily ascending trend over a further year and a half.

Defensiveness   High-threat tends to evoke a great deal of denial, thereby ob-scuring some of the results of studies in this area (Collins & Burger, 1970; Harrison & Budoff, 1972). The presence of denial suggests underlying difficulties in the ways re-tarded individuals feel about themselves.

Edgerton (1967), in his study of a group of mildly retarded adults living in the community on their own after discharge from a state institution, clearly delineates the role of defensiveness in propping up shattered self-concepts. These individuals in-vested a great deal of energy in covering up the stigma of their earlier institutionaliza-tion, denying their inadequacies and blaming the hospital rather than their retardation for their lack of education. As one of the women said plaintively yet defiantly, "I've got a tendency of an ailment but it isn't what it seems" (p. 219). Those who did not know how to tell time often wore a watch but pretended that it had stopped in order to have an acceptable excuse to ask the time. Others pretended that their glasses were broken so that they might ask for help when they needed to read in public. They accumulated material possessions to simulate mementos of a normal past and they assiduously avoided phrases which might reveal their hospital history. Edgerton con-cludes,

> So the desperate search for self-esteem continues. The ex-patients strive to cover themselves with a protective cloak of competence. To their own satisfaction they manage to locate such coverings, but the cloaks that they think protect them are in reality such tattered and transparent garments that they reveal their wearers in all their naked incompetence. In a sense, these retarded persons are like the emperor in the fairy tale who thought he was wearing the most elegant garments but, in fact, was wearing nothing at all (p. 218).

We should mention a rather clever study before leaving this topic. Cleland, Pat-ton, and Seitz (1967) asked a group of 316 retarded individuals to pretend to insult someone who had made them angry; they asked the same thing of 112 business school students. The most common insults of the retarded group related to the intelligence of the offender, whereas the normal group favored attacks on his character.

Although we have little understanding as yet of the nature of the self-concepts of retarded individuals of various ages, sexes, and social settings, there are sufficient intriguing studies to warrant further interest in this area. Before we can solve the substantive questions, however, we will need to develop more reliable methodologies and to discover the relationships among various measures of the same target concept.

SUMMARY

The present chapter summarizes several lines of research which, despite their relative insularity, provide a fairly coherent picture of some aspects of personality develop-ment in mildly retarded children. Underlying all these lines of research is an apprecia-tion of the social influences on the retarded child. When differences have been found between normal and retarded groups, rarely has the assumption been that the discrep-ancy is a product of the retardation per se. Perhaps, indeed, we should be formulating more explicitly some of the consequences of limited cognitive development for person-ality. Be that as it may, it is the social consequences of the intellectual handicap which have received the lion's share of attention. Although group contrasts have been iden-tified, however, there is abundant evidence of individual differences among retarded children, although this has not always been apparent in the reports of contrast-oriented research.

We have seen, for example, that as a group the retarded tend to be more anxious than nonretarded children; that both their positive and their negative reaction tendencies toward adults tend to be heightened; that many have come to expect failure as a way of life and have learned to defend themselves against it; that they are developmentally slow to internalize conceptions of success and failure as the product of their own doing and in fact are exceptionally sensitive to cues in their environment; that they tend to be more passively conforming than other children; and that, conflicting evidence notwithstanding, their self-concepts may be more negative and certainly are more defensive than those of nonretarded children.

The challenge, then, is there: If life in our society has these kinds of effects on retarded children, how may we modify matters so that the untoward effects are minimized? Can we not arrange their environments so that failure and confusion are not their constant companions? How may we fortify them against the blows they face? The current trend toward fuller integration of the handicapped into the general population has some possibilities in this direction, but it may also harbor some pitfalls. It is not the fault of these children that they are retarded—though their retardation must be taken into account.

10

Severe Emotional Disturbances Associated with Mental Retardation[1]

Severe emotional disturbances in retarded children range from short-lived, episodic reactions which emerge only under unusual stress to long-term, continuous, bizarre and intractable psychotic behaviors. Although intellectual handicap and emotional maladjustment are clearly not related to each other in any simple fashion, the incidence of some degree of emotional disturbance is apparently a great deal higher in retarded children than in others of average or superior intellect. We have already discussed in Chapter 9 what might be called the natural consequences of mental retardation which in turn result in varying degrees of inappropriate behavior and distress and which are more or less common to a large proportion of the mentally retarded population. In this chapter, we will discuss more severe degrees of disturbance which are very prominent in the behavior of a few children and present difficult diagnostic dilemmas and questions of treatment. We will focus on conditions which first emerge during early childhood, although severe behavior disorders also appear in retarded adolescents and adults whose emotional development until that time has not been remarkably deviant. We will eliminate from consideration those disturbances known variously as "sociopathic" or "psychopathic character disorders" which primarily designate asocial patterns. It is not that any of these disorders is less important in the mentally retarded population than in the nonretarded but simply that they have received very little attention in the literature concerned with retardation, so that there is little to report about them.

[1] Historic reviews of this area may be found in Beier (1964) and Garfield (1963).

The reader should be forewarned that the field of psychiatric disturbances in young children is exceptionally fraught with controversy. As this chapter will describe, there are intense disagreements concerning the wisdom of differentiating among various forms of childhood psychosis or of determining the primary and secondary roles of emotional disturbance and mental retardation when both are present. Arguments about the etiology of childhood psychosis are especially strong and confusing. Specialists are unable even to agree on the frequency of emotional disturbance in mentally retarded populations, partly because their diagnostic criteria vary widely.

THE CONCOMITANCE OF EARLY CHILDHOOD PSYCHOSIS AND MENTAL RETARDATION

Estimates of the frequency in young mentally retarded children of emotional disorders sufficient to carry a psychiatric diagnosis range from 100 percent (Webster, 1970) to perhaps 25 percent (Menolascino, 1965a), and some would place the figure even lower. Most of these disorders are not of a psychotic nature. "For the most part there is nothing specific about the psychiatric disorders associated with intellectual retardation" (Rutter, 1961, p. 194). Yet there are a few disorders such as hyperkinetic behavior and early childhood schizophrenia, including early infantile autism, which are more common in the retarded population than the nonretarded. There are, too, some behaviors such as stereotyped repetitive movements and self-destructive behaviors which are mainly associated with severe and profound retardation. Truly severe depressive reactions are, however, rather infrequent (Berman, 1967; Gardner, 1967).

The frequency with which one discovers emotional disturbance in a population of course tends to vary with the nature of the sample.[2] In a high-powered diagnostic clinic such as the Langley Porter Neuropsychiatric Institute in San Francisco, for example, despite pleas to professionals in the community for referrals of uncomplicated cases, Philips (1966) reported that "It was uncommon . . . to see a retarded child who presented no emotional maladjustment of moderate to severe degree as part of his clinical picture" (p. 112).

Preschool children identified as retarded also generally constitute a biased sample since the mildly retarded are usually overlooked. Webster (1970) reports examinations of 159 children who were seen as part of the application procedure for the Boston Preschool Retarded Children's Program. Only six cultural-familial mentally retarded children were found in the series. He states, "Efforts to find a child who was simply retarded, one who was developing just like other children except more slowly, were in vain. Even those retarded children who showed the best emotional development were not comparable to nonretarded children of the same age" (p. 17). Webster designated 35 percent of the children as mildly disturbed, 48 percent as moderately disturbed, and 17 percent as severely disturbed, about half of the last group exhibiting childhood psychosis without neurological findings. Menolascino (1965a) reported a much lower estimate in a series of 616 children under eight years of age studied intensively because of suspected retardation: 69 percent were diagnosed primarily as retarded, 24.5 percent of the group were seen as retarded and sufficiently disturbed to warrant a formal diagnosis, and 6.5 percent were disturbed but not retarded. Note that the slightly wider range of this age group included a number who for various reasons were not suspected of retardation until school age.

---

[2] Even normal children, from time to time, exhibit scattered symptoms, which in a clinical setting, would be judged pathological (Ryle, Pond, & Hamilton, 1965).

Epidemiological surveys can provide somewhat more objective estimates. It is especially interesting, then, that a high proportion of psychiatric disturbance was found in nine- to eleven-year-old retarded children studied on the Isle of Wight (Rutter, Tizard, & Whitmore, 1970). As we have already reported, 30.4 percent of the retarded children were apparently disturbed according to the reports of their parents and 41.8 percent according to teacher report, in contrast with only 7.7 percent and 9.5 percent, respectively, in the nonretarded group. Precise figures are probably unimportant. The point is that psychiatric disturbance is, for several reasons, a frequent concomitant of mental retardation.

General Description of Childhood Schizophrenia

Most of the remainder of this chapter is devoted to a discussion of the most severe form of emotional disturbance in children, childhood schizophrenia. It is first necessary to distinguish between psychotic and nonpsychotic behaviors. Menolascino (1972), for example, labels as *primitive* (nonpsychotic) the kinds of behaviors seen in severely and profoundly retarded children, most of them under the age of eight and ambulatory. These children make very rudimentary use of their sensory modalities, such as mouthing and licking toys, excessive tactile stimulation including peculiar hand movements near the eyes, skin picking, rocking, and the like. Although superficially they appear psychotic, they will make eye contact and will interact if invited to,

Fig. 10-1 *(J. & M. Menapace)*

although they have no real verbalizations. Essentially, says Menolascino, they have "no functional personality structure" (p. 85), but it would be an error to deem them psychotic.

It is in their willingness to interact when approached that these primitive children differ from *abnormal,* or psychotic, children, whose manner, gestures, and posture are bizarre. Their speech is uncommunicative, they make little or no discrimination between animate and inanimate objects, they exhibit little if any relationship with peers, and they show marked negativism.

Onset and Prevalence of Psychosis in Nonretarded and Retarded Children

In some children, the onset of the psychosis is quite abrupt, in others it is more insidious, and in still others it seems to have been present from birth (Kanner, 1957). In the first group, many of the children have been outstanding students, models of good conduct. Suddenly, their school grades drop sharply and they become confused, restless, anxious, and bizarre in speech and action. Sometimes such episodes, which in many instances follow an illness or an emotional upheaval, last only a few days or weeks, but in others recovery comes slowly or not at all. In some children, remissions are followed by further episodes while the patient slowly deteriorates from one cycle to the next.

In the second group of children, the psychosis begins so imperceptibly that its onset is unnoticed except in retrospect. The child gradually loses interest in his surroundings. He plays less often, broods more often, and becomes increasingly seclusive and preoccupied with abstract ideas and his own fantasies. The older schizophrenic child may become absorbed by unusual ideas or may begin to collect things that seem worthless to others but which assume intense value for him.

In the third group, a severe emotional disorder becomes apparent within the first few months of life, by age two and one-half at the latest. This type of childhood psychosis, early infantile autism, is distinguished by extreme self-isolation, lack of relationships with parents and others, language impairment, and an obsessive insistence on sameness in the environment. As will become clear later in this chapter, there is evidence that *early infantile autism represents a distinct disorder* in which specific, but incompletely understood, organic and/or genetic factors are implicated. It seems appropriate, nonetheless, for the present at least, to classify it as one form of childhood schizophrenia. Indeed, the rubric "childhood schizophrenia" or "childhood psychosis" probably conceals a number of distinct syndromes, grouped together simply because too little is known to permit a differentiation (Mosher & Feinsilver, 1971). Early infantile autism shares with other forms of childhood schizophrenia a bizarre quality of behavior and disturbed relationships with the environment. Once the very early years are past, it is extremely difficult to differentiate between an autistic child and a child with another form of childhood psychosis.

Childhood schizophrenia is an infrequent disorder, or group of disorders, although the true prevalence rates are unknown. Diagnostic practices vary from one area to another, and there is often disagreement even among experts as to a proper diagnosis. The assignment of a particular diagnostic label is, too often, more a reflection of the orientation of the diagnostician than the distinctive behavioral patterns of the child (Pollack, 1958). Treffert (1970) estimates 3.1 schizophrenic children per 10,000 in the United States, with less than a quarter of these (0.7 per 10,000) being autistic. In contrast, Lotter (1966) estimates 4.5 cases of autism per 10,000 in Great Britain. All authorities agree, however, that the incidences of both the childhood psychoses in general and early infantile autism in particular are considerably higher in males than in females (Bender & Faretra, 1962).

Behavioral Indices[3]

The behavioral features of childhood schizophrenia are not the same as those observed in adults and adolescents who become psychotic after a period of apparently normal development. Hallucinatory behavior, for example, is very uncommon. The older the child when he first appears psychotic, the more like adult psychotics is his behavior likely to be.

Undifferentiated Childhood Psychosis   Rosen, Fox, and Gregory (1972) describe the psychotic child as experiencing severe defects in his ability to relate to other people. His thoughts and feelings may be dull and barren. There is likely to be blocking, retardation, or inhibition of speech sometimes so severe that a child is completely mute. Activity level is likely to be abnormal, some children being practically immobile, some restless and excited, and some alternating between these extremes. Most characteristic, perhaps, is the withdrawal of the child's interest in the environment. He simply does not respond as do other children to the people and objects available to him.

Lauretta Bender (1947), who regards childhood schizophrenia as an organic condition, has called attention to abnormalities at every level and in every area of integration or patterning within the central nervous system. In a study of 100 schizophrenic children, she described irregularities in six characteristic areas of functioning:

1   Vasovegetative functions were distinguished by excessive lability (flushing, perspiring, or pallor), by disturbances in eating, sleeping, and elimination, by growth discrepancies, and by delay or acceleration of puberty.

2   Motor functioning was irregular, awkward, immature, bizarre, and often characterized by rotating or whirling play.

3   Perceptual malfunction was noted in distinguishing the important from the unimportant and in utilizing unusual relationships and symbols.

4   Emotional functioning was characterized by an inability to form close ties with other persons and by fear states, panic, bewilderment, apathy, and anxiety.

5   Intellectual processes were "gyrating," excessive concern being given to philosophical problems and excessive reaction being shown to threatening symbols. Language was fragmented, dissociated, and bizarre. In the early years, numerous children were mute. Many continued for a long time to refer to themselves in the third person.

6   Social relationships were paradoxical. On the one hand, some children were attractive and intriguing, and some appeared gifted because of their abstract interests and facility in symbolic expression. On the other hand, all were incapable of achieving close social relationships.

All investigators agree that one of the outstanding features of childhood schizophrenia is the prevalence of autistic thought processes.[4] These are egocentric modes of

---

[3] See also Creak (1964) and O'Gorman (1967) for behavioral descriptions of childhood schizophrenia.

[4] This use of the term "autistic" should not be confused with the diagnostic term "early infantile autism."

thinking which are preoccupied with fantasy and are little concerned with the demands of reality. Primitive, archaic preoccupations and symbols predominate. All of us engage in autistic thinking at least occasionally; our dreams and daydreams are clear examples of autistic processes. Normal preschool children frequently have vivid imaginary playmates (Manosevitz, Prentice, & Wilson, 1973), and autistic thinking is a normal, very early stage in the development of intelligence. Piaget (1926), for example, sees intelligence as arising in the beginning from sensorimotor phenomena which are pleasure seeking but relatively undirected by external reality factors, and therefore early imagery is egocentric, concrete, and incommunicable. It is not, then, the presence of autistic thinking which is pathological, but its persistence and prominence.

For many psychotic children, security comes only through their possessions and through a compulsive routine and sameness in the environment. The window shade must be drawn by exactly the same amount each night, the same places at table must be occupied at each meal, and the same route must be taken on each outing. When all is not the same, panic ensues, with outbursts of anger against the agent responsible. Many schizophrenic children depend in an exaggerated fashion upon a favorite toy, blanket, or pet. The following account illustrates not only this security mechanism but an utter estrangement from the world of people in a child with early infantile autism.

> He heard them reasoning and pleading, but he felt that theirs were foreign voices. He couldn't understand their strange language. If only they could go back—back so that he and his jiggler [a doorknob on a piece of string] could become themselves again. And then he knew he was saved. He remembered his jiggler. He reached in his pocket and squeezed it.
>
> Friend, friend—lovely, lovely jiggler, he thought.
>
> He felt the strength and wholeness return to him. The jiggler chased the shakiness right out of him.
>
> He was still afraid, but he squeezed the jiggler and felt connected to the old scene. He walked off the bus. The jiggler felt like it hooked the new scene [a day school for disturbed children] to the old one [home]. He told himself that this was just a part of the places he knew—not a new place—really a newer part of the old place. That way he wasn't new either. That way he remained himself—Jordi. (Rubin, 1960, p. 16)

Tantrums and self-mutilation are frequent in psychotic children. One may bite himself to the point of bleeding and scarring, whereas another may bruise his head against the walls or furniture. Sometimes the behavior is triggered by frustration, as when the parents attempt to impose simple limits. It is reminiscent of the undirected anger of a year-old infant who has not yet learned to direct his aggression toward the frustrating agent. Sometimes, though, psychotic children do aggress against parents, teachers, or other children with primitive hitting, biting, and kicking. "Some of these children absolutely tyranize [sic] their parents, never sleeping through the night, tearing curtains off the window, spilling flour in the kitchen, etc., and the parents are at a complete loss as to how to cope with this situation" (Lovaas, 1973, p. 2).

Early Infantile Autism   A few characteristics are more or less specific to children assigned a diagnosis of early infantile autism. Onset is extremely early, usually within the first year of life. The autistic baby fails to reach out to be picked up and remains stiff and unaccommodating in an adult's arms. Preschool autistic children act as if other persons were not there and prefer solitude to company. They tend to react as if people were inanimate objects. If their arms are held by an adult, for example, they will tear at the offending hand, though normal children would be more likely to turn to the adult's face in an appeal for release. In contrast with their solitariness and avoidance of others, autistic children may relate well to objects. They can play with some toys for hours, especially manipulative and/or rotating toys, but they are likely to employ them unimaginatively, ignoring the use for which they were intended (Tilton & Ottinger, 1964). Unlike normal children, their play does not mirror the actions of those around them; they do not play "house" or "school." Play behavior is, however, also likely to be disturbed in other young psychotic children.

Although in most ways young autistic children are indistinguishable from any other schizophrenic child, their speech is more likely to be severely impaired or absent. Some children, in fact, seem to be deaf. Nearly two-thirds of the children seen by Kanner (Kanner & Eisenberg, 1955) learned eventually to speak, but their speech was concrete and essentially uncommunicative. Often they merely parroted words (echolalia). Frequently they answered a question with the same question and showed a characteristic delay in learning to shift the "you" of the question to the "I" of the answer. Some, on the other hand, were remarkably good at making lists of names of objects, capitals, or dates and at memorizing long passages. They might be called upon to recite in front of company, and their parents spent hours teaching them such parlor tricks. Ordinary conversation, however, was far beyond them.

Between the ages of five and six, most autistic children living at home gradually begin to establish contact with those about them (Kanner, 1957; Van Krevelen, 1960). In the usual instance, language becomes somewhat more communicative, noises and sudden motions are less likely to produce panic, and contact with a few persons who satisfy their needs begins to be tolerated. The children may still be obsessively preoccupied with their own symbols, but they may begin to read and even to play alongside a group of other children. The bizarre and unpredictable nature of their behavior tends to subside during middle childhood, although their illness seldom disappears. Many become indistinguishable from chronic mentally retarded individuals (Eveloff, 1960).

Deviant Behavior in the Severely and Profoundly Retarded   Among children with IQs roughly below 25, a very high percentage show bizarre symptoms which are compulsively repetitive or self-mutilative (Menolascino, 1972). These behaviors appear to be much more prevalent among institutionalized children than among others living at home, and it is probable that they relate to tension and to a lack of interesting and active pursuits (Klaber & Butterfield, 1968; Forehand & Baumeister, 1970a). They are apparently more common in blind retarded persons than in sighted ones, and in the nonambulatory than in the mobile (Guess, 1966). One's best hunch is that even self-mutilative behaviors can be a form of occupation when normal stimulation is absent for too long a period. They probably should not be regarded as psychotic in the usual sense. (See Chapters 15 and 19 for treatment methods.)

Test Results

With psychotic children of preschool age, it is often difficult to elicit cooperation on standardized psychological tests. The psychotic child may so consistently ignore the examiner's "games" that he seems deaf. This essential untestability is often strongly suggestive of psychosis, especially of early infantile autism (Kolvin, Humphrey, & McNay, 1971). With such children, some success at evaluation can often be achieved through the introduction of materials which are self-administering, since children may reveal by their spontaneous responses that they understand the relationships involved. The formboard and puzzle-type items of the Arthur Point Scale of Performance Tests (Arthur, 1947) may, for example, intrigue them, as may the Block Design and Object Assembly subtests of the WISC (Sattler, 1974). It has been our experience that the picture vocabulary tests and the Bender-Gestalt Test (Bender, 1938) also appeal to many seriously disturbed children.

School-age psychotic children are in general more amenable to testing, especially if they are given sufficient time to approach the situation slowly. It may be necessary to carry out the evaluation in a number of short sessions when the child seems to be in relatively good contact.

The incidence of low IQs among psychotic children is quite striking. Reviewing the literature, Pollack (1967) concluded that one-third to one-half of schizophrenic children obtain IQs below 70, and less than one-quarter obtain IQs above 90. Schizophrenic children with positive neurological symptoms tend to obtain lower IQs than those in whom the signs are absent (Gittelman & Birch, 1967; Goldfarb, 1961). Furthermore, the earlier the age of onset of the psychotic pattern, the lower the tested intelligence tends to be (Pollack, 1960). Kolvin et al. (1971), for example, found that 51 percent of children whose psychosis began in the first three years of life were either untestable or obtained IQs below 50, whereas only 3 percent of children with a later onset fit either criterion. In the former group, 43 percent obtained IQs of 50 to 89 and only 6 percent obtained IQs of 90 or above; the comparable figures were 40 percent and 56 percent in the later-onset group.

Indeed, according to Goldfarb (1970), "The best single measure of integrative functioning is the intelligence test" (p. 789). Despite the difficulties in testing, when appraisals are carried out by skilled clinicians, the IQs tend to remain relatively stable over time, especially in those attaining IQs below 60 (Goldfarb, Goldfarb, & Pollack, 1969; Rutter, 1968). As we shall see, the IQ is also the best single predictor of subsequent development.

When psychotic children are matched for CA and IQ with brain-damaged children, no characteristic pattern of subtest scores apparently distinguishes between the performances of the two groups (Bortner & Birch, 1969; Rowley, 1961). Lockyer and Rutter (1970), however, report a pattern of high scores on some WISC subtests (Block Design, Object Assembly, and Digit Span) and very low scores on Comprehension. Des Lauriers and Halpern (1947), in a study of 100 schizophrenic children in New York's Bellevue Hospital, found a wide range of IQs on the Stanford-Binet and the WISC. No special patterns of responding to particular test items were diagnostic, but there were unpredictable breaks in their sequence of successes. (See also Sattler, 1974.)

Schizophrenic children's human-figure drawings are said to show disturbed spatial relationships, elongations and the deliberate omissions of various parts of the body, overemphasis on the extremities, a tendency to project a spiral motion into the lines, and transparencies showing introjected objects within the body (Mehr, 1952). Bender (1932) found that the copies of simple line designs of the Bender-Gestalt test by the typical schizophrenic patient were recognizable by their bizarre quality, the frequent splitting apart or exaggerated cohesion between the figures, the addition of lines, or the creation of new figures. Goldberg (1957) found that the Bender-Gestalt productions of schizophrenic boys closely resembled those by cultural-familial retarded boys of the same age, however, and both were significantly different from the scores of a group of normal boys. During the past several decades, there have also been numerous attempts to employ projective methods such as the Rorschach inkblots and the Thematic Apperception Test to discover patterns of responses of psychotic children. These tend to reveal the same bizarre quality, the variability, and the poor correspondence with reality noted in the drawings (Goldfarb, 1949; Piotrowski, 1937; Rabin & Haworth, 1960).

Treatment[5]

Attempts at psychoanalytic psychotherapy with severely disturbed children have appeared sporadically in the literature since the 1920s (Witmer, 1919-1922). Another group of workers has directed attention to a careful structuring of the environment, establishing firm limits and schedules (Goldfarb, 1961). Still others have used intensive "mothering" (Gelinier-Ortigues & Aubry, 1955).

The most reliable and effective results, however, have been obtained by workers using behavior-modification techniques. Ferster (1961; Ferster & DeMeyer, 1961) first experimented with sustaining autistic children's behavior on operant mechanical devices and broadening their response repertoires by means of carefully controlled reinforcement schedules. Wolf, Risley, and Mees (1964) used operant techniques to reduce tantrums and self-destruction in a child, and Dodge and Harris (1969) succeeded in dramatically increasing the appropriate social behavior and verbalizations of two autistic children. All this work has been greatly extended and sharpened by the work of Ivar Lovaas and his students (Lovaas, 1973; Lovaas & Bucher, 1974). They have used various forms of negative reinforcement to halt self-destructive behavior, have taught rudimentary language skills to young autistic children, have discovered techniques to teach perceptual discrimination tasks, and have enriched and normalized the reinforcement conditions to which the children will respond. Although their subjects have remained bizarre and deviant, to an extent their behavior has been socialized and small improvements in adjustment have been achieved. Operant techniques also seem to offer the best opportunity to bring a stop to injurious behaviors seen in severely and profoundly retarded children (e.g., Tate & Baroff, 1966) and to establish a pattern of attention to the possibilities offered by the environment. With psychotic children and with the profoundly retarded, where the situation often seems so hopeless, even small steps are welcome, especially when they center on particularly critical areas which make living with them so difficult.

Prognosis[6]

The prospects of psychotic children's attaining a normal adjustment are rather bleak. Many of these individuals require long-term hospitalization or supervision. Few actually attain an adequate overall social adjustment.

The most important prognostic signs are apparently the IQ level and the presence or absence of meaningful language during the preschool years. In one series of forty-two cases (Kanner & Eisenberg, 1955), for example, eighteen of the nineteen children

---

[5] See Chap. 18 for a discussion of parent training and Chap. 19 for a discussion of psychotherapy with retarded individuals. Ullmann and Krasner (1969) have presented an extensive discussion of the use of behavior-modification techniques with psychotic children.

[6] For a review, see Laufer and Gair (1969). It should be noted that the follow-up studies available so far do not include children treated with behavior-modification techniques.

who had not developed language before age five were found some years later to have remained in a state of isolation and marked retardation. Of twenty-three psychotic children who had used speech, however, only ten remained psychotic and thirteen were functioning more or less effectively.

A number of studies substantiate the prognostic significance of poor test performance. Rutter, Greenfield, and Lockyer (1967), following sixty-three psychotic children ten years after they were first seen at Maudsley Hospital in London, found that the untestable children and those with IQs below 60 had developed very poorly. Similarly, Levy (1969) followed one hundred children eight to twenty years after discharge from the Children's Hospital of the Menninger Clinic. Of the sixteen children who had earlier attained IQs below 90, only four could be said to have achieved an ordinary or even a marginal adjustment. Nine of the sixteen were still in institutions when reevaluated. In contrast, only four of the eighty-four children who had attained IQs above 90 were still in an institution.

A study by Bender (1970) of the life course of fifty patients who had developed autism in early childhood revealed no unique pattern. In adulthood, they displayed many variants of schizophrenia with many varieties of organic defect. At ages twenty-one to forty-two, thirty-three of them were still chronic and institutionalized, whereas twelve had achieved community adjustment which varied from complete dependency on their families to varying degrees of emotional, social, and financial self-sufficiency. Five patients had died, all of them in a group of nine whose life course seemed to be one of organic defect and deterioration.

Other follow-up studies of childhood schizophrenia are similarly bleak (Goldberg & Soper, 1963; Lempp & Vogel, 1966; Pollack, 1967). Pollack (1960) suggests that in addition to the low IQ and language disturbances, three other characteristics are unfavorable prognostic indicators: gradual onset of symptoms, a long duration of the illness prior to hospitalization, and flat or inappropriate affect.

RELATIONSHIP BETWEEN MENTAL RETARDATION AND EMOTIONAL DISTURBANCE

An enormous amount of professional effort has been exerted in the attempt to make a differential diagnosis in individual cases between "primary" mental retardation with "secondary" emotional features, and the reverse. Most of the diagnostic focus in such attempts has been in deciphering etiological factors. When there is sensory or other neurological impairment, the picture becomes accordingly much more complicated.

As Bialer (1970) points out, when it appears possible to make a differential diagnosis, a number of consequences ensue. First, predictions about the outcomes of various forms of treatment or education differ, depending upon the postulated causative sequence. If the mental retardation is seen as psychogenic, then psychotherapeutic measures seem reasonable, perhaps with the expectation that treatment should result in intellectual as well as emotional improvement. If the behavior is seen as stemming from central nervous system malfunction, on the other hand, a program of drug therapy might be tried, as might special educational programs emphasizing perceptual organization.

A second consequence of a differential diagnosis is the kind of facility to which a child is referred for treatment, e.g., a special class for retarded or disturbed children or a psychiatric or nonpsychiatric residential center. The expectation is that a child wrongly diagnosed will deviate from the group to which he is assigned and may not be tolerated and, more important, that the treatment will be inappropriate. Furthermore, despite the fact that so many children have handicaps in more than one sphere, relatively few facilities are oriented toward treatment of other than a single category of disability. There is danger that the child will become "a living football, bouncing back and forth between the state school and nearest state hospital, or . . . being shunted from agencies serving the retarded to agencies serving the disturbed, each claiming the other should have the responsibility" (Bialer, 1970, p. 617).

There is considerable debate about whether in fact such differential diagnosis is either feasible or desirable. As we shall see, mental retardation and emotional disorder are often so closely intertwined that many authors feel that accurate differential diagnosis is simply impossible (Benda, 1954; Bialer, 1970; Cantor, 1960, 1961; Milgram, 1972). Others maintain that it is both possible and imperative (Bernstein & Menolascino, 1970; Garfield & Wittson, 1960a, 1960b; Halpern, 1970). The diagnostic manual adopted by the AAMD does not encourage differential diagnosis (Halpern, 1970), although the Committee on Nomenclature of the American Psychiatric Association (1968) encourages the simultaneous diagnoses of mental retardation and other disorders. A scheme proposed by a World Health Organization committee (Rutter et al., 1969) favors solving the problem with a tri-axial classification scheme for psychiatric disorders in children: the first axis concerns the clinical psychiatric syndrome, the second notes the presence or absence of mental retardation, and the third concerns associated or etiological factors.

Given the current state of our knowledge and the evidence of the intimate relationship between mental retardation and emotional disorder, the diagnostic goal in most cases should be not to discover whether emotional disturbance or mental retardation is "primary," but rather to determine the depth and nature both of the child's emotional troubles and of his intellectual deficit. The advice of Eisenberg (1958) is well taken. He recommends that whenever deviant symptoms are present in both intellectual and emotional behavior, the wise clinician will concern himself not with unraveling the two but with learning how the condition came about in this particular child and what can be done to help him. This advice is nowhere more pertinent than in dealing with the puzzling kinds of reactions found in children who have suffered misfortune at the hands of their psychological environment.

Perhaps it would be well to repeat here the assertion that mental retardation is a symptom and not a syndrome. If a child is functioning at a retarded level, then he is retarded, for the time being at least, whether the symptom is associated with permanent organic damage or malfunction, with a chronic illness, with a familial disorder, with cultural deprivation, or with psychosis. For some children, especially those with severe organic damage, there is hardly any likelihood of their even attaining normal development. With children whose mental retardation appears to have a significant emotional component, however, the prognosis is usually less certain. Some psychotic children vacillate between periods of lucidity and others of marked impairment, some regress to a permanent state of apathetic debility, and a few recover to more-or-less adequate functioning levels. Some mildly disturbed children previously of borderline or low-average intelligence may temporarily function at a retarded level during a period of stress and then regain their earlier status when a better emotional equilibrium has been reached. To refuse to describe these children as mentally retarded because the retardation can be related to emotional factors would be to draw a misleading and incomplete picture of the nature of their behavior.

Emotional Disturbance as a Cause of Mental Retardation

Although some authors (e.g., Rutter, 1971) maintain that mental retardation seldom stems from purely psychogenic disorders, many others disagree. A high level of anxiety is known to interfere with complex learning, to inhibit curiosity, and to cause a child to be unresponsive to the opportunities offered by the environment. (See Chapter 9.) A number of psychoanalysts interpret many instances of mental retardation as defective ego development resulting primarily from anxiety and other psychogenic factors (e.g., Woodward et al., 1958, 1960).

To maintain that mental retardation is caused by emotional factors, it is not necessary to demonstrate very large decrements in intelligence. Indeed, such cases are probably infrequent and are associated with gross distortions in the environment such as the extreme isolation of "attic children." Yet there are probably many mildly re-tarded children who, under more propitious circumstances, would have developed at a borderline or low normal rate, or whose adaptive behavior would have been adequate even when accompanied by low IQ. The high incidence of mild mental retardation in lower socioeconomic groups and of emotional disorders as well (Hollingshead & Red-lich, 1958; Srole et al., 1962) suggests that psychosocial factors probably indeed play an important role in both sets of behaviors. Cultural-familial retarded children are offspring of parents who are borderline or subnormal in intelligence. Ill prepared to manage for themselves, these parents may be quite unable to care adequately for their children. As a consequence, many of the children's psychological needs may be satis-fied in a capricious fashion at best.

In other families, the parents may appear disturbed and/or unable optimally to meet the retarded child's needs, but the source of the child's problems, in turn, may be unclear. Although Kanner (1943), who was responsible for the first major interest in early infantile autism, assumed that there might be a biologic base in the autistic child's inability to make affective contact, nevertheless he indicted even more strongly the cold, obsessive parents who, he said, give a "mechanized service of the kind which is rendered by an overconscientious gasoline station attendant" (1949, p. 424). Current writers give much more emphasis to the atypical behavior of the baby than to that of the mother, although an obvious interaction occurs. "The clamouring, demanding baby may be a nuisance, but at least he is unlikely to be left alone and he is unlikely to develop autism" (Tredgold & Soddy, 1956, p. 195). Indeed, one recent study of parental practices of families with autistic, normal, or retarded children found the first two groups of parents very similar to one another; it was the parents of retarded children who were "coldest" and most restrictive (DeMyer et al., 1972).

The apathetic baby or the stiff, unresponsive one does not encourage the mother to respond with tenderness or affection. The ambivalence which a mother feels toward the demands of child care may become exaggerated when her efforts go unrewarded by a smile, a stretching out of the arms, or a snuggling to her shoulder. She is likely to become confused and inconsistent, sometimes trying desperately to reach her child and at other times rejecting him with anger or simply ignoring him as the child ignores her. Presumably, many women with conflicts concerning motherhood have been won over by their infants, but the healthy give-and-take of mother and child does not take place with the autistic baby.

It is, in fact, hard to imagine a more trying experience than being the parent of an acutely psychotic child. A finding that mothers of schizophrenic children are them-selves disturbed is not necessarily an indication that their disturbance is the cause of the child's disorder. The reverse may more often be true. These mothers must tolerate continuous, unrestrained asocial behavior in their children. Wanton destructiveness, messy eating habits, nonexistent toilet training, tantrums, and the interruption of normal social relationships with family friends are all part of the daily routine. Willing babysitters are usually impossible to find. In addition, the mother of a psychotic child may be constantly exposed to the notion that she is to blame both for the child's suffering and her own. Bettelheim (1967), for example, proposes that the parents of an autistic child harbor wishes to destroy the child, who retreats to his "empty fortress" in defense.[7] Such wholesale accusations are probably both inaccurate and cruelly unfair.

Organic Brain Dysfunction as a Cause of Psychiatric Disorder

A close association of retardation due to organic brain dysfunction and the presence of psychosis in children has emerged from recent studies. There is a strong suspicion that many instances of early infantile autism and other forms of childhood schizophrenia result from the same etiology as the intellectual deficits which usually accompany these disorders.

Research in this area is extremely difficult because neurological examinations are generally rather imprecise. The state of the central nervous system (CNS) must be inferred indirectly from the individual's behavior for the most part, and there may or may not be physical symptoms of underlying damage. Only in some cases will there be "hard signs" of neurological disorder, such as abnormal electroencephalographic (EEG) tracings, changes in the eyes, or abnormal reflexes. The astute neurologist may notice "soft signs" such as muscular incoordination, but even these may be absent when actual brain damage exists. Moreover, it is usually impossible to relate overt symptoms to specific kinds of CNS lesions in young children.

Yet the evidence is strong that brain abnormalities responsible for intellectual retardation are also responsible for severe behavior disorders in a substantial proportion of cases. Lauretta Bender (1947) has for many years maintained that there is an organic etiology underlying schizophrenic reactions in children, and others (e.g., Escalona, 1948; Peck, Rabinovitch, & Kramer, 1949) have suggested that the observed impaired relationship between the mother and the autistic child is a result of the mother's reaction to the child's atypical development. Positive neurologic findings in the form of EEG records and seizures were also reported some time ago in many schizophrenic children (Eveloff, 1960).

Subsequent research has further substantiated a relationship between childhood psychosis and organic factors. Gittelman and Birch (1967) investigated the relationships among IQ, neurological dysfunction, and family pathology in ninety-seven noninstitutionalized childhood schizophrenics. In 80 percent of the patients CNS pathology was found with relatively little evidence for psychogenic factors in the etiology of their disorders. Other investigators have similarly found demonstrable or strongly suspected CNS pathology in proportions of psychotic children ranging from more than half to 92 percent of cases (Hinton, 1963; Menolascino, 1969; Pollack, 1967; Rutter, 1965).

Some of the most provocative new evidence comes from studies of children suffering prenatal infection by rubella. (See Chapter 5.) Extremely high rates of autistic reactions are reported in such cases. Chess, Korn, and Fernandez (1971) studied 243 children surviving the rubella syndrome. At ages two and one-half to four years,

---

[7] See also Tustin (1973).

approximately 80 percent of them showed neurological and/or behavioral disturbances including mental retardation. (See Table 10-1.) Of the eighteen cases of autism (7.4 percent versus general population estimates of .007 percent to .045 percent) every one also had a hearing loss and sixteen were in addition retarded. Note that 72.8 percent of the children in the sample did have some degree of hearing loss and 42.4 percent were retarded, but of those with hearing loss alone, only 1.2 percent were autistic.

Evidence confirming the frequency of autism has been found in two other studies of post-rubella children. Of the 103 such children attending the California School for the Deaf, 28 were emotionally disturbed and characterized by a set of behaviors very much like those described by Werner and Strauss in brain-damaged children (hyperactivity, emotional lability, impulsivity, explosiveness) (Vernon, 1969). (See Chapter 11.) Eight of the children were diagnosed as psychotic. How many additional children had been excluded from the facility for such behavior is unknown. Desmond et al., (1970), following sixty-four survivors of prenatal rubella, found eight of them to be autistic at age eighteen months. Although such very high figures were not found in earlier studies, some deaf children in earlier samples had probably been dismissed as "untestable" rather than being identified as psychotic.

Schain and Yannet (1960) have maintained that the basic difficulty in early infantile autism lies in the limbic system. Rimland (1964) has presented extensive evidence that defects in the reticular system of the brain stem may underlie autistic behavior. Other workers have postulated somewhat different basic disorders underlying autism, disorders usually thought to be associated with CNS damage. O'Connor and Hermelin (1967) and Frith & Hermelin (1969) indict an inefficient employment of visual cues. Others have maintained that autistic children sustain a level of arousal that is either chronically too high (Hutt & Hutt, 1969), too low (Rimland, 1964), or alternating between the two (Ornitz & Ritvo, 1968). Schopler and Reichler (1971) have suggested that there is a deficit in the child's "availability via his various receptor systems," but laboratory studies designed to test the distortion of receptor hierarchies in autistic children have failed to support that notion (Schopler, 1966; Lovaas, Schreibman, Koegel, & Rehm, 1971). There is, however, some confirming evidence that autistic children are unable to attend to all the elements of a complex stimulus but instead attend one at a time to its separate components (Lovaas et al., 1971; Schreibman & Lovaas, 1973).

Table 10-1   Autism in Post-Rubella Syndrome Children

Nature of impairment	Autism present	Autism absent	Total
Hearing and MR	7	19	26
Hearing, visual, and MR	9	45	54
Visual and MR	0	6	6
Visual and hearing	1	12	13
MR only	0	4	4
Visual only	0	4	4
Hearing only	1	83	84
No sensory or intellectual impairment	0	52	52
Totals	18	225	243

Source: Adapted from Chess, Korn, and Fernandez (1971, p. 117).

There is the very strong likelihood that psychotic syndromes are really heteroge-neous disorders, only some of which are due to organic dysfunction (Churchill, Al-pern, & DeMyer, 1971). It is much too early to conclude that there is an invariate relationship between CNS disturbance and emotional disturbance. Among twenty-five children who had been diagnosed by a number of experts as schizophrenic, Goldfarb (1961) and his coworkers identified seventeen whom they labeled "organic" on the basis of "hard" or "soft" neurological signs. These children were inferior to the re-maining "nonorganic" children on several variables, including a number of percep-tual, psychomotor, and orientation items and a mean difference of almost 30 points in IQ. Especially fascinating was the finding that the mothers of the children without organic deficit seemed either actively or passively to encourage disordered communi-cation in the children (possibly producing a psychogenic disturbance), whereas the mothers of the "organic" children were more realistic and straightforward with them (Goldfarb, Braunstein & Scholl, 1959). The vast behavioral heterogeneity of children exhibiting psychotic syndromes is further suggestive of a diverse group of disorders whose superficial commonalities blind us to their differences.

There is, then, substantial evidence that CNS damage, perhaps a particular kind of CNS damage not yet understood, is responsible for a large proportion, but probably not all, of the behaviors called psychotic and previously thought to be more or less completely psychogenic. Rutter (1971) suggests that simple loss of brain function through early damage probably is less often involved than is some sort of continuing malfunction or active disturbance. He cites evidence that rates of disturbed behavior are especially high in children and adults with continuing seizure patterns. This is an intriguing notion, but as yet the evidence is rather meager.

The Possible Role of Language Deficit in Psychosis

Language abnormalities are a prominent part of the syndrome of early infantile au-tism and as we have seen, they constitute a particularly unfavorable prognostic index. Although this association has often been noted, it has not really been systematically studied. The implications of the association of deafness and autism in post-rubella children could, perhaps, lie in the resulting interference with language development. Although theorists differ in the importance which they place upon language in the establishment of cognitive processes, some sort of intimate connection can hardly be denied (Lockyer & Rutter, 1970; Mittler, 1968; Olson, 1970; Rutter, 1974), nor can we overlook the critical role of language in establishing relationships between the child and those around him. Even so, the relationship cannot be a simple one. Not all deaf or aphasic children are psychotic, and language impairment alone obviously cannot account for early psychosis.

SUMMARY

Severe emotional disturbance in young children is a puzzling condition which is very frequently intertwined with intellectual deficit. Although one can describe the behav-ior of these intensely unhappy and maladjusted children, questions of etiology and treatment are far from solution. It is, however, clear that in a great many such chil-dren, organic factors play an extremely important role and that laying the blame for the child's condition wholly on the parents' shoulders is both inaccurate and poten-tially cruel.

11
Mental Retardation and Other Consequences of Brain Damage

Damage to the brain of a growing human being can contribute to an almost infinite list of behavioral abnormalities at all levels of severity. In some instances, the consequences may be hardly detectable. The damage may be so well compensated by intact components of the brain that it has little meaningful effect on behavior. It may result in relatively circumscribed deficits which pass unnoticed in everyday functioning but interfere with some aspects of schoolwork. In the extreme, it may wreak havoc with the ability to cope with everyday problems and the capacity to engage in congenial relationships with others. Indeed, it may threaten survival.

In Chapter 5, the anatomy and physiology of the brain were considered, as were some agents capable of crippling normal development. Chapter 6 presented a few specific clinical disorders. Some of the genetic syndromes considered in Chapter 4 represent instances of faulty cerebral formation, but more of them actually bring about conditions damaging to an otherwise intact central nervous system (CNS) such as the presence of toxic substances or tumors. There are, then, a substantial proportion of retarded children whose intellectual and behavioral deficits are ultimately traceable to damage to the CNS.

In view of the billions of cells which constitute the brain and the delicacy of its electrochemical functioning, and in recognition of the many conditions which can potentially do irreparable harm, perhaps it is accurate to say that no one is completely intact. The concept of a continuum of severity of brain damage is useful, but there is no simple correspondence between the degree of behavioral impairment and the number of cells damaged. A great many other factors affect the relationship between the extent of damage and the behavioral symptoms which result. The timing of the insult, the part of the brain affected, the degree of continuing active disturbance, and the diffused or localized nature of the damage, all play complicated roles. Sometimes quite puzzling cases are found, from children known to have been subjected to potentially very damaging conditions but who appear essentially normal, to children whose behavior is grossly distorted but in whom no neurologic evidence of damage can be discovered. The child's psychosocial and educational experiences can also profoundly affect the eventual degree of impairment. (See Chapter 7).

It has become increasingly apparent that no single prototype of the brain-damaged child exists, that differences among damaged children far exceed their similarities. From a psychological and educational standpoint, emphasis has shifted from a search for common characteristics to a search for better means of describing individual differences and present needs. Indeed, many psychologists and an even greater proportion of educators have been forced to conclude that "diagnosis" in the sense of discovering the etiology of a disorder is not very helpful in dealing with individual children. From an historical perspective this is a distinct shift. The older literature is replete with studies searching for prototypical responses among brain-damaged mentally retarded children and is equally replete with failures.

Today's emphasis is on the functional evaluation of individual children, on discovering their particular deficits and vulnerabilities. Yet one must recognize that this individualized process, both neurological and psychological, is largely an art, not a science. Experienced neurologists who are sensitive to a broad spectrum of subtle symptoms can often identify signs of organic damage and/or malfunction, but they are frequently unable to link these signs to particular sites in the brain which have suffered trauma. Likewise, skilled psychodiagnosticians can often identify meaningful problem areas which are interfering with a child's developmental progress, but they are usually less able than the neurologists to suggest links between what they observe and underlying somatic conditions. This state of affairs need not be totally discouraging when one is dealing with an individual child. Except for the rare instances of progressive or operable disorders, such as continued ingestion of lead or a growing tumor, the treatment of choice should be behaviorally oriented. Surprising improvements can be accomplished without full knowledge of the relationship between the behaviors observed and what is going on in that hidden and protected "black box" which is the brain.

Interest in brain-damaged children has encouragingly moved toward understanding individual differences among them. There has been a less encouraging corresponding shift in interest away from mentally retarded brain-damaged children to children of normal or superior intelligence in whom damage is known or suspected. An historical survey of studies concerned with brain-damaged or learning-disabled children found that during the period 1941-1945, 82 percent of the articles dealt with retarded children, but that by 1966–1970, a mere 16 percent did so (Hallahan & Cruickshank, 1973). Various labels have been proposed for the brighter brain-damaged children, including "minimal brain damage" (MBD), "minimal brain injury" (MBI), "minimal cerebral dysfunction" (MCD), or "perceptual handicap." Educators tend to employ the labels "learning disability" (LD) and "language and learning disability" (L/LD). The afflicted children are distinguished from the retarded not by the extent or nature of the damage suffered but by the fact that they attain intelligence-test scores higher than two standard deviations below the mean. Such arbitrary classificatory schemes seem pointless to many.[1] In any event, mentally retarded children have been to a considerable extent lost sight of in the rush toward defining, exploring, and ameliorating the problems shown by brighter children with known or suspected neurological handicaps.

HISTORICAL PERSPECTIVE[2]

Knowledge regarding the relationships between CNS impairments and the behavioral deficits to which they can lead is of surprisingly recent origin. It was not until the 1920s that definitive studies of the effects of brain injury appeared, and most of these early studies had to do with previously normal adults who had suffered trauma. Although Pierre Paul Broca had demonstrated in 1861 that a lesion in part of the brain (the third frontal gyrus) could eradicate expressive language, only after World War I was a definitive syndrome described (Gelb & Goldstein, 1920; K. Goldstein, 1927; Head, 1926). Systematic observations of young war veterans with head wounds revealed not only that they had lost specific functions which were related to the locale of their injuries, but that many of them were functioning less intelligently in general. They also tended to exhibit a rather common set of abnormal reactions, including a general reduction in ability to think abstractly, overly meticulous habits, overreaction to minor frustrations, and a tendency to respond to extraneous stimuli. It was suspected that some of these symptoms were direct effects of the injury, although others seemed to represent secondary effects attributable to response to the loss of former abilities.

These studies of young adults had relatively little impact upon the thinking about mentally retarded children before the 1930s. Until that time, the usual practice was to include in one large, relatively undifferentiated group all retarded children who did not exhibit one of the more distinct clinical syndromes such as Down's syndrome. During the 1930s, however, investigators working with retarded children began to emphasize the differences between two general groups. One group was roughly equivalent to that which today we call cultural-familial mental retardation, or mental retardation due to psychosocial disadvantage. These mildly retarded children came from marginal families and were relatively free of neurological symptoms.[3] The other group was the equivalent of that which today would be termed brain-damaged. These children had a history of probable brain injury before, during, or after birth and many had observable neurological symptoms. They ranged from the mildly to the profoundly retarded and came from families in all walks of life.

Two pioneer researchers, Heinz Werner and Alfred A. Strauss, were profoundly influenced by the work of Goldstein and his colleagues. These two men, immigrants to the United States to escape Hitler's Germany, eventually found themselves at the Wayne County Training School at Northfield, Michigan. Beginning with an early study by Strauss (1933) and a series of experiments dealing with perception and perceptual-motor functioning in brain-damaged and cultural-familial retarded and nor-

---

[1] See Hobbs (1975a, 1975b) for discussions of this problem.

[2] Historical accounts of work with brain-damaged children may be found in Hallahan & Cruickshank (1973) and Strother (1973).

[3] The reader will recall, however, that contemporary studies of cultural-familial groups reveal a high incidence of minor neurological symptoms (Chap. 8).

mal children, they discovered many similarities between the brain-damaged children and the adults whom Goldstein had described. When the children were given a marble-board task in which they were to copy a design from one board onto another and then to draw it, the brain-damaged children were guided much less by the form of the outline and responded in a more disorganized fashion than did cultural-familial children (Werner & Strauss, 1939). Asked to sing a melodic pattern played on the piano, the responses of the brain-damaged children were more disorganized and harsh, lacking melody or harmony. Using a behavior-rating scale, Strauss and Kephart (1940) confirmed their impression that the brain-damaged children were more disinhibited, erratic, impulsive, socially unaccepted, uncontrolled, and uncoordinated.

In this way, Strauss and Werner developed a picture of what they called *exogenous* (brain-damaged) as opposed to *endogenous* (cultural-familial) mental retardation. This overly simplified and somewhat erroneous dichotomy had a powerful effect on the thinking of all those who followed. Indeed, the cluster of behaviors they described has come to be known as the Strauss syndrome. Among the symptoms emphasized (Strauss & Lehtinen, 1947) were excessive activity, distractibility, short-lived aggressive and destructive behavior, poor controls, and heightened variability. So convincing were Strauss's writings and so dramatic were the cases observed that for a time many workers regarded these behavioral symptoms as absolutely diagnostic of brain damage even in the absence of supporting neurologic or historical data. The "driven" quality of activity, the distractibility, and good-natured aggressiveness of children regarded as typical of the brain-injured group are illustrated in the following case report by Strauss and Lehtinen (1947). Although this little boy eventually functioned at a normal intellectual level, his poor control at the beginning of treatment prevented his success in any concerted intellectual endeavor, rendering him functionally retarded despite his second-grade achievement.

J. de T. y T., son of a wealthy Spanish family. Father a prominent attorney, mother educated according to the standards of the upper social class. . . . An only child. Pregnancy and delivery were both normal but the child was blue [a sign of asphyxia] at birth and the usual procedures were applied. He walked and talked somewhat later than usual and had no serious childhood diseases. He was an extremely disobedient and obstinate child with destructive tendencies, very easily excited. He seemed to be fearless. Not accepted by other children because of his constant teasing and tormenting. Cared for by a personal nurse. When six years old, he was entered in a private school but could not be admitted to a class with other children. Two teachers were employed for him alone since one teacher refused to stand it without relief for the entire day.

At 8 years and 6 months of age he was admitted to our clinic. He had a second grade school achievement; psychometric testing was impossible because of extreme restlessness and distractibility. He was always "on the move," exploring everything in the house, particularly technical equipment, electric switches, door bells, elevators, etc. Asked questions incessantly, like a machine gun. Very affectionate with all persons in the house. When taken to bed, he did not sleep until midnight but asked another question every five minutes. On the days following his admission he was still very restless and disinhibited but meticulous and pedantic in the arrangement of his belongings and everything handled by him at the table or in the classroom. Play in the garden consisted in trying to destroy flowers or bushes but without ill-humor or anger. Always smiling and good-humored. At dinner time he ate enormous quantities of

food and drank a glass of water or milk with one gulp. In church he was very distractible, wishing to give money to all the collection boxes. . . . He was discharged after one
and one half years with an intelligence quotient within the normal range and admitted
to a private school. Then attended class with children of his age and in an examination proved to be ninth in placement among forty children (p. 2).[4]

Through the influential writings of Strauss (Strauss & Lehtinen, 1947; Strauss &
Kephart, 1955), this syndrome became accepted as the prototype of brain injury in
young children. A child exhibiting such behaviors was considered brain-damaged
whether or not any corroborating evidence could be found. Attention was thereby
drawn away from the sizable number of brain-damaged children who do not show
such behaviors and who may, indeed, be quite the opposite: underactive, lethargic,
and/or withdrawn.

A number of other workers modified and extended the position of Strauss and
Werner and developed theories of their own, particularly in the area of perceptual-
motor skills. Among them were William M. Cruickshank (1967; Cruickshank, Bentzen, Ratzeberg, & Tannhauser, 1961), Marianne Frostig (Frostig, Lefever, & Whittlesey, 1961; Frostig, Maslow, Lefever & Whittlesey, 1964), Gerald Getman (Getman &
Kephart, 1956; Getman, Kane, Halgren, & McKee, 1964), and Newell G. Kephart
(1971). Although these theorists differed from one another in detail, strong similarities to the work of Strauss and Werner can be found in their conceptions, including an
emphasis on perceptual-motor abnormalities.

A few other workers have emphasized the relationship between behavioral characteristics and specific kinds of brain lesions. Arthur Benton (1955, 1962) has paid
particular attention to right-left discrimination problems in children and to the association between defective finger recognition (finger agnosia) and the presence of brain
damage.[5]

The work of Ralph Reitan (e.g., 1966) has also concentrated on the relationship
of a broad variety of psychological abilities to brain damage. Although most of his
investigations have concerned adults with more-or-less circumscribed lesions of the
brain, Reitan and Thomas J. Boll (1973) have extended the work to include brain-
damaged children of normal and retarded intelligence. Reitan's major research has
utilized a battery of tests adapted from a series developed by Ward Halstead (1947), in
combination with the Wechsler intelligence scale appropriate for the subject's age.
Reitan does not seek to demonstrate a prototypic response common to brain-damaged
individuals, but rather he looks for specific behavior patterns which are associated
with specific types of brain damage. His studies with adults, for example, have indicated rather consistent relationships between impaired verbal abilities and lesions of
the left cerebral hemisphere, and between impaired nonverbal abilities and lesions of
the right cerebral hemisphere. In children, such relationships are much less clear,
although Reitan and Boll (1973) were able to discover a few consistent differences
between minimally brain-damaged (MBD) children referred for school learning problems and MBD children referred for behavioral problems.

Another prominent researcher, until his untimely death in 1972, was Herbert G.
Birch, whose far-ranging interests and outstanding research skills made him a sort of

---

[4] From A. A. Strauss, and Laura E. Lehtinen. *Psychopathology and education of the brain-injured
child.* New York: Grune & Stratton, 1947. Reprinted by permission.
[5] For a latter-day study of this kind, see Lefford, Birch, and Green (1974).

Renaissance Man of psychology. Among Birch's contributions were his pinpointing of the difficulty some brain-damaged children have in integrating sensory input from two modalities (e.g., Birch & Belmont, 1965; Cravioto, Birch, & Gaona, 1967), their perceptual domination by immediately present properties of a stimulus rather than its conceptual properties (Birch & Bortner, 1967), a possible prolongation of cortical inhibition after a response (Birch, Belmont, & Karp, 1965), and impaired patterning of movements in damaged newborns (Turkewitz & Birch, 1971). Birch's account of the effects of poverty and malnutrition (Birch & Gussow, 1970) has been cited elsewhere. Two important conceptual distinctions are also among Birch's contributions to contemporary views. In 1964, he called attention to the distinction between the fact of "brain damage," which consists of any structural or physiologic alteration of a pathologic nature present in the nerve tissues of the brain, and "organicity," the observable behavioral patterns which are manifested only by certain individuals with particular kinds of brain damage and experiential histories and are in no sense the prototype of all the disturbances which accompany injury to the brain. Birch (Birch & Diller, 1959) also distinguished between two kinds of behavioral alterations due to damage to the cerebrum: *subtractive* dysfunctions, simple losses or deficiencies in one or more behavioral functions, and *additive* dysfunctions, often accompanied by seizures, spasticity, perseveration, or perceptual distortions, with behavioral disturbances due to active ongoing distortions of CNS processes.

Glen Doman and Carl Delacato (see Doman, Spitz, Zucman, Delacato, & Doman, 1960), proposed that remediation of the damaged brain through surgical or behavioral methods is far preferable to symptomatic treatment. They advocated a treatment regimen which entailed (1) training children to perform activities such as creeping and crawling in order to remediate damaged areas of the brain, (2) manipulating children into passive body patterns corresponding with damaged brain functions, (3) forcing them to favor one side of the body (hand, foot, eye) to strengthen hemispheric dominance and laterality, (4) administering carbon dioxide treatment to improve blood circulation in the brain, and (5) sensory stimulation to promote body awareness. Institutes for the Achievement of Human Potential, established under the direction of Doman and Delacato and their colleagues in a number of locations in the United States and abroad, became meccas for many parents desperate to find an effective treatment. Public acceptance of this unusual theory also was for the most part immediate and enthusiastic, fed to a large extent by optimistic reports from the sponsors (see, e.g., LeWinn, Doman, Doman, Delacato, Spitz, & Thomas, 1966). Unfortunately, others found little evidence to substantiate either the theory or the very demanding treatment regimen (Robbins & Glass, 1969). The dispute reached such heights that a group of prestigious professional organizations felt it necessary to issue a joint statement describing the lack of scientific proof of the Doman-Delacato position and decrying the pressures exerted on parents to conform to the program. That statement and a summary of the scientific evidence on both sides have been presented by Hallahan and Cruickshank (1973). In the ensuing years, enthusiasm both in and out of the professional community declined markedly. Recently, however, a study (Neman, Roos, McCann, Menolascino, & Heal, 1975) with sixty-six carefully selected, institutionalized, mentally retarded children demonstrated some improvement in mobility, visual perception, and language ability after a seven-month program, two hours a day, for the most part seven days a week. The program consisted of mobility exercises including patterning, creeping, and crawling; visual-motor training; and sensory stimulation exercises, and was carried out by personnel of the American Academy for

Human Development, an organization related to the Institutes for the Achievement of Human Potential. Matched control groups were given either an equally extensive but less structured program which included the sensory stimulation exercises, or no treatment. Although no subjects improved dramatically, the results of this study, sponsored by the National Association for Retarded Citizens, suggest that the program may have some benefit when carried out intensively and expertly with appropriate children, though probably not to the degree for which claims have from time to time been made.

DEFINITIONS AND CATEGORIES

As the discerning reader has discovered, the term "brain damaged" is an omnibus category applicable to any individual in whom the normal structure or function of the brain has been distorted. Such a category is of course unwieldy, but it is not an inaccurate reflection of our state of knowledge. There is a great deal more that we *do not* know than that we *do* know about brain-damaged children!

Although many workers use *brain injury* and *brain damage* interchangeably, we prefer the latter to the former term simply because it seems to connote the result of a (usually unidentified) process, rather than the injurious process itself. The reader will encounter, in other sources, a number of related terms such as *cerebral dysfunction* or *neurological disability,* any of which is also acceptable. In any event, it is the child as he or she is, not the label, that must be the focus of concern for those who seek to give assistance.

Within the large group of children who are brain-damaged and mentally retarded, it is possible to make a number of distinctions. First, the relative prominence of symptoms is inversely related to *IQ level.* Many of the moderately retarded and practically all severely and profoundly retarded children have sustained very serious brain injury; institutional populations and pupils in classes for the trainable mentally retarded consist largely of brain-damaged children. Among the mildly retarded, on the other hand, prominent symptoms of brain damage are much less common. Nevertheless, it seems reasonable to suspect that many mildly retarded children are actually the victims of brain damage. Studies which fail to equate groups on intellectual measures often confound etiology with other gross aspects of mental functioning. One of the attractions of work with brain-damaged children of normal intelligence is that with this group one can select nondamaged children who can be matched simultaneously on CA, MA, and IQ, whereas this is impossible with children whose IQs are below approximately 55 or 60.

With regard to etiology it is possible to make the distinction, as we have in previous chapters, between *genetic* and *nongenetic* disorders, but for present purposes such categories are not very useful. Children with Lesch-Nyhan syndrome suffer a genetic disorder intrinsic to the brain, but most children with phenylketonuria are born with essentially intact central nervous systems, their faulty enzymes having been irrelevant so long as their mothers were supplying needed substances. Only after birth, when the child becomes dependent on his own metabolic processes, do the buildup of toxic biochemicals and subsequent damage occur. That some disorders arise from the child's genetic makeup rather than some external source makes little difference.

The *timing of the injury* is also an important determining variable, though not a simple one. Among mentally retarded brain-damaged children, many were affected *in utero,* others sustained injury during the perinatal period, and a smaller group suffered later insult. (See Chapter 5.) There is some controversy whether a given degree of brain injury early in life results in greater or less impairment than "equivalent" damage in adulthood. During the period when organs are emerging and growing most rapidly, they are most vulnerable. This fact argues for greater susceptibility of the fetus and infant, who are undergoing the highest rates of growth and differentiation (Lenneberg, 1968). The individual who has enjoyed a period of intact development prior to the injury has established some normal patterns and also has a backlog of experience on which to draw. On the other hand, there is the possibility that the immature brain may be able to make adjustments or compensations which are impossible in the older person and that cells which are still undifferentiated at the time of injury may take over functions of the damaged ones.

The weight of the evidence seems to indicate that early brain damage results in greater impairment than later damage (Boll, 1973; Hebb, 1949). The situation is still cloudy, however, because in the absence of clear-cut symptoms, the actual presence of brain damage can only be surmised. Even if potentially damaging circumstances have been observed, it is difficult to say with certainty whether or not damage has occurred. A substantial proportion of children known to have experienced anoxia at birth, for example, have not shown serious signs of impairment later on (Graham, Ernhart, Craft, & Berman, 1963). Was this because the anoxia did no damage or because damage which did occur was compensated for by undamaged areas? There is also evidence that children who are susceptible to difficulties during the perinatal period have developed abnormally prior to birth, so that the problems are confounded. (See Chapter 5.) When children with disabilities are brought to professional attention, the histories given by the parents may be similarly confusing. They may have been unaware of their children's earlier slow development and may be prone to attribute major deficits to minor events such as a high fever or a fall from a bed, which were actually irrelevant and would have been overlooked in a normal child.

A distinction which often remains equally elusive is that between damage which is *diffuse* versus that which is *localized* or circumscribed. In most retarded children, though possibly not so many brain-damaged children of normal intelligence, the damage is diffuse. Most brain damage resulting in mental retardation is now believed to happen before birth. Because prenatal damage tends to be the result of generalized assault and because the brain as a whole is developing so rapidly during this period, diffuse damage is a likely result (Lenneberg, 1968). At any given time some components of the brain, especially those undergoing the most rapid period of differentiation, are more vulnerable than others. Diffuse damage apparently produces more pervasive symptoms, more highly disturbed behavior, and greater intellectual deficit.

Wortis (1956) some time ago suggested that the symptoms ascribed by Strauss to lesions localized in the new brain may actually be the result of diffuse damage. Others have ascribed the Strauss syndrome to lesions in the brain stem, the diencephalon, or both, rather than to the cerebral hemispheres (Benton, 1962). Even a circumscribed lesion, however, may cause disruption and reorganization of the vascular system in areas of the brain relatively remote from the original site. Most of what we know about the effects of circumscribed lesions comes from studies of adults who had been normal previous to head trauma, tumor, or stroke. It is not at all safe to generalize from these findings to children (Connors, 1973). Even the relatively reliable effects known to result from damage to the right or left hemisphere in adults do not seem to be applicable to children (Reed & Reitan, 1969).

Although there are many unanswered questions about the effects of development on symptoms of brain damage, it seems abundantly clear that behavior is significantly related to the child's *current age* (Graham & Berman, 1961). Since infants and children exhibit such different ranges of behavior, changes with increasing age are inevitable. Even the characteristic hyperactivity and inattentiveness of the Strauss syndrome seem to subside as children grow older (Dykman, Peters, & Ackerman, 1973). The time elapsed since the injury is obviously important as well. The young child has had a shorter time to compensate for a birth injury than has an adult. Some effects may wax and wane, perhaps because of changing levels of stress, asynchrony in growth, or developmental plateaus which allow children to consolidate their resources and more effectively to compensate for disabilities. It has been suggested that there may be critical phases during which the effects of injuries may most easily be observed (Masland, 1958; Thurston et al., 1960). Subtle perceptual distortions may, for example, be very difficult to observe in infants but readily apparent when children begin to read. Distortions in speech will become apparent as children learn to talk (Meyer, 1968). Awkwardness in riding a bicycle might be obvious in a seven-year-old but undetectable by the time the child is thirteen and has had six years of maturation and practice.

Children's *temperamental endowment,* quite aside from whatever brain damage they have sustained, will substantially color their behavior. Thomas, Chess, and Birch (1968) found that most non-brain-damaged children who had been temperamentally "difficult" infants later showed behavior disorders, whereas few "easy" children did. At the same time, they found that some parents were able to manage the difficult children better than were others. It is easy to attribute all a child's problems to the single fact of his being brain-damaged, whereas in truth, even without that added burden, he might have been "difficult."

In the same way, the child's *intellectual potential* prior to the injury is a factor of some importance. Although there is obviously no way to judge potential directly, a comparison with parents and siblings may indirectly suggest the degree of impairment a child has suffered. As we have already mentioned, brain-damaged retarded children tend to come from families across a wide spectrum of the socioeconomic and intellectual scales, and intrafamily IQ discrepancies are typically much larger than those found in cultural-familial families.

Finally, the reader should be reminded of the several studies quoted in Chapter 8, which demonstrate *social class differences* in the abilities of families to support optimal development in children who have experienced perinatal problems. Retardation following such events is considerably more common in children growing up in lower-class families. There remains the possibility that middle-class children who at school age exhibit specific learning disabilities of various kinds would, if their families had been less capable of providing for their needs, have exhibited much more striking disabilities. The "minimal brain damage" suspected in such children may be physiologically not very different from the damage sustained by many mildly retarded children who were not so fortunate in their life experiences. Should this be the case, it suggests that at-risk children in problematic families deserve considerably more preventive intervention than they are likely to receive under our present system.

There is much still unknown about the differential effects of various kinds of dysfunctions and about the environmental factors which are a part of the child's history. Our ignorance far exceeds our expertise. Yet, an incalculable amount of time has been devoted by professionals over the years to the search for a precise etiological diagnosis and, that remaining elusive, simply to deciding whether or not to assign a child a diagnosis of "brain-damaged." Unfortunately, most of this effort has been completely wasted. Ross (1968) has called this "the Rumplestiltskin fixation," the conviction held by many that "if could they but give the disease a name the patient would be saved" (p. 22). Clearly, mere diagnostic labels are not very informative, least so to the psychologist or the educator who is planning a preventive or remediational program. As Barbara Bateman (1973) put it, "Etiological truths do not necessarily have educational implications. Someday they might, although betting at that window is not heavy" (p. 246). Further rejecting the notion that generalized trait descriptions (e.g., hyperactivity, short attention span) are helpful to the educator, she suggests that the most cogent question to be asked is, "What does this child need to be taught?"

AREAS OF SPECIAL VULNERABILITY

Most professionals probably agree with Bateman that one needs to be very specific in assessing the needs and abilities of individual brain-damaged children. It is surprising that the available body of research has been oriented almost exclusively toward group rather than toward individual differences. The typical study revealing differences between brain-damaged and non-brain-damaged children has found considerable overlap, only some of the brain-damaged subjects showing the disability in question to any marked degree. In essence, these studies have succeeded in identifying areas of vulnerability rather than predictable symptoms. This section will outline some of what is known about these special areas of vulnerability. Most children with significant degrees of damage will probably show some difficulties in one or more areas, but the pattern of assets and deficits they exhibit will be very much an individual matter. The psychologist's task, then, is not to classify but to describe, as specifically as possible, the strengths and weaknesses of the child and, with the cooperation of the adults important in the child's life, to devise the best possible management and treatment program.

General Intellectual Deficit (IQ)

Depression of performance on general intelligence tests is one of the primary signals of the presence of serious brain damage. Studies of children with known cerebral damage consistently show a large proportion to be functioning at an intellectual level significantly lower than comparison groups of non-brain-damaged children with intellectual or emotional difficulties (Birch, Belmont, Belmont, & Taft, 1967; Bortner & Birch, 1969; Jordan, 1964; Reitan & Boll, 1973). It is no accident that the early studies of brain damage in children concentrated on mentally retarded populations, for retardation is a familiar consequence of cerebral trauma.

Two special aspects of intelligence-test performance have received attention in a number of studies: discrepancies between verbal and performance items and scatter or range of scores. In general, brain-damaged children have been expected to do poorly on performance items, since these are heavily weighted with perceptual-motor skills, which are thought to be more vulnerable to brain injury than verbal skills. Although some of the evidence has upheld this prediction (e.g., Baroff, 1959; Gubbay, Elles, Walton, & Court, 1965; Holroys & Wright, 1965), it is clear that the discrepancy is by no means a reliable indicator. The Birch et al. (1967) and Bortner and Birch (1969) studies mentioned above found no reason to substantiate the verbal-performance discrepancy in children, nor did they find any particular patterns of intellectual functioning to be systematically associated either with neurological evidence of brain damage or with a history of high-risk factors. In a study of boys with minimal brain dysfunction, Dykman et al. (1973) found that they differed from a control group on Verbal and Full-Scale WISC IQs, but *not* in Performance IQ.

Studies of verbal-performance discrepancies in adults have revealed a distinct relationship between the direction of the discrepancy and the cite of a lesion in the right or left hemisphere. Lesions in the left hemisphere, where many language functions tend to be localized, are often accompanied by deficits in verbal IQ, whereas lesions in the right hemisphere tend to be accompanied by deficits in performance IQ. Diffuse (bilateral) lesions apparently tend to be similar in effect to right-hemisphere lesions. (See Matarazzo, 1972). These are, of course, group differences, and exceptions clearly exist. Moreover, these differences are by no means so regular in children and, in fact, are quite unreliable diagnostic indicators during childhood.

Studies of scatter (range of scores) have not been at all encouraging. Those comparing brain-injured with cultural-familial retarded children have typically found greater scatter on only some kinds of items. Moreover, tests which have produced greater scatter with one brain-damaged group often have not done so with other such groups (Berko, 1955; Satter, 1955). Birch et al. (1967), studying all known cases of educable subnormality in eight- to ten-year-old children in Aberdeen, Scotland, found no evidence of greater scatter among the subgroup with brain damage.

One must conclude, then, that as a group the brain-damaged do not show any specific patterning of intelligence-test responses. Group comparisons no doubt mask individual patterns of disabilities. An alert clinician will remain sensitive to the consistent patterns he sees in a child's performance, looking for cues to special kinds of disabilities, while realizing that intelligence tests have not been constructed to reveal "pure" weaknesses or strengths.

The clinician is often doubtful of the reliability of intelligence tests of brain-damaged children, especially when there is speech or motor involvement which interferes with the child's ability to respond in the usual fashion or when behavior problems are present. An interesting study by Nielsen (1971), however, indicates that the IQs obtained in such cases are probably as stable as those of nondamaged children. In this retrospective study, 128 cerebral palsied children with medical or psychological problems were retested after a mean interval of four years, using a variety of tests in a clinical setting. Although the test-retest reliability for those children originally tested before age twenty months was low, as is also true for normal children, the scores of those originally tested at age two and older were respectably reliable, the correlations ranging from .76 to .88 for various age groups. The lack of sensivity of intelligence tests to the classical "signs" of brain damage, then, does not invalidate their usefulness for the purposes for which they are usually employed.

Sensory and Motor Handicaps

Impairment of sensory and motor functions is a consequence of damage to some areas of the brain. In infants and young children, clumsiness and abnormalities in sucking, grasping, posture, muscle tonus, and locomotion may be among the earliest signals of such damage. A follow-up of those one-year-olds who had been in very poor condition at birth (scores of 0–3 on a 10-point scale)[6] of a total sample of 10,000 cases found that one-fifth showed abnormal or suspicious gait, posture, muscle tonus, or other neuro-

---

[6] Scores were derived from a rating technique developed by Virginia Apgar (Apgar, Holaday, James, Berrien, & Weisbrot, 1958; Apgar & James, 1962). The scale is a simple appraisal of five aspects of vital functioning (heartrate, respiration, muscle tone, reflex responsiveness, and skin color).

Fig. 11-1   The form may not be perfect but the ball seems on its way to a strike. *(University of Washington Child Development and Mental Retardation Center)*

logical signs (Kennedy, Drage, & Schwartz, 1963). At age four, many of the children with low scores (0-6) at birth were found to show poor fine and gross motor control (Drage, Berendes, & Fisher, 1969).

Cerebral palsy, blindness, and deafness are handicaps relatively easy to detect, but other difficulties may be more subtle. The visual field may be limited, for example, or the child may have hearing loss in some frequencies and not in others. Some of the subtler problems can sometimes be detected by tests of motor "impersistence" which require the child to carry out a number of commands, such as keeping his eyes closed or his mouth open, protruding his tongue while his eyes are open or shut, etc. (Garfield, 1964; Garfield, Benton & MacQueen, 1966). Tests requiring the child to walk a pattern may also reveal distortions, suggesting disturbances or delay in the integration of body positions and movements with visual organizations (Keogh & Birch, 1968). Some tests such as the Lincoln-Oseretsky Motor Development Scale (Sloan, 1955) or the Southern California Sensory Integration Tests (Ayers, 1972) have been specifically designed to assess motor behavior and integration, but most psychologists tend to leave the detailed assessment of sensory and motor functions to other professionals better qualified in those areas and to limit their evaluations to sensory-motor behavior as seen primarily in drawing tasks. This division of labor sometimes blinds the psychologist to evidence of subtle sensory or motor problems.

Perceptual Development[7]

Since the days of Goldstein, Werner, and Strauss, deficits in perception and in perceptual-motor behavior have been a favorite focus of those studying brain-damaged indi-

---

[7] The interested reader is referred to Hallahan and Cruickshank (1973) for a well-reasoned account of the theoretical and empirical work in this area, including efforts at remediation.

viduals. Perception involves an interpretive response about the nature of the environment, as opposed to sensory acuity which involves the ability to detect the presence of a stimulus such as a tone or a picture. Seeing an object is sensory; identifying it is perceptual.

A number of major theories of cognitive development (e.g., Bruner, 1957; Bruner, Olver, & Greenfield, 1966; Gibson, 1969; Hebb, 1949; Inhelder & Piaget, 1964; Wohlwill, 1962) emphasize the basic importance of accurate perception in concept building, although the theorists differ among themselves in the ways in which they link perception to cognition. None would deny the importance of accurate input in the formation of an individual's relationship with his environment. Disturbances in perceptual development are expected to wreak havoc with cognitive processes. Many studies have indeed revealed perceptual deficits in brain-injured children and adults.

The importance of perceptual processes in children's academic achievement is emphasized by a group of experts, members of the Hobbs group mentioned in Chapter 2 (Wepman, Cruickshank, Deutsch, Morency, & Strother, 1975) who recommend that the term *specific learning disability* be applied to those children whose low achievement can be traced to perceptual or perceptual-motor handicaps, regardless of etiology. In so doing, they propose to define a relatively identifiable subgroup of those children unable to master basic academic skills, ruling out those with educational problems due to "behavior disturbances, severe mental retardation, poverty, lessened educational opportunity, visual impairment, hearing loss, or muscular paralysis" (p. 306). In the process, however, they also shift the educational perspective from a neurologically assumed basis (e.g., "minimal brain dysfunction") to an assumption that perception underlies many of the puzzling handicaps seen in otherwise apparently intact and normally intelligent children with trouble in reading.

Unimodal Perception   Among brain-damaged children, some show deficits in visual, auditory, spatial, kinesthetic, and/or tactual perception. One study by Boll (1972), for example, comparing twenty-seven brain-damaged children with twenty-seven normal controls, found the most serious impairments in the brain-damaged children to be in concept formation, followed (in order) by visual perception, auditory perception, motor speed, and tactile form perception, in all of which they differed significantly from the controls.

The usual means of probing for errors within a perceptual system is to use a discrimination task or a matching-to-sample task which requires the subject to make an uncomplicated verbal or motor response to indicate a choice. Cundick and Robison (1972), for example, presented fifty sets of geometric designs to twenty-four brain-damaged six- to eleven-year-olds and to twenty-four controls matched in sex, age, and verbal ability. The subjects were shown a design and asked to pick an identical one from an array of four. Both with and without the model design present, the brain-damaged subjects were significantly poorer at this task than were the controls.

Integration Across Modalities   Some provocative studies of auditory-visual integrations suggest that although the separate systems may remain intact, defects in cross-modal functions may occur which are sensitive indicators of brain damage (Birch & Belmont, 1964, 1965a; Birch & Lefford, 1963; Deutsch & Schumer, 1970). Conners and Barta (1967), for example, asked brain-damaged children and children with severe emotional disturbances to touch a form which was out of sight and to match it to one of twenty-seven forms varying in shape, size, and angle of orientation.

The brain-damaged children were slower and explored the forms more carefully, but they were less accurate.

Refining techniques used by Birch and his colleagues, Sterritt and Rudnick (1966) asked children to match auditory patterns of pencil taps with visual patterns of dots and of a blinking light. They substantiated the finding by Birch and Belmont (1965b) that deficits in this kind of intersensory integration were related to reading problems. They further discovered that with respect to reading disability, the significance of the purely visual performance declined with age, although performance on the cross-modality tasks took on added importance. Similar kinds of cross-modal deficits have been shown to persist in seven-year-old children who had been severely malnourished before the age of thirty months (Cravioto, 1972; Cravioto et al., 1967). This series of studies lends support to the hypothesis that high-order integrative functions are more vulnerable and/or more difficult to compensate for than relatively less complex, uni-modal responses.

The most common cross-modality indices of organicity have been tests requiring the subject to copy a visual stimulus. The Bender-Gestalt Test (Bender, 1938) and the Visual Retention Test (Benton, 1955) are two such tests in which the child is asked to reproduce a series of figures either while they are present or after they have been removed. A number of studies have confirmed the poorer performance of brain-damaged subjects on such tasks (Friedman & Barclay, 1963; Jones, 1964; McConnell, 1967; Pacella, 1965; N. M. Robinson, 1953). Contradictory evidence has, however, been obtained by other investigators (Dony, 1973; Friedman, Strochak, Gitlin, & Gottsgen, 1967; Parsons, McLeroy, & Wright, 1971), although some investigators have found positive results using one scoring system or test but not others (Sternlicht, Pustel, & Siegel, 1968). This confused state of affairs probably substantiates the important differences in perceptual-motor vulnerability among the conglomerate of individuals labeled brain-damaged. Certainly not all brain-injured subjects can be expected to perform poorly on such tasks. In some of those who do have difficulty with a particular task, perception of the visual stimuli may be distorted; in others, difficulties with motor control may be implicated; in still others, the fault may lie in integrative functions which translate visually perceived stimuli to guidelines for motor action.

Selective Perception   The difficulties some brain-damaged individuals have in perceiving or attending to components of complex stimuli were documented in the early studies of Goldstein and of Werner and Strauss. They continue to command attention today. Some authors (e.g., Hallahan & Cruickshank, 1973; Zeaman & House, 1963[8]) have proposed that the difficulties are essentially an aspect of attention, although others (e.g., Werner & Strauss, 1941; Strauss & Werner, 1941) have characterized them as an aspect of perception. The ability to focus on one stimulus while ignoring others apparently develops normally in the intact person as a product of early experience (Riesen, 1947; von Senden, 1932). For reasons not yet well understood, many brain-damaged children have difficulty in separating a significant stimulus from its distracting background (Birch & Lefford, 1964). They seem not to outgrow the initial chaos of infancy, or what William James (1890) termed the "great blooming, buzzing confusion" (p. 488).

Werner and Strauss (1941; Strauss & Werner, 1941) demonstrated this disability by comparing two groups of retarded children, one cultural-familial and one brain-

[8] See Chap. 13.

damaged, with a group of younger normal children of the same mental age. The children were given simple tasks which involved the recognition of objects or figures embedded in a distracting background. Many more of the brain-damaged children responded to the background. When shown a cup superimposed on a series of diagonal lines, for example, a great many of the brain-damaged children said "lines," although non-brain-injured children, whether or not they were mentally retarded, usually said "a cup." Werner and Strauss also gave the children a marble board (similar to a Chinese Checkers board) on which they were to copy a pattern presented on a model board which had a distracting background pattern. Only 15 percent of the non-brain-injured group seemed to respond in any way to the background, whereas 84 percent of the brain-damaged children showed the effects of this distraction.

In a very thorough investigation Cruickshank, Bice, Wallen, and Lynch (1965) used a large group of cerebral palsied children, of whom 211 were spastics and 114 athetoids, together with a group of 111 nonhandicapped children. Among other tasks, they asked the children to draw on paper a design they had felt on a marble board. The spastic children made significantly more references to the background than did the normal children. Although in this respect the athetoid children did not differ significantly from the normal children, they gave other evidence of having been somewhat more distracted by the background than were the normal children. Using another modification of the Werner-Strauss approach, a tachistoscopic flashing of figures presented in a structured background, Cruickshank et al. found that the spastic children performed most poorly, whereas the athetoid children made more correct choices than the spastic children and gave virtually the same low number of background responses as the normal children. Rubin (1969) modified this procedure by minimizing the distracting conditions and forcing subjects to choose between a correct background and a correct figure. Although the brain-damaged subjects did well at this task, such findings do not negate the original tendency for the subjects to give a background response when unimpeded, as Hallahan and Cruickshank (1973) have pointed out.

A series of recent studies using measures of incidental memory (Chapter 14) lend support to an alternative interpretation of these findings. Individuals who do not restrict their attention to the central stimulus they are expected to learn seem to pay close enough attention to the incidental stimuli that they learn them at the same time. The more attention is focused on the central stimulus, the less attention is given to incidental stimuli. In young, normal children, central and incidental learning are correlated positively; in older children, the correlation is a negative one (Hagen, 1967). The discrepancy between central and incidental learning measures thus becomes an index of maturity. Hallahan, Stainback, Ball, and Kauffman (1973) compared noninstitutionalized mildly retarded spastic cerebral palsied children who had MAs of seven to eleven with normal controls of the same MAs. They found selective perception to be a function of MA. There were no significant differences between the brain-damaged and the normal subjects at a given MA level. One must, then, be somewhat circumspect in evaluating the long-held conviction that the phenomenon of selective perception is closely related to cerebral dysfunction.

Perceptual Organization and Analysis   Some brain-damaged children are less well organized in their perceptual responses than children with an intact CNS. An early technique used to assess perceptual organization was the Lowenfeld Mosaic Test (Lowenfeld, 1949, 1954), which requires the child to devise a design using as many of a large collection of colored pieces as he or she likes. Colm (1948) observed that brain-damaged children tended to use one kind of block rather than several and to pile them up or line them up rather than make a free design. Others (Carr, 1958; Shotwell, & Lawrence, 1951), comparing matched groups of cultural-familial and brain-damaged children, found that the latter plunged into the task with little planning, worked longer, and used a greater number of pieces, but were less satisfied with their products.

Chaotic organization was also reported by several authors to characterize the responses of brain-damaged children to the marble-board test developed by Werner (Bensberg, 1950; Oki, Sakai, Kizu, Higashi, Otsuka, Asano, 1960; Strauss & Werner, 1941). Non-brain-injured children were able to organize the patterns they were copying into a continuous figure and to place the marbles one after the other in an orderly fashion. The brain-damaged children, in contrast, seemed constantly to be striving to attain order, sometimes counting the holes, marking their place with a finger, and so on. Despite these efforts, they tended to skip around the board in copying the patterns. Consistent but far less striking results were obtained by Gallagher (1957) with brain-damaged and cultural-familial children. Along the same line, Belmont, Belmont, and Birch (1969) observed that, in general, EMR children with signs of CNS damage imposed inappropriate organization on their percepts and could not analyze them as adequately as other EMR children, the major factor apparently being in the analytic processes rather than inattention, perception, or poor motivation.

Brain-damaged children seem to be more strongly affected by concrete stimulus properties than other children, so that they are unable to utilize the concepts and organizational skills they have. Birch and Bortner (1967) studied object-matching behavior in 104 cerebral palsied and 188 normal children under two conditions. In the first, subjects could choose to match on the basis of concrete stimulus similarity, common function, or common class membership. In the second condition, the similarity between objects was reduced. Although the cerebral palsied children had difficulty expressing concepts of function and class membership in the first condition, when the concrete stimulus similarity was high, they could express these concepts when the similarity was eliminated. The child who is overly attracted to concrete stimulus properties has difficulty detaching attention from them in order to utilize other cognitive abilities. The problem, then, is at least as much one of selective perception or attention as it is one of perceptual organization.

Perseveration   Some brain-damaged children have trouble in shifting effectively from one stimulus or one kind of response to another and in ceasing a train of action once embarked on it. This problem seems to be especially acute with difficult tasks. Werner (1946) required children to draw a series of dot patterns which had been presented by tachistoscope. Brain-damaged children did about as well as cultural-familial children on simple designs, but on a series in which the designs were more difficult they repeated the earlier, simpler responses on 20 percent of the trials. The familial children made no such perseverative responses at all. Perseveration in a test such as the Bender-Gestalt occurs when a subject who is copying the series of dots lengthens the series, sometimes until he runs off the page. On the Rorschach inkblot test, it is said to occur when the same response is given to several cards.

Perceptual-motor Training   Hallahan and Cruickshank (1973) carefully reviewed forty-two studies in which methods to train perceptual-motor skills were applied to groups of retarded or nonretarded brain-damaged children. Only seven to ten of the forty-two studies were passable from a methodological point of view, most of them suffering from lack of control groups and flaws in reporting or analyzing the data. Among the methodologically sound studies, the results for the most part failed to indicate that the training procedures were effective. The training programs also failed, however, to provide remediation specifically tailored to the deficits exhibited by individual children. Since the weight of the evidence indicates that variation among brain-damaged children is at least as broad as that among normal populations, these data should probably not be viewed as definitive. What works for one child may slow down the progress of another. It would certainly be premature to conclude that deficits in perceptual-motor functioning are intractable in brain-damaged children. There is, in fact, from the scattered successes some evidence that quite the opposite is the case.

Deficits in Attentional Responses

Several kinds of behavior are subsumed under the rubric "attention." Earlier, we encountered *selective attention,* or the ability to attend to relevant and/or salient features in the environment with a corresponding decrease of attention to irrelevant features. *Sustained attention* refers to the ability of the individual to remain alert and attentive (to "pay attention") over a continuous period of time. A closely related aspect of behavior is *resistance to distraction,* the ability to maintain focus despite competing "noise" in the environment. *Habituation* refers to the normal tendency of the individual to withdraw attention from material which is overly familiar or redundant. Each of these aspects of attention is at least partly developmental in nature, and on each there is evidence that some brain-damaged retarded children differ from normal children.

Sustained Attention   The inability to remain alert and attentive for a protracted period obviously interferes with learning. "Poor concentration" is, however, a frequent complaint of teachers of perfectly normal children, especially boys. In the epidemiological study on the Isle of Wight (Rutter, 1971) cited in Chapter 9, 30 percent of boys with IQs 100-119 and 50 percent of boys with IQs 80-99 were said by their teachers to concentrate poorly, as were 76 percent of those with IQs below 80. One is hardly justified, then, in assuming that "poor concentration" or "short attention span" is necessarily a sign of brain damage!

Inattention can, of course, stem from a variety of sources. The child may be preoccupied with other matters, internal or external. The material to which he is expected to attend may be inherently dull, or it may be too easy or too difficult to provide a good cognitive "match" which would engage him (Hunt, 1961; Lewis, Goldberg, & Rausch, 1967). Although infants and young children are normally expected to have brief attention spans, one study which provided especially interesting "lessons" for eight- to twelve-month-old infants found them able to remain more or less continuously attentive for at least a half hour, except for those who were preoccupied with learning to walk (Hernandez, 1968). "Attention span," is, then, a relative affair, dependent not only on the cortical integrity, arousal, and/or maturational state of the individual, but on the nature of environmental events and of competing interests.

Although the phenomenon of continuous attention is a complicated one, there is considerable evidence that brain-damaged children have special problems in this area. One measure of continuous attention used by a number of investigators was developed by Rosvold, Mirsky, Sarason, Bransome, and Beck (1956). Their Continuous Performance Test (CPT) includes two tasks. The first requires the child to press a response key every time an X appears in a series of letters, and the second requires him to respond only when an X appears immediately after an A. Rosvold et al. found that the brain-damaged children made more errors on both tasks than did controls, but especially on the AX task. The effectiveness of the CPT at identifying brain-damaged children and adults, especially those with diffuse lesions, has been confirmed by other investigators (Crosby, 1972; Mirsky, Primac, Stevens, & Cosimo, 1958; Schein, 1962). Campanelli (1970) administered the CPT to three groups of children of normal intelligence: twenty normal children, twenty epileptics with focal lesions in the cortex, and twenty epileptics with diffuse, subcortical lesions. Under control conditions, the performance of the two epileptic groups was similar but significantly inferior to that of the normals. Under a stressful condition (poor illumination), however, the performance of the group with diffuse subcortical lesions dropped dramatically, whereas the other two groups showed only moderate decrements.

To the extent that brain-damaged children are observed to have shorter attention spans or poorer concentration, then, one may expect that *one* controlling factor may be interruption in internal control processes. This does not, however, imply that the situation is hopeless. If the environment encourages the re-establishment of attention, especially if the child is reinforced for attending and if he finds the material interesting and challenging, the effects of periodic interruptions should be minimized. The technique suggested by Strauss and Lehtinen (1947) and Cruickshank et al. (1961) of isolating children for desk work by means of cubicles seems to be effective at increasing the amount of work accomplished if not the overall level of academic achievement (Hallahan & Cruickshank, 1973). Possibly the best approach is one too seldom attempted—*earning* attention by making lessons so fascinating that the child wants to attend and assuring that they are well matched to his current level of attainment.

Resistance to Distraction   One of the cardinal qualities of the Strauss syndrome was "distractibility," or attention to stimuli extraneous to the task at hand. It has thus been advised that the home and school environments be kept as simple and nonstimulating as possible so that the child can concentrate more easily. This dictum should be taken with a grain of salt.

The presumed inability to inhibit responses to extraneous stimuli has been subjected to considerable investigation. Typically, a learning task or a test of attention such as the CPT is presented under conditions of minimal distraction and again in the presence of visual distractors such as a mirror, a flashing or moving light, or auditory distractors such as conversation, cafeteria noise, "white noise," music, or nonsense syllables. Although such stimuli often do detract from performance, particularly on difficult tasks or when the session is lengthy, brain-damaged retarded children have *not* tended to respond differently from cultural-familial children (Brown, 1964; Crosby, 1972; Jones, 1964; Whitman & Sprague, 1968), nor have low-active and high-active retarded children differed (Lucker, 1970). Retarded groups do, however, tend to perform less well across all conditions than do normal children.

Under some conditions, the presence of a "distractor" may actually facilitate attention in retarded children (Belmont & Ellis, 1968; Crosby, 1972), perhaps by enhancing the overall level of arousal or signaling the child to remain attentive. A number of studies have shown that retarded children become less active motorically in the presence of distracting visual stimuli, whereas they do not change much with auditory distraction (Cromwell & Foshee, 1960; Gardner, Cromwell, & Foshee, 1959; Spradlin, Cromwell, & Foshee, 1960).

Most of the evidence, then, suggests that when inattention is shown by brain-damaged children, it is likely to be based primarily on internal sources and not on a heightened sensitivity to external events. Turnure (1970) has suggested that a child's glancing about the room often is a search for cues or for help and that such glances should not be interpreted as distraction from the task but as a signal that a highly "teachable moment" has arrived. Even so, unstructured and highly interesting environments probably do interfere with learning since when interruptions occur the children may fasten their attention on something besides their lessons. Increasing the interest level and attractiveness of the task at hand seems a logical, though unproven, approach. Operant conditioning techniques can also be effective at increasing attention span. (See Chapter 15.)

Habituation   Once an infant has become familiar with a stimulus and, in Piagetian terms, has assimilated it to an existing scheme (see Chapter 12), he ordinarily becomes less responsive to it. This habituation occurs as a function of repeated stimulation and of the complexity of the stimulus in relation to the child's developmental level. The time spent responding to increasingly familiar stimuli thus decreases with age and is also shorter in infants whose mothers are responsive and stimulating, variables associated with enhancement of cognitive growth (Lewis, 1969). During the first six months of life, for example, infants will increasingly attend to a stimulus in the form of a realistic face, but during the second six months, various distortions in the face elicit greater attention (Kagan, Henker, Hen-Tov, Levine, & Lewis, 1966; Lewis, 1969). Infants with suspected cortical dysfunctions, even those who at birth had Apgar ratings in the normal range of six to nine, habituate less quickly than those with perfect scores of 10 (Lewis, 1971a). Conway and Brackbill (1969) showed that one-month-old infants whose mothers had been heavily medicated during labor were weak in habituation long after the medication itself had disappeared. Miranda and Fantz (1974) presented three visual tasks of different levels of difficulty to Down's syndrome and normal infants. The normal controls showed a preference for novel stimuli in every case several weeks earlier than the Down's syndrome infants, in whom cortical functions are known to be abnormal.

Thus, measures of habituation to familiar stimuli provide a sensitive index of some aspects of cognitive functioning. Perhaps this explains an otherwise puzzling finding of a longitudinal study of normal children (Kagan & Moss, 1962) that playing a long time with one toy in infancy is a negative predictor of later intelligence. Rather than interpreting such behavior as persistence, we should probably see it as a failure to exploit, or assimilate, the possibilities which a toy has to offer, in the time it takes for brighter children to do so.

Activity Level

Hyperactivity, i.e., restlessness or an inappropriately high level of motor activity, is seen in perhaps 4 to 10 percent of elementary school children (Huessy, 1967; Stewart, Pitts, Craig, & Dieruf, 1966). Normal children are often active, of course, and many adults seem to be hypersensitive to such behavior. Perhaps half of the mothers of boys six to twelve years of age consider their sons "overactive" (Lapouse & Monk, 1958)! Extremely overactive children, though, seem incessantly in motion, "into everything," destroying objects, and often endangering themselves or others by their inquisitiveness and impulsivity. Parents complain of having to be constantly watchful, even at night, for many of these children seem to require little sleep and may climb out of their cribs in the early hours of the morning. Teachers are driven to distraction by the children's always being out of their seats, their talkativeness, restlessness, and inability to settle down to work. This pattern of activity, labeled "hyperactive" or "hyperkinetic," is extremely aversive to adults. It may not be the excessive movement itself which is so disturbing, though, but rather its inappropriateness, its seeming lack of purpose, and the lack of adaptability which accompanies it (Talkington & Hutton, 1973). Such behavior, unlike some of the other symptoms we have discussed, is sure to be noticed. The uninhibited quality of the hyperactive child was captured by Strauss and Lehtinen in the following description of what they termed a typical case.

> Bobby, a boy of 8 years, has come to the outpatient department of the training school for his first mental test . . . Bobby is almost immediately attracted to the French doors, the telephone, the radiator, and the windows. He explores his surroundings but more often settles on one object, such as the radiator control, which he immediately turns on with the questions, "What's this?" "What is it for?" "Why do you have it here?" etc. He is invited to take the seat at the desk and generally complies very willingly, for he frequently has had good home training. He may sit quietly for several minutes if the examiner can provide enough for him to do and a sufficiently rapid change of stimuli to hold his attention.
>
> Frequently this type of child, trying to remain obediently in his seat, will perform acrobatics. He tries to sit in his chair with his feet on the desk. The next moment his feet are on the chair and he is hanging head downward over the back, or he attempts to engage the examiner in a game of hide and seek, where he hides by slumping down in his seat until only a shock of hair is visible above the desk. Occasionally a child attempts to climb on his desk or even on the examiner's desk. . . .
>
> The test materials and test questions become only starters for new lines of association, questions, and chatter rather than a challenge to comply with the examiner's request. He breaks into the test with irrelevant questions and persists with these until he receives an answer. . . . The behavior of Bobby is especially disturbed because he is young and has had comparatively little time or experience to learn inhibition (Strauss & Lehtinen, 1947, pp. 98–99).[9]

The frequency of this kind of behavior in brain-damaged children is unknown, but it certainly appears often enough to warrant attention. For Strauss and Werner, hyperactivity (which they saw as part of a cluster of problems including perceptual distortions, inattention, disorganization and impulsivity) was thought to be the single most important and reliable index of brain damage. Because their position has so colored professional views, the presence of brain damage has often been assumed on the basis of hyperactivity alone, and that sizable group of children who are brain-damaged but not hyperactive have often failed to be so identified. Many contemporary researchers, conscious of this confusion, have begun to study children *behaviorally* selected as hyperactive, regardless of etiological classification.

Etiology   There is clearly no agreement in the present-day literature about the etiology of hyperactivity, nor any reason to believe that a common etiology underlies

[9] From A. A. Strauss and Laura E. Lehtinen. *Psychopathology and education of the brain-injured child.* New York: Grune & Stratton, 1947. Reprinted by permission.

all or even most cases of this behavioral symptom. Numerous theories have been advanced as explanations. (See Alabiso, 1972; Cromwell et al., 1963; Van Osdol & Carlson, 1972.)

A number of authors have suggested that genetic predispositions may be involved (Omenn, 1973b; Vandenberg, 1973; Wender, 1973). Several signs point in this direction. The effects of some drugs which paradoxically are calming to some hyperactive children though stimulating to normal children (see below) suggest a biochemical disorder which might well have an hereditary basis. Waldrop and Halverson (1971) have reported an unusually high incidence of minor physical anomalies such as fine "electric" hair, low-seated ears, wide-set eyes, and curved fifth finger in hyperactive boys. These anomalies are congenital and have been associated with known genetic defects, although they are sometimes seen in otherwise normal individuals. Also suggesting hereditary factors, an increased incidence of psychiatric abnormalities and childhood hyperactivity has been observed in the families of hyperactive children (Cantwell, 1972; Morrison & Stewart, 1971), but no such excess of psychopathology among the foster families of hyperactive adopted children (Morrison & Stewart, as reported by Omenn, 1973b). Similarly, Wender (1973) reports an unpublished study by Safer, who examined the full and half-siblings of a small number of hyperactive children placed in separate foster homes. Safer found that half of the fostered-away full siblings were independently diagnosed as hyperactive, although only 15 percent of the half-siblings were so diagnosed.

Another prominent theory relates hyperactivity to a dysfunction of the reticular activating system (e.g., Hebb, 1955; Lindsley, 1966).[10] The previously cited study by Campanelli (1970) supported this hypothesis, and there is substantial evidence of the same nature from other researchers working with both animal and human subjects (Alabiso, 1972). The theory proposed by Strauss and his coworkers (see Cromwell et al., 1963) has been related to the role of the reticular activating system. This theory has to do with a proposed sequence in which sensation leads to perception which in turn triggers mediational processes and then motor output. When the normal sequence is blocked or ineffective, the reservoir of energy which powers it is not fully utilized. The unutilized energy attaches to motor responses which appear behaviorally as hyperactivity.

Still another etiological view is that of Bakwin and Bakwin (1966). These authors restrict their theory to children who are hyperactive but show no indication of major CNS disorder or psychosis and whose intelligence is reasonably close to that of their parents. They regard hyperactivity as an inborn developmental retardation, either from genetic or environmental causes or both, the child's activity level essentially resembling that of a normal child of a younger age.

There is also evidence that hyperactivity in some children may be the result of environmental assault. Lead poisoning has been shown to result in hyperactivity in some children (David, 1974; Needleman, Davidson, Sewall, & Shapiro, 1974) and is probably only one of several environmental agents (possibly including some food additives) which may be implicated (Omenn, 1973).

The etiology of hyperactivity as a problem behavior can also lie in the parent-child relationship, as has been pointed out by Thomas et al. (1963). They found a high activity level to be a stable and not uncommon characteristic in the normal group of

---

[10] Another subcortical formation, the diencephalon and its largest subdivision, the thalamus, has also been associated with hyperactivity (Woodburne, 1967).

100 children they followed longitudinally. The children who got into difficulty often were extremely active and at the same time had parents who were made uncomfortable by their behavior and were unsuccessful at controlling them.

Still others view hyperactivity as a function of emotional disturbance, without any necessary cortical dysfunction. Although most authors accept this possibility as one explanation of the presence of hyperkinetic children in whom no neurological problems have been discovered, a few authors (e.g., Shaffer, McNamara, & Pincus, 1974) go farther. They maintain that hyperactivity is a nonspecific correlate of a "conduct disorder syndrome." Brain-damaged children may exhibit conduct disorders and thus be hyperactive, but the explanation of the hyperactivity is the conduct disorder and not cortical dysfunction. This is distinctly a minority view.

This brief discussion does not by any means exhaust the etiological possibilities which have been advanced. Damage to the prefrontal lobes (Alabiso, 1972), a compensatory stimulus-seeking by children who fail to react meaningfully to ordinary stimulus input (Gellner, 1959), impairment of the normal progression from motor-touch associations to visual and verbal associations (Zaporozhets, 1960) are among these, and the list could be greatly extended.

Measurement   Hyperactivity is an elusive concept. It implies an excessive amount of motoric activity, but what is "excessive"? Bakwin and Bakwin (1966) have pointed out that activity level is an age-related characteristic, decreasing in normal children as they grow older, and that it is also related to sex and socioeconomic and ethnic background. To be judged hyperactive, therefore, a child must be significantly more active than is typical for other children of the same age, sex, and socioeconomic and cultural background.

A number of ingenious techniques have been developed to measure activity in infants and children (see Cromwell et al., 1963), although each tends to measure a somewhat different aspect than the others with the result that the measures may not correlate highly (Shaffer et al., 1974). Some investigators have observed the number of blocked-off squares a child traverses while moving about a room; some have used pressure pads or "electric eyes" which do the job automatically; some have attached a gadget to the child, such as a Boy Scout pedometer or a modified self-winding watch; and some have used a stabilometer attached to desk seat or crib to tabulate restless movements. Human observers capable of recording simultaneously a variety of behaviors offer many advantages, but such use of manpower is costly and cumbersome. Rating scales are also a possibility, though one must be wary of unwitting bias in the reports of parents, caretakers, and teachers who may overreact to normal levels of activity.

A basic dictum of empirical research, the necessity for careful definition of the behavior to be measured, has been far too often ignored in studies of hyperactivity. One finds adequate specificity primarily in studies of operant conditioning treatment procedures. They are, certainly, equally necessary in studies of any other type of treatment.

If a child is felt to need treatment for hyperactivity, the most valid way to evaluate the treatment is to specify exactly what the child did to earn the diagnosis (e.g., left his seat often at school, moved his arms more frequently than desired, etc.) and then measure those . . . behaviors, under treatment versus no-treatment conditions. (Sulzbacher, 1974, p. 44)

Just as everyone else varies in energy and activity according to the setting, the time of day, or the mood of the moment, so do brain-damaged children. One must remember to look at them when they are not causing trouble as well as when they are. Some sit for hours in front of a television set, perhaps squirming a bit more than other children, but certainly not "hyperactive."

Sulzbacher (1973) reviewed 208 studies of drug effects which employed a comparison of a placebo with an active drug and the safeguards of a double-blind design. Neither the evaluator nor the subject knew during a specific period whether the placebo or the drug was being administered. He found that when the evaluation rested on clinical impression, only 12 percent of studies reported no experimental differences between placebo and active drug; when the evaluation was based on a rating scale, 43 percent of studies reported no differences; but when direct measurement of behavior was relied upon, 59 percent of studies reported no differences. Without careful measurement of the target behaviors which the treatment is designed to change, it is impossible to know the precise effects of the drugs. What is recorded as a clinical impression of improvement, for example, may actually reflect oversedation of the child, a reduction both in desirable and undesirable behaviors. When the experimenter is aware of the treatment being administered, favorable results are reported considerably more often than in the double-blind design (Glick & Margolis, 1962).

Management Fortunately, most hyperactive children seem to outgrow this behavior pattern by the middle school years (Dykman et al., 1973; Menkes, Rowe, & Menkes, 1967; Weiss, Minde, Werry, Douglas, & Nemeth, 1971; Routh, Schroeder, & L'Tuama, 1974). Only one study contradicts this finding (Stewart, 1970). One approach, then, is simply to wait long enough, though such advice is unlikely to be graciously received by the parents of a three-year-old! It is also true that although the troublesome symptom of hyperactivity may be outgrown, in the sense at least that restlessness is expressed in ways that are less gross and disturbing, the long-term outlook for a truly good adjustment is doubtful (Menkes et al., 1967; Weiss et al., 1971).

Two major methods for reducing hyperactive behavior have been developed: administration of stimulant drugs or major tranquilizers and the use of behavior-modification techniques. Although the use of long-term pharmacotherapy is a somewhat controversial issue, certainly some hyperactive children respond well. Individual differences in response to medication must be carefully monitored. A drug which works well for one child may simply increase the problems of another. Dosages must be individually calibrated and adjusted from time to time. Unfortunately, most children are not very well monitored while on a drug regime (Solomons, 1973), and many physicians are worried about the dangers of this situation, as well as the unknown side effects of long-term use of some drugs during the developmental period. Sulzbacher (1974) has pointed out that one must be careful when evaluating a drug program to be sure that decreases in undesirable behaviors are not accompanied by severe decreases in desired behaviors as well.

The two most popular stimulant drugs, dextroamphetamine and methylphenidate (Ritalin), have a "paradoxic" calming effect on some hyperactive children (Snyder & Meyerhoff, 1973). In children with whom they are effective, they seem not to affect overall energy-expenditure patterns, but rather to increase attention, tractability, and learning in situations which demand productivity and compliance. They also tend to leave undisturbed informal behavior patterns, such as those seen on the playground, where a high activity level is appropriate (Ellis, Witt, Reynolds, & Sprague, 1974). For children in whom the stimulants are not effective, tranquilizers of the antianxiety and antipsychosis types sometimes are (Millichap, 1973).

A number of studies using behavior-modification techniques (e.g., Edelson & Sprague, 1974; Patterson, Jones, Whittier, & Wright, 1965; Sprague, 1973; Switzsky & Haywood, 1973) have also reported success in controlling overactivity. Christensen (1972) combined behavior-modification techniques with the administration of methylphenidate or a placebo to a group of hyperactive, emotionally disturbed boys in special education classes. Activity level was monitored by a stabilometer, and subjects were informed of their behavior by lights on their desks. The results of this study are seen in Figure 11-2. They show very strikingly the independent action of these two management techniques. Both the conditioning and the drug were effective, but to-

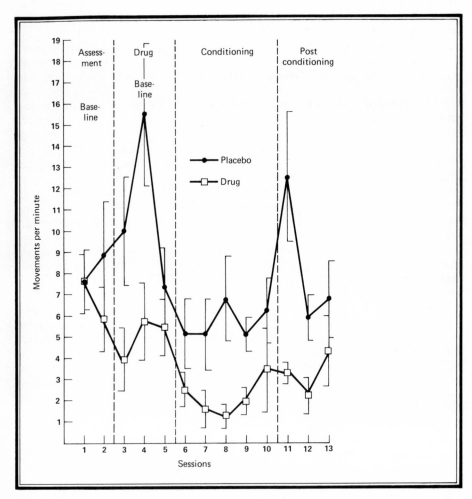

Fig. 11-2 Effects of operant conditioning and of operant conditioning combined with methylphenidate on hyperactive behavior. *(From Christensen, 1972)*

gether they were significantly more so. Later, working with a group of boys in an institution, Christensen (in press) found that with this group behavior modification was significantly more powerful in its effects than was the same drug he had used previously.

Other environmental changes can also reduce hyperactivity. Increased auditory and/or visual stimulation often decreases activity level in hyperactive individuals, whereas reduced stimulation produces increases (Forehand & Baumeister, 1970; Switzsky & Haywood, 1973). Just why this is so is not known. It is unclear whether some types of increased stimulation help the children to focus internal processes, whether they compete with other response tendencies by distraction from other pursuits, or some other explanation. Whatever the reason, this finding is consonant with the time-honored techniques of quieting a fussy baby or distracting a wayward child from an unacceptable course of action by stimulation such as tickling or showing a new or favorite toy.

A number of educators (e.g., Cruickshank et al., 1961; Haring & Phillips, 1972) have suggested that a highly structured environment, especially one in which the consequences of a child's behavior are carefully controlled, is likely to reduce hyperactive, unacceptable behavior. Adherence to predictable daily routines, firm limits on behavior, and avoidance of excessive stimulation or fatigue, are among the features of such a planned environment. At home, parents are probably well advised to child-proof the house, to establish regular schedules and routines, and above all to pay attention to reinforcing actions on their part which may inadvertently be strengthening the very behaviors they wish to avoid.

In the course of a visit to the People's Republic of China, Eleanor Maccoby (1974) observed that hyperactivity is a rare occurrence among children there. Her description of this highly structured society and the equally structured educational programs lead one to suspect that reinforcement of desired behaviors in China is explicit, prompt, and regularly administered. She concluded, "If hyperactivity as we know it really is rare in China, either the Chinese must have fewer children than we do who suffer minimal neurological damage, or they must provide an environment more conducive to a high degree of purposeful organization of young children's behavior. Both things may be true" (p. 5).

In summary, hyperactivity is a frequent but certainly not an invariable companion of brain damage. Just why it occurs is presently debatable, but that it exists and can be extremely disruptive to a family or a schoolroom is agreed to by anyone who has ever come in contact with hyperactive children. Such children do not grow up in isolation. They interact with adults and other children, and the treatment they are accorded has a great deal to do with the course of events. Pharmacological and behavioral techniques are being developed for managing such children, but our comprehension of the causes of their abnormal behavior is far from complete.

Impulsivity

Another element of the Strauss syndrome is impulsivity, the tendency to rush into action without considering the consequences. J. Kagan (1965a) has studied the tempo of performance in normal children, distinguishing between "reflective" response styles and "impulsive" ones. On his Matching Familiar Figures Test, the subject is asked to match a model figure with the identical one within an array of similar stimuli. Kagan has concentrated primarily on fast/inaccurate and slow/accurate responders. He found stable individual differences on this variable and also discovered that the impulsives were poorer both at inductive reasoning (Kagan, Pearson, & Welch, 1966) and at reading (Kagan, 1965b).[11] Although the modifiability of conceptual impulsivity has been demonstrated in undifferentiated groups of EMR pupils (Duckworth, Ragland, Sommerfeld, & Wyne, 1974), so far as we know this dimension has not been explicitly studied with groups of brain-injured retarded children. There is, indeed, some reason to doubt that the "impulsivity" which Strauss and Werner felt to be so characteristic of brain damage would be agreed to by all observers. Reaction times on tasks given such subjects are often *slower* than those of other children (e.g., Conners & Barta, 1967). Cromwell, Wolf, and Palk (reported by Cromwell, Baumeister, & Hawkins, 1963) found that hyperactive subjects were actually slower to respond to stimuli than other children. Again, we are reminded of the need to break down complex areas of human functioning into their distinct components as we attempt to zero in on specific problem areas.

Language Disabilities

A number of indicators point to the necessity for a thorough understanding of language deficits in brain-damaged children. Among them are an almost universal conviction that cognitive development and language development are closely intertwined, theoretical interest in the biological bases of language development (see Lenneberg, 1967), interest in the effect of focal brain lesions which are known to produce language deficits (Osgood & Miron, 1963), and the development of language-training programs for retarded children (McLean, Yoder, & Schiefelbusch, 1972). All these indicators of interest, together with the very rapid rise of research in psycholinguistics in general and in language development in particular (see Dale, 1972), lead one to expect that language disorders in brain-damaged children would be a subject of lively research interest. Unfortunately, such work as exists with retarded children has generally failed even to attempt a differentiation by etiology,[12] much less to distinguish among various groups of brain-damaged children. There is the repeated finding that the acquisition of language is typically slower in retarded children, but that it proceeds in a normal developmental sequence (e.g., O'Conner & Hermelin, 1963; Lenneberg, 1967). The role of the dominant hemisphere in language development has also been established in adults (Reitan, 1966). Aside from such general observations, however, knowledge is very limited about the CNS factors which are involved in language development, or about specific kinds of damage which result in specific language deficits.

Speech and language disorders[13] are a frequent concomitant of mental retardation, although "no unique configuration or pattern of speech and language problems has been demonstrated in the mentally retarded as a group or within any subcategory or syndrome under the aegis of mental retardation" (Keane, 1972, p. 5). Sixteen surveys of various populations reviewed by Keane revealed that an extremely high percentage (52 to 72 percent) of retarded children in institutions but far fewer (8 to 26 percent) of children in special public school classes are identified as having speech defects. These surveys made no pretense, however, of tapping the more basic retardation of language acquisition which accompanies intellectual deficit.

---

[11] Block, Block, and Harrington (1974) suggest, however, that Kagan has confused speed of response with the more important accuracy variable. They found that although accuracy had important personality concomitants, latency (speed) did not.

[12] Some exceptions to this rule have been listed by Jordan (1966).

[13] *Speech* refers to oral communication. *Language,* on the other hand, may be verbal or nonverbal; it consists not only of communication but of an abstract system of symbols and meanings and the rules of grammar that link them.

Diagnosticians should be alert to language deficiencies in brain-damaged children, for there is no doubt that damage to the cerebral cortex can lead to severe language handicaps. The language-defective child is at a serious disadvantage, both cognitively and socially. Furthermore, there is some reason to believe that language intervention must be begun early to be truly effective, for there are at least some aspects of language which apparently must be established during circumscribed periods of development (Lenneberg, 1967). (See Chapter 7.)

By far the most popular language assessment instrument is the Illinois Test of Psycholinguistic Abilities, the ITPA (Kirk, McCarthy, & Kirk, 1968; Paraskevopoulos & Kirk, 1969). This instrument is based for the most part on the model of language proposed by Charles Osgood (1957). Using a multidimensional scheme, it samples (1) auditory and visual input (reception), (2) vocal and motor output (expression), and (3) representational manipulation of symbols and automatic, habitual processes (organization or mediation). Even this simplified three-dimensional model generates more combinations of linguistic functions than can conveniently be tapped in a test designed to be given at a single sitting. Its twelve subtests are necessarily an incomplete sampling of Osgood's model. The test also fails to tap progression in the use of abstract language or any analysis of the child's extended or spontaneous use of language.

A number of criticisms have been leveled at the ITPA (e.g., Weener, Barritt, & Semmel, 1967). Although designed for use with children from ages two and one half to ten, its usefulness is hindered by the fact that the 962 subjects in the standardization sample were carefully screened to include only "normal" children with IQs of 80-120 whose school achievement was close to grade level and in whom there was no evidence of major behavioral, sensory, or family problems. The scaled scores are interpreted, however, as though there was a normal, unrestricted distribution, with the result that deviations from the mean are exaggerated. Since clinical populations include children with decided language problems, learning disabilities, mental retardation, emotional disturbances, and neurological handicaps, interpretation of scores is problematic. Reliability of some subtests is too low to generate confidence in intrasubject differences in performance. The authors do, however, provide some help in judging when differences between subtest scores should be interpreted as significant. Particularly at the lower age levels, the separate subtests do not measure factorially separable dimensions (Ryckman & Wiegerink, 1969). The total score correlates very highly with Stanford-Binet and WISC IQs (Hulzinga, 1973), suggesting that the test is measuring "psycholinguistic" functions which are not very different from those termed "intellectual."

Despite these criticisms, the test does appear to be useful in assessing some of the dimensions for which it was intended. It has certainly received wide usage. Nevertheless, it is far from the ultimate instrument needed to further our understanding of language development among brain-damaged children.

Emotional Disturbance

In view of the many areas of vulnerability to which brain-damaged children are prey, it is little wonder that a great many of them show signs of emotional disturbance as well. Some aspects of deviant emotional behavior may stem from faulty CNS control systems or physiological dysfunctions. In any event, many brain-damaged children are extremely difficult for their parents and teachers to handle. In essence the children create an unaccepting and often punishing environment for themselves which in turn adds to their problems.

That this field is fertile for research was demonstrated by the famous Dutch neurobiologist, H. F. R. Prechtl (1963), who followed eight mildly damaged newborns who had been observed by the hospital staff to be hyperexcitable and a control group of ten apparently normal newborns. The mothers of the damaged babies were not told of their condition. The infants continued to show signs of hyperexcitability and hypersensitivity, but their mothers tended to shoulder the blame for the trouble. After six months, of the eight mothers only one had positive attitudes toward her infant; the rest were rejecting or overanxious. In contrast, nine of the ten control mother-baby pairs established harmonious relationships. Although demonstrating the need both to inform parents and to support them in their attempts to deal with "difficult" children, this study also demonstrates that the consequences of brain damage extend beyond the children themselves and are in turn determinants of the disturbances which they exhibit.

It is not only the family members who experience difficulty with the brain-damaged child. Jacobs and Pierce (1968) studied the social position of 155 mildly and moderately retarded children in public school special classes. They found that those most frequently rejected by their peers exhibited characteristics often associated with CNS deficits: short attention span, hyperactivity, emotional lability, and impulsivity. Other children, like adults, find these children unpredictable, abrasive, and sometimes frightening. As a result, the child who exhibits such behavior is likely to have to deal with rejection and loneliness, as well as with his other handicaps.

A valuable review by Shaffer (1973) makes clear that in addition to these interpersonal problems, there are probably structural and functional defects which affect the degree of emotional disturbance which a brain-damaged child experiences. In a part of the oft-cited Isle of Wight survey (Rutter, Graham, & Yule, 1970), the incidence of psychiatric disorders in children with brain damage was found to be increased when the damage was associated with seizures. Children with temporal lobe epilepsy or with idiopathic epilepsy (i.e., without evidence of CNS damage) also showed a high incidence of psychiatric disorders. Overall, emotional disturbance was five times as frequent in brain-damaged or epileptic children as in normals, and three times as frequent as in children with physical disorders other than CNS damage. Postnatal head injury in childhood sometimes is followed by emotional disturbance, especially poorly controlled aggression and hyperactivity, whereas in adults, head injury is more likely to be followed by somatic complications which are uncommon in children, such as dizziness and headaches (Black, Jeffries, Blumer, Wellner, & Walker, 1969).

Both internal and external factors, then, combine to exacerbate the emotional disorders seen in brain-damaged children. The lot of these children may indeed be an unhappy one, and both they and the adults who care for them may suffer bitterly.

PART III
COGNITION, LEARNING, AND MEMORY

12

Piaget's Theory of Cognitive Development

For many centuries, theorists have attempted to explain in lawful terms the differences among men and the ways in which their consistent patterns of behavior arise. Each theorist has regarded human development in a somewhat different way. In the past, a number of rather grand and comprehensive theories sought to explain a very wide range of behavior. For a time, it appeared to many that psychoanalytic theory as propounded by Sigmund Freud and extended by his students could explain the origin and functioning of almost all facets of human behavior. During a golden age in the history of learning theory (1920-1950), many held high hopes for all-encompassing theories based on learning paradigms. Recently, we have seen the development of more modest theoretical endeavors, focusing on rather circumscribed aspects of behavior, eschewing "grand schemes" in favor of detailed explorations of critical areas of human functioning.

The grand schemes failed in part because knowledge of human development has multiplied greatly during recent decades. With the extension of an empirical grasp of matters which range from the macroscopic level of entire cultures to the submicroscopic level of the gene, the behavioral scientist faces the increasingly difficult task of making his theory at least consonant with this body of knowledge.

This chapter and the three which follow will be devoted to an examination of some existing theories of cognitive development, learning, and memory. This chapter will review the work of Jean Piaget, who has proposed the most comprehensive contemporary theory of cognitive development. Chapter 13 will deal with empirical studies of learning and Chapter 14, with similar studies in the field of memory. Chapter 15 will describe the theories and practical applications of operant conditioning and of social learning and imitation.

There is, in our opinion, no contemporary psychological theory which is superior to all others in its relevance to mentally retarded children. It is probably wise, therefore, to employ a number of concepts in considering the processes of psychological development. Just as it is meaningful to characterize a mentally retarded child from etiological, behavioral, social, and educational perspectives, one need not be impatient if several theoretical systems prove useful in understanding behavior. One need become impatient only when the systems do not further an understanding of retarded individuals or when they fail to fit the current knowledge base.

JEAN PIAGET

Jean Piaget, born in 1896 in Neuchâtel, Switzerland, has pursued for more than a half-century one of the most interesting, unique, and productive careers in the history of science. His central concern has always been the ontogeny of intelligence in humans. Probably more than any other scientist, he has seen the scope and complexity of the problems in this area, and his theoretical and empirical excursions have been correspondingly broad and deep. He has succeeded in evolving and elaborating a set of constructs which have in many instances provided amazing insights into the development of the functions and structures of the human mind. No other theorist or group of theorists has set forth nearly so comprehensive a theory of the development of intelligence.

Piaget has been characterized as "a zoologist by training, an epistemologist by vocation and a logician by method" (Inhelder, 1953–1954). His early interests and training were concentrated in biology and zoology. He has, however, displayed throughout his life a deep and abiding interest in the bases of knowledge. Particularly in his more recent work, he has attempted to integrate logicomathematical and psychological methods. As we shall see, a good many characterizations of the thought systems which he believes to describe school-age children and adults have been borrowed from the logicomathematical field. When one is confronted with Piaget's ideas concerning the development of intelligence, it is necessary to keep in mind this triple orientation—biological, epistemological, and logicomathematical—because it is continuously reflected in every aspect of his theories: in the way he formulates them, in the illustrative examples he gives, and in the vocabulary he uses to talk about them.

Piaget has been working with children since the early 1920s, addressing himself always to the broad question of the way in which they acquire knowledge. Some of his early studies on such topics as children's language, the development of moral judgment, notions of physical causality (e.g., the movement of clouds and rivers and the displacement of water when an object is immersed), and ideas about the origins of dreams, of trees, and of the sun and moon, are fairly well known although they represent an early and relatively primitive stage in the development of Piaget's systematic position. The phenomena he studied at that time are particularly appealing because they relate to the everyday experiences of children and often echo the questions children ask of adults. It is only recently, however, that Piaget's more systematic work, dealing less with the content of children's thought and more with their thought processes, has been assimilated in any detail by the psychological audience in English-speaking countries. Since the early 1960s there has been an efflorescence of interest among developmental psychologists and educators, particularly since the publication of J. McV. Hunt's influential *Intelligence and Experience* (1961) and since the translation into English of Piaget's later works, but the spillover into work with the retarded has been much more modest.

CONCEPTS IN PIAGET'S THEORY OF COGNITIVE DEVELOPMENT[1]

As we pointed out in Chapter 1, Piaget characterizes intelligence as an adaptive process. Moreover, he posits that adaptation is the most basic characteristic of all life and that the adaptations involved in intellectual functioning are only special cases of this fundamental biologic principle. In this, Piaget does not differ widely from many other theorists who have concerned themselves with intellectual functioning. He has, however, gone considerably beyond this basic position, specifying in detail the processes of adaptation. According to his system, "adaptation must be described as an equilibrium between the action of the organism on the environment and vice versa" (Piaget, 1950). Thus, the environment is seen as constantly forcing the organism to adjust itself to the reality situation and, reciprocally, the organism is seen as constantly imposing on the environment a structure of its own.

Assimilation and Accommodation

The process by which the organism fits the environment to biologic systems already in existence Piaget calls "assimilation." The organism assimilates the environment or its perception of the environment to its own systems. The processes which involve the modification of the organism to fit the environment Piaget calls "accommodation." The organism accommodates itself to external reality.

At all levels of biologic activity the organism is constantly adapting—both assimilating and accommodating. In eating, for example, food is adapted to the organs and systems of the body by the digestive processes (assimilation), but the individual must also adapt himself to the nature of the entering material (accommodation) by opening his mouth more or less wide, chewing with more or less energy, and so on.

In mental activity the invariant processes of assimilation and accommodation are also easily identified. Every intellectual act, according to Piaget, presupposes an interpretation of the environment (mental assimilation), a structuring of the situation according to some existing system. For example, messages can be understood only in terms of one's existing language and not in an unfamiliar foreign tongue. Every mental act also involves some adaptation of existing systems to the reality conditions which prevail at the time (mental accommodation). The environment is never infinitely malleable. An individual riding a bicycle, no matter how experienced he is, must guide it to avoid obstacles and must pump harder when going uphill. Similarly, the individual who is confronted with a purely mental problem must adjust his cognitive patterns to

---

[1] We are greatly indebted to John H. Flavell for his excellent book, *The Developmental Psychology of Jean Piaget* (1963). We have not quoted Flavell extensively, but it should be recognized that we have nevertheless profited greatly from his exposition of Piaget's theory. The interested reader might well begin his study of Piaget's work with the extremely readable book by Ginsburg and Opper (1969), however, to be followed by the more detailed descriptions by Hunt (1961) and Flavell and/or the writings of Piaget.

conform to some extent to the exact statement of the problem, the context in which it is posed, the form in which the answer is expected, etc.

Equilibrium

Piaget defines adaptation as the state in which assimilation and accommodation are in equilibrium, which amounts, he says, to saying that there exists an equilibrium in the interaction between the organism and its environment. The individual is not adapted when either assimilation or accommodation predominates. Mental activity in which the individual distorts the cues of the environment to fit an idiosyncratic or egocentric cognitive system, as is the case in autistic thinking, imaginative play, and dreaming, is not adapted. Here assimilation predominates over accommodation. Mental activity in which an individual struggles for the first time with a new part of the environment (say, an adolescent attempting to learn to dance or endeavoring to grasp a principle of Euclidean geometry) is not adapted. Here accommodation predominates over assimilation.

Piaget proposes that every mental act, as well as every other action of every living organism, can be analyzed according to the balance or equilibrium which exists between assimilation and accommodation. This has proved to be a particularly fruitful way of viewing mental activity. Piaget has pointed out, for example, that in play, assimilation predominates, whereas in imitation, assimilation is subordinate to accommodation. When playing, children typically force reality to fit the cognitive systems they are using; a dog becomes a mother, a doll becomes a father, and a stick is now a gun, now a horse, now a sword. When imitating, children struggle to adjust their response patterns to fit the model: the adolescent girl tries to talk, dress, and move just like her favorite television actress; the adolescent boy, like his favorite basketball player.

Schemes

The point has been made that mental assimilation involves incorporation of sensory data into existing behavioral or intellectual patterns and that mental accommodation involves adjustment of these patterns to the sensory data. These patterns are seen as structures of the individual's mental equipment. Piaget calls them schemes.

The concept of the scheme is defined for the most part in behavioral terms. It most closely approximates an organized response sequence, but the term also has important physiological structural implications. Piaget, for example, often refers to the scheme of sucking in his discussion of infant development. He is here alluding to the organized sucking behavior of the infant, but he is apparently also referring to the underlying organized structures of the brain which control this behavior.

All schemes show a tendency toward repeated application. Once an individual has found a cognitive strategy or, if you will, a scheme for dealing with a particular environmental situation, he or she has a tendency to use this scheme again when in a similar situation. Moreover, the individual tends to practice the newly formed scheme even when situational environmental factors do not call for it. (Good examples of this tendency are seen in children's play.) The tendency to exercise or practice schemes, which Piaget calls "functional assimilation" or "reproductive assimilation," causes them to become better integrated, more stable, and more enduring. At the same time, however, it is responsible for alterations in the schemes.

First of all, the schemes are changed because the individual, when practicing the pattern of behavior, gradually extends its field of operation. This is, of course, the well-known principle of generalization. Piaget, in fact, refers to this process as "generalizing assimilation." Second, the schemes are changed because the individual encounters differences among environmental situations. This is, of course, the process of discrimination, or recognition of differences. Piaget labels it "recognitory assimilation."

Another characteristic of schemes is their tendency to combine or interlock with each other, forming increasingly complex higher-order schemes. Piaget speaks of the process of uniting two or more separate and distinct schemes as "reciprocal assimilation," which refers to the notion that each scheme assimilates the other. Reciprocal assimilation can be seen in the early developing intercoordinations among the separate schemes of vision, hearing, reaching, and prehension. The infant first looks, hears, reaches, and grasps, but gradually things heard become things to look for, things looked at become things to reach for and grasp, etc.

The various categories of assimilation are not, of course, the only means by which developmental changes are effected in schemes. Accommodation, too, is a very important factor. As the individual adjusts to the environment, he inevitably is presented with new data which produce changes in the schemes. As the young child struggles to imitate the sounds of a new word, he feeds new data into his cognitive system, and the schemes involved are thus gradually changed.

PERIODS IN THE DEVELOPMENT OF INTELLIGENCE

All the Piagetian concepts discussed so far concern intellectual functioning at all levels of development. They are the functionally invariant, stage-independent aspects of cognitive functioning and structure. Piaget's is, however, above all a developmental theory of intelligence. He postulates a definite sequence of developmental steps, a sequence which is said to be the same for every individual.

There are four major periods in the ontogeny of intelligence in Piaget's system, each of which is divided into a variable number of subperiods, stages, and substages. The development of intelligence—whether it involves the further elaboration of response patterns within a period, subperiod, stage, or substage, or the progression from one of these to the next in the sequence—is, of course, accomplished by gradual changes in and intercoordination of schemes which are produced by the reciprocal processes of assimilation and accommodation.

The Period of Sensorimotor Intelligence (Birth to Two Years)[2]

The first period in the development of intelligence is that of sensorimotor intelligence, which begins at birth and lasts for about two years. It is divided into six more-or-less distinct stages, each of which is subdivided into several substages.

Stage 1: Practicing the Reflex Schemes (birth to one month) At birth children already possess a number of built-in schemes, which are the various neonatal reflexes such as the sucking reflex, the grasping reflex, and the Moro reflex. During this first period newborn infants simply exercise or practice these reflexes, which in the process become more stable and efficient.

Assimilation and accommodation are not easily distinguishable during this period, but faint precursors of both are operating. Newborn infants exist in a state of

---

[2] The interested reader will want to consult Piaget (1951, 1952a, 1954) and Wolff (1960).

extreme egocentrism: they simply repeat again and again whatever behavioral patterns are in their repertoire and "know" nothing of the objects with which they interact.

Stage 2:   The First Acquired Adaptations and the Primary Circular Reactions (One to Four Months)   During this stage the reflex schemes undergo many changes because of the interaction between the infants and their environment. As these changes occur, the schemes become increasingly a function of learning rather than "wired-in" response patterns. In addition, the infants add to their repertoire a variety of new simple adaptive acts.

The primary circular reactions are linked to the tendency of infants to repeat the response patterns in their repertoire. The concept is thus very closely related to the notion of reproductive assimilation. The essence of the primary circular reaction lies in the fact that when infants unexpectedly encounter something new and interesting connected with their own bodies, as a result of some act, they try to reproduce the experience by reenacting the original movements, attempting to rediscover the behavior which led to the interesting result. With the beginning of the process of reciprocal assimilation, audimentary coordinations are established among a variety of schemes, e.g., sucking and vision, prehension and sucking, vision and hearing.

Stage 3:   The Secondary Circular Reaction (Four to Eight Months)   During this stage children become more oriented toward the world around them. They show the first signs of recognizing familiar objects and of intentionality in their behavior. The secondary circular reaction is the same as the primary one except for one very important difference. Instead of being primarily oriented toward their own bodies, infants become concerned with the effects of their actions on the environment. "Thus, the Stage-2 infant simply grasps, touches, looks, listens, etc.; the Stage-3 infant swings, strikes, rubs, and shakes objects with intense interest in the sights and sounds which these actions elicit in the objects" (Flavell, 1963, p. 102). During this stage, in addition, there is further and at times startling progress in the intercoordination of schemes.

Stage 4:   Coordination of Secondary Schemes (Eight to Twelve Months)   During this stage infants become increasingly oriented toward the world outside themselves. The secondary circular reactions which were developed in Stage 3 begin to be intercoordinated, forming more and more complex structures which provide the bases for new and more complicated behavioral sequences. These new higher-order response patterns are unquestionably goal-directed. Stage-4 infants begin to anticipate what is to come and, with this ability, for the first time clearly attempt to influence the future. It is important to note that the ability to anticipate coming events crucially involves the ability to use signs or signals.

Consider the following example, one of several given by Piaget (1952, pp. 240–250). The mother starts to put on her hat, and the infant indicates his anticipation of her impending departure by crying. This behavior illustrates a number of things about Stage-4 children. Children respond to the mother's behavior as a signal, anticipating that she is about to leave and showing displeasure by crying and thus perhaps attempting to influence her not to leave. All of this means, of course, that Stage-4 infants have made considerable progress toward an objectification of reality.

Stage 5:   The Tertiary Circular Reaction (Twelve to Eighteen Months)   The essence of intellectual development in Stage 5 is children's increasing interest in and pursuit of new experiences. Hitherto they have attempted to sustain or recapture new experiences fortuitously encountered, but now they begin to seek the novel by experimentation. The tertiary circular reaction has much in common with the primary and secondary circular reactions. The core of the concept is still the repetitive application of behavioral sequences, but whereas younger children repeat only response patterns that they have met unexpectedly, Stage 5 children actively seek to discover or invent new response patterns which will bring about a novel effect. They seem to want to explore the potentialities of each situation. Assimilation and accommodation are now clearly differentiated. Accommodations are no longer merely forced upon children; they actively seek new accommodational experiences by experimenting with the environment. This is, of course, an extremely important development. It marks the beginning of a type of adaptation which, as Piaget has pointed out (1950, p. 104), anyone would admit to have the character of true intelligence.

Stage 6: The Invention of New Means through Mental Combinations (Eighteen Months Onward) During the final stage of the sensorimotor period, children make their first primitive rudimentary excursions into the conceptual-symbolic realm. They begin to be able to represent symbolically events which are not present in the perceptual field and to manipulate and combine these images or symbols internally. They seem to think about the effects of certain response patterns and to evaluate the probable relative effectiveness of proposed actions. Thus, there appear the first indications of foresight and the ability to plan. It is at this stage that we first see such phenomena as the insight experiences which have been described in human beings and in other primates. It is important to note, however, that the behavior of infants at this time is the end result of the development in the previous five levels.

The Period of Preoperational Thought (Two to Seven Years)[3]

This period is bounded on the one end by the period of sensorimotor intelligence and on the other by the period of concrete operations. During the period of sensorimotor intelligence children's intellectual functioning involves primarily overt acts; they "know" by doing. Sensorimotor intelligence, however, can never attain anything resembling an all-embracing representation of any aspect of the world. Piaget says that "sensorimotor intelligence acts like a slow-motion film, in which all the pictures are seen in succession but without fusion, and so without the continuous vision necessary for understanding the whole" (1950, pp. 120–121).

The goals of the sensorimotor period are extremely narrow. Sensorimotor children are interested only in whether their responses produced the results they desired; they are not concerned with the way in which they obtained these results. Intelligence during this period is thus in no way reflective; there is not as yet anything like a pursuit of knowledge or of truth. Finally, sensorimotor intelligence deals only with the most concrete aspects of the world of reality; the spatiotemporal distances between children and the objects with which they deal are always very short. The ontogeny of intelligence after the sensorimotor period involves the development of internal representational systems which allow children to withdraw from the actual objects of the

---

[3] Whether this period is considered as independent of the following one, or whether the two are considered to be subperiods of a larger one covering the age span two to eleven years, is largely an arbitrary matter. Piaget himself has not been entirely consistent in this matter. We are here following what has come to be the consensus of American usage.

real world and to deal increasingly with internally organized conceptual systems which represent reality.

During the preoperational period children take their first giant strides toward becoming an individual capable of swift, internal, symbolic manipulations of reality. According to Piaget, the paramount requisite for the inner representation of reality is the ability to distinguish between *signifiers* and *significates*. A signifier is an internal representation, such as an image or a word that symbolizes or stands for some aspect of reality. The significate is children's understanding of that aspect of reality. Sensorimotor children at Stage 6 can use a few rudimentary signifiers, but they never recognize them as such. The visible end of a hidden object serves as an index to children that the object is present, and putting on their pajamas may be a signal to the infants that they are about to be put to bed, but in neither of these situations do the children understand the difference between the signifier and the significate. In contrast, older children who are playing at feeding their toy dog understand that the piece of wood they use to represent the dog biscuit is that which symbolizes and that the biscuit is that which is symbolized. Here preoperational or higher-level children demonstrate their ability to evoke internally an aspect of the world which is not perceptually present and to recognize that this is what they are doing. The capacity to do this, to differentiate the signifier and the significate, Piaget calls the "semiotic (symbolic) function." He distinguishes two kinds of higher-level signifiers, the *symbol* and the *sign*. Symbols are the private, primarily nonverbal signifiers which the individual cannot share. Signs are the largely verbal signifiers which have acquired a conventional social meaning; they enable children to communicate with other persons. Piaget asserts that the private symbols emerge first and are followed by the social signs. Thus, it is not the incorporation of verbal signs which first produces representational thought. The acquisition of language is, of course, extremely important in the development of conceptual thinking, but it does not provide the first or the sole basis for this development.

The early forms of representational thought which are attained during the preoperational period represent truly significant gains in children's intellectual functioning. First, they have for the first time the beginnings of an ability to grasp by a swift, single internal means a gamut of distinct and spatiotemporally separate events. They possess a faster, more flexible, and more mobile cognitive apparatus. Second, they are for the first time capable of the pursuit of knowledge or of truth as such. Third, they have for the first time the beginnings of a cognitive system which can transcend time and space and even reality itself. They can think of the past, the present, and the future; the here and the not-here; the real and the hypothetical or fantasied. Fourth, they can for the first time begin to share with others and to test the social appropriateness of their feelings, attitudes, and beliefs.

Although representational intelligence is certainly far superior to sensorimotor intelligence, it must not be assumed that developments in the preoperational period lead to the full flowering of representational intelligence. Definite limitations are inherent in the structures and function of preoperational intelligence. In the first place, preoperational thought processes are basically egocentric. During this period children do not develop the ability to adopt various points of view about a problem. They cannot assume the cognitive position of another person or see their own point of view as merely one of many that might be entertained. Thus, they feel no need to defend their views or to justify their logic. Rarely if ever are they tempted to think about their own thought processes. They may often be aware of the fact that they are thinking, but they are not concerned with whether or not their thought processes are consistent, whether they adhere to social and logical norms, and so on. Second, even though preoperational children develop the ability to function in the representational world, their signifiers tend to be relatively concrete mental representations of the corresponding significates. Children in this period are convinced that everything is what it seems to them to be.

Third, preoperational children tend to focus their attention on the most compelling attribute of the stimulus situation. Piaget refers to this as the tendency to "center." Children in this period lack the ability to "decenter"; they cannot review and integrate a variety of stimulus characteristics. If preoperational children are presented with two identical clay squares which they see to contain equal amounts of clay and one of them is molded into a rectangle before their eyes, they are likely to maintain stoutly that the taller now contains more clay. They have centered on one aspect of the stimulus (height) but have failed to compensate for the change in this dimension by taking into account the changes in other dimensions (width and depth). A fourth limitation of preoperational thought involves the inability of children to move back and forth along a train of thought. Piaget emphasizes this concept of "irreversibility," which he considers probably the single most important characteristic of the cognitive processes of the preoperational period. A reversible thought process can move back and forth along a chain of thought elements without distorting any of them, but the thought of preoperational children cannot reverse itself without major distortions. The thought of this period is more or less isomorphic with the events in the environment. In the problem of the clay squares cited above, preoperational children cannot grasp the fact that the quantity has remained the same because they cannot mentally transform the clay backward into its original state.

A fifth difficulty in the thought of this period is that children are unable to reason rationally. The reasoning of preoperational children proceeds from the particular to the particular in an irreversible sequence. They jump to cause-and-effect conclusions on the basis of a simple juxtaposition of elements in the situation (e.g., putting on a raincoat makes it rain). There are many other limitations of preoperational thought which Piaget has discussed at one time or another. Among them are a relative lack of equilibrium in the cognitive structures; rigid and primitive concepts of justice and morality; a lack of clarity in distinguishing between the thought realms of play and reality; notions about the basic nature of the world which are often animistic and artificial; and naïve and immature ideas about such fundamental concepts as time, space, number, and quantity.

The thought forms of the preoperational period represent a great improvement over those of the sensorimotor period, but in many ways they are much like those of the earlier period. The main difference lies in the fact that they are internalized and representational. A recapitulation of the development which has taken place in the more externalized sensorimotor sphere occurs in the new internalized representational preoperational sphere.

The Period of Concrete Operations (Seven to Eleven Years)[4]

Children during this period operate at the level of representational thought just as do preoperational children, but there is one overwhelming difference: concrete-operation-

---

[4] Piaget's ideas concerning both the period of concrete operations and the period of logical operations are couched in the highly technical language of mathematical logic. The reader is urged to consult Flavell (1963) or Ginsburg and Opper (1969) which explain these concepts in clear terms. The interested reader should also turn to Piaget (1942; 1949; 1950; 1957).

al children possess well-organized cognitive systems which enable them to deal much more effectively with the environment.

> Much more than his younger counterpart, [the child] gives the decided impression of possessing a solid cognitive bedrock, something flexible and plastic and yet consistent and enduring, with which he can structure the present in terms of the past without undue strain and dislocation, that is, without the ever-present tendency to tumble into the perplexity and contradiction which mark the preschooler. Restated in Piaget's lexicon, the concrete-operational child behaves in a wide variety of tasks as though a rich and integrated assimilatory organization were functioning in equilibrium or balance with a finely tuned, discriminative, accommodatory mechanism. (Flavell, 1963, p. 165)

When cognitive actions are mediated by such enduring and tightly organized structures, Piaget calls them "cognitive operations." There are a large number of such operations. Arithmetic operations (addition, subtraction, multiplication, and division), for example, when not accomplished by rote, are cognitive representational activities of this sort.

Another very important aspect of cognitive growth during the period of concrete operations is the ability to establish hierarchical classifications and to comprehend the relations among the levels of the hierarchy. Preoperational children, given an array of things to classify, typically use an incomplete method of arranging the objects. They may, for example, make a "small partial alignment" in which they use only some of the objects and assemble them in inconsistent ways, without any overall guiding plan. In an intermediate stage, children may produce classes in the form of collections of objects and may even subdivide these classes, but they fail to comprehend the principle of *class inclusion,* which has to do with "the relations of the parts to the whole, or the whole to the parts, and the parts to the parts. They may seem very obvious, but so do many principles which children fail to understand" (Ginsburg & Opper, 1969, p. 125). By the time children reach about age seven to eleven, however, they can construct hierarchical classifications *and* have mastered the problem of class inclusion; they can handle both whole and part simultaneously, and they are indeed the master of concrete operations.

The prototypes of the cognitive operations with which Piaget is most concerned during this period are a variety of logicomathematical structures. These structures (Piaget calls them "groupings") are used as models of cognitive functioning in the concrete-operational period. We lack the space to concern ourselves here with the specific models which Piaget has proposed, but we can consider the more general characteristics of grouping. Groups are logical operations which establish the equivalences among things or concepts. Although the things or concepts may be transformed in certain ways, they usually remain the same. Thus they are conserved and the principle of conservation is therefore an important attribute of the thought of concrete-operational children. When faced with the clay problem presented above, they are certain that the two pieces retain the same quantity no matter how they are molded. They will probably even think that an adult is silly to suggest that they might change by posing such a question.

The properties of the groupings which make it possible for children to be "conservative" in the clay situation and many others are very important for Piaget. A grouping is a structure which is composed of two substructures familiar to mathematicians and logicians: the *group* and the *lattice*. An abstract system used in logical algebra, a group is composed of an arbitrarily specified number of operations bearing on the elements of an object or a concept, such that the properties of composition, associativity, identity, and reversibility hold true. The term *composition* refers to the principle that two or more distinct actions or elements within the group can be combined into one. In the clay problem, the elements of height, width, and depth can be combined into the element of quantity; in concrete-operational children all these are thus part of the same cognitive system. The term *associativity* refers to the principle that the same point can be reached by different cognitive routes. In the clay problem it makes no difference whether one combines height and width and then combines the results of this operation with depth or whether one combines width and depth and then combines the results with height. The term *identity* refers to the principle that in every system there is always only a single element (often the zero element) which when combined with any group element leaves that element unaltered. In the clay situation we can form a rectangle from the square without changing one element (the height) at all. In the area of symbolic logic, to make a statement and then to repeat it leaves the statement unaltered. The term *reversibility* refers to the principle that for each group element there is a single element, referred to as the "inverse," which when combined with the group element produces the identity element. In the clay situation any alteration in any of the elements (height, width, or depth) can be undone by applying the inverse operation. It should be clear, of course, that any of the four properties of groups can be applied cognitively or representationally as well as concretely.

Another kind of abstract structure in the logicomathematical system, the lattice is composed of a set of elements just like the group, but in this case a relationship holds between two or more of the elements. The lattice thus consists of the elements and their relationship. In the clay problem, height, width, and depth are elements, and the amount of clay is another element which subsumes the others and expresses their relationship. The concept of the lattice is useful in representing the properties of concrete operations or groupings, since it expresses such factors as classifying, ordering, enumerating, measuring, and placing or displacing in space or time.

We should make one point clear before we continue with our discussion of this period. It is not the fact that concrete-operational children possess in their cognitive apparatus each of the properties discussed above that is most important at this stage of intellectual development. Younger children are able to make use, at least in rudimentary form, of almost all these transformations and relationships. What preoperational children cannot do is to use them all together, combined into an organized system. Each of these properties, Piaget says, "is really new despite its affinity with the corresponding intuitive relation that was already formed at the previous level," only because of all of them involved in a grouping "—reversibility, . . . identity, etc.—in fact depend on each other and, because they amalgamate into an organized whole" (1950, p. 141).

As children succeed in integrating all the properties of groupings into the organized total structures or systems which are the bases of concrete-operational thought, fundamental changes occur in their behavior. All these changes can be characterized by the developing ability of children to coordinate an increasing variety of points of view. In the clay situation, which involves conservation of quantity, they are able to coordinate their inner representations of objects as the objects are changed during a length of time. In the period of concrete operations children also develop the ability to conserve weight, volume, etc. The coordinations which occur make it possible for them truly to consider and appreciate the point of view taken by another person. Thus, children of this period begin to deal logically with other persons. They can understand and even formulate logical rules. Piaget (1951) has noted that concrete-operational children tend to play games which have coherent and logically organized rules.

Concrete-operational children's communications with other persons increasingly become less egocentric and more socialized. J. McV. Hunt (1961) has written:

> With the development of the concrete operations . . . thought acquires a markedly increased degree of mobility that shows in the child's new ability to shift back and forth between part-part and part-whole relationships for classes and subclasses, and thought acquires a new independence of the child's individual focus. . . . The increased mobility of thought permits the child to sustain . . . [and] to share a topic and also to share the obligation to keep the meanings of words used constant. . . . Only thus can a communicative interchange take place in which there is progressive unfolding of a topic, the chief thing missing in egocentric speech. (p. 217)

The Period of Formal Operations (Eleven Years Onward)[5]

During the period of concrete operations children develop very complex and tightly organized cognitive systems which enable them to deal effectively with an extremely wide range of problems, but they are still far from being able to function efficiently in the abstract realm of the theoretical. The thought processes of concrete-operational children are still relatively closely linked to the surrounding world of objects and events. Concrete operations are, as the label states, concrete; their starting point is always the real as opposed to the possible.

The most important characteristic of formal operational thought is that it tends to start with the possible—the hypothetical or theoretical—rather than with the real. As Flavell (1963) has stated,

> the adolescent begins his consideration of the problem at hand by trying to envisage all the possible relations which could hold true in the data and then attempts, through a combination of experimentation and logical analysis, to find out which of these possible relations in fact do hold true. Reality is thus conceived as a special subset within the totality of things which the data would admit as hypotheses. (p. 204)

Formal operational thought can be characterized as fundamentally propositional and hypotheticodeductive.

Let us illustrate the characteristic approach of formal operational thought by contrasting it with that of lower levels. Suppose we present a problem such as the following to children of different ages.[6] Each child is presented with five bottles (labeled A, B, C, D, and E) containing colorless, odorless liquids which appear to be identical, and is told that if some of them are mixed with liquid A in a certain but unspecified manner, the result will be a liquid which is a pretty red. Preoperational

[5] The complexities of this period have been slighted in this discussion because they are of least relevance to retarded individuals. The interested reader will want to consult Flavell (1963), Ginsburg and Opper (1969) and Inhelder and Piaget (1958).

[6] Several problems much like this have been used by Piaget and his coworkers (Inhelder & Piaget, 1958, pp. 107–122.)

children attack this problem in a quite unsystematic way, trying first this and then that, but appearing to have no overall plan. They lack the cognitive organization which would enable them systematically to generate and test hypotheses. Concrete-operational children are strikingly different in their approach to the problem. In a much better organized manner they test a series of hypotheses, for example, trying A × B, A × C, A × D, and A × E, in that order. They may even try more complex combinations, but they do not pursue these higher-order combinations in an organized manner. Formal-operational children attack this problem in a very orderly manner. They soon recognize that an adequate solution demands checking all the feasible combinations. They examine all possible combinations of two, all combinations of three, all combinations of four, and finally all five together. When they attain the correct combination, they may still pursue their overall plan to see if there is more than one combination which produces the required result. The approach of formal-operational children demonstrates, of course, that they tend to think of all the possible combinations before they begin to experiment. They are able to design effective, or-derly experiments and to isolate critical factors by varying each one and only one at a time, holding the others constant. They are accurate observers and draw logical con-clusions from the results they obtain.

An important feature of adolescents' thought is the use of reasoning to examine the possible logical relations between the elements with which they have to work. Given two elements, each of which may exist in two states, a complete consideration of their possible relationships requires sixteen logical operations, called "the sixteen binary operations;" most of these are unfamiliar to the reader who has not studied logic. Not all the operations are required for a given task, but adolescents are capable of calling upon the array as needed, and of entertaining the notion that hypothetical relationships might exist which run quite contrary to their concrete experience.

Other problems which Piaget and his coworkers have used with bright adoles-cents illustrate their superiority at handling, on an abstract level, the formal operations expressed in the group substructure of groupings. In solving these problems, the indi-vidual using logical operations handles relationships in a sophisticated fashion. Four transformations in the system of symbolic logic are of special importance in Piaget's conceptual description of this stage of intellectual development. They form the ele-ments of a structure which is called the INRC group (for *i*dentity, *n*egation, *r*eciprocal, and *c*orrelative transformations). Their precise nature, a direct translation of the rules of logic, need not concern us here. They do, however, permit the individual to manipu-late relationships between elements representing concepts, forces, entities, structures, and so on in complicated ways without losing sight of the complex whole in which the elements are a part. For Piaget, these transformations permit the epitome of intellec-tual activity.

IMPLICATIONS OF PIAGET'S THEORY FOR THE FIELD OF MENTAL RETARDATION

Although the significance of Piaget's insights concerning the development of cognitive processes have been kept no secret from the professional community who deal with retarded individuals (e.g., Bovet, 1970; Reiss, 1967; Schmid-Kitsikis, 1973; Wohlwill, 1966; Woodward, 1963), actual research efforts have been rather sparse. Particularly lacking have been efforts to attempt to remediate cognitive deficiencies of retarded children by various educational means. In view of the very rich and detailed research literature which has explored cognitive functioning in normal children according to the systematic framework of Piaget, it is difficult to account for the lag in such research with retarded subjects. The lag is all the more striking when compared with the very high degree of activity in more traditional theories of learning and memory as they apply to this group. (See Chapters 13, 14, and 15.)

The explanation, we believe, stems in part from rather severe obstacles in Piaget's own formulations and interests. He has been little concerned with individual differences among children and has published very little explicitly about retarded children. His theory is also, from the point of view of those working with retarded individuals, rather lacking in specificity concerning how relationships are established between environmental conditions and the advancement or retardation of cognitive attainments.

Relevant Concepts in Piaget's Theory

If Piaget's theory has not particularly encouraged research with retarded individuals, it has contributed strikingly to an understanding of their plight. Let us examine some of the elements in the theory which are particularly relevant to the problems of retardation of intellectual development.

Stage-analytic Developmental Orientation The single most important quality in Piaget's general theory is that it is truly developmental in orientation. Almost all other theories of intelligence have had a developmental orientation of sorts, but at the same time they have "featured a mind which remains qualitatively invariant as it slowly manufactures knowledge from experience over the childhood years, a mind which changes in size but not in shape, so to speak" (Flavell, 1963, p. 381). If the human mind is likened to a very complex computer, this is tantamount to saying that the essential data-processing characteristics of the mind remain invariant from birth onward and that changes occur primarily in the storage (memory) units.

Piaget, on the other hand, has given us a picture of a central nervous system which, as a result of its intercourse with the environment during the formative years, forms new levels of integration which are both quantitatively and qualitatively different from previous levels out of which they evolved. His view of the human mind is analogous to a computer which changes its data-processing characteristics (perhaps by adding a more sophisticated component or a new coordination among its old ones) as well as the amount of data it retains in its storage units.

Piaget's system, then, is not simply developmental. It is by far the most comprehensive and detailed stage-analytic theory of cognitive development in existence; in addition, it is one of the best documented. This is particularly true of the three periods which are most relevant to the field of mental retardation, those of sensorimotor, preoperational, and concrete-operational intelligence.

An important aspect of his orientation is that it forces us to shift from looking at what retarded children are not to looking at what they are. The result is that a much richer picture emerges even of the profoundly retarded adult, lying in a crib and shaking a rattle. Even more significantly, the mildly retarded twelve-year-old whose thought processes are just emerging from the preoperational period can be appreciated in terms of the capabilities he or she has. He or she can be seen not merely as resembling a seven-year-old, which is somehow better than resembling a six-year-old and not so good as resembling an eight-year-old; rather, he or she can be seen as a child in transit from one whole way of thinking to another.[7]

Fixation and Viscosity in Mental Retardation   Because Piaget sees the mind as a dynamic system which, en route to maturity, passes through qualitatively different levels of integration, he views intellectual development as an unfolding process, marked by the progressive disappearance of earlier systems of thought in favor of new higher-order systems. He thus tends to think of mental retardation as the result of the child's failure to progress beyond inferior levels of stages of integration. The greater the degree of retardation, the lower the level or stage of organization at which the individual is fixated. This does not imply, of course, that Piaget believes that all normal children develop at the same rate but rather that the rate of development alone is not a sufficient explanation of mental retardation.

Inhelder (1968) has proposed a scheme by which to order retarded adults according to stage. Her research demonstrates that the severely and profoundly mentally retarded adult ("idiot"[8]) can be viewed as fixated at the level of sensorimotor intelligence; the moderately retarded adult ("imbecile") should be seen as incapable of surpassing the preoperational intuitive period; the mildly retarded adult ("moron") can be characterized as unable to progress beyond the level of concrete operations; and, finally, the borderline adult is able to use only the simpler forms of formal operations.

As Lovell (1966) has pointed out, attainment of the stage of concrete operations is not a necessary precondition for a great deal of what might be thought of as simple associations "at the first level of abstraction, involving learning but not much understanding" (p. 87). Reviewing the literature, Clarke (1963) found that moderately retarded individuals are capable of considerable motor learning, space perception, discrimination and generalization of uncomplicated stimuli, and the mastery of a number of simple job-related skills. Clarke himself taught nine-, seventeen-, and twenty-three-year-old moderately retarded subjects several sorting and discrimination tasks and found that not only were learning and retention good, but that transfer of training to new situations was also good, especially in the children. This suggests that, so long as one remains within the level for which the individual possesses adequate schemes, he or she is able to function quite well. Understanding the nature of preoperational (intuitive) thought processes is, however, essential for designing learning situations which are appropriate for persons functioning at this level, so that their successes may be maximized. Self-care and many kinds of productive labor are well within their reach so long as conditions are properly engineered.

Inhelder's notion of *fixation* of thinking implies not only that retarded individuals are slower in development, but that during the latter part of the developmental period when one could have expected continued cognitive growth, they gradually decelerate, become fixated at a terminal stage, and exhibit no further progress. Inhelder also characterizes mental functioning in retarded persons as exhibiting a *viscosity* (literally,

---

[7] Wohlwill has aptly observed, "the difference between the child who is crawling on all 'fours' and the child who starts to walk represents a qualitative difference. You don't find intermediate stages of going around on 'threes'" (1966, p. 104).

[8] Inhelder, of course, used the terminology acceptable in the 1940s when the first edition of her work was published.

a stickiness) which not only retards progress but causes traces of old patterns, which should have been discarded in favor of new coordinations, to persist even when the child is capable of a more advanced conceptualization. She observed the viscosity in retarded individuals who, for example, remained in a state of transition between two stages for a much longer period than do normal children, oscillating between different levels of construction, not only on different tasks, but at different times on the same task.

> It is possible to be simultaneously confronted with two heterogeneous systems in the same individual. At this point, the emotional and social factors add their influence to this situation. According to the degree of confidence or distrust which the child feels for the examiner, it is possible to make him advance or regress between these two coexisting states. . . . Lack of interior mobility is the cause (thus the oscillation does not result from a greater mobility than that found in the normal child, but it does show the existence of these "viscosities"). (Inhelder, 1968, p. 292)

Although those who were completely dominated by oscillations constituted only 10 percent of the total group of 159 retarded subjects she examined, Inhelder sees this phenomenon somewhat as characteristic even of retarded children who show the predominance of one level of functioning or another. It is, furthermore, involved with what Inhelder terms "a state of 'false equilibrium' (capacity for some logical constructions, but inability to complete them), while normally developed intelligence is recognized by its ability to attain the equilibrium which is assured by the groupment of all the perceptive and intuitive facts involved" (1968, p. 298).

The fragility of this "false equilibrium," together with other psychological factors, contributes to the susceptibility of the retarded individual to influence by emotional and social factors. In some subjects, Inhelder noted a high degree of suggestibility; in others, she maintains, emotional tension and particularly lack of self-confidence, interfered with performance. These factors, however, play a minor and unelaborated role in Inhelder's (and Piaget's) formulations.

Although the body of research literature is not large, most of Inhelder's observations have tended to be confirmed by other investigators. With respect, first, to the terminal levels attained by individuals of various levels of intelligence as measured by standard tests, Lovell (1966), on the basis of extensive work with mildly retarded young people in England, found that, by ages thirteen to fifteen, only some of them had attained concrete operations. He maintains that almost all adolescents with IQs roughly 75 to 85 do eventually attain this period but do not succeed with the next step, the period of formal operations. On the other hand, moderately retarded individuals (IQs 30 to 50) rarely if ever attain concrete operational schemes, responding instead on an intuitive, perceptually dominated preoperational level (Kershner, 1973; Lovell, 1966; Woodward, 1962). Still further down on the scale, Woodward (1959) was able to match the behavior of severely subnormal children with Piaget's six substages of sensorimotor intelligence.

Inhelder observed that there was predictive value to the direction in which the child's oscillation during the evaluation session varied. She found that, of children who seemed to improve during the session because initially they were functioning below their current optimum, growth and consolidation of gains at the higher level tended to occur during the next year; of those whose performance seemed to deteriorate during the session, no progress was observed during the year. Bovet (1970) distinguished between retarded children who in the initial tests performed in at least one area at a higher level than in others, versus children whose performance was homogeneous. The former attained at the end of a year an even level corresponding to their best performance in the initial tests; they had, presumably, been on the verge of advancement to the next stage. The children whose initial performance had been even to begin with made poor progress.

It should be clear, of course, that across different content areas, attainment of concrete operations even in normal children varies in timing. Some concepts are more difficult for them than others. Conservation of substance, for example, generally comes before conservation of weight, and not until then, conservation of volume (which requires elemental formal operations). This order holds true for retarded individuals (Inhelder, 1968), and therefore discrepancies in responses to various types of problems is the expected, rather than the exceptional, case.[9]

With respect to Inhelder's notion of viscosity, it is difficult to establish objective means by which to test for the existence of this phenomenon. One finding does appear prominent among studies of retarded subjects: there appears to be a lag (up to about two years) in the mastery of Piagetian tasks compared with nonretarded groups matched for mental age on a standardized intelligence test (Gruen, 1973; Gruen & Vore, 1972; Keasey & Charles, 1967; Kirk, 1968; McManis, 1969a, 1970; Stephens & McLaughlin, 1974; Stevenson, Friedrichs, & Simpson, 1970; Stevenson, Hale, Klein, & Miller, 1968; Vitello, 1973).[10] This lag implies retardation (possibly a difficulty in shifting from one stage to the next) over and beyond that measured by concepts such as mental age and IQ.

A particularly interesting group of studies is being carried on at Temple University by Beth Stephens and her colleagues (Mahaney & Stephens, 1974; McLaughlin & Stephens, 1974; Moore & Stephens, 1974; Stephens & McLaughlin, 1974). They are following seventy-five normal (IQ 90-110) and seventy-five retarded (IQ 50-75) individuals at two-year intervals, with particular emphasis on the development of reasoning, moral judgment, and moral conduct. At the initiation of the study, the subjects were six to eighteen years old; at the second retest the same young people were ten to twenty-two. This design permits comparison over time of responses by the same individuals and also cross-group comparisons at various chronological and mental ages. For the most part, the results of these studies have tended to show that although increments are considerably slower among the retarded than the normal subjects, it is probably inaccurate to say that at these ages they are irrevocably fixated at a given level. In behavioral tests of moral conduct, for example, there seemed to be little or no increase as the retarded subjects approached middle adolescence and some items actually showed a decrease, but as the subjects moved into late adolescence, they began again to increase in scores. This interlude or pause (perhaps a product of "viscosity") did not appear in normal subjects (Moore & Stephens, 1974). In the area of moral judgment, irregularities also occurred, affecting judgments concerned with the distinction between the effects of an act and its intent. In most areas, retarded subjects of all three age groups demonstrated improved performance over time on such matters as the tendency to assign accountability to an entire group for the misdeeds of one of its members, choosing among forms of punishment, etc.

[9] See Wilton and Boersma (1974) for a review of conservation research with mentally retarded children.

[10] Brison & Bereiter (1967), however, found no such discrepancy between MA-matched retarded and nonretarded groups in conservation of substance.

Another study by this group presented the subjects a broad array of reasoning problems, together with some standard intelligence test items. Little evidence for true fixation was found; the data indicate that development does continue in retarded adolescents, although at a decelerating tempo, and furthermore, that in subjects of average intelligence, formal thought processes appear to develop beyond the eighteenth year. Nevertheless, this study showed significant deficits in the retarded subjects which were not accounted for by chronological or mental age and which appear "to involve the categorization, the flexibility, and the reversibility required in tasks involving conservation and classification" (Stephens & McLaughlin, 1974, p. 126).

Specific Deficits   Some investigators have sought to identify specific, rather than overall, deficits, in the judgment and reasoning of retarded persons. According to Piaget, each new attainment presupposes adequate resolution of the tasks of the previous period. Several writers (e.g., Wohlwill, 1966) have suggested that, although for most retarded individuals the current level of functioning is in the preoperational or concrete operations period, the original source of difficulty may lie in the child's previous experience during the sensorimotor period. There is, as yet, no definitive evidence concerning this hypothesis.

The work of McManis (1969b, 1969c, 1970), while identifying essential similarities between retarded and normal children matched for mental age, seems to pinpoint some special difficulty with seriation which stands in the way of retarded subjects' achieving success with transitivity tasks (e.g., if $A<B$ and if $B<C$, then $A<C$). Gruen (1973) indicates that the relative difficulty with such tasks lies in the retarded subjects' inability to make the logical inferences required. Gruen suggested, however, and Lutkus and Trabasso (1974) appeared to confirm, that retarded subjects also have difficulty with memory for the initial stimuli with which they must make comparisons. Once having mastered the initial discriminations, their performance was only slightly poorer than that of normal children of similar mental age.

Except for these scattered studies, there is no real indication that specific deficits exist in any sizable proportion of mentally retarded individuals. Furthermore, neither Piaget nor Inhelder gives any theoretical reason to expect such deficits. We must be particularly wary of falling into the trap of anticipating that all retarded children will function alike—a trap baited rather attractively by the disinterest of Piaget and his followers in the problem of individual differences.

Environmental Correlates of the Rate of Attainment of Functions

As we have already indicated, Piaget has paid relatively little attention to the environmental conditions necessary for development, but because this area is of vital interest to workers hoping to prevent or to remediate retarded development, a few studies have attempted to investigate aspects of the problem.

A first question, quite naturally, relates to the effect of social class on the attainment of Piagetian tasks. Not surprisingly, relationships do appear with social class in a rather orderly way (Gaudia, 1972; Wei, Lavatelli, & Jones, 1971; Harris, 1970). Kagan and Tulkin (1971), for example, found upper-middle-class infants more responsive than lower-middle-class infants to scheme discrepancy, and they possessed "richer nests of hypotheses" to use in evaluating stimulus input. In other studies, however, social class differences appear to be very small (e.g., Goodnow & Bethon, 1966). In Chapter 7, we reviewed a number of studies by Hunt and his associates which also bear on the relationship between cognitive functions such as object constancy and imitation and the infant's experience. Of special interest is a study by Wachs, Uzgiris, and Hunt (1971), which not only discovered developmental differences as early as seven months of age according to gross levels of social class, but which also related specific kinds of stimulation (or overstimulation) to the acceleration or deceleration of attainments. One should note that other investigators (Golden & Birns, 1968; Golden et al., 1971) have not found class-related differences on Piagetian tasks so early, though according to their data, differences are clearly present by the end of the third year.

Cross-national differences have been reflected in attainment on Piagetian tasks. Reviewing a number of cross-cultural studies, Uzgiris (1970) found that children in non-Western cultures generally conform to the pattern of developmental sequences proposed by the Piagetian framework, but that they lag somewhat behind the children in Switzerland, England, France, and the United States, where the bulk of Piagetian research has been carried out (Bovet, 1970; Greenfield, 1966; Maccoby & Modiano, 1966). The use of familiar materials appears to reduce the lag somewhat (Price-Williams, 1961). Children from rural backgrounds appear to be influenced very favorably by school attendance (Greenfield, 1966), although the effect of schooling per se within a Western nation such as the United States, appears less important (Goodnow & Bethon, 1966; Mermelstein & Shulman, 1967). Greenfield (1966) and Uzgiris (1970) propose that both schooling and urban residence promote abstract functions by encouraging communication in situations removed from the original context of the event. Rural residence, they maintain, fosters "attention to the particular, the unique, the given in immediate experience. Schooling . . . (helps) the child see a greater number of possibilities for grouping any set of objects by teaching him an analytic approach toward perceptual wholes" (Uzgiris, 1970, p. 30).

One must, of course, distinguish between substantive and superficial relationships. Simply varying the instructions (Carlson & Michalson, 1973) or minor details of the tasks (Vitello, 1973) may substantially affect the responses of retarded children. Minimizing the problem of understanding instructions may, in selected circumstances, change rather markedly the age at which a given mastery appears. H. B. Robinson (1964), for example, discovered that the size-weight illusion (the smaller of two objects of the same weight seems heavier) appeared a great deal earlier than predicted by Piaget when the children were first trained to comprehend the instructions.

Through deliberate training for retarded children who are developmentally on the brink of a new coordination, progress may also be achieved and may indeed be quite stable (Lister, 1969; Litrownik, Franzini, & Harvey, 1974; C. Robinson, 1974; Smedslund, 1961). Even extensive experience will have little effect, however, if the child is not developmentally ready. Keasey and Charles (1967) studied conservation of substance in twenty-one retarded and twenty-one normal children matched for mental age and found that the normal children had a much better grasp of the concept despite the fact that the retarded subjects had, on the average, over eleven years more of life experience.

Although the precise correspondences between experience and cognitive development remain elusive, there is the clear implication that crucial and probably specific correspondences do exist and can eventually be discovered. Experimental designs like those of Wachs, Uzgiris, and Hunt (1971) or Hunt, Paraskevopoulos, and Schickedanz (1973) are especially exciting because they establish the possibility of decoding the infant's environment to establish patterns of rearing which affect cognitive development.

Applications of the Piagetian Framework to Psychological Assessment

It may well be that one of the most practically valuable extensions of Piaget's work will be the development of new and more useful tests of intelligence. Almost all the currently available assessment techniques deal principally with the content rather than the functioning of the intellect. Most assume that an individual simply improves at certain tasks—remembering numbers, for example, or writing codes—from early childhood onward, not that different tasks are needed to emphasize different types of intellectual functioning at different points in the life span. Typical items are concerned with the information an individual has readily available, his ability to define words, and so on; practically no attention is paid to the method by which the child arrives at his answer.

None of the popularly used intelligence tests is truly developmental in orientation. It is true that some of them, following the pattern established by Alfred Binet, are turned at different age levels to the behavior of children of those ages, since items were chosen for such tests on the basis of the performance of children of different ages.[11] Other tests do give additional credit for higher-level responses. The items, however, have largely been chosen on a trial-and-error basis and not because they are representative of central intellectual processes characteristic of different age levels. It is assumed, moreover, that the same basic intellectual operations generally are manifested at all levels and that essential changes occur mainly in the complexity of the material with which these operations can cope. The child who defines "peculiarity" as "something queer" receives the same credit as one who defines the same word as "the state of being peculiar, or distinctive," although each has arrived at the answer in quite a different way. These two children might arrive at correct answers to arithmetic problems by different routes, but their processes of solution would be considered irrelevant on most current tests. It may be true that the better tests measure to some extent different developmental stages of intellectual functioning, but they were not intended for this precise purpose and, furthermore, they do not do the job very well.

Age Norms   Piaget has indicated tentative age levels which correspond to each period of intellectual development, but he has made no deliberate effort to study representative groups of children in order to establish valid norms. His estimates are based on observations of diverse groups of children—his own infants, some retarded children, some nonretarded or even exceptionally bright—and they make little pretense of precision. It is not surprising, then, that there have been a number of exceptions to his findings when representative groups of children have been evaluated (e.g., Braine, 1959; Elkind, 1961; Mehler & Bever, 1967; H. B. Robinson, 1964).

Piagetian Tasks versus Standardized Tests   In developing assessment techniques for use with retarded children, researchers have first compared performance on the Piagetian tasks with mental ages on standard, individual tests of intelligence (e.g., McManis, 1968; Sterns & Borkowski, 1969). Inhelder's fundamental research with

---

[11] See Chap. 17. It is a pity, as Inhelder (1968) points out, that theorists such as Binet, whose conceptualization of cognitive functioning was so rich, should for practical reasons have developed tests so sterile in this respect.

retardates also made use of such data. Generally, the relationships between Piagetian tasks and mental ages have been found to be moderately high (DeVries, 1974; Freyberg, 1966; Wachs, 1970), even though the two approaches seem to be measuring somewhat different things. Factor analytic techniques applied by McLaughlin and Stephens (1974) to the responses of seventy-five retarded and seventy-five normal persons on a variety of Piagetian tasks, one of the Wechsler scales and the Wide Range Achievement Test, made it clear that the Piagetian assessments measured something quite distinct from the abilities measured by the other tests. There were no major factors which included both Wechsler and Piagetian measures; in other words, no substantial commonalities of any kind were found which cut across the intelligence tests and the Piagetian tasks. Among the Piagetian tasks themselves, however (reasoning, moral judgment, and moral conduct), there were low to moderate relationships, relationships which intensified in both normal and retarded subjects after a period of two years.

New Piagetian Scales of Cognitive Development A number of workers have attempted to standardize some of Piaget's tasks. The best known of the resulting tests was published by Uzgiris and Hunt (1975) and consists of several ordinal scales of psychological development (e.g., object constancy, vocal imitation, gestural imitation) during infancy. By the time of its publication, it had already had rather extensive use in experimental form and it will probably become a standby among the assessment devices available for use with infants. It has also proved useful with older (ages four to ten) retarded children (Wachs, 1970). Another very well developed scale for use with infants has been published in France by Casati and Lézine (1968). It, too, consists of separate ordinal scales focusing on areas such as searching for hidden objects, the use of intermediary tools, exploration of objects, and combination of objects.

By far the most ambitious project has been undertaken by Father Adrien Pinard and Ms. Monique Laurendeau at the Institut de Psychologie of the University of Montreal. This very extensive battery, which requires some ten hours of testing, is being standardized with a representative sample of 700 French-speaking Canadian children ages two to twelve. The complete experimental battery consists of sixty-two subtests. The scales on causal thinking (1962) and on the child's concept of space (1970) are the first segments to have been published. The emphasis has been

> . . . first and always on the qualitative value of the responses given by the child, without any direct consideration for . . . speed. The examiner tries, rather, to obtain the child's maximal performance, to reach the limit so to say, of his reasoning abilities through a systematic questionnaire; the standardization of this questionnaire insures objectivity and uniformity, but it nevertheless remains flexible and subtle enough to prevent rigidity and lack of precision. Five of these questionnaires bear on the notion of time, movement, and speed; four study the notions of number and quantity; six attempt to reach the various notions intervening in the representation of space (topological space, projective space, and Euclidian space); five more have for their purpose the evaluation of the notions of causality and chance. Of the seven last questionnaires, almost all are exclusively verbal, three are concerned with the child's beliefs (realism, animism, and artificialism) and four with the logic of relations, connections, and deduction. (Pinard, 1959, p. 5)

Another rather ambitious test-construction project has been undertaken at the Institut des Sciences de l'Education of the University of Geneva, under the joint direction of Inhelder and Vinh-Bang (1957, 1959). Approximately thirty tasks, drawn from the various content areas considered by Piaget, have been individually administered according to a standardized format to approximately 1,500 children ages four to twelve years. "Although details are lacking, the impression is that the outcome has been positive. . .: Piaget's tasks do appear to scale satisfactorily and his previous developmental conclusions based on these tasks are in the main confirmed" (Flavell, 1963, p. 362).

Other scaling attempts cover a variety of purposes. The New York City Board of Education in 1965 published a Piagetian readiness test called "Let's Look at Children." Decarie (1965) constructed a Piagetian object concept and object relations test for early childhood, with scores relating to mental age, the quality of the environment, and chronological age. For children three to six years of age, a standardized test of imitation of gestures was developed by Berges and Lézine (1965). Over a broader and somewhat older age range, Tuddenham (1970) has published a Piagetian test, and Stephens, Mahaney, and McLaughlin (1972) published a normative scale of mental ages for the achievement of Piagetian reasoning assessments.

Implications of Piaget's Theory for the Education of Retarded Children[12]

Piaget and his followers have had little explicitly to say about the problems of the special education of the handicapped. Nevertheless, there are important implications in Piaget's position for teaching mentally retarded children.

Recognition of the Childlike Logic of the Retarded Child's Reasoning The perspective of children is often extremely difficult for adults to grasp, despite the fact that in their own distant past, reality appeared that way to them as well. Teaching fractions by cutting an apple into halves or quarters is not very effective if the child believes the amount of apple changes so that there is more or less of it than there was before. The attainment of just that ability to conserve is a sizable accomplishment for a moderately retarded adolescent.

The recognition of children's distorted view of reality and of their faulty logic have important implications for diagnosis, placement, and curriculum design. Teachers need to be aware that, in many functions, retarded children typically lag behind equal-MA normal children who are younger. The wise teacher will replace his or her concept of the children's mental ages with a careful appraisal of their current mental functioning. Piaget's data seem, for example, to indicate that teaching the multiplication tables can be nothing but a mindless exercise before children are capable of concrete operations. If it is introduced too early into the curriculum, children may use intuitive, preoperational processes to grasp in an inferior way the lessons they are assigned, and they may never comprehend the systematic nature of multiplication unless it is retaught later (possibly with greater difficulty). What seems so self-evident to adults is not necessarily self-evident or simple to children.

What the educator needs to do is to try to improve his own capacity to watch and listen, and to place himself in the distinctive perspective of the child. Since the meaning expressed by the child's language is often idiosyncratic, the adult must try to

---

[12] See also Furth (1970) and Ginsburg and Opper (1969, pp. 218–232). We are particularly in the debt of the latter authors for some of the ideas contained in this section.

understand the child's world by observing his actions closely. There are no easy rules or procedures for the educator. . . . What is needed chiefly is considerable sensitivity. (Ginsburg & Opper, 1969, p. 220)

Nevertheless, there is a great deal that children can learn at a straightforward level that does not require concrete operations, many skills children can acquire without much deep understanding (Lovell, 1966).

The Teacher's Job   Piaget's work has important implications for teaching methods. First, his theory maintains that we learn by doing, that we learn about the world we live in by actively interacting with it. Especially during the earlier developmental periods, which characterize most school-age retarded children, verbalization is said to follow and not to precede conceptualization. Under these circumstances, the best teaching methods encourage the pupil to interact concretely with the material to be mastered. A teacher seeking to clarify the principles involved in fractions would, for example, best approach this task by having the student divide an object into various combinations of component parts (Aebli, 1951), rather than by giving a verbal explanation or even a demonstration.

Second, Piagetian theory maintains that one of the basic ways in which an individual learns is through continuous interaction with his peers. Flavell writes:

One can learn the meaning of perspective—and thereby acquire the rationality and objectivity which only a multiperspective view can confer—only by pitting one's thoughts against those of others and noting similarities and differences. The extension of this view to education consists of plumping for group activities in the classroom— projects to be undertaken in common, discussion sessions, and the like. (1963, p. 369)

Finally, the notion that the attainment of almost any new behavioral sequence involves a step-by-step process implies that the teacher must be sure that each step in the attainment process has been mastered before the next step is considered. The teacher may seek to accomplish this task by a variety of techniques. None of them will be unique to Piaget's system, but his theory presents a rationale which is somewhat different from and more explicit than those underlying such techniques as they are employed today.

The Impetus toward Equilibrium: Development Through Self-regulation of the Cognitive Structures   Piaget's theory implies that children are the learners, but that the teachers do not necessarily teach. Teachers function for the most part as expert stage-managers, inviting the children to action with the materials and setting up situations that the children will feel to be a cognitive challenge that they are capable of meeting. What Hunt (1961) has termed the "problem of the match" is the selection of a task which is neither so familiar and easy for children that they are disinterested nor so difficult and/or novel that they cannot "get a handle on it." Children are more apt to try hard and to function on an effective and growth-inducing level when they are interested and challenged, as they will be if the "match" is appropriate. Children are their own best regulators, especially healthy and curious children looking for a challenge. Some retarded children may be so beaten by an unremitting history of defeats that they tend to prefer problems that are too easy, or to give up before they start. The teacher must strive to provide situations that they can master with a little effort to begin with, and a greater effort as their self-confidence is bolstered by success.

Contemporary Schools   A number of contemporary schools have established programs which are consistent with Piaget's educational prescriptions. There has been, for example, a significant trend toward individuation of instruction, meeting children in each subject at their level and helping them to grow from there. The breaking up of the classroom into smaller independent groups from time to time affords the opportunity for the kind of social interactions which challenge children's intuitive perceptions and provide the most effective means by which they can dislodge themselves from an earlier, false equilibrium to move toward more mature cognitive organizations.

The need for activity and involvement with material props, the emphasis on peer-group interactions and individual effort, the necessity to capture children's interest for real learning to take place—all these can be seen in the "open classrooms" which are becoming more popular. As children talk together, challenge and entice one another, as they defend their opinions and offer reasons to justify their views, as they manipulate objects and control their own learning environment, genuine development is likely to occur. The open classroom is recommended by Ginsburg (1972; Ginsburg & Opper, 1969), especially for culturally deprived and/or mildly retarded children.[13] There are, of course, some dangers to such schools. Unless they are very expertly handled, they can become chaotic playgrounds which are equally frustrating and stifling to the learning process as the traditional schools they were designed to replace. They may be particularly hazardous for children with histories of failure who enter them with deeply ingrained patterns of avoidance.

Piaget leaves us with many paradoxes. For those interested in retarded children, his disinterest in individual differences is frustrating, yet he has provided important insights into cognitive functioning. By his emphasis on the stages of the development of logical thinking, Piaget seems to say that children are exceedingly refractory to learning anything which requires more mature functions than they are ready to adopt, but at the same time he has greatly enriched the possibilities of meaningful structuring of children's cognitive world.

Piaget has ignored many of the most pressing questions which anyone responsible for the care of retarded children must ask: How do the children differ in cognitive capacities? What factors are responsible for the differences? What may be done to facilitate solid growth and to maximize eventual attainment? It is a tribute to the genius of Piaget that we so persistently seek the answers from him. We wish he would turn *his* giant mind to *our* concerns, but it is not to be so. His overriding interest is in genetic epistemology, in the blending of the biopsychological sciences and the rigorous structure of philosophy to elucidate the growth of the mental functions which permit one to know and understand. We must, then, find our answers elsewhere—but Piaget has furnished many intriguing leads and the chance to apply a whole new way of thinking to the appraisal and the treatment of retarded children.

---

[13] The issue of open-versus-structured classrooms is controversial. Analyzing data from Head Start programs, Datta, Mitchell, and McHale (1972) reported that better results were obtained in structured programs.

13

Learning Processes
in the Mentally Retarded

One of the most fundamental ways in which retarded children differ from normal children of the same age lies in the slowness and inefficiency with which they acquire knowledge and skills. For some writers, intelligence is practically synonymous with learning capacity. (See Chapter 1.) Detailed investigations of learning in retarded children can answer a number of questions relevant to understanding their basic handicaps, predicting the sorts of tasks which they will do more or less well, planning their educational experiences, and designing environments to enhance their performance.

Within the discipline of psychology, one of the most prolific and precise areas of investigation has been that of learning theory. Working from a variety of theoretical viewpoints, psychologists have conducted painstaking programmatic work which has resulted in a number of tightly reasoned cores of research. None of the research cores can explain all the changes in behavior which constitute learning, but each of them provides a rather exactly formulated and carefully tested description of some important aspects of learning.

It would be reasonable then to suppose that studies of learning in retarded individuals, emanating from these laboratories, would do much to elucidate differences between retarded and normal individuals and would further explain many of the individual differences observed among retarded persons. As we shall see, progress in

This chapter was written with the collaboration of Joseph C. Campione.

the former direction has been considerably greater than progress in the latter. The reason certainly does not lie in any apathy for work with retarded subjects, but rather in the focus of interest. Indeed, between 1954 and 1974 at least 1500 studies of learning processes were conducted with retarded individuals (Zeaman, 1974). This area of research continues today to be one of the most active in the entire field of mental retardation.

AN HISTORICAL PERSPECTIVE OF LEARNING RESEARCH

Although experimental learning research began during the latter part of the 19th century, learning theory came into its own in the period of the 1920s, 1930s, and 1940s, with the work of a number of intellectual giants. These men constructed comprehensive theories which they confidently expected eventually to extend to the understanding of all types of learning and to other aspects of psychological functioning as well.[1]

Theory Building: 1920-1950

Ivan Petrovich Pavlov (1927), the distinguished Russian physiologist, is best known to Western readers for his studies of what has come to be known as "classical conditioning." His most famous conditioning paradigm involved the *unconditioned reflex* of salivation which occurs when an *unconditioned stimulus,* a bit of meat powder, is placed in a dog's mouth. When some arbitrary stimulus, such as a light or a ringing bell, is repeatedly presented just ahead of the meat powder, this stimulus acquires the capacity to evoke a salivation response in the absence of the powder. The light or bell has then become the *conditioned stimulus* and the response it evokes has become the *conditioned response.* Note that in this paradigm the strengthening factor, or reinforcer—the meat powder—precedes the response and is not contingent on the dog's behavior. Although Pavlov's work on conditioned reflexes had great international influence on the field of learning theory, in the Soviet Union his much more extensive neuropsychological theory has remained of paramount importance and today forms the basis of much Soviet cognitive theory.

Another intellectual giant of the 1920-1950 period was Edwin R. Guthrie (Smith & Guthrie, 1921), who studied *contiguity of stimulus and response.* He maintained that all that was necessary for learning was a combination of stimulus conditions with a movement, or response; reinforcement was not required. According to his analysis, that which was done last in the presence of a stimulus or combination of stimuli tends to recur when the stimulus conditions are next presented. One of Guthrie's classic experiments (Guthrie & Horton, 1946) involved placing cats in a puzzle box, the door of which they could open by touching a pole in the center of the box. The cats developed extremely stereotyped but individualistic behavior. Those who first bit the pole continued to bite it to open the door; those who touched it with front paws, hind paws, haunches, or nose continued to use that part of the body. Although contiguity theory has few active adherents today, it effectively called attention to the repetitiveness and stereotypy which characterize much of human behavior.

Clark L. Hull (1943) developed the most rigorous and elaborate theory of all, one in which the notion of *drive reduction* was of great importance in establishing the

---

[1] For a comprehensive description of the positions of these theorists, see Hilgard and Bower (1974).

strength of the bond connecting a stimulus with a response. In a typical Hullian experiment, a rat might be taught to run a complex maze with greater and greater efficiency for a food reward in the goal box. For Hull, the animal's drive state and drive reduction by the food (the reinforcer), the stimulus cues in the maze, and the complexity of the response to be learned, were all essential variables which could be not only varied but quantified. Although it has been shown that the theory of drive reduction has limited human applicability, a great deal of modern theory and methodology owes its origins to Hull and one of his principal proponents, Kenneth W. Spence (1956).

Edward C. Tolman (1932, 1948) was a theorist of a different order, for whom the notion of *purposive behavior* and the development of *cognitive signs* or expectancies were prominently involved in learning. He described the brain as similar to a "map control room" rather than to an "old-fashioned telephone exchange" (1948, p. 192). In some of his experiments, rats were required to run a complex maze from several different starting points. That they could reach the goal via differing routes was evidence to Tolman that they had acquired "cognitive maps" rather than specific stimulus-response sequences.

B. F. Skinner (1938), the theorist of this period whose work remains most prominent today, has emphasized the emission of *operant responses* and their relationship to *reinforcement conditions*. For him, the unobservable intervening variables of drive, purpose, and cognitive structure are largely irrelevant and, indeed, unwarranted inferential notions which have little place in a behaviorist theory. In some of Skinner's experiments, pigeons were taught to peck at a disk in their experimental box to receive a food reinforcer, a pellet of grain. The scheduling of the delivery of the reinforcer exerted powerful influence on the rate of pecking, which could be maintained at a low or a high level, at a constant rate or in spurts, depending upon the nature of the scheduling. Skinner's work will be described in detail in Chapter 15.

Other theorists such as Wolfgang Köhler, John B. Watson, Edward L. Thorndike, and O. Hobart Mowrer also developed self-contained systematic theories of grand design. The period was one of excitement, passion, and optimism.

Several aspects of the views of the 1920-1950 period are notable. First, all the theorists were *behaviorists* who maintained that any scientific enterprise must be firmly based in what it could observe and measure—namely, behavior—and that armchair philosophical speculations about the nature of man's learning were likely to be far wide of the mark. Theory building and data gathering, they insisted, must go hand in hand. They tended to reject notions such as innate instincts, consciousness, and imagery, and devoted themselves rather to conceptualizations which could be tied closely to the behavior they observed.

Second, theorists were interested in *universal laws* of behavior applicable to all species. For a number of practical reasons, however, some species such as the laboratory rat, the cat, the pigeon, or the dog were more convenient to study than others. The investigators preferred the lower animals to man for this purpose because their behavior patterns were simpler and the control of experimental conditions was much easier. Animals could, for example, be deprived of food for twenty-four hours to increase their drive states, whereas human subjects were likely to object to such treatment. When human beings were studied, they were much more likely to be accessible college sophomores than infants, children, or mentally retarded persons.

Third, the mainstream of experimental psychology was strongly *associational*. Learning was conceived by most theorists as the acquisition of connections among stimuli and responses in various combinations. The theorists firmly opposed a rationalistic view which held that reason, not raw sensory experience, was the governing mechanism of the mind. (See Hilgard & Bower, 1974, chap. 1.) As we shall see, contemporary learning theory centers upon mediating mechanisms and organizational configurations in the learning process, a rather intermediate position between associationism and rationalism. During the 1920–1950 period, however, the emphasis was on the logging of the empirical associations between stimulus events and responses.

Fourth, the various associational theories were seen as *mutually exclusive* and therefore competing. Each theorist tended to reinterpret the work of the others in terms of his own point of view (Hilgard & Bower, 1974). There was great emphasis on conducting critical experiments which would enable the researcher to demolish someone else's theory while fortifying his own. Some of the controversies had to do with establishing the relative importance of the four basic components of the learning process: drive state, cue (stimulus) conditions, response, and reinforcement. Guthrie, for example, maintained that stimuli and response factors were paramount in the learning process, that a drive state merely served to activate the response and the reinforcer served merely to remove the learner from the situation, thereby preserving the connection between the behavior and the stimulus. For Hull, all four components were necessary parts of the learning paradigm, whereas for Skinner, cue, response, and reinforcer (which might or might not be drive reducing) were important. Another controversy centered around the accretional view of learning of Pavlov, Hull, and Skinner. These men saw each reinforced trial as serving by small steps to strengthen the acquisition of a response. This view was opposed to the one-trial or jump-wise learning of the type maintained by Guthrie to be a simple product of contiguity or by Köhler (1925) to be the shift from initial trial-and-error learning to insightful problem solving. Some of the critical issues of that period remain unresolved today.

A fifth characteristic, which seems obvious to us now, was not recognized at that time. Each of the theorists had actually studied learning in a somewhat *different set of situations* and built his theory upon his own experimental paradigms. Although the laws each theorist derived from his experiments were thought to be universal, in fact each had unwittingly contrived a theory based on a limited number of very specific situations.

Research after 1950

During the 1950s difficulties arose as psychologists began to apply learning theories to a wide range of human behaviors and found the theories wanting. Investigators with a drive-reduction orientation were hard put, for example, to explain why human beings sometimes seek stimulation such as roller-coaster rides to increase rather than decrease drive state. More important, however, the theories began to falter when questions were asked about more complex forms of learning and development which had to be derived inferentially from observed behavior. None of the theorists we have mentioned would, for example, have been able to explain the acquisition of language in light of the complexities now recognized, nor would they have been able to approach the kind of phenomena described by Piaget (Chapter 12).

As a result, psychologists began to study much more circumscribed areas of human cognitive functioning. Since the 1960s, learning research has been characterized not so much by competing theories as by groups of researchers who have focused on distinct facets of human functioning which they are able to explore in depth. With the exception of the considerable number of investigators who have followed B. F.

Skinner and who attempt to explain broad areas of human functioning by means of the principles of operant conditioning, much of the work has been rather more circumscribed and inferential, but no less rigorous, than that which came before.

Research with Retarded Subjects

When one examines the history of work with retarded subjects, the shift from the grand theories to more specific ones and the shift in emphasis from simpler forms of learning to more complex ones are both clearly visible. Much of the research with retarded populations, which began to proliferate in the mid-1950s, was conducted by theorists intent upon testing the universal characteristics of the learning processes. Some thought of retarded individuals primarily as another group of organisms with whom to test theoretical principles as they had previously been tested with the laboratory rat and the college sophomore. Individual differences among retarded subjects were of little importance for them. Furthermore, because they were interested in principles of learning which were applicable across species, they often employed simple learning tasks such as classical conditioning and simple discriminations which were least sensitive to the cognitive deficits shown by retarded persons and also least likely to reveal developmental progressions in nonretarded children. Although much of the exploratory work at that time did deal with differences between groups of normal and retarded subjects of various IQ and/or MA levels, refined descriptions of subjects were virtually nonexistent.

Recent learning research has become more sophisticated in its orientation toward retarded subjects as interesting in their own right. Much of it has searched for specific deficits or processes which characterize the learning of retarded as opposed to that of nonretarded persons. Some fairly clear and cohesive general patterns have become apparent. There remains, however, an unfortunate tendency to regard the retarded population as rather homogeneous. Even so, at a minimum, researchers now routinely report subject characteristics such as CA, MA, and IQ levels, sex, school or residential placement, and, occasionally, diagnostic classifications. Such data permit quantitative analyses of learning behavior according to maturity level (CA or MA), though relatively few studies are addressed to discerning possible step-wise qualitative changes or developmental stages in learning behavior.[2]

SOME DISTINCTIONS OCCURRING IN LEARNING RESEARCH

To comprehend the significance of the studies to be reported subsequently in Chapters 13, 14, and 15, a few basic features of learning research need to be kept in mind.

Learning versus Performance

The aim of learning theorists has been to account for the way in which behaviors are acquired or modified or, alternatively, for the extraction of information from the environment. *Learning* is conceived as an underlying process of change in the abilities or propensities of an organism which occur as a result of its experience. Learning, like intelligence, cannot be measured directly. It can be inferred only from observed behavior or *performance*. Since many extraneous factors such as distraction, fatigue, or transitory illness can interfere with a child's performing responses he has learned, one must be careful to keep in mind this distinction.

[2] For an analysis of the literature, see Zeaman (1974). The most explicit treatment of individual differences in learning is to be found in Estes (1970).

Learning Not a Unitary Process

Although the early theorists tended to conceive of various aspects of learning as simply different facets of a single process, investigators at present maintain that this is not necessarily the case. Although most would admit to the possibility that unifying neurochemical or neuroelectrical mechanisms may some day be discovered, they are content for the present to hold to the more conservative view that the various processes elicited by different types of situations are not all the same. Studies now being conducted with retarded subjects illustrate this preference for in-depth exploration of limited area and task-specific processes.

Learning versus Memory

The distinction between *learning* and *memory* is a fine one which is becoming progressively less clear because of changes in research emphasis (Melton & Martin, 1972). Information must be learned before it can be remembered, and the manner in which it is learned affects subsequent memory. Memory for information previously acquired is usually involved in new learning, as is illustrated by the relative ease of learning to type one's own language as compared with learning to type material in an unfamiliar tongue. Nevertheless, some research paradigms are traditionally assumed primarily to reflect learning and others primarily memory. This separation will be followed in the present chapter and the next two.

Classical versus Instrumental Conditioning

We have already mentioned several types of conditioning, or learning, studies which differ in their arrangement of reinforcer and response. In the *classical conditioning* studies of Pavlov, the reader will recall, the reinforcer, the unconditioned stimulus, preceded the response. In an *instrumental learning* paradigm, the reinforcer follows the response and is contingent on it. The rat must, for example, complete the maze to reach the food box.

A further distinction is sometimes drawn between *instrumental conditioning* conducted according to a Hullian design, with discrete trials followed by a reinforcer, and *operant conditioning*, in which the response happens as a freely occurring event whose frequency is to be manipulated. The pigeon may peck at the disk from time to time even before any reinforcement occurs, or the nontalking child may occasionally vocalize. The experimenter sometimes administers reinforcers on a predetermined schedule which has no simple one-to-one correspondence with the operant response. (See Chapter 15.)

In the discussion which follows, the reader will note that classical conditioning experiments with retarded subjects will not be reported, primarily because such experiments are not currently an area of active interest. (See, however, L. E. Ross and S. M. Ross, 1973.) Earlier investigations generally discovered that retarded subjects acquired classically conditioned responses about as readily as other subjects did, but that they were slower to extinguish the conditioned response (i.e., to "unlearn" the response in the absence of reinforcement). This slow extinction may represent an inhibitory deficit of the central nervous system. On the other hand, it may reflect the fact that the nonreinforced trials are neither so tightly controlled nor so attention demanding as are reinforced trials (Estes, 1970, pp. 58-61).

Voluntary Learning Strategies versus Trial and Error

Some of the most interesting work with retarded subjects has focused upon their passivity as learners, their lack of propensity to utilize helpful aids to learning. One such aid to memory is rehearsal of previously presented material which is to be repeated in sequence. Other aids include both elaboration of stimuli to be associated so that they acquire a meaningful connection and deliberate hypothesis testing. Younger and duller subjects, and even normal adults in new situations, tend to resort to poorly guided trial-and-error methods, with typically slow rates of acquisition. Skilled learners, on the other hand, employ a variety of strategies which lead to efficient learning and memory.

Acquisition of Higher-order Structures: Effects of Prior Learning

As learning progresses, subjects tend to organize or order their knowledge according to higher order structures or groupings which provide useful shortcuts to the learning and retrieval of information.

> Suppose, for example, that the list of words read to a subject in a free-recall experiment included the first ten digits, the primary colors, and the names of the New England states. A sufficiently sophisticated learner would need only to rehearse and transfer to long-term memory the category names, or code designations, of the three classes in order to be prepared to reproduce the entire list on request (Estes, 1970, p. 15).

Such higher-order structures greatly reduce the learning task and permit efficient approaches to new situations. The child who has learned to regard color as one dimension and form as another, for example, is prepared to handle a discrimination problem involving form and/or color in a more sophisticated manner than a child who does not have such categories at his disposal.

RESEARCH DESIGNS WITH RETARDED SUBJECTS

The investigator who would deal with retarded subjects must solve a large number of theoretical and methodological problems before proceeding with research.

Selection of Subjects

Although overall comparisons of normal and retarded children are certainly interesting, and in fact constituted much of the research of the 1950s and 1960s in this field, a number of potentially relevant variables must be taken into account if one is to discover anything more than the unsurprising finding that retarded individuals perform less well than nonretarded individuals of the same CA. At a minimum, the experimenter usually attempts to control for differences in CA, MA, and IQ levels. CA is taken as a compound index of both maturation and experience, MA as an index of the level of maturity attained, and IQ as a measure of the rate of the subject's previous learning. The problem, of course, is that because groups of normal and retarded children differ in IQ, they must also differ in CA or MA or both. Many research designs have therefore used a minimum of three groups: a retarded group of given CA and MA and two normal groups, one equivalent to the retarded group in CA but differing in MA and IQ, and the other equivalent to the retarded group in MA but differing in CA and IQ. As Estes (1970) has noted, however, of two subjects of differing CA with the same MA, the younger subject would be expected to learn more quickly since his rate of learning to this point has been more rapid than that of the older subject. The reader is referred to Goulet (1968) for an analysis of similar problems in learning research and to Kappauf (1973) for a more detailed methodological analysis.

Many other variables would be controlled in the ideal experiment, if it were possible to equate groups on background factors such as social class status, nature and degree of parental attention, enriched or deprived experience levels, and the types of educational curricula to which they have been exposed, and on psychophysiological factors such as activity level, integrity of the central nervous system, and so on. The fact that in practice the normal and retarded groups can rarely be equated on even a single one of these dimensions seriously limits the possibilities of generalizing the findings of most studies.

Selection of Tasks and Experimental Conditions

The learning task to be presented must also be selected with care. It must be neither so easy that all subjects can master it rapidly nor so difficult that it will be mastered by few. The set of tasks must be analyzed into component processes and the presentation so arranged that differences in performance can pinpoint both the precise processes which are occurring and any specific deficiencies which appear. In addition, the investigator must identify the environmental conditions or experimental procedures which influence the processes, such as the salience of various cues, the nature of the instructions, and the effectiveness of the reinforcers.

Research Strategies

The general strategy of much of the contemporary research to be reported here includes three steps. An initial phase of the research demonstrates deficient performance in a process such as attention to the relevant dimensions of a discrimination task or rehearsal of items in a memory task. Second, the subjects are given specific training in the target process. If their subsequent performance on the original task improves, this outcome reinforces the theoretical conclusions regarding the importance of the process and at the same time indicates a practical area in which remediation is both desirable and possible. Although many investigations have stopped at this point, a third step is highly desirable: to test whether the subject has learned a specific skill tied to a particular context or whether he has acquired a general problem-solving principle. To study this question, a different task involving the same process is administered. The data obtained so far indicate that the usual extent of generalization is very small. Minor changes in the experimental task or in the instructions frequently and disappointingly lead to marked decrements in performance which suggest that the retarded subjects have not grasped either the general principle or the utility of the strategy in the original task.

SPECIFIC AREAS OF RESEARCH

The remainder of this chapter will describe a few areas of investigation of learning processes which have been particularly fruitful with retarded subjects. It is by no means a comprehensive review, but rather a selective sampling of important themes. Areas to be highlighted include deficits in attentional processes in discrimination experiments; the typical slowness of retarded subjects to acquire learning sets, i.e., to profit from past experience; difficulties in problem solving, hypothesis testing, and information seeking; and the failure to use mediators to aid in paired-associates learning.

Discrimination Learning: The Significance of Attention

Much of the learning research with retarded subjects has been devoted to discrimination tasks, which can be modified sufficiently to allow analogous work with populations ranging from subhuman subjects to college students.[3] The basic procedure is to present a series of sets of two or three stimuli from which the subject is to choose the correct one on the basis of feedback about the correctness of his or her choices on previous trials. A series of training trials with objects differing in, say, form, color, and size, continues until the subject consistently chooses the correct stimulus (e.g., the red one, the square one, the larger one). The number of trials or errors prior to problem solution serves as a measure of learning efficiency. Given the historical interest in this method, over the years there has accrued an impressive amount of theoretical refinement, making it possible to pinpoint some of the crucial processes involved.

By far the most systematic approach to discrimination learning has been that of Zeaman and House (1963; Zeaman, 1973). Their work has demonstrated the importance of the subject's attention being directed to relevant elements of the stimuli to be discriminated. These investigators began by noting that the usual method of data plotting, an averaging of the performance of an entire group of subjects over a series of trials, masks the individual performance characteristics. The traditional learning curve (see Figure 13-1) rises quickly at first and then more slowly. Its form has usually been taken as evidence that learning proceeds in small steps with each reinforcement of the response until the correct choice becomes dominant. The reader will recall that arguments concerning the small-step versus jump-wise nature of learning constituted one of the crucial areas of disagreement among the early learning theorists.

When the data of Figure 13-1 were replotted using individual data and backward learning curves,[4] a much different picture emerged. (See Figure 13-2.) The learning curves, rather than gradually rising from the guessing level of 50 percent correct to 100 percent, hovered around the 50 percent level for a varying number of trials before jumping rapidly to 100 percent.

The Role of Attention This apparent discontinuity led Zeaman and House to propose the operation of two processes, one which controlled the duration of the initial segment of the curve and one which was involved in the rapid jump to problem solution. As indicated in Figure 13-2, the difference between retarded children with MAs two to four years, and those with MAs four to six years (mean CA of both groups was twelve years) lies in the length of the initial, flat portion of the curve. When improvement begins, it occurs rapidly for both groups. House and Zeaman (1958)

---

[3] For a detailed description of procedural matters involved in discrimination-learning paradigms, see Shepp and Turrisi (1966).

[4] The graph is rearranged so that the last point of every individual curve is identical in position and has the same height. The curves are superimposed as in forward learning curves, but the shapes of the curves in the region of attaining the criterion are visually emphasized.

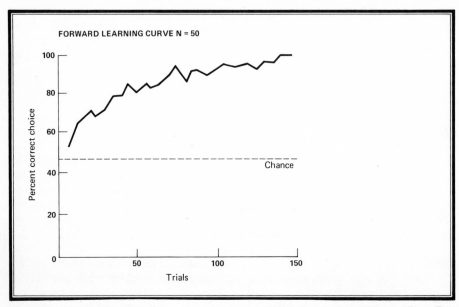

FORWARD LEARNING CURVE N = 50

Fig. 13-1 Average discrimination curve of a group of mentally retarded subjects. *(From Zeaman & House, 1963, p. 161)*

found that within the two- to four-year MA range, at least, retarded children were poorer performers than were normal children. Furthermore, among retarded subjects they found that, independent of MA, higher IQ was related to more efficient discrimination performance (Zeaman & House, 1966).

The length of the flat portion also depends upon the nature of the stimuli being discriminated. In any discrimination experiment, at least one dimension or attribute of the stimuli provides information as to the correct choice and is therefore *relevant,* whereas other dimensions provide no information and are therefore *irrelevant.* "Junk stimuli" (e.g., toy car versus toothbrush) which differ along many relevant dimensions are much easier than color-form discriminations (e.g., red and green circles and squares) on which a single dimension is relevant. These data led Zeaman and House to hypothesize that the process influencing the length of the flat portion of the curve was *attentional* in nature. They suggested that the child must learn a chain of two responses. He must come to attend to the relevant dimension (e.g., color) and then learn which value or cue (e.g., red) along that dimension is correct. Until the child learns to attend to the relevant dimension, his performance cannot possibly improve. Zeaman and House concluded that retarded children enter the situation with a low probability of attending to the relevant dimension and learn but slowly which dimension is in fact relevant (flat portion of curve). Once the child begins to attend to the relevant dimension, however, his choice of the correct cue or value comes very rapidly.

According to this theory, procedures which influence the probability of the child's attending to the relevant dimension will enhance his problem-solving efficiency. One such procedure is to alter the problem so that the relevant dimension is one to which the child naturally attends more readily, i.e., one which he prefers. For both normal

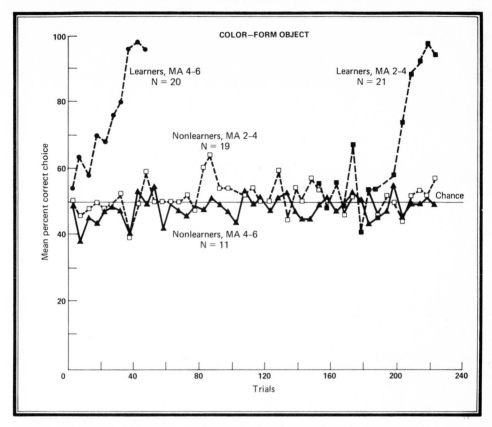

Fig. 13-2 Effects of intelligence on discrimination learning are shown in the average performance of four groups classified by mental age and achievement. Backward curves are plotted for the two groups of learners. *(From Zeaman & House, 1963, p. 163)*

(Smiley & Weir, 1966) and retarded children (Heal, Bransky, & Mankinen, 1966) speed of learning is directly related to preference for the dimension. Preference hierarchies seem to vary with intelligence. Retarded children highly prefer position and, as expected, learn position discriminations quickly, in some cases even faster than do equal-CA normal children (Schusterman, 1964).

Transfer of Training Because learning proceeds so quickly once attention is correctly focused, the importance of the adroit management of attention in home and school learning situations is clear. The effects of direct training of attention responses have been extensively examined in transfer of training models. These experiments are conducted in two phases. Their form is illustrated in Table 13-1. During the initial phase of the experiment, subjects are trained to solve a problem in which one dimension, say, the color dimension, is relevant. After such training, it is safe to assume that the probability of the subject's attending to color is high. Because there is a natural "warm-up" effect when subjects learn the second of two similar problems, the second

**Table 13-1   An Illustration of the Types of Stimulus
Arrangements and Reward Contingencies Used in Dimensional
Transfer Experiments**

Original learning	
+	
red square	blue circle
+	
red circle	blue square
	+
blue square	red circle
	+
blue circle	red square

Transfer			
Intradimensional shift		Extradimensional shift	
+		+	
yellow T	green X	yellow T	green X
+			+
yellow X	green T	yellow X	green T
+		+	
green T	yellow X	green T	yellow X
	+		+
green X	yellow T	green X	yellow T

phase of the experiment includes two transfer conditions. Half the subjects are given an intradimensional (ID) shift, in which new stimuli are used but the relevant dimension, color, remains the same. The remaining half of the subjects are given new stimuli with an extradimensional (ED) shift, in which a previously irrelevant dimension, form, becomes relevant. Note that the two groups are equated in terms of nonspecific warm-up effects. According to the theory, the ID shift should be much easier than the ED shift, since the subjects in the ID shift groups should begin the transfer problem with a high probability of attending to color. The subjects in the ED shift group, however, should enter the transfer phase with a high probability of attending to the now irrelevant color dimension and a correspondingly low probability of attending to the now relevant form dimension. This predicted difference has been obtained many times (e.g., Campione, Hyman, & Zeaman, 1965) and is one of the strongest sets of evidence concerning both the Zeaman-House theory and the utility of direct training of attention responses.

The importance of attention in more complex discrimination problems has also been demonstrated. As one example, consider an oddity-learning problem.[5] In one variant, the child is presented on each trial with three objects, two the same and one different (e.g., two red circles and a green circle). He must learn to choose the odd object. An abstract concept of oddity must be acquired because no simple attribute-specific response can lead to problem solution. For young normal and for retarded children, the oddity task is a very difficult one. If the experimenter provides training on the relevant attention response before the oddity is introduced, however, there are reliable increases in both the speed with which the problem is learned and in the number of children who can solve it (Brown, 1970; Martin & Tyrrell, 1971).

[5] A detailed review and theoretical synthesis of this literature has been presented by House, Brown, and Scott (1974).

Learning to Learn

In addition to research involving specific transfer according to identifiable dimensions, there has been considerable interest in nonspecific transfer or general "learning to learn," termed *learning set* by Harlow (1949). Harlow reported that monkeys given a series of similar problems, each presented for only a few trials, showed successive improvement until they were able to solve each new problem with maximal efficiency, i.e., no more than one error. If the series was composed of simple discrimination problems, a set was established for solving simple discrimination problems. If discrimination reversal problems were used, they established the learning set for discrimination reversal, and oddity problems, the set for oddity. The improvement is an example of nonspecific transfer or a complex attentional response involving a problem-solving set. On discrimination tasks like those described previously, the nonspecific transfer may overcome even the specific negative transfer of an ED shift.

Because learning-set formation represents the effects of prior learning on current learning, it is widely regarded as an important index of learning ability. The procedures used in studies of retarded populations have varied widely, but the data indicate that the formation of the set to solve a particular kind of problem proceeds more slowly in retarded children than in normal children. Also, retarded persons in institutions perform less well than those living at home but matched for MA and IQ (Harter, 1967; Kaufman & Prehm, 1966), perhaps suggesting that in many institutions the number or variety of learning situations is limited.

Some of these results can be illustrated by a pair of experiments reported by Harter (1965, 1967), who investigated the rate of acquisition of learning set as a function of both IQ and MA. Her subjects received a series of two-choice discrimination problems. Each problem was presented for exactly four trials and involved an entirely new pair of stimuli. In both experiments, rate of learning set formation improved with increases in both MA and IQ.[6] Harter (1967) also reported that noninstitutionalized children were more adept at learning-set formation than an institutionalized group matched on mean MA (5½ years) and mean IQ (65). Figure 13-3 shows backward learning curves for the various groups included in that experiment. As is the case with learning a single discrimination problem, differences between the groups seem to lie primarily in the amount of time for improvement to begin, rather than in the rate of improvement once it starts. The higher MA subjects, who learn more rapidly, begin by employing strategies which take into account the outcome of a previous trial. The lower MA subjects, however, make more use of strategies which are not contingent upon information presented on trial 1, such as a simple position (left or right) perseveration. The slower learning of retarded children, then, seems to reflect the fact that they begin with inappropriate response sets and tend to be unresponsive to the information provided by the experimenter. These differences in initial preference for position versus visual aspects of the stimuli have been documented in several other learning situations (Gerjuoy & Winters, 1968).

A reverse type of learning set, dubbed *failure set* by Zeaman and House (1963), is of particular importance for retarded children, who meet failure often in their everyday lives. (See Chapter 9.) In any type of learning situation, the one most fundamental requirement, basic to all others, is that the child's earliest attempts to succeed be

---

[6] Although Harter concluded that MA and IQ independently contributed to learning-set formation and that CA was irrelevant, see Kappauf (1973) for a reinterpretation.

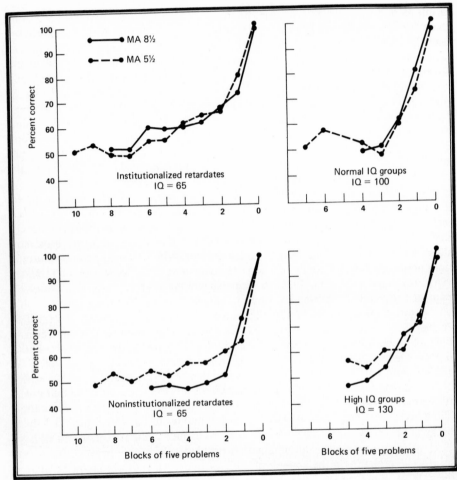

Fig. 13-3 Backward learning curves of the percentage of correct responses on trials 2, 3, and 4 over successive blocks of five learning-set problems preceding criterion (consistently successful) block. *(From Harter, 1967, p. 133)*

positively reinforced. Otherwise, not only may these early approximations be extinguished (see Chapter 15), but the child may readily develop an aversion to the situation and an expectation of failure. Children who perform for many trials without solving a difficult problem are sometimes then unable to solve easier problems which they could have mastered rapidly before the failure experience. Results of this type suggest strongly that learning tasks should be presented in an easy-to-hard sequence. The child's solving an easy problem first will permit crucial reinforcement of his initial attempts as well as some nonspecific transfer to subsequent problems. If the hard problem is given first, however, the effects of failure may make it difficult to return to the easy-to-hard sequence, as even the easy problem may have become temporarily insoluble.

Problem Solving: Hypothesis Testing

In this section we will describe a number of paradigms which have been investigated recently with retarded subjects. Although the number of experiments is rather small, the data indicate some relatively marked and extremely interesting deficiencies.

According to some theorists (e.g., Restle, 1962; Levine, 1966), a discrimination-learning problem can be regarded as a problem involving a number of hypotheses, only one of which is correct. For example, if the only two dimensions along which the stimuli differ are color and position, each with two values, the four (2 × 2) hypotheses would be the following: red is correct, blue is correct, left is correct, right is correct. If the child is given feedback on each trial, eventually he can exclude all but one hypothesis, the correct one. He can solve the problem after two trials, but only if he has attended to both dimensions on the first trial and has remembered which hypotheses were eliminated on that trial.[7]

Question Asking   The child may be told at the outset the possible solutions to a problem and required to select the information he wants by asking a series of questions, as in the familiar Twenty Questions game. He might be shown a matrix containing sixteen pictures and told to discover as quickly as possible the picture of which the experimenter is thinking. He may ask any "yes-no" questions he wants. Obviously each question should be chosen to eliminate as many alternatives as possible. Suppose, for example, the sixteen pictures consist of four men, four women, four automobiles, and four airplanes. An optimal starting question would be, "Is it a person?" Whatever the answer, eight alternatives are eliminated. Questions of this type, which refer to more than one alternative, are called *constraint-seeking* questions, as contrasted with *hypothesis-testing* questions which refer only to an individual item.[8] Using an optimal strategy, it is possible to solve a sixteen-picture problem in exactly four questions. Asking a series of hypothesis-testing questions will require, on the average, eight questions, assuming that the child does not forget an earlier question and re-ask it. Young and/or retarded children tend to do poorly on this type of task because they ask hypothesis-testing questions. Indeed, the Twenty Questions task is sufficiently difficult that even college students under favorable conditions do not perform perfectly (Eimas, 1970). Choosing an informative question requires some foresight or planning and anticipating the utility of the question. Too, once the relevant information has been obtained, the child may or may not be able to use it to infer the correct answer.

To digress slightly at this point, it is interesting to note that on the Twenty Questions task, there are clear differences between impulsive and reflective children. (See Chapter 11.) Impulsive children tend to give quick, frequently incorrect answers, whereas reflective children respond more slowly and more accurately (Kagan, 1965). Their patterns are what might be expected on the basis of S. H. White's (1965) *temporal stacking* hypothesis. White has proposed that different types of responses occupy different response-time zones. Lower-level, specific stimulus-response linkages are

---

[7] Viewed in this way, it becomes clear that memory processes play an important role in discrimination-learning problems. Difficulties with the memory portion of the task are typical of young normal children (Eimas, 1970). Also reflecting the importance of memorial processes in retarded children, an extension of Zeaman and House's original theory, called Attention-Retention Theory (Fisher & Zeaman, 1973) is concerned with what have traditionally been called "memory processes."

[8] The discerning reader will note similarities between this contrast and Piaget's distinction between preoperational (intuitive) and concrete operations (systematic) functions. (See Chap. 12.)

readily available and emitted quickly, whereas more complex cognitive responses become available only later. As a consequence, mature responding requires that the child inhibit the initial response, and reflective children, who presumably do inhibit these first-available responses, do well on question-asking tasks. White argues that the ability to inhibit lower-level responses is a process which develops progressively in children, although Heal and Johnson (1970) have summarized data which suggest that retarded individuals have a marked inhibitory deficit. Simply requiring young nonretarded children to slow down their responses elicits better question-asking performance (Olson, 1966). Effective classroom procedures for modifying impulsivity in young, mildly retarded children have been developed by Duckworth, Ragland, Sommerfeld, and Wyne (1974).

Pattern Matching   The classic Twenty Questions task has some obvious disadvantages for work with retarded subjects, since the task is quite difficult and requires the child to verbalize his questions. Variations (Neimark & Lewis, 1967; Olson, 1966) can be made relatively simple and can avoid oral questions. Spitz and Nadler (1974), using the Neimark-Lewis type of task, have found that mildly retarded adolescents are markedly poorer at asking informative questions than are normal children of the same MA. A sample of the type of problem used by Spitz and Nadler (1974) is shown in Figure 13-4. The child is shown the bird (B) and dog (D) patterns, but the openings in the cat (C) figure are covered. By moving the levers covering the C pattern openings, the child is to determine whether the pattern in the C figure matches the B or D pattern. Interest here centers about the particular openings the child chooses to "interrogate." In the example shown in Figure 13-4, there are one informative choice (bottom lever) and two uninformative choices. Spitz and Nadler used a learning-set proce-

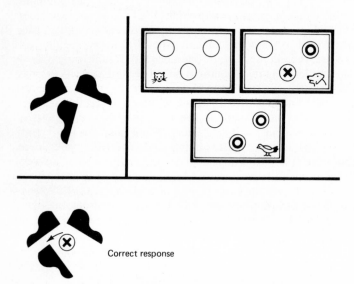

Correct response

Fig. 13-4 The upper section shows an example of a one-bit problem. Only the lower lever must be interrogated to discover which pattern is correct. The lower section shows the lever in the correct response position, identifying the B pattern. *(From Spitz & Nadler, 1974, p. 405)*

dure, giving each child a series of problems with few trials per problem. In the example problem, called a "one-bit problem," a single choice is sufficient if the correct opening is interrogated. Spitz and Nadler found a dramatic difference between normal and retarded children on these simple one-bit problems, many of the retarded children being unable to master them, much less the more difficult two-bit problems. Similar results have been reported by Gruen and Korte (1973), who compared equal-MA groups of normal and retarded children. On a three-bit task, their retarded subjects simply gave random responses. Spitz and Nadler's data indicate that the trouble does not stem from an inability to use information once it is available, but rather from an inability to ask the correct question originally. Once retarded subjects uncovered the correct opening, they were able to identify the correct pattern.

McKinney (1972) investigated training a number of information-gathering strategies in mildly retarded children. The concept-identification task he employed is similar in principle to the ones discussed above. McKinney found that training can indeed be effective in improving performance but that the best results are obtained when the strategy is suitable in difficulty level for the child's stage of development.

To summarize, retarded subjects perform poorly in these tasks, failing to plan a strategy or course of action prior to making a response, with a resulting dramatic impairment in problem-solving efficiency. Training can sometimes remedy the difficulty to some extent, but there are few data yet available on its long-term effects or on generalization to other problems.

Paired-Associates Learning: Mediational Strategies

In the typical paired-associates task, the subject is shown a series of pairs of stimuli such as three-dimensional objects, pictures, or words. One of each pair is designated the stimulus item and the other the response item. On the first trial, the subject sees both items, but on succeeding trials he is shown the stimulus item first and is asked to indicate the response item before it is shown. The study of paired-associates learning has a long history and can serve as an analogue for many familiar tasks such as vocabulary learning, learning a foreign language, attaching names to faces, and generally forming associations or connections among items.

Although there have been many paired-associates studies with retarded individuals, we will restrict our attention to those addressed to mediational processes which consist of active, usually covert, strategies which people employ to establish a connection between the stimuli. A variety of elaborative strategies are typically employed by normal children above the age of five or so. (Kendler, 1963). Since the mid-1960s, interest in mediational processes in paired-associates learning has increased dramatically.[9] It has become clear that learning associations between pairs of items (e.g., chicken and flag) is much easier if the items are embedded in a meaningful sentence (e.g., "The chicken is carrying the flag.") This is an example of an elaborative strategy in which information is added to facilitate learning.

Some of the early emphasis on mediational processes in the retarded stems from Luria's (1961) hypothesis that retarded children are deficient in the use of language systems to regulate, or mediate, complex behavior. (See Chapter 1.) Many studies have therefore asked whether young and retarded children can and do effectively mediate. Another series of questions has had to do with the relative effectiveness of verbal as

---

[9] Goulet (1968) has reviewed studies with retarded subjects. A more detailed review of the mediation literature can be found in Borkowski and Wanschura (1974).

opposed to visual-imaginal elaborations. Some theorists such as Piaget have assumed that, with development, there are fundamental changes in the form of the internal representation of events. Bruner (1966) argues that there is a change from ikonic (visual or imaginal) to symbolic (linguistic) representation. Therefore, we might expect younger children and retarded persons to perform better with visual, as opposed to verbal elaborations, whereas older children should do better with verbal elaborations.

With regard to the first question, it appears that retarded children can indeed benefit from elaborative techniques to increase mediation, although the amount of intervention required to induce them to use the techniques depends upon developmental level. The younger the child, the more explicitly he must be prompted before he employs a mediational strategy (Rohwer, 1973). Unlike college students, who spontaneously employ elaborative strategies (Bugelski, 1962), young children must be provided with numerous examples and told exactly what to do. Instructions to use mediators, either sentences or interacting images, can also facilitate performance in retarded subjects. For example, Jensen and Rohwer (1963) investigated paired-associates learning in retarded adults under two conditions. Control subjects were given only the standard treatment, but in the mediational condition, the experimenter provided a sentence containing both stimulus and response items. Subjects in the second group learned faster than those in the first, indicating that they were able to use the mediators effectively once they were provided.

In a number of other experiments (e.g., Milgram & Riedel, 1969), the stimulus and response items have been linked by visual images such as a picture of a chicken carrying a flag. The use of such interactive pictures leads to faster learning than presenting the pictures side by side. With respect to the comparison of visual (imagery) and verbal strategies, however, predictions based on the reasoning of Piaget and Bruner do not apparently hold true. Visual elaborative techniques are indeed effective with retarded subjects, but the learning rate is no greater, and is sometimes less, than if a mediating sentence is provided.

These experiments demonstrate that the poorer performance of retarded subjects is not due to an inability to use mediators, but rather due to a failure habitually to produce them. (See Chapter 14.) Why the control subjects failed to produce their own mediators is a critical and important question to which the answer is not yet clear. The simplest explanation is that they do not think of using any type of strategy, elaborative or otherwise, when faced with a learning task. Alternatively they may be unable to provide effective mediators when left to their own devices.

In several experiments, normal and retarded children and adults have been explicitly instructed to generate their own mediators. Generally, the quality of the mediators they produce is higher for normal than for retarded children (Martin, Boersma, & Bulgarella, 1968; Milgram & Riedel, 1969). Surprisingly, however, quality ratings are not correlated with learning efficiency, and therefore the generation of poor mediators is not clearly implicated as the primary cause of the deficiency. In fact, retarded subjects instructed to generate mediators perform as well as others for whom better-quality mediators are supplied by the experimenter (Gordon & Baumeister, 1971; MacMillan, 1972).

The evidence indicates, then, that retarded subjects can employ elaborative strategies but simply do not think to use them. Data which lend support to this interpretation come from experiments involving tests for transfer of the strategy after it has been trained. (See Borkowski & Wanschura, 1974.) Given that, after instruction, the subject has employed the strategy and improved his performance, what happens when the experimenter reintroduces the task without specific instructions to continue using the strategy? Frequently, the subject reverts to nonstrategic behavior. This is particularly likely for retarded subjects of low IQ. The abandonment of the strategy even after it has been explicitly trained supports the idea that poor performance in untrained subjects is due to a failure to employ the strategy rather than to an ineffective ability to generate mediators.

Failure to observe long-lasting effects of training is somewhat discouraging. Transfer has, however, been obtained in some instances in which training has been both extensive and consistent (Borkowski & Wanschura, 1974). Turner and Thurlow (1973), for example, tested for transfer after subjects had received experimenter-supplied mediators on either one or two training lists. Subjects who had received the more extensive training on two lists showed some transfer, but those given training on only one list did not. With regard to consistency of training, Wanschura and Borkowski (1974) gave retarded children a series of paired-associates training lists. In one group, mediators were provided for all items (100 percent aid); in a second, mediators were supplied for half the items on each list (50 percent aid); and in the third, control, condition, no mediators were provided at all. Two weeks later, the 100 percent aid group showed some evidence of transfer of the mediational strategy, whereas the 50 percent aid group did not. The magnitude of the transfer was, however, very small.

Using an entirely different kind of approach, D. M. Ross and her associates have presented more encouraging evidence that young, mildly retarded subjects can indeed learn to use mediational strategies in paired-associates tasks and can retain a significant portion of their gains for at least a week. Using a story and table-game procedure in fifteen sessions spread over five weeks, D. M. Ross and S. A. Ross (1973b) obtained evidence of retention of the previously formulated mediators over a one-week post-training period. In another study (Ross, Ross, & Downing, 1973), they found that mediational skills gained through the story and table-game procedures could be gained by young, mildly retarded children as effectively by observing a model as through direct involvement. With a different procedure, embedding the mediational "lessons" in a special primary music program, Ross (1971) had earlier demonstrated considerable transfer of mediational training as well as retention over a one-week period of both verbal and nonverbal paired-associates learning.

Thus, the evidence suggests that under standard conditions, retarded children usually perform poorly on paired-associates tasks. Their performance can be facilitated, however, by the experimenter's providing verbal or visual mediators or instructing the subjects to do so for themselves. The effectiveness of such procedures is enhanced, however, when a variety of approaches are used over a number of sessions in a gamelike atmosphere, permitting a significantly greater amount of generalization than when the training is confined to a single type of task.

SUMMARY

In this chapter we have reviewed a number of studies of learning in retarded subjects which, taken together, reveal a rather consistent picture. On the one hand, retarded subjects tend not to be alert to cues already available which would help them solve problems. They do not readily attend to the relevant dimensions in a discrimination-learning problem (unless the relevant dimension is the position of the stimuli); they do not tend to ask strategic questions to gain information they need in a Twenty Question or pattern-matching task; and in the formation of learning sets they often fail to take into account the outcome of a previous trial. They are, then, less sensitive to precise cues in the environment, perhaps because their perceptions are less organized or systematic so that they are beset by useless "noise" in the situation, perhaps because they fail to grasp the relevance of the information available or for some other reason. We have also seen that retarded subjects are less prone to employ active strategies such as the invention of mediational sentences or images, even though they are capable of doing so, remaining instead rather passive. Training in all these aspects of learning behavior can be effective, but generalization of effects is disappointingly limited. As we shall see in the next chapter, this general picture in learning tasks is consistent with what has been discovered in the area of memory as well.

14

Memory Processes in the Mentally Retarded

The importance of memory, the storing and retrieving of learned material, is obvious. Memory of previous events is required if one is to profit from past experience. Information which has been learned is not very useful unless it can later be recalled and in fact recalled at precisely the time it is needed. An intelligent person may be thought of as one who has a well-developed knowledge system and who is capable of retrieving relevant items of knowledge when a problem is presented.

Memory items have been included in almost every comprehensive individual intelligence test since the beginning of the testing movement. At age twenty months on the Bayley Mental Scale of Infant Development, the baby is required to recall, after a short delay, under which of two cups a toy has been hidden, and a similar three-choice item is placed at age two years on the Stanford-Binet. Another common item on both Stanford-Binet and Wechsler tests requires the individual to reproduce a series of spoken digits, sometimes in the order presented and sometimes in reverse order. Such items were originally included both because memory was recognized as a component of intelligence and because they correlated well with other test items, but in fact the true significance of memorial processes was not appreciated until well into the 1960s. Indeed, memory was considered by many psychologists to be an isolated, circumscribed facet of behavior. Reports of *idiot savants,* markedly retarded except for islands of astounding memorial skills, were taken as proof that memory was somehow in-

This chapter was written with the collaboration of Joseph C. Campione.

dependent of and different from the problem-solving abilities ordinarily considered intelligent.

As a consequence, much of the early research with memory in normal and retarded children lacked systematization or theoretical guidance. Focusing mainly on a rather superficial measure, the number of items which could be recalled, the studies did indicate that retarded children generally recalled somewhat fewer words or numbers than did normal persons, but they did little to indicate why this might be the case.

In the early 1960s, a substantially increased interest in memory theory began to emerge. Whereas previously memory had been regarded as a necessary, but rather uninteresting, component of learning, a number of theorists began to reverse the importance of these processes and to regard memory as indeed the essence of learning. Today, this area of research is extremely active, and knowledge about memory in retarded subjects has increased dramatically. The focus has shifted away from a concentration on the product, the number of items recalled, to a concentration on process, the activities of the subject as he strives to remember. There is a growing understanding of the ways in which memorial processes develop in normal and retarded children and of the active methods they can employ to achieve success and efficiency.

THEORIES CONCERNING MEMORY

Stages of Memory

At the simplest level, memory can be conceived as including three stages: encoding, storage, and retrieval. *Encoding* refers to the acquisition of the original input, the registration of experience through sensory receptors, and its initial coding by the central nervous system. *Storage* involves holding information which has been encoded; information in storage has been retained or learned. *Retrieval* refers to finding or obtaining access to material which has been stored, dredging it up so that it may be put to use.

It early became apparent that the human mind was much more than a passive acceptor of information, but rather was actively involved. Broadbent (1957), for example, noted the importance of attention, which depended not only upon the characteristics of the stimuli (it is difficult to avoid noticing a thunderstorm), but also upon the selectivity which the subject exerts (as illustrated by the filtering one engages in to follow a single conversation at a noisy party).

The Atkinson-Shiffrin Model

Since the 1960s, a number of theories or models have been proposed which take into account the several stages of the memory-learning process and the active role of the memorizer. One of the most popular and useful is that proposed by Atkinson and Shiffrin (1968). In the Atkinson-Shiffrin model, shown schematically in Figure 14-1, information is assumed to pass through a series of "boxes" or "stores" before it can be committed to permanent memory. Incoming information comes first into a *sensory store,* which features a large capacity but from which information is very rapidly lost, in perhaps a quarter-second. The sensory store registers the immediate impact of the experience, but for just a fleeting instant. Only that information to which the subject attends passes into the next box, a *short-term* store (STS), where a small amount of information can remain for a relatively short time (up to about thirty seconds) before being lost through fading or decay, unless there is a deliberate attempt to maintain it

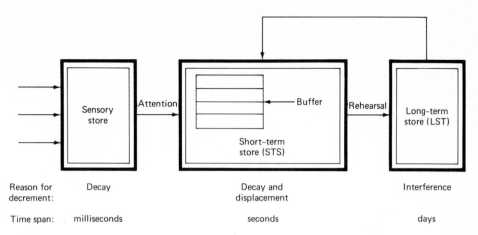

Fig. 14-1 The Atkinson-Shiffrin model. *(From Mussen & Rosenzweig, 1973, p. 524)*

at this level. Rehearsal is a frequent strategy employed to retain information in STS. One usually looks up a telephone number and repeats it over and over to one's self until, having dialed, one hears a ringing signal. If the operator intercepts to ask for the number wanted, the caller may have to look it up all over again.

According to the Atkinson-Shiffrin model, the STS contains a buffer mechanism capable of handling only a few items of information. It is rather like a file box with a few slots which are quickly filled. There is constant turnover in the material being retained in the buffer, as some information passes into the *long-term store* (LTS), some is displaced by subsequent items attended to, and some simply decays because the person ceases to rehearse it.

Although information resides in STS, it is continuously transferred to LTS. The longer the information remains in STS and/or the better it fits in with material already in LTS, the more likely it is to be transferred to LTS and remembered permanently. Information in the LTS is, then, capable of influencing what is remembered. If the STS buffer is like a little file box, the LTS is more like a huge filing cabinet, organized and cross-referenced in complex ways. Transfer from STS is facilitated by a good filing system in LTS, which provides a ready niche into which the information may easily slip. This process points up the importance of coding processes which are brought to bear on the incoming information, so that it can readily be tagged and related to the meaningful organization existing in LTS.

In the Atkinson-Shiffrin model, there is no provision for true forgetting or erasing of information in the LTS. Whether or not the material is retrievable, however, is a different matter. Like the misplaced book in the stacks of a library, it may be stored, potentially *available,* but not easily located and therefore not *accessible.* Whether the subject is able to call up from LTS a bit of stored information depends on a number of factors. Among these are the effectiveness of the coding system under which it was stored (which is in turn dependent to some degree upon the conditions under which the material was learned and also the effectiveness of the cross-referencing system in the LTS) and the appropriateness of the environmental conditions under which the subject tries to remember, such as the form of the question asked or the number of clues provided (Tulving & Pearlstone, 1966).

To summarize, the system which processes information is thought to include a sensory register, a short-term store which includes a buffer mechanism, and a long-term store. Human beings are active memorizers, not just passive recipients of information. Their activities while they are attempting to remember, past experiences, and organizational propensities all affect the way in which they are able to store and retrieve material.

The Craik-Lockhart Model

A more recent formulation has been proposed by Craik and Lockhart (1972) who, like Atkinson and Shiffrin, see human beings as actively attempting to find ways of manipulating information to maximize retention. Abandoning the multistore model, Craik and Lockhart suggest that incoming information is subjected to varying *levels of analysis.* The deeper the level of analysis, the more persistent the memories. The most superficial and least durable level involves the simple physical or sensory features of the experience and is therefore highly dependent on the properties of the stimulus. Successively deeper levels of analysis include attaching a name, recognizing a pattern, or extracting meaning from the stimulus. The subject may choose to rehearse the material at a superficial level or to pursue any of a variety of other ways of handling it, such as relating the new information to previously learned information or using one of the elaborational mediation techniques discussed in Chapter 13. The learner is in charge, he is actively at work processing material, and the durability of the learning varies according to the level of analysis he pursues.

These two models, though prominent, by no means exhaust the theoretical formulations which investigators have developed in recent years. They illustrate the complete faceabout which many theorists have made. As one can see, these "memory" models might serve equally well as "learning" models. Although there are associational elements in all of the recent theories, there is also an emphasis on rational and organizational modes of operation which are quite unlike the stimulus-response theories introduced in Chapter 13 and the beginning of Chapter 15.

WHAT IS DEFICIENT IN THE MENTALLY RETARDED MEMORIZER?

Memory is an area in which retarded individuals have long been regarded as deficient, but the explanations seeking to account for this deficiency have varied widely. Some have postulated a defect in biological makeup, whereas others have looked for ways in which they make poor use of essentially intact equipment. The distinction can be likened to that between hardware and software in the computer field. Hardware refers to the basic, built-in capabilities of the computer system; software refers to the manner and content of the programming. The theories have not looked for individual differences within mentally retarded populations, although there is every reason to believe that such differences exist. In Chapter 2, we discussed the existence of two major groups among the mentally retarded. One group seems to represent the lower end of the normal distribution, persons in whom an unlucky set of circumstances and probably an unlucky selection of genes produce slow development, but in whom there are no major discernible biological defects. The "hardware" of this group, mainly found among the mildly retarded, should resemble that of a normal group, although the schedule of development is delayed and final attainment level reduced. The second group has sustained damage to its "hardware" from some overriding genetic defect or trauma and therefore differs qualitatively from a normal group. The second group should include a variety of biological defects, since the type, degree, and timing of damage varies considerably. (See Chapter 11.)

With few exceptions, learning and memory theorists have ignored the existence of these two groups. Admittedly, it is difficult if not impossible to determine to which group many individuals belong, and there is considerable overlap between them. Be that as it may, the theoretical distinction remains, as Zigler (1967) pointed out in an article distinguishing *defect* and *developmental* difference theories. Yet one must recognize that the theorists tend not to make the distinction, and few investigators have attempted to differentiate among their subjects. The reader should, however, be aware that the probability exists that in any heterogeneous group of retarded persons there exists a variety of both "hardware" and "software" deficiencies.

Structure versus Control Deficiencies

An important distinction among the theories attempting to explain the problems encountered by the mentally retarded, considered as a more-or-less homogeneous group, is that between *structural* and *control* features of memory processes.

Structural Features: "Hardware" Some aspects of a system are considered fixed and unchangeable, and it is in terms of such structural differences that many theorists have tried to specify a locus of the deficiencies in retarded individuals. Often it has been assumed that the underlying mechanisms are neurological in nature. Structural deficiencies by their very nature are not directly modifiable by training.

Most of the structural-deficiency theories have had to do with what we now call the STS, rather than the LTS, a notion put forth first in different terms by Galton (1887). Ellis (1963), although he has since modified his view (e.g., Ellis, 1970), once postulated that the major memory deficiency in mentally retarded persons lay in lowered central nervous system integrity which results in faster loss from STS by retarded children than by normal children of the same age. He suggested that the basis for normal STS function was a brief reverberatory trace or circuit, which he termed "stimulus trace." The postulated stimulus trace ordinarily decays very quickly, but while it persists it may produce changes in the brain which result in storage of information. He suggested that in the mentally retarded, the stimulus trace is both shortened in duration and lessened in intensity, with consequent deficits in learning and retention.

Another theorist postulating structural deficiencies in mentally retarded individuals is Spitz (1963), who has marshalled evidence to indict sluggishness, or torpidity, of cortical cells. If it requires a longer time to induce changes in the electrical, chemical, and physical condition of stimulated cortical cells in mentally retarded persons, they should learn and remember less than normal individuals given the same amount of stimulation and/or effort. Spitz further maintains that once such changes have been introduced, they tend to persist and to be resistant to new information input. The cortical function of the retarded individuals in this formulation is sluggish and inflexible.

A third possible structural deficiency notion has to do with the capacity of the STS buffer. Spitz (1973a) has presented evidence that the mature mildly retarded individual can remember only about four or five bits or chunks of information at once, whereas the typical mature normal individual can remember about seven. One might assume that in mentally retarded individuals, the buffer system's "little file box" has fewer slots than in normal individuals, thus reducing the amount of information which can be processed.

These three examples of structural-deficiency hypotheses have in common a postulation of an underlying, unchangeable property of the central nervous system. Although it might be possible to teach a retarded child indirect means of compensating for such a deficiency just as one can teach a blind child to read through his fingers, it should be impossible to change the system directly, just as it is impossible to restore sight to a child whose optic nerves have been destroyed.

Control Processes: "Software"   Control processes, optional components of the memory system, consist of those activities instigated by the subject for the purpose of remembering. These activities, or strategies, can be extremely varied, and range from the simple to the sophisticated.[1] Rehearsal, grouping of bits of information, and use of elaborative mediators are all examples of control processes which can enhance retention.

Control processes, being optional or voluntary, are assumed to be amenable to training procedures. It is clear that normal and mentally retarded children can be taught to employ a rehearsal strategy, for example, although they may not continue to employ this strategy after the prompting has ceased. Theoretically, then, if a deficiency is identified as dependent on the use of a control process, it should be modifiable, whereas a structural deficiency should not. In practice, the distinction lies in the ease with which improvement can be brought about through training.

As we have seen, contemporary memory theories emphasize the use of control processes. The use of mnemonic strategies is quite uncommon in preschool children but increases dramatically during the elementary school years. Eventually, the children have at their disposal a broad repertoire of devices from which they can choose as the demands of the situation dictate. During the elementary school period, children also become more capable of distinguishing the features of a task which suggest that one strategy should be more appropriate than another (Hagen, Jongeward & Kail, 1975).

Production versus Mediation Deficiencies

A distinction very similar to that between structural features and control processes is the one drawn between production and mediation deficiencies (Flavell, 1970; Maccoby, 1964). The practical distinction again lies in the ability of the subject to profit from training. As with a structural deficiency, a *mediation* deficiency is said to occur when a subject is unable to use a mediational strategy even when instructed to do so. A *production* deficiency, on the other hand, involves the subject's failure to produce or employ a strategy or a control process, even though he is capable of producing and using it.

In an example drawn from the previous chapter, the failure of retarded subjects to use elaborative strategies to facilitate paired-associates learning stems from production deficiencies. When the elaboration is supplied for the children or when they are instructed to invent one, their performance markedly improves. Many types of learning and memory deficits in mentally retarded individuals appear to be production deficiencies. Brown (1974b) has argued that differences between normal and retarded

---

[1] See Yates (1966) for a discussion of some mnemonic techniques.

subjects are obtained mainly when some active strategy is required. Retarded subjects tend to remain relatively passive in response to generalized instructions to remember. When specific strategies are pointed out, their performance improves, although it may not reach the level of normal subjects. As we shall see, "pure" memory tasks, where no active mnemonic strategy appears to be required, do not tend to differentiate between groups of normal and moderately retarded children.

SPECIFIC AREAS OF RESEARCH

In the remainder of this chapter, we will review some of the kinds of memory tasks on which normal and retarded children have been compared. In most areas, there is a marked performance differential, but in some there is not. Where differences exist, the question of production versus mediation deficiency must be considered as well as the results of specific training or intervention. Finally, we shall deal with the limitations of specific training and indicate some newer areas of research which provide further insights into the nature of the memory deficits in the mentally retarded.

Much of the research to be described will involve short-term memory tasks which require the use of fairly complex rehearsal strategies. Most theoretical formulations concerned with deficits in retarded groups have assumed that the primary locus of difficulty is in short-term rather than in long-term memory. Furthermore, much of the most careful research has involved short-term memory, and the theoretical development is detailed and highly developed. The results obtained with rehearsal training have also proved to be reasonably representative of the general patterns obtained with other strategies.

The Use of Rehearsal

As we have seen, rehearsal plays a crucial role in memory. Without it, material may be quickly lost from STS. In most normal children, spontaneous rehearsal is clearly evident by third grade (Frank & Rabinovitch, 1974). Available research data indicate that retarded subjects do not tend spontaneously to rehearse in situations which call for rehearsal, and thereby they lose a great deal of information which they are capable of remembering.

When normal adults are given the task of remembering a series of visual or auditory stimuli such as digits, words, or pictures, they show a typical bowed serial-position curve. Performance is good on the final items presented, a so-called recency effect, and on the initial item or items presented, a so-called primacy effect, with performance poorest on the middle items. Recall in such experiments probably involves retrieval from both STS and LTS. Retrieval of the final items is high because these terminal items have not yet faded from STS. Recall of initial items, on the other hand, is due to the use of rehearsal processes which have resulted in more of these items having been transferred to LTS (Atkinson & Shiffrin, 1968; Waugh & Norman, 1965). The typical rehearsal strategy used by older children and normal adults can be characterized as *cumulative rehearsal.* When new items are added, the subject rehearses both the current item and the previous one(s), such as [4], then [4,1;4,1], then [4,1,7; 4,1,7], etc. Obviously this process cannot be extended endlessly, and we will return to this issue later.

Failure to Rehearse   Ellis (1970) investigated the performance of retarded adolescents on a probe serial-recall task. Briefly, the subject sat facing a panel containing a horizontal array of windows. On each trial, he saw a series of digits exposed one at a time beginning in the left-hand window. After the items were presented, a probe digit was shown and the subject was asked to indicate the window in which that digit had appeared.[2] Ellis found that on this task, his retarded subjects showed a strong recency effect and a much reduced primacy effect. He inferred that one of the factors decreasing the primacy effect was the failure spontaneously to adopt a rehearsal strategy. He also discovered other evidence which supported this reasoning. For example, for normal adults, increasing the time between successive digits facilitates performance because it allows more time to rehearse previous items. Ellis found that an increase in time between items did not enhance performance of retarded subjects, suggesting that they did not use the time to rehearse the items.

Ellis' conclusion here differs from the short-term learning deficit which he had proposed in 1963. The inference of a rehearsal deficit in the memory processes of retarded persons suggests not a structural limitation but a failure to employ a control process. If so, training retarded subjects to rehearse should reduce if not eliminate the difference between their performance and that of normal subjects. Moreover, preventing normal adults from rehearsing should result in performance resembling that of the retarded. Such results have been obtained, and we will briefly outline some relevant experiments.

Training Rehearsal in Retarded Subjects and Preventing It in Normal Subjects   Brown, Campione, Bray, and Wilcox (1973) used a keeping-track task on each trial of which subjects were shown four pictures, each representing a different category (e.g., animals, foods, clothing, vehicles). One category contained two items, two contained four items, and one contained six. In an apparatus like that used by Ellis, the subjects were shown an exemplar of each category, one at a time. They were then given a category and asked to recall which items from it they had just seen. The focus of interest was the influence on performance, if any, exerted by the number of items in the categories. If a subject rehearses the items as they are presented, he can simply refer to the set of four items on the current trial to answer the probe. If he does not rehearse, he is forced to choose among the items in the probed category, and, in that case, accuracy should be greater when the category has only two, as opposed to four or six items. Consistent with the rehearsal-deficit notion, the performance of moderately retarded subjects deteriorated as the number of items increased (Brown, 1972a), whereas with normal adults, such was not the case (Yntema & Meuser, 1962).

Brown et al. (1973) conducted a pair of training experiments. In the first, one group of moderately retarded subjects was given explicit rehearsal training and the other served as an untrained control group. As can be seen in Figure 14-2, the rehearsal (trained) subjects performed much better than did the nonrehearsal (untrained) subjects, and the patterns were dramatically different. The level of accuracy for the rehearsal subjects was independent of the number of items in the probed category but the performance of the nonrehearsal subjects deteriorated as the number of items increased. This result indicates, of course, that training retarded subjects to rehearse leads to much improved performance and also suggests that their difficulty in remembering represents a production deficiency, the failure spontaneously to employ rehearsal.

[2] Probe techniques are employed to overcome the "output interference" which occurs if a subject is asked to recall all the items in a list and forgets some during the process of recall.

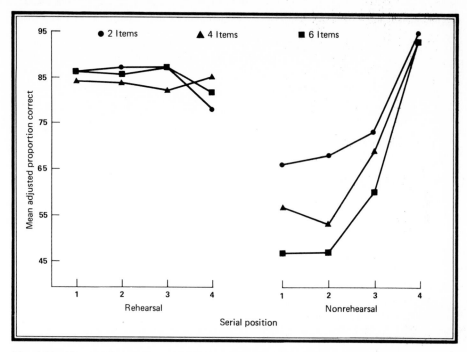

Fig. 14-2 The mean adjusted proportion of correct scores for the retarded subjects in the rehearsal and nonrehearsal conditions as a function of number of items and serial position. *(From Brown, Campione, Bray, & Wilcox, 1973, p. 126)*

Going one step further, if the differences originally obtained in normal and retarded subjects were primarily because of differences in the use of rehearsal, then preventing normal adolescents from rehearsing should result in both poorer overall accuracy and patterns similar to those obtained with untrained retarded subjects. In the second experiment reported by Brown et al., normal junior high school students were divided into two groups, one (free strategy) allowed to perform without restrictions and a second (repetition) prevented from using a cumulative rehearsal strategy. The results of this experiment are shown in Figure 14-3. The free-strategy group performed well, and the pattern is the same as that of the rehearsal-trained retarded subjects, i.e., performance is constant across category size. The repetition subjects, conversely, performed like untrained (nonrehearsal) retarded subjects with poorer performance and accuracy levels varying with the number of items in the probed category. Thus, retarded persons can be trained to perform like normal adolescents, and normal adolescents can be induced to perform like retarded persons.

Although improvement in the performance of mentally retarded persons is encouraging for both theory and application, the situation is more complex than indicated thus far. Although it is relatively easy to rehearse a small number of items, what happens when the series contains, say, nine items? Belmont and Butterfield (1969) have investigated performance in such a situation, using the same type of task as did Ellis (1970). The main modification was to allow subjects to determine for themselves when they were ready to view the next item in the series. Normal adults show patterns

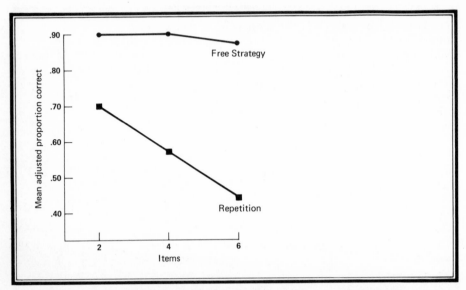

Fig. 14-3 The mean adjusted proportion of correct responses for normal subjects as a function of number of items. *(From Brown, Campione, Bray, & Wilcox, 1973, p. 128)*

of pauses between successive items. Generally, the first six items are rehearsed in groups of three, the last three items are viewed briefly, and the question light is hit immediately with the expectation that the last three items can be remembered without additional processing if the interval is short enough. With this paradigm, the pattern of pauses reflects the subject's strategy for dealing with incoming material. Retarded individuals in this situation fail to show pause patterns which reflect the use of active strategies; their pause times are the same following each item.

Belmont and Butterfield (1971) found, though, that retarded subjects can be trained to use the appropriate strategy, and that when they are so trained, their performance improves dramatically. The task employed by Belmont and Butterfield is a more difficult one than that of Brown et al. (1973); although performance of retarded subjects improves with rehearsal training, it does not reach normal adult levels.

An excellent paper by Butterfield, Wambold, and Belmont (1973) indicates both why this may be true and why "simple" rehearsal is an extremely complex cognitive process. In a series of experiments designed to improve short-term memory performance, Butterfield et al. used a six-item list of letters. Subjects were instructed to look at the first three items, one at a time, then to pause to rehearse them cumulatively (active memory), to look quickly at the final three items (passive memory), and then rapidly to expose the probe stimulus. This was the *acquisition* strategy. The subject was then faced with the task of *retrieving* the stored information. The optimal retrieval strategy is to search through passive memory first to see if the probe item was in one of the last three positions. If active memory, containing the first three items, is searched first, and if the item looked for is not found, the remaining information will have faded from the passive memory system.

Butterfield et al. (1973) conducted a series of three experiments in which they trained subjects more and more explicitly in the process involved. In the first study, they trained the 3-3 acquisition strategy. They found that their retarded subjects performed much better (64 percent trials correct) than before training (36 percent correct), that they retained the strategy one week later, but that after two weeks they had regressed to pretraining levels. The correspondence between strategy usage and recall accuracy was not, however, exceptionally close. Getting the material into memory correctly did not guarantee getting it out correctly. In a second experiment the retrieval portion of the process was trained. When subjects were explicitly instructed to search the last three items first, average performance improved to 77 percent correct. In a final experiment, with still more explicit training of the retrieval strategy, performance rose to 82 percent correct. The high levels of performance obtained in the last experiment are the same as those of nonretarded adolescents given 3-3 training by Belmont and Butterfield (1971).

By way of summary, the original notion of a defective short-term memory (Ellis, 1963) has been replaced by the notion of a deficiency in the use of spontaneous rehearsal processes, a deficiency which involves both acquisition and retrieval strategies. Retarded individuals appear to use neither spontaneously, although they can be trained to do so. Several major problems are also indicated. First, training leads to performance which is often far from perfect and the effects of training typically dissipate rather rapidly with time. This problem can probably be overcome by very extensive training or overlearning (Brown, Campione, & Murphy, 1974). Second, and of equal importance, simply training the various components does not guarantee that they will be joined together properly unless the overall sequence itself is explicitly trained. "They do not properly sequence rehearsal and essential non-rehearsal learning techniques, and they neither intercoordinate multiple retrieval strategies nor coordinate these retrieval strategies with strategies of acquisition" (Butterfield et al., 1973, p. 667). This process of sequencing and coordinating various processes is referred to as *executive control,* a topic to which we shall return.

Organization

Often, when one is faced with the task of remembering, the amount of material is simply too much to deal with. However, the limit to the amount of information one can recall seems to be in the number of chunks, or bundles, of information rather than in the amount of information per se (Miller, 1956). It is no harder to remember six information-rich chunks than six chunks which contain relatively little information. By organizing the incoming information according to some rule or structure, we can increase the information value (e.g., number of items) of each chunk, thereby increasing the number of items we can retain. The mature memorizer attempts to make use of any organization inherent in the material and, in fact, seems to invent organization when there is none obviously available. In this section, we will deal with the role of organizational processes when retarded persons are asked to recall a list of items (letters, words, pictures, or digits).

In studies investigating *clustering* or grouping (Bousfield, 1953), the items presented for study have come from a small set of categories. As an example, a sixteen-item list might consist of four animals, four tools, four articles of clothing, and four foods. Bousfield observed that even if the items were presented in a random order, the subjects' recall was not random but clustered by category. If the first word recalled were *dog*, the next word was likely to be another animal. Recall of organized lists is better than recall of random lists, and the extent to which subjects organize or cluster their recall correlates with overall recall scores.

Retarded and young normal children show little evidence of clustering their output in a free-recall situation (e.g., Bousfield, Esterson, & Whitmarsh, 1958). Spitz (1966) reviewed a number of relevant studies with retarded subjects, including one which he conducted with Gerjuoy. Four groups of subjects were included: college students, retarded adolescents, and two groups of normal children matched with the retarded adolescents on either MA or CA. Only the college students and the equal-CA (fourteen-year-old) normal children showed real clustering, and for them, recall and clustering were significantly correlated. For the retarded and equal-MA (MA = 9.8 years) children, there was no evidence for clustering.

It is possible, however, to induce clustering in retarded subjects by presenting lists in blocked, as opposed to random order (Bilsky & Evans, 1970; Gerjuoy, Winters, Pullen, & Spitz, 1969). All the animals are presented together, then all the foods, etc. Gerjuoy and Spitz (1966) included this procedure and another one in a three-group experiment. The first group of retarded (control) subjects received a random order of presentation and standard free-recall instructions. For a second group (presented clustering), the items were presented in blocked order with free recall, and for the final group (requested clustering), the items were presented in random order but the subjects were instructed to recall by category (e.g., "Tell me all the animals you can remember from the list.") The latter two groups recalled significantly more than the control group, and both showed increased evidence of clustering. The experimental methods were equally effective in getting the subjects to see the organization and to use that organization to mediate enhanced recall. Again the problem seems to lie in the failure spontaneously to use inherent organization unless induced to do so.

Once the ability to use organization has been demonstrated, the question of maintenance arises. With young children the use of induced strategies often stops as soon as the experimenter ceases prompting the subject (Flavell, Beach, & Chinsky, 1966). Although there is some evidence for maintenance of organization strategies in retarded subjects, that evidence is far from strong. Bilsky and Evans (1970) found that training with blocked lists led to increased clustering on a subsequent random list of the same items, but this effect did not carry over to new lists (Bilsky, Evans, & Gilbert, 1972). Nye, McManis, and Haugen (1972) did find generalization to new lists following fifteen days of extensive training, but performance was still much better with the original items. As in the paired-associates and rehearsal areas, the likelihood of obtaining any transfer seems to depend upon the amount of training and, as we shall see in Chapter 15, on the variety of problems presented during training.

Another example of a failure by retarded subjects to employ organization spontaneously can be found in a series of experiments conducted by Spitz (1973b). To illustrate, Spitz presented strings of digits containing different degrees of redundancy. For example, the list *1 3 8 1 3 8* is 50 percent redundant since only the first three digits must be known to generate all six. Although normal adults detect the redundancy quickly, retarded subjects do not. If the redundancy is made more salient during acquisition trials *(1 3 8 1 3 8)*, their performance improves dramatically (Spitz, Goettler, & Webreck, 1972), and the facilitation lasts for a period of at least seven days (Spitz & Webreck, 1972). In these tasks, as in the clustering research, adults seem spontaneously to use natural redundancy to reduce the information load and to enhance retention. In retarded persons, this activity is apparently lacking, with the result that their input is chaotic. As Spitz concluded, "chaotic input makes for chaotic retrieval," and of course for poorer memory.

Attention and Task Demands: Intentional (Central) versus Incidental Memory

The reader will no doubt have heard some songs played many times without attending closely to them. One finds that the songs become more familiar and some of the words may be recalled but not to the degree or with the speed that such memory would occur if one deliberately attended. Several researchers have investigated such incidental memory. In the typical experiment, the subject is told precisely what is expected of him, but sometimes he is tested for information without having been explicitly informed that such a test would be forthcoming (Postman, 1964). Among other things, such experiments with incidental memory provide information about whether attention and the intent to remember something are in themselves important determinants of performance.

Following a study by Maccoby and Hagen (1965), a number of experiments have been designed to investigate the development of selection strategies in both short-term memory and learning situations.[3] In the memory experiments, the subjects view a sequence of cards, with requirements generally the same as in the probe task used by Ellis (1970) to investigate rehearsal mechanisms, but here each card contains two items, one *central* and one *incidental*. For example, each card might show an animal and a household object. On each trial, after the cards are presented, the subject might be shown a picture of an animal and asked to indicate its position in the sequence. In this case, the animals constitute the central items and the household objects are the incidental items.

After this phase of the experiment, the subjects are shown all the animal pictures and asked to select the household object which was paired with each animal picture. The typical finding is that whereas recall of central information increases with age, during childhood the amount of incidental recall remains approximately constant (Druker & Hagen, 1969) or actually decreases with age (Maccoby & Hagen, 1965). There is strong evidence that as children mature, they become more likely to trade off central and incidental information. They direct more of their attention to the central or relevant information at the expense of the incidental information (Druker & Hagen, 1969). The plight of the younger child is even worse than this would suggest. He fails to attend almost exclusively to central information, and, moreover, when the incidental information, to which he seems to attend, can actually aid performance, he fails to exploit this advantage unless he is explicitly instructed to do so (Brown, Campione, & Gilliard, 1974). Finally, the tendency to concentrate primarily upon central information seems to depend upon the development of acquisition strategies such as rehearsal (Hagen, Meacham, & Mesibov, 1970). As one might expect, retarded subjects behave very much like younger children on these tasks (Hagen & Huntsman, 1971).

Control of Forgetting

In all the previous examples, we have emphasized activities or strategies designed to enhance remembering and learning. An equally important skill, however, is that of

[3] For a more detailed discussion of this research, see Hagen and Hale (1973).

forgetting, or ceasing to attend to, information which is no longer needed. Maintaining out-of-date information can overload the memory system or result in interference, making new learning more difficult.[4] Normal adults show excellent control over what to remember and what to forget (Bjork, 1970; Block, 1971). According to Bjork, at least part of the process depends on a smoothly functioning rehearsal system. Information is rehearsed as it comes in, but as soon as the subject realizes that the information is no longer necessary, he ceases to attend to it and expends all his efforts on new material.

Although this may seem a simple activity, mildly retarded adolescents do not appear to execute it spontaneously. Brown (1971) used the keeping-track task described earlier, but skipped probes on some trials. With adults, this variation made no difference, but with the retarded, performance declined with the number of consecutive nonprobed trials. The subjects did not abandon the old information and concentrate on new material as adults do. As a result, the outdated information remained a source of interference. Fortunately, this problem is easy to remedy. In a second experiment in which retarded subjects were given a signal to forget (a red X) following some unprobed trials, performance was the same as with a probe following each trial. Expressly telling the subjects to forget the previous information enabled them to control forgetting.

Similarly, using a probe-type short-term memory task, Bray (1973) presented a series of digits, each digit being shown on a colored background. A change in background color served as the signal that the subject would not be tested on the preceding items and could forget them. With considerable pretraining and explicit instructions, the forget signal was clearly effective, and the subjects behaved essentially as though the items had never been presented.

Areas of Equality between Normal and Retarded Subjects

Although most of the research has been addressed to areas of poor performance by retarded subjects, a better understanding of memory in retarded individuals would result if we could also identify areas in which they perform well. This is not a new idea, one example being Ellis' (1963) suggestion that retarded individuals are deficient in short-term memory but not in long-term memory. Belmont (1966) has concluded that the evidence supports the notion that long-term memory in retarded persons equals that of the nonretarded *if* the degrees of original learning are the same.

Brown (1974a) has suggested that the likelihood of finding a deficiency on a particular task depends upon the amount of strategic intervention required. If no active strategies are needed, differences between normal and moderately or mildly retarded children and adolescents are likely to be very small, if they exist at all. She concludes that the differences therefore do not lie primarily in structural limitations. Similarly, Belmont and Butterfield (1969) have reviewed a large number of comparative studies which indicate that the retarded do not simply forget (have information fade) more rapidly.

Although it is clear that tasks requiring strategies do demonstrate differences between normal and retarded persons, there are few studies of the corollary that nonstrategic tasks should be much less sensitive to comparative differences. Belmont (1967) obtained comparable performance from nonretarded children, retarded adoles-

---

[4] For an extreme case, see Luria's (1968) description of a great mnemonist.

cents, and college students in a memory task requiring judgment of the length of a line. More evidence comes from experiments investigating recognition memory for pictures. In such experiments, subjects view a long series of pictures and are asked to indicate whether or not they have seen each item previously during the experiment. Since up to 2,500 pictures are used with adults, there is little the subject can do on presentation except look at them. This ability appears to be well developed even in preschool children (Brown & Campione, 1972; Brown & Scott, 1971), and performance in young retarded subjects appears comparable (Brown 1972b, 1973; Martin, 1970).

As a final example, adults are relatively good at identifying when and where they have previously seen an item. Because instructions warning subjects that they will be asked such questions do not improve performance (Hintzman & Block, 1971), it appears that such time-and-place information can be stored without any active intent. We might then expect to find excellent performance by retarded individuals in such tasks, and this appears to be the case (Brown, 1972b, 1973).

Types and Effects of Training

Training studies, as we have seen, have demonstrated that many deficiencies in retarded individuals are of the control-process or production type and are consequently at least partially remediable. Even using the appropriate strategy does not lead the retarded to perform as well as normal controls, however, at least not unless the training is extensive and planned in minute detail. The main points are that training does frequently have a pronounced effect and that very positive results have been obtained.

The training attempts have differed considerably in terms of how explicitly the subjects are induced to use the strategy. At one extreme are approaches which use no specific instructions but which rather aim at altering the environment to increase the likelihood that the subjects will use the strategy. Blocked input in clustering studies is one example. At the other extreme, the rehearsal-training procedures used by Brown et al. (1973) were very explicit. The subjects were told exactly what to do, the experimenter illustrated use of the strategy, the subject and experimenter executed the strategy together for a number of trials until the subject could do it alone, and there were frequent reminders provided throughout the sessions. Butterfield and Belmont (1975) have looked at a number of training studies with both normal and retarded children in terms of this variable. Explicit training works much better than attempting to induce the target behavior by manipulating the environment. Of ten studies they reviewed involving explicit training, performance increases averaged 64 percent, whereas the comparable figure for seven induction studies was only 34 percent.

Although training certainly can be effective, a number of problems still remain. The durability of the training effects is not great. As we have seen, often the effect ceases as soon as the experimenter stops prompting the subject, although with very extensive training the result can be maintained for up to six months, so long as the task is not changed. The amount of transfer to new tasks is remarkably small, however, even when the type of transfer is of the simplest type. When transfer has been obtained, as in the Turnure and Thurlow (1973) and Wanschura and Borkowski (1974) experiments in paired-associates learning and the Nye et al. (1972) experiment on clustering, the transfer task has been in fact the *same* as the training task, although the specific materials may have been different. Broader transfer to *different* tasks is the goal of instruction, but there is no real evidence of such transfer in the training studies we have reviewed. Thus, the results of training retarded subjects appear to be both lacking in durability and extremely task-specific.

Metamemorial Functioning and Executive Control

We have seen a general pattern that retarded persons do not proceed planfully in learning or memory situations, remaining relatively passive rather than employing strategies to deal with the material. It seems to be the "plan to use a plan" (Miller, Galanter, & Pribram, 1960) which is deficient (Brown, 1975). Although training can reduce the magnitude of the problem in specific tasks, more general approaches must be found if we are not to be in the position of having to train many different strategies on each task and each situation likely to be met by the retarded individual, a formidable undertaking even if it were possible.

Some candidates for a general approach include metamemorial functioning (Flavell, 1971) and executive control (Butterfield & Belmont, 1975). Although there are few data available with retarded populations, their role in normal development has been studied, and we would like to suggest here the role they may play in determining performance.

Metamemorial Functioning   Metamemorial functioning refers to the subjects' awareness and control of their own memory processes. Young children are relatively unaware of their own memory capacities or of specific task demands (Kreutzer, Leonard, & Flavell, 1974). For example, when shown a list of ten items and asked how many they will be able to remember, young children often say ten (Flavell, Friedrichs, & Hoyt, 1970; Markman, 1973). They are also unable to distinguish easily between lists which would be hard or easy to remember (Moynahan, 1973). As children mature, they become more accurate in predicting their performance and in judging difficulty. As illustrated in the common "tip of the tongue" phenomenon (Brown & McNeill, 1966), adults are very accurate at identifying occasions on which they "know they remember" even when they cannot retrieve the answer. They know the items are available in memory storage even though they are not currently accessible.

Such introspective knowledge is important because it signals the subject when some kind of activity is called for. Unless an individual realizes that a particular memory task is difficult, there is no reason for him to attempt anything extra to help him remember. This ability is a very general one, and a deficiency here could underlie many more specific defects. Poor metamemorial performance is associated with relatively nonstrategic memory behavior in normal children, and it is at least possible that the nonstrategic approach of the retarded may reflect their lack of awareness of their own memory processing. The few data available tend to indicate that this is an area in which the retarded do perform poorly (Brown, 1975).

Executive Control   Even if it is possible to train the "intent to be strategic" in retarded persons and even if the various strategies necessary for effective performance were trained, the problem would still not be solved. There would remain the hurdle of inducing the subject to decide which strategy to use on a particular task, i.e., to exert executive control. As the Butterfield et al. (1973) series of experiments demonstrated, even if two strategies (acquisition and retrieval) are trained on the same task, the retarded adolescent has difficulty in putting them together appropriately unless the entire sequence is explicitly trained.

With the young normal child as with retarded adolescents, many production deficiencies are found (Brown, 1974a; Flavell, 1970). As the normal child grows older, the production deficiencies vanish, but such does not occur with the retarded. Whether more general processing, such as that involved in adequate metamemorial functioning and executive control, can be trained remains an open and important question. If not, we may have discovered the source of a "structural" limitation responsible for inferior performance on a wide variety of tasks.

CONCLUSIONS

In both the learning and memory areas, a major problem for retarded persons stems from failures to employ active mnemonic and problem-solving strategies. In many of the tasks we have considered, efficient performance depends upon planning and active involvement. As information is presented, the subject must manipulate and transform it in accordance with the nature of the task. In some cases, the best approach is to attend selectively to only part of the input; in other cases, the use of incidental information can be of help. In paired-associate tasks, the optimal strategy may be to add additional contextual information, to elaborate upon the material. In some memory tasks, the subject should rehearse the material to maintain it in memory rather than let it fade unattended. In some of the same tasks, the subject should also attempt some control over his forgetting, to cease attending to outdated material. Although this list can be extended, the point is clear. Efficient information-processing requires the flexible use of an impressive array of strategies. The failure to accomplish this is a major source of many of the deficiencies shown by retarded subjects.

There may, of course, exist structural limitations on the use of a strategy. For example, a retarded individual may never be able to rehearse as many items as a normal adult. In dealing with material which can be organized by a normal individual, unless the child has reached a stage at which he can comprehend the organizational principle, any attempt to use an organizational strategy is doomed to failure.[5]

In any event, the most reasonable conclusion appears to be that problems in the intention to use a strategy and in executive control are of major importance. Retarded individuals cannot easily be trained to show spontaneous transfer, nor can they be readily induced to sequence strategies. This conclusion is similar to that of a number of other reviewers. Summarizing some Soviet research, Shif (1969) has argued that when retarded children learn something, that learning is "welded" to the form in which it was learned originally, precluding the flexibility necessary for more general improvement. Similarly, Spitz (1963) concluded that "once material is learned well by retardates, it is unlikely to be serviceable in instances which are not directly related to the original learning experience" (p. 33). Thus, there are deficiencies in the use of strategies, deficiencies which can be overcome in specific situations through explicit training, but the manner in which one can induce more generalization remains a problem of extreme theoretical and applied interest.

---

[5] If we embrace Piaget's approach (Chapter 12), attempts to deal with memory phenomena divorced from cognition represent only a false and misleading separation (Brown, 1975).

15
Learning Principles Applied to Nonlaboratory Behavior (Operant Conditioning and Observational Learning)

In this chapter, we will discuss two bodies of research, operant conditioning and imitative learning, which have contributed enormously to the success of teachers, parents, therapists, and others concerned with the care and education of retarded children. The principles derived from laboratory research as outlined in Chapters 13 and 14 have their counterparts in the home and classroom, of course, as well as considerable value in understanding the cognitive processes of mentally retarded individuals. Their applications to real-life situations are, however, in a more primitive stage than those derived from the laboratory-based theories of operant conditioning, developed by B. F. Skinner, and social learning, developed by A. Bandura.

These two approaches constitute something of a technological revolution in the education and management of retarded children. They have pointed the way to the development of effective tools which are relatively simple in rationale and appropriate to a broad variety of situations. A flood of publications applying the principles in a multitude of settings has occurred in recent years, a convincing display of their effectiveness and flexibility. Reform efforts in whole institutions have been centered around principles of operant conditioning (Thompson & Grabowski, 1972), and the same principles have become mainstays in educational settings (see Chapter 18) and parent training (see Chapter 19). The high degree of enthusiasm among proponents of this view at times tends to mask the distinct limitations of this approach, as though the grand panacea had been discovered at last. As we shall see, neither approach is such

This chapter was written with the collaboration of Joseph C. Campione.

a panacea, though each can furnish a remarkably effective means of arriving at some goals which are of central importance to the socialization and education of children.

This chapter will be devoted to an explication of the principles involved in the two theories, descriptions of a few examples of applications of the principles to real-life situations, and finally, an example of an eclectic approach to special education which combines operant conditioning, imitation, modeling, and other principles described in Chapters 13 and 14.

BEHAVIOR MODIFICATION (OPERANT CONDITIONING)

As long ago as 1898, E. L. Thorndike (1898, 1913) pointed to the determining effects of the consequences of behavior on learning and forgetting. Today recognized as the first of a long line of "reinforcement" theorists, Thorndike maintained that the probability of the occurrence of a response is largely a function of the events which follow it. He argued that a satisfying state of affairs which accompanies or follows a response tends to strengthen the response, whereas the response is weakened if it is accompanied by or followed by a noxious state of affairs. Building mainly upon the positively reinforcing effects of favorable consequences of behavior, B. F. Skinner (1938, 1966) has extended and refined Thorndike's theory until it bears little resemblance to its initial formulation. In turn, Skinner's work has been greatly expanded and refined by his own followers. The finer points of his theory need not concern us here. A limited set of rather easy-to-grasp principles constitutes a basic approach which can be applied in any situation in which adults find themselves responsible for children.

Principles of Operant Conditioning

Operant conditioning consists of the modification of the strength of operant or emitted responses, i.e., responses which are not necessarily elicited by an identifiable prior stimulus. (The reader whose eyes are following this page is emitting a number of operant responses as he reads, turns pages, fidgets in his chair, smokes a cigarette, or chews gum.) The cardinal principle of operant conditioning is that the strength of an operant response is influenced (reinforced) by its consequences, the stimuli it produces. The consequences may be a natural outcome of the behavior (e.g., page-turning is reinforced by the availability of new material to read) or may be artificially or extrinsically introduced (e.g., a grade in an examination based on the text). The manipulation of reinforcement contingencies thus becomes the central focus of efforts to change behavior. This apparently simple statement of course requires amplification.

Modification of Response Strength   The desired direction of behavior change may be an increase in the strength of a response (learning) or a decrease in its strength (extinction). The only responses with which this theoretical approach is prepared to deal are those which are directly observable or which can be made observable (as in the case of brain waves which can be recorded on an EEG). The strength of a response can be indexed in a number of ways, the most common being the rate of emission of that response. Other measures of response strength include intensity, latency (rapidity), and resistance to extinction.

Reinforcers   Stimulus consequences which affect the strength of an operant are called reinforcers. Reinforcers can be either positive or negative. If the strength of a response is increased as a result of *producing* a stimulus, that stimulus is by definition a positive reinforcer. If the strength of the response is increased by the *cessation* or *removal* of a stimulus, that stimulus is by definition a negative reinforcer. Typical positive reinforcers are food ("M&M's"), social approval ("Good boy!"), and the opportunity to engage in a desired behavior ("You can watch TV as soon as you put your toys away"). One of the most effective negative reinforcers is a cessation of positive stimuli, the well-known "time out" period. More aversive negative reinforcers can be employed, such as saying "no" or actively punishing, but since they are often accompanied by positive reinforcers such as attention and interest, their effects tend to be unpredictable. Not all stimuli are reinforcers; some have no effect on the strength of an operant and are therefore neutral.

Choosing effective reinforcers is an essential part of operant conditioning. What is positively or negatively reinforcing for one child may be quite the opposite for another, or it may be neutral. Some reinforcers such as food tend to lose effectiveness with satiation and must be replaced midstream, complicating matters unduly. Food reinforcers are generally used only when others are ineffective and may be paired with less satiable reinforcers such as social approval so that a shift may eventually be made. Another way of avoiding satiation is to use symbolic (token) reinforcers such as checkmarks, gold stars, or colored chips which may later be exchanged for any of a variety of reinforcers of the subject's own choosing.

Learning "New" Responses   Responses which are most readily amenable to reinforcement are behaviors which occur relatively often in the subject's repertoire. Some responses occur so infrequently that waiting for their natural occurrence would be unfeasible, and other responses do not appear at all. Operant conditioning techniques do not result in the formation of completely new responses but are capable of producing novel combinations of previously available responses or of perfecting responses being made inefficiently. A variety of approaches may be used to elicit infrequent behaviors or new combinations which can then be reinforced.

Situational variables may be manipulated to *elicit* infrequent responses. In a toilet-training experiment (Azrin & Foxx, 1971) to be described later, for example, large amounts of fluids were given in order to increase the frequency of elimination. If temper tantrums are the target behavior, the parent may deliberately thwart the child to elicit a response.

A second technique typical of the operant conditioning approach is *response shaping,* or the method of *successive approximations.* The desired response may be approached by stages. If a rat is being trained to press a lever, for example, he may be reinforced at first simply for taking a step or two in the direction of the lever, then for arriving in the vicinity of the lever, and eventually only for pressing it. This technique is very familiar to parents. The child's first spontaneous vocalization which approximates a word is often greeted with great exultation, but as he or she grows older, increasing degrees of proficiency are required.

The child's propensity for imitative learning is often employed to teach new responses through *modeling.* Toilet training is usually initiated after a child has seen other family members using the toilet and wants to do so himself. The furor over the aggressive content of television programs reflects the public's recognition of the power of imitative learning. We shall have more to say about this technique in conjunction with a later discussion of social learning.

Verbal instructions (one type of modeling) constitute another technique for eliciting responses, although they do not play a prominent role in operant theory or research. Instructions can focus a subject's attention on the most relevant cues in a modeled response or can help the subject to combine responses already in his or her repertoire ("Wipe the extra paint off your brush before it touches the paper").

Still another technique associated with operant conditioning is *guided learning, prompting,* or *cuing* accompanied by *fading* as the subject acquires the capability of making the response independently. The mother who holds her hand over the child's as she guides a spoon to the plate and then to the child's mouth is using such a technique; later she will give less and less help, letting the child do as much as possible alone. Teaching social conventions offers a prime example of prompting ("Say 'Thank you'").

Chaining is another technique for teaching complex behaviors by adding successive links or steps. It works most effectively if the final component is elicited and reinforced first (e.g., eliminating on the toilet) and links are added in a backward direction (e.g., reinforcement only for pulling down one's pants *and* eliminating, then going independently to the bathroom *and* pulling down one's pants *and* eliminating on the toilet.)

Rather than focusing directly on reducing the frequency of a problem behavior, a more indirect but often more effective approach is *response substitution,* reinforcing a response which is incompatible with the undesirable one, which in turn is left unattended. Reinforcement may be given in the morning for a dry bed but nothing said about a wet one; positive social responses to classmates may be praised but offensive ones ignored. The undesirable response is decreased because it remains unreinforced and because the incompatible response increases in frequency.

Learning Discriminations   Often the aim of teaching is not simply to increase or decrease the strength of an operant, but to restrict its appearance to an appropriate set of circumstances. Talking out in class may be unacceptable, but responding to a teacher's question is highly acceptable. Running in school halls may be prohibited, but running on the playground is encouraged. In these situations, the appropriate circumstances (the teacher's question, the playground) become *discriminative stimuli* which signal the subject that reinforcement will be available if he makes the response. The formation of such discriminations indicates that although operants are controlled by their consequences, they are also influenced by preceding stimuli or cues. According to Skinner, the discriminative stimulus, a "go ahead" signal, does not elicit the response but simply indicates the availability of reinforcement.

Manipulation of Reinforcement   Manipulation of reinforcement obviously occupies a central place in operant conditioning theory. One important variable is the *number of times* a response has been reinforced. Up to some limit, the greater the cumulative frequency of reinforced emissions, the stronger the response becomes.

A second important variable is the *timing* of the reinforcement. In general, the more immediately reinforcement follows the response, the greater its effectiveness. Unless reinforcement is prompt, other responses made during the delay interval may be strengthened by the reinforcer with little effect on the target behavior.

Turning to a more complex issue, the *schedule* of reinforcement can have a powerful effect on the rapidity of acquisition, the frequency the response is emitted, and its resistance to extinction.[1] Reinforcement can be delivered either *continuously,* after every instance of the target response, or *intermittently,* after only some proportion of

[1] The reader is referred to Ferster and Skinner (1957) or Honig (1966) for a more detailed account of scheduling.

the responses. The schedules can be based either on the number of responses emitted (*ratio* schedules) or on the interval of time which has passed since the previous reinforcement (*interval* schedules). Furthermore, either a ratio or an interval schedule may be *fixed* (regular) or it may be *variable* (varying within a range but averaging a given ratio or interval). On a fixed ratio 5 (FR-5) schedule, for example, only every fifth response is reinforced. A continuous reinforcement schedule is also an FR-1 schedule. On an interval schedule, the subject will receive reinforcement for the first response emitted a specified time following the previous reinforcement. A fixed interval one-minute (FI-1) schedule would allow no reinforcement during a one-minute interval following a prior reinforcement. For purposes of the present discussion, we will ignore variable schedules as an unnecessary complication.

The schedule of reinforcement influences performance both during acquisition (reinforcement) and during extinction, when reinforcement is no longer provided. One clear result is that FR schedules consistently lead to high rates of responding, whereas FI schedules result in much more variable effects (Weisberg, 1971). Interval schedules lead with animals to a "scalloping" effect, in which the rate of responding falls following a reinforcement and then increases up to the point at which the next reinforcement is administered (Honig, 1966). With severely retarded subjects, FI schedules seem to result in one of two alternative patterns: low rates of responding with pauses following each reinforcement or higher rates without pauses (Ellis, Barnett, & Pryer, 1960; Orlando & Bijou, 1960; Spradlin, Girardeau, & Corte, 1965). The factor(s) which determine an individual's pattern of response have not yet been isolated (Weisberg, 1971). In any event, ratio schedules appear to have the virtue of more consistent and predictable results than do interval schedules.

It is of course possible to modify the reinforcement schedule at different points during training. During the early stages, an FR-1 schedule is advisable to establish response strength and prevent premature extinction effects. The schedule may later be thinned out (e.g., FR-1 to FR-5 to FR-10) until the response continues to be made frequently with very infrequent reinforcement. Ellis (1962) thinned out a schedule to FR-128 with success.

Resistance to extinction also varies as a function of the reinforcement schedule, with intermittent reinforcement resulting in far greater response rates than continuous reinforcement, following cessation of reinforcement. The potential benefits of this result are clear. A response may be maintained at high strength with only occasional reinforcements. The adult who has painstakingly shaped and reinforced a desirable response in a child can look forward to a release from intensive involvement or can shift his intensive efforts to another operant target while only occasionally reinforcing the first one. At the same time, however, the strength of intermittently reinforced responses makes clear why it is so difficult to extinguish problem behaviors which have a high demand value. Many parents are able to ignore tantrum behavior *most* of the time but slip occasionally, especially when the tantrum occurs in a public place such as a grocery store. Occasional positive reinforcement, even in the guise of punishment, simply strengthens the behavior.

Limitations of the Operant Conditioning Approach

The discerning reader will have noted that although this approach provides an extremely effective tool for modifying behavior, there are a number of problems which the theory and its accompanying technology fail to solve (MacMillan & Forness, 1973).

First, the theory simply ignores many variables which form the central foci of other points of view. There is, for example, nowhere a treatment of the mediational strategies which have occupied so large a role in learning and memory research, nor is there a workable treatment of the symbolic processes involved in learning. The approach is much more amenable to increasing the rate at which a child solves a homogeneous set of arithmetic problems than to charting his progress with tasks at increasing levels of complexity.

Although the theory has been applied to such complex matters as the development of verbal behavior (Skinner, 1957) and abnormal behaviors of many kinds (Ullmann & Krasner, 1975), it discards as speculative and superfluous such constructs as drive, intelligence, anxiety, or self-concept. As MacMillan and Forness (1973) point out, the behavioristic paradigm cannot deal successfully with such concepts as the equilibration process described by Jean Piaget (see Chapter 12), the inherent interest of a child in the challenge of problems which constitute a good "match" with his developing schemes (Hunt, 1961), the value of exploration or curiosity for its own sake (Harlow, 1950), the motivation for competence (see Chapter 9), or self-administered (covert) reinforcement (Jensen, 1968).

MacMillan and Forness (1973) also point to what they call "reinforcement overkill," by which they mean that the reinforcers typically used in operant conditioning studies are more primitive, concrete, and extrinsic to the task than are the natural consequences of the act on which sustained maintenance will depend. Toilet training, for example, must eventually be reinforced not by praise and cookies but by physical comfort and the social acceptability which is denied the incontinent.

There is also the problem, not fully handled in most behavior-modification studies, of generalization and maintenance of the behavior once the intensive phase of training is completed. Without systematic provision for intermittent reinforcement, the behavior tends to disappear, especially if there is a return to the original condition in which unacceptable behavior was a pathway to attention. Furthermore, behaviors typically generalize to new situations only when a specific effort is made to effect the transition. As MacMillan and Forness (1973) conclude, "Behavior modification must not be oversold, lest as limitations appear, the entire approach be discarded in response to one's disenchantment" (p. 208).

Applications of Operant Conditioning with Retarded Individuals

The proliferation of studies employing an operant approach with retarded children and adults has been impressive to say the least. A review of this body of literature is far beyond the scope of the present chapter.[2] Among the operant behaviors which have been targeted in investigations with retarded children have been the following:

Verbal behaviors   (imitation, question answering, vocabulary)
Academic learning   (arithmetic, sight vocabulary)
Nonacademic classroom behaviors   (attending, sitting, taking turns, talking only at appropriate times)
Peer-oriented behaviors   (cooperation, group activities)
Self-help behaviors   (toileting, feeding, dressing, locomotion)
Work-oriented habits   (productivity, promptness, task completion)

[2] The reader is referred to reviews by Birnbrauer (in press), Forness & MacMillan (1970), Gardner (1969), Watson (1967) and Weisberg (1971). One of the most useful guides for teachers and parents has been provided by Krumboltz and Krumboltz (1972).

Attention-getting behaviors   (whining, demands, tantrums)
Aggressive behaviors   (fighting, window breaking, swearing)
Self-injurious behaviors   (head banging, scratching)

The present section will describe in detail a few studies which illustrate the practical application of operant conditioning.

Straightforward Reinforcement of Existing Responses: Developing Appropriate Verbal Responses in an Echolalic Subject   Researchers working with autistic and/or nonverbal children have demonstrated that some speech can be instituted through imitation when the imitations are consistently reinforced (Lovaas, Berberich, Perloff, & Schaeffer, 1966). Such procedures require arduous eliciting and shaping techniques, however. In an echolalic child, one who can say words but uses them inappropriately in simple repetition of what he has heard, the procedures can be shortened (Risley & Wolf, 1967). Ausman and Gaddy (1974) worked with an echolalic seventeen-year-old blind girl who could repeat complete sentences and entire commercials but could not answer a question except by repeating it, did not initiate appropriate conversation or make requests, and referred to herself in the second person. The procedure involved a long series of trials in which the subject heard a question and its answer and then was required to give the answer in response to the question. The procedure made use of her tendency to repeat but shifted the model stimulus from the question to the following answer. With seventy-six days of training, she was able to learn thirty-one such responses to a 100 percent level, her responses during training remaining so high after the first few sessions that it was obvious that she had grasped the underlying principle rather quickly. Outside of the training sessions, she began to ask for items she wanted, responded more appropriately to questions, and responded to many questions not included in the training protocols, presumably on the basis of social reinforcement.

More Complex Reinforcement Procedures: Toilet Training   Incontinence is one of the most persistent problems in institutions for severely retarded persons. Because of the necessity for constantly cleaning residents, beds, clothing, and floors and the pervasive odors of urine and feces, attendants tend to react negatively toward residents who soil themselves and assignments to their wards carry low status. Achieving toilet training of these residents serves several purposes: greater comfort for residents, more positive interaction with attendants, improved hygiene, and the possibility of residents' going out of the ward for various purposes.

Accordingly, a number of studies have instituted intensive regimes to achieve toilet training in severely and profoundly retarded children and adults. (See Watson, 1967.) The simplest procedure is to place the child on the toilet at times when the likelihood of elimination is high and then to reinforce elimination which takes place there. Although this method does result in some improvement (Baumeister & Klosowski, 1965; Levine & Elliott, 1970; Azrin & Foxx, 1971), it also presents a number of problems. It is hard to anticipate when the subject may need to eliminate, and the cleaning and changing after an accident provide considerable positive reinforcement. Furthermore, an adult usually has to eliminate only a few times a day, so that the procedure may stretch out endlessly.

To meet some of these problems, Azrin and Foxx (1971) combined portions of a number of approaches. To increase the elimination rate, the experimenters gave a large volume of fluid each half hour. Moreover, to ease the detection task of the ward attendants, the residents wore moisture-sensitive pants which sounded a tone when wet, and a device was inserted inside the toilet bowl to emit a signal when the subject eliminated there (Azrin, Bugle, & O'Brien, 1971).

During the eight-hour training sessions, the subjects remained in the vicinity of the toilet area. They were placed on the toilet every thirty minutes and remained there for a period of either twenty minutes or until they had eliminated. Candy and social reinforcement were given for elimination into the bowl or, during intertrial intervals, for remaining dry. If inappropriate elimination occurred, the resident was required to obtain fresh clothing, undress, wash himself in the shower, mop the floor, and wash the soiled pants. This "overcorrection" procedure was followed by a one-hour time-out during which positive reinforcement was unavailable (Foxx & Azrin, 1972, 1973). After training was completed, a maintenance program was carried out by the ward attendants, who periodically gave social reinforcement if the resident was dry and the overcorrection sequence if he was not. If no accidents had occurred in a four-week interval, the explicit maintenance program was dropped. The intensive-training phase required a mean of six days (range one to fourteen days) to reduce the frequency of accidents by at least 80 percent for each subject. Reaching the criterion of no soiling for four weeks required a mean of 8.5 weeks, all subjects attaining the criterion by 15 weeks. Some nighttime control was also achieved.

Another set of procedures deals with the self-initiating phase, namely, recognizing early cues and withholding elimination until reaching the toilet. Van Wagenen, Meyerson, Kerr, and Mahoney (1969) also used moisture-sensitive pants which emitted a tone, whereupon the experimenter said "no" in an attempt to delay urination until the child reached the toilet. Although it was possible to fade out the verbal command, Van Wagenen et al. had difficulty eliminating reliance on the tone. In a subsequent study, Mahoney, Van Wagenen, and Meyerson (1971) broke the training into still smaller steps. In the first phase, the experimenter controlled the tone, which was a signal to the residents to go to the toilet, lower pants, and assume the appropriate posture. In this way, the initial part of the sequence could be taught without the stress of trying to inhibit urination. After the initial phase, administration of liquid was increased and reinforcement was withheld until the resident eliminated into the toilet. Finally, the tone was eliminated as well, and seven of the eight subjects continued to respond appropriately. This procedure is less demanding than the Azrin-Foxx method, but there was no maintenance program and long-term effects were not investigated.

Aversive Reinforcers In the preceding examples, the major emphasis was on building appropriate responses through positive reinforcement. With some forms of self-injurious behavior, however, positive reinforcement procedures have tended to be relatively ineffective (Bucher & Lovaas, 1969; Gardner, 1969). As a result, a number of investigators have used active punishment procedures to halt the injurious behaviors while administering positive reinforcers for acceptable substitute behaviors. The most frequent aversive stimulus employed has been electric shock, usually paired with negative social reinforcers ("No!" "Stop!"). Baer (1970), Hamilton and Standahl (1969), and Roos (1974) discuss some of the ethical and practical considerations involved in the use of aversive procedures. (See also Chapter 19.)

The effects of shock are often immediate, with response rates decreasing greatly as a result of even one training session, though the effect does not automatically generalize to other settings (Lovaas & Simmons, 1969). The Lovaas and Simmons experiment compared standard extinction (nonreinforcement) and punishment procedures. The extinction procedure was predicated on the assumption that self-destructive behavior is usually maintained by the social consequences of the act (e.g., attention, restraining efforts). Residents were placed in a small room for 1½ hours a day and were left there unattended though observed from an adjoining room. For the two subjects investigated, there was a marked reduction in the rate of self-injurious behavior, though the reduction was relatively gradual, one subject emitting some 9,000 self-injurious acts during the extinction period. For neither subject was the rate of these behaviors reduced in other settings.

In a subsequent portion of the experiment, painful electric shock was made contingent on self-injurious behavior. Although the drop in response rate was extremely rapid, again the effect generalized neither to other settings nor other experimenters. When one of the subjects (John) was shocked in a second setting, however, the response rate dropped immediately in that setting. A slightly different technique was used with the other subject (Linda). With her, during original punishment training, shock and a loud "no!" were administered. Again, the response decrement was very rapid but did not generalize to other situations. However, responding "no!" (previously an ineffective procedure) was sufficient to drop response rates to zero in situations other than the original training setting. By this means, the necessity for administering shock was greatly reduced. Surprisingly, rather than bringing about negative side effects, the procedure decreased the occurrence of other undesirable behaviors such as whining and avoiding adults, even though the behaviors were not explicitly punished. Such positive side effects have also been reported by other investigators (Risley, 1968; Tate & Baroff, 1966).

As Birnbrauer (in press) has pointed out, the effects of shock are situationally specific, but not necessarily more so than the effects obtained with other types of reinforcement procedures. Generalization can, however, be obtained by applying the reinforcement procedures in several settings, and similar results can be obtained with other severe behavior problems (Corte, Wolf, & Locke, 1971; Weisberg, 1971).

Token Economies   A token economy involves positive reinforcers in the form of chips, checkmarks, stars, or the like, which at specified intervals may be exchanged for the subject's choice from an array of back-up reinforcers. The aim of such procedures is much like that of direct reinforcement with the food, manipulable toys, or privileges which the subject may choose, but it has the additional advantage of not interrupting the learning session while the subject eats his raisin or plays with his new toy. Furthermore, tokens are not as susceptible to satiation effects as a single primary reinforcer would be.

Birnbrauer and Lawler (1964) employed one of the earliest token economies with twenty-seven severely mentally retarded subjects in academic classes in a state school. In the beginning, candies were used as reinforcers, but within a month the tokens were given as occasional substitutes. In time, the only reinforcers were chips which could be exchanged for candy bars and other edibles, balloons, whistles, and trinkets. A ten-minute time-out procedure was also used. By the end of the school year, nonacademic behavior had improved tremendously. Thirty-three of the thirty-seven pupils hung up their coats upon entering the classroom, took their seats quietly, and waited for the assignment. Eleven of the children were working alone and persistently on prereading assignments of as much as thirty minutes in length. During a test period when tokens were omitted for fifteen subjects but social reinforcement and time-outs continued, five subjects showed no change, six increased error rates but remained cooperative, and only two both increased error rates and became disciplinary problems. Similar results were obtained by Zimmerman, Zimmerman, and Russell (1969) and indeed this procedure has been very popular in classroom studies (O'Leary & Drabman, 1971). Token economies need not, of course, be limited to the classroom. Token rewards for a variety of desirable behaviors have been given in residential facilities (e.g., Bath & Smith, 1974; Girardeau & Spradlin, 1964), in teaching work habits and work skills in a sheltered workshop (Tate & Baroff, 1967), and even in maintaining ward attendants' desirable behavior toward residents (Bricker, Morgan, & Grabowski, 1972).

Vocational Habilitation   Although principles of operant conditioning are clearly applicable in the area of vocational habilitation, research in explicit vocational training procedures has lagged behind research in other areas of training with the retarded (Gold, 1972). At least part of the reason may be the low expectancies for retarded workers held by many employers and potential employers. Even in sheltered workshops, because most depend for income on commercial contracts, the tendency has been to find simple jobs suited to the abilities of retarded workers rather than to devise ways of training the clients to perform more complex or varied tasks. In fact, as Gold (1972) has noted, the use of the term *training* in the vocational habilitation literature "almost without exception refers to exposure rather than treatment, or, it refers to placing clients on a job situation where it is hoped training occurs" (p. 100).

One focus of research in this area has dealt with the modification of rates of existing behaviors, i.e., increasing productivity, through *manipulation of reinforcement schedules*. As indicated earlier, reinforcement is most effective when it is prompt, but in most work settings, payment is given once a week or even less frequently. A number of investigators (Evans & Spradlin, 1966; Schroeder, 1972; Zimmerman, Stuckey, Garlick, & Miller, 1969) have shown that better timing and scheduling of reinforcement results in enhanced production rates for simple tasks of which workers are already capable. Schroeder (1972), for example, employed an automated arrangement which allowed immediate reinforcement. On a fixed interval (FI) schedule, productivity lessened as the interval was lengthened from one minute to one hour, but for some subjects, productivity increased on a fixed ratio (FR) schedule as the ratio was increased from 1:5 to 1:300. Schroeder also found, however, that when considerable effort was required for the task, increasing the FR led to a decrease rather than an increase in productivity.

Another set of research studies has attempted to teach new and more complicated tasks, usually on the basis of a careful *task analysis* in which the target behavior is broken down into its component acts. For example, in a series of experiments, seven severely retarded males were trained in the operation of a drill press. Since the task involves a long series of responses, it was necessary to train each one separately. Crosson and deJung (1967, cited in Gold, 1972) isolated approximately one hundred separate operants in the drill press task, since, as Crosson (1969) argued, "the more severe the retardation of the individual to be trained, the more discrete the behavior specification should be" (p. 815). Some of the operants were already within the clients' repertoire but specific training was necessary for "new" operants. Crosson and deJung singled out a number of "new" operants for practice during a pretraining session prior to incorporating them into the overall sequence. This training involved the use of modeling, varieties of verbal and nonverbal instruction, and physical assistance, with prompt reinforcement of correct responses. As the clients' accuracy increased, these assists were gradually faded until the response occurred without aid. Reinforcement was then made contingent upon longer and longer chains of responses until the entire sequence could be performed, and the reinforcement schedule was then thinned to the point at which it was compatible with other aspects of the overall program. All seven clients were able to reach a criterion of two errorless trials with less than three hours of training and showed good retention two and twelve months following training. Thus, the training procedure was successful in bringing about both acceptable performance and long-lasting effects.

Another example of successful training was reported by Gold (1972) employing a bicycle brake assembly. Clients were trained to assemble a fifteen-piece bicycle brake. The parts were placed in fifteen bins arranged in the order in which they were to be added to the assembly, one at a time. For half the workers, each part was painted red on the surface facing the client when the brake was assembled. All clients were trained to a criterion of six errorless trials in a block of eight consecutive trials and were then given a transfer task involving a twenty-four-piece brake. On the second task, sixty-three of the sixty-four clients reached criterion. The provision of the color cue halved the number of training trials required. Clients' performance remained accurate one year later.

In both the Crosson and Gold experiments, the use of a well-developed training procedure resulted in fairly rapid acquisition of the target behavior along with impressive evidence for long-term retention. Clearly, sheltered workshop clients and other retarded workers can be trained to perform much more difficult tasks than had previously been assumed.

OBSERVATIONAL LEARNING

Imitative learning, patterning behavior after an observed model, is a salient characteristic of human behavior. Each of the major learning theorists has tended to deal with this phenomenon in his own way (McLaughlin, 1971, chap. 4), but none has been able to ignore it. Under the right circumstances, the provision of models provides a very appropriate means of facilitating learning in mentally retarded persons, a means which thus far certainly has been neither explored nor exploited to its fullest.

Most of the recent empirical work in this area has followed a theory proposed by Albert Bandura (1962, 1969). Bandura himself has not often worked with mentally retarded subjects, but others have applied his framework with sufficient success to make clear that imitative learning constitutes a powerful tool for work with this group.

Bandura's Theory of Observational Learning

Bandura (1969) points out that human subjects in social settings can acquire new behaviors simply by seeing them made by a model. He calls this "no-trial learning." In Skinner's model, learning cannot be assumed to take place until after the response has been performed *and* reinforced. Bandura maintains that even if the observer does not make the response himself and even if at the time neither he nor the model is reinforced for the behavior, he may nevertheless learn the response so that he can perform it later as it is called for. The way he does this, Bandura says, is to acquire internal representational responses which mediate subsequent behavioral reproduction or performance. Unlike Skinner, then, Bandura depends upon covert, *mediational* processes to explain imitational learning. Bandura, in fact, proposes that there are two distinct kinds of mediational responses involved: *imagery formation,* which is assumed to occur via a process of sensory conditioning or perceptual responses which form long-lasting images of the behavior, and *verbal coding* of responses, which enables a tie-in with the extensive verbal component of cognitive behavior in human beings. The verbal coding of responses greatly facilitates retrieval and reproduction of imitative behavior and in fact the "model" observed by the subject may be completely verbal, a set of instructions or even a story.

Although Bandura sees imitation as an active, not a passive process, he maintains that for the establishment of the mediational responses, images and verbal codings, reinforcement is not a necessary condition. Imitative behavior is acquired simply through stimulus contiguity. Performance is quite a different matter, however. The imitative responses are much more likely to be translated into behavior when there is motivation or incentive (reinforcement).

Bandura (1969) has specified three interrelated subprocesses which are a part of imitative learning, each of these with its own controlling variables. The first subprocess is *attention.* The subject must attend to the model and must, furthermore, discriminate among the distinguishing features of the model's behavior. A very large number of variables determine how effectively the subject attends to the model. Some of these variables have to do with characteristics of what is observed. Attention is facilitated by a display which is novel, interesting, and includes a variety of models; by models who are seen as competent, powerful, high in status, of the same sex and age as the observer, and who are observed to be rewarded for behaviors they perform. Other variables have to do with the observers. Observers with high dependency, low self-esteem and low competence, and a history of positive reinforcement for exhibiting matching behaviors are likely to be highly attentive to the behavior of models. Stimulus-input conditions are also related to the subject's success at attending. Verbal instructions may make more salient the relevant aspects of the display the subject is watching. If the behavior to be modeled is not presented too quickly, does not exceed the level of complexity the subject is prepared to handle, and is made salient, attention will be enhanced. Finally, incentive conditions will to some extent determine the level of observational learning and attentiveness, though incentive is not a necessary condition of such learning.

A second subprocess of observational learning, according to Bandura, is *retention* of the observed behavior. Observational learning can be retained over long periods of time without overt response. Retention depends in part upon the efficient symbolic coding or mediation of the event (Gerst, 1968) and upon covert rehearsal operations (Bandura, Ross, & Ross, 1963). Decrements in retention may also occur if the complexity of the model exceeds the observer's capacity to code and store.

A third process concerns *motoric reproduction.* The observer may be able to imagine and to code behaviors of which he is motorically incapable. Motor responses are most readily acquired and performed when the observer already possesses the component skills and need only synthesize them into new patterns.

Actual performance, however, depends on *incentive or motivation.* A person may have learned a modeled behavior but may not activate the response into overt per-

Fig. 15-1   Modeling with prompting and rapt attention. *(University of Washington Child Development and Mental Retardation Center)*

formance because of negative sanctions or the absence of positive incentives. In other words, the subject may be inhibited from responding (as, for example, through fear of failure or because the response has been prohibited) or may simply have no reason to make the response, although watching a model under favorable circumstances may encourage him to do so.

To recapitulate, the failure of observational learning to occur following exposure to a model may result from a wide variety of factors, including "sensory registration difficulties, ineffective imagery formation, inability to code observed events, retention decrement, motor deficits, or unfavorable incentive conditions" (Ross, 1975). Many aspects of Bandura's theory have been thoroughly documented with nonretarded subjects (Bandura, 1969).

Observational Learning by Retarded Subjects

Despite the complexities of observational learning revealed by Bandura's elegant analysis, this kind of learning is neither unusual nor esoteric. Given a highly visible motor response of which he or she is capable, such as thrusting the tongue in and out, even a very young baby is capable of rather precise imitation, and imitative learning is a pervasive part of learning throughout life, whatever the individual's mental maturity. This phenomenon is, then, of particular interest to those involved with retarded individuals. Given propitious circumstances, there are reasons to believe that mildly retarded persons at times may be more likely to imitate than other persons. The more severe the retardation, of course, the simpler the model the individual can attend to and perform. What are some of the limitations of retarded individuals as imitators, and what are some of their propensities?

In Chapter 13, we considered some of the difficulties which retarded individuals exhibit in attending to the salient dimensions of a display. The Zeaman-House data indicate that it takes retarded individuals longer to center in on relevant dimensions, though once they attend effectively, they are capable of learning rather rapidly. We have also noted their difficulties with following verbal instructions, with spontaneously employing mediational processes including rehearsal, and with verbal coding. Their relatively limited motoric capabilities, too, should stand in the way of the performance of some responses.

On the other hand, to the extent that retarded individuals are taught or enticed to attend properly, to utilize effective mediational processes, and to perform component motoric responses, there is reason to believe that they should be more inclined to imitate than other persons. Bandura and Walters (1963, p. 10), for example, summarize some of the early evidence which indicates that children with strong dependency habits, those with a history of failure, and perhaps institutionalized children, are all more prone than other children to be subject to social influence. Strichart (1974), too, concludes that imitation occurs most often in situations where a noncompetent observer is asked to imitate a competent model. It goes without saying that mentally retarded children are generally less competent than other children of their age. In Chapter 9, we discussed both the outerdirectedness and the conformity which characterize the behavior of retarded children, who tend to distrust their own resources and to look to rules, to advisers, and to models for cues as to how to behave.

With respect to designing research and educational strategies with retarded children, the provision of models is then very attractive. Propitious conditions for retarded children as observers should probably include highly structured settings in which attention can be easily directed and the imitative responses elicited unambiguously, and simplification of the visual array so that the salient features are exaggerated or otherwise made outstanding. Additional saliency of relevant features can be attained by making the behaviors novel, by giving verbal instructions, by rewarding attending behavior, and so on. Opportunities should probably be given for periodic rehearsal, although there is no evidence that retarded children are deficient in long-term memory per se. (See Chapter 14.) To the extent that the models are made to appear attractive, strong, competent, and capable of attaining significant rewards, though remaining similar to the observers in such features as sex and age, the propensities of the retarded observer to imitate can be capitalized upon.

Modeling and imitation techniques are only now beginning to be utilized explicitly and extensively in work with retarded subjects, though retarded children like other children have been learning by this means since time immemorial. In treatment programs for severely and moderately retarded subjects, a combination of modeling and reinforcement has been used in teaching new motor and verbal skills (Lovaas, Freitas, Nelson, & Whalen, 1967; Whalen & Henker, 1969). Modeling has been used to modify the aggressive and friendly behavior of institutionalized retarded adolescents who often attack other residents, although the effects of the same technique on nonaggressive retarded subjects is more marked (Fechter, 1971). Telephone usage (Stephan, Stephano, & Talkington, 1973), basic communication responses (Talkington, Hall, & Altman, 1973), the use of verbal communication with parents (Seitz & Hoekenga, 1974), and concept acquisition (Yoder & Forehand, 1974) are among the kinds of skills which have been taught retarded subjects via this method. Only with very severely retarded subjects has there been any failure to achieve spontaneous imitative learning (Altman, Talkington, & Cleland, 1972).

New Techniques

A. P. Goldstein (1973) has developed a technique, Structured Learning Therapy, which uses a series of videotapes to facilitate social learning. Although the procedure has so far been applied to a variety of subjects including chronic psychiatric patients (Gutride, Goldstein, & Hunter, 1973), neurotic outpatients (Goldstein, Martins, Hubbins, Van Belle, Schaaf, Wiersma, & Goodhart, 1973), and lower-class workers (Sorcher & Goldstein, 1973) to teach appropriate social behaviors in common situations, this approach has not yet been modified for use with retarded individuals, despite its promise.

Another technique growing out of Bandura's theoretical position but not yet attempted with retarded individuals is the modification of inappropriate behavior by *modeling with guided participation*. Ross, Ross, and Evans (1971), for example, were able to modify a six-year-old boy's extreme social withdrawal from peers by a seven-week treatment program in a naturalistic setting. A model who was highly valued by the boy demonstrated social interactions, provided the subject with graded opportunities for practice, and participated with him in other social interactions, never exceeding his expanding tolerance for the newly acquired social behavior. Ross, Ross, and Evans suggest that the same kind of demonstration-practice-joint-participation method would be extremely suitable for helping children with learning disabilities to overcome their expectancy of failure, and D. M. Ross (personal communication) suggests that the method should be equally suitable for many retarded children with the same sorts of expectancies.

Imitative learning, then, is a process which the mentally retarded tend to employ at least as readily as do nonretarded persons, provided that the situation is designed to fit within the limits of their capabilities. Imitation provides a simple and natural teaching technique. We can expect to see far more exploitation of this approach within the next few years.

AN ACADEMIC PROGRAM COMBINING PRINCIPLES DERIVED FROM SEVERAL THEORIES

As an example of an academic program combining learning principles derived from several theories, we may examine in some detail an energetic program of research and curriculum development summarized by Dorothea M. Ross and Sheila A. Ross (1972). The program has involved a number of basic studies on the training of cognitive skills. Effective training procedures have been combined into a detailed curriculum for educable mentally retarded (EMR) children approximately five to ten years of age (Ross & Ross, 1974). The training program is based on a number of assumptions about the functioning of the EMR child, including an assumed deficiency in the use of central mediational processes like those discussed in Chapters 13 and 14. Ross and Ross argue that such processes can best be trained through a broad-based program involving a variety of training techniques, active involvement of the child, and the use of clearly defined reinforcement procedures.

Ross and Ross's principal training strategy involves small groups of children selected on the basis of ability level. Some elements of the basic procedure were mentioned in Chapter 13 with reference to a study by Ross, Ross, and Downing (1973). In that five-week training study, experimental sessions three times a week consisted of games which involved, among other things, the learning of paired associates. Subjects were given points (token reinforcers) for winning games, the points being exchangeable for prizes.

In the *intentional training* condition, the teacher explained the use of mediational links such as forming a sentence with the two words to be associated. At subsequent points, mediational links were provided for the subjects, then they were instructed to supply their own, and finally, no instructions at all were given. In the *observational learning* condition, no specific mediational instructions were given but the subjects were exposed to an adult model who participated in the memory game and, exhibiting the use of his own mediational strategies, usually won. Subjects in the control group played similar games but were never given instructions regarding mediational strategies, nor did they observe an adult modeling such strategies. One week after the training sessions ended, another paired-associates task was presented by a new experimenter in a new setting, a condition which should decrease the likelihood of obtaining transfer of the strategy. Even so, the experimental groups performed equally well and significantly better than the control group. Both experimental groups were observed to use mediational links (combined total was sixty-one instances), but the control group exhibited none.

The impressive acquisition of the mediational strategy and its transfer contrast sharply with the studies reviewed in Chapter 13, in which very little evidence of transfer was obtained even when the task was presented immediately after and in the same context as the training task. A number of possible reasons for the discrepancy exist. First, the Ross, Ross, and Downing (1973) study provided more extensive training than those reporting weak evidence of transfer. A second and more interesting possibility concerns the method of training. Soviet investigators have emphasized the importance of the task context in determining the development of strategic behaviors. For example, Zinchenko (Smirnoff & Zinchenko, 1969) has argued that mnemonic strategies are first formed as special purposive acts requiring intensive conscious control. During the next stage of development, the mnemonic is transferred to materials of various contexts and finally, as a consequence of repeated use, it becomes "to a certain degree, automatized and acquire(s) the form of a generalized skill" (p. 469). What experience, then, might facilitate such development? Smirnoff and Zinchenko (1969) and Yendovitskaya (1971) have argued that mnemonic activities first emerge in meaningful situations, where memory becomes a means toward some desirable goal. Istomina (cited in Yendovitskaya, 1971) has compared retention of a five-item list of words under conditions where memory itself was the goal (a standard laboratory task) or where memory was necessary to achieve another, more meaningful goal. Performance was far superior in the latter case. The suggestion is that the training situation employed by Ross, Ross, and Downing (1973) involved the subjects in a more meaningful situation and used a more extensive array of contexts, both factors which should result in greater acquisition and transfer.

The general form of the training employed in the Ross, Ross, and Downing study has been the main ingredient in the curriculum devised by Ross and Ross (1972, 1974). Small-group games involving both intentional and observational learning opportunities are provided. In some cases, one of the children serves as a *peer model* for the others in the group; in other cases, sixth-grade nonretarded children *(high-status models)* are recruited. In still other cases, *symbolic modeling* is provided by the children's use of dolls to mimic sequences or actions carried out by storybook characters.

The specific areas in the experimental curriculum tested by Ross and Ross (1972) are listed in Table 15-1. Detailed plans are provided within each area. Subjects in the

**Table 15-1   Summary of Specific Training Areas in the
Ross and Ross (1972) Curriculum**

I.   Basic academic skills
     A.   Reading
     B.   Vocabulary
     C.   Verbal expression
     D.   Arithmetic
II. General learning skills
     A.   Listening and following directions
     B.   Planning
     C.   Problem solving
III. Social behavior
IV. Gross and fine motor skills
     A.   Physical education
     B.   Fine motor skills
V.   Fine arts
     A.   Painting
     B.   Music

---

basic curriculum study were sixty EMR children, ages five to ten, with IQs 40 to 80. Half the subjects were given the experimental curriculum and half a more traditional EMR curriculum. The experimental group showed significantly greater increases in IQ than the controls and furthermore, eleven of the thirty experimental subjects were transferred to regular classes during the year in contrast to the retention of all control children in special classes. These initial results are quite encouraging, although there is an obvious need to replicate the study. Several questions remain unanswered, including the maintenance of the increases over time, the degree to which the differential return of the children to regular classes was related to teachers' expectancies about the effects of the program, and the subsequent success of the children who returned to regular classes.

SUMMARY

In each of the areas we have described, it is clear that training can be used effectively with retarded individuals. In the case of relatively simple behaviors, straightforward use of operant principles is often highly effective. When the target behaviors become more complex, the use of a combination of different procedures appears preferable. The more successful attempts appear to involve detailed task analyses, the use of a variety of explicit training procedures in contexts meaningful to the subjects, and carefully programmed schedules of reinforcement. The amount of research in the training area appears to be increasing rapidly, the results are frequently positive, and there is good reason to be encouraged about the prospects for an extremely useful technology in this area.

PART IV
PROFESSIONAL PRACTICE: PSYCHODIAGNOSIS, EDUCATION, AND PSYCHOTHERAPY

16
Psychological Assessment in Mental Retardation[1]

Psychologists who are asked to assist in the appraisal of the intellectual status and adjustment of a child suspected of being mentally retarded are in a highly sensitive position. They may be dealing with parents who are first becoming aware of the child's problems; they may be called upon to aid in decisions and programming which will significantly affect the future course of a child's life; they may encounter a situation in which the child, family, teachers, or others, are distraught, frustrated, anxious, and/or perhaps seriously disturbed. Very frequently, psychologists enter the scene at a critical point when changes are taking place—in adults' perception of the child and consequently the child's self-perceptions, when a new course of action is being contemplated, when a crisis has been reached in the home or classroom, or when the child is emerging from the privacy of home to the public life of school. Because matters are in a state of flux and uncertainty, professional opinion is likely to be particularly influential. The matter of psychological assessment is never to be taken lightly, but at these critical times it is even more crucial that psychologists take care to utilize the best of their skills; to remain rational, cautious, and sympathetic; and to do the very best job of which they are capable in behalf of the child.

[1] See Sattler (1974) for a rational and detailed introduction to psychodiagnosis, particularly the appraisal of children's intelligence.

WHERE PSYCHODIAGNOSTICIANS WORK
AND WHAT THEY DO

Some psychologists see a great many retarded children; some see very few. The four most frequent professional settings in which psychologists do tend to see a large proportion of retarded children for evaluation are the following:

1. The Schools

School psychologists see many children whose teachers have observed their slow development and low achievement level. The responsibility for recommending whether children should be placed in special classes is often the school psychologists'; often they will work with the regular or special teachers to devise suitable individualized programs. These professionals tend to see more cultural-familial mentally retarded children than do other psychologists. Most moderately or severely retarded children will already have been identified by the time they reach school, although further evaluation may be necessary before placing them in special classrooms.

2. Independent Practice

Many psychologists work privately and independently, usually combining assessment and psychotherapeutic practice. Often they see clients on referral from other professionals, but sometimes they are approached directly by families who are troubled by their children's slow development. They tend to see mainly children from middle-class families since such families tend to seek private consultation and are able to pay for it.

3. Diagnostic Clinics

Diagnostic clinics, usually (but not always) publicly subsidized, generally consist of multidisciplinary teams which offer the possibility of an integrated service for retarded children and their families, a cooperative attempt at understanding, planning, and treatment by several specialists, no one of whom could achieve as complete a picture alone. Some teams constitute a bare minimum (typically, a physician, a psychologist, and a social worker); others include many more of the disciplines concerned with mental retardation. In large medical centers which combine teaching and research with a diagnostic and treatment center for mental retardation, one is likely to find representatives of audiology, dentistry, education, medicine (genetics, neonatology, neurology, obstetrics, ophthalmology, orthopedics, pediatrics, psychiatry, etc.), nursing, nutrition, occupational therapy, physical therapy, recreation, social work, speech and communication, vocational rehabilitation, etc. Of course, no single clinic is likely to encompass all these disciplines. The more elaborate the clinic staff, the more complicated the cases which are likely to be referred to and accepted by them for study. The best diagnostic clinic, however, is useless unless its findings are translated into a program of action. Some clinics undertake long-range, continuing contacts with families but many do not, instead recommending appropriate steps to be taken by other agencies. Since community services typically are unable to carry out all the recommendations made by the clinic staff, particularly when the child lives outside a large urban center of population, a great deal of ingenuity in planning is often called for—and a great deal of frustration often results both for clinic staff and for the children's families.

4. Institutional Settings

Psychologists working in institutions for the mentally retarded are generally concerned with quite different problems and populations. They may be asked to assist in admission procedures, in placing children in appropriate programs within the institution (see Chapter 21), and in helping to plan for post-institutional placement. They are also likely to be active in devising and carrying out therapeutic and educational programs and in consulting with caretaking personnel to upgrade the quality of care. The children and adults they see today are likely to be moderately to profoundly retarded, since few mildly retarded individuals currently are being placed in self-contained residential settings. Psychological services to community residential programs thus far have been very sparse, although hopefully this situation is changing.

Whatever the setting in which psychologists work with retarded individuals and their families, their activities naturally vary according to the needs of the clients, the nature of the contact, and the functions they are expected to cover. Rarely in fact do psychologists work completely alone. Even if they are in private practice there are likely to be other professionals—frequently school personnel, social welfare workers, and/or physicians—who have either referred the child to the psychologist or who are otherwise engaged in ongoing relationships with the child and his family.

The skills of psychologists working in clinical situations include those unique to the profession and those overlapping with the competencies of members of other disciplines. Psychodiagnosis involving more-or-less standardized assessment instruments is among the unique skills of the clinical psychologist; this chapter and the next are therefore devoted to matters related to this activity. In most situations, psychologists find that their special training in research is also a skill not shared to a significant degree by other members of the team.

The areas of overlapping skills are, however, much more numerous. These include behavioral assessments in nonstandardized situations (e.g., observation in the classroom or clinic playroom); assessment of the home and school situations and some understanding of the dynamic relationships found there; skills in working with parents, interpreting to them their child's problems and abilities, working out a program of treatment/management; and psychotherapy for the child or the parents, individually or in groups.[2]

Today psychologists have at their disposal a large number of objective instruments with which to assess many aspects of children's behavior.[3] Probably the most important and certainly the most thoroughly developed instruments are those which measure intellectual development. These tests are of unique importance for the psychologist who deals with retarded children, since it is in the cognitive sphere that retarded children are set apart most strikingly from normal children.

This chapter will present a general discussion of psychological diagnosis, or psychodiagnosis, giving particular attention to the problems involved in the assessment of intellectual status. In Chapter 17, the reader will find a discussion of the concepts of mental age (MA) and the intelligence quotient (IQ), and some assessment techniques which are useful in evaluating adaptive behavior. The emphasis in these chapters on the appraisal of intelligence and of adaptive behavior should by no means be taken to

[2] Chapters 17 through 21 are also relevant to the competencies of psychologists.
[3] See also Buros (1972), Cromwell (1967), Johnson and Bommarito (1971), Lambert, Wilcox, and Gleason (1974), Meyers (1973), and Silverstein (1970).

imply that other kinds of appraisals are unimportant with retarded children. Personality evaluation, achievement testing, and investigation of perceptual and motor difficulties are, indeed, as important with retarded individuals as with anyone else, and often these areas are critical to an understanding of the individual and his situation.

LIMITATIONS OF THE "DIAGNOSTIC" APPROACH

Diagnosis in the traditional sense involves the identification of a disease on the basis of its symptoms. As clinical procedure has evolved through hundreds of years of medical practice, the mainstay of the diagnostic process has come to be the system of syndrome classification on which it rests. This classification system requires the isolation of specific conditions which are a unique combination of etiology, symptoms, and prognosis. In some instances, identification of the syndrome rests mainly on the present pattern of symptoms; in others, special features of the medical history make classification possible. Matching the patient's condition to the correct category in the diagnostic system can supply missing information about etiology, treatment, and prognosis which could not have been deduced from the symptoms alone. Underlying this approach is the assumption that given causes are regular and predictable in their effects. In most branches of medicine, this scheme has worked fairly well, although there are many conditions about which full information is lacking.

For the psychodiagnostician, however, such an approach is not satisfactory. As yet, there are no known behavioral patterns based on physiological or psychological etiology which can be said to be certainly diagnostic of any given underlying condition. There is some hint that focalized lesions in the brain may produce characteristic test behaviors in children and adults, but these behaviors are not found exclusively in brain-injured individuals. Although there are various schemes for classifying psychiatric abnormalities, the usually broad and ill-defined categories are seldom expressions of specific etiologic entities. This is true in part because the human personality is capable of learning so many different ways of handling adversities and conflicts. For example, one retarded child who is exposed to pressure and rejection in his second-grade class may respond with a dogged determination to learn as well as the next fellow. Another second-grader with precisely the same mental abilities may refuse to try to learn at all.

Although an emphasis on etiology is a good way to organize the vast amount of data available about mental retardation, it is likely to be misleading. First, it tends to obscure the fact that genetic, physical, and psychological factors exist only in constant interaction with one another. Second, the scheme implies that most mentally retarded persons can now be classified according to etiological categories; as a matter of fact, it is the exceptional rather than the routine case which permits a confident, specific diagnosis. Third, it suggests that most of what is important about a retarded child is subsumed as part of a syndrome; this impression is patently false. Fourth, it predisposes one to conclude that identifying syndromes and underlying etiological processes is the way to solve important problems in the broad field of mental retardation. Such an approach would weaken the important progress which is currently being made in prevention, treatment, education, and rehabilitation and even in psychodiagnosis itself.

The "pigeonhole" diagnostic approach, therefore, has very limited utility; instead, the psychologist devotes his major efforts to answering the specific questions which brought the child to his attention in the first place, to pinpointing current difficulties, and to formulating more-or-less precise plans of action. For purposes of research and management, there is, of course, a need for systematic behavioral categories, comparable over time, space, and divergent populations. The schools, courts, welfare agencies, and insurance companies all seek systems which will help them to determine an individual's competence and the degree to which he can be held responsible for his actions.

It seems clear, however, that the time has come to turn to a descriptive approach to appraisal. A great deal of effort has been wasted in defining, debating, and redefining grossly oversimplified labels. A more complex multidimensional system would seem to be called for, a system which will permit the orderly description of each child in terms of a broad selection of behavioral propensities, skills, and abilities, the settings with which he or she must cope, and the services needed. One of the most important recommendations of the group of specialists working under Hobbs' leadership was that standard profiling systems be developed to describe individual children in just this way. Hobbs (1975b, Chap. 4) has described initial efforts in this direction undertaken by a number of agencies. The inclusion of both intellective and adaptive behaviors as part of the current AAMD definition of mental retardation (Grossman, 1973) is a small step in the direction of establishing a multidimensional descriptive system.

A thoroughgoing psychological evaluation involves complicated procedures and requires considerable time. Assessment instruments have been devised to yield a maximum of meaningful information in the shortest possible time, but there is no magic involved. The psychologist needs to sample many kinds of behaviors and to be sure that the picture obtained is representative of the child's usual behavior at home, in school, with playmates and so on. If the child's intellectual competence in school and other life situations appears higher than one would expect on the basis of the test score, that information, much more than the IQ, should be used in appraising the child's status.

To be frank, there is much for the psychologist to be modest about with regard to his assessment tools and the accuracy of his predictions. Although the tests of general intelligence are for the most part reliable and valid indicators of how well children will do in school, and to some extent their achievement in other areas, they are not foolproof. In addition, there is much more about children which psychologists would like to be able to describe with the same precision. This state of affairs is not, however, unique to psychological assessment; the tentativeness of diagnostic efforts is characteristic of many other professions in this field as well. Yet, using the tools of their trade, imperfect though they may be, and an extensive background of clinical experience, psychologists can, in cooperation with their colleagues and with the child's family, develop a reasonably coherent description of the child. If, on that basis, a supportive program can be devised, it will often more than justify the investment of time and funds in the diagnostic enterprise.

PROGRESS IN TESTING

Since the inception of psychological testing at about the beginning of the twentieth century, the precision and the utility of many psychological tests, particularly some intelligence tests, have been greatly improved. Although the use of tests, particularly group tests,[4] has tended at times to grow beyond all reasonable proportion and even to

[4] Group tests are seldom appropriate for retarded individuals, although they may sometimes be used for screening purposes, to be followed by individual assessment. See Chap. 1.

violate the rights of individuals in some situations (Matarazzo, 1972), individually administered intelligence tests have proved to be important assessment devices when used by well-trained, sophisticated, and somewhat cautious specialists.

This success has been the result of several factors. First, the test results have been regarded as samples of behavior and not as powerful x-rays of psychological functioning. The psychologist is fully aware that a child's performance in the testing room is not exactly the same as it would be under different conditions, that his score today is not necessarily the same as his score on the same test might be tomorrow, and that his score on one test bears only a partial resemblance to the score he might have received had a different test been given him. Test results are useful only to the extent that they are related to or predictive of important behaviors outside the test situation, and instruments which have not withstood research scrutiny have gradually been discarded over the years.

A second reason for the relative success of psychological testing has been the careful standardization of administration and scoring procedures. To the extent that the tests are presented each time under conditions which are the same for all, the responses of one child can be compared with those of another or with his own responses at some other time even if the tests are administered by different examiners, in different parts of the country.

A third factor in the success of psychological testing has been the development of meaningful norms with which each individual's performance can be compared. Normative distributions have been established by administering a test to large numbers of persons who are representative of the types of subjects with whom the test will be used. Since social and educational conditions vary somewhat from time to time, normative research must be repeated when it becomes outdated. Often, it is helpful to have norms for different populations with which the child will be in contact. The Nebraska Test of Learning Aptitude (Hiskey, 1941–1955) presents norms for both deaf and hearing children. Sometimes local or regional norms are also helpful, as, for example, Stanford-Binet performance of black children in the Southeastern part of the United States (Kennedy et al., 1963).

Anyone who doubts the contribution made by the development of standardized intelligence tests should consider the state of affairs which existed before these tests were available. Terman, in 1918, published a dramatic illustration of what may happen when even a knowledgeable expert attempts to assess intellectual status without the benefit of empirical guidelines. He had been called to examine a young man charged by the State of California with the murder of a six-year-old girl. The man had readily confessed to the crime, and the central issue in the case concerned the question of whether he was intelligent enough fully to comprehend the consequences of his actions and, thus, whether or not he could have "intended" to kill the child. The expert called to testify for the prosecution was a well-trained physician who had had extensive experience in mental hospitals but who was not acquainted with the then new intelligence tests. He had interviewed the defendant a number of times and was clearly well informed about the young man's intellectual behavior. The following are typical excerpts from his testimony, which bear upon his reasons for concluding that the defendant was of normal intelligence.

> I made any test that I could think of and which seemed appropriate at the time. I talked with him, had long conversations with him and checked up on how he answered my questions. At subsequent visits I would repeat those questions and see if he

gave the same answers. . . . [At one point] he picked up a paper. When he came to a picture of Uncle Sam I asked him what it was. He said it was a picture of Uncle Sam. . . . (p. 153)

On . . . [another] occasion I put him through some intelligence tests. I had brought with me a magazine and I turned through various pages; showed him some of the pictures; for example, I turned to a picture [representing cows in a building, with a patent stanchion] and I asked him, "Do you know what this is?" He said, "Sure, a dairy." I asked him if he had any cows at home and he said that they had some, a few. . . . (pp. 157-158)

At various times during these visits I made upon this man . . . some other tests; some tests to show his knowledge of moral responsibility, or his relationship to other people and his estimate of his ethical obligation to others. I suggested to him a suppositious offense. I said, "Suppose a Negro committed a crime upon a little girl, and as a result of that the little girl died. What ought to be done with him?" . . . His answer was that he ought to be put in jail for one hundred years, and fed on bread and water. (p. 158)

In summary, the physician stated:

Comparing him to a normal person living in such a family, living in such a house, living in such a location, having had a small term of education and no more than this boy has had, I would say that he is within two or three years either way of the normal for that style of person. In some ways he might exceed it and in others he would fall deficient. (p. 159)

Terman administered the 1916 revision of the Stanford-Binet, on which the nineteen-year-old defendant earned an MA of $7\frac{1}{2}$ years and an IQ of 50. On the Yerkes-Bridges Point Scale, he earned an MA of about 8 years. Terman described a case history which today would be considered rather typical of retardation due to psychosocial disadvantage. Whether or not this man was capable of recognizing the consequences of his behavior is a question we cannot answer, but we can be certain that he was not functioning at a normal intellectual level. Because he lacked standardized procedures or carefully documented normative data, it was impossible for the physician properly to interpret the information he had so laboriously collected.

Although professionals in all disciplines are now much more knowledgeable about mental retardation in general, their subjective estimates of the intellectual level of children still may vary considerably. Although there is often substantial similarity in the informal ratings of retarded individuals by pediatricians or by speech pathologists and the IQs obtained by psychologists, agreement is far from perfect, the correlations in one study ranging from .63 to .86 (Kurtz, 1965). With very young children, even lower degrees of agreement are found: pediatricians' estimates and scores on the Cattell Infant Intelligence Scale for a large group of two-year-olds correlated only .32 (Bierman, Connor, Vaage, & Honzik, 1964).[5] In this study, the pediatricians were more likely to underrate children with poor physical status and poor speech, especially boys.

---

[5] As we shall see, infant tests are rather unreliable indices of intellectual development, so this finding is difficult to interpret.

PROBLEMS IN ASSESSMENT AND THE APPROPRIATENESS
OF TESTS

Describing the behavioral patterns of a living human being is a difficult job at best. The difficulty arises from several sources. To begin with, each child is to some extent different from every other child. His unique combination of constitution and experience has produced behavioral patterns which to some extent are his alone. Adding to the difficulty is the fact that there exists nothing resembling a really comprehensive theory of psychological development. We do not fully understand the interplay of different aspects of behavior, and we undoubtedly ignore significant facets of intellectual and emotional behavior because we do not grasp their importance.

Still another problem arises from the fact that there are few if any assessment techniques which fully accomplish the tasks for which they were designed. Even the intelligence tests, by and large our most carefully developed instruments, are not equally effective with all persons. Emotional problems, restricted experience, uncooperativeness, and many other factors can depress performance. Children may appear retarded in a test situation who are in fact not retarded, though the reverse situation is rare. Too great a reliance on test scores alone can lead to very unfortunate outcomes, such as unjustified commitment to state institutions and inappropriate school placement.

Another problem relates to the appropriateness of the instrument for the child being evaluated. An obvious rule (though one evidentally violated at times by inexperienced psychologists) is that a verbal test of intelligence is completely unsuitable for a child who has had significantly less exposure to English than other children of his developmental level. With a native-born child, the psychologist may be unaware that English is not the major tongue spoken at home. In such cases, it is of course necessary to use the child's habitual language or a measure minimally dependent on language. Because of failure to employ such safeguards, the number of Mexican-American children placed in special classes, for example, is probably higher than it should be (Mercer, 1970); when tested individually with appropriate measures, such children tend to fare much better. Chandler and Plakos (1969) retested forty-seven Mexican-American children from special classes, grades three through eight; all spoke Spanish and had trouble using English. With a Spanish version of the Wechsler Intelligence Scale for Children, administered in a relaxed atmosphere, the group showed a mean gain in IQ of about thirteen points, from 68.6 to 81.8; thirty-seven students attained IQs of 75 or over, indicating that they had been previously misplaced. Although these differences hold true for children whose initial language is not English, dialectical differences (e.g., Negro nonstandard dialects) are apparently less powerful in their effects (Johnson, 1974; Quay, 1974).

It has been frequently argued (e.g., Ginsburg, 1972) that children raised in poverty environments are in a situation analogous to children with limited English fluency, that their experience has not fitted them to be tested on the same content as other children, and that they do not understand or accept the testing situation in the same light. This is, in other words, the contention that psychological tests are not "culture fair," that they consistently underestimate the abilities of some cultural groups. There is ample evidence to justify this suspicion. Children of economically disadvantaged families, those from rural areas, and those from some ethnic minorities tend to do poorly on the intelligence tests in common use. To some workers, the fact that the children do poorly is evidence that the tests are culturally biased against them, especially since in the past many normative samples have excluded nonwhite and/or rural children. To others, the same fact is evidence that the children are on the whole less intelligent. The latter group includes both those who tend to interpret the difference on a genetic basis and those who maintain that the environmental handicaps of disadvantaged minorities have suppressed the development of the children.

The simple fact that one group performs more poorly than another does not in itself prove bias, of course (Schmidt & Hunter, 1974). A test can be judged fair or unfair only on the basis of what it does. In the case of intelligence tests, the primary goal has been the prediction of academic success; in the case of selection tests, the goal is the prediction of success on the job. A test is biased against a group, then, if it consistently predicts lower achievement or performance by that group than actually proves to be the case (Cleary, 1968), or if it consistently excludes from selection more members of that group than would have been selected if their actual performance on the job or in school could have been foreseen (Thorndike, 1971).[6]

One must distinguish carefully between the unfairness of a test and the unfairness of society itself. In the United States, the same ethnic minorities which do poorly on intelligence tests, relative to the white middle class, do equally poorly in other ways— in school, in job success, in income. As we saw in Chapter 8, conditions associated with poverty deal many cruel blows to healthy development.

There is, of course, truth to the contention that psychological tests are sometimes biased, both in content and in the ways children react to them. To the extent that the content of a child's experience affects his performance on a standard test item, that is, to the extent that he would do better if a conceptually equivalent but more familiar item were presented, then the standard item will underestimate his conceptual ability. This point was demonstrated in a discrimination experiment with kindergarten children (Covington, 1967). The children were exposed repeatedly to stimulus items from a perceptual-discrimination test. The lower-status children improved their subsequent test performance significantly more than did the upper-status children, suggesting that an important element in their earlier poor performance had been a simple lack of familiarity.

If familiarity were the only difficulty, it would be a relatively simple matter to revise the tests. Unfortunately, it is not so easy. A classic attempt was the development of an intelligence test called the Davis-Eells Games (Eells, Davis, Havighurst, Herrick, & Tyler, 1951), which consisted of cartoon items equally familiar to lower-class and middle-class children. The lower-class children still achieved lower scores and, moreover, the scores did not yield as useful correlations with criterion measures such as school performance as did traditional tests.

Cultures do vary widely in the enhancement of intellectual skills and in attitudes toward taking tests. Each cultural group systematically seeks to encourage certain mental abilities and ways of behaving and to discourage others. Some African children, for example, have little experience with pictures and are said to have a very difficult time translating ordinary two-dimensional pictures into three-dimensional concepts (Hudson, 1960), their performance being highly dependent on the materials used (Omari & MacGinitie, 1974). Certainly, this deficit would be a handicap in many standard test items such as Picture Absurdities on the Stanford-Binet or the Block Design items of the Wechsler scales. The same Africans have by Western standards

---

[6] See Cleary, Humphreys, Kendrick, and Wesman (1975) for an even-handed discussion of the educational uses of tests with disadvantaged students.

very unusual skills in making auditory discriminations and would probably obtain superior scores if intelligence tests tapped this quality. Several investigators have pointed out that the Zuni Indians tend to do poorly on intelligence tests. In their cooperative society, it is considered rude to show one's peers at a disadvantage. When taking an intelligence test, a Zuni child may fail some items deliberately because he is afraid that the next child will be unable to answer (Cronbach, 1960).

It is not only between geographically separate cultures that such contrasts exist. Differences in motivation and in experience have been cited as accounting for the almost invariable finding that children of higher socioeconomic groups obtain better scores on intelligence tests. Havighurst commented on class differences:

> When the middle-class child comes to a test, he has been taught to do his very best on it. Life stretches ahead of him as a long series of tests, and he must always work himself to the very limit on them. To the average lower-class child, on the other hand, a test is just another place to be punished, to have one's weaknesses shown up, to be reminded that one is at the tail end of the procession. Hence the child soon learns to accept the inevitable and to get it over with as quickly as possible. Observation of the performance of lower-class children on speed tests leads one to suspect that such children often work very rapidly through a test, making responses more or less at random. Apparently they are convinced in advance that they cannot do well on the test, and they find that by getting through the test rapidly they can shorten the period of discomfort which it produces. (Eells et al., 1951, p. 21)[7]

As it stands, then, the argument about culture-fair tests involves reasonable arguments on both sides. It is clear that an examiner must be particularly cautious when selecting tests for a child whose experience has not been in the social mainstream and who may be threatened or simply unmotivated by the test situation. Children with limitations of fluency or with impairments of neurological, sensory, or motor functions require special handling to ensure that handicaps irrelevant to intelligence are not allowed to interfere with performance. To expect tests not in any way to favor one cultural group or another is, however, to deny both the complexity and the importance of environmental determination of intellectual development and the unavoidable truth that intelligent behavior will always tend to be defined and evaluated in relation to what the culture, and, of course, the test maker, choose to foster and to prize.

COMPETENCE AND TRAINING OF THE PSYCHOLOGIST

Individual testing requires very careful professional training. Most individual intelligence tests use a variety of items and several different kinds of materials. The standardized procedures must be followed precisely in word and gesture if the normative data are to be useful. Many test questions can be answered in a variety of ways, and the psychologist must be intimately acquainted with the scoring criteria in order to know whether further questioning is necessary. Finally, the interpretation of test behavior is a delicate task, requiring clinical experience, thorough grounding in personality and learning theory, extensive formal study, and supervised training. For ethical

---

[7] By permission from Eells, K. W., Davis, A., Havighurst, R. J., Herrick, V. E., and Tyler, R. W. *Intelligence and cultural differences: A study of cultural learning and problem solving.* The University of Chicago Press. Copyright, 1951, by the University of Chicago.

as well as legal reasons, the psychologist must make certain that he is qualified and is properly licensed or certified and/or working under acceptable supervision, according to the laws of his state or country.

Although there is much that is scientific about the way in which tests are developed, the psychodiagnostician is "first, foremost, and last an artisan" (Matarazzo, 1972, p. 14), a craftsman making use of a broad base of scientific information but depending a great deal on his own judgment, his knowledge about people and the worlds in which they live. He needs to be able to call upon a thorough education and on academic training in a variety of skills to (1) identify the purpose of the appraisal and the specific decisions which are contemplated, (2) select, administer, and interpret appropriate assessment techniques in the context of a broad view of the child's life situation, and (3) protect the child's rights and interests, those of the family, and those of the society.

All individual intelligence tests assume that the child's responses represent his or her very best effort. As we have seen, this high degree of motivation is not always easy to elicit. Many retarded children are chronically unhappy, shy, impulsive, or distractible. They may be made particularly tense by their strange surroundings or by their parents' fears about what the tests will reveal. Testers must have such command of the procedures and materials that they can give their full attention to the child, keeping him or her comfortable, interested, encouraged, and motivated to succeed. At the same time, sensitive clinicians will carefully note the qualitative as well as the quantitative aspects of the child's responses. Obviously, carrying out all these tasks simultaneously requires practice with many children under supervised conditions. Binet and Simon, who developed the first useful intelligence test, expressed it thus:

> It will not suffice simply to read what we have written in order to be able to conduct examinations. A good experimenter can be produced only by example and imitation, and nothing equals the lesson gained from the thing itself. . . . Theoretical instruction is valuable only when it merges into practical experience. Having made these reservations, let us point out the principal errors likely to be committed by inexperienced persons. There are two: the first consists in recording the gross results without making psychological observations, without noticing such little facts as permit one to give the gross results their true value. The second error, equally frequent, is that of making suggestions. An inexperienced examiner has no idea of the influence of words; he talks too much, he aids his subject, he puts him on the track, unconscious of the help he is thus giving. He plays the part of the pedagogue, when he should remain psychologist. Thus his examination is vitiated. It is a difficult art to be able to encourage a subject, to hold his attention, to make him do his best without giving aid in any form by an unskillful suggestion (Dennis, 1948, pp. 418–419).

The question of examiner influence is an important one. That different examiners can obtain very different results is an established finding (Cattell, 1937; Cieutat, 1965; Schwarz & Flanigan, 1971). Most studies indicate, however, that well-trained examiners tend to obtain relatively comparable results. Bateman (1969) found less than a half-point difference in Stanford-Binet IQs of mentally retarded children tested under standard positive "clinical" conditions and those tested under "production-line" conditions. The stability of IQs of retarded persons over time (see Chapter 17) also suggests rather limited examiner effects.

A number of investigators have studied the question of whether children achieve higher IQs when tested by an examiner of the same or a different race. (See Moore & Retish [1974] for a list of such studies.) Most have found no significant differences according to the race of the examiner, although there is a tendency for *inexperienced* examiners to show differences in the expected direction. LaCrosse (1964), for example, found only slightly greater variation between Stanford-Binet IQs obtained on retest by an experienced examiner of a different race than those obtained when the children were twice tested by the same person. The controversy is not entirely settled, but it is clear that experience is a far more powerful variable than is racial difference.

Yet, it is clear that the interchange between the examiner and subject is indeed sensitive to influence. Masling (1959) demonstrated that a friendly, warm subject is likely to receive greater encouragement and follow-up questioning from the examiner than is an unresponsive subject. Conversely, studies by Thomas, Hertzig, Dryman, & Fernandez (1971) and by Sacks (1952) demonstrate that a positive, encouraging attitude on the part of the examiner can generate significant gains in obtained IQ. An extremely important study by Zigler and Butterfield (1968) with culturally deprived children who did or did not attend nursery school demonstrated that the significant IQ gains made by the nursery school children were because of the reduction in debilitating motivational factors rather than because of the changes in their "real" rate of intellectual development.

Standardized intelligence tests are probably more resistant to examiner differences than are projective tests and others which are relatively unstructured. Dangel (1972), for example, gave differing referral information (positive, negative, or neutral) to three graduate students who tested fifty-four mentally retarded children. Despite differences in the examiners' expectations, there were no differences in WISC IQs, scoring errors, or follow-up questions to clarify responses. Dangel concluded that unstructured measures were more subject to examiner difference, however, as were items requiring relatively more examiner-subject interaction and more examiner judgment in scoring. Younger subjects may be more influenced by differences in examiners than are older subjects.

THE REFERRAL

One of the most important of the psychologist's functions is accomplished at the onset of his contact, when he seeks to determine exactly what prompted the child's being brought to him. His efforts at this time may well determine the usefulness of his findings. He may receive from a professional colleague a request such as, "Please test Susan Brown, age six." Often the request is no more specific than that, but it may be elaborated to read, "Organic? Schizophrenic?" or some equally cryptic question.

It is important to ensure that permission has been granted by the person(s) legally responsible for the child and also to seek further information before undertaking such a referral. Otherwise, the psychologist robs himself of the opportunity to be alerted to qualities in the child of special interest or importance and might even completely ignore the real questions which need to be answered. It is possible that when the psychologist gets in touch with the pediatrician who referred Susan, for example, he may find that the physician suspects the existence of a brain tumor, that he has been called to testify in court because Susan was hit by an automobile two months ago, that he is considering recommending institutionalization to the parents, or that Susan is being given medication which may account for her over- or underactivity. The physician may intend to show the report to the parents, to a school principal, or to the court, in which case the psychologist will wish to phrase his conclusions in slightly different words so that they will be easily understood by the reader.

When the request has come from the parents, the psychologist will probably want to arrange an interview with one or preferably both parents before seeing the child. Such an interview is especially desirable if the psychologist is not working in a clinic setting in which the parents have talked with other members of the clinic team. The psychologist will want to explore with special care the reasons behind the request for testing, the parents' specific concerns about the child, and the decisions they are facing at the moment. It is often appropriate to administer at this time a standardized questionnaire concerned with the child's social development. (See Chapter 17.) In describing their son or daughter, the parents may reveal a great deal about the emotional atmosphere in which the child is living. Moreover, the child may act very differently in the psychologist's office than at home.

The psychologist faces questions which are as varied as the individuals he sees. There are, however, some rather typical questions asked about mentally retarded children which have special reference to their retardation.

Description

Many questions call primarily for a description of the current behavior of a child suspected or known to be mentally retarded. The request may relate to the child's intellectual development, general behavior, or specific areas, such as perceptual distortions or language disorders. Usually, the psychologist will employ several different approaches in order to gain a notion of the kinds of things the child does better and worse and the evenness of his or her performance.

Sometimes the psychologist must administer poorly standardized tests because nothing better is available. This is particularly true when the child suffers a physical or communicative handicap, rendering the usual tests useless. When poorly standardized tests are used skillfully and the results are used conservatively, an evaluation adequate for the needs of the situation may be accomplished.[8]

The IQ scores derived from testing are merely summary indices of the child's performance. Whether the psychologist will wish to report the numerical IQ depends upon the sophistication of the person to whom the report is made, its possible future use, and the extent to which the psychologist considers it an adequate estimate of the child's functioning level. The young psychologist quickly learns that indiscriminate reporting of IQs can be damaging. In speaking with parents and other persons who cannot be expected to use the information with proper caution, the experienced psychologist prefers to describe the child's behavior in more general terms and to supplement this description with estimates of mental age or appropriate school placement. Thus, in speaking with the mother of Lorraine, a ten-year-old with an IQ of 75, the psychologist was able to talk about the child's development as resembling that of a

---

[8] Students are urged to read Haeusserman (1958), Jedrysek, Pope, Klapper, & Wortis (1972), Mittler (1970b), and Taylor (1959), sensitive discourses on techniques for testing young physically handicapped children.

seven- or eight-year-old, or "just about what would be expected of a second or third grader."

Quite apart from numerical scores, a testing situation is a rich source of information, only a small sample of life to be sure, but a period of an hour or more during which the child is in the company of a sympathetic and professionally trained adult. The psychologist will be alert to observe many facets of the child's behavior aside from successes or failures on the test items. He will see, for example, that Johnny is sullen and withdrawn, unwilling to be drawn into a "game" atmosphere, whereas Anna thoroughly enjoys herself. Sam does well until he reaches the harder items, after which he stops making an effort, but George tries so hard that he never admits that he does not know an answer. Sandra is up and about the room after every item and can be brought back to her chair only with an effort; Jonathan sits passively, waiting for the examiner to produce the next item. Kathy has an air of security and happiness; Joe seems sad; Scott appears angry. Each child is different, but each tells the psychologist much about himself or herself through the language of behavior.

Test items may give important clues unrelated to the primary purpose of the task. When asked, "What's the thing for you to do if another boy hits you without meaning to do it?" Bert says, "I don't care; I'd hit him back," and Hank, whose response is also unacceptable, says, "I'd tell the teacher." Sandy gives two reasons why children should obey their parents: "Because they'll hit you and because they'll yell real loud." Joey defines "nuisance" as "my brother." Elaine says the color of rubies is "bloody."

The psychologist should remain aware that, no matter what the superficial nature of the referral, personality variables are likely to be implicated (Cromwell, 1967), both on the part of the child and the family members or others who care for him. Mildly retarded children are seldom referred for special placement, for example, if they make modest progress in the classroom and relate well enough to the teacher and the other children that the situation seems relatively satisfactory to all concerned. Others no more retarded in intelligence or school achievement are referred for distractibility, "talking back" and other forms of attention getting, sullenness, etc. Sometimes the child is referred because the parents or even the grandparents are having difficulty accepting his retardation; sensitive intervention can often reduce the disruptive tensions and frustrations.

Classification

The clinician may be asked to classify a child as "retarded" or "normal," "trainable" or "educable," or to place him in the appropriate niche in some other classification system. Fortunately, such questions rarely occur by themselves, but their most frequent legitimate use, aside from research, occurs in connection with decisions about admission to special classes or residential facilities, or establishing legal eligibility for special programs such as Social Security Childhood Disability supports. This yes-or-no kind of judgment is often vexing, especially in the borderline levels of intellectual ability and in cases in which emotional maladjustment or environmental deprivation seem to interfere with intellectual functioning.

With the development of intelligence tests and the apparent simplicity of interpreting IQs, which early were thought to be constant throughout life, it became very popular to label as subnormal all persons attaining an IQ of less than 70 on a standardized test. Psychologists are still suffering the effects of this custom and are continually being exhorted to relinquish their "mechanical" administration and interpretation of tests (e.g., Ginsburg, 1972; Mercer, 1970). As a matter of fact, there are probably not many bona fide psychologists today who interpret even a routine test without regard to the consistency of the findings, the personal adjustment and prior experience of the child, the testing conditions, or any of the numerous other factors which have repeatedly been shown to affect test scores. If it were not for the exigencies arising from the need to establish consistent criteria for admission to schools and other programs, psychologists would probably tend to avoid altogether the application of labels, which are apt to be inaccurate in a borderline case and misinterpreted in any case. The misuse of tests and test scores by insufficiently trained individuals, is, however, a very serious continuing problem. Although seeking actively to eradicate abuses, it remains the responsibility of the psychologist to employ good judgment in applying labels when he must, to refuse to apply them when he cannot do so in good conscience, and to note clearly the bases upon which each classification was made.

> Mark and Barbara, ages 6 and 9, were the oldest of four children whose father had recently died. Their mother proved to be inadequate to the task of keeping the family together, and eventually the juvenile court was forced to take custody of the children. School records listed Mark's IQ as 65 and Barbara's as 59. The reports did not reveal that these scores were obtained on a group intelligence test administered throughout the school shortly after their father had died, when tension was high in the family. At that time, both children were failing in their studies, although they had not previously been noted as being unusually slow. On the basis of this report, proceedings were begun to commit Mark and Barbara to a state institution, while the two younger children were kept in a foster home for observation. Unlike many, the institution to which they were sent provided a probationary evaluation period. Since both children were resistive and sullen when they first came to the school, the psychologist did not try to administer any test until he had spent a considerable amount of time in winning their confidence. Two months after admission, Mark attained an IQ of 93 on a Stanford-Binet, and Barbara's IQ under the same favorable conditions was 87. They were placed in a foster home together with their siblings, and even though their future is not bright because of their social situation, they at least have a better chance than in an institution which did not fit their needs.

Twenty-four cases likewise erroneously committed to an institution were reviewed by Garfield and Affleck (1960). They found in some instances that serious emotional problems, a history of deprivation, or uncooperativeness in the testing situation had existed but had been ignored in the test reports.

As better measures of adaptive behavior are becoming available (see Chapter 17), it should soon be possible to carry out a standardized evaluation of both the aspects of behavior subsumed under the AAMD definition of mental retardation. Such a development will be most welcome, for it will provide an objective means to summarize the clinical impressions of the psychologist about the degree to which impaired intellect is proving a practical handicap to the child. Even then, however, judgments will remain difficult, for mechanical interpretation of two scores would be little improvement over the mechanical interpretation of one.

Fortunately, we are no longer burdened with the notion that retardation must be a permanent affliction; instead, it is seen now as perfectly possible that a child may be accurately regarded as mildly or even moderately retarded at one time in his life and not at another. Intellectual handicap is likely to be most blatant during the school years. Environments change; people change; expectations change. It is important to keep alternatives open and to provide for periodic reevaluation.

Preplacement or Pretreatment Appraisal

A psychological evaluation is often a prerequisite when a program of action is being contemplated. Sometimes there is need to establish a baseline against which to measure later progress; at other times the psychologist is asked for help in selecting among alternative placements or in designing a program of remediation. The psychologist may be asked to establish whether a child is eligible for a program (e.g., speech therapy may be limited to children whose language development lags significantly behind their cognitive development). To answer such questions, the psychologist obviously will need an armamentarium of instruments as well as considerable experience with the potential helping facilities within the child's community. Planning a remedial program involves many specific decisions. Initial explorations will evaluate the child's current status in a number of areas and may attempt to formulate some cause-and-effect hypotheses—e.g., lack of auditory discrimination skills interfering with reading ability, competitive tensions leading to bedwetting, unwitting reinforcement of misbehavior by the teacher, etc. Ultimate and intermediate goals can then be defined, and steps toward achieving them outlined, as well as steps for checking the validity of the hypotheses. In each of these processes, behavioral assessment is essential.

Etiology

Although the psychologist is often asked to speculate about the etiology of a child's handicap, his instruments and skills are not very useful to this task. This state of affairs exists for a number of reasons. First, by virtue of the organic unity discussed in Chapter 7, children suffering from different kinds of stress show symptoms in all spheres of their life processes. Second, symptoms produced by organic causes often resemble learned maladjustive behavior patterns and vice versa. Third, conditions which begin quite differently may later result in very similar pictures. Finally, some difficulty in distinguishing between apparently diverse groups may stem from actual similarities in etiology, such as organic factors underlying autism (seen as emotional disturbance) or retardation apparently due to psychosocial disadvantage.

For all these reasons, test patterns of emotionally disturbed, cultural-familial, and brain-injured groups of children are very difficult to differentiate. Bortner and Birch (1969), for example, compared the WISC responses of 131 emotionally disturbed and 116 brain-damaged children, ages seven to eleven years. They found more instances of subnormal intellectual functioning in the brain-damaged group, but according to other indices the intellectual organization of the two groups was markedly similar. Most other studies also show little validity for scatter or subtest patterning as diagnostic aids (Silverstein, 1970). Such results cast considerable doubt upon the validity of etiological judgments based on test scores or of using etiological diagnoses as valid criteria for separating the groups in school or for designing different curricula for them.

Despite all these factors which demand caution, test behavior does at times suggest clues deserving further investigation. Symptoms of brain injury, overprotection, rejection, isolation, and lack of stimulation are often but not always apparent in a child's behavior. In conjunction with medical and social findings, the psychologist can sometimes make a valuable contribution if he proceeds with modesty and caution.

Research and Evaluation

The psychologist has an important role to play in research and evaluation. Most of the research reported in this entire volume has made use in some way of objective standardized procedures. There is a temptation, because the intelligence tests have been so carefully standardized, to utilize them to the exclusion of any other instruments. Much of the controversy about the effectiveness of Head Start programs, for example, stems from the paucity of instruments sensitive to possible changes in children's social behavior, their self-concepts, their curiosity and creativity, and their motivation to learn. To some extent, this is like a person looking under the lamppost when he knows he dropped his keys around the corner—one looks where one can see.

Prognosis

Finally, the psychologist may be asked to predict the child's future behavior. This indeed is the most difficult kind of question of all. No simple rules suffice; complexities abound when we deal with the very plastic growth patterns of children. In general, however, the older the child, the lower his intelligence, and the more limited the time span, the more accurate the prognostic statement is likely to be. (See Chapter 17.) It is particularly important with young and/or mildly retarded children, therefore, to provide for retesting at appropriate intervals.

Deficiencies which are extremely handicapping during childhood, particularly in the school situation, may be much less debilitating during the adult years when other skills can be used to maintain an adequate economic and social adjustment. Many mildly retarded individuals can maintain their own families and live independently in the community. Within a given range, the child's motivation, personality pattern, and nonintellectual abilities may be more important for prediction than his or her IQ; his or her life situation and the opportunities it provides may be even more critical. (See Chapter 22.)

Consideration of the future development of retarded children cannot easily be sidestepped, for many far-reaching practical decisions must often be made while they are still young. Sometimes the psychologist is asked to help parents who are concerned with school placement, institutionalization, and a host of other management questions such as, "Is it worthwhile to try to teach him to read? Will he ever be able to do so for his own enjoyment?" "In connection with writing our wills, how extensive will be the supervision he will need as an adult?" Social agencies commonly desire predictions of intellectual growth when placing infants and young children in adoptive homes. Other questions may concern a child's ability to respond to psychotherapy, speech therapy, or other special treatment. Guarded predictions on the basis of the child's present behavior may be better than no predictions at all, but the clinician is well advised to shut as few doors as possible, leaving the way open for periodic reevaluation in light of the child's actual progress.

REPORTING THE FINDINGS

Having formulated accurate, perceptive, and wise responses to the referral questions, and even having written a report which communicates the findings in plain, straightforward language, the psychodiagnostician has not completed his task. Unless the findings are communicated effectively to the people who count in the child's life, the entire effort has been but a useless exercise. The psychologist may not be the appropriate professional to interpret the findings to the persons responsible for the child, especially if a colleague is working with them on a continuing basis, but it is his responsibility, nonetheless, to do what he can to aid the feedback process by making sure his findings are understood by the person who will ultimately make the contact and by making himself available if further questions arise.

Frequently, direct interpretation of the findings to parents is likely to be helpful. A typical situation arises when a school has requested help in arriving at a placement decision or in formulating an individualized plan of remediation. Superficially, a report to the school authorities and/or the teacher would seem to suffice, but in fact the parents are the most stable figures in the child's life and the most invested in his or her well-being. As the child grows older and changes schools, as teachers resign and are replaced, as the family moves, real continuity can best be achieved when the parents are full participants. Sometimes it will be up to them to inform unfamiliar school personnel about their child's special needs and strengths.

The feedback interview is a potent clinical interaction involving many unspoken and irrational elements. (See Chapter 20.) Those intimately involved with the child, especially parents, teachers, even therapists, may have attitudes toward the child or toward their own role adequacy which interfere with communication. Unless these feelings are handled, the psychologist may be speaking to deaf ears.

> The psychologist must assume that this person (or couple) has built up a set of needs and personal constructs about the child's behavior. Otherwise, they would not have sought the clinician's assistance. . . . The psychologist must unfold a sequence of communication that has the best possibility of changing attitudes and behavior in a way that would represent the best interests of the child and all concerned. (Cromwell, 1967, p. 82)

PROVIDING A SUPPORTIVE EXPERIENCE FOR THE CHILD

Thus far we have discussed the psychologist's responsibility to the child only as it is expressed in what he communicates to other persons. Equally important are the attitudes he communicates to the child himself. There is no reason to subject a child to the feeling that he has failed to perform adequately in the examination situation or that he has failed to earn the respect and support of the tester. Most children are all too painfully aware of their shortcomings. It is usually possible to give reassurance by offering tactful praise and taking care to present a number of tasks the child can accomplish well. Although the competent examiner will not allow the child to be satisfied with a performance which represents less than his best effort, the child deserves to know that his best effort is indeed quite satisfactory.[9]

Finally, let us take this opportunity to remind the reader of a maxim too often forgotten: the retarded child is simply a child. The worker who seeks to understand any child needs to ask, "What is this child like? What sorts of factors contribute to his being this way? What can be done to help him overcome his weaker points and maximize his capabilities?" The retarded child's competence and happiness depend not only on his own capacities and limitations but on his opportunities for development and the attitudes and skills his environment teaches him. Although he exhibits a special disability, it constitutes only a part of the picture of his life adjustment.

---

[9] Ways of helping a child gain confidence within the framework of standard testing conditions have been outlined by Terman and Merrill (1973).

17

Mental Age, the Intelligence Quotient, and Assessment of Adaptive Behavior

Every year, many thousands of retarded persons are administered individual intelligence tests, and a growing number are also evaluated by means of a variety of measures designed to tap adaptive behavior. Decisions based on these data can affect children for the rest of their lives. The services offered to or withheld from them and their families may depend very largely on the degree to which these children are seen as deviant from the norm in intelligence and adaptive behavior. It is absolutely imperative that anyone using these kinds of data understand the statistical concepts involved, recognize the limits within which the tests may be of use, and learn to employ them judiciously.

The present chapter discusses some of the basic essentials needed to interpret intelligence tests and measures of adaptive behavior. After introducing the concepts of mental age (MA) and the intelligence quotient (IQ), we will discuss a number of questions about the continuity of intellectual development and the stability of the IQ. Fortunately, the history of intelligence testing is a long one (see Chapter 1), and there is a considerable body of data on which to draw. With regard to the assessment of adaptive behavior, on the other hand, we are seeing only the beginning of a comparable effort; the final section of the chapter describes the state of that art.

MA, IQ, AND CONSTANCY OF INTELLECTUAL DEVELOPMENT[1]

The concepts MA and IQ owe their origins to the development of tests of the Binet type, but each has been modified to some extent over the years. Only by understanding the operations on which each is based can one grasp the essential fact that each is a form of *test score,* no more and no less. Reasonably, one expects test scores to change a bit from one testing or one instrument to another; one should expect changes in MA and IQ. Just as test scores are summaries of a limited range of behavior related to the particular areas sampled by the test, so MA and IQ measures are restricted in scope. Their value is that they are, indeed, often related to important kinds of behaviors about which one needs to know and that, as such measures go in the realm of human behavior, they are relatively stable and effectively predictive. Their faults tend to be as much a product of the unrealistic expectations with which they have been invested as in their own limitations. The good carpenter knows what each of the tools will and will not do; so must it be for the professional in the field of mental retardation with regard to these tools of the trade.

Definitions and Usage

Mental age is a notion introduced by Alfred Binet[2] (Binet & Simon, 1908) as a yardstick by which to measure a child's current intellectual development. A specific MA is meant to express the average intellectual attainment of children of that chronological age (CA). This concept is used routinely in intelligence tests of the Binet type in which items are arranged by age levels, with the goal that groups of randomly selected children will attain average MA scores which equal their average CAs.

When such a test is administered, the child is given all the items in the range of his abilities, including the highest level at which he can pass all the items *(basal age)* and the lowest level at which he fails all of them *(ceiling age).* The MA is obtained by adding to the basal age credit for each item passed above it. A bright child and a dull child of different CAs may attain the same MA, of course, although their mental development has been quite different. Actually, the brighter child will, as a rule, succeed more frequently with abstract and verbal reasoning items and the dull child with performance items or those requiring the repetition of previously learned material (Achenbach, 1970; Merrill, 1924; Meyers, Dingman, Attwell, & Orpet, 1961; Thompson & Magaret, 1947).

Following a suggestion by L. W. Stern, Terman (1916) introduced a further refinement, the *intelligence quotient* or IQ. This measure is obtained by dividing an individual's MA by his CA and multiplying by 100. For example, a child whose CA is four years, two months (fifty months) and who attains an MA of fifty months, obtains an IQ of 100. If he attains an MA of only three years, four months (forty months), his IQ is 80. With an MA of five years (sixty months), his IQ is 120. Just as the MA is an index of the child's intellectual maturity, so the IQ becomes a measure of his brightness or rate of growth. The IQ we have just described is known technically as a *ratio IQ,* since it represents the ratio of MA to CA.

---

[1] The reader is referred to Johnson & Bommarito (1971), Buros (1972), and Sattler (1973) for information about individual tests of intelligence. The scope of this book has dictated an emphasis on the appraisal of intellectual development, although techniques of personality assessment constitute a vital adjunct in testing retarded children.

[2] Binet actually used, instead, the term *mental level* (Hunt, 1974).

Only age scales, like the Stanford Binet, yield age scores. Other tests yield point scores. The various Wechsler tests, for example, utilize homogeneous subtests; the subtest point scores, translated into standard scores, are added separately within verbal and performance divisions of the test and the totals are converted, by means of a table, to a Verbal IQ, a Performance IQ, and a Full Scale IQ. (See Chapter 1.)

The most popular individual intelligence tests are the Stanford-Binet Intelligence Scale (Terman & Merrill, 1973), the Revised Wechsler Intelligence Scale for Children (WISC-R) (Wechsler, 1974), the Wechsler Preschool and Primary Scale of Intelligence (WPPSI) (Wechsler, 1967), and the Wechsler Adult Intelligence Scale (WAIS) (Wechsler, 1955). These tests have all abandoned the simple ratio IQ in favor of a measure introduced by David Wechsler in 1944, the *deviation IQ*. The deviation IQ is a form of standard score in which the obtained distribution of IQs (which is usually slightly irregular) is converted to a normal distribution with a mean of 100 and a standard deviation which is the same at every age. The Stanford-Binet uses a standard deviation of 16; the Wechsler scales, a standard deviation of 15. It is unfortunate that the scales do not employ identical standard deviations, but the differences are ordinarily of minor psychological significance.

The deviation IQ method has the advantage of establishing IQs which are more nearly comparable and more stable from one age level to another than can be attained with the ratio IQ (Pinneau, 1961). In the 1937 revision of the Stanford-Binet, for example, actual standard deviations were high at some ages and low at others. The deviation IQ expresses the relative standing of a child with respect to the scores of children of his own age and is easily convertible to a percentile rank,[3] a simple and widely accepted statistical expression. Furthermore it permits easy comparison of standard scores on one test with those on another, provided that their means and standard deviations are made comparable.

Table 17-1 compares Stanford-Binet ratio IQs and deviation IQs at two mental ages, 4-0 and 8-0, for children of varying CAs. As can be seen from the two rows in which CA = MA, the 1972 standardization found the greatest mean changes from the test as originally constructed for the preschool age range. A child of 4-0 earning an MA of 4-0 now attains a surprising IQ of only 88. For retarded children, the differences are generally smaller than for children of above-average ability.

Table 17-1 Ratio IQs versus Deviation IQs on the 1972 Stanford-Binet

CA	MA	Ratio IQ	Deviation IQ*
3-0	4-0	133	115
4-0	4-0	100	88
6-0	4-0	67	58
8-0	4-0	50	48
6-0	8-0	133	129
8-0	8-0	100	95
12-0	8-0	67	68
16-0	8-0	50	52

Source: Terman and Merrill (1973).

[3] The reader may wish to refer to the normal curve illustrated in Chap. 2, on which percentile figures are shown.

Concepts analogous to the MA and the IQ have been found useful by workers dealing with other aspects of human variation. Gesell (1949) used the ratio concept of *developmental quotient* (DQ) in his infant-assessment scale, and Bayley (1969) used deviation quotients to express an infant's *mental development index* (MDI) and *psychomotor development index* (PDI). E. A. Doll (1936, 1964) used the concepts *social age* (SA) and (ratio) *social quotient* (SQ) in a developmental approach to the assessment of adaptive behavior. Gruelich (1950) used the term *skeletal age* to express the maturity of children's bone structure. In reporting such scores as these, it is important to guard against confusion with the terms MA and IQ, which should be reserved exclusively for the description of intellectual behavior.

How One Uses an MA   Although different children with the same MA may vary widely in the quality of their intellectual development, the MA concept has been retained because of its basic utility in answering certain questions. Little sophistication is required to grasp the concept, and it is therefore extremely useful in talking with parents and other lay persons. Parents have observed their own and other children at different ages and can usually more readily accept this way of discussing the needs and limitations of their handicapped children. Adults are generally rather good at modifying their behavior according to the child's developmental level, and this way of thinking can help them to behave appropriately. One is often interested primarily in the actual level of maturity the child has attained. In arranging special classes, homogeneous grouping by standards of mental maturity is sometimes more helpful than grouping by CA or brightness. Determination of the point at which a teen-ager is ready for training as a gardener or stock clerk may be more accurate if MA is considered.

With normal adults the MA concept means little; age changes are slow and irregular following the adolescent years. With retarded adults the concept is more appropriate, however, since in some ways their intellectual capacities can be meaningfully compared with those of children. The MA also avoids the implication that the intellectual development of retarded persons is limited to the same period of the life span as tends to be true for normal persons. In fact, there is evidence that this growth period is extended in the moderately and mildly retarded (Fisher & Zeaman, 1970).

The MA also offers special advantages for research. In equating or dividing groups by intellectual level, or in discovering the relationship (correlation) between some other variable and mental ability, the MA is usually the preferred unit of measurement. Most variables are expressed as scores on a single dimension which, unlike the IQ, has no built-in correction for age. If, for example, one wishes to correlate intellectual status with reading achievement according to school-grade equivalent, MA is clearly more appropriate than IQ.

How One Uses an IQ   The development and popular utilization of the IQ as a single, simple, objective index of the rate of intellectual growth has been a mixed blessing. When properly understood and carefully used, an IQ can be valuable in assessing a child's rate of progress, but it refers to only those aspects of mental ability tapped by a particular test. (See Chapter 1.) Its measurement is subject to error from a number of sources, some of them capable of drastically affecting scores. There is little doubt that IQs have been seriously misused because of persistent and erroneous notions about their supposed permanence or their magical power to predict future performance. Such a simple index of present behavior as the IQ cannot possibly reflect

Fig. 17-1   These moderately retarded teenagers are happy on playground equipment normally used by younger children. *(J. & M. Menapace)*

all the many aspects of the complex developmental phenomenon known as intelligence.

Nowhere has the IQ proved to be a more mixed blessing than in matters concerning the welfare of mentally retarded children. To be sure, the development of intelligence tests provided a means for more objective assessment. Tests have been very useful in helping to identify children who need special training and in establishing more orderly methods for admission procedures in institutions. Many retarded children have been helped to lead more productive lives because of the early identification of their problems. Other children whose school failures were not due to overall intellectual deficits have also been identified and treated accordingly.

On the other hand, the apparent simplicity of the IQ led to an enthusiastic but largely misguided movement to label or classify children primarily on the basis of their scores on intelligence tests. Accurate classification of intellectual deficit was thought to be all that was required to achieve an understanding of retarded children, their individual characteristics being grossly underestimated. Furthermore, undue belief in IQ constancy led to a diminution in research and treatment. Professional interest in many complex problems declined over a long period, not to be rejuvenated until the mid-1960s. Fortunately, a more realistic view now prevails. Although some persons (seldom those who work directly with retarded children) advocate abandoning the IQ concept altogether because it has been so badly used and so grossly abused, this minority view has not received much support. Most psychologists today continue to use the IQ as an index of intellectual development and, when judiciously employed, it can greatly facilitate helping a child better utilize his or her potential as a human being.

Continuity of Intellectual Development and the Constancy of the IQ

One source of the IQ controversy has been the problem of the continuity of intellectual development. When the question is phrased in terms of mental tests, it becomes the problem of the constancy of the IQ. Several different notions have been included and, more often than not, confounded by those who have discussed the continuity-constancy problem. Difficulties have stemmed largely from confusion of the construct intelligence with the tests themselves. Questions pertinent to the problem are discussed in the following sections.

How Do General Mental Ability and the IQ Develop and Decline Over the Life Span?   Everybody knows that mental growth is most dramatic in the early years of life. There is a much greater difference, for example, between a child's behavior at ages one and two than at twelve and thirteen. There may be minor spurts at various stages during childhood (Epstein [1974] suggests spurts at ages three, seven, eleven, and fifteen), but by and large the curve of growth shows a continuing, steadily decelerating rise (Bayley, 1955, 1956a), declining from the very rapid rate during infancy to a relatively slow increment in adolescence.

The fate of mental ability during adulthood has been a subject of greater controversy. It had previously been held that normal mental growth decelerated so dramatically in adolescence that, for practical purposes, beyond age sixteen it could be ignored. Terman and Merrill (1937), for example, provided an arbitrary adult CA of fifteen years in calculating the ratio IQ for the 1937 revision of the Stanford-Binet; the present revision allows for increments only to age eighteen (Terman & Merrill, 1973). Widely accepted studies by Jones and Conrad (1933), Miles and Miles (1932), and the adult norms of the Wechsler scales (1939, 1955) had seemingly demonstrated on cross-sectional samples that mental growth showed a sharp decline after the early twenties.

A major fallacy in cross-sectional studies is that they do not take into account sociocultural changes, such as broadened educational opportunities and the advent of television, which affect whole populations growing up in different eras. Most authors of intelligence tests have found that each successive revision requires an upgrading of the norms. One study (Schaie, Labouvie, & Buech, 1973) which compared cross-sectional samples of adults tested one time only in 1956, 1963, or 1970, found each successive cohort scoring higher than the one before it. These investigators found that for abilities heavily dependent on education and acculturation, including verbal meaning, reasoning and arithmetic, there was a negligible amount of genuine longitudinal change even past middle age, although there were declines in fluency dimensions such as word fluency and psychomotor speed.

Longitudinal studies following individual adults (Bayley, 1955; Bayley & Oden, 1955; Green, 1969; Kangas & Bradway, 1971; Owens, 1966) have found, in fact, continued mental growth rather than decline on such items as vocabulary and comprehension, which depend upon continuous learning. Items which test visual and motor factors do seem to show a decrement, some beginning to decline as early as age twenty-five. Overall mental ability probably does not ordinarily decrease seriously, however, until people become quite elderly.

Available studies of retarded individuals over time are less definitive, but they suggest that, for institutional populations at least, the rate of growth during childhood and adolescence fails to keep pace with the level predicted from early IQs. During this period, there is a progressive decrease in the IQ because CA is increasing proportionally faster than MA. For mildly and moderately retarded groups, however, the period of mental growth is extended so that there are subsequent increases in IQ to age twenty-five or thirty-five (Fisher & Zeaman, 1970; Guertin, 1949; Ross, 1971a; Sternlicht & Siegel, 1968). Although it is tempting to blame the earlier decreases on the effects of institutionalization, there are no directly comparable studies of equivalent noninstitutionalized groups. Some retests of institutionalized individuals after periods of twenty-five to thirty-five years have shown small but consistent decreases (Earhart & Warren, 1965; Silverstein, 1969), but these may merely indicate that individuals who remain in institutions that long are those who have not shown continued growth.

As we shall see in Chapter 22, a few studies have shown improved test scores in adults who had been placed in special education classes as children and who, when studied, were functioning in the community. Several interpretations of this finding are possible. First, there is the possibility that the difference is mainly a statistical artifact reflecting regression toward the mean.[4] Second, as was suggested with institutional populations, this group may continue to gain in mental maturity longer than do nonretarded persons. There is evidence that in a number of other ways their adjustment improves during young adulthood. And finally, it may also be that school has an unduly depressing effect on the mental functioning of many children (those who are such spectacular failures that they are placed in special classes), and that once this stressful period is behind, the individual is able to function more adequately. One cannot pick among these alternatives on the basis of research evidence, and indeed there may be some truth to all three.

Do Individuals Maintain Their Relative Status Compared with Others of Their Age? The overall question about continuity or constancy in the development of general mental ability essentially concerns the progress of a general factor (g factor) during the life span. (See Chapter 1.) Studies of IQ constancy naturally depend upon the reliability of the tests and the consistency of their content from one age level to another. Constancy tends to be higher when subjects are older rather than younger at the time of original testing, when the interval between test and retest is shorter, and when the better standardized tests are employed (Bayley, 1949; H. E. Jones, 1954).

If we eliminate infant tests, we find substantial correlations between early and later tests of intelligence. Wilson (1974), for example, reports a correlation of .70 between Bayley test scores at age two and Wechsler test scores at age six in a large sample of twins. A very long-term follow-up of the California segment of the original preschool standardization sample for the 1937 Stanford-Binet is the best study available of an unselected population. By means of diligent and heroic efforts, Bradway (Bradway, Thompson, & Cravens, 1958; Bradway & Robinson, 1961) was able to keep track of 111 of these subjects into adolescence and early adulthood and 62 of them into their middle adult years (Kangas & Bradway, 1971). On the last occasion, she

---

[4] A group selected by its low scores, when retested, will attain scores more like the mean of the population, negative measurement errors having predominated at the time when the group was chosen.

Table 17-2   Correlations among Test Scores at Four Administrations over a Thirty-eight-year Period

Test	1941 N = 110	1956 N = 109 - 111		1969 N = 48	
		S - B (Form L)	W A I S (Full Scale)	S - B (Form L-M)	W A I S (Full Scale)
1931 S-B*	.65	.59	.64	.41	.39
1941 S-B (L)		.85	.80	.68	.53
1956 S-B (L)			.83	.77	.58
1956 WAIS (FS)				.72	.73
1969 S-B (L-M)					.77

*Mean of Forms L&M
Source: Kangas & Bradway (1971, p. 335).

chose 48 of the willing and geographically most convenient subjects for retest. The Stanford-Binet was administered in 1931, 1941, 1956, and 1969; WAIS's were administered as well in 1956 and 1969. Table 17-2 lists the intercorrelations among these six tests. They are rather impressive. Consistent with the other studies we have reported, Bradway's data further reveal progressive increments in Binet IQs during adulthood which suggest continued mental growth during this period, with somewhat less marked increments in both Verbal and Performance IQs from the 1956 to the 1969 WAIS tests.

Studies of mentally retarded children generally report very stable IQs, much more stable than those of children with average or superior IQs (Goodman & Cameron, in press). The lower the IQ, the more stable it generally is found to be. Part of the stability stems from a statistical artifact of test construction which makes low scores more stable than high ones, especially on an age scale like the Stanford-Binet (McNemar, 1942). Collmann and Newlyn (1958) reported a test-retest correlation of .93 for 182 retarded children who were tested on admission to a residential school and again after one year. Over longer periods, of course, one cannot expect quite as stable results, but even after periods as long as thirty-five years, and even with changes in the actual tests administered, institutionalized retarded subjects seldom show changes of as much as 10 to 14 points (Alper & Horne, 1959; Earhart & Warren, 1964).[5] For an even more severely handicapped group of children and adults (mean IQ 11), a remarkable correlation of .98 was found on retest with the Stanford-Binet or the Kuhlmann-Binet (Kuhlmann, 1939) after a period of sixteen months (Ross & Boroskin, 1972). With another profoundly retarded group (mean IQ 15), a test-retest correlation of .80 was found with a period of nine years separating the two tests (MacAndrew & Edgerton, 1964).

Despite the strong tendency for scores on well-standardized scales to remain relatively constant over a period of years, the IQs of some individuals do change dramatically. Honzik, Macfarlane, and Allen (1948) tested a group of normal children repeatedly over a period of several years. Some test patterns remained stable, some

[5] One must be somewhat wary of using the WAIS with retarded adults, since the IQs it yields for this group tend to be somewhat higher than those of other tests (Fisher, 1962a, 1962b; Walker & Gross, 1970).

showed irregular changes, and others demonstrated consistent trends toward higher or lower test scores. Often the changes coincided with changes in family situation, social adjustment, and mental health. McCall (1970; McCall, Applebaum, & Hogarthy, 1973), too, found relatively consistent trends over time in a large number of normal children, with one-third of them showing progressive IQ changes of more than 30 points between ages two and one-half and seventeen, though these tended to occur in brighter rather than in duller children. Even the high follow-up correlations reported by Bradway et al. (1958) concealed some large discrepancies. Between the first and second tests, 22 percent changed by more than 15 points and between the second and the third, 7 percent by more than 15 points.

Shifts in IQ come from several sources. The direction, if not the extent, of the changes may often be predicted from the sort of environmental modifications which have taken place. Other major sources of shifts come from errors of measurement due to errors in test construction, transient conditions such as fatigue or ill health, and unreliability of interpreting and scoring items. We must conclude that although the majority of children, especially retarded children, tend to remain rather stable in IQ over a period of time, a minority show surprising changes. This conclusion provides a strong argument for caution in predicting future performance for the *individual* child on the basis of IQ alone.

How Stable Are Specific Mental Abilities? Relatively little evidence is available on the stability of specific abilities or factors of intelligence. The low reliability of the brief individual subscales on the Wechsler tests, or groupings derived from age scales such as the Stanford-Binet, precludes the possibility of finding extremely high stability of such scores. Meyer (1960) found, however, that scores on subtests of the Tests for Primary Mental Abilities were stable enough that subtest scores obtained in grade eight predicted the same subtests taken by the same children in grade twelve better than did total scores, particularly for subtests dealing with numbers and space. The complete matrix of correlations reported by Kangas and Bradway (1971) reveals that, except for the 1931 IQs, correlations between the Stanford-Binet and the WAIS Verbal IQs were consistently higher than correlations between the Binet and WAIS Performance IQs, or even the WAIS Full Scale IQs. This is thoroughly understandable, since at ages six and above, the Stanford-Binet is a highly verbal test, whereas below that age it includes many more performance-type items. As we shall see, most infant development tests are poor predictors for normal groups, but one first-year item cluster composed principally of vocalizations has been found to correlate with girls' later intelligence, increasingly so with age, and more highly with verbal than performance scores (Cameron, Livson, & Bayley, 1967).

How Predictive Are Infant Assessments? Assessment of infant behavior is exceedingly difficult to accomplish reliably and well, and for normal groups of children the correspondence is very poor between scores obtained on developmental scales during infancy and later IQs (e.g., Anderson, 1940; Bayley, 1949, 1958; Ireton, Thwing, & Gravem, 1970). Tests during the first three to six months of life are particularly weak predictors; in fact, such early scores tend to show a tiny reverse correlation with later scores (Bayley, 1949).

Despite these difficulties, there is substantial need to evaluate development during infancy. Major impetus has come from adoption agencies wishing to place babies as soon as possible but wanting to identify beforehand those likely to be significantly handicapped so that prospective parents can make an informed decision. Another cogent reason for early evaluation is to discover lags in development in order to institute prompt remedial measures and to evaluate the progress of treatment. Some neurologists are convinced that early infancy is the best time to discover abnormalities, before compensatory mechanisms have had time to come into play (Knobloch & Pasamanick, 1962).

For these practical purposes, fortunately, the evidence suggests that infant tests may have some utility. In contrast with normal and high scores, low scores during infancy are much more reliable predictors (Erickson, 1968; Knobloch & Pasamanick, 1967; Smith, Flick, Ferriss, & Sellmann, 1972; VanderVeer & Schweid, 1974). Illingworth (1969) followed 192 healthy infants who had been examined for adoption as early as five months. At age seven, the mean IQ of children rated "retarded" as infants was 84, whereas the early "doubtfuls," "average," and "above-average" groups attained mean seven-year IQs of 100, 107, and 109, respectively. In a sample of 639 full-term children (Werner, Honzik, & Smith, 1968), the Cattell IQ obtained at age twenty months was a reasonably good predictor of IQ at age ten ($r = .49$) and of school achievement ($r = .44$). For children with Cattell IQs below 80, a combination of test scores and pediatrician's ratings of intelligence yielded a multiple correlation of .80 with ten-year IQs. Most children rated low on either of these two variables had serious school achievement problems at age ten.

On the other hand, several studies agree that one child out of four or five judged definitely retarded even up to the age of two or three years will not be so judged later on (Hermann, 1967; Holden, 1972; Koch, 1963). During the first several years of life, the course of development is more predictable in some diagnosable syndromes than others (Fishler, Graliker, & Koch, 1964). Down's syndrome children, for example, typically evidence a marked drop in IQ during the first three or four years; in contrast, cerebral palsy victims tend to show variable scores, but some improve in IQ when the importance of sensorimotor functions on the tests is attenuated at later ages with the introduction of more conceptual and verbal items. Even when they feel quite confident of their assessment, then, clinicians are well advised to be circumspect in stating it— and at the same time to do all they can to optimize the child's chances for healthy development.

How Sensitive Are Mental Ability and the IQ to Personal-social Adjustment?[6]

A great many psychological variables have been shown to influence test scores and, presumptively, nontest behavior as well. Sontag, Baker, and Nelson (1955, 1958), as part of a long-term study at the Fels Institute in Ohio, compared children who showed the most significant increases in IQ between ages three and ten with those who showed the most significant decreases. Those who increased in IQ obtained higher ratings on several scales related to achievement motivation and lower ratings on those related to femininity and passivity. The "go-getters" were those whose mental growth was fastest; the more passive, lackadaisical children actually decreased in relative standing. In another longitudinal study (Wiener, Rider, & Oppel, 1963), a group of children whose IQs had decreased over a period of a few years exhibited an increase in emotional disturbance. Such influences do not stop with the end of childhood. Owens (1966),

[6] See also Chapters 5, 7, and 8 for discussions of environmental effects on intelligence.

following a group of men tested in 1919, 1950, and 1961, found that types of mental ability were related to major components of living patterns. Socioeconomic success was positively related to verbal, reasoning, and total scores, for example, but physical vigor was positively related only to numerical score.

Children's behavior in standardized situations can, of course, be temporarily affected by psychological factors. Frustration reduces the constructiveness of most children's behavior (Barker, Dembo, & Lewin, 1941), and a broad variety of personality variables including anxiety, expectancies of failure, negative self-image, conformity, and suggestibility have all been shown to relate to IQ. (See Chapter 9.)

To summarize this section on matters related to the continuity of intellectual development and the constancy of IQ, both real changes in the rate of development and changes in the test scores are to be expected within any group, but the frequency and degree of such changes are typically smaller among retarded populations than normal ones. When tests are properly used—when they are administered accurately, when care is taken to select a test appropriate for the child, and when his best effort is secured—then there is reason to have cautious confidence in the predictive value of the test results, especially with children who appear retarded. Such results must not, however, be taken out of context of other indices about the child's developmental progress, nor must any score be allowed to rest unchallenged as "the diagnosis" which will determine, once and for all, opportunities open to the child and/or his family. IQs, like any other test scores, represent only a brief sample of behavior. Both their values and their limitations deserve recognition and respect.

Interpretation of IQs

Functioning versus Potential Intelligence The psychologist is frequently asked to estimate a child's "potential intelligence" (e.g., Hausman, 1969), but it is often unclear just what the questioner intends by the request. No one can, of course, assess "potential," if what is meant is the upper limit set by the child's constitutional endowment, the promise left unfulfilled. It is, however, legitimate to inquire whether a test score represents optimum performance at the moment. A child who is failing in school may, if he is comfortable, attain a test score which is much better than his school performance would have led one to expect. In this case, he could be said to be functioning in school at a level "below his potential." An irregular test performance, too, may suggest that the child is not doing his best on the test and may also indicate that he is not doing as well as he might in other life situations. Test behavior is thus not an index of potential capacity (if only the child's life had been different), but of his functioning intelligence in an examining situation made as encouraging and facilitative as possible.

One does not ask a yardstick to measure the height a child might have attained had he encountered the best of all possible worlds. If he is short for his age, the yardstick cannot reveal whether he has attained the maximum height permitted by his genetic endowment or whether his growth has been hampered by illness, malnutrition, or neglect. By pointing out certain discrepancies such as a short leg length compared with torso, the yardstick may hint at certain relationships, but these are the legitimate objects of investigations of a different sort.

The Meaning Conveyed by the IQ The most important question to ask about a reliable score is its meaning. To what present or future behaviors are MA and IQ typically related? Intelligence tests of one sort or another have been available for most of the twentieth century, and a wealth of clinical experience has been accumulated. Of course, not all intelligence tests measure precisely the same abilities. If they did, we would be the worse for it. The major tests in use, however, yield IQs which seem to be related to general mental ability. What do the scores from these tests tell us?

To begin with, *general mental ability,* as the term has been used, is something of a misnomer. All the items in most tests require understanding of verbal directions (some specialized tests do use pantomime), and many require the use of words in the response. Even on performance items with simple instructions, unspoken verbal mediational strategies can facilitate the problem-solving process. (See Chapter 13.) Particularly on the Stanford-Binet, the weighting of verbal abilities is very high at the upper age levels (Hofstaetter, 1954; McNemar, 1942).

In Chapter 1, we discussed at some length the factor analytic approach to the definition of intelligence and made clear that a number of different group abilities are tapped by the popular intelligence tests. Analyzing the WAIS, for example, Berger, Bernstein, Klein, Cohen, and Lucas (1964) described a general factor of intelligence, but they also discovered three important group factors which they called Verbal Comprehension, Perceptual Organization, and Memory/Freedom from Distractibility. Silverstein (1969), analyzing the Wechsler scales for children as well as adults, found a general factor, a strong verbal factor, and a slightly less robust performance factor. These studies represent a consensus of the many investigations of the structure of the Wechsler tests (Matarazzo, 1972).

The Stanford-Binet and the verbal scales of the Wechsler tests are highly related to school achievement. This was the purpose for which Binet devised his original scale, and it remains a very important reason for using the tests today. Most reported correlations between IQ and school grades, teachers' ratings, and school achievement scores have ranged from .45 to .75. Correlations tend to be highest with the predominantly verbal school subjects, including English, history, and the social sciences (Littell, 1960). With retarded children, the relationship of test scores to school achievement serves a very practical purpose during the school years, although for some populations such as rural children and retarded children in special classes, academic achievement is often lower than would be predicted by MA (Schwarz & Cook, 1971).

With the emphasis in most tests on verbal reasoning capacities, other important elements of general mental ability are underrepresented, including "insight, foresight, originality, organization of ideas and so on" (Cronbach, 1960, p. 182). As a result, the IQ is inefficient in predicting performance in nonscholastic situations, and even in scholastic situations requiring what Guilford has called "divergent thinking." (See Chapter 1.) The ability to achieve an independent, productive adult life is only partly dependent upon verbal-scholastic ability.

Matarazzo (1972) has summarized the typical validity coefficients of IQ with adaptive behavior measures and other variables. (See Table 17-3.) Most of these coefficients are substantial. The lower-order relationship between job success and IQ is accounted for by the fact that these figures are usually calculated within a single occupation with a somewhat narrow IQ range and are based on difficult-to-define supervisors' ratings. The extremely high relationship between IQ and prestige of occupation results from studies which have related the mean IQs of persons in an occupational category to ratings of the social prestige of the occupations by other individuals. The status of an occupation seems to in large measure be a function of the perceived level of intelligence of the people so employed.

Table 17-3　Typical Validity Coefficients of IQ

Exemplars	r
IQ with Adaptive Behavior Measure	
IQ X educational attainment (in years)	.70
IQ X academic success (overall grade point)	.50
IQ X occupational attainment	.50
IQ X socioeconomic status	.40
IQ X success on the job	.20
Related Variables	
IQ X independently judged prestige of occupation	.95
IQ X parents' educational attainment	.50

Source:　Matarazzo (1972, p. 296).

Guidelines for Interpretation of IQs　We have discussed so many qualifying factors that the reader is probably justified in asking, "Why bother to interpret an IQ at all?" Yet years of clinical and research experience have taught psychologists approximately what to expect of individuals who obtain different IQs. Although such guides are not dependable in every case, they are helpful in planning for most children and groups.

In general, we recommend this rule of thumb: *The greater the intellectual handicap, the wider the area of behavior it determines.* The more profound the retardation, the more likely that the deficit will limit to a narrow range the behaviors that are possible for the child. A child with an IQ of 10, for example, is so severely deficient that none of his other attributes can significantly alter his situation. The IQ of a child who scores in the low seventies, on the other hand, tells us little about the nature of his play activities, his skills, or his potential for social development.

Because retarded children, like all other growing creatures, are constantly changing and developing new skills, hard-and-fast rules are not feasible. A few broad guidelines may aid in knowing what to expect of children at various ages and levels of retardation. Whatever the child's intellectual level, it is upsetting to all concerned if the parents' expectations greatly exceed or lag behind actual developmental levels. In fact, many parents expect too little of their retarded children, doing much for them which they could happily learn to do for themselves. (See Chapter 20.) As we shall see in Chapter 18, the same may be said for many special education teachers.

Mental age is usually a fairly good guide to the overall maturity of the child in social and communicative skills. A child of 10 with an IQ of 40, for example, can usually talk coherently in short sentences, sing little songs, and partially dress herself in about the same manner as a four-year-old nonretarded child. Like a four-year-old, she may battle with her playmates over sharing toys and turns, have a relatively brief attention span unless she is vitally interested in what she is doing, and be unable to learn many things. Nursery school type experience in the company of other retarded children might well be profitable and enjoyable for her. In contrast, the ten-year-old with an IQ of 80 is usually much more like a second-grader. He may have made some progress in learning to read and print, enjoy simple games with definite rules, and easily make his ideas understood. He may have pals among the boys who live close by and can probably range through the neighborhood on his bicycle and do some errands.

The less pronounced the intellectual handicap, the less the relative retardation in motor areas. Within the mildly and moderately retarded ranges, one can predict in

Fig. 17-2 This mildly retarded ten-year-old is mastering a task appropriate for a first-grader. *(J. & M. Menapace)*

general that the brighter children will show relatively less retardation in learning to walk, run, and climb, and in fine motor coordination than they show in intellectual development, although as a group they will show significant retardation in these behaviors too (Thurstone, 1959). Among mildly retarded children, it is not too unusual to find well-coordinated athletes and many others within the normal range in motor skills. Among the more severely retarded, damage to the central nervous system is often involved to such an extent that some deficit in motor proficiency is readily apparent.

Retardation is often more pronounced in behaviors which require verbal-abstract reasoning than in socially adaptive areas. Teen-age girls may learn to make their own clothes with only minimal supervision but be unable to follow the directions on a pattern; printed bus schedules may be incomprehensible, but taking the bus to and from a job may present no problem if the individual is accompanied once or twice.

Levels of Retardation According to MA   As we have seen, the diagnostic manual published by the AAMD (Grossman, 1973) describes four levels of retardation. Each level is defined in terms of one standard deviation range on the normal probability curve. The descriptive terms are only convenient labels. If a given child falls near

Fig. 17-3 This severely retarded ten-year-old is preoccupied with a toy intended for a two-year-old. *(J. & M. Menapace)*

the borderline of any two categories, or if his behavior is particularly variable, he may change levels as frequently as his behavior is evaluated.

Table 17-4 lists the Binet-IQ levels and the MA expectations of an adult in each category. Table 17-5 lists some Stanford-Binet items, simply for illustrative purposes, so that the reader may develop a feel for the thought processes represented by the various developmental levels. The reader is also urged to recall Piaget's descriptions of the sensorimotor level (zero to two years), preoperational level (two to seven years), and level of concrete operations (seven to eleven years). (See Chapter 12.)

Table 17-4   Mental Retardation Categories

Degree of retardation	Binet IQ levels	Adult MA range
Mild	52–56	8 years, 6 months to 10 years, 10 months
Moderate	36–51	6 years, 1 month to 8 years, 5 months
Severe	20–35	3 years, 9 months to 6 years, 0 months
Profound	Below 20	Below 3 years, 9 months

Table 17-5 Selected Stanford-Binet Items by Age Level

AGE XI	Explaining two of three absurdities; e.g., "The judge said to the prisoner, 'You are to be hanged, and I hope it will be a warning to you.'"
	Defining three of five abstract words; e.g., *connection, conquer.*
AGE X	Vocabulary. Definitions of eleven words on a graduated list scored at several age levels; e.g., through the difficulty level of *Mars, juggler, scorch.*
	Giving two reasons why children should not be too noisy in school and two reasons why most people prefer an automobile to a bicycle.
AGE IX	Drawing from memory one of two designs shown together for ten seconds.
	Making three of four rhymes; e.g., "Tell me a number that rhymes with tree."
AGE VIII	Expressing similarities and differences between three of four pairs of objects, such as *baseball* and *orange.*
	Solving four of six practical problems such as, "What makes a sailboat move?"
AGE VII	Finding the absurdity in four of five pictures.
	Copying a diamond correctly at least one of three trials.
AGE VI	Vocabulary. Definitions of six words; e.g., *tap, gown.*
	Expressing a difference between two of three pairs of objects; e.g., *bird* and *dog.*
AGE V	Adding two features to an incomplete drawing of a man.
	Copying a square correctly one of three trials.
AGE IV	Pointing correctly three times in six to the appropriate drawing on a card, e.g., "Show me the one we cook on."
	Answering both "Why do we have houses?" and "Why do we have books?"
AGE III	Stringing four beads in two minutes.
	Copying a circle correctly one of three trials.
AGE II	Replacing a circle, square, and triangle in a form board, one trial in two.
	Naming three of eighteen drawings of common objects.

Source: Terman and Merrill (1973, pp. 67–99).

Other Strategies in Mental Testing

The tests discussed above have two major difficulties. First, they are empirically derived heterogeneous ("grab-bag") scales composed of items chosen for their practical utility. They fail to reflect contemporary advances in the systematic understanding of cognitive growth. Second, they tell us little about the ways in which the individual perceives and manipulates his world. For the most part, the opportunity to discover the means by which the child derived his answers is ignored.

For very young children, several tests now exist which are built on the developmental theories of Jean Piaget. (See Chapter 12.) Unlike the familiar infant and preschool tests, these are sequential, ordinal scales constructed to reflect specific stages in the development of aspects of sensorimotor intelligence. There is no particular reason why such scales could not be standardized on representative samples, as have the more familiar general tests of intelligence. Lézine (1969) and Uzgiris and Hunt (1975) have in fact begun such an effort. It is more difficult to develop scales for use with older children than with infants and toddlers, since Piaget's descriptions of later developmental stages do not yield the same closely spaced increments and regularities.

The work of Glaser (1963; Glaser & Nitko, 1971) offers an approach akin to traditional educational testing in the skills areas. *Criterion-referenced* tests (as opposed to *norm-referenced* tests) formulate specific goals and assess a child's progress toward them. In judging whether a child is ready for school a number of needed skills and strategies can be identified and scales developed to measure them. One such attempt has been undertaken in the area of semantic mastery (Hunt & Kirk, 1973). For this approach to work, it is not necessary to know how the "average" child performs. It matters only that the test bears a valid relationship to the criterion. Criterion-referenced tests have a valid place in the armamentarium of psychologists called upon to plan management and educational programming for children. In some ways, the tests of adaptive behavior we will examine bear a closer relationship to criterion-referenced tests than they do to norm-referenced tests.

Summary

As the reader is already aware, the designation of mental retardation rests, by definition, on two criteria: performance on a test of general intelligence at least two standard deviations below the mean, and equally deviant adaptive behavior as assessed clinically or by means of an objective scale. The first part of this chapter has reviewed the derivation and implications of the two major indices, MA and IQ, yielded by tests of intelligence. The MA is a measure of the intellectual maturity attained by the child or the retarded adult by the time he is tested; the IQ is an index of the rate of his progress and can serve, within broad limits, as a predictor of his rate of growth in the future.

We have tried to suggest some general and practical guidelines for the interpretation of both these measures, but they must, of course, be adapted by each professional to the situation in which he works. The test scores, handy summaries of a child's behavior during perhaps an hour's exposure to a standardized, highly structured situation, do a rather good job of predicting school achievement for mildly retarded children and they do an even better job of predicting developmental progress among the moderately and severely retarded. They do not even attempt, however, to answer a great many important questions about the quality and adequacy of an individual's behavioral adjustment.

These test scores will be seriously misused if they are taken out of the context of a broad range of information about the child and his or her environment. Responsible test users are cautious and modest. They have no secret password to the child's mental development and they ask neither too much nor too little of the test score. They have data which can be exceedingly valuable if viewed in terms of the brief investment of time required of both tester and child, but which furnish only a single piece of the puzzle presented by any complex individual, whose history is unique and whose future is uncharted.

MEASUREMENT OF ADAPTIVE BEHAVIOR

There are many nonintellectual facets of the lives and personalities of retarded children for which we need assessment tools as technically sound as the best of the intelligence tests. In the field of personality, reliable and valid instruments for normal children are few and far between. For retarded children, with their comparatively limited capacities for abstraction, verbal expression, and creative ideation, there are still fewer appropriate instruments. Psychologists must rely on these instruments, on their own informal observations, and on reports by families, teachers, and others to put together a comprehensible portrait of retarded children and the dynamics of their relationships with important people in their lives. There is considerable room for error in this process and, at the same time, little opportunity for objective checks on the validity of conclusions.

It is a critical responsibility of the psychodiagnostician, though, to evaluate the child's "adaptive behavior." Some objective or clinical assessment of adaptive behavior is, in fact, required in the AAMD classificatory process. (See Chapter 2.) Unfortunately, assessment in this realm is more primitive than in intellectual evaluation, but since the publication of the 1959 AAMD manual, energetic attempts have been made to develop objective scales for appraisal of adaptive behavior. Prior to scale development, however, there are many other questions to be answered, just as there were earlier for the makers of tests designed to tap intelligence.

Defining Adaptive Behavior

After struggling for some time with the problem of defining adaptive behavior, a broadly representative group of professionals in the field of mental retardation developed the following definition under the auspices of the Adaptive Behavior Project, sponsored by the National Institute of Mental Health (Nihira, Foster, Shellhaas, & Kagin, 1968):

> Adaptive behavior refers primarily to the manner in which the individual copes and . . . therefore, 'an impairment in adaptive behavior' would imply unsuccessful or incomplete coping. This concept of 'coping' is represented by three major facets:
>
> **1** *Independent functioning* . . . the ability of the individual to successfully accomplish those tasks or activities demanded of him by the general community and in terms of the typical expectations for specific ages.
>
> **2** *Personal responsibility* . . . both the willingness of the individual to accomplish those critical tasks he is able to accomplish . . . and his ability to assume individual responsibility for his personal behavior. This ability is reflected in decision-making and choice of behaviors.
>
> **3** *Social responsibility* . . . the ability of the individual to accept responsibility as a member of a community group . . . reflected in levels of conformity, socially positive creativity, social adjustment, and emotional maturity . . . some level of civic responsibility leading to complete or partial economic independence. (Leland, Nihara, Foster, Shellhaas, & Kagin, 1968, p. 14)

In attempting to shortcut the endless debates preventing agreement on a definition, other investigators have looked at the behaviors tapped by the existing scales designed to assess adaptation. This process is analogous to defining intelligence as "what the tests test" (Boring, 1923), a circular definition but one which often allows a hidden consensus to emerge without semantic sparring. Leland, Shellhaas, Nihira, and Foster (1967) analyzed a dozen rating scales and isolated twelve major areas of adaptive behavior:

1 Self-help skills, e.g., dressing, grooming, eating, toileting, (represented in nine scales)
2 Communication skills (nine scales)
3 Socialization of interpersonal skills (twelve scales)
4 Locomotion (five scales)
5 Self-direction, e.g., initiative, attending (nine scales)

6 Occupational skills (eight scales)
7 Economic activity (five scales)
8 Neuromotor development, e.g., motor control, mannerisms (four scales)
9 Personal responsibility, e.g., trustworthiness, care of own property (five scales)
10 Social responsibility, e.g., care of others' property (four scales)
11 Emotional adjustment, e.g., prevalent mood, control, reaction to criticism (seven scales)
12 Health (1 scale)

Comparing this list with the previous three-part definition, we can see that the first eight scales correspond more or less with "independent functioning," the seventh overlapping somewhat with "social responsibility." Both personal and social responsibility are relatively ignored by most of the scales. The trend among the testers has clearly been to emphasize independent functioning, particularly in the form of skills mastery, rather than broader forms of responsibility.

During the developmental era, children's environments are changing and expanding, as are the kinds of demands made of them. Recognizing this, the AAMD definition suggests that deficits in adaptive behavior will be reflected in the following areas, according to age and cultural group:

During infancy and early childhood in the following:

1 Sensory-motor skills development
2 Communication skills (including speech and language)
3 Self-help skills
4 Socialization (development of ability to interact with others)

During childhood and early adolescence in the following:

5 Application of basic academic skills in daily life activities
6 Application of appropriate reasoning and judgment in mastery of the environment
7 Social skills (participation in group activities and interpersonal relationships)

During late adolescence and adult life in the following:

8 Vocational and social responsibilities and performances (Grossman, 1973, p. 12).

Developmental versus Inventory Approach

Closely allied with the concept of adaptive behavior is the concept of *social maturity*, a developmental phenomenon increasing with age, denoting one's ability to cope within an expanding social environment. A maturity concept implies age increments. In terms of measurement, two competing priorities present themselves. The developmental orientation suggests that items be arranged according to age level and be selected to sample socially adaptive responses typical of children of that age ($Mean_{SA} = Mean_{CA}$). By analogy, this is, of course, a scale of the Binet type—a few representative items, selected to present a statistically balanced series and also to be highly correlated with scores on the total scale. In contrast, the orientation toward adaptive behavior which is broadly inclusive of skills and responsibilities in several domains, demands the inventory type of scale which is usually arranged by subscales. The analogous intelligence test is a Wechsler scale, although in this instance the subscales tap everyday behaviors rather than responses to novel stimuli. (Herein lies the connection with criterion-referenced scales mentioned previously.) It is worth noting that the first widely popular test, the Vineland Social Maturity Scale (Doll, 1936, 1964) is an age scale composed of only a few items at each level. Like the Binet (but unlike most other adaptive behavior scales) it was standardized on a population which was geographically isolated and probably biased, but which was, in fact, intended to be an approximation of a normal sample. Tests of this nature can, as the Vineland does, yield measures similar to the MA and the IQ (here, Social Age [SA] and Social Quotient [SQ]), although until converted to deviation scores, these are subject to the same weaknesses as the old ratio IQ. The essential point is that this approach is based on normal development and gauges an individual's adaptive behavior against age norms.[7]

The inventory approach is a good deal more popular, to judge from existing contemporary scales. Its strengths include the ease with which important target behaviors can be included, but even more, the much greater ease of standardization. An age scale must be standardized on a normal population, and a decent sampling of subjects in as diverse a country as the United States is an expensive proposition. Most inventory scales have settled for testing institutionalized retarded populations, severely limiting the interpretive possibilities and thereby foregoing the use of the scale to discriminate between normal and retarded individuals.

For technical reasons, too, the creation of an age scale is a difficult task involving an uncommon amount of juggling to select items which give a balanced distribution, including a mean at each age level which matches the CA of the subjects and an equivalent standard deviation at each age level. Although computers make this process easier than it used to be, and a deviation IQ can adjust for minor discrepancies, the need can be circumvented entirely in inventory scales where item placement is of minor importance.

One of the most useful and best standardized instruments has achieved a compromise between age-level and inventory approaches. The Alpern-Boll Developmental Profile (Alpern & Boll, 1972) was standardized on more than 3,000 unselected children, ages birth to twelve years. It consists of 217 items tapping five separate areas: physical development, self-help, social development, preacademic and academic skills, and communication skills. Age-equivalent scores can be obtained in each of these areas as well as an overall developmental index.

Source of Information

To use a comprehensive inventory to assess everyday behavior, the examiner will ordinarily need to rely on reports from others who are well acquainted with the individual being studied, such as his parents, teachers, or ward attendants. The possibility

---

[7] Perhaps we should also mention another venerable age-graded instrument, the Porteus Maze Test (Porteus 1924, 1959). This instrument consists of a series of mazes said by its author to be better than ordinary tests of mental ability in predicting practical, social behavior. There is some support for this contention (Cooper, York, Daston, & Adams, 1967) but also some room for doubt (Tobias & Goelick, 1962).

of bias on the part of such respondents can be reduced by sticking to specific behavioral descriptions and by training those who make such ratings routinely.

There are a few measures of adaptive behavior which involve direct observation by experienced raters (Balthazar, 1971) or which attempt to predict overall adaptive behavior on the basis of psychometric tests (Caldwell, 1970; Gunzburg, 1968; Porteus, 1959). The former are, however, generally too time-consuming for the usual case study and the latter, although useful in their own right, are somewhat different in kind from the scales we are considering here.

Available Scales

The scales in the following list have been designed to measure adaptive behavior/social competence. The Alpern-Boll Developmental Profile, the Bristol Scale, and the Vineland Scale are the only ones of this group standardized originally on normal subjects, although a standardization of one form of the AAMD Adaptive Behavior Scales has now been accomplished with nonretarded public school children as well as subjects in special classes for the handicapped (Lambert, Wilcox, & Gleason, 1974).

>   AAMD Adaptive Behavior Scales (Nihira, Foster, Shellhaas, & Leland, 1969)
>   Adaptation for Profoundly Retarded (Congdon, 1973)
>   1972 Revision—School Form (Lambert et al., 1974)
>   Alpern-Boll Developmental Profile (Alpern & Boll, 1972)
>   Balthazar Scales of Adaptive Behavior (Balthazar, 1971; Balthazar, Roseen, & English, 1968)
>   Bristol Social Adjustment Guides (Stott, 1963)
>   Cain-Levine Social Competency Scale (Cain, Levine, & Elzey, 1963)
>   Fairview Behavior Evaluation Battery for the Mentally Retarded (R. T. Ross et al., 1970-1974)
>   Gardner Behavior Chart (Dayan & McLean, 1963; Wilcox, 1942)
>   Hospital Adjustment Scale (McReynolds, Ferguson, & Ballachey, 1963)
>   Newman-Doby Measure of Social Competence (Newman & Doby, 1973)
>   Preschool Educational Attainment Record (E. A. Doll, 1966)
>   Progress Assessment Chart of Social Development (Gunzburg, 1968)
>   Social Competence Rating (Banham, 1960)
>   Vineland Social Maturity Scale (E. A. Doll, 1964)

Relationship of Adaptive Behavior to Other Variables

An important theoretical problem is the relationship between measured intelligence and adaptive behavior. The strong consensus (Cromwell, 1967a; Johnson, 1970; Leland et al., 1967, 1968; Olechnowicz, 1973a) is that the two should be—and are—moderately related over a wide range of retardation. This is to be anticipated, since intelligence is a major ingredient in a child's pattern of coping. At the lowest end of the scales, there is probably a much closer correspondence than at the higher ranges (R. T. Ross, 1971a; Ross & Boroskin, 1972).

Verbal expressiveness (Halpern & Equinossi, 1969; Ross & Boroskin, 1972), age and experience with the environment, teacher expectation (Newman & Doby, 1973), and ethnic background (Adams, McIntosh, & Weade, 1973) also correlate with measures of adaptive behavior. Emotional disturbance, in addition, interferes with coping capacities (Olechnowicz, 1973a). Although most authors today agree that it is often

Fig. 17-4 Learning to wash one's own hair is a component of adaptive behavior. *(University of Washington Child Development and Mental Retardation Center)*

futile to try to distinguish completely between the constellations of emotional disturbance and mental retardation (see Chapter 10), this complication should be recognized.

Environmental Context

The success of coping behavior cannot be judged outside the existing environmental framework. The AAMD definition supports the current trend to consider adaptive behavior in the context of the general environmental demands. "Here the key concept seems to center around the ability of the retarded individual to be sufficiently 'invisible' within his community that members . . . do not become unnecessarily concerned about his presence" (Leland et al., 1968, p. 14). The question is not, however, so easily resolved. If one is able to create an environment, such as a sheltered workshop, in which a retarded individual can cope very adequately, how is his adaptive capacity in the general community to be judged? In a restricted institution, how is one to guess whether a child could make a telephone call independently or order his dinner in a restaurant and eat it properly? A six-level classification of adaptive behavior levels recognizes this dilemma (Leland et al., 1968) and defines the level of adult adaptive impairment according to the degree of environmental complexity and the amount of continuing support and supervision necessary.

Levels of Impairment in Adaptive Behavior

Limitations of space unfortunately preclude a detailed presentation of typical behaviors to be anticipated at different ages and varying levels of retardation. One rough guide is to be found in the AAMD guidelines (Grossman, 1973), of which some excerpts are listed in Table 17-6.

Table 17-6   Illustrations of Highest Level of Adaptive Behavior Functioning

CA and level of impairment indicated	
3 years: *Mild* 6 years: *Moderate* 9 years: *Severe* 12 years and above: *Profound*	*Independent functioning:* Feeds self with spoon, with considerable spilling or messiness; drinks unassisted; can pull off clothing and put on some; tries to help with bath or hand washing but still needs considerable help; indicates toilet accident and may indicate toilet need. *Physical:* May climb up and down stairs but not alternating feet; may run and jump; may balance briefly on one foot; can pass ball to others; transfers objects. *Communication:* May speak in two or three word sentences; names simple common objects, understands simple directions, knows people by name. (If nonverbal, may use many gestures to convey needs or other information.) *Social:* May interact with others in simple play activities, usually with only one or two others unless guided into group activity; (prefers) some persons over others.
12 years: *Mild* 15 years and over: *Moderate*	*Independent functioning:* Feeds, bathes, dresses self; may select daily clothing; may prepare easy foods for self or others; combs/brushes hair, may shampoo and roll up hair; may wash and/or iron and store own clothes. *Physical:* Good body control; good gross and fine motor coordination. *Communication:* May carry on simple conversation; uses complex sentences. Recognizes words, may read sentences, ads, signs, and simple prose material with some comprehension. *Social:* May interact cooperatively and/or competitively with others. *Economic activity:* May be sent on shopping errand for several items without notes; makes minor purchases; adds coins to dollar with fair accuracy. *Occupation:* May do simple routine household chores (dusting, garbage, dishwashing; prepare simple foods which require mixing). *Self-direction:* May initiate most of own activities; attend to task fifteen to twenty minutes (or more); may be conscientious in assuming much responsibility.

Source: Grossman (1973, pp. 28, 31).

Focusing on adult behavior, for purposes of simplification, the following behaviors can be expected at various levels of impairment. The reader is urged to note that even at IQ levels below 50, the individual may be capable of considerable useful activity. It may be helpful to imagine for a moment a normal six-year-old given the strength and stature of an adult and practice in skills he can master. We run the risk of underestimating the contributions which such an individual can make to his own well-being and that of his fellow men.

The *mildly retarded* are likely to be capable of maintaining themselves in laboring jobs but will frequently need a benefactor to help with their social and financial affairs. Even with special education, they will usually have completed only the equivalent of elementary school academic work. Appropriate jobs include cleaning, harvesting, assisting skilled workers, and the like, although some may master semiskilled tasks. The women, more than the men, may be capable of adequate married life because homemaking skills and social relationships can be less demanding and stressful than is often the case with public work. Providing an optimal environment for children may, however, be beyond their capacities. For some individuals, sheltered-workshop situations are particularly appropriate. Motor incoordination, slowness, and lack of reading skills are likely to make competitive employment difficult.

With the *moderately retarded*, self-care usually becomes the focus of attention. This range corresponds approximately to the "trainable" group while in school. Many moderately retarded individuals who are able to remain with their families are well accepted in the neighborhood, and a few can hold regular full-time jobs, such as mowing lawns, routine laundry, and simple assembly. Most of these adults do useful work around the house with little or no supervision and can be left at home alone for several hours. Speech is usually understandable, although simple and concrete. Hardly any of these adults marry and very few bear children. The majority apparently have little heterosexual social contact and few friends of their own.

Severely retarded persons are very likely to have sustained neurologic damage which further restricts their social behavior. These persons need special training in learning to talk and care for their own simple cleanliness and health needs; they do not profit from academic training. Habits of dressing, eating, and finding one's way around a neighborhood require careful, prolonged, and supervised practice. Very little independent behavior is observed; lethargy and apathy are frequent. Sometimes, in the way of little children, adults of this level are openly friendly and attach themselves to persons with whom they come in contact, but are incapable of communicating on any but a momentary concrete level.

Profoundly retarded persons are frequently very restricted in their ability to move about and usually cannot protect and care for themselves. Many, having sustained severe neurologic damage, are confined to a bed or wheelchair. They may learn to walk and to vocalize a greeting, and some can be trained to use the toilet and feed themselves. Total supervision is required. Little learning of any kind will be exhibited, although the individual may come to recognize familiar faces and obey familiar commands.

Summary

Despite the urgency of the need for well-standardized scales to measure social competence—preferably, scales standardized on normal samples—measurement in this area is only beginning to attain a technical status warranting serious consideration. A number of scales are now available, the AAMD Adaptive Behavior Scales being the leader in quality at this point, and there is considerable interest and activity in this area. Nevertheless, clinical assessment demands astute judgment on the part of the psychodiagnostician, and a willingness to forego precise categorization in favor of attention to the details of the individual's achievements and shortcomings in his daily life. Priority is given to optimizing adjustment through specific, goal-directed plans— whether by modulating the demands of the environment, making a change of placement, or teaching needed skills. Defining the problem, planning a line of attack, carrying it through and evaluating progress—these are the hallmarks of the psychodiagnostician attempting to contribute to the well-being and satisfaction of retarded individuals and those responsible for their education and care.

18
Special Education and Training of the Retarded Child

Special education in the United States today takes place amid a vortex of change and controversy, pressure and prejudice. There are court mandates to seek out every retarded child in order to offer him education/training suited to his needs—and there is a simultaneous hue and cry about children erroneously or unnecessarily labeled retarded and consigned to unsuitable placements. There are demands for more special classes—and at the same time, moves to eradicate self-contained classrooms for the mildly retarded in favor of placement in regular classrooms supported by special services to minimize the differential treatment of retarded pupils. There are preventive efforts to reach downward into the playpen and the preschool years, together with efforts to extend upward the years of organized intervention by postschool occupational and rehabilitation programs.

There is both encouragement and discouragement. Few studies show compensatory preschool efforts or special education programs to be of very significant benefit to children in comparison with ordinary management. Yet the courts are told that

> . . . retarded children of any intelligence quotient are capable of benefiting from education. . . . Education is even more important to the development of the retarded citizen than it is to normal citizen, for the latter may develop skills willy-nilly and informally, but the retarded citizen cannot, without sustained educational attention. (Lippmann & Goldberg, 1973, p. 27)

Above all, there is community involvement and citizen participation. The optimism and pessimism, the promise and disappointment, are all evidence that, as never before, people care about retarded children and the adults they become, and are willing to help—if only they can figure out how.

The purpose of this chapter is to afford an overview of the current status of special education. The school ranks second only to the home in its impact on children. Psychologists helping families plan for their retarded children need to be well informed about available local alternatives and to understand what each has to offer. They have much to learn from educators. Teachers of mentally retarded children have a background of intimate, long-term experience with educational methods and with these children which is rarely available to others. Psychologists, in turn, can contribute to teachers and counselors their knowledge of processes involved in learning and thinking, their skills in behavioral assessment and research, and their training in understanding the individual in a broad social context. Joint collaboration of psychologists and educators—indeed, of all adults concerned with retarded children—is a growing and laudable phenomenon.

History[1]

Society has always had to deal with the mentally retarded in one way or another. Some cultures have feared and persecuted them, some have ignored them, still others have destroyed them. With the first insights of modern science and the rise of the doctrine of the brotherhood of man, there emerged an attempt to protect the feebleminded at least from starvation and physical suffering. Institutions were built during the seventeenth century, and, about 1800, with the initial attempts of Jean Itard to educate a single defective boy, education of the retarded began. Not for a long time, however—essentially, not until after World War II—did special education become widely available.

The fact that special programs devoted to the education of the retarded have become widespread so recently should not be surprising. Education for the masses did not, after all, become common in the countries of the Western world until the middle of the nineteenth century. When education was a privilege of the elite, the retarded were often excluded from classrooms for which they were ill-fitted. Many poor families never considered sending their children to school. In 1870, only 57 percent of children ages five to seventeen were enrolled in schools in the United States; by 1970, the figure was 87 percent—the missing 13 percent including both dropouts (most of them with learning problems) and exclusions. It was not, in fact, until 1972 that the successively widening waves of educational opportunity were finally guaranteed by the courts to all in the age range eligible for public school. As late as the mid-1950s, there was still spirited debate between those who felt it the school's obligation to provide appropriate educational experiences for all (Goldberg, 1958) and those who maintained that, it being the job of the school to educate, only children capable of profiting from academic pursuits (i.e., "educable" retarded children) need be furnished public classes (Cruickshank, 1958; Newland, 1953). At least this is one issue which appears to be settled.

---

[1] For much more detailed historical accounts, see E. E. Doll (1967) and Wallin (1966). This review is restricted to events affecting school programs. See Chap. 2 for a broader review of social changes affecting the field of mental retardation.

The Beginning

In 1799, a boy of about twelve was captured in the forest of Aveyron, France. Jean Itard, a physician who was working with the deaf, believed this animal-like creature to be physiologically normal but essentially unaffected by civilization. To vindicate his point of view against those who maintained that intellectual functions were innate and impervious to training, he spent five years in a dedicated effort to convert the child to an educated, civilized creature, yet the "Wild Boy of Aveyron" died at the age of forty with little improvement. Some years later, at the behest of the French Academy of Sciences, Itard wrote an account of his experiment; his little book is now a classic in its field. His emphasis on sensory training is still seen today in many preschool and readiness programs for normal as well as retarded children.

Itard's most famous student was Edouard Seguin, who left France after the revolution of 1848 and emigrated to the United States, where he became superintendent of the Pennsylvania Training School for Idiots. Seguin (1866) believed that mental defect could be divided into two types, a superficial type in which the peripheral nervous system has been damaged or weakened and a profound type in which the central nervous system has always been defective. The educational methods for both types were the same, however, since muscle and sense training were seen as essential both for strengthening the peripheral nervous system in the first type and for developing the nerve cells of the cortex by bombardment through the receptors in the second type. He advocated muscular activities and gymnastics in the open air, but only activities which satisfied the child's needs and desires. All the senses were to receive formal training as part of ongoing activities. His philosophy of education was in many ways quite modern. He emphasized the whole child, the need for individualized teaching, the importance of a good relationship between teacher and child, and the physical comfort of the child.

Another famous educator of the retarded was Maria Montessori (1912), a student of Seguin. In her early work in asylums for the mentally ill in Rome, she came to the conclusion that the problem of mental deficiency was essentially educational and not medical. In her Orthophrenic School for the Cure of the Feebleminded, she achieved spectacular success in teaching a number of retarded pupils to read and write as well as normal children did. Later, she founded a school for young normal children which was destined to become even more celebrated. Like Seguin, Montessori ascribed great importance to sense and muscle training in early education, and she also emphasized practical life activities like those of the home. The most unique aspect of her system was the method known as "autoeducation" (self-teaching), in which the child used twenty-six different items designed to train the senses: visual discrimination and perception of dimensions, temperature, touch, color, and so on. The teacher merely supervised the child's activities. Montessori's work is seldom now connected with its original target groups, disadvantaged and retarded children, but instead tends to be popular with middle-class parents.

There were many other innovators who advanced work with the retarded, many of them known also to educators of nonretarded children and especially of preschool children. Preschool educators have understood for a long time children's need for active involvement in their learning, the necessity to let them follow their own inclinations to a large extent, the need for training large and small muscles, and the importance of individual differences. Preschool education has generally proceeded at a gentle pace, its materials concrete and its goals firmly rooted in daily activities, yet,

Probably no field of education has ignored its past so cavalierly as have educators of the mentally retarded. . . . Teachers of the normal still glean inspiration from Rousseau, Pestalozzi, Herbart, Froebel, Parker, and Dewey, but who among us knows Seguin, Howe, Wilbur, W. E. Fernald, Farrell, or Anderson? Even the recent revival of Montessori came to us largely from general education—and characteristically, it is the disciple, Montessori, rather than the master, Seguin, who is revived. . . . One finds today papers and systems advocating many of the techniques used by W. E. Fernald or E. R. Johnstone fifty years ago. The newest methods, perhaps unawares, revamp the devices of Seguin and Goddard in terms of modern statistics. (E. E. Doll, 1967, p. 181)

Recent History

1915 to 1960   Since the 1920s, the history of education of the retarded has become less closely identified with individuals and more with educational philosophies, methods, and administrative practices. Educators have increasingly recognized the curricular needs of the school-age retarded child. The training of teachers and the actual establishment of special classes in the public schools were, however, slow to materialize. Except for a short period in the mid-1800s, even the residential institutions have until recently provided little in the way of explicit education for the retarded children living there.

Prior to 1920, there were few special teachers of any kind, and most of those with special training taught the blind or the deaf. In 1914, Charles Scott Berry began to train a few teachers at the Lapeer State Home and Training School (for the mentally retarded) in Michigan. Soon after, the first college program was organized by Professor Charles M. Elliott at what is now Eastern Michigan University at Ypsilanti. Other colleges and universities began slowly to follow suit, but after World War II, the rate was much increased.

From 1915 to 1930, special classes in public schools grew rapidly, but from 1930 to 1940, there was a halt and even a decline in this trend. The financial burdens of the Depression, dissatisfaction with the premature establishment of inadequately planned classes with untrained teachers, and misinterpretation of the assumptions of progressive education, typified by the notion that any basically good teacher could teach any group of children, combined to dampen public enthusiasm. Most retarded children therefore remained without special attention, many of them attending school year after year without learning very much (Cruickshank, 1958), others simply excluded from the schools. After World War II, special classes were again promoted enthusiastically. Whereas only about 87,000 retarded children were enrolled in special programs in 1948 (U.S. Office of Education, 1954), about 213,400 were enrolled ten years later (Mackie & Robbins, 1960).

During the 1950s, the major impetus for expansion of services came from parents' groups, who combined forces to demand special facilities for their handicapped children. (See Chapter 2.) Because these groups tended to be composed primarily of middle-class parents with children moderately to severely retarded, it often happened that classes for this minority of "trainable" retarded children were established prior to classes for "educable" (mildly retarded) children, the bulk of whom came from families of low socioeconomic status who were not so adept at political processes nor so aware of their children's special needs. Many classes for trainable children were actually begun on a voluntary basis by parents' groups and later incorporated into the schools.

1960 to 1970   During the administrations of Presidents Kennedy and Johnson, the nation's attention turned toward the problems of the poor and the retarded, including not only the mildly retarded but the borderline retarded as well. This new commitment was not only an expression of a more liberal and compassionate national sentiment, but also a reflection of a renewed conviction of the power of education to solve the nation's problems. In 1958, Samuel A. Kirk had published an account of an intensive preschool program for young mentally retarded children, a precursor of the compensatory preschool programs for disadvantaged children which were to come. Publications by Hunt (1961) and Bloom (1964) convinced many citizens of the plasticity of the developing intellect and the importance of early experience. The startling entry of the United States into the space age, and the hope of breaking into the cycling morass of poverty and communication, together with the unabashed acceptance by and concern of the Joseph P. Kennedy family for their severely retarded daughter, all reinforced changes in the overall climate. The time was ripe for educational initiatives for the handicapped as well as the normal child.

In 1961, John F. Kennedy appointed the President's Panel on Mental Retardation,[2] and its report (1962a) presented the problem of mental retardation as a matter of grave national concern and federal responsibility. A number of delegations to Europe under the auspices of the Panel found that in other countries, especially in the Netherlands (1962c) and the Scandinavian nations (1962b) there were programs for the retarded which far exceeded those in the United States both in humanitarianism and effectiveness.

Meanwhile, legislative efforts progressively broadened the base of federal support for special education which, like other educational matters, had previously been considered the exclusive province of the states (Martin, 1968). Although there had been legislation in 1957-1959 to provide limited funds for research and for training leadership personnel in the education of the retarded, it was not until 1963 that expanded authority for training, research, and demonstration projects was legislated.

The real landmark year was 1965, which saw a broadscale launching of programs to aid the disadvantaged, including the passage of the Elementary and Secondary Education Act of 1965 (ESEA), with its special programs of assistance to disadvantaged and handicapped children, as well as new instructional-materials centers for innovation and research, and strengthening of state education agencies. In addition, 1965 was the first year of Project Head Start, and signaled increased support for other compensatory programs, especially preschool programs, aimed at the prevention of sociocultural deprivation. That year also witnessed legislation extending professional preparation for teaching the retarded, funding research and demonstration centers, and making direct grants to states for educating handicapped children in residential schools. This was followed in 1966 by the creation of the powerful Bureau of Education for the Handicapped and by federal grants to states for special education, and in 1967 by further significant extensions of services and supports on a wide front. Support for these programs, and for other efforts in the area of mental retardation/special education continued steadily, and much better coordination was eventually achieved among programs primarily of a medical/diagnostic nature, health and educational programs targeted at high-risk populations (e.g., Project Head Start, Model Cities), and special education programs under state auspices. In 1970, state and federal councils were established for the purpose of comprehensive planning of services to the

---

[2] Its successor became the President's Committee on Mental Retardation.

developmentally disabled (mentally retarded, neurologically impaired, etc.), and funds were made available for a wide variety of specialized services to alleviate the disabilities.

Another important bill, passed in 1969, provided for a National Center on Educational Media and Materials for the Handicapped; fourteen regional Instructional Materials Centers were subsequently developed to provide ready access to valid materials and information. An omnibus bill passed in 1970 and renewed in 1973, the Education of the Handicapped Act granted aid to states and considerable money for special target programs, including early childhood education, the development of regional resource centers, and a program to help children with specific learning disabilities. Training of personnel, research and demonstration programs, and media services were also supported by this act (Dinger, 1973).

The 1970s By the beginning of the 1970s, special education was indeed a going concern, although some retarded children were still not being reached. Some 15,000 to 17,000 new teachers for the retarded were being graduated each year. By 1970, approximately 728,000 retarded children, 78 percent of the 936,000 who had been identified, were receiving special instruction in the public schools, in addition to some 2,240,000 pupils with different handicaps who were receiving special attention (Metz, 1973). In fiscal 1973, federal funds committed in behalf of the retarded altogether amounted to $879 million, of which $91.4 million was budgeted by the U.S. Office of Education (Office of Mental Retardation Coordination, 1972). In addition, among the states' own expenditures for education, a median of about 3 percent was spent on special education, with some states spending more than 8 percent (Dinger, 1973). These statistical indices reveal the magnitude of the investment the nation was by then willing to make for its young retarded citizens.

If the 1960s were a decade of executive action, legislative breakthrough, and vastly increased funding, the early 1970s were much more the era of the judiciary. Court decisions established the right of every chronically ill or disabled child to education, treatment, and habilitation (Gilhool, 1972; Lippman & Goldberg, 1973). The courts had broken ground with the historic 1954 Supreme Court decision, *Brown v. Board of Education*, maintaining that "separate but equal" facilities were unacceptable. Equally important were a series of decisions by federal and state courts which established the educational rights of retarded children. Two cases in particular should be singled out.

The first, in 1970, *Diana v. State Board of Education*, was filed in California in behalf of nine Mexican-American children ages eight to thirteen, in whose homes Spanish was the major language. Although before being placed in special education classes, they had obtained IQs from 30 to 72 with a mean of 63, upon retesting with a Spanish-language examination their scores were an average of 15 points higher. The lowest score was 3 points below the cutoff line for admission to special classes, but seven of the nine scored above it. As a result, the court ordered that all children be tested in their native language prior to placement in special classes, that all Mexican-American and Chinese-American children in special classes be reevaluated, and that other measures be taken to effect a transition for misplaced children and to develop and standardize a new means of appraisal.

The second case had equally far-reaching implications. It dealt with the rights of children previously excluded from special education. The decision in this 1972 Pennsylvania case, technically the *Pennsylvania Association for Retarded Children, Nancy*

Beth Bowman, et al., v. Commonwealth of Pennsylvania, David H. Kurtzman, et al., required that the Commonwealth of Pennsylvania search out all children requiring special education and provide services suited to their needs. The order included preschool programs where other children of the same age were afforded public education. It also required a periodic reevaluation of all retarded children every two years at most, the notification of parents before changing the educational assignment of any retarded child, and the right to a hearing (Lippman & Goldberg, 1973). More than half the states had before this decision been able to exclude children with very low IQs from the educational system, and at least three-fourths had been legally able to place children without parental permission, though most in fact abided by parental wishes (Rodrigues & Lombardi, 1973).

Other cases attacked and in some instances forced the dissolution of special tracking systems, awarded compensation for damages caused by misclassification, and in general strengthened the human rights of the retarded and other handicapped children within the public schools of the United States.[3] To translate these rights into reality will, however, require wholehearted cooperative ventures involving local school districts as well as private, state, and federal agencies and associations (Vaughan, 1973). It remains to be seen to what degree, and with what speed, the humanitarian objectives developed by voluntary efforts and by the action of administrative, legislative, and judicial bodies will be achieved.

There is reason for optimism. The trend away from reliance on institutional solutions has produced a broad array of programs to support the ability of the family to care for the retarded child at home, opening new avenues of community participation. The schools represent an important component of that array, but in addition there are many other services on which families and schools can call for assistance. There is a firm commitment to retaining retarded children and adults within the community whenever possible. Another reason for optimism at this point is the widespread movement within schools toward individualized instruction, team teaching, and open classrooms, all in one form or another designed to encourage each child to proceed at his own pace. So long as the class need not move in unison, education suited to the special needs of each child can be provided within the regular classroom. This ideal may not work completely, but contemporary educational philosophy permits considerable leeway for individual differences and makes possible the use of a variety of instructional materials and approaches within the same four walls.

There are still hazards in our schools for many children, however. Recognized by a newly coined phrase, "The Six-Hour Retarded Child," there are many children for whom school is the most trying and failure-ridden period of life. For whatever reason, they are unable to function adaptively in school, although outside they "may be exceptionally adaptive to the situation and community in which [they live]" (President's Committee on Mental Retardation, 1970b). These children—mostly inner-city, minority-group members, and poor—are ill-served by the schools. Whether the emphasis should be on changing the schools, helping the children to adapt to them, or both, it is obvious that the schools and the children are too often cruelly mismatched.

The 1959 AAMD definition encompassed most of these children in its definition of borderline retardation, and in so doing it recognized society's special responsibility to discover ways of reaching the children and enabling them to profit from and enjoy their school experiences. The 1973 AAMD definition creates the danger that these

---

[3] See Chap. 22 for a discussion of other legal rights of retarded individuals.

children will not be recognized explicitly enough and that special innovations will be reduced. At one stroke, the definition reduces from about 16 percent to 3 percent the proportion of children who, by reason of IQ, are considered potentially retarded. We must be sure that this shift is not made at the children's expense, for they remain vulnerable to the same woes and failures as before (Meyers & Lombardi, 1974).

TRADITIONAL ORGANIZATION OF SPECIAL EDUCATION

Most school systems in the United States use schemes of classification which, though based on IQ level, do not correspond precisely with the system advocated by the American Association on Mental Deficiency (Grossman, 1973). Most popular are the terms *educable mentally retarded* (EMR) and *trainable mentally retarded* (TMR). EMR children generally are defined as having IQs from 50 or 55 to 75 or 80. They are expected eventually to achieve academic work at least to the third-grade level and occasionally to the sixth-grade level by school-leaving age. TMR children with IQs of 25 or 35 to 50 or 55 are not expected to achieve functionally useful academic skills. Self-care and social adjustment within a restricted environment are the goals of their school experience. Children with still lower IQs previously tended to be known as *custodial mentally retarded,* but fortunately that terminology is no longer in use. Presently they tend to be known as *"right-to-education children,"* although hopefully a less awkward term will soon emerge. Some educators have recognized the learning problems of the *dull-normal* or *slow-learning* child (IQ = 75 to 89), but the present consensus tends to be that special education is neither necessary nor desirable for this group, except for those with specific learning disabilities. (See Chapter 11.)

There are strong moves afoot to integrate retarded children as much as possible into regular classrooms with the support of special services. Before we consider the pros and cons of that trend, however, perhaps it would be well to consider the traditional pattern of more-or-less self-contained classrooms for the retarded.

Education for the Educable Mentally Retarded Child

For EMR children, whose rate of intellectual development is commonly one-half to three-fourths that of the average children, stress on purely academic accomplishments is quite inappropriate. Programs are designed instead to enhance social competence, personal adequacy, and occupational skills. Academic skills are taught as tools, since adults in our society need to be at least minimally literate, to be able to handle money, and to keep track of time.

Most educators recommend that, to maximize individual attention, special classes be small. For younger retarded children, the usual recommendation has been eight to twelve students, and for adolescent EMRs, twelve to eighteen, but most classes have been somewhat larger than this. A program individualized to attack the specific weaknesses of each child is much to be preferred to a mechanical group approach (Bateman, 1967). Educators are also searching for ways of matching children's aptitudes with methods (as opposed to levels) of instruction (Reynolds & Balow, 1974), but so far progress has been slow. In any effective instructional program, tasks must be arranged sequentially, each step being checked carefully, and placed so that both success and challenge are assured. A heavy burden is thus placed upon the teacher.

Special classes are usually grouped to correspond roughly with regular school grades. Classes are more plentiful though, at some ages than others. The *infant stimu-*

Fig. 18-1 This Down's syndrome boy is enrolled in a special preschool. *(From Smith & Wilson, 1973, p. 58)*

lation class, a very recent innovation, usually provides highly individualized work with a few retarded or physically handicapped children, birth to three years. In most such programs, parents attend many of the sessions and receive instruction in developmentally stimulating ways to play with their babies. The *preschool class,* for children three to six years old with mental ages of two to four years, is designed to introduce group experiences. As with the infant stimulation programs, there are few of these classes, partly because so many mildly retarded children escape recognition until they reach first or second grades. A few have been organized especially for very young emotionally disturbed, retarded children (Woodward, Jaffe, & Brown, 1971). As preschool programs for nonretarded children of all socioeconomic groups develop, it is likely that many more EMR children will be spotted at an earlier age, but it does not necessarily follow that segregated classes for them will be established as long as they can be retained with their age-peers.

The *elementary primary class,* for EMR children six to ten years of age, is generally a preacademic program. Because the mental ages of the pupils range from only three or four to about six years, they profit from the kinds of readiness programs found in the ordinary structured kindergarten. Emphasis in most classes is on the develop-

Fig. 18-2 An intermediate special class for EMR children. *(J. & M. Menapace)*

ment of self-confidence, enriched language development, and good habits of health, safety, work, and play. A great many EMR children at this level remain in regular classes, sometimes the targets of heroic efforts to "bring them up to standard."

The *elementary intermediate class,* for children nine to thirteen, is the most common one in the public school system. EMR children in this age range have a mental age of about six to nine years. By the time they have reached the third or fourth grade, it is clear that even with the most energetic remedial efforts, EMR children will not catch up with their classes, and many become a problem in the regular classroom. Especially in traditionally organized classes, where they are expected to sit quietly and answer when called on, they may create a disturbance because of failure to follow material they do not understand, and they may exhibit poor social skills and immaturity. When they transfer to a special class, they often are burdened with negative self-concepts, dislike for school, and self-defeating avoidance patterns. While overcoming these handicaps, emphasis is put on mastering the tool subjects of reading, writing, and arithmetic, learning about the local environment, and exploring personal goals and interests.

Secondary school classes for EMRs at the junior and senior high level are becoming more popular but still fail to meet the demand. At this level, the discrepancy between the achievement of EMRs and nonretarded students becomes much more marked, as the nonretarded students master formal operations and conceptualize subject matter far removed from their concrete experience. Special programs tend to emphasize vocational education and domestic skills and were in fact first established as occupational classes in the late 1930s and early 1940s (Douglas, 1944; Hungerford, DeProspo, & Rosenzweig, 1948). Instruction in tool subjects is continued, with emphasis on practical, everyday uses such as reading the telephone book, newspapers, and job application forms, and making change. Occupational education is generally aimed less at acquiring salable skills, most of which can better be learned on the job, than at the development of appropriate job-related attitudes and behaviors including courtesy, punctuality, and ability to follow directions. This aspect of the program is particularly important since most vocational failures among this group occur not because of low mental ability but because of poor adjustment on the job. (See Chapter 22.) The better secondary school programs also emphasize many other facets of citizenship and of physical and mental health.

Postschool programs are found in the public schools and in nonschool agencies such as sheltered workshops, state employment agencies, and rehabilitation agencies. They recognize the continuing needs of the mildly retarded for training and guidance in our complex society. Vocational placement and supervision, leisure-time activities, and social group programs enhance the adjustment of many mildly retarded adults. Particularly fast-growing have been the federally sponsored vocational rehabilitation services (Morgenstern & Michal-Smith, 1973).

Training for the Trainable Mentally Retarded Child

Trainable mentally retarded children (TMRs) constitute a relatively small group; perhaps one child in five hundred is in this range. These children do not profit from retention in a regular classroom except under unusual circumstances, and for this reason as well as their frequent physical problems, especially seizures, cerebral palsy, and toileting difficulties, many have been totally excluded from school. For many TMRs, especially those living in small towns and rural areas and those presenting management problems, the only solution has been care at home or admission to a residential facility. Many urban communities have, on the other hand, provided special classes for many years.

Recently, with the judicial establishment of the right of every child to appropriate public education or training, and with the expansion of other facilities supporting the ability of parents to maintain their retarded offspring in the community, educational services for TMRs are increasing rapidly. In urban settings, self-contained classrooms are favored, but where the population is more dispersed, a variety of other solutions have been tried including home-based programs and five-day boarding facilities.

Educational services for TMRs serve a number of goals different from those for EMR children. In fact, if the term "education" carries the traditional implications, it is a misnomer and should be avoided (Burton, 1974). Except for the very rare case, TMR children will not achieve any measure of social or economic independence as adults, although they may certainly engage in economically useful work and often can get along quite well in a family setting. The goals of the curriculum of a TMR class are the development of skills which normal or mildly retarded young children learn at home as a matter of course. Trainable children need special tutoring to develop habits of self-care, including acceptable cleanliness, health, and eating behavior. They need help in developing communication skills, work habits, the ability to follow directions, and the rudiments of social participation. Many have physical, sensory, and perceptual handicaps which require special attention. Since traditional academic skills are unlikely to be functionally useful to them, arithmetic instruction is limited to elementary number concepts such as making change, and reading is likely to be concerned with recognition of signs such as "Stop," "Salt," "Men," and "Women."[4] Practical home-

---

[4] A whimsical sign painter created consternation in a clinic for retarded children when he labeled the bathrooms "His" and "Hers."

Fig. 18-3 Simple counting exercises are appropriate for some TMR adolescents. This one shows the features of Down's syndrome. *(J. & M. Menapace)*

making chores and manual activities help make these children valued members of their families.

Special programs for trainable children have not been spectacularly successful as measured by standardized tests of intelligence or academic achievement. When TMRs in school have been compared with those at home, the differences have been negligible, though actually there are few studies sufficiently sophisticated to control for confounding variables. On the whole, there is little evidence that the usual informal, total group instruction in self-care and socialization has been very effective (Dunn, 1973). It is important to keep in mind, however, that selected accomplishments may make a great deal of difference in the quality of family life without showing up on standardized tests. Each step can become a major victory, and it is clear that with teaching based on behavior modification and similar techniques, significant victories are entirely possible. (See Chapter 15.) In addition to welcome relief from child care, the parents may develop more realistic expectations of their children's limitations and their capacities for growth. The fact that many severely retarded children are admitted to institutions at the age at which they outgrow school classes (Saenger, 1957) is perhaps proof enough of the effectiveness of these programs, and it argues for out-of-home services even if, in nonurban areas, these require extremely small classes and heterogeneous age grouping.

Programs for Severely and Profoundly Mentally Retarded Children

Prior to the recent court decisions, it was rare to find any public school programs for severely or profoundly retarded children, and even within institutional facilities, training was often minimal or nonexistent. Now the picture is changing, but in view of the very small number of these children living in most communities, organizational problems are extremely difficult. The needs of some children may be met in predominantly TMR groups. Home visitation programs may be required for some, particularly those in outlying areas, but in large centers of population, special classes for this ability group are possible. Within residential facilities, one may expect a marked increase in formal training programs carried out by ward personnel and by special teachers.

An example of a suitable curriculum has been published by Myers, Sinco, and Stalma (1973); others are being devised to meet the needs of the teachers and paraprofessionals seeking to provide meaningful learning experiences for children whose physical handicaps are generally severe, whose communication skills are minimal, and whose behavior may be extremely infantile. An especially imaginative, integrated program for socialization, motor skills, verbal communication, and personal development has been described by Olechnowicz (1973b) and her coworkers in the Day Center of the Psychoneurological Institute in Warsaw.

ISSUES AND CONTROVERSIES

As has already been mentioned, the field of special education is undergoing a period of rapid growth and reassessment. Prominent among the issues of contention are the establishment of equitable procedures for placement, the organization of special programs for EMR children, and affective versus cognitive teaching approaches.

Selection and Labeling[5]

There is a widespread conviction that labeling a child as mentally retarded by placing him in a special program should be avoided if possible, especially if the child is really only a slow learner or suffers from a specific disability which has lowered his general school performance. In addition to whatever other handicaps a child may have to endure, the label "EMR" is seen as another cross to bear. As Binet and Simon (1905b) put it long ago, "It will never be to one's credit to have attended a special school. We should at the least spare from this mark those who do not deserve it." As we discussed in Chapter 1, however, the evidence for the negative effects of labeling is heavily confounded with other variables and, furthermore, somewhat contradictory.

Although the IQ might seem to be the single criterion for special class placement, that is not in fact the case. Referral to an EMR class usually follows intensive observation by at least one teacher who concludes that the child is failing and shows little

---

[5] This issue is discussed in more general terms in Chap. 1, together with recommendations of the Hobbs (1975b) project.

academic aptitude and generally also that he is adjusting poorly to the regular class-room. With the concurrence of the school principal, an evaluation is usually made by the school psychologist which includes not only the test results but all of the school records. If special placement seems appropriate, the parents are also consulted. At a very minimum, then, three concerned adults with knowledge of the child's behavior at home, in school, and on objective tests, are likely to be actively involved in making the decision.

This is not to say that room for error does not exist. A teacher with little patience for deviance who finds a child difficult to handle may conclude prematurely that he must be retarded. Some testing is conducted by inexperienced, unsympathetic, or overworked personnel who administer inappropriate tests or fail to gain the best effort of the child. Parents who are unsure of themselves may be coerced by those in the educational establishment into acquiescing to a placement with which they do not agree.

Much of the controversy about labeling and segregated classrooms stems from recognition of the large numbers of minority children in special classes and from the struggle to eliminate racial segregation from the schools (Blanton, 1975). The overrep-resentation of minority group children in special education classes does not, in itself, of course, prove that they have been misclassified. As indicated in Chapters 7 and 8, the unfairness which exists in society began its attack on these children long before school entry, and many of their handicaps are real. Nevertheless, there is further evidence which suggests that misperceptions of minority children may indeed play a role in placement. Mercer (1973) found that school psychologists in Riverside, California, were more likely to recommend for placement Mexican-American children and those from poor families than other children of the same IQ. In a startling study (Franks, 1971), the racial composition of programs in Missouri for children with specific learn-ing disabilities was found to be almost exclusively (96.8%) Caucasian, whereas Negro children constituted 34.2 percent of the enrollment in EMR classes. In Scotland, Broadhead (1973) found many children of the same IQs in classes for ESN (EMR) children and classes for children with minimal brain injuries (MBI), the poorer chil-dren tending to be in the ESN classes, the middle-class children tending to be in MBI classes. One is pressed to explain these discrepancies without the strong suspicion that differential perceptions are at work, that the child of a poverty family, especially if he is of minority background, is assumed to be retarded, whereas the poor achiever of white middle-class background is treated more supportively.

No one, of course, denies that such unequal treatment is inherently unfair. No one denies that each child deserves appropriate placement and suitable education. The controversy centers about the best means of assuring equitable procedures. Some would advise discarding intelligence tests altogether, although the Broadhead and Mercer studies demonstrate that the unfairness was not inherent in the test scores but in other aspects of the placement procedure. Others would, as we shall see, advise for other reasons as well that special class placement be discarded altogether for mildly retarded youngsters, substituting individualized instruction within regular classrooms. Still others (ourselves included) maintain that, whatever the means provided by the schools for adapting the instruction given mentally retarded children to their special needs and capabilities, the best insurance against unfair practice is the provision of a cadre of well-trained, experienced, and sympathetic professionals, including psycholo-gists, who in conjunction with parents are committed to making and periodically reviewing decisions which are in the best interests of the children.

Organizational Patterns: Special Classes versus "Mainstreaming"

The concept of "normalization" or "mainstreaming" in educational placement of handicapped children is today much in vogue. With respect to retarded children, this concept is interpreted as the integration of EMR children into groups of nonretarded children, minimizing their distinctiveness or difference. Like any other popular movement, such a change of practice can be exaggerated and premature. This particular movement carries with it both the danger that the special needs of the retarded will be ignored and that school districts will welcome an opportunity to withdraw funding support for special personnel and resources. Before we discuss some evidence about the effects of "mainstreaming," let us consider some alternative organizational patterns which have been used in the past.

Alternatives   The *residential school* is the oldest arrangement for the education of retarded children, except for a few private day schools, but today children in the United States are rarely admitted to residential facilities for educational reasons alone. Most children are placed there only if their presence at home has become detrimental to the family or if the home does not provide a wholesome environment. Within institutions, education and training play an important role. (See Chapter 21.)

The *community special school* became a popular arrangement for a time in some of the larger cities of the United States and is still popular in some other countries such as England (Viggiani, 1969) and the Soviet Union (Hoe, 1969). Some of these schools are devoted completely to retarded children, while others serve children with a broad range of handicaps. Special schools enable children to remain with their families and to benefit from the varied resources of the community. Like the residential schools, however, they tend to isolate retarded children from their nonhandicapped peers, and their centralized location necessitates fatiguing travel for many.

The *special class* in a neighborhood public school has become the most popular arrangement for the majority of retarded children in the United States. Frequently, several classes are placed in one school so that the children can be grouped homogeneously according to age and mental ability. Proximity to home is an advantage, and for mildly retarded children this arrangement may enable them to associate with other (possibly younger) normal children in informal play and in school activities such as art, music, and physical education. Moderately and severely retarded children, however, seldom mingle successfully with normal children, and for them the relative advantages of the neighborhood school are reduced.

A great many retarded children are enrolled in traditionally organized *regular classes* with nonretarded children and given no special services. In some school systems, retarded children are promoted every year until they reach high school, at which time they are allowed (often encouraged) to withdraw.[6] In others, they are retained in the lower grades. Often their presence is tolerated only because space in special classes is unavailable. Many mildly retarded children actually progress academically about as rapidly in regular elementary school classes as in special classes, though the subject matter may be unsuited to their interests and cognitive processes. This discrepancy becomes even greater in junior and senior high schools. Their low level of achievement

---

[6] In 1970, 2.4 percent of U.S. elementary school children but only 1.4 percent of high school students were identified as retarded (Metz, 1973).

places an additional burden on their teachers, who tend to concentrate on their slower pupils in an attempt to bring them along with the group (Dunn, 1968).

Why Special Classrooms?   Before examining the evidence about the consequence of special-class versus regular-class placement, some assumptions underlying the advocacy of special classrooms should be made explicit. (See Bruininks & Rynders, 1974.) First, it has been maintained that special classes make possible *homogeneous grouping,* narrowing differences in mental ability and thereby in interests and skills, to a manageable range. Presumably, removing the extreme child, the "sore thumb," reduces the range in the regular classroom. There is evidence, though, that within special classes, the range of educationally relevant characteristics (e.g., reading and arithmetic skills) is at least as great as in regular classes (Bruininks & Rynders, 1974; MacMillan, 1971). This heterogeneity comes about both because educational skills are imperfectly correlated with MA or with IQ (which form the basis for grouping) and because in special classes, the CA range is typically wider than in regular classes.

Another assumption for EMR classes was the belief that *specialized curricula* suitable for retarded children would be in line with their interests and with the goals of vocational and social adequacy. An earlier review by Simches and Bohn (1963) was rather discouraging in this regard. Although considerable progress has been made to develop specialized curricula, a great many EMR classes still utilize a "watered-down" regular program, especially in such skill areas as reading and arithmetic. They simply follow the pattern of the general curriculum at a slower pace.

Another assumption has to do with *special training needs for teachers* of the retarded, with respect, for example, to the use of different materials, an orientation toward individualization, and an understanding of the special learning handicaps and personal-social problems of retarded children. Training of special education teachers has been stepped up considerably in the last decade, and many more classrooms are staffed by qualified teachers. Whether such teachers actually do a better job with retarded children, however, is yet to be demonstrated. The logic is there, but not the evidence.

It has also been assumed that retarded children will profit from *adult attention.* Class sizes have been reduced accordingly and are now generally twelve to eighteen students per class. In TMR classes, an additional aide is often provided to help the teacher. The efficacy of this assumption has yet to be tested. Analogously, in the United States, it is thought essential that preschool classes be kept small and several adults are generally available. In preschools in other countries, however, child-adult ratios are considerably larger, without apparent adverse effects (Robinson & Robinson, 1974).

Regular versus Special Classrooms   Of the many studies about the effects of school placement in self-contained versus unembellished regular classrooms, few are worth summarizing. Most of the evidence has been taken from comparisions of children arriving in special classes and those remaining in regular classes in the ordinary course of events. Such evidence is at best equivocal. The children who are most likely to be singled out for special placement are those who are difficult to handle (more often boys than girls), who are learning little from exposure to the regular programs, and who have remained in the same grade for several years. It is hardly surprising that retarded children in regular classes generally have higher academic achievement than

Fig. 18-4 *(University of Washington Child Development and Mental Retardation Center)*

those in special classes (Hoeltke, 1967; Stanton & Cassidy, 1964; Thurstone, 1959). It is worthy of note, however, that in neither setting is the EMR child likely to achieve the level of academic work or verbal development which would be predicted from his MA (Meyen & Hieronymus, 1970; Quay, 1963; Stanton & Cassidy, 1964). Neither type of class, then, as typically constituted, may be doing a good enough job with these students.

Despite the fact that children with poor social and academic adjustment are referred more quickly for special classes than are nondisruptive children, most of the evidence, though much of it equivocal (Guskin & Spicker, 1968), points to superior social adjustment of EMR children placed in self-contained classrooms. Their self-concepts appear more positive and they are rejected somewhat less strongly by nonretarded pupils than are retarded children in regular classes who are often classroom isolates (Goodman, Gottlieb, & Harrison, 1972; Gottlieb & Budoff, 1973; Johnson, 1950; Rucker, Howe, & Snider, 1969; Towne, Joiner, & Schurr, 1967). They may also be less suggestible in the sense that they are less excessively outer-directed (Trippi, 1973). Zito & Bardon (1969), however, found that Negro EMR adolescents in special classes anticipated failure to achieve their goals, although regular-class Negro retarded students more often anticipated success.

A recent study (Bruininks, Rynders, & Gross, 1974) points up some methodological problems inherent in studies of peer acceptance. They found that when retarded children were rated by nonretarded children of the same sex, EMR children enrolled in regular classrooms with the support of resource centers were rated *higher* in urban areas and *lower* in suburban areas than nonretarded children. When boy and girl ratings were combined, the differences disappeared. Presumably, children of the same sex are more sensitive to important variables about one another. The retarded pupils in suburban classrooms are more discrepant from the modal academic and intellectual performance than are urban retarded pupils, and the importance of school achievement in the value hierarchies in suburban families is probably greater than in the central cities, where the special attention given the children may have enhanced their status.

There are, however, a few studies with sufficient methodological sophistication to be given considerable weight. The best known of these is a study by Goldstein, Moss, and Jordan (1965), who identified 126 children entering school with IQs below 85. Half were randomly selected for placement in special classes, although the others were not given special experience. Over the four-year period of the study, the children in the special classes appeared to be somewhat better off in emotional adjustment and peer acceptance. The major finding of the study was that, academically, the group with IQs above 75 did better in regular classrooms, whereas the EMR group with lower IQs made more progress in special classes.

Another random-assignment study (Drews, 1967) compared homogeneous grouping versus heterogeneous grouping of slow, average, and superior students. The slow learners were not necessarily retarded but were three to eight years behind in reading and language skills. Slow learners in homogeneous classes made significantly more class contributions and received higher ratings from both teachers and peers than did those in heterogeneous (regular) classes. Reduced class participation was also observed by Grosenick (1969) after EMR boys were transferred to an integrated classroom. Similarly, Gampel, Harrison, & Budoff (1972) found that EMR pupils were more restricted in verbal behavior in an integrated classroom.

Retention in Grade The old-fashioned alternative of retaining retarded children in the same regular grade for more than a year is not, on the basis of the evidence, a good solution. Where yearly grade promotion is the norm, children retained in grade achieve significantly less the second year than they did the first, seldom catching up as expected (Dobbs, 1965; Kraus, 1973). This is not the same as retaining a child in an ungraded classroom; for example, taking four years to complete an ordinary three-year sequence. Evidence about this kind of retardation is unfortunately not available.

The evidence suggests, then, that social competence and social adjustment are the areas in which retarded children may profit most from special classes. In addition, the studies which show that special-class children are less often rejected by nonretarded peers than are EMR children in regular classes indicate that labeling has some positive value after all, that the picture is not entirely one-sided. The child explicitly identified as retarded may be judged by more lenient standards, accepted or at least tolerated as is. Yet, typically, neither group of EMR children is at all popular with nonretarded peers. The overall import of these studies is that life can be dreary and lonely for the retarded child, but that the child is less likely to be isolated in a special class than in a regular class.

Special Classrooms versus Integrated Patterns The notion of mainstreaming—placing retarded with nonretarded children for all or most of the school day—is a new and overpowering phenomenon which is sweeping the field of education for the physically handicapped as well as the mentally retarded. In the headlong rush toward mainstreaming, the old patterns and old personnel are rapidly falling by the wayside, often with insufficient care given to safeguarding the contributions that special classes have had to offer to disabled children.

The beginnings of this movement date to the late 1960s, coincident with the trend toward normalization in all services to retarded individuals. Leadership was given by Lloyd M. Dunn (1968), long an advocate of self-contained special classes. He introduced his switch of position with the following statement:

> I have loyally supported and promoted special classes for the educable mentally retarded for most of the last 20 years, but with growing disaffection. In my view, much of our past and present practices are morally and educationally wrong. We have been living at the mercy of general educators who have referred their problem children to us. And we have been generally ill prepared and ineffective in educating these children. Let us stop being pressured into continuing and expanding a special education program that we know now to be undesirable for many of the children we are dedicated to serve. (p. 5)

Dunn based his argument on a number of factors, among them the apparently slower progress of slow learners and disadvantaged children placed in homogeneous classrooms and the high proportion of such pupils who were of ethnic and racial minorities. He argued that the label of disability worked to children's disadvantage, both in their own eyes and in the lowered expectations of their teachers. He also noted that schools are now much better prepared to deal with individual differences among pupils at all levels of mental ability.

As it is interpreted by responsible educators, mainstreaming is not an abdication of special education. True, the individualized and flexible regular classrooms of today are better able to accommodate the deviant child than were the authoritarian, lockstep classes of yesterday, though one is deceived if it is assumed that all vestiges of that traditional atmosphere have disappeared. Still, regular classroom teachers usually lack both the materials and the skills to do the job alone. Many forms of integration are possible, and many are being tried. Some schools provide a continuum from totally self-contained EMR classrooms to day-long exposure to the regular classroom, the goal being to move the child as rapidly as he can manage well from one to the other. Children exhibiting disruptive behavior may be retained in the self-contained classroom only until their behavior can be brought reliably under control. Introduction to nonretarded children is often first accomplished in physical education, art, music, and similar "contact" classes. Some schools provide a resource room in which a trained specialist provides help to the children who visit there a few hours a day. Other schools provide visiting master teachers who carry out meticulous educational assessment, prescribe work to be carried out under the supervision of the regular teacher, and consult with her to select materials and to handle day-to-day problems as they arise. The limits to what may be called "mainstreaming" are as broad as the flexibility and imagination of school personnel permit. The common strain in all the plans is the provision of specialized help to both children and their classroom teachers. The task is much more difficult than it seems at first glance.

Borginsky (1974) collected data throughout the United States about the programs provided for mentally retarded children in public schools in 1970, shortly after the mainstreaming movement began. He found that more than half the children were in special classes all day, nearly a quarter were receiving no specialized services, and the remainder were involved in a variety of other arrangements. These figures are shown in Table 18-1.

We have already examined some of the assumptions on which the establishment of special classrooms was based. Mainstreaming rests on an entirely different—and somewhat contradictory or tangential—set of assumptions (Brenton, 1974). First, it is assumed that *the special classroom is an isolating experience* for retarded children. As we have seen, often the regular classroom is in fact more isolating. Placing children side by side does not guarantee that they will become friends or even that they will interact with one another. As any visitor to a school which houses children of different ethnic, socioeconomic, or racial groups soon becomes aware, a great deal of voluntary segregation occurs in the most "integrated" schools. Particularly when mildly retarded children are distinctly deviant in the regular classroom, as most often happens in suburban schools and schools serving mainly middle-class neighborhoods, they may be lonely indeed. To achieve real acceptance by their classmates, retarded children usually need a great deal of support from their teachers, who must be able to accept retarded children honestly and to communicate to the other children that despite their learning problems, they can be valued and trusted friends. Many retarded children also need to be explicitly taught social skills which they are sorely lacking.

Second, the move toward mainstreaming assumes that retarded children are *better able to achieve, both academically and socially,* at a level commensurate with their abilities, *when they are exposed to models whose achievement in both areas is more expert than their own.* There may well be truth to this argument. It may be one explanation for the typically higher academic achievement of EMR children in regular classes. Imitation of competent models can be very effective in retarded children if, and only if, they are able to add to their repertoires the targeted skills possessed by the models and to grasp the central features of the situation. (See Chapter 15.)

A further assumption of mainstreaming is that the *regular classroom bears a greater resemblance to the "real world"* with which retarded individuals must cope than does the protected special classroom. To us, this argument bears an uneasy resemblance to the "school of hard knocks" philosophy, but it may have more relevance to the adaptation of physically handicapped children without marked intellectual difficulties. Mentally retarded children must, of course, learn to function in a world where most people are brighter than they are. Outside of school, they do this every day.

Table 18-1   Provision of Instruction to Mentally Retarded Children in Local Public Schools, Spring, 1970, By Percentages

School	Separate classes		Individualized Instruction			
				Specialized personnel		
	All day	Part day	Regular teacher	Own school	Another school/agency	No services
Elementary	53	5	12	3	5	25
Secondary	50	28	8	6	5	15
Total	53	11	11	4	5	22

Source: Borginsky (1974). Percentages add to more than 100 because some pupils received more than one type of service.

When they learn to do so without sacrifice of their own self-confidence, a great deal has been accomplished. Yet, as we have seen, the few studies which have observed EMR children in regular classrooms tend to suggest that they are rather vulnerable in this respect.

Finally, the arguments for mainstreaming include the notion that *exposure to handicapped children helps other children to understand and accept them,* to respond with less fear and prejudice against people who are different from themselves. This is most likely to happen when teachers explicitly prepare their pupils for the intoduction of a handicapped child and when they provide interpretation on occasions when the handicapped child behaves in ways which the other children did not expect.

The research evaluating the effects of mainstreaming is so far naturally very meager. Few studies have shown as positive an improvement in the social status of EMR children as one might hope with integrated classroom procedures (Gottlieb & Davis, 1973; Iano, Ayers, Heller, McGettigan, & Walker, 1974). Gampel, Gottlieb, and Harrison (1974), however, found that EMRs in integrated classes behaved more like their normal peers than did those in segregated classes. They were somewhat less restless, gave fewer negative verbal responses to their peers, and received fewer negative verbal responses from them in return. Another study which reported very positive results was conducted by Edgerton and Edgerton (1973), who studied a school in Hawaii which formerly had sent its retarded children elsewhere for special class placement, following a formal labeling process. Under a new plan, EMR children were placed in regular classrooms but spent an hour a day in a resource room which also served nonretarded children who went there for a variety of purposes. In comparison with the old plan, the investigators found considerable improvement in morale among the retarded children and significantly enhanced academic progress. It is important to note that in this instance not only were integration achieved and support given, but labeling was avoided. Most programs are unable to achieve this double goal. It seems doubtful that in the long run truly low-achieving children can escape being labeled in an informal way by their classmates, their teachers, and themselves.

There is considerable flux in the organization of school programs for EMR children. Hopefully, the older, rigid forms of segregation will be modified by comprehensive plans in which each child—whatever his ability and his social skills—can be placed in classrooms and study groups suited to his current needs and challenging his abilities.

Affective versus Cognitive Approaches

A number of the studies we have mentioned suggest that too little is expected of children in special classes. Their teachers assign a higher priority to personal and social adjustment than to preparing them to cope as children and as adults with the demands of their environment, and indeed they tend to demand less achievement than their pupils could deliver (Fine, 1967; Schmidt, & Nelson, 1969). There is evidence (e.g., Hart, 1964) that a moderate degree of anxiety reflecting realistic stress actually favors academic progress, though excessive anxiety unquestionably has negative effects on learning (Tymchuk, 1974).

> Where much of the stress (drive to learn, achieve or perform) has been removed from the learning situation, as in special classes where the primary objective is to remove pressures and make the child "happy," little learning can take place despite the instruction that may be provided. (Johnson, 1962, p. 68)

Teacher expectations about pupil performance are powerful influences (Blanton, 1975; Guskin & Spicker, 1968), and it is easy to expect too little of retarded children, especially those from poverty backgrounds who may be socially less acceptable to the teachers (Lenkowsky & Blackman, 1968) and who typically have many real-life problems to face at home. Parental and teacher expectations and pressures are suggested by the fact that middle-class children in EMR classes tend to achieve at a higher level than do children of low social class (Schwarz & Shores, 1969). The parent-teacher relationship is sometimes a vulnerable one. Each party can fall prey to the temptation to blame the other for the child's slow progress. Professional consultation services may help teachers to cope with disturbed student behavior and disturbing parent demands (Berlin, 1966), while preserving a realistic challenge for the child.

Within the past several years, numerous materials useful for cognitive-oriented activities in EMR classes have become available. It is, however, much easier to devise curricula for skill-building (reading, arithmetic), where precise behavioral goals and progressive steps can be serially specified, than to meet more elusive cognitive goals related to problem-solving strategies, mediational strategies, planfulness, concrete operations (in the Piagetian sense), and so on. Curricula for nonretarded children tend to assume that such cognitive skills will be acquired as a matter of course, but one cannot make that assumption with mentally retarded children. Special approaches are necessary both for this reason and because materials calibrated to ages and rates of learning in normal children are demeaning to the older student who is, perhaps, learning to read at age ten from a Dick-and-Jane primer depicting six-year-olds, and who needs more repetition and drill at each step of the way than those books provide.

Beyond the elementary years, largely devoted to acquiring skills such as reading, basic arithmetic, and spelling, appropriate curricula for retarded and nonretarded groups substantially diverge, the retarded needing greater emphasis on immediate practical matters useful in everyday coping (Meyen & Hieronymus, 1970). A class in government might well ignore the Constitution (aside, perhaps, from the Bill of Rights) and the conduct of foreign affairs in favor of an emphasis on local politics, means of coping with fragmented social agencies, the reasons one must pay taxes, laws about personal conduct, one's rights if arrested, etc. Because EMR progress cannot be judged in terms of the full range of curricular aims for nonretarded students, it is tempting to let matters slide along at a comfortable pace, minimizing frustration. To avoid this trap while supporting healthy personal and social adaptation, teachers may need outside support in formulating explicit goals and timetables and may profit by an explicit contract between school and family (Gallagher, 1974), regularly administered achievement tests (Gallien, 1968), and/or periodic teaching assignments with nonretarded children of equivalent mental age.

PREVENTION OF MENTAL RETARDATION: COMPENSATORY PROGRAMS

The War on Poverty created many programs designed to aid poor families and to advance the development of their children. Prominent among these were the compensatory educational programs, some of them mainly addressed to school-age children and some to preschool children. Of the latter, Project Head Start was by far the largest. There was great optimism at the outset, followed by discouragement and pessimism when the results of the programs were not as dramatic as had been unrealistically hoped. Although most of the group programs made an immediate and positive impact on the children's development, the long-term effects of brief and/or partial intervention were negligible (e.g., Bronfenbrenner, 1974; Datta, 1972). It became clear that compensatory activities need to begin early and to be continued. Without such efforts, most of the gains achieved during the preschool programs tended to wash out during the first three grades of school. The continuing effects of home and school environments typical of poor neighborhoods could not be prevented by an "inoculation" of preschool experience. Only small experimental programs have thus far produced really superior achievement in disadvantaged children—i.e., mean IQs of 120 or higher, sometimes with an advantage of 30 to 40 points over controls (Heber, Garber, & Falender, 1973; Robinson & Robinson, 1971; Sprigle, 1972). Head Start projects have produced more modest test results. They have, though, increased the children's interaction patterns, increased task orientation, improved self-concept, and increased trust in others (Datta, 1969).

A wide range of studies has suggested that structured preschool and primary grade programs designed to meet carefully specified behavioral goals are more effective in enhancing cognitive development in disadvantaged children than are programs which have less well-defined goals and are run in a more traditional manner. This is especially true with children with low pretest IQs, those who are older, and those from nonurban areas (Datta, Mitchell, & McHale, 1972). Their intellectual development is enhanced by the orderly environment of a well-run center, low pupil-teacher ratios, an academic orientation, and an emphasis on language.

One line of investigation deserves special mention because it is a distinct departure from the usual group approaches and because it has shown signs of being effective, economical, and long-lasting (Gordon, 1970; Klaus & Gray, 1968; Levenstein, 1974; Madden, Levenstein, & Levenstein, 1974; Weikart et al., 1974). This intervention approach, reviewed in detail by Bronfenbrenner (1974), consists of frequent home visits by personnel, often poverty-group mothers with only moderate training, whose goal is to enhance the effectiveness of the relationship between the mother and her infant or young child. The visitor may be introduced as a toy demonstrator (as in the Levenstein study) or by some other title, but in fact it is the mother's way of using the materials, her view of herself as the central educator, and her recognition of her child's potential as a learner, which are the foci of attention.

The research data have consistently indicated that children from the most deprived backgrounds show the greatest developmental deficits. Bronfenbrenner (1974) points out that children from the most deprived backgrounds also profit least from intervention programs. He questions whether this may to some degree be attributable to their parents' being so overburdened with the tasks and frustrations of sheer survival that they have neither the energy nor the psychological resources to participate fully in programs designed to benefit their children. He argues persuasively that parents who are provided the means effectively to interact with their children must be the key persons in any intervention effort.

Three kinds of compensatory studies deserve further mention. The first involves early stimulation of prematures and helping the parents to enhance development during the first year of life (e.g., Barnard, 1973; Scarr-Salapatek & Williams, 1973). (See also Chapter 5.) Although these studies have shown rather temporary effects, they are important because low-birthweight infants typically fare poorly in families of low socioeconomic status.

A second type of study has provided group stimulation for infants and young children from extremely high-risk families, with encouraging results. Kugel and Parsons (1967) studied thirty-five cultural-familial retarded children in sixteen families, who showed no gross neurological findings. They entered the program between the ages of three and six years. The children received nursery school type stimulation while the mothers received training in how to keep house and feed a family, group experiences, and a variety of social services. More than half (twenty) of the children were identified as having abnormal EEGs, suggesting that a significant amount of the deficit observed in such children is organic in nature. Even so, this subgroup gained an average of about 12 points in IQ during the study, while the fifteen children with normal EEG's gained an average of about 19 points. In both subgroups the changes were greater for the younger than the older children.

Another study (Heber, Garber, & Falender, 1973) is more significant because of its intensive and prolonged work with the children and also because of its more sophisticated methodology. The children were enrolled between three and six months of age and the intervention program was continued through the preschool years. It included both a full-day stimulation program which emphasized a cognitive-language orientation implemented through a structured environment and a maternal rehabilitation program. Many of the mothers and fathers were retarded and all lived in poverty. By age eighteen months, significant differences could be detected between the developmental status of the experimental and control groups; eventually the two groups stabilized with a difference of about 25 to 30 IQ points. At age fifty-four months, for example, the mean IQs were 124 and 94. One interesting sidelight is provided by a study of mother-child interactions (Falender, 1973). The experimental children, ages forty to sixty-six months, were much more active in relation to their mothers than were the controls, expecting and in turn receiving a significantly higher level of verbal behavior.

A third group of preventive studies have concentrated on sensorimotor behavior. As an example, Adelson and Fraiberg (1974) studied ten infants, blind from birth, and found them lagging in self-initiated mobility and locomotion. An intervention program resulted in advances in mobility for this group in comparison with other blind infants. Two preschool programs (Lillie, 1968; Morrison & Pothier, 1972) demonstrated that advances in motor development can be obtained, especially when goals are explicitly defined and activities prescribed to correct deficiencies.

Overall, then, the outlook for compensatory programs suggests moderate optimism for intensive programs, especially those involving the parents as well as the children. Under the auspices of the federal Education of the Handicapped Act, support for preschool programs for retarded children is gaining momentum. The inclusion of handicapped children in Project Head Start is also becoming a standard practice. There are no panaceas, however, and programs are extremely difficult and expensive to do well on a large scale.

SPECIALIZED TEACHING APPROACHES

The extensive treatment of learning and memory in retarded individuals (Chapters 13 and 14) makes it superfluous to repeat here the evidence developed through laboratory research. Such findings have obvious relevance, of course, for the design of learning experiences. The tools of behavior modification, in particular, are nowhere more relevant than the classroom (Chapter 15). Given properly engineered conditions, specific training in the mental processes involved, tasks they can perform, the opportunity for plenty of practice, and reward for achievement, retarded children can learn effectively and remember well (e.g., Haring & Kunzelmann, 1966; Kaufman, 1971). Beyond this simple generalization, it is well to remember that the retarded population is a hetero-geneous group with highly variable learning characteristics, not predictable in a simple fashion from a knowledge of mental age alone (Scheerenberger, 1967).

The number of specialized curricula available to the teacher is increasing. Among the programs published are some which are utterly worthless and some which can be very valuable. Some curriculum guides are training manuals for obviously useful skills, and in such cases "face validity" may suffice, at least for an initial trial. But any program which extends beyond a commonsense approach deserves a healthy skepti-cism—witness, for example, the debacles of instruction when slow learning and EMR children were required to learn the abstract conceptualizations of the "new math." The teacher should demand evidence that a program works; the publishers should take the time and effort to pretest products which may promise more than they can deliver.

Whatever the curriculum, however, there is no substitute for the trained, talented, dedicated, and energetic teacher. A major and usually overlooked teaching ingredient is the degree of conviction of the teacher that what she is doing is right, important, and effective, and the sense of urgency she communicates, the message that every day's work is significant and that time is short.

Although detailed matters of curriculum design are beyond the scope of this book, it is perhaps worth mentioning a few approaches which have proved useful for the classroom. Most successful educational approaches have featured clear step-by-step definitions of desired behavior, deliberate attention to the teaching and reinforce-ment conditions, and continuous evaluation of progress.

Engineering attention, as we saw in Chapter 13, is an important means of over-coming some of the deficiencies which retarded individuals show in learning situ-ations. This can be done in part by moving the child gradually from easy items (where cues are very prominent) to harder ones, providing multiple relevant cues for problem solving, and using a novel approach rather than negative reinforcement when failure does occur (Scott, 1966). Overlearning and rote learning probably also have their place (Prehm, 1967) as a means of overcoming difficulties in retention and in generalizing from one situation to another.

From the most basic lesson, such as getting a profoundly retarded child to look his mother in the face (Linde & Kopp, 1973) to teaching EMR adolescents to drive a car[7] (Kubaiko & Kokaska, 1969), the message for teachers comes through loud and clear: the task must be broken into achievable steps within the ability of the child, carefully modulated, monitored, and positively reinforced.

In some ways, programmed instruction provides the epitome of this process. This approach can be useful in the educational process, although it is usually not found to be more effective than ordinary classroom methods (Greene, 1966). Programmed in-struction may be particularly suitable for skills such as spelling which require extended practice (Malpass, Hardy, Gilmore, & Williams, 1964) and at least equal to traditional classroom techniques in teaching reading and arithmetic (Bijou, Birnbrauer, Kidder,

---

[7] Many (e.g., Egan, 1967; Gutshall, Harper, & Burke, 1968), are dubious about the wisdom of encouraging retarded persons to drive, especially in view of their relatively inferior performance as a group. So long as state laws permit licensing retarded drivers, however, one must conclude the oppor-tunity for training is probably called for, and that instruction may also serve a screening function.

& Tague, 1966; Blackman & Capobianco, 1965). With programmed learning as a part of a comprehensive program, teacher time may be released to work with small groups of children. Although some very sophisticated computerized programs are available (Suppes, 1974), they are beyond the means or the needs of most classrooms. Some form of simple gadgetry may be helpful to keep the child's interest and to make possible immediate feedback and delivery of reinforcement, but one cannot assume that simple knowledge of results or moving ahead in the program automatically will be reinforcing for retarded children (Greene, 1966).

Another way of making goals and progress more explicit for everyone concerned is to draw up contracts with definite commitments within a given time span. Contracts may vary from an agreement on the part of the child to finish a single arithmetic assignment before recess to a much more comprehensive agreement on the part of the teacher, the parents, and the child, to accomplish a series of behavioral goals during a schoolyear, with rewards for successful completion of the contract and penalties for failure to do so (Gallagher, 1974).

An extremely important approach has entered the classroom through applications of social learning theory. (See Chapter 15.) Prominent among these are the techniques of modeling, imitative learning, and social (direct and/or vicarious) reinforcement.[8] Parents can be trained to use these techniques (Seitz & Hoekenga, 1974); "foster grandparents" can use them (Gray & Kasteler, 1969); and they are eminently suitable for small group and individual instruction in the classroom (Ross & Ross, 1973a). One of the arguments for mainstreaming is that EMRs will be provided with normal models, the advantage being for the less mature child (Amaria, Biron, & Leith, 1969; Gampel, Gottlieb, & Harrison, 1974) but with the model also having the opportunity to profit from playing a mature role.

Out of the social learning laboratories have come a variety of small-group games to teach numbers (Ross, 1970), listening skills (Ross & Ross, 1972), and generalized cognitive skills (Ross & Ross, 1973a). The effectiveness of these techniques suggests that an EMR child's performance reflects not only a slower intellectual development, but the social-play deprivation which so frequently is secondary to the intellectual problem (Ross, 1970). Ross and Ross (1974) have published a systematic and comprehensive curriculum for kindergarten and primary-level EMRs which makes considerable use of reward and modeling. (See also Chapter 15.)

Techniques aside, the special teacher needs to be acutely sensitive to the motivational and personality problems of her pupils (Hulicka, 1969), recognizing that limited mental ability has powerful indirect as well as direct effects on learning. Many children come to school with reserves they are not using because of motivational barriers (Zigler & Butterfield, 1968); gratifying progress can be made by attending first to the barriers themselves. MacMillan (1974) has cogently described the motivational problems of retarded youngsters as they affect classroom behavior, particularly the child's expectancy for failure, his positive and negative reaction tendencies, and his outer-directedness. (See also Chapter 9.) With respect to the need for dealing with the child's expectation of failure, MacMillan suggests that the teacher be prepared to go to great lengths in the beginning to establish feelings of self-worth and competence, for example, by engineering tasks within the child's capabilities, using prompting to elicit the correct answer, or giving extrinsic or tangible rewards even for low degrees of success.

---

[8] See Sarason & Sarason (1974) for a teacher's guide to modeling and role-playing techniques.

As the child becomes accustomed to success experiences, greater challenges may be presented. The teacher from time to time may also want to challenge a child's correct answers, to teach him to rely on his own good judgment.

Many schools have recently found, somewhat to their surprise, that children make excellent tutors for younger and/or slower students. One of the most unexpected aspects of this innovation is that under such a partnership, both children gain—tutor and tutee, the former perhaps even more than the latter. Wagner (1974) suggests that the tutorial relationship, in addition to individualization, special and consistent attention, immediate feedback, and modeling, provides direct peer support and cooperation which an adult can not contribute in the same way. Furthermore, the tutor may be able to see problems from the point of view of the tutee more readily than can the adult. At any rate, tutorial programs seem to work beautifully with tutors varying widely in academic ability and achievement (Wagner, 1974).

In summary, special education is undergoing rapid change, and it is also developing an array of teaching tools and an army of competent teachers. All this bodes well for the future. Although we may be in danger of giving too little attention to the child of borderline academic competence, we are making healthy strides toward offering effective programs to children who require special attention.

19
Psychotherapy with the Mentally Retarded

Among the services which mentally retarded individuals and their families are most sorely lacking are those of the mental health professions. There are, though, many avenues by which these professions can contribute to alleviating emotional distress, decreasing socially maladaptive behavior, and strengthening adjustive behavior patterns. Often the worker needs to look beyond the needs of specific individuals and families, toward more broadly conceived preventive efforts, community organization, education, and consultation which result in an improved mental health milieu.

Indirect mental health services benefiting retarded citizens can take many forms. Among these are, for example, participation in setting priorities and organizing mental health resources within a community; providing information to parents' groups, elected officials, planners, and the general public; training staffs of voluntary and tax-supported agencies in the fields of health, education, and social welfare; and provision of interagency and interprofessional collaboration on joint cases (Hume, 1972). Emotional disturbance in retarded persons often is more a social phenomenon than an intrapsychic problem. There is an exciting opportunity for mental health professionals to affect the entire social environment of retarded children and adults, optimizing their chances for wholesome development in an accepting and growth-enhancing network of settings. It may be much more effective, for example, to spend several hours consulting with or training nursery school teachers, foster parents, or institutional attendants, than to try to undo in psychotherapy damage resulting from misdirected upbringing.

Direct mental health services to retarded persons and their families include the more traditional clinical activities, such as early case finding, assessment and evaluation, crisis intervention, individual and group psychotherapy, behavior modification, and other treatment methods including the use of psychotropic drugs (E. Katz, 1972).

Psychotherapy forms the focus of the present chapter. Although no single definition would please all theorists or practitioners, we can use the term with reasonable accuracy to characterize a more-or-less regular series of interchanges between a professionally trained resource person, the therapist, and one or more patients or clients who come to him because of their problems in living. Within this very broad definition there is wide variation. Some workers distinguish, for example, between "counseling," oriented toward a set of problems of coping with the environment, and "psychotherapy," oriented toward thoroughgoing personality change. Psychotherapy, as we use the term, may occur in an office or in a play setting, may involve one individual or several in a group, may be sought at the instigation of the retarded client or of someone else, and may include verbal and/or nonverbal means of communication, manipulation of the reinforcement contingencies (behavior modification), and other means of behavior change. Often the therapist will focus at least as much of his efforts on work with parents and teachers as on work with the child himself.

Only in recent years have professionals who work with retarded persons begun to consider psychotherapy a suitable endeavor.[1] Publications as late as the 1940s typically implied that psychotherapy was neither feasible nor profitable for mentally retarded persons. A very limited number of psychologists and psychiatrists ventured against the tide to undertake one or another form of psychotherapy with a few retarded children. Probably no more than two dozen papers appeared in the literature of the 1930s and 1940s. Although these papers were generally poor from a methodological point of view, they were sufficiently enthusiastic to establish the notion that at least some retarded children could profit from at least some forms of psychotherapeutic experience. During the 1950s and 1960s reports of psychotherapy with retarded children began to appear with increased frequency.

With today's emphasis on normalization and on services to enable retarded individuals to live amicably in their families and communities, there is concomitant recognition of the disruptive problems which occur even within capable and empathic families and of the psychological discomfort which so often accompanies intellectual deficit. (See Chapters 9 and 20.) Within specialized facilities for the mentally retarded there are now many more active efforts to ameliorate these problems through direct psychotherapy and through work with parents and teachers concerning the management of problem behaviors. In community facilities which serve a wider range of clients, similar psychological services are now also more often made available than previously, a change encouraged in part by the Mental Retardation and Community Mental Health Centers Construction Act of 1963. Yet, even today, families and children are turned away from too many treatment facilities simply because the children are found to be retarded or brain damaged, without regard for their needs or amenability to treatment. Appropriate counseling services for the families of retarded children and for the children themselves are still difficult to find.

Although psychological services including psychotherapy provide no sure-fire solutions, they can often help create an avenue for change which will make it possible for

---

[1] The interested reader is referred to a collection of reprinted papers edited by Stacey and De Martino (1957) and to reviews by Bialer (1967) and Sternlicht (1966).

retarded individuals to continue living at home rather than away, to live in a relaxed community residential facility instead of in a regimented institution, or to remain in an integrated class instead of a segregated one, as well as to make strides toward the best use of their abilities for growth, independence, and self-respect. Prompt treatment instituted at early stages can avert more serious problems which might otherwise develop. Some authors (see Chapter 10) maintain that among retarded children, behavior pathology is the rule rather than the exception. To the extent that professional guidance can help, it follows that every family and every retarded person deserves access to services that will help to optimize development and psychological well-being.

BARRIERS TO PSYCHOTHERAPY WITH THE MENTALLY RETARDED

There are a number of hindrances to psychotherapy with the retarded. Some lie in shortages of personnel and facilities, some in the unexplored and often erroneous notions held by uninformed professionals, and still others in the limitations of retarded persons themselves.

Shortages of Personnel and Facilities

Psychotherapy requires extensive specialized training and unusual emotional maturity on the part of the therapist. Ordinarily a therapist sees children and/or their families for a series of sessions ranging from a few weeks to several years. Therefore, psychotherapy is often very expensive for a family which obtains the services of a therapist in private practice or for a community which supports public clinics. Moreover, there are not now nor are there likely soon to be enough qualified therapists to treat the millions of parents, children, adolescents, and adults who could profit from their services. It is true that opportunities for training are expanding, that paraprofessionals are being used to a greater extent, and that therapeutic techniques are being modified to make them of shorter duration and/or capable of treating several individuals at one time. There is no possibility, however, that these measures alone will prove adequate to meet the tremendous needs of the general population.

Under these circumstances, clients must be selected. Therapists tend to work primarily with individuals who seem to have the best chance of adequate adjustment and of contributing to the common good. They understandably tend to favor the brighter child over the duller one, the young person over the older one, and the less seriously disabled over the severely crippled. Conflicting with this tendency are cultural values which proclaim the equal worth of every individual, rich or poor, bright or dull, dependent or productive. The formulation of answers to this dilemma is a problem which has been faced more often by default than by determination.

Attitudes of Therapists

Psychotherapists react to handicapped children much as other persons do, often seeing them as uninteresting, unattractive, and perhaps even somewhat repulsive. The greater the clinician's experience with retarded individuals and their families, however, the greater tend to be his sympathy for them, his respect for their needs and goals, and his appreciation of their individuality.

As we indicated in Chapter 2, the notion of the incurability of mental retardation at one time so dominated thinking about the retarded that efforts at rehabilitation appeared useless. If retarded children could not be made normal, it seemed pointless to engage with them in the demanding, intensive, emotional relationship upon which psychotherapy rests. Today, of course, mental retardation is seen as a symptom which may arise from many sources, including a variety of psychological factors, and there is greater appreciation for the basic human right of all individuals, whatever their level of capacity, to as normal and rewarding a life as possible.

Therapists of many persuasions were long influenced by such leaders as Sigmund Freud (1904) and Carl Rogers (1951), who were discouraged with the feasibility of psychotherapy with retarded persons. It was of course quite true that traditional forms of therapy, including orthodox psychoanalysis and client-centered psychotherapy, re- lied heavily on verbal communication, perspective, insight, the ability to derive under- lying patterns from apparently very disparate kinds of behavior, and the ability cogni- tively to control maladaptive behaviors. Even nonretarded children are limited in such abilities, of course, and a variety of therapeutic approaches have been devised which demand much less in the way of verbal and abstract abilities on the part of children and retarded clients.

Limitations of Retarded Clients

Contemporary approaches to psychotherapy are much broader and more flexible than the traditional techniques used originally with adolescents and adults of average or superior intelligence. Many of them are entirely suitable for retarded clients, despite their limitations in intellectual ability and social adaptation. Let us cite some examples of limitations often found in retarded persons and indicate their implications for modi- fications in the therapeutic process, keeping in mind how widely retarded individuals vary in their behavior, their problems, and their talents.

Verbal Ability   Verbal ability is, of course, one of the central aspects of intelli- gence which is commonly impaired in retarded persons. In some, poor verbal ability probably has a constitutional basis, but others have in essence retreated from verbal interchange. A child who has been often punished for "stupid talk" may avoid either talking or listening. Whatever the source, difficulty in formulating and understanding ideas through words requires that psychotherapy with many retarded persons include a substantial nonverbal component. Little intellectual maturity is required to grasp the meaning in facial expressions, postural changes, gestures, and tone of voice. Very small children need no words to distinguish a teasing tap (which may be quite hard) from a disciplinary spank (which may be quite light) in order to tell whether to laugh or to cry.

Poor Impulse Control   It has been often maintained that retarded individuals are impulsive and relatively unable to substitute socially appropriate activities for more primitive ones when they are frustrated or restricted. The behavior modification research cited in Chapter 15 easily refutes this notion as a blanket rule. In some children, inability to control or delay emotional expression originates less in weak mechanisms for handling impulses than in the strength of the impulses engendered. Children who become enraged with slight provocation may actually be chronically angry children, angry at the seeming futility of much that they do, angry at the fact that they are cut off irrevocably from the normal world which, in their eyes, is paved with streets of gold. They are ill-equipped to handle the additional minor provocations of having to tie their shoes with clumsy fingers or eat their broccoli before dessert, so that their tantrums appear completely out of proportion. Instead of retreating from these children because of their difficulties in impulse control, therapists might well direct their efforts toward finding solutions to such problems.

Passivity in Problem-solving Situations In Chapters 13 and 14, we considered the tendency of retarded children to remain passive in learning and memory situations which call for the use of active strategies. As we saw, the difficulties seem to lie much less in structural limitations than in the selection, activation, and use of effective strategies. Although this tendency may be remediable to some extent, generalization to new situations is often very limited. By implication, the therapist will be called upon for guidance in helping the individual to activate the strategies he possesses for working out solutions to the problems he faces.

In summary, differences between retarded and normal children, whatever their source, need not be insurmountable barriers to successful psychotherapeutic endeavors. Instead of rejecting the prospect of work with retarded individuals because of these barriers, the therapist may instead find them a challenge calling for his ingenuity and active participation.

GOALS OF PSYCHOTHERAPY WITH THE MENTALLY RETARDED

The goals to be achieved in psychotherapy with retarded individuals, like those in psychotherapy with other clients, vary from the very specific and immediate extinction of a dangerous or irritating symptom to a far-reaching personality reorganization conceived in the broadest sense. Sometimes the goal is quite modest. A boy who spits and bites may learn verbal means of expressing anger, or a little girl may learn to overcome her fear of the classroom. At other times, the goal may be more ambitious. A withdrawn youngster may be moved toward recovery from childhood schizophrenia, or a young woman who has been institutionalized since early childhood may be enabled to achieve independent existence in the community.

Many of the studies of psychotherapy have gauged their success or lack of it by changes in IQ. Successful psychotherapy need not always, however, produce a rise in tested intelligence. Some maladjusted children are already achieving intellectually about as much as they ever can; their principal problems lie in other areas. Other children have been able to function at a higher level in the supportive atmosphere of the testing situation than in their everyday lives; their schoolwork might improve without a change in IQ. Some children, of course, may show dramatic IQ increases when they are able to overcome central problems which have been barriers to intellectual attainment (Bernstein & Menolascino, 1970). Nevertheless, to gauge the success of psychotherapy by any single dimension is shortsighted.

Other commonly used indices of progress in psychotherapy have been reduction in the observed frequency of specific undesirable behaviors, improvement in social adaptation as measured by ratings by teachers or ward attendants or standardized measures of adaptive behavior, and more positive responses to questionnaires tapping self-esteem. Obviously, the range of outcome variables needs to be as broad and as uniquely adapted to the individual cases as the reasons which bring individuals to psychotherapy. One must remember that, particularly with retarded children, small improvements can make a tremendous qualitative difference in adaptation. Simply reducing the frequency of tantrum behavior may make it possible for a child to live at home; achieving toilet training may free as much as two hours of a mother's day. Progress need not be dramatic in absolute terms, but this does not reduce the necessity to demonstrate reliable behavioral gains for a course of psychotherapy to be judged successful.

INDICATIONS FOR PSYCHOTHERAPY

Just because a mentally retarded child or adult is exhibiting behavioral problems with emotional overtones is not necessarily sufficient indication that direct psychotherapy is the intervention of choice. With young children, in particular, a more effective avenue may lie through parent counseling (Moody, 1972). Sometimes a recreational play experience like those provided in integrated school settings is called for, particularly for children from disadvantaged groups whose behavior reflects patterns more acceptable within that subculture than outside it (Leland & Smith, 1972). Many other kinds of supportive services can be considered for adolescents and adults who may be lonely and self-defeating in their groping attempts to cope with the demands of their environment. Sometimes a change in a living situation or the provision of a kindly benefactor to furnish guidance and protection can effect a more significant change than can a therapist whose relationship is limited to encapsulated contacts.

The office of the psychotherapist is often not the first stop, but the last in a long series of efforts by the retarded individual or by his family. "Thus, the clinical situation has to deal not only with a child who is demonstrating maladaptive behavior and inappropriate coping responses, but one who has been demonstrating such behaviors over a period of time and already has a history of failure experiences and inappropriate social interaction" (Leland & Smith, 1972, p. 39). Some form of psychotherapy may well be indicated to help the child to modify the outcome of this discouraging history, while environmental supports are simultaneously being strengthened.

PSYCHOTHERAPEUTIC TECHNIQUES SUITABLE FOR USE WITH THE MENTALLY RETARDED

Over the years, the term "psychotherapy" has come to encompass a wide range of techniques, situations, and goals. These are grouped together only in that they relate to conscious efforts by therapists to improve the mental health and/or the social behavior of the troubled persons with whom they are dealing. Psychotherapy is not unique; there are many kinds of helping relationships in which people engage. To some extent, the same sorts of human relationships occur in psychotherapy as may be found between parent and child, minister and parishioner, teacher and pupil, friend and friend.

Perhaps at this point it would be wise to caution the reader that this section is not intended to serve as a manual on the conduct of psychotherapy with retarded children. It cannot and should not be a manual for at least two important reasons. First, at this stage in the growth of the field, no one way of conducting psychotherapy has been shown to be superior to many alternative ways. Wide diversity exists in disturbed children, in the causes of their difficulties, in the skills and propensities of therapists, and in the settings under which therapy occurs. To attempt at this time to formulate "right" and "wrong" ways of conducting psychotherapy would be premature and possibly even detrimental to the discovery of better ways of doing things. Second, in many instances psychotherapy can create a powerful, intensive, and ultimately dangerous situation if the therapists are not highly skilled and fully aware of what they are doing. Extensive training in psychotherapy is essential if the therapists are to be effective and avoid unintentional harm to the very children they are trying to help.

Nonverbal Techniques

As we have seen, many retarded children are relatively deficient in their use of language. For this reason, a number of techniques which minimize the necessity for verbal communication have been developed.

Play Therapy   Since play is a natural part of childhood, a familiar and intrinsically attractive activity, it has been extensively used with disturbed children whose intellectual ability varies from superior to moderately retarded. Healthy children use play in a number of ways which promote their emotional growth. Through play, they are able to express the conflicts, tensions, and fears which are an inevitable part of growing up. It provides a medium in which children can test their competence and their capacity to control the world. They can rehearse future patterns and sometimes threatening behavior: going to the dentist, going to school. They can, too, begin to see themselves through the eyes of others as they take on many roles. Morever, with the gentle forgivingness of childhood, they can engage with friends in spirited verbal and physical battles, relationships of leading and following, in which mistakes are easily forgotten and relationships easily repaired.

For the disturbed child, however, play has often lost its efficacy. Sometimes the depth of the child's problems is simply too great. Psychotic children, for example, are usually unable to utilize toys in any but primitive and stereotyped ways, not at all in the imaginative and differentiated manner in which other children use them. Sometimes play has been discouraged by overly anxious or irritable adults who cannot tolerate noise, messiness, or exhibition of feelings and fantasies. Sometimes the child has had no opportunity to acquire playmates or has been rejected by them. For many children, then, therapy can facilitate the ordinary healthy properties of play, and, moreover, it has advantages lacking in unsupervised play, including the therapist, who without reservation accepts the child and his behavior within broad limits of time, space, safety, and preservation of property. "What *is* it? What *is* it? In here I just spill out all over myself," observed one disturbed young client. And then, as he relaxed happily, having covered himself with sand and with oozy black finger paint, "You sure ain't no don't person" (Axline, 1948, p. 216).

Leland and Smith (1962, 1965, 1972) have developed a systematic approach which adapts the degree of structure in the play materials and in the therapeutic method to the characteristics of the retarded children and the goals of therapy. Their approach uses a combination of learning theory and behavior modification principles "to force the child to think." "The theory . . . is based on the premise that all behavior is lawful, that behavior tends to be tension-relieving, and that aberrations of behavior tend to be self-reinforcing, that the way to deal with these aberrations is through a process of building and/or unblocking cognitive functions, that this may be done through a . . . situation where reward becomes the permission to carry out behavior of the patient's choice, and punishment becomes intrusion in this sphere" (1965, p. 38).

In their four therapeutic models, materials may be unstructured (U) or structured (S), as may be the therapeutic approach. A "U-U" approach is seen as best serving the needs of the most primitive, emotionally disturbed child whose intellectual and/or

Fig. 19-1 Finger painting provides an opportunity for the expression of ideas, tactile experience, and the joy of action. *(J. & M. Menapace)*

adaptive behavior is very low.[2] Therapeutic goals are limited to simple recognition of self, to grasping the notion that impulses can be controlled, and to learning to function within simple limits. At the other end of the continuum (the "S-S" approach) are therapeutic situations most like special education classrooms, which are most suitable for children with "high training potential." Intermediate steps ("U-S" and "S-U") are more like occupational, recreational, or music therapy in the first case, and like traditional psychotherapeutic play activities with structured toys in the second. The U-S approach furthers the work of self-cognition, impulse control, and social limits; the S-U approach helps the child to build relationships with other people and things, to understand in a more complex way the social and cultural realities, and to develop personal goals and preferences. The Leland-Smith approach, through insufficiently subjected to empirical research, has the virtue of prescribing different approaches to different children, and of developing explicit behavioral goals for each step. Not all children are seen as capable of making the entire progression. Some, of course, start ahead of others.

Play materials can also be used selectively in another sort of approach. Sternlicht (1966), for example, describes the use of balloons in group therapy with retarded female adolescents as a diagnostic and therapeutic tool, as a media for artistic activity, and as a tension-reducing instrument. A similar use was made of a "Bobo" toy by Connie, whose therapy is described at the end of this chapter.

[2] Note, however, that Schopler, Brehm, Kinsbourne, and Reichler (1971) found that a group of young autistic children responded more favorably to a structured approach.

Artistic Expression   A number of workers have utilized artistic media as adjuncts to psychotherapy with retarded adults and children. Among the media commonly used have been various visual art forms (Ludins-Katz, 1972), finger painting (Kadis, 1951), music (Nordoff & Robbins, 1971), and dancing (Knight, Ludwig, Strazzulla, & Pope, 1957). In many respects, such techniques resemble play in their symbolism, their intrinsic attraction, and the opportunity they provide for the expression of feelings and ideas without direct verbalization. In addition, most of them have the advantage of providing a tangible product which the child can claim as his own, as evidence of something he himself has accomplished. For a talented individual, his art objects may win him deserved recognition, which in itself may be extremely therapeutic. Even the child with little talent can be proud of his productions, however, if his therapist is sensitive to the facets of his work which indicate growth and progress or make it uniquely his own.

Verbal Techniques

Although the retarded individual may be relatively inarticulate, verbal ability is seldom so limited that it cannot be a powerful avenue of contact and of growth. Comparisons with normal children too often blind us to the fact that retarded children are endowed (except for the most severely damaged) with language, humor, and understanding. It is thus worthwhile to consider some of the many relatively less abstract kinds of verbal interchange which are utilized in counseling normal persons and are equally suitable for communication with retarded children.

Catharsis   Just as play and artistic expression can permit emotional release, so, too, can children find relief in the simple verbal ventilation of their feelings, in describing fantasies and memories which have been troubling them, and in confessing whatever sins weigh upon them. Catharsis is said to resemble the release of pressure from the steam cooker. Healthy children normally find ventilation in their everyday lives, but troubled children may have no open avenues or at best inadequate and retributive ones.

Reassurance   The therapist can sometimes effect changes in children simply by helping them to recognize their own areas of competence and by interpreting reality. Many are so deeply consumed with shame and discouragement about their shortcomings that they completely disregard their assets. Every child has some ability or some feature for which he can be praised and for which he can value himself.

Support   In some instances, particularly at the beginning of therapy, therapists may want to do things for the child which later he will be able to do for himself. They may, for example, obtain a job for an adolescent client or they may arbitrate a disagreement between the child and teacher, paving the way for the child to begin to take action for himself when he sees clearly that such things may be accomplished without great turmoil.

Advice   Carefully formulated advice is for some therapists a useful adjunct, although others (particularly those of Rogerian persuasion) abjure it. Retarded individuals will need advice off and on during their entire adult lives, and it is important for them to learn to ask for it when it is needed, evaluate it within the limits of their ability, and use it as intelligently as possible.

Alternative Guidance   One reason maladaptive behavior sometimes persists in retarded individuals is that few alternatives for attaining the same objectives occur to them. In the "alternative guidance" approach (Wanderer & Sternlicht, 1964), the therapist provides a "source of data, a library of alternatives" for the client's consideration, an array from which he can make his own choice rather than following someone else's suggestions or being trapped in his habitual patterns. The therapist thus serves partly as tutor, but because the patient makes his own decision, the "negative aspects of directive counseling (fostering of dependency and the destruction of the patient's self-image) [can] be eliminated" (Sternlicht, 1966, p. 328).

Directed Discussion   The usual procedure requiring the client to determine the direction of the conversation must sometimes be modified with retarded individuals (Moody, 1972; Sternlicht, 1966; Thorne, 1948). Many appear to respond mainly to the immediate situation and neglect to talk about important events which are taking place in their lives. Once the topic has been introduced by the therapist, however, they may quite easily participate in active and genuine discussion.

Reflection and Clarification of Feeling   A number of authors (Rogers, 1951; Thorne, 1948) have recommended reflection and clarification of feeling to help children to recognize and understand what they have just said and felt. These techiques do not require abstract interpretations but can be closely attuned to their own frames of reference.

Interpretation   Some workers have complained that retarded individuals have little capacity for developing insight, and yet understanding obviously can range from very concrete and immediate to very abstract and distant formulations. Mildly retarded children and adults are usually quite capable of recognizing simple patterns of behavior and of grasping some notion of how they might have developed, provided that interpretation is founded on a number of concrete examples. A child may, for example, recognize that she has outbursts of temper every time other children leave for home visits since she resents the fact that her own family seldom takes her out. The effectiveness of such interpretations is not necessarily reduced by their concreteness.

Role Playing, or Psychodrama[3]   This technique calls for the acting out of a spontaneous skit by one or more children. A general situation is outlined beforehand, but the plot and characters are allowed to develop rather freely. The therapist ordinarily is an observer and leader of discussions about the roles played, but at times he may participate actively in the scene. The effectiveness of psychodrama is assumed to lie in the opportunity it provides for testing or rehearsing new or alternative patterns of behavior in a sheltered, guided situation. In addition, it furnishes the opportunity to see oneself through the eyes of others, put oneself in the role of another, and share ideas about different ways of reacting to or handling a situation. The published accounts of role playing with retarded patients tend to be enthusiastic (Taylor, 1969). Pilkey, Goldman, and Kleinman (1961) obtained evidence that participation in role playing improved the ability of retarded adolescents to predict self-evaluations made

---

[3] The term psychodrama was used by J. L. Moreno (1946), whose writings are considered classic in this field.

by other adolescents and the ways in which they themselves were seen by those teen-agers. Other investigators (Seeley, 1971; Tawadros, 1956) have found that role playing enhanced social problem-solving skills in retarded adolescents.

Group Psychotherapy

With Retarded Children   In recent years, by far the most popular variant of psychotherapy has been group therapy.[4] A single therapist usually meets at regular intervals with six to ten children at once, although many groups consist of two thera-pists and a slightly larger number of children. Specific psychotherapeutic approaches have varied widely. Some therapists have limited interaction to rather formal discus-sions; some have been extremely permissive and passive, encouraging the clients to select their own topics and make their own rules. Some have employed play therapy and some have incorporated activities such as handicrafts, trips, games, movies, lec-tures, and role playing. Some have formulated interpretations in a psychoanalytic framework; some have limited themselves to reflection and clarification of feeling; some have responded in a more eclectic framework.

Group therapy does offer several advantages for work with retarded clients. First, it is an economical approach because several children can be seen at one time. Second, group therapy sets up a concrete microcosm of human relationships which can be examined, varied, controlled, and rehearsed. It thus provides one way of minimizing the demands which are made upon the abstract verbal abilities of the child without sacrificing the kinds of experiences which can be discussed and understood. Third, most disturbed children experience intense difficulty in their relationships with their peers. They may be overly withdrawn, overly aggressive and surly, or overly accom-modating. In a one-to-one contact with a kindly adult therapist, these difficulties may appear only in very attenuated form, whereas the group therapy situation offers an opportunity to work directly on real problems. Fourth, group therapy provides proof that there are other troubled persons "in the same boat." In areas seldom mentioned in everyday conversation (sexual feelings, resentment of one's parents, feelings of confu-sion and incompetence), it is a dramatic revelation to find others sharing the same concerns. Fifth, in group therapy a child who is afraid of close emotional contact can be absorbed at a gradual pace, setting his own speed. The shy child may use the group as a buffer against the intensive relationship with the therapist which an individual situation would demand. Finally, group therapy affords an unparalleled opportunity for the training of therapists. It also permits the participation of paraprofessional personnel (cottage parents or aides) in the planning and execution of therapeutic programs.

There are, of course, difficulties as well as advantages inherent in group psycho-therapy. A group demands of its leader even greater sensitivity, stability, and flexibility than does a single child. He must be alert to the responses of each child, which occur simultaneously and covertly. A word addressed to one child has diverse effects on the others. A shy child who suddenly bursts into four-letter invectives needs a different response than the habitual delinquent whose tirades are continual. One child may cause outbursts in others, and general chaos may ensue if the leader is not firm in

---

[4] The following is a sample of published accounts of group therapy with retarded children and adolescents: Borenzweig (1970), Mann (1969), Mehlman (1953), Mowatt (1970), Rosen and Rosen (1969), and Slivkin and Bernstein (1970).

setting limits and establishing order. In short, the task of the group therapist demands great skill and strength.

A major difficulty presented by the group situation is the selection of members. Ordinarily, a group should probably be relatively homogeneous in age and mental level, though not necessarily in sex. Following suggestions made by Slavson (1950), there has usually been an effort to achieve a balance within the group. Members who are aggressive, uncooperative, overly active, and demanding of attention may be balanced and mutually helpful to those who are submissive, withdrawn, or lethargic. Yet problems of group membership may arise also from the necessity to exclude members who prove unsuitable. It sometimes happens that one member who is especially vocal, aggressive, and frightening to the others dominates the proceedings to the extent that the others are not heard from at all, though they may feel resentful of the leader who does not protect their rights. Therapists find it distasteful to exclude children who have so often been rejected in the past, but acceptance of their unacceptable behavior gains them nothing and robs the rest of the group of its just due.

A number of novel approaches have been used with retarded groups. One of the most intriguing was conducted by Ricker and Pinkard (1964), who used audiovisual feedback to improve self-perception and thereby social skills of retarded young adults. In one of the carefully matched groups, counseling on improving social skills was conducted in conjunction with sound movies of the subjects themselves in varied social situations within the sheltered workshop in which the experiment took place. In the second group, counseling was combined with movies of retarded persons (not themselves) and in the third, group counseling took place without such stimuli. The results seemed to favor the first group, although the second also showed some improvement.

Another variant of group psychotherapy is the "remotivation" technique developed for use by nursing personnel and ward aides (A. M. Robinson, 1964). This approach follows a carefully defined sequential procedure with the aim of awakening interest in the environment and establishing basic social skills.

With Parents[5]   Problems of parents of retarded children are often deep and continuing. In families of children with disturbed behavior these problems are likely to be exacerbated, and frequently further contribute to the child's difficulties. A group setting can provide a highly supportive atmosphere in which parents can share their feelings and engage in active problem solving. Parents' groups affiliated with the National Association for Retarded Children, for example, have often formed at the parents' own instigation. Blatt (1957) has suggested that three types of groups be made available to parents: (1) a rather formal, educationally oriented counseling group focused on childrearing and child development, for parents whose defenses are rather fragile and brittle; (2) a group-counseling approach for parents able and willing to explore their feelings and attitudes about their children, as well as their own behavior; and (3) a psychotherapeutic group for parents who wish to explore their own emotions and feelings, rather incidentally related to the retarded children. Sometimes parent-counseling groups are used in conjunction with a school program (Blatt, 1957); sometimes they run parallel with group counseling of the children (Mowatt, 1970); sometimes they are conducted independently of programs for the children (Beck, 1973). Occasionally, siblings are offered the same kind of help (Grossman, 1972).

---

[5] See Sternlicht (1966) for a summary of group work with parents and Beck (1973) for a "how to" manual.

Whether or not the child receives direct treatment, the offer of help to family members rests on two facts: First, the upbringing of a retarded child demands emotional and cognitive resources which tax the abilities of parents and siblings, creating stresses and uncertainties which affect the entire family. Second, there is recognition that in large part, the child's overall development and his mental health are dependent upon the environment in which he lives. There are 168 hours in every week, of which few can be spent with a therapist even in an intensive program. There must be cooperation and consistency among the child's thearapist and the others responsible for him if substantial progress is to be made. Sometimes, indeed, the child need not be treated directly at all, or for only a brief period, if the family can be helped to understand, tolerate, and encourage changes in him and to provide experiences conducive to his growth.

Behavior Modification[6]

Chapter 15 deals at some length with the theoretical underpinnings and the techniques involved in behavior modification. Their utility in reducing inappropriate behaviors and in increasing acceptable and constructive behavior is remarkable. It is only because these techniques have been discussed at length elsewhere that they have not been given more prominence in this chapter. "In fact, it is felt by some that (the) impact [of behavior modification principles] will be as great as that of any other single contribution [by psychology] since the introduction of mental testing in the early decades of this century" (Gardner, 1970, p. 251). Although operant principles are probably most dramatic and reliable when utilized with rather discrete categories of behaviors, they are basic to understanding the effects of any environment on the child's behavior, including the therapeutic environment. As in the Leland-Smith approach, behavior modification can be incorporated into several different forms of psychotherapy, or may be used virtually alone.

> The focus of treatment (using these principles) is the overt behavior that is creating difficulty or concern for those responsible for the child. Explanation of psychological problems is not in terms of internal events. Rather, stated simply, the causes of the behavior are viewed as those environmental events which are effective in influencing the occurrence or nonoccurrence of the behavior. (Gardner, 1970, p. 252.)

When maladaptive behaviors are viewed as learned rather than symptomatic of deep, dynamic conflicts, "neurosis" or "psychosis," it follows that the disruptive behaviors may be unlearned and others, more acceptable and productive, substituted for them. Behavior therapy, i.e., psychotherapy using behavior-modification principles, utilizes (1) a behavioral analysis to discover the precise nature of the maladaptive behavior and the frequency of its occurrence, (2) examination of the current consequences of the behavior which are likely to be maintaining it, (3) manipulation of those consequences to reduce their reinforcing qualities or even to substitute aversive consequences to reduce the behavior, and (4) increasing the positive reinforcement for incompatible and more desirable behaviors.

---

[6] In addition to Chapter 15, see Gardner (1970), Graziano (1971), Lovaas and Bucher (1974), Miron (1972), and Thompson & Grabowski (1972) for discussions of behavior therapy with retarded individuals.

Management of Reinforcement Contingencies   In some disturbed children, particularly severely retarded children, habitual behaviors may be so severely self-destructive or injurious to others that they need to be stopped "cold." Lovaas (1973) reports that during a ninety-minute session, one child hit himself more than 2,700 times! Use of primary aversive stimuli has had considerable success in such cases. (See Chapter 15.) Therapists do not, of course, employ such means when other measures will work, but in emergency situations a few mild shocks may reduce much more damaging and painful stimuli which the child is administering to himself.

Most behaviors can, however, be controlled by positive reinforcement. Dodge and Harris (1969), for example, reported the modification of autistic behavior in two young boys by systematic social and primary reinforcement in a well-planned and rich environment. After an initial period of observation of a seven-and-one-half-year-old boy, social reinforcement was given liberally for appropriate behaviors and inappropriate behaviors were ignored. In addition, he received individual training in academic work and active play three hours a week. Inappropriate behavior decreased from 49 percent of the time to 2 percent; appropriate behavior increased from 27 percent to 72 percent; and appropriate verbal behavior increased from 1 percent to 45 percent and from one-word utterances to six or eight words.

Parent Training   These are but two of a rich array of studies which show that a broad variety of maladaptive behaviors can be modified by adroit management of the reinforcement contingencies. Sometimes, indeed, the parent can become the primary therapist (Hawkins, Peterson, Schweid & Bijou, 1966; O'Dell, 1974). In any event, it is almost always essential that the parents be helped to modify their behavior so that therapeutic progress can be transferred and generalized.

One of the most active and promising new therapeutic strategies with retarded children is parent training or parent counseling of a behavioral nature (Tavormina, 1974; Watson & Bassinger, 1974). One popular approach follows a model described by Patterson (1971), in which parents are trained first to observe and record the child's behavior, and then deliberately to modify their own behavior to bring about an increase in desirable behaviors and a decrease in undesirable ones. Parents and the target child, sometimes together with other siblings and family members, may be seen together to determine which specific behaviors will receive top priority for modification, to explore the kinds of reinforcers which are most effective with the child and most compatible with the parents' modes of operation, and to provide practice with the techniques involved. The therapist may model for the parents the behaviors he expects them to acquire, including observing and recording the child's behavior, shaping and modeling techniques, and means of positive and negative reinforcement. Often the parents have been unaware of their own roles in maintaining the very behaviors they wish to eliminate or of how infrequently they reinforce the behaviors they appreciate. They may not have noticed under what conditions the troublesome behaviors appear, and they may be particularly surprised when they discover how inconsistent they have been in their behavior toward the child. Careful planning and reassurance may enable them to achieve consistency, firmness, and effectiveness that have been previously lacking.

Ordinarily the therapist will see the parents and child regularly for a period of several weeks, making use of the parents' home records to evaluate progress, to work out more effective reinforcers, and to know when to select new target behaviors as the initial ones come under control. The therapist may even visit the home to help transfer what has been learned in the office to its real-life setting and to furnish insights of a trained observer concerning the environment and the parents' interaction with the child. Continued but more sporadic contact may be called for over a period of months or even years.

In essence, this form of behavior therapy is a form of teaching or training parents to apply the principles of learning theory in their upbringing practices. The principles are not extremely complex, but their application is not always easy, given the complexities of parent-child relationships, the waxing and waning of patience and fortitude, and the often trying nature of the children's behavior. Simply reading a book will seldom enable parents by themselves to solve deeply entrenched situations. Furthermore, the parents often need to be reinforced for their progress, just as their children do, and to receive guidance in designing the approaches they will take. When things do not go entirely well, they may need support to follow through with the program. For example, when a regime of nonreinforcement for an unwanted behavior such as tantrums is instituted, the frequency and intensity of the tantrums may sharply rise at first, particularly if the parents have inconsistently reinforced them in the past, as most parents have. The rise will be only temporary if the behavior continues to be ignored, but the initial period can be trying indeed for the parents and others in the child's surroundings.

Psychotropic Drugs[7]

For some children, the adjunctive use of psychoactive drugs has proved very effective in a program of therapy and behavior management. That drugs are used widely, probably too widely, too long, and in too large doses in some cases, is unquestionable. Lipman (1970), for example, reports that, of a sample of nearly 150,000 retarded residents in 109 institutions, at the time of the survey 39 percent were receiving major tranquilizers, 8 percent minor tranquilizers and 4 percent antidepressants or energizers. These drugs were in addition to the several others used as anticonvulsants and completely independent of the hormones, vitamins, and other compounds being used for other purposes.

This is not the place for a discussion of the indications or the effectiveness of drugs for various purposes. A potential clearly exists that for some retarded adults and children, psychotropic chemotherapy and psychotherapy may be combined to good effect. There is too often, however, a professional chasm between the physicians who prescribe these drugs for the purpose of changing behavior, and the mental health workers who use other means of attempting to alter maladaptive behavior. Overcommitment probably exists on both sides to the use of one or the other mode of operation.

EFFECTIVENESS OF PSYCHOTHERAPY WITH THE RETARDED

It would be very hazardous to conclude at this point that psychotherapy with retarded children is either more or less effective than it is with normal children. It is not foolproof with either group, nor is the picture wholly discouraging with either one. With the exception of behavior-modification techniques, the general status of research methodology and indeed of clinical practice in this field is still primitive. Few defini-

---

[7] For useful reviews, see Freeman (1970), Lipman (1970) and Sprague and Werry (1971). See also Chap. 11.

tive statements can be made about the relative effectiveness of various kinds of treatment or with children of different etiologies or levels of retardation.

Despite the great shortcomings in the research literature, at this point it appears safe to say that psychotherapeutic practices of several kinds have been shown to be successful with some children, under some conditions, and with some therapists. The most highly developed are the approaches based on operant principles of learning, but other approaches show promise as well. This in itself refutes the notions of a generation or more ago that psychotherapy could not be successful with retarded children. There appears to be no substantiation for the notion that factors intrinsic to children's retardation give them a poorer therapeutic prognosis than that of disturbed children with normal intelligence, so long as one is realistic about what to expect of the child. The following report illustrates this point rather dramatically.

THE CASE OF CONNIE

Connie was a vivacious, eighteen-year-old, mildly retarded girl in a state school. Her shapely figure, light-brown curls, faint freckles and turned-up nose made her a star attraction at school dances. She was a recent transfer from another state school, one in which she and her older sister Carol had lived for the past ten years. Carol had recently been placed in a work assignment in a nearby town, and Connie had been transferred to the new school because it was nearer the the county in which her parents resided. As a matter of fact, Connie had had very little contact with her parents since she was six years old. At that time, the alcoholic father was in prison for robbery and the two girls were so badly neglected by their mother that the court placed them in a foster home. The first foster mother became ill, however, and the second foster father left the state to find a better job. The welfare worker was not able to find another suitable family, and the girls were therefore sent to the state school. Connie's record there contained occasional reports of fighting with other girls, but her school achievement and general behavior were well within acceptable limits. Connie and Carol became very close during these years. After Connie's transfer, she became progressively more anxious and had episodes of misbehavior which were followed by contrition, apology, and calm.

When her therapist first saw Connie, she was tied hand and foot to her bed and was covered with angry bruises, her eyes swollen and her clothing ripped. Her condition was her own doing. From irritability and moroseness in the early morning hours, she had slowly reached the point of banging herself with a chair and throwing herself against the wall. Now she was sedated and restrained. Although she complained of the rough treatment she had received at the hands of the three cottage parents who had subdued her, there was also a note of relief in her voice.

Therapist: There must be some pretty good reasons for what has happened today. I don't know what they are yet; I guess you don't either. We might get somewhere by talking things over together a few times a week . . . maybe so, maybe not. Talking about how you feel, what's going on in your life. Would you like to try?

Connie: (Sleepily) I guess so. This is a . . . I'm a mess. But Mrs. S. and Mrs. M. (cottage parents) tied me down.

Therapist: They can help you when you get wound up; so can you. We'll talk about that, too.

Interviews with Connie, held three times a week at first and later twice a week, extended over an eight-month period. As concrete evidence of the staff's offer of help to Connie in establishing controls, the psychiatrist prescribed a mild tranquilizer. Connie and her therapist together talked with her cottage parents, establishing that Connie could be admitted to a seclusion room for a brief period at her own request if she felt the need for greater control. It was made clear that she would not be allowed to get completely out of hand again. Meanwhile, the staff tried to obtain Connie's return to her original school so that she might be near her sister, but this proved impossible.

Within the safety provided by these explicit provisions, Connie was able to talk freely about her anger. First, she faced the rage she felt at having been summarily removed from her sister and a school situation which (then) seemed much rosier to her. As she talked, her targets spread to include her parents, who had failed her, and, to some extent, her friends and cottage parents for more prosaic faults. Connie began to recognize that she had been punishing herself when she was angry with the people on whom she had depended—her parents, foster parents, welfare worker, and finally the staff of her former school—who had each, albeit involuntarily, made it appear that she was not worth keeping. The angrier she felt, the more despicable she considered herself to be, and so the vicious circle had gone on. With tangible proof that her therapist and the staff did value her and could accept her anger, she was able to evaluate some of the realistic and the exaggerated elements in her resentment.

C: It wasn't fair to send me here. They didn't have to do that. To be near my mother! Hah! (She gives an experimental tap to an inflated plastic clown which rights itself.) That's a pretty silly toy.

T: A lot of kids really bang on that when they are feeling angry, like you are.

C: Little kids?

T: Little kids and big kids. It's like a punching bag. (T swats it.) See?

Connie spent the next ten minutes punching the toy up, down, and into the air. As she did, her grin revealed both her relish at this activity and her feeling that she was being a little childish.

C: That's silly, but it feels sort of good.

T: It does feel good, when you can really bat that old clown around.

C: And it don't hurt, that's the best part of it. He's just like a pillow. (Pause) Next time I think I'll use my own pillow instead of a wall!

T: There *are* ways to be angry around here, and not have to bottle it up!

C: It don't look like it much. You can't talk back to your cottage parents; you always have to do just what *they* say—wear what *they* say, go to bed when *they* say, scrub the john when *they* say, yeah, yeah.

T: Sounds like you're doing a good job of being angry right now!

Later on, Connie used other toys (a dart game, an infant's hammering set) and then moved toward a more symbolic expression of her feelings. She came in one day with several "little moron" riddles and, evidently missing the irony, took great pleasure in stumping her therapist. With the aid of the librarian, she found some riddle books intended for younger nonretarded children. Eventually, she found another girl with whom she began a friendly competition to discover jokes the other had not heard.

Connie soon had a boyfriend, Frank, two years older than she. He sometimes accompanied her to therapy sessions and remained for a short while, apparently enlisting the therapist's support for his contention that he should find a job and establish

himself before getting married. There were no immediate plans for his work placement. Their frequent quarrels were usually caused by Connie's teasing Frank until he
slapped her, or walked off, angry. Then Connie would apologize and he would return,
still somewhat annoyed. She began to see that she was using Frank as an innocent
target for her hostility, confident that he would stop her before she lost control. In the
process, however, she was hurting his feelings and endangering their relationship.
Gradually, this pattern subsided.

Unexpectedly, Connie's mother appeared at the school, stating that she had
missed her baby terribly and that she would soon take Connie home to stay. She
remained for only an hour and then departed, leaving her daughter frantic. Connie
visited several members of the staff, demanding to be sent home immediately. Each
advised her to wait and see what steps her mother took next. The social worker wrote
to the welfare department in Connie's home town, asking for clarification. Meanwhile,
Connie discussed this development with her therapist. After repeating her demand to
be sent home, she fell silent.

C: I don't believe her. She just said that. Why didn't my dad come with her?
Why didn't my welfare lady write? She didn't mean it. She never did come before. She
never did send any presents, not even my birthday. Why did she do that? It's a long
bus ride down here. Why did she do it?

T: Think she might have been mixed up about her feelings, too?

C: I guess so. That must be it. She maybe is sorry that everything did happen
the way it did. It's been a long time. She might got to thinking about how nice it would
be if everything changed. I think about that sometimes. You know, I maybe wouldn't
like it there, anyway.

T: Maybe things wouldn't be so good, even if you went home?

C: No. Mom said that Dad isn't drinking any more. If he don't, maybe it would
be different. But if he is—he used to beat on us, me and Carol, and Mom, too, at night.
And then we don't have much money; you should'a seen the clothes I took with me to
my foster home. They just threw them away, all but a little doll. All these years, I been
thinking about going home, but it wouldn't be nothing so great. I would like to see our
dogs, though. Maybe if I get out and get a job, could I have a dog? I'd like a little dog.
I'd raise it from a puppy. I'd be good to it.

T: Good idea. There were some good things about it—but otherwise going
home doesn't look like so much to you now?

C: Well, I don't know. Maybe things have changed like she said. Tell you what,
do you think I could go home on a visit? Just to *see?*

T: I am sure that if things have changed enough that your welfare department
will okay your going home, that it *would* be for a visit, at least the first time. Just to see
how you like it, how things were. Your bed and your place here would stay right here,
waiting for you, until you came back and had a chance to think things over. No rush
about it.

C: It wouldn't be the end right away? Oh, I was scared! I didn't let on, but I
was scared!

As it turned out, Connie's mother had acted on impulse, and there was actually
no plan to take her home. After an investigation, the welfare department reported that
it still considered the home unsuitable. Connie accepted the information with surprising equanimity. There was no further word from her mother.

During all this time, Carol had continued to write to Connie, to send her gifts and
spending money from a pay check which must have been meager to begin with. On her

own initiative, Carol arranged for Connie to spend a week with her. The visit went somewhat less well than they had hoped. Carol's living conditions were not very glamorous, she gave freely of advice about Connie's behavior, and their disagreements troubled Connie deeply. This was an opportunity to explore with her the unrealistic pictures she had drawn of Carol and of life on the "outside." Reality in both instances was far less romantic than she had fantasized. Connie admitted that she had expected that Carol would someday take her home, provide her with a job, and look after her. Her schoolwork improved and she began to feel more self-reliant.

After six months, Connie felt that she no longer needed medication, and her tranquilizers were stopped. She began to miss appointments, finding it difficult to say that she no longer felt the need for her sessions. It was as though breaking off the relationship with the therapist was reminiscent of the many broken relationships in her past. After regular appointments were terminated, Connie continued to visit the therapist when difficulties arose. By and large, her future looked considerably more hopeful than it had previously.

PART V
PRACTICAL PROBLEMS OF RETARDED INDIVIDUALS AND THEIR FAMILIES

20
Problems in the Family of a Retarded Child

The path of parenthood is never completely smooth. Patience, understanding, ingenuity, good humor, and strength are demanded in large measure from the parents of any youngster. For the family of a retarded child, however, the situation may be more complicated and more hazardous, and the rewards of parenting more likely to be lost sight of. The child's handicaps; his slow development; the special arrangements needed for his physical care, training, and companionship; the disappointments and the lost dreams—all combine to create pressures which tend to disrupt family equilibrium. Added to these pressures may be financial problems, tensions created by the child's immature self-control, handicaps in communication, and the parents' own lingering doubts about their upbringing practices. They may also wonder about an unwitting role they might have played in bringing about the handicap. At the same time, the parent-child relationship may be altered by the child's slow development and isolation from a neighborhood peer group. In some instances, he will remain emotionally and economically dependent upon his family throughout his life. Thus, the relationship between a retarded child and his family is potentially more complex and ambivalent than the ordinary one, and more intense and prolonged. The parents of most retarded children need at least occasional help in dealing with their family situation, in recognizing and accepting their child's handicaps, and in handling successive day-to-day problems of living both with the retarded child and with his normal brothers and sisters.

For entirely too long, the emphasis in professional services to families has been diagnostic. The best diagnostic services in the world are useless if they become an end in themselves and do not culminate in a realistic plan, if the recommended remedial facilities are nonexistent or financially out of reach, if parents and siblings are asked to rise to uncommon heights of wisdom in devising means of coping with their problems. Fortunately, recent years have seen a rapid expansion of community services which recognize the shared and continuing responsibility of the society and the family for the care of the handicapped child. Yet too few professionals even now are aware of the facilities available in their own communities. Only a very few are able or willing to stay with the case, recognizing the ongoing progressions of life situations which the family must handle over the years.

Although we fall far short of the need, our society makes available a variety of services to support childrearing in families with normal children. Most parents can turn to professionals such as physicians, nurses, teachers, and guidance clinics; to standard community services including baby-sitters, recreation programs, and welfare departments; and to friends and family members from time to time when various kinds of sustenance are needed. These resources are less likely to be available to the family with a retarded child, because of professional ignorance and because of the various ways in which the handicapped child is out of step with his normal peers. It therefore becomes the responsibility of workers concerned with retarded children to provide a network of support on which the family can depend, specialized services to meet needs which are circumscribed, and continuing points of contact to be called upon as new situations arise. What every family of a retarded child deserves is a sort of ombudsman, an ally and advocate, to serve as a sounding board and release valve, to clarify next steps and new decisions as choice points are reached, to inform about resources and services, and to intervene when necessary. Because of their unique circumstances and because of personal preference, various families will find different ombudsmen among the professionals potentially available. For some, it can be one or another member of the staff of a diagnostic-service clinic (Paulson & Stone, 1973); for others, it may be a sympathetic family physician; for still others, the executive director of the local parents' group, someone in the school system, etc.

Although each family is unique, there are many commonalities in the problems faced by families with retarded children. This chapter will be devoted to delineating some of these problems and suggesting means by which families may be helped to deal with them. At the outset, however, it must be recognized that hard, scientific data about such families and their problems is practically nonexistent. The most comprehensive review available (Wolfensberger, 1967) makes clear how impressionistic, how poorly controlled and poorly designed, are almost all the so-called studies in this area. Reasons for this lack are not hard to decipher. They begin, of course, with the futility of trying to find too many common threads among the families of retarded children, who constitute a group only by virtue of a common quirk of fate. Second, most of the professionals who have worked with families have had limited research training and share a clinical orientation, with the tendencies toward superstition, impressionism, and overgeneralization which characterize so much of the clinically oriented literature. Finally, most of the settings in which studies have taken place have furnished biased populations and have practically precluded the use of matched control subjects. Certain kinds of wisdom about selected groups can be valuable, but myths can be established in such circumstances, too. The reader should be aware that most of the literature is based on material gleaned from parents seen in outpatient facilities, mainly white, middle-class mothers of young, severely handicapped retarded children.

QUALIFICATIONS OF A COUNSELOR

Considerable pain and lasting damage can be inflicted by insensitive counselors who abruptly announce a diagnosis or give professional advice characterized by a lack of respect for the parents and for the child.

> A professional must be very conscious of the fact that his intervention may have the profoundest effect, perhaps for their life-time, not only upon clients but also their entire family groups. Unless he approaches his task with awe and the willingness to be most cautious and circumspect with his counsel, he is not ready to work with parents of the retarded, if, indeed, in any kind of helping relationship. Social workers, clinical psychologists and physicians are sometimes heard to assert that any member of their profession is qualified to render counseling to parents of the retarded . . . this is clearly not the case (Wolfensberger, 1967, pp. 354-355).

Wolfensberger goes on to suggest that the professional discipline of the counselor is largely irrelevant, but that preparation for the task is far from simple. He lists the following qualifications:

> (1) knowledge of the broader medical, social, educational, habilitational, and behavioral aspects of retardation; (2) knowledge of resources in the broadest sense, including agencies, services, long-range local prospects, reading materials, and "gadgets" useful in home management; (3) competency, acquired through training, in counseling principles and techniques in general; (4) experience in the applied-clinical area of retardation; (5) freedom from stereotypes about retardation; (6) possession of genuinely positive attitudes toward retardation, the handicapped, and their parents; (7) an orientation to the current community centered management approach; (8) a sensitivity to the reality needs of the family; (9) willingness to go beyond traditional approaches to help parents, even at the cost of personal convenience; and (10) great patience. (1967, p. 355)

Such knowledge, skills, and attitudes cannot be acquired in the classroom. They require specific training in mental retardation and counseling and acquaintance with the politics and planning for the retarded, with literature written for parents and child-care workers, and, above all, knowing what it is like to live with a retarded child, both the hazards and the rewards. First-hand knowledge of community and residential facilities and parent groups is extremely helpful, as is extensive visitation in the homes of retarded children.

The counselor who is to have continued contact with a family serves as a representative of the subsociety made up of families with retarded children and the people and places which serve them, a world of which the family may have been almost completely unaware and is probably both fearful and misinformed. Willy-nilly, the family has become a part of that subsociety. As a contributor to that group, the effective counselor serves as an ally and as a guide to resources which may spell for the family the difference between successful coping and defeat. The counselor must be able and willing to establish a mutual respect relationship with the child and with the family and be willing to focus on the development of a healthy parent-child relationship. He must actively recognize the chronic nature of mental retardation and be willing, therefore, to establish a routine for services over a prolonged span of time, rather than only at times of crisis.

COMING TO TERMS WITH THE FACT THAT A CHILD IS RETARDED

Every family of a retarded child must eventually face the fact that he is mentally handicapped. The circumstances of this recognition may be sudden or gradual. The realization may come at birth or may be avoided even until the child has been in school for a while. For almost every family, however, the truth must be acknowledged to some degree by the time the child is seven or eight years old.

Most parents develop an understanding of their child's condition in a gradual and painful manner. Many spend a great deal of time, energy, and money in a fruitless search for some more acceptable diagnosis or for an elusive cure. The process seems to follow a rather regular pattern. Various authors have categorized the successive stages of parental reaction in different ways, identifying as few as three or as many as six distinct steps in coping with the situation (Wolfensberger, 1967). Each of the schemes for conceptualizing the changes in parental reactions over time makes some intuitive sense. Rather arbitrarily, we have adopted the five-step framework suggested by Rosen (1955), but the superior wisdom of this breakdown, versus some other thoughtful categorization, has surely not been demonstrated.

According to Rosen, the first stage is characterized by an awareness that a serious problem exists; the second, by recognition of the retardation for what it is; the third, by a search for the cause; the fourth, by a search for a solution; and the fifth, by acceptance of the problem, a goal which he maintains is seldom attained in full. Rheingold (1945) had earlier described much the same sequence in successful interpretive interviews with parents, although today we recognize that a much more protracted period is needed than a single contact can provide.

Awareness of a Problem

By the time most families reach a diagnostic clinic or a psychologist's office, they are aware that something is the matter with their child, but their attention may be focused on a rather circumscribed aspect of development. Frequently, they have been sent by a family physician, pediatrician, audiologist, social worker, minister, or teacher to whom they have gone for help. The parents of many retarded babies and young children suspect deafness, because vocalizations and speech are delayed and the child does not respond appropriately when he is spoken to. Others complain of disciplinary and behavioral problems, failing to recognize the general immaturity which underlies the enuresis, negativism, destructiveness, or shyness with which they are most concerned. Some are troubled because their child lacks friends. Physical disabilities, clumsiness, and slow progress in school bring other worried parents for help.

Ordinarily, at least one parent can admit by this time that he is very seriously concerned about the child's unusual behavior. Often, however, the other parent and, more frequently, the grandparents and other relatives categorically deny that there is anything wrong. Usually, they maintain that the child "will grow out of it," fastening their hopes on scattered bits of behavior or professional opinions which, taken out of context, seem to show that the child is really alert and bright. Even in emotionally healthy parents, temporary denial is a natural and sometimes useful defense against the massive impact of the situation (Michaels & Schucman, 1962), but when denial is carried to extremes it can become harmful to all concerned.

Jean and Jill were shy, well-behaved twins. They presented few problems at home but did poor first-grade work. Concerned with their slow progress and lack of enthusiasm for school, their father consulted a psychologist. On the Stanford-Binet, the girls attained IQs of 62 and 65, respectively. The father wished to place them in a special class in the public school, as the teacher and the psychologist had recommended, but this course was opposed by his wife and his mother-in-law, the matriarch of the family. They maintained that the children's teacher had not been interested in them and that a better school was in order. The girls subsequently repeated first grade in a private school. By the end of their second year, both were thoroughly discouraged by their failure to keep pace with the other children and clung to each other for support.

Needless to say, it is important that whatever the parents' initial concern, it be regarded seriously. Sometimes the parents are right. One of the most frequent misdiagnoses is in children with peripheral hearing loss, particularly high-frequency loss which interferes with language comprehension and may produce inattentive or hyperactive behavior superficially resembling mental retardation or emotional disturbance (Hodgson, 1960). Cerebral palsy may also mask relatively adequate cognitive development. Even when the parents are wrong, however, they may cling to their hypothesis, finding it easier and less threatening to accept a diagnosis of physical than mental impairment. A multidisciplinary approach, calibrated to the specific case, can be helpful in focusing on the problems which do exist and enabling the parents to dismiss those which do not. For children with multiple handicaps, a broad range of diagnostic work may be necessary to identify unsuspected noncognitive handicaps as well as strengths. Yet the value of a detailed comprehensive examination must be weighed in each case against the expense in money and professional time and also against the dangers of reaching conclusions prematurely by seeming to have done a "definitive" workup.

Recognition of the Basic Problem[1]

Parents who are not themselves retarded often perceive their child's mental subnormality with a profound sense of confusion and shock.[2] Their dreams of the future shattered, their own feelings of adequacy seriously shaken, many experience a grief reaction during which, for a time, they may withdraw from others and even from the child in preoccupation with their own sorrow. Just as grieving for the death of a loved one serves a healthy function, this reaction probably affords an opportunity to face the problem and its implications profoundly and intimately and to emerge with thoughtfully considered attitudes. In part, the parents may be mourning the loss of a hoped-for fantasy child (Solnit and Stark, 1971). It is often a mistake for the counselor to interrupt this process too quickly with reassurance and comfort. At the same time, it is wise to be sensitive to the complicated feelings which assail the parents and not to expect every set of parents to react in the same way. It is, of course, essential that both parents be seen by the counselor, preferably together, and it is sometimes necessary later on to see other family members as well.

---

[1] Readers who will be in a position to interpret diagnostic findings to parents are strongly advised to read, at a minimum, the articles by Rheingold and by Sarason reprinted in Wolfensberger and Kurtz (1969).

[2] Note, however, that in one study (Meyerowitz, 1967) of parents of mildly retarded young children in school, even at the end of two years, no more than one in four evaluated their children's academic achievement as "below average," whether the children were in special classes or not.

The unstable nature of early developmental indices means that there is usually little value initially in making foreboding statements about the distant future. Most parents need time to adjust to the tasks of the present. Long-range forecasts, moreover, stand a very good chance of being wrong. (See Chapter 17.) Nevertheless, even when competent medical and psychological examinations fail to permit a confident diagnosis, honesty is essential, as it is in any client relationship. One group of mothers of brain-injured infants who were not told of the condition, for example, were beset for many months by worry, self-blame, and anxiety. The entire mother-child relationship was disturbed while they assumed the burden as though it were entirely their fault that all was not well (Prechtl, 1963).

Once they face the issue, moreover, and are assured of assistance, parents can be very accurate judges of their children's level of development (Kurtz, 1965, Wolfensberger & Kurtz, 1971). If given an opportunity they can usually bring into focus the comparisons they have already made between the retarded child and his siblings or other children of comparable age (Rheingold, 1945). Mothers may, perhaps, by virtue of their closer day-to-day association with the child and other children, be more accurate than fathers (Capobianco & Knox, 1964). The counselor can be of help by listening sympathetically and helping the parents to interpret their own observations, using the results of psychological testing and observation mainly to confirm their judgment.

Complete avoidance of diagnostic labels is usually unfair to the parents. They will inevitably hear others call their child "retarded," "defective," "mongoloid" and the like. Often they need help in understanding the diagnostic terms which are appropriate and in discarding those which are not. Few parents have any very clear notion of the meaning of the words "mental retardation" and even less understanding of more technical terms. The image of the drooling idiot is strong in the minds of many; others equate mental subnormality with insanity and with unpredictability of action and lack of impulse control. To most, the diagnosis has a ring of finality, the consignment of the child to society's rubbish heap. These popular images are much too harsh, and encouraging parents to voice their expectations and fears can often help them to be more realistic in facing their child.

The Search for a Cause

Once they recognize the extent to which their child is retarded, most parents seek the cause of the tragedy which has beset them. At least two kinds of motivation seem to underlie this search. The first and more rational is a hope that, in discovering the etiology of the disorder, they may find a way to cure it or to prevent its occurrence in any future children they may have. Additional motivation can stem from an ardent wish for relief from a heavy burden of responsibility and guilt (Korkes, 1955). In one way or another, a great many parents feel that the blame for the child's handicap rests with them. They may, for example, be concerned because they allowed the baby to roll off a bed or failed to call a physician when he was ill. These are common events of childhood which would have been forgotten had the child not been subnormal and which unfortunately may be overemphasized by the clinician who also has the professional and personal need to make a diagnosis. Other parents feel that, if only they had been more resourceful or wealthy, they might have avoided the damage. Still others harbor the memory of an unwanted pregnancy. In some parents, the most primitive kinds of thinking determine beliefs about the etiology of the handicap. Sometimes the retarded child becomes the focus of all past wrongdoings of which the parents feel ashamed.

Chip, a severely retarded hyperkinetic boy of eight, was seen in a diagnostic clinic upon referral by a public health nurse who had visited the home to care for his aged grandfather. The mother had never sought medical advice because she and the father both believed Chip to be God's punishment for her having given birth before their marriage to an illegitimate daughter who was then eighteen years old. This girl was living at home and doing fairly well. As a consequence of her guilt, the mother was unable to discipline Chip and he was like an untamed animal. He had not been toilet trained; he grabbed food from the plates of others; he was disobedient and destructive.

Diagnostic procedures revealed that Chip was the victim of a progressive carbohydrate-storage disease which eventually would be fatal. The opportunity to achieve a measure of discipline and a healthy relationship with Chip had been lost, although previously he probably would have responded well to training. It seemed a measure of poetic justice that, despite the fact that the father had participated vigorously in censuring his wife, the disease was an hereditary disorder to which each parent had involuntarily contributed one recessive gene.

In a small percentage of cases, the parents are realistic in their belief that they are, at least in part, to blame for the child's condition. An unsuccessful attempt to abort an unwanted pregnancy, misuse of drugs during gestation, a negligent automobile accident resulting in head injury to the child, failure to recognize the severity of an illness with high fever or dehydration, even beating a child about the head in a fit of temper—these are burdens with which some parents have to come to terms. They are perhaps not so uncommon as we are apt to believe. In 3 percent of one clinic population, for example, the parents admitted to abortion attempts (Wortis, 1965). Even when parents have not been at all instrumental in the original condition, guilt can continue to assail those who harbor destructive impulses toward the child.

Most parents find some relief when they learn of the many families who share their problems, of the multiplicity of factors which can interfere with the delicate balance of normal development, and of the overwhelming likelihood that their child was damaged before birth by causes over which they had no control. Wolfensberger has suggested that not all guilt is necessarily disruptive, that "perhaps a bit of guilt may go a long way in motivating a parent to provide the extra attention, effort, and even love a child may need . . . some parents may need to be helped to a realistic and manageable dose of it" (1967, p. 331).

Although the number of recognized syndromes is proliferating rather rapidly, except for Down's syndrome the majority are very rare. Most parents will seek a cause, but few will find one of which they can be certain even with the most expert medical assistance.

In most instances, identifying the precise cause of the retardation would make little difference to the child. Etiology generally matters little when future plans are being made. Except in conditions in which there is progressive deterioration or a significant emotional component, or in which there is question of the risk to possible future children, costly procedures which are designed to discover not how a child is but why he is that way may be largely wasted. The child will gain much greater benefit from attention focused on his current status and planning what can be done to help him than from speculation about the cause of his handicap.

The Search for a Cure

Medical science is advancing so rapidly that many parents hope to find a miraculous cure, if only they can locate exactly the right specialist. They spend precious resources shopping from one clinic to another, grasping at straws, and fastening on minor discrepancies in the advice they receive. It is highly doubtful that any seriously damaged child can ever be made completely normal. The treatments which have proved helpful in conditions such as phenylketonuria and congenital hypothyroidism must be initiated very early in life, before the central nervous system has been damaged. Early diagnosis and prompt treatment are critical in such diseases, but even then the treatments are by no means sure. There is, perhaps, greater reason for optimism in the case of children who are physically normal but functioning at low level because they are emotionally disturbed or have had insufficient opportunities for learning. Even with these children, however, today's prognosis seldom can be very hopeful.

On the other hand, there are many specialized treatments which can help some children to make better use of the assets they possess. Within the past several years, community clinics offering preschool programs, speech therapy, physical therapy, and help for the deaf and visually impaired have become much more widely available than before, although even now some are restricted to children with single, remediable handicaps. Families needing psychotherapy may find services available to the adults and the nonretarded siblings, but less frequently is psychotherapy offered to the retarded child. (See Chapter 19.)

Acceptance of the Child

Although Rosen labels the final stage of parental growth as "acceptance" of the child, and the word is frequently used in the literature about childrearing, an explicit definition is hard to find. It usually seems to involve a warm respect for the child as he is, appreciation of his assets, tolerance for his shortcomings, and active pleasure in relating to him. The accepted child is viewed as having a smoothly functioning role in his household. In fact, two indices of acceptance are the degree to which the mother functions in her usual manner, continuing her association with her friends, and the degree to which both parents meet the needs of their normal children as well as those of the retarded child (Wortis, 1966). Even in model families, however, parents and children have their difficulties, their moments of anger, and outbursts of unaccepting behavior. We can certainly expect no more of the parents of a retarded child than we can of parents in general. Even this limited goal is, of course, more difficult to achieve when a child is retarded, and especially if there are accompanying handicaps which increase frustrations every day.

If it is difficult to define, or even to recognize, acceptance when it occurs, contrariwise, personnel working with retarded children profess little difficulty in identifying its reverse, rejection. Indeed, blaming parents as rejecting is a common phenomenon in any setting designed to serve children, either handicapped or normal, not only in clinical settings in which one is looking for the dynamics of problem behavior, but in day-care centers, schools, scout groups, anywhere, in short, where the adults are in possible competition with parents or are tempted to take sides in difficulties between parents and children. We need to respect differences and to remember that most parents of handicapped children manage their affairs and keep their equanimity rather well (Barsch, 1968).

Gallagher (1956) defines rejection as "the persistent and unrelieved holding of unrealistic negative values of the child to the extent that the whole behavior of the parent towards that child is colored unrealistically by this negative tone." He identifies four ways in which the rejection can be expressed: (1) strong underexpectations of achievement, (2) setting unrealistic goals, (3) escape, as through desertion or unwarranted institutionalization, and (4) reaction formation, defined as masking the rejection by espousing precisely the opposite view. Furthermore, he distinguishes usefully between *primary rejection*, which stems from the basic unchangeable nature of the child, such as sex or ability level, and which is based in the personality dynamics of the parent rather than the behavior of the child, and *secondary rejection*, which "represents the expression of negative attitudes based upon unfortunate behavior manifestations of the child himself. . . . A deaf child may hoot or honk or make other unusual or unpleasant noises; a brain injured child may seem to be about to run up the wall and across the ceiling." Anyone would find it hard to accept such behavior. Gallagher concludes,

It is the writer's firm opinion that cases of secondary rejection far exceed the cases of primary rejection, and serious danger is done to the education program of many children by the erroneous conclusion that since the parents have revealed strong negative attitudes, nothing much can be expected from them in the way of cooperation. (p. 276)

There is an obvious reciprocal relationship between retarded children and their families. The more favorable the relationship, the more stable, tractable, and self-possessed the children are likely to be and the greater the contentment and stability of those who live with them. Such, in essence, was the finding in an extensive survey by Saenger (1957), who followed up retarded adults with IQs below 50 who as children had attended special classes in New York City. (See Chapter 22.) He discovered that the presence or absence of personality problems in these retarded adults showed "an exceedingly high relationship to the extent of parental acceptance, family cohesion, and degree of overprotection, as measured [by an] index of family relations" (p. 97). Of the cases from families whose relationships were characterized as satisfactory, only one-fourth of the parents reported that their retarded children presented serious problems of adjustment, such as stubbornness and overdependence. In contrast, of the families in which tension and rejection of the retarded children were marked, more than three-fourths of the retarded children were reported as presenting adjustment problems.

Of course, many factors influence the parents' ability to adjust to the situation of having a retarded child, some involving their own nature and some their external circumstances. Although research evidence is very scanty, clinical studies suggest that the parents' strengths, their satisfactions in other areas in their lives, their economic circumstances, and the particular needs of the child are among the most influential factors. Saenger found that acceptance or rejection of the retarded adults was related primarily to the general emotional adjustment of the parents and to some extent to their ethnic group. Wortis (1966), examining case histories of families with excellent adjustment, found them for the most part to be favored by circumstances such as educational and financial advantages and the lack of psychiatric problems in their retarded children.

An important factor in determining the relationship between parents and child is the parents' intelligence (Michaels & Schucman, 1962). For bright families in which intellectual attainment is highly valued, the discrepancy between the ideal child and the retarded child is greatest in precisely that quality. Contrasts with brothers, sisters, and neighborhood playmates are highlighted. On the other hand, families from marginal intellectual groups are often able to accept even severely retarded children more casually (Iano, 1970; Wortis, 1966). Their lower intelligence may protect them somewhat from planning for much more than the immediate future. Their focus on the children may be oriented toward their present emotional responsiveness and compatibility rather than toward the children's potential for achievement. With retarded older children and adults, the presence in the lower socioeconomic level home of a boy who fails to contribute to the family coffers exerts a strain on family relations to a greater degree than does the presence of a retarded girl, a sex differential which is missing in middle-class homes (Farber, 1959; Saenger, 1960). Nevertheless, to a family which has depended to some extent on welfare agencies, the prospect of another dependent family member is perhaps less an attack on a system of values than an economic threat, a threat which to some degree can be reduced by financial assistance to the family or by subsidized employment.

John, (age seventeen, IQ 60) was the youngest child of retarded parents. The older children, all married, worked in a nearby sawmill. John stayed home with his widowed mother, whose IQ was approximately 55. He helped her with the chores, did handyman jobs for neighbors who could afford to pay him a little money, and was his mother's boon companion. Although mother and son were dependent on the welfare department for their subsistence, the mother was extremely proud of her handsome boy and would have been lost without him.

The early years of rearing the retarded child may well be more stressful than later ones (Kramm, 1963). Parents seen in diagnostic clinics may show a broad variety of signs of disturbance during this period (Erickson, 1969). Cummings, Bayley, and Rie (1966), who compared responses to self-administered personality tests of 240 mothers, 60 mothers each of retarded, chronically ill, neurotic, and healthy children ages four to thirteen, found that mothers of the retarded and the neurotic children showed greater depression and more difficulty in coping with anger toward the child, and a lower sense of maternal competence, than mothers of normal children. In addition, the mothers of retarded children were more preoccupied with the child.

As the child grows older, the picture often develops considerable promise. In fact, Saenger (1957) estimated that only two of ten mothers of severely retarded adults experienced significant ambivalent feelings, and only one of ten whose children remained at home expressed hidden or open rejection. The relationship between any child and his parents fulfills many reciprocal needs, some of which can actually be enhanced if his development is retarded. The mutually dependent relationship of a child and his family can be very rewarding. Indeed, a mother who has no career outside her home may continue to play a maternal role with her dependent child long after her normal children have grown away from her, or a retired father may find companionship and a continued purpose in living.

A seventy-five-year-old widow of a government official made tentative applica-tion at a state institution for her fifty-seven-year-old severely retarded son. Her other children were married and leading successful careers. She had continued to care for this son at home, but now she felt that she must make arrangements for his custody after her death. She said, "My friends are wealthy, but what do they have? Their children don't need them; nobody does. I am still a young woman compared with them, for I am still really a mother."

The Counselor's Role

The counselor working with families who have traversed the earlier stages of adapting to the child's retardation can be helpful in different ways than before. One way of conceptualizing the changes in adjustment which occur over time is to look at the different sorts of crises which families face with their children. Wolfensberger (1967) and Menolascino (1968) have distinguished among three different crises: the *novelty shock crisis,* the demolition of parental expectancies which occurs with the birth of an abnormal child; the *crisis of personal values,* the reaction to the mental deficit and its manifestations which are unacceptable in the parents' hierarchy of values; and the *reality crisis,* which involves the day-to-day management problems which make living with the child difficult. According to these authors, parents undergoing novelty shock can profit best from information and support; those in the value crisis may need prolonged counseling and personal therapy; and those in the reality crisis need help with down-to-earth issues concerned with care of the child and perhaps in deciding upon residential placement.[3]

In some ways, this model expresses the kinds of tasks described by Rosen (1955) in the four stages preceding acceptance of the child, but also highlights issues which may continue to intrude upon the smooth functioning of the family. Sometimes changes in the family structure or status such as divorce or loss of employment precipi-tate the necessity to face again these old issues; sometimes changes in the child such as the emergence of sexual behavior do so. The sensitive couselor will help parents to become aware of their feelings and to come to new understandings so that the reality problems may be given prominence.

In helping parents to face reality issues, there are a number of ways in which counselors can be of specific help. First, they can serve as sounding board and ally. In so doing, they can communicate to the parents a respect for the capacities of the child which they may have lost sight of, rekindling the expectation that whatever the level of functioning, the child will be a worthy and contributing family member (Linde & Kopp, 1973).

Second, they can serve as teacher, if necessary, or at least see to it that the parents receive help in acquiring management techniques which for retarded children need to be made explicitly a part of childrearing practices. Some agencies provide direct tutor-ing in these skills (e.g., Hirsch & Walder, 1969). Principles of behavior modification

---

[3] A somewhat similar differentiation has been made by Farber (1960b; Farber & Ryckman, 1965), who differentiates between the *tragic crisis* and the *role-organization crisis,* the first of these combining elements of the first two crises mentioned by Wolfensberger and Menolascino, and the latter having to do with establishing workable roles in the family.

are extremely useful in controlling unwanted behavior patterns and teaching new ones. (See Chapter 15.) Suitable reading materials can often be very helpful.[4]

Third, counselors can make certain that parents are in touch with appropriate community services, not only those which presently exist but those which are in the making. Parents of a young, moderately retarded child may, for example, be enormously cheered by the prospect of yet-to-come sheltered workshops and half-way houses, which will presumably be there when they are needed. One service often overlooked but highly valued by many mothers is in-home training by a public health nurse (Ehlers, 1966; Logan, 1969). A large proportion of families, especially minority group parents, are not in touch with existing services (Justice, O'Connor, & Warren, 1971).

Fourth, counselors can strongly encourage parents to make contact with local parents' groups. Especially during the early years, even those who are not ordinarily "joiners" may find strength in the understanding which others in the same boat are able to give them.

Fifth, counselors can, by virtue of their continuing relationship, assure the parents that they need not make decisions prematurely, that bridges need not be crossed until rivers are reached. Even parents who are realistic about their child's current development are often unrealistic about the future (Wolfensberger & Kurtz, 1971), but there will be plenty of time to deal with such future problems. The question of residential care, for example, need not be determined right away, not unless or until the child becomes unmanageable or until the parents become enfeebled or die.

PROBLEMS CREATED BY A RETARDED CHILD IN THE HOME

Problems of all shapes and sizes beset families whose retarded children live at home. They tend to vary with the degree of the child's retardation, the accompanying emotional and physical handicaps, and the values, interests, and external circumstances of the other family members.

Practical Problems

A number of practical problems make living with a retarded child especially demanding. The budget may be strained to provide special medical care, transportation, or remedial procedures. Baby-sitters and day-care facilities will still be required at an age at which most children can be left alone and may be virtually unobtainable for a child who is difficult to manage (Sells, West, & Reichert, 1974). Minute-by-minute supervision is required for much longer than is necessary with normal children. Ordinary toddlers are into everything because they are physically mobile and as yet lack the good sense to avoid dangers and preserve property, but by the age of perhaps thirty months, they have acquired many reasonable limits. In contrast, moderately to severely retarded six-year-olds who are physically healthy and boisterous may need constant surveillance.

---

[4] An annotated bibliography of publications through 1969 can be found in Gorham, Timberg, and Moore (1970). Especially useful are Bensberg (1965), Blodgett (1971), Dittman (1959), Egg (1964), Linde and Kopp (1973) Morgenstern, LowBeer, and Morgenstern (1966), and Younghusband, Birchall, Davie, and Kellmer Pringle (1970). Some of these are pamphlets which present useful orientations to what is known about retardation; others are manuals for progressive programs of training which parents will probably want to keep.

Fig. 20-1 This father and his Down's syndrome daughter are off to a good start. *(From Smith & Wilson, 1973, p. 49)*

Other practical problems must be solved. The family may find it difficult to entertain friends at home, visit their friends, or attend the cinema or church together. Transportation to special classes may be expensive and time-consuming even when the classes are free. Dietary controls for children with disorders such as phenylketonuria and Prader-Willi syndrome are likely to be especially difficult to manage (Keleske, Solomons, & Opitz, 1967; Wood, Friedman, & Steisel, 1967). Some families are troubled by coping with temper tantrums, critical neighbors, and diminished time and resources for the other children in the family. Arranging for suitable leisure-time activities and companionship for the child are also difficult, especially as the child reaches adolescence and adulthood. One group of 201 British familes with a severely retarded child at home, for example, listed the following irksome problems (Holt, 1958): limitation of family activities (41 percent), constant supervision (31 percent), additional expenses (29 percent), exhaustion of the mother (19 percent), and frequent attention at night (15 percent). In an Australian sample of families with moderately retarded children (Jackson, 1969), half felt hindered in arranging for holidays and outings. With reasonable planning and systematic attack, however, these problems can be overcome.

An acute problem revolves around the mother's almost inevitably increased responsibilities for the retarded child (McAllister, Butler, & Jen-lai, 1973). In normal families, the natural response to a strain on the budget is for the mother to go to work, and contemporary lifestyles often include the mother's pursuing her own career ambitions even if financial needs are not severe. Fathers of retarded children may be pressed by money problems and possible neglect by overworked wives (Hutchison, 1966). Furthermore, the increasing rate of divorce among the general population affects families with retarded children as well as it does other families, leaving many mothers to fend alone for their children as well as themselves. We know of no studies which have investigated one-parent families of retarded children, but it is altogether reasonable to assume that they are on the increase.

Further stresses may emanate from discrepancies in the parents' reactions. There may be a tendency for fathers to perceive children more in terms of practical problems such as financial concerns or obtaining a high school diploma, whereas mothers react more in terms of the emotional issues, familial and extra-familial relationships (Gumz & Gubrium, 1972). There is some indication that fathers tend to react by extremes of great involvement or total withdrawal if the retarded child is a boy, whereas sex of the child has little influence on the mother's relationship with him (Tallman, 1965). In fact, however, there has been very little research about the role of the father, a very serious gap in understanding family relationships.

Tendencies toward Overprotection

The relative inability of the retarded child to cope with his environment may be exaggerated if his parents fail to encourage the maximum growth consistent with his handicap. Overprotection tends to perpetuate the child's dependence on his parents, prevents his mastering skills of which he is capable, and may lead to a decrement in IQ (Sharlin & Polansky, 1971).

Overprotection, nevertheless, is rather common among parents of children with any sort of chronic condition, although the same parents may require too much independent behavior of nonaffected siblings (Farber, 1960a). Overprotective behavior toward the retarded probably stems from a variety of sources. First, the busy mother may find that it is easier to continue to feed, bathe, and dress the child who is slow to learn to do these things alone. The mother who suffers a few weeks of mess while her normal baby masters the use of a spoon is soon rewarded by the child's delight and her own new freedom from doing the task. The same process is likely to take months, however, with the slow learner.

Second, the prolonged infancy and heightened dependency of retarded children make it especially difficult for their parents to set limits when later on they become reasonable (Forbes, 1958). Today's parents are encouraged to gratify their infant's every whim. Extended infancy establishes a closely dependent and in some ways mutually gratifying relationship. The pattern can be easily overlearned by both mother and children.

Third, overprotection may be a defensive maneuver to conceal irritation with the child who has made the parents' lives so problematic (Grebler, 1952). Many parents are ashamed of the fact that they are more spontaneously drawn toward their normal children. Painful emotions can be assuaged somewhat and perhaps repressed altogether if the mother goes "beyond the call of duty" in caring for her child. Keeping him a baby and protecting him from possible danger reassures her that her hostility has not annihilated her child, but she may cripple him in more subtle ways (Levy, 1943). Her behavior tells him implicitly, "You are part of mother; you are fragile; you are special" (Sharlin & Polansky, 1971). The unspoken message continues, however, "I, your martyred mother, will shield you from this dangerous world because I love you so much and you must love me also." Levy (1943) found this pattern most striking in mothers whose own childhoods had been conflicted and deprived.

Saenger (1957), in the survey we have cited, attempted to evaluate the extent of overprotection in families of adults who had attended New York City classes for retarded children with IQs below 50. Subjective estimates by the interviewers suggested overprotection in about four out of every ten families in this group. About three of ten parents seemed to try actively to encourage independent behavior. Saenger found several external variables to be related to the frequency of overprotection. It was more common, for example, in families whose children sustained a physical handicap, had the appearance of Down's syndrome, or had a vacant expression, suggesting to Saenger that in these instances, overprotection might serve to compensate for real or expected rejection based on the appearance of the child. Overprotection was also related to the cultural background of the parents. Jewish parents were more frequently overprotective; Italian parents were least so.

In Saenger's group, most of the parents seemed to be of normal intelligence. Children whose retardation is cultural-familial are less likely to be overprotected. Their parents are less able to provide abundantly for their needs, the parents may recognize the retardation only vaguely, and they need not adopt defenses to handle the guilt which other parents feel. On the contrary, they may expect too much of their young and fail to furnish needed supervision. Many a mildly retarded child has received an additional handicap from falls, poisons, street accidents, or illnesses which could have been avoided or treated more adequately had the parents been more alert.

Assessing overprotection is a difficult and subjective matter. One hint can be gleaned from a comparison of the retarded children's social maturity with their overall intellectual behavior. Adaptive behavior ratings much lower than mental age suggest, in the absence of crippling physical or sensory deficits, that they might be capable of more mature behavior. Children who continually ask for help, show poor large-muscle coordination, have unusual difficulty in leaving their mothers in the waiting room, or draw back from more difficult items in an intelligence test may have had little opportunity for independence.

There are but a few studies which have directly observed the interaction between mothers and their retarded children, but these suggest that the patterns, at least with young children, are not very different from the interactions between mothers and their normal children. Mothers of retarded children may give more direct commands and establish more assertive control (Kogan & Tyler, 1973; Kogan, Wimberger, & Bobbitt, 1969; Marshall, Hegrenes & Goldstein, 1973). This pattern has also been found in teachers in special elementary school classrooms (Stuck & Wyne, 1971), perhaps because the children otherwise fail to respond. What may appear to be "authoritarian" attitudes (Cook, 1963) may in fact be a realistic reaction to the response tendencies of the child.

Effects on Family Integration

Although no one would question the assumption that the presence of retarded children tends to place additional stress on their families, little about this process is very well documented. Clinical experience suggests that this stress situation is much like any other which a family may face. Indeed, it may be a lesser threat to the family's mode of living than chronic illness, imprisonment, or death of a family member, or the economic defeat which accompanies a loss of a job or the collapse of a business venture. It is, in fact, not unusual to find families in which retarded children exert an integrative effect, mobilizing the resources of the family members and encouraging their psychological growth.

Sometimes, too, the retarded child in a marginally adjusted family becomes a focus for the tensions family members have been developing with each other (Mahoney, 1958). "If only Johnny were normal, we wouldn't have all this trouble," the family seems to say, ignoring the strife which antedated Johnny. Johnny is a scapegoat, and although this may be a very unhappy situation for him, the rest of the family, by blaming his handicap, may be able to escape for a time some of their other difficulties.

> Russell, age fifteen, was a mildly retarded boy who was admitted to a state school because of his persistent problems in the community. He strayed from home for long periods of time and engaged in petty theft, rode railroad cars, and was a constant truant. His father was a paranoid schizophrenic who managed to hold a job but terrorized his wife and children. As long as Russell remained at home, the father was aggressive primarily toward him, whipping him when he was caught in a transgression and complaining loudly to anyone who would listen. Russell's mother derived some satisfaction from caring for her dependent husband and son, and Russell gave her some protection when the father became abusive toward her. The twelve-year-old brother, Harley, was allowed to go and come as he pleased. After Russell's admission to the state school, however, Harley began to bear the brunt of the father's attention. The father began investigating his friends, demanded that his teachers be more strict with him, and punished him for minor misbehaviors. When Harley began to keep to himself and to have night fears, the mother finally gathered the courage to move out of the house with him. At this point, the father became so blatantly psychotic that his hospitalization was necessary.

The presence of a retarded child is not, however, ordinarily conducive to family integration. Farber (1959) and his associates have suggested that the presence of such a child in a family arrests the usual family cycle. The cycle may be thought of as beginning at marriage and progressing through successive stages determined by the age of the youngest child in the family. This is a sensible way of looking at things, because it is the youngest child who limits the behavior of the parents to the greatest extent. The retarded child, who becomes in essence the youngest child whatever his position in the birth order, may never be more socially mature than the normal preadolescent, and therefore the family cycle may never progress beyond this stage. Never is there a time when parental responsibilities will have been completely fulfilled. Occupational retirement takes on a different meaning, and arrangements must be made for care after the parents are no longer capable of doing so. When there are no normal children, the satisfactions of grandparenthood may be denied to the parents as well.

To investigate the effects of the retarded child on marital integration, Farber (1959) compared indices of the present adjustment of 240 families having a severely retarded child with estimates of the adjustment they had achieved early in their marriages. Farber and Blackman (1956) had previously found that marital integration tends to remain about the same during the early and middle stages of marriage when all the children are normal. In this investigation it was also found that the degree of marital integration early in marriage was significantly related to that which character-ized the marriages at the time of the study, although overall, there was a decline. Families whose integration scores had been high early in the marriages fared better after the birth of a retarded child than did families whose prospects had been poor.

Effects on Siblings

Most studies of the effect of retarded children on their brothers and sisters have been concerned with the question of institutionalization (Chapter 21). The majority of these studies, it should be noted, have been rather subjective and/or much too small to be very helpful, and most have also failed to compare the siblings of handicapped chil-dren with unaffected families.

Farber (1959, 1960a) used no control groups, but he gathered interesting data about the siblings of severely retarded children. He reasoned that the effect of retarded children on their siblings should be different from that on their parents. He conceived of the family consisting of a number of three-person relationships, or triads, each composed of the parents and one child. Each family contains as many triads as it does children, the center of organization thus residing primarily in the parents. The effect of the retarded child under such conditions would be felt by the siblings primarily as it was transmitted to them by the parents. The brothers and sisters would be less deeply affected by the arrest in the family's life cycle, which is relevant to parental behavior, and more deeply affected by short-term, immediate situational values. His data tended to substantiate these ideas.

The variable which seemed of greatest importance to the siblings was the degree of dependence of retarded children, that is, how much they were able or permitted to do for themselves. The more dependent the children, and also the younger they were, the more adverse was their effect on their siblings. It was thus apparently the amount of responsibility assumed by the normal siblings which was the adverse factor so far as they were concerned. The major part of the burden in the home evidently fell on the normal sisters, who were expected to serve as baby-sitters and to take over part of the housework from the mother. Normal girls who interacted frequently with their re-tarded sibling tended to be involved in more tense relationships with their mothers than those who had little to do with the subnormal child. These findings were just the opposite of those discovered with the parents. The adjustment of the adults tended to be immune to the degree of dependence of the retarded child.

Confirming Farber's results is a study by Fowle (1968) of the siblings, ages six to seventeen, of severely retarded children. Two carefully matched groups of thirty-five families were compared: one in which the retarded child had been placed in an insti-tution within the past five years and one in which the child remained at home, attend-ing a community day facility. Fowle concluded that the role tension (maladjustment) of both boy and girl siblings tended to be greater in the latter group, but that the oldest sister was more adversely affected by the presence of a retarded sibling than was the oldest brother. In both groups, tensions were greater in sisters than brothers.

Grossman (1972), who studied eighty-three college-age siblings of retarded chil-dren, came up with a picture somewhat at variance with Farber's findings, although in the main the studies support one another. She found that the most important variable in this *ex post facto* study was the family's general ability to cope with stress. In general, the students from private universities, whose parents were well-off financially, had been protected from most of the adverse circumstances of having a retarded sibling. They were still close to their parents, and their ability to deal adaptively with their situation was closely tied to the parents' acceptance of the sibling and their willingness to communicate about his handicap. Many of the retarded siblings by then had been placed in residential facilities, but the longer the time they had spent growing up in the family, the better able were their siblings to cope, to like their siblings, and to see them as human beings. There were few important differences according to the sex of the college student, except that for the boys, the greater the sibling's physical handicap, the more explicitly they seemed able to handle their feelings.

In the community-university group, however, where most came from less advantaged backgrounds, the adverse results of the sibling's care were more apparent. The girls had been saddled with unusual responsibilities for child care, and they had had greater difficulties with the more physically handicapped, although not necessarily the more retarded, siblings because of this. They had also found it difficult to cope with mildly retarded siblings, with whom their relationships were probably more ambiguous. Those from large families, where responsibilities were shared, were in a somewhat better position. The boys did not show these differential effects; they had been relatively uninvolved with the retarded sibling whatever his characteristics. Even so, they too revealed the adverse effects of the families' limited resources, and they might have profited had a greater number of their siblings been placed in residential care.

In Grossman's study, older siblings in both groups exhibited more adaptive coping than did younger siblings, who were probably less able to understand the situation and relatively more deprived of parental attention. All in all, however, Grossman concluded that about half the college subjects had essentially profited from the presence of the retardate. They seemed more tolerant, more compassionate, and more focused both occupationally and personally than other young adults. Most of the others, though, seemed to have suffered from the experience. They tended to be guilty about the anger they felt at their parents for the personal costs they had borne, were more fearful of being tainted or damaged themselves, and were more deprived in general of the resources they had needed. Grossman concluded that in an unselected group of young adults, the proportion reacting negatively might well have been higher, since the relatively privileged group in the private university were overrepresented in her sample, and of course, young people who had not made it to college at all were completely unrepresented.

In some family situations, then, the presence of a retarded child adversely affects the development and happiness of his siblings. Most frequently, these situations develop when the retarded sibling claims so much of the parents' attention that there is not enough left for the other children, who are asked to assume unusual responsibilities. Occasionally, this occurs with a hyperkinetic child who requires an undue amount of supervision. Sometimes, however, it is not the realistic demands made by the retarded child but the irrational elements in the parents' behavior which work the hardship on the nonhandicapped child.

A mother of four children devoted practically her every waking moment to Eileen, her first born, a severely retarded daughter. Household help looked after the younger children, who did not lack attention but grew up resenting what they felt to be the usurpation of their rightful place. In her old age, the mother said proudly, "Everything Eileen knows, I taught her. I gave her everything I could."

Eileen, who at age 58 was painfully shy of strangers, did show the effects of her additional training. Despite her tested IQ of 20, her conversation and facial expression resembled those of a less retarded woman, and she played the piano rather nicely. One could not, however, miss the irony in her spinster sister's comment. "And we," she added, "gave her our mother."

SUMMARY

Families with retarded children have life-long reality problems with which they must learn to cope. The counselor has a great deal to offer in terms of support, understanding, and guidance. Fostering a viable parent-child relationship, mobilizing reasonable self-esteem and motivation in both parents and children, and enabling the family unit to make use of available resources to solve myriad practical problems are some of the tasks which demand of the professional a long-term commitment to a helping relationship. Most families are able to adapt positively and effectively to this chronic situation, but they deserve the wholehearted support of the community in doing so.

21

Residential Facilities for the Mentally Retarded

Today's family with a retarded child can call upon a richer set of alternative services than ever before for aid in diagnosis, upbringing, education, therapy, recreation, financial assistance, and counseling. We are riding a wave of change which is transforming both the array of community facilities and the nature of residential services for the retarded. It reflects, hopefully, a new commitment on the part of society to establish a meaningful partnership with families, to accept within its ranks far greater proportions of retarded citizens. The contemporary philosophy is one of normalization, "making available to the mentally retarded patterns and conditions of everyday life which are as close as possible to the norms and patterns of the mainstream of society" (Nirje, 1969, p. 181). As a result of all these changes, the complexities of decision making by parents are, of course, greatly increased and are spread over a broader portion of the life span.

It is unfashionable to advocate widespread residential placement these days, but it would be a mistake to underestimate the continued presence of this view, especially among obstetricians and pediatricians who are unacquainted with the actual conditions in the institutions they recommend (Wolfensberger, 1970). Even where there are no illusions about the conditions, many physicians still feel that for the good of the children and/or the welfare of their families, institutions furnish the best solution. They have been particularly prone to give this kind of advice when the diagnosis can be made at birth. Kramm (1963) studied fifty families of children with Down's syndrome and found that forty-four had been advised to seek placement when they first were told of the diagnosis, thirty-one of them told to do so immediately.

Very frequently it will be the duty of the physician to convince the parents that the child would be better off in the state school than at home and to help with the procedures necessary to have the child admitted to the public institution. Even though the buildings may be old and crowded and the food scorned by Duncan Hines, the child will find himself among his equals and will be able to compete with them, whereas in the home community he will always be either overprotected or cruelly rejected from social contacts (Reed, 1963).

It is generally agreed that there are some children who can profit from residential placement and that there are families for whose welfare it is essential that a retarded child be removed from the home. It is also agreed that even if it were economically feasible, a practice of institutionalizing all or even most retarded children would frequently ignore the welfare of both the child and the family.

Because it is the retarded child's parents who must decide whether to seek residential care for him or her, it is essential that there be readily available answers to their many questions about the advantages and disadvantages of out-of-home living for their child. There is seldom a simple answer. Group care can rarely match ideal family care, but few families are ideal and some can have a detrimental effect on development. There are always other persons to consider in addition to the retarded child. Very substantial differences exist among facilities, and solutions appropriate at some periods of life may be inappropriate at others.

HISTORICAL BACKGROUND OF THE RESIDENTIAL INSTITUTION[1]

Institutional care in the United States dates back more than a century, to the mid-1800s. Although it was hard work to convince a skeptical citizenry, a small band of concerned and humanitarian professionals managed to establish modest residential educational facilities, rather like boarding schools, in which they hoped to teach skills necessary to function in school and society (Wolfensberger, 1969). When the results failed to match expectations, and few residents actually did return to their families or to independent living, there was an inevitable backlash. In the disappointment which by the 1880s had become widespread, a trend was initiated to provide long-term, large custodial facilities, intended not to rehabilitate but merely to protect retarded persons from the dangers and demands of the larger society and to afford them the opportunity to live peacefully together. Subsequently a second change of sentiment took place. About the turn of the century, society began to feel that it was the nonretarded who needed protection from the tainted (the mentally retarded, the mentally ill, and criminals). Augmented by the new empirical intelligence tests which helped reveal "how extensive stupidity really was" (Baumeister, 1970, p. 10), the eugenics movements resulted in a number of measures designed to limit the retarded population. Segregation into institutions, sterilization measures, exclusion from the public schools, and restrictions on the right to marry were proposed and, to varying degrees, carried out in desperate attempts to protect the human race from anticipated deterioration and degeneracy.

As a result, during the first third of the twentieth century, the growth of institutions was dramatic. Almost every state built large custodial "hospitals." These institu-

---

[1] See Baumeister (1970), Kanner (1964), and Wolfensberger (1969) for more complete historical surveys. See also E. E. Doll (1970) for a history of private residential facilities.

tions, since they were founded on the perceived needs of the society rather than of the individual, adopted a variety of economic measures. They were located on isolated rural land which could sustain farming operations largely manned by the residents. Patients were rigidly segregated by sex, age, ability level, and sometimes by race as well. Because of the medical orientation, most directors were physicians and the untrained caretakers were supervised by nurses. With the exception of teachers for the limited educational endeavors, few professionals were employed to render treatment and rehabilitation. The geographic isolation, the high patient/staff ratios, low pay, and generally authoritarian hierarchies progressively lowered morale and tended to "institutionalize" the employees. "The residents were dehumanized, deprived of many legal rights, frequently subjected to physical and psychological abuse and personal indignity, and their welfare generally neglected" (Baumeister, 1970, p. 15). It was to these dismal warehouses that parents were advised to send their children, "for their own good!"[2]

That many parents took such advice is evident from the sharp increase in institutional populations between 1915 and 1935. The number of residents per 100,000 persons in the U.S. population nearly quadrupled, from 20 to 75, during those 20 years. By the early 1960s this figure had reached a level of about 100 per 100,000. Part of the more gradual rise after 1935 corresponds with increasing longevity of residents due to enhanced medical technology, including the use of antibiotics. but unsatisfied public demand was reflected in long waiting lists. By 1969, a comprehensive survey by the Office of Mental Retardation Coordination (1972) showed approximately 190,000 residents in public institutions for the retarded, 33,000 in private institutions, and an additional 32,000 patients with a primary diagnosis of mental retardation in state mental hospitals. Together these constituted a small fraction of the 2 million to 6 million retarded persons in the United States (see Chapter 2), but a very sizable proportion of the severely and profoundly retarded.

Recent years have seen striking changes in the tenor of the professional literature concerning institutions, accompanied unfortunately by a much more modest degree of change in the institutions themselves. During the late 1960s and early 1970s there appeared in the United States and in Great Britain numerous descriptions of the inhumane conditions which prevailed in many establishments, including the back wards of some institutions which furnished exemplary programs for other segments of their populations (e. g., Blatt, 1968; Blatt & Kaplan, 1966; Butterfield, 1969; Cleland & Dingman, 1970; Helsel, 1971; Morris, 1969; Wolfensberger, 1969). Without exception, the reports documented the overpopulated, segregated, geographically isolated, barren, and dehumanizing nature of the majority of the large institutions. At the same time, encouraging signs of progress followed the report of the President's Panel on Mental Retardation (1962a) and the subsequent legislation and programming to improve the quality of life for the retarded individuals (e. g., Cleland & Swartz, 1970; Helsel, 1971).

USE OF PUBLIC INSTITUTIONS FOR THE MENTALLY RETARDED

Populations of State Institutions

Certain gross indices reveal the kind of use to which residential institutions are put. Residents enter institutions at somewhat younger ages now than before, as is shown in

---

[2] Similar conditions prevailed and to some extent still prevail in mental hospitals and in juvenile and adult correctional facilities. They are not unique to institutions for the mentally retarded.

Table 21-1   Percent Distribution of Age at First Admission and Age of Resident Populations in State Institutions, 1950–1970

Year	Total	Under 5	5–9	10–14	15–19	20–24	25–34	35 and over
				Age at admission				
1950	100.0	15.9	21.3	23.3	18.5	6.7	7.1	7.2
1960	100.0	16.7	27.6	26.1	17.1	3.7	3.4	5.4
1970	100.0	13.8	28.2	25.8	19.7	3.7	3.9	4.9
				Resident population				
1950	100.0	1.5	5.6	10.9	14.7	13.1	21.8	32.4
1960	100.0	2.1	8.9	14.5	15.7	11.0	16.8	31.0
1970	100.0	3.9	11.5	15.6	19.4	10.2	14.8	24.6

Source: Office of Mental Retardation Coordination (1972), pp. 23–24).

Table 22-1, and as a consequence of this and of increased efforts to place less severely retarded older individuals in noninstitutional residential facilities or to return them to their families, institutional populations are becoming younger.

Furthermore, as community facilities have improved, the large institutions have tended to be used for the severely and profoundly retarded, for whom participation in the life of the larger community is less practical. Although nationwide figures are unavailable, changes over a seventeen-year period for one large institution, Pacific State Hospital in California, are illustrative though probably somewhat more marked than the nationwide average, since during this period California instituted an active program of community services and out-of-hospital placement. Half the patients at Pacific State Hospital in 1967 were profoundly retarded, nearly twice the percentage in 1950. (See Table 21-2.)

A comprehensive study of more than 20,000 retarded residents in twenty-two public institutions in the thirteen Western states (Payne, Johnson, & Abelson, 1969) revealed that more than two-thirds were classified as severely or profoundly retarded; the average IQ was 31.

Not unexpectedly, children in institutions show a very high incidence of handicaps aside from basic intellectual deficiencies. In one institution, 82 percent of the children had one or more medical conditions distinct from mental retardation (Smith, Decker, Herberg, & Rupke, 1969). Among the severely and profoundly retarded, perhaps 25 to 30 percent have seizures (Jasper, Ward, & Pope, 1969). The Payne et al. (1969) survey of residents in state institutions found that special diets were required by a third, and two-thirds received drug treatment. (See Chapter 19.) Many residents had

Table 21-2   Percentages of Residents at Pacific State Hospital, by IQ, 1950–1967

Year	Total	0-19	20–49	50 +
1950	100.0	27.2	48.9	23.9
1960	100.0	29.9	49.7	20.4
1967	100.0	49.7	37.7	12.6
1974	100.0	53.0	40.0	7.0

Source: Tarjan, Wright, Eyman, & Keeran (1973, p. 373) and Eyman (1974).

extensive sensorimotor impairments: 26 percent were unable to walk, 65 percent had impaired speech, and 32 percent were chronic bedwetters. A large number required help in dressing, grooming, brushing teeth, and toileting.

Mortality

Mortality among the institutionalized retarded has always been a matter of concern, especially for the more severely handicapped and especially during the first year after admission. Analyzing data over a twenty-three-year period, Forssman and Akesson (1970) found overall mortality rates for mildly and severely retarded individuals in institutions to be 1.7 and 4.1 times, respectively, the rates for the general populations of the same ages. Because of the marked increase in the most vulnerable populations, improving mortality rates is an uphill battle. In all U.S. public institutions for the retarded, between 1961 and 1970 there was a slow drop from 19.1 to 18.3 annual deaths per thousand residents (Office of Mental Retardation Coordination, 1972b).

A famous group of studies conducted by the psychoanalyst Rene Spitz (1945, 1947) revealed how murderous minimal custodial care *can* be. These studies involved two groups of infants, one reared in a prison nursery by their own mothers, who devoted a great deal of time and emotional investment to their care, and the other in a more aseptic but impersonal and understaffed foundling home. Not only were the foundling-home infants markedly retarded, but their mortality rate was staggering. Thirty-four out of ninety-one children died within a two-year period of various causes, including an epidemic of measles. In the prison nursery, a search through hundreds of records over a 14-year period revealed only three deaths, two of them the result of congenital defects.

During the period immediately after admission, when adjustment to the new environment makes risk the greatest, and when the individual may, realistically or not, experience most sharply the pangs of rejection, mortality is especially high (Tarjan et al., 1973). Equally vulnerable children kept at home are, of course, also subject to high mortality rates. One study (Pense, Patton, Camp, & Kebalo, 1961) of children admitted to state schools in New York before age five, found a 33 percent mortality rate during the first four years after admission, whereas equally young children on the waiting lists of these schools suffered a mortality of 10 to 20 percent. No doubt, the more severely damaged and vulnerable children were admitted somewhat more readily, but a differential probably exists nevertheless.

Factors Predisposing to Institutionalization

Overall, no more than 4 percent of retarded individuals with IQs below 70 are found in institutions, but this figure represents a mixture of many subgroups. Among some, institutionalization is the rule; among others, it is rare. One major study in New York City revealed the following very interesting information about the factors related to the likelihood of a child's being institutionalized (Saenger, 1960), and it has been supplemented by other investigators.

Level of Retardation   As we have already seen, institutions are being utilized for the most retarded segments of the population. Saenger found that of profoundly retarded school-age children in his sample, 88 percent were institutionalized, whereas of those with IQs from 50 to 69, only 10 percent were living in institutions. Moreover, children whose adaptive behavior, as assessed by the Vineland Scale, was lower than their IQs were found by Fotheringham (1970) in Canada and by Kershner (1970) in the

United States to be more readily placed in institutions than groups of the same IQs whose adaptive behavior was rated higher.

Ethnic Background and Economic Status   Within each IQ category, children in residential facilities tend to belong to the economically and socially least adequate families (e. g., Fotheringham, 1970; Fotheringham, Skelton, & Hoddinott, 1971; Saenger, 1960). Ethnic background also contributed in Saenger's study to the likelihood of a child's being placed outside the home. During the two-year period of the investigation, "one out of every two known Puerto Rican low grade retarded children were committed . . . as compared to one out of every four Negro, one out of every ten White Catholic and White Protestant, and one out of every 20 Jewish children" (1960, p. 9). The foreign-born were more likely to keep the child at home than were native-born Americans. It should be noted, too, that the culturally disadvantaged groups, especially Puerto Ricans and Negroes, were less likely to receive the community services they so badly needed than were the Jewish and Protestant groups.

Behavioral Problems   In Saenger's study, the incidence of behavior problems was also an important factor leading to placement. Other workers have confirmed this (Craft & Miles, 1970; Fotheringham, 1970; Fotheringham et al., 1971; Olshansky & Schonfeld, 1964; Shellhaas & Nihira, 1970). Among those with IQs above 50 in Saenger's study, behavior problems outside the home were particularly important, especially those involving breaches of the law. Sexual offenses among girls frequently resulted in placement; a high proportion of girls admitted during adolescence are sent because of sexual or nonsexual delinquencies (Churchill, 1964). Maney, Pace, and Morrison (1964) found "conspicuous behavior problems outside the home" to be related to the need for institutionalization among the mildly retarded, including arrests, trouble getting along with teachers, truancy, and running away. Often, the offenses which lead to institutionalization are not the type that would lead to actual incarceration for other citizens. In many such cases, admission is used to avoid a court trial and/or a jail sentence, which usually would be much shorter than the eventual stay in the institution. Sometimes the behavior which precipitates admission is not even against the law. Occasionally, parents or neighbors are simply fearful that, with approaching sexual maturity, the individual may misbehave. Accordingly, most institutions show a peak in the age distributions of mildly retarded residents during later adolescence.

Among individuals with IQs below 50, Saenger found that the impetus for institutionalization tended to be problems in the home rather than in the community. Presumably, these retarded persons spent little unsupervised time outside the home. Stone (1967), studying the placement intentions of 103 sets of parents with Down's syndrome children, found that the availability of community programs, professional help, and parents' groups seemed to help parents adapt to having the young child at home, but with the increased stress of management as he grew older, placement was more likely to be considered necessary for the family's welfare.

Family Characteristics   Several researchers have found signs of stress and maladjustment in families who seek placement for their children (Fotheringham, 1970; Graliker, Koch, & Henderson, 1965; Kerschner, 1970), and among those who leave them in institutions when they might have been discharged (Mercer, 1966). A frequent reason for seeking admission has to do with a threat to the welfare of the family, such as extreme conflict among the siblings, disagreement between the parents over the treatment of the child, and the general unmanageability of the child in the home (M. K. Allen, 1972). Infants and preschool children early in the birth order are likely to be placed outside the home more readily, as though families who had already "practiced" on other children are more likely to feel capable of coping (Graliker et al., 1965). In Saenger's sample, the institutionalized children more often had retarded parents and siblings, parents with severe economic and/or emotional problems, and single-parental families than did those who remained in the community. Active parental rejection rarely seemed to play a major role in the decision to institutionalize a child. Far more often, the parents or the court were forced to the decision by conditions lying essentially outside their control.

PATTERNS OF LIVING WITHIN INSTITUTIONS

Institutional Components

Institutions are far from the monolithic entities they seem to be. Most, in fact, are conglomerates of several different kinds of milieus. In England, an "institution" may consist of a main nucleus which is a large multibuilding structure, but at the same time may administratively include hostels and other smaller settings some distance away (Morris, 1969). Even on a single campus, very disparate programs may be provided for different age and ability groups.

Round-the-clock *nursing care* for nonambulant patients, most of them severely and profoundly retarded, constitutes the most expensive type of care, requiring facilities and personnel much like those needed by a general hospital. Multiply handicapped children also, of course, often need specialized personnel and equipment. The percentage of institutionalized individuals actually requiring intensive nursing care is small; in England, McKeown and Leck (1967) found only 0.4 percent in Birmingham hospitals needed constant medical treatment, and about half needed only basic nursing maintenance. Morris (1970), also in England, found only 8.8 percent truly bedfast, whereas an additional 7.7 percent walked with difficulty; Payne et al. (1969) found approximately a quarter of the residents in institutions in the United States were unable to walk.

Another more common institutional program is simple *custodial care,* which sometimes involves little more than furnishing a safe place to stay, something to eat and to wear, and minimal supervision. Such programs provide only the necessities to maintain life more or less pleasantly, without organized efforts toward rehabilitation or training. Typically the residents themselves do much of the work. Their labor can be of mutual benefit to themselves and to the institution. Indeed, those who participate sometimes gain a feeling of accomplishment, a sense of being needed. Exploitation is common, however, and wages, if any, are typically a mere token. Children who cannot care for themselves are bathed, fed, and otherwise cared for primarily by more competent residents. These unlucky ones sometimes lie or sit all day, their vacant lives uninterrupted except by rapid spoon-fed meals, baths, and bedtime rituals.Their major diversion is likely to be a radio or a television they do not comprehend. At its worst, this sort of program is characterized by unrelieved deprivation; there is nothing to see, nothing to hear, nothing to feel, nothing to touch, no one to consider one's own.

The philosophy of the founders of hospitals and colonies for the mentally retarded in the early 1900s was aimed at precisely this custodial goal. Reflecting the

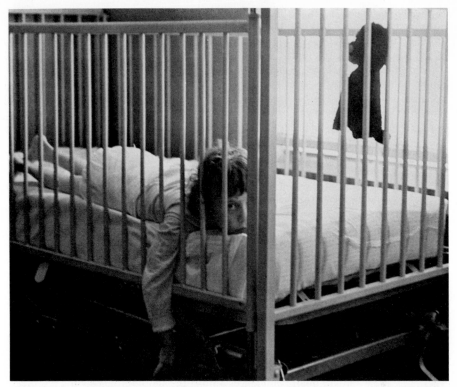

Fig. 21-1   This profoundly retarded twelve-year-old requires total nursing care. *(J. & M. Menapace)*

fatalistic view that nothing could be done about mental deficiency, the primary need was seen as housing and nourishing large numbers of persons as economically as possible. The apparent thrift, however, is shortsighted. The less severely handicapped children who could profit significantly from training will, under such conditions, never have the slightest chance to develop the rudimentary skills needed for life outside an institution. Keeping severely retarded children in custodial settings is uneconomic as well as inhumane, primarily because they could live less expensively and in most instances much more pleasantly in their own homes or in foster homes. Because of recent court decisions involving the right to education (Chapter 18) and the right to treatment (Chapter 22), the legality of minimal custodial care is questionable. Yet, without large infusions of funds, it will probably continue to exist as a blot on a society which regards itself as humanitarian.

Another type of program is what might be called *custodial care in a therapeutic milieu.* In such settings, an effort is made to train children to take care of themselves as much as they can, with or without the goal of returning them to the community. Recreational programs, bright and cheerful surroundings, and stimulation of many kinds can be provided. Trained ward personnel and specialists cooperate in working toward developmental goals. Such efforts have much more to offer a retarded child than do minimal custodial programs, but their advantages over arrangements in the community have not been demonstrated.

Finally, there are programs which undertake *intensive rehabilitative and educational activities,* often with mildly retarded children, adolescents, and young adults, although the full spectrum of the population may be served. Intensive programs are inevitably quite expensive in the short run, but they are potentially more economical when they enable retarded people to provide at least partially for their needs and to return to the community to live independently or in residential programs requiring minimal supervision. The best programs attempt not only to train their students in particular skills, but also to accustom them to environments as much like those outside the school as possible. Academic and vocational training are blended with attention to personal and social development. To meet specific needs, physicians, physical therapists, speech therapists, and counselors are provided. Experience in the community, including vacations, field trips, and trial placements is encouraged. Finally, counselors and social workers help smooth the individual's reentry into the community and provide supervision until he or she is well established.

In the early 1900s most institutions in the United States were called "colonies," "hospitals," or "asylums," but by 1958 there was a significant increase in the popularity of "schools" (Windle, 1962), concomitant with a turn toward educational and rehabilitative goals. Now, with the growth of community facilities for education and training, and the higher proportions of severely subnormal children in institutions, there is a return to the term "hospital" and a use of the newer term "center" (Windle, 1973). "Hospitals" tend to be the more massive institutions, typically with 500 to 1000 residents or more and greater proportions of younger and profoundly retarded. "Centers" tend to be smaller with populations of fewer than 500 residents.

The Quality of Life

There are, to be sure, dramatic differences among the states in philosophy, resources, expenditures, and in number and type of retarded served (Butterfield, 1969), and there are further differences among the institutions in a given state and even, as we have seen, within a single institution.

Commitment of Resources   According to the Office of Mental Retardation Coordination (1972), in 1970, the average daily maintenance expenditure per resident in U.S. public institutions for the retarded was $11.64, up from $4.20 in the space of only ten years. In real dollar terms, this was an increase of 212 percent, concrete evidence of the remarkable increase of public commitment. The number of full-time staff members per 100 residents increased, from an average of 31.3 in 1960 to 57.3 in 1970. These figures include professional and administrative staff as well as caretakers, but the majority are ward attendants who render direct care to residents and are really the personnel on whom the quality of a program stands or falls. A word of caution is in order. Although these ratios look rather encouraging, better than one staff member to two patients, only about a third of the caretaking staff is on duty at one time during the day, because of as many as three shifts, vacations, days off, illness, holidays, and inservice training.

The physical isolation of most state institutions is in itself a considerable problem. Approximately half, even of those built since 1950, are more than 25 miles from the largest city they serve (Rosen & Bruno, 1971). This results in problems to families who want to visit, acute difficulties in recruiting and keeping professional personnel and volunteer workers, and the near impossiblity of preparing residents to cope with urban living. Further accentuating the "out of sight, out of mind" situation, within the institution the profoundly retarded tend to be located outside of what has been called the "normalization zone," close to the entrance and/or the administration building. Even in institutions founded since World War II, more than three-quarters of the wards for profoundly retarded are thus hidden (McGavern, Cleland, & Swartz, 1974).

Crowding and Restriction Overlarge wards and dormitories constitute another persistent problem. In the United States, 40 percent of residents are housed in rooms holding more than thirty persons (Baumeister, 1970); in England, approximately the same proportion are in wards with sixty or more, although a good many of these have two or three dormitories (Morris, 1969). Morris's survey found that 60 percent of the residents were housed in dormitories where no personal possessions at all were displayed; that figure is probably not far off the mark in the United States. She found, further, that few residents had their own toothbrush, shaving kit, or hair brush, and that most wore everyday clothing supplied on a common use basis by the hospital. Economic measures of this kind render an individual completely devoid of privacy or a sense of personal identity. Ordinarily, there is no bit of space inviolable to invasion by staff or other residents.

> For the profoundly retarded whose capacity for mobility through space is limited, one finds a not infrequent positioning in spots of relative privacy, i.e., under their bed, in the same chair or corner day after day, or similar unoccupied spots where "squatter's rights" are open. (Cleland & Dingman, 1970, p. 156)

Inevitably in large institutions, in order to produce the least amount of work for the staff and to maintain the most conventional codes of behavior, rules and routine dominate the day. Sleeping, waking, toileting, bathing, and eating are strictly regimented. The new resident quickly learns to conform, and in many institutions conformity is the chief lesson taught (Braginsky & Braginsky, 1971). This attitude is often reinforced by the community and by parents. Institutions such as Pacific State Hospital, which have experimented with allowing patients greater freedom even in such areas as dating and other heterosexual behavior, have found that many rules are unnecessary; the patients themselves establish codes which are decidedly puritanical (Edgerton & Dingman, 1964; Tarjan, 1973). Staff fears that chaos would result from a relaxation of rules are probably unfounded, but the general attitude continues to be, "Give them an inch; they'll take a mile."

Interinstitutional Differences Klaber (1970) carried out an exceptionally valuable study of six public institutions, which illustrates some factors which distinguish effective environments in which residents are happy and developing well, from those in which the quality of life is detrimental. Five institutions were of medium to very large size and were virtually self-contained; institution E was a new, well-staffed facility for fewer than 300 residents, where many needs were met by community resources. In each institution, Klaber observed matched groups of severely retarded boys; he also assessed attendants' attitudes and institutional patterns of staffing.

Institution E in this study clearly stood out as the most effective in terms of the residents' behavior and development. The most important variable distinguishing institution E from the others was apparently the amount and quality of the interaction of the boys with their caretakers. The attendants there were most responsive to the children; they spent more time in active child care, talked more with the children and played with them, and spent less time in passive supervision or in activities completely unrelated to ward care. In contrast with the other institutions, where the boys interacted mainly with their peers, in institution E they not only interacted more often with the aides but also with other staff members and volunteers. Klaber, Butterfield, and Gould (1969) demonstrated that children transferred to institution E from one of the other custodial institutions gained more social independence than a group who had remained behind.

In spite of the distinct differences among the institutions, commonalities were persistent in some areas. Even in institution E, the boys spent a substantial amount of time doing nothing (not even watching television), though not as much as in the other institutions. Repetitive, self-stimulating behavior was also frequent in all six settings.[3] Although the behavior of the attendants differed from one institution to another, their attitudes were very similar. None of the attendant groups had anything positive to say about the parents of retarded children, for example, and their views of professional educators were also negative. On the positive side, they clearly viewed mental retardation not as an illness but as a problem residing in the relationship of the child to the social environment.

Except in educational services, professional staff members tended to be minimally qualified for their positions. In only one institution, for example, was the social work department directed by a person holding a master's degree; most social workers were either untrained college graduates or had an incomplete social work education. The major problem was not in recruiting qualified people but in keeping them. Among the highly competent professionals who had left the employ of the institutions, the general feeling was that rigidity and the lack of appreciation of their contributions were major problems.

Although Klaber's study covered only 6 of the 190 state institutions in the United States and its observations were restricted to young, severely handicapped males, it illustrates the problems and the potentials of institutional care for this group. Life need not be dismal and barren. Morris (1969) summarizes the feelings of British nurses with, "Some say they are not nurses but glorified domestic workers or, alternatively, jailers." Clearly this need not be the case. At present, however, all too commonly, it is.

EFFECTS OF INSTITUTIONALIZATION ON THE CHILD AND THE FAMILY

Effects on the Child

Predicting the effects of admission to an institution is not easy.Children's responses to long-term residential care are a complex matter, having to do not only with the environment offered by the institution, but also with preplacement life experiences, their own behavior patterns, their age and sex, and the length of their stay (Balla, Butter-

---

[3] Kaufman and Levitt (1965) found such behavior to peak prior to meals and rest periods as well as mid-afternoon. They interpreted it as related to the degree of tension and to reduced opportunities for discharge by other means. Klaber and Butterfield (1968) also established that rocking was related to tension and discomfort and was inversely related to ward effectiveness. At a primitive level, stereotyped self-stimulation may simply represent something to do when other activities are lacking.

field, & Zigler, 1974). Surprisingly, even such obvious indices as institution or living-group size, annual expenditures, patient/staff ratio, and level of resident retardation are not clearly related to either the quality of child-care practices or the responses of children (Balla et al., 1974; King, Raynes, & Tizard, 1971).

Institutional Variables   Numerous studies have compared groups of children reared from early life in institutional settings and at home. Some studies have looked at normal groups (e.g. Kohen-Raz, 1968; Paraskevopoulos & Hunt, 1971; Rajalak-shmi, 1968) and some at retarded groups (e.g. Carr, 1970; Centerwall & Centerwall, 1960; Kaufman, 1967; Kirk, 1958). Generally the at-home children have been shown to have the advantage in mental development, especially in language, and to exhibit fewer stereotyped, self-stimulating behaviors. These differences have persisted even after the home-reared children have subsequently been admitted to an institution (Matejcek & Langmeier, 1965; Shipe & Shotwell, 1965).

Other studies of nonretarded children have not found such results when the institutions were particular stimulating. Infants in well-staffed institutions evidently develop rather normally (Dennis, 1960; Paraskevopoulos & Hunt, 1971; Rheingold, 1960, 1961; Tizard & Rees, 1974). Moyles and Wolins (1971), who studied several hundred children in various high-quality group-care programs in Austria, Israel, Poland, and Yugoslavia, found no evidence for developmental deficiencies and no correlation between the age of entry or length of stay and performance on the Raven Progressive Matrices, a nonverbal intelligence test. Although Kohen-Raz (1968) found that infants in institutions fared worse than home-reared babies, he also found that kibbutz infants (who receive attentive group care and daily contact with their own parents) performed on the same level as did infants in private middle-class Israeli homes.

Variations in institutional practices account to some extent for developmental differences. Tizard (1964), for example, removed sixteen severely subnormal children from a large and crowded institution and transferred them to a small family-type unit. Subsequently, they made significantly greater advances in verbal and social development than sixteen matched children who remained behind in the institution. A study by Stedman and Eichorn (1964) of ten Down's syndrome[4] children at home and ten in a special enrichment unit of a state hospital found that despite the stimulation, the institution group had significantly lower IQ and SQ scores. Subsequently, however, both groups attended a special nursery school and the institutionalized children received special language training on their ward. After one year of this regime, both groups showed improvement, the institutionalized group advancing enough to equal the at-home group in mental and motor behavior, though not in social competence (Bayley, Rhodes, Gooch, & Marcus, 1971).

Dennis (1960), who studied children living in three institutions in Iran, found that development was greatly retarded in two of the institutions in which there was a minimum of handling of the infants. In the third institution, where the children had much more handling and opportunity for exercise, the babies' motor development resembled that of home-reared children. Visiting one of the first two orphanages years later, Hunt (1974) arranged for additional personnel and found that with increased

---

[4] Down's syndrome children are a particularly interesting group for research because so many used to be placed at birth, on the arbitrary advice of professionals, rather than because of special attributes of child or family.

handling, motor behavior improved rapidly, but not other aspects of development. Along the same line, Paraskevopoulos and Hunt (1971) compared the development of infants in two Athenian orphanages (one with an infant-caretaker ratio of about 10:1, and the other with a ratio of 3:1) with infants reared at home. Infants in the first orphanage showed considerable retardation compared with the other two groups, but in some respects, even the infants in the second orphanage (the well-known Metera Baby Center) were at a slight disadvantage compared with the home-reared group.

Home Variables   One is tempted to forget that not all homes provide equally suitable environments. For some children, the institution may, in comparison with the home, be a step in the right direction. Tizard and Rees (1974) studied sixty-five children, age four and one-half years, who had spent their first two to four years in a particularly stimulating institution. Twenty-four had been adopted and fifteen restored to their natural mothers at a mean age of three, whereas twenty-six remained in the institution. The mean IQs of all groups were at least average. The adopted children had significantly higher IQs and were more friendly and less restless than the others, but the children who had been restored to their own mothers (whose various problems had led to the initial placement) did somewhat more poorly than even the children remaining in the institution.

There are some retarded children, most of them in their preadolescent or adolescent years, in which a decided improvement occurs after admission to an institution (Clarke & Clarke, 1954; Clarke, Clarke, & Reiman, 1958). Many of the subjects in the Clarkes' studies had presented problems which seemed to be related to the inadequacies or inconsistencies of supervision or discipline in the home. They were lonely children who often made life difficult for their neighbors and their families. Some had been allowed to roam the streets, predictably making a nuisance of themselves and becoming involved in petty thievery. A large proportion responded well to the new environment. Those with a very adverse socioeconomic background improved in IQ to a significantly greater extent, made a better adjustment within the hospital, and were placed in the community earlier and more often than were those whose background was not quite so inadequate.

Cognitive Development   Numerous studies comparing home-reared children with institutional children have centered on intellectual functioning. Although the picture is far from clear, the poorer institutional programs can certainly have a debilitating effect on intelligence (Klaber, 1970; Tizard & Tizard, 1971). As we saw in Chapter 17, longitudinal studies of tested intelligence in institution populations have revealed progressive decreases in IQ. The drop in IQ may be in part an artifact because those residents who have increased in IQ may more readily have been placed in the community (Silverstein, 1969). There is also some indication that institutional life may be more deleterious to young children than to adolescents and adults (Sternlicht & Siegel, 1968). Other measures of cognitive functioning, such as associative learning (Baumeister, 1968), tend to show progressive deficits in institutionalized groups as well.[5] In contrast, Penney and Willows (1970) found that the longer retarded children had been in an institution, the better their scores on a task requiring mediation. The latter authors felt that schooling and ward instruction teach children to attend to relevant elements or cues in a situation.

[5] See Chap. 13 for an explanation of associative and mediational processes in learning.

Verbal Development   Verbal development is especially vulnerable to the effects of deprivation when children grow up in an institutional setting (Bayley et al., 1971; David & Appell, 1973; Lyle, 1960; Pringle & Bossio, 1958; Tizard & Tizard, 1971). Living in even a well-staffed institution is in some ways like living in a very large family. (See Chapter 7.) A large proportion of the speech to be heard is that of other children, which is likely to be poorly articulated, unresponsive, and unlikely to call forth a verbal reply from the children who hear it. Skeels, Updegraff, Wellman, and Williams (1938), who introduced a preschool training program into an understaffed and poorly equipped orphanage, found striking retardation in the verbal development of the twenty-one children, ages eighteen to sixty-six months.

> Language and speech were greatly retarded. Not only was the vocabulary meager and based upon very limited experience but the structure was far below that ordinarily expected. Coupled to these two serious handicaps were such faulty enunciation and poor speech habits that the language of the children was in the great majority of cases either entirely or practically unintelligible. Although children who were already acquainted were able to make each other understand in some few simple interchanges, any constructive conversation seemed out of the question. Voices were unpleasantly monotonous, mumbling was common. With little provocation, talking voices would become loudly demanding. Finally, and of great significance in the teaching situation, was the fact that these children were not accustomed to listening to the words of adults or of other children in order to acquire ideas. Words as a medium of communication were poor commodities in this environment. In fact, the urgency for communication seemed to confine itself to situations of extreme discomfort (anything looked upon as discomfort by the child seemed to him extreme) and in such situations a loud crying was the favorite resort. On the other hand, there was a considerable amount of what might be called "verbalization," which consisted of imitation of the sounds of words of others, more with the idea of filling space than with definite communicative purpose. A phrase or word said by one child would be repeated by several not as a game, not in hilarity, but more as an activity arising from nothing and resulting in nothing. (pp. 23-24)

Personality   Much has been written about the adverse effects of institutionalization on the personality of the child, especially the very young child, yet research in this area is sparse. Personality variables are difficult to measure systematically in any group of subjects, but especially among retarded ones. (See Chapters 9 and 16.) One classic group of studies was carried out by William Goldfarb (1943, 1945, 1955), who dealt with a small group of children who had spent almost all their first three years in an orphanage and had then been transferred to foster homes. He compared them with other children who had spent their first year or so at home and had then been transferred directly to foster homes. He found that the first group were less bright, less mature, more impoverished, more apathetic, and less ambitious. Their behavior was poorly controlled and impulsive, presenting a constant discipline problem at home and at school. They constantly demanded attention but profited little from it and seemed in many respects to lack firm bonds with other people. There are, to be sure, limitations in these studies. Goldfarb dealt with only a few cases, he was not unaware of their history when he later tested and interviewed them, his groups may not have been precisely equivalent, and his work has not been replicated.

Authoritarian and repressive attitudes in institutional caretakers are designed to minimize management problems. To compensate for the paucity of personnel, and to deal with difficult relationships, conformity and submissiveness are encouraged (Braginsky & Braginsky, 1971; Morris, 1969; Stein & Longenecker, 1962). It is not surprising, then, to find that social quotients (SQs) derived from the Vineland Social Maturity Scale are negatively related to the length of time in an institution (Doll, 1945; Myklebust & Burchard, 1945).[6] We have already seen that a prominent index of the effectiveness of an institution lies in the self-sufficiency of the children (Klaber, 1970). Formal training in this area can be of some help (Mitchell & Smeriglio, 1970), but ordinary school programs within the institution are apparently insufficient to halt the decline in adaptive behavior (Bayley et al., 1971; Cain & Levine, 1963).

Butterfield (1967a) has summarized a very important group of studies conducted by Zigler and his coworkers. These studies indicate that institutions do typically provide an environment which is socially depriving and that some institutions are more depriving than others. Two longitudinal studies by this group (Balla et al., 1974; Zigler, Butterfield, & Capobianco, 1970) concluded that the institutional experience was more socially depriving for children from relatively good than from relatively poor homes. IQ changes were related to degree of preinstitutional deprivation.

> The view of personality development that these studies support is that if children experience sufficient positive interaction with adults, they gradually become more oriented toward achieving independence and less needful of frequent, indiscriminate support from adults and peers. A corollary of this view is that if children, whether retarded or normal, do not receive sufficient positive adult contact (as they probably do not in institutions), they will remain immaturely oriented toward receiving attention from adults. They will not become sufficiently motivated toward achieving independence to make a satisfactory adjustment as an adult. Furthermore, this view suggests that retardates are even more susceptible to the detrimental effects of insufficient or inadequate adult support than are normal children. The reason for this is that retardates, because of their lesser intelligence, are more frequently incapable of meeting conventional standards of achievement and are more likely to learn that they cannot rely upon themselves.[7]
>
> The studies . . . suggest that one of the hallmarks of a desirable institutional environment is the provision of intimate positive contact between adult caretakers and residents. (Butterfield, 1967a, p. 128)

Another small group of studies have had to do with the effects of institutional experience on self-concept and expectancy of failure. (See Chapter 9.) Guthrie, Butler, and Gorlow (1963) administered personality tests to mildly retarded adolescent females, one hundred in an institution and eighty-three living in their homes. They found that the former tended to regard themselves as worthless and were more self-oriented. They did not admit to feelings of anger in situations which would normally anger people, quite possibly because even reasonable expressions of anger by residents are not permitted in most institutions.

---

[6] Fotheringham et al. (1971), however, failed to find a loss in SQ after one year. There is the possibility that children with comparatively low SQs are admitted at an earlier age.

[7] See Chap. 9 for a discussion of "outer-directedness" in retarded individuals.

A few other studies, in contrast, indicate that the sheltered environment of the institution may have some beneficial aspects. Rosen and his coworkers (Rosen, Diggory, Floor, & Nowakiwska, 1971; Rosen, Diggory, & Werlinsky, 1966) concluded that retarded persons in institutions were more confident of success than those at home, though the two groups were more like each other than like normal controls of the same age. Yando and Zigler (1970) found increased autonomy in problem solving in institutionalized children. In the same vein, Payne (1971) found a tendency for continued residence to lead to a reduction in failure expectancy in mildly retarded children, possibly because the demands made on them in the protected environment were more appropriate to their level of ability than those they had experienced before.

The picture is certainly not all negative. Kirkland (1967), while pointing out that institutions are inaccurate models of the kinds of settings to which many residents will later be called upon to adjust, lists a number of aspects which *may* be beneficial, at least on a temporary basis.

> For example, the impersonality of the institution may offer the emotionally damaged retardate a rest from too-intense relationship demands.
>
> For the child whose former environment provided no stable predictability, the routines of the institution may be, for a limited time, specifically therapeutic. Predictability of the environment is necessary if one is to learn the concept of cause and effect. . . .
>
> The child whose personality is disorganized, who has not developed internal controls because of inconsistent demands at home, may benefit for a while from the rather clear, and usually rather inflexible standards set forth for his guidance. . . .
>
> Certain aspects of behavior can be taught more easily in group situtations, such as accepting the need for and carrying out rules and regulations, sharing, taking turns, standing in line, taking orders from a variety of people—in other words, training in conformity. . . .
>
> The so-called "familial" retardate, who by definition has experienced social, educational and physical deprivation, may benefit in a special way from a limited period in an institution . . . he has probably suffered repeating losing battles in all kinds of competitions, except perhaps in the area of disruptive behavior. Consequently, he has often developed a picture of himself as inadequate, incompetent, and often, "bad". . . .
>
> He sees many others much more limited than himself, and finds himself, for the first time, at the top of the status ladder. He is counted on for the most responsible jobs assigned to residents. His assets are recognized and valued, rather than his limitations being always noticed. . . . (Kirkland, 1967, pp. 6–7)

Effects on the Family

Siblings   The adverse effect of retarded children on their siblings is often given as a reason for seeking placement. What little research there is, however, indicates that the picture is not entirely one-sided. Sometimes, indeed, siblings of institutionalized children are found to display a greater number of mental health problems than those of similar retarded children who are living at home (Tizard & Grad, 1961). This finding should not be surprising in view of the relatively high incidence of problems of all sorts in the families of institutionalized children, but it is not invariable. Fowle

(1968), for example, found just the opposite to be true, that siblings with retardates in institutions showed fewer signs of maladjustment.

Evidence collected by Farber (1959; Farber & Jenné, 1963) suggests that brothers and sisters tend to be affected differentially. In general, the adjustment of normal brothers in these studies deteriorated when their retarded sibling left home. Evidently, the handicapped children had served as a kind of buffer, absorbing so much of the parents' attention that the brothers became more involved with friends outside the home. When the handicapped child left, however, the brother's role in the family was expanded, and tensions seemed to settle on him. Farber, and also Fowle (1968), found, in contrast, that normal sisters were sometimes helped by placing the retarded child outside the home. They had previously handled undue responsibility, taking over many of the tasks ordinarily performed by the mother and thus being forced into very close contact with her. With the cessation of the extra responsibilities, mother and daughter had fewer opportunities to come into conflict and the daughter was free to pursue relationships outside the home.

Parents   In the case of the parents, the situation is complicated. Dittmann (1962) has written perceptively about the intense conflict experienced by many parents who decide to send their children to a residential facility. Very frequently, the child has displayed severe behavior problems such as hyperactivity, tantrums, running away, or delinquency. Once the child has left home, however, the parents may begin to idealize him and to feel that their decision was a bad one. In some instances, parents even abandon the retarded child because they cannot bear to face their feelings.

Occasionally, the removal of the retarded child opens a Pandora's box of family troubles: when the scapegoat is gone, all sorts of problems reemerge from their hiding places.[8] The mother continues to pay less attention to the father than he would like (or vice versa); the adolescent sister is still unpopular. The empirical evidence is mixed as to whether placement is, on the average, followed by an improvement in family functioning (Fotheringham et al., 1971; Fowle, 1968; Kershner, 1970).

The deep affection felt by the family toward a retarded child is not lightly to be shrugged off. It is all too easy to overlook the plain fact that a child is loved. A poignant essay by Edith P. Gramm about the birth and subsequent placement of her retarded son reflects the regrets of a mother who has done her best and can do no more.

> [A nurse] told me we were lucky to be alive, and when he unsquinted his eyes for a second, I caught a flash of the most incredible blue and I thought she could never know how lucky. No baby would ever be loved as I would love Peter. One day I would write a little story for him, and I would call it *Peter Beautiful*. In it he would hear all those things about himself that make each of us feel wonderful and blithe.
>
> I would never strike him nor scream at him. Other mothers who did were harassed, but nerves would never drive me to unkindness. . . .
>
> Last summer we were forced by our conscience, by my broken nerves (I have struck my Peter Beautiful, and I have screamed at him), and by the pressure of advising, censorious neighbors who considered this thirty-odd pounds of prettiness a menace to their stalwart young pugnacious "normals"—we were forced by all this to "put him away."

[8] See the case of Russell, Chap. 20.

I won't pretend it was because we were advised to do so by every physician we saw. Nor can I rationalize that it was because he was becoming a very evident danger to himself. There is nothing rational about parenthood. It is primitive and emotional. (Gramm, 1951, pp. 271-272)

EFFORTS AT INSTITUTIONAL IMPROVEMENT

When the American public is aroused about a problem which is suddenly perceived as unfair and intolerable—even if the problem is chronic and long-standing—people demand, and usually get prompt action. The report of the President's Panel on Mental Retardation (1962a) and the subsequent exposés of hospital conditions mobilized a number of efforts at reform. As we have seen, the states have more than doubled the appropriations to institutions; staffs have been enlarged; to some extent the institutions have been retrieved from their solitary isolation and have become a part of the continuum of services to the retarded.

In 1964, the AAMD published *Standards for State Residential Institutions for the Mentally Retarded,* a monograph which provided an objective means by which the adequacy of physical plant, staffing patterns, and programming could be evaluated. With the guidance of the AAMD, a subsequent study of 134 of the then 168 existing institutions was undertaken, largely involving self-evaluations by staffs of the institutions. The findings (Hubbard, 1969) were stark indeed. More than 50 percent of the institutions were rated as below standard; 89 percent failed to meet AAMD attendant/resident ratios; 60 percent were overcrowded. A survey by Rosen and Bruno (1971) further confirmed the problems in residential services. Still, the evaluation process had a mobilizing effect and some innovative solutions began to be found (Helsel, 1971).

Among the first steps taken on a nationwide basis was the establishment of an accreditation system under the Joint Commission for Accreditation of Hospitals. Accreditation in itself solves no problems, but it serves the useful purposes of setting explicit goals, putting pressure upon hospital superintendents and state legislatures to meet standards, and providing a rough index to parents who are considering placement for their children (Helsel, 1971). Proposals by the President's Committee on Mental Retardation (1970a) were also influential.

Financial assistance was made available through the Hospital Improvement Project (HIP) of the National Institute of Mental Health for innovations in programming. Funds provided for Hospital Inservice Training (HIST) were mainly directed at upgrading the skills of attendants. Other funds were made available through several government agencies. The Rehabilitation Services Administration furnished grants-in-aid to states to develop rehabilitation and vocational programs; the Summer Work Experience and Training (SWEAT) enabled high school students to become acquainted with institutions; the Administration on Aging established the foster grandparents program (see below); the National Institute of Child Health and Human Development granted funds for construction of research centers; the Office of Education provided educational and library service funding; and the Surplus Property Program made land available. Various financial assistance programs, including the Social Security Administration and the military services, by paying full tuition for individual residents whose families had been paying reduced fees, freed other funds for institution use. At the same time, community services were being rapidly improved by federal and state provisions of funds and personnel.

Among the programs stemming from these new resources were the applications of behavior modification techniques in a variety of settings. (See Chapter 15.) To cite but one example, several innovations at Faribault State Hospital in Minnesota, transformed a largely custodial institution to an educational-therapeutic environment (Thompson & Grabowski, 1972). Other projects have been described by Mackay and Sidman (1968) and Watson (1970).

Another group of projects was aimed at providing increased mothering (or grandparenting), attention, nurturance, affection, and physical contact, through the participation of volunteers and of foster grandparents, low-income elderly persons employed part time, who thereby gain not only financial rewards but the feeling of being needed and useful. Results on both sides have been positive (Coyte, 1969; Saltz, 1973). The foster grandparent program has also been used to ease the transition from home to institution (Friedsam & Dick, 1968).

The role of the attendant is the key to improvement of care. A number of efforts have been directed toward upgrading the skills and status of attendants, many of whom have minimal general education and little or no prior exposure to retarded individuals. Many function at a low-normal range of intelligence (Butterfield, 1967b). Low pay, low status, lack of contact with professional personnel (Cleland & Dingman, 1970), geographic isolation, and authoritarian lines of command within institutions which have emphasized physical rather than parenting responsibilities—all these have combined to reduce the effectiveness even of the most dedicated souls. Improved selection can help (Butterfield, 1967b), but major efforts are needed to mobilize the resources of these caregivers, to dignify their positions, to provide support for their developmental efforts with the residents, and to pay them at a level commensurate with their importance to the effectiveness of their institution. Pioneering efforts at inservice training for attendants were made by the Southern Regional Education Board (SREB). Cleland and Swartz (1969) have written a text for attendant personnel which encourages innovation, insight, and responsibility. Numerous other efforts are currently under way.

Finally, one must recall that a child's parents continue to be a vital resource for his or her care. Opening institutions to parents and to the public at large is, in the long run, the most effective guarantee that quality programs will be provided. Deplorable institutions do not attract parents or the public, but effective ones do. Whatever the distances involved, parents tend to visit their children in institutions where they see them developing well, where they are happy and relatively self-sufficient (Klaber, 1968). A disturbing finding of Klaber's (1970) study of attendants' attitudes was the overwhelming negative picture of parents which even those in effective institutions held very strongly. Mutual respect and cooperation among the adults who care for and care about the child is far to be preferred.

ALTERNATIVE FORMS OF RESIDENTIAL FACILITIES

One of the most exciting developments in recent years is the move toward providing a broad spectrum of residential facilities for retarded individuals unable to live at home. Long-term care in a public institution for the mentally retarded is not by any means the only form of out-of-home care. With varying degrees of rapidity, the states are developing a number of community-based alternatives, ranging from foster placement which most closely approximates a natural home setting, to mini-institutions housing a number of individuals and utilizing community services to meet needs which self-sufficient institutions formerly had to supply.

By 1974, for example, trend-setting California had placed three times as many individuals needing out-of-home care in community facilities as in institutions (Individualized Data Base Project, 1974). Most other states are moving in that direction, but have been much slower to develop community placements. Facilities are emerging rapidly and the number of innovative programs is very large. The overall picture is one of considerable diversity, experimentation, and optimism. There is as yet, however, very little evidence about the suitability of the alternatives for various groups of retarded persons nor about their effectiveness in supporting social and intellectual development. For this reason, our coverage of these forms of placement must be much more meager than is warranted by either the degree of activity or by their probable influence on future patterns of care.

Private Institutions and State Hospitals

Even prior to the current emphasis on community facilities, many retarded persons were placed in private institutions for the retarded and in state hospitals for the mentally ill. In 1970, there were 33,000 in the former and 32,000 in the latter whose primary diagnosis was mental retardation. Individuals were frequently placed in these facilities while they awaited space in public institutions for the mentally retarded.[9]

Private institutions for the retarded are usually small. In 1970, there were 708 such facilities in the United States, with an average population of forty-seven residents. These included both nonprofit and proprietary homes. Most cater to children and many provide for the severely and profoundly retarded. The cost of such private care is generally well beyond the means of a family with moderate income.

In contrast, about half of the retarded patients in state mental hospitals are adults ages fifteen to twenty-four, and about three-quarters of them are only mildly or moderately retarded. Many had been involved in disturbances in the community for which they might otherwise have been jailed. Only about 4 percent in 1970 were under the age of fifteen, but better than 31 percent were age fifty-five or older (Office of Mental Retardation Coordination, 1972).

Alternate Uses for Public Institutions for the Retarded

To provide reasonable services, placement of anyone in an institution should be explicitly time- and goal-oriented. One potential use for institutional facilities is short-term admission for a period of weeks or months (e.g., Savage, Weltmen, & Zarfas, 1967). An admission of this nature can provide an opportunity for detailed diagnosis; it can permit skilled personnel to center on a particular behavior which the parents have been unable to handle such as toilet training or control of hyperactivity; it can furnish temporary placement while the family is under acute stress, while the mother is ill, or simply while the family takes a vacation or a respite from full-time care; and

---

[9] It was a heartrending experience for one of the authors to test several children who had been placed temporarily, while acutely disturbed, in available space on adult wards of a state mental hospital. Now that they had "simmered down," these children desperately and realistically wanted a transfer to the state school for the retarded. They tried their utmost to "pass" the intelligence test. How could they know that if they "passed," they would be declared ineligible?

it can serve as a trial placement to enable family and institution to determine the suitability of long-term residential placement for a child. Such programs have been much talked about, and they are desired by parents (Sells, West, & Reichert, 1974), but unfortunately they have seldom been put into practice. With the increased availability of skilled diagnostic services, the need for inpatient diagnosis has been reduced, but the potential for other purposes remains.

Regional Centers

One of the first attempts to improve upon monolithic institutions was by decentralizing the facilities into smaller centers, usually under 200 beds, closer to families and interwoven with other community services such as local health care facilities, public schools, and recreational facilities. Some of these centers have also accepted non-boarding participants for programs such as day-care and sheltered workshops. Connecticut, California, and Nebraska have been leaders in regionalizing facilities to meet local needs. In England, many of the hospitals which were already decentralized to some extent, included small facilities and hostels under the administrative wing of a nearby hospital for the retarded (Morris, 1969).

Group Homes

Under either private or public auspices, group homes have proliferated in the past several years. Included are "boarding homes," "hostels," "halfway houses," and modified motels and hotels. They accept children who attend public schools or, more frequently, adults who are employed in the community or who attend sheltered workshops. Some also provide day care and/or night care for the more severely handicapped. They can be used as a means of transition from institutional life to independent living, or they can furnish a more-or-less permanent placement. Many of these facilities have been established under the impetus of the same parents who earlier had sparked the drive for special education classes in the public schools. Determined to keep their offspring at home as long as possible, these parents have now reached an age where they must consider placement when they can no longer provide a home. The very existence of group homes is reassuring to many parents, both young and old, who must consider the life-long nature of their child's need for supervision (Helsel, 1971). Benoit has suggested that continued at-home living for many retarded adults can in fact be detrimental. He found that out-of-town participants in a rehabilitation program progressed more rapidly than did an apparently equivalent local group whose "parents were always around to reinforce immaturity. . . . If their sons and daughters can handle an eight-hour job to a supervisor's complete satisfaction, they ought to be able to boil an egg or take a suit to the cleaners" (1973, p. 24). Benoit advocates a social center staffed only by a director, in which the residents do all the work necessary to meet their needs and in which there is explicit anticipation of departure, either to live alone or on a sharing basis or even in matrimony.

Community living centers of fifteen to forty residents have been established in Canada (Bridges, 1970) and in Britain (Kushlick, 1970). In the Netherlands, there are small homes for six to eight retarded persons with high social integration and homes for fifteen to twenty-five persons requiring more specialized care (Germeraad, 1966).

Dunn (1969) has advocated the establishment of a network of small, special-purpose facilities to replace general-purpose facilities. He suggests that some should be oriented toward short-term or long-term medical services, whereas others might be oriented toward development of the severely retarded or might operate as boarding schools (e.g., for mildly retarded children from rural areas), rehabilitation centers, or hostels. Rather than trying to provide all services in all facilities, he suggests that residents, personnel, and budgets might profit from such an arrangement, provided that transfers from one facility to another were made easy.

As yet, there have been very few studies of community facilities. An observational study by Bjaanes and Butler (1974) has demonstrated significant differences between board and care facilities (thirty to fifty residents) and community homes (four to six residents). The former much more closely approximate the goal of normalization, with more independent behavior and more exposure to the community. A series of studies by Tizard and his colleagues (King et al., 1971) also points to better care in group homes than in large institutions, in terms of continuity of care and reduced social distance between resident and staff.

Nursing Homes

There exist in most communities nursing homes, convalescent homes, and intermediate care facilities oriented toward long-term care of nonretarded patients. A number of institutions have experimented with transferring retarded residents to these homes. A three-year evaluation in Wisconsin (Mueller & Porter, 1969) revealed that such units preferred individuals who were ambulatory, capable of self-care, and fifty years of age or older. Even moderately and severely retarded residents were well accepted, were able to engage in productive work and to feel a greater degree of independence. They also enjoyed more privacy in this kind of setting than in the institution. Lyon and Bland (1969) observed twenty-five patients who had been transferred from an institution to fourteen different nursing homes. They concluded that most patients were functioning at a much higher level than they had exhibited in the hospital. They received better care, were encouraged to help with nursing home tasks (for which some were paid), and in general seemed happier and more satisfied.

Foster Homes

For normal children in the United States, foster home care has replaced the large orphanage. Both the principle of normalization and the assumption that home care provides the best environment for most children support the use of foster homes for retarded children and for adults as well. A nationwide survey (Morrissey, 1966) indicated that half the state institutions had a program of family care, but only five states made extensive use of it at that time. A much larger number are now using family care, which has become more feasible with the provision of other community resources for the retarded. Although foster home care is in most instances much less expensive than institutional care, the method of channeling of funds often prompted social workers, whose budgets for foster care were almost invariably insufficient to meet the need, to seek institutional placement for retarded children. Various budgetary reforms have reduced this factor in recent years but have not eradicated it.

A problem of all foster family projects, for normal as well as for retarded children, has been the insufficient provision of supportive and supervisory services by the sponsoring agencies. Manpower has usually been too limited to provide careful selection of inservice training for foster parents or to make frequent supervisory visits practical. One study which carefully drew up developmental plans for the retarded children, in cooperation with the foster mothers, demonstrated appreciable progress as compared with a standard control group of foster mothers and children (Mamula, 1971).

It is surely not enough simply to place children and hope that good-hearted foster families will be able to provide sufficiently for their special needs. Insufficient recognition has been given to the turmoil a retarded person can bring to even a stable home (Komisar, 1965). The rates of payment for care in most states are very low. Indeed, there seems to exist a basic philosophy that the services of a foster family should be like those of a "real" family, i.e., virtually free. Attraction of adults talented at parenting and professionalization of the role cannot be expected until foster parents are recognized as the skillful and hardworking individuals they must be if foster care is to remain a viable practice.

Support for Own-Home Care

The decision for out-of-home placement at times derives from a shortsighted view of the responsibility of the community to provide only for children whose families have failed. Sometimes rather simple aids would enable a family to function successfully. Direct financial grants to hard-pressed families could pay for baby-sitters, medical care, even a few "frills" which would render the burden of the child's care less overwhelming. In Sweden, parents receive an extra allowance if they have a severely retarded child, whether or not specific financial deficits have been established. Homemakers or home aides for families with severely retarded infants have been tried in the United States (Arnold & Goodman, 1966; Kuralt, 1966). Periodic visits by a public health nurse or an educator can be of enormous benefit to some families in their efforts to cope with child management. Five-day boarding schools for school-age children and young adults, as are used in the Soviet Union (Dolgoborodova & Danilkina, 1968) are another possibility, especially where the mother works and/or where special classes require transportation over great distances. The variations on this theme are potentially broad indeed. We need not continue to be so rigid in drawing the line between in-home and out-of-home services.

CONCLUSION

Wolfensberger (1967) has suggested an orientation for counselors helping parents to make a decision about placement. In addition to a number of specific points to be considered, he proposes the following basic principles:

> **1** An individual's worth and the degree of his humanity is not to be measured primarily by his intellectual endowment, worldly achievement, or number of handicaps.
>
> **2** By its very nature, the procreative contract imposes responsibilities and hardship. Even extraordinary demands may still be within a range of hardship that parents should expect to tolerate as part of parenthood. . . . Appropriateness of placement into public care is, ultimately, a decision to be made by society, not by an individual parent. . . .
>
> **4** If a decision is to be made that has detrimental effects upon the retardate and beneficial effects upon others, then the retardate's loss must be more than only equally offset by the others' gain.

5 If a family seems capable or potentially willing to integrate the retardate into the home, they should be given all possible help and services so as to make their success more likely. . . .

8 Consideration of the retardate's physical welfare cannot be viewed as categorically preempting considerations of his emotional well-being. For instance, a child may be happy at home, but may be accident-prone or lack a certain optimal level of medical attention even to the point of definitely lowering his life expectancy. This situation should not be viewed as categorically less desirable than one where the child may enjoy better health and a higher life expectancy, but will live in a state of emotional deprivation and unhappiness. (p. 373)

These principles constitute a position of advocacy for the rights of the child in placement decisions being made on his behalf. It is to be hoped that with the growth of diverse facilities and flexibility in their use, each family's position will continue to be improved. Parents not only can increasingly count upon skilled services for aid in carrying out their responsibilities and in maintaining their equilibrium while doing so, but need not fear so deeply that a decision made now binds them irrevocably to that path in the future. "Normalization" counts for parents as well as children.

22

The Retarded Adult
in the Community and
The Law and
the Mentally Retarded

Although the major concern of this volume has been the mentally retarded child, it would be shortsighted to ignore the adult into whom the child will grow. Until recently, though, the professional community has behaved as though retarded children grew up into some never-never-land. To be sure, there have been sporadic studies of former institutional residents, and of adults who as children had been identified by the schools as retarded, and most of these studies have been relatively encouraging, but provision of community services has been meager to say the least. It was as though the only retarded citizens worthy of special attention were the children, and as though the only efforts worth making were those during the early formative years. Fortunately, this attitude, like so many others in the field of mental retardation, is undergoing a healthy revision.

The lag in services for mentally retarded adults had a number of sources, among them the "baby boom" of the 1950s which overtaxed resources and an emphasis on institutional solutions to needs for supervision or guidance. The parents' groups which were responsible for so much of the activity of the 1950s and 1960s were at that time composed mainly of members with moderately and severely retarded children of school age and below, and naturally their interest focused upon children's services. These same parents have adult offspring now and their focus has broadened accordingly.

In addition, however, the earlier reticence to provide programs for adults reflected a degree of pessimism based on an awareness of the large numbers of retarded adults to be reached and on discouragement about their possibilities for self-sufficiency in an increasingly technological and competitive society, a society in which urbanization has made life more complex for everyone and had nearly eradicated the loosely woven extended family which could often accommodate a dependent member. The population of the village or small town might amiably tolerate and help to look after the familiar retarded adult who often did useful small tasks. That adult in the big city is lost. No one knows him; he cannot compete for friends; he is lonely and prey to misuse.

Automation in farms and factories has changed, but not eliminated, the possibilities of unskilled and semiskilled employment. Many mildly retarded adults are in fact employed and functioning members of society. Yet, the dull and/or poorly educated segment of the population, including many persons of borderline intelligence, is greatly overrepresented among the ranks of the unemployed. Minimum-wage laws have benefited many in our society, but they have priced out of many work situations some (by no means all) retarded workers, whose actual output may not be worth the legal hourly wage.

As we shall see, however, the situation is by no means as grim as earlier predictions would imply, particularly for the retarded adult who is identified as such and may therefore be protected from the vagaries of the employment market. In fact, there is considerable reason to feel optimistic about the eventual social adjustment of most retarded persons as they mature beyond the early adult years. The moderately or severely retarded person as well, given a favorable living situation and supportive community services, has a far from bleak outlook for a reasonable social adjustment.

ADJUSTMENT OF MODERATELY AND SEVERELY RETARDED INDIVIDUALS IN THE COMMUNITY

The few follow-up studies of adults who as children had IQs under 50 demonstrate that, under certain circumstances, they may be well integrated into their communities. A survey of 1,144 persons who had been considered uneducable in Birmingham, England (City of Birmingham, 1956), found no fewer than 14 percent of the women and 26 percent of the men gainfully employed; only 4 percent were living in institutions. It should be pointed out that in Birmingham at that time, work was plentiful and there was an effective program of aftercare.

Delp and Lorenz (1953) followed seventy-five adults who had attended classes in a special occupational center in St. Paul, Minnesota. The median IQ at the time of follow-up was 36. Twenty-five members of this group were in institutions and nine were dead. Of the forty-one adults living in the community, twenty-seven "fitted in well" and ten were "tolerated." Most of them could dress themselves, choose their own clothing, and help purchase their own things. Five men had regular full-time or part-time jobs and five did odd jobs. Another twenty-five persons did worthwhile tasks around the house; only two required more than a little supervision.

In a large and comprehensive study, Saenger (1957) investigated the adjustment of 520 severely retarded adults who had been randomly selected from the 2,640 pupils formerly enrolled in classes for the trainable retarded in New York City between 1929 and 1955. Admission to classes had been restricted to those able to take care of their bodily needs, and the group is thus not entirely typical of moderately retarded adults in general. Because the study was so carefully executed, it is worthwhile reporting the results in some detail.

Two-thirds of all former pupils were living in the community when they were located, 26 percent were institutionalized, and 8 percent had died. In appearance, about half of the at-home group were alert and lively and about half seemed outspokenly happy and contented. The oldest group (thirty to forty years) tended to be emotionally better adjusted than did the younger subjects, suggesting the beneficial effects of prolonged experience and/or maturation, although selective factors could not be ruled out. When behavioral problems were reported by the parents, they tended to be those which are typical of a young child, such as restlessness, temper tantrums, and obstinate behavior. A few individuals were reported to be shy and clinging. Among those who had been institutionalized, behavior problems were much more common and constituted the chief reason for placement. Further descriptions of the at-home group are provided in Table 22-1.

All in all, this is reassuring evidence that even in a very large city, and even in the absence of supportive community services, many severely handicapped adults led useful and contented lives, satisfying both to themselves and to their families. Even so, as a group they were lonely, alone, and unoccupied much of the time. The older ones, especially, had few friends of their own. Recreational programs and sheltered workshops could have helped to fill much of the void.

More recent studies by Katz (1968) and Kidd (1970) in the United States, and by Gunzberg (1968) in England, after the advent of extensive social, educational, and occupational services, are even more encouraging. As we observed in Chapter 21, community residential facilities could no doubt maintain many other moderately and severely handicapped adults when their families can no longer give them the kind of sheltered environment which Saenger's families had provided.

ADJUSTMENT OF MILDLY RETARDED INDIVIDUALS IN THE COMMUNITY

There are now a wealth of follow-up studies[1] which demonstrate that the overwhelming proportion of mildly retarded children grow into adults who are capable of blending into the society at large. Under favorable conditions, a great many of them become responsible and productive citizens. The preponderance of these mildly retarded individuals have come from disadvantaged social backgrounds, and most investigators have found them to be virtually indistinguishable from others of similar social status. These findings confirm the view that for many retarded persons, the most difficult period of life is that spent in school, where verbal and abstract intellectual skills are accorded so high a premium. For many, the immediate postschool adjustment is also problematic (as it is for many disadvantaged and minority young people), but with continuing maturity, experience, and the acquisition of vocational and other coping skills, the outlook tends to brighten.

Overall Adjustment

As we discussed in Chapter 2, estimates of the prevalence of mild retardation in the postschool population are much lower than those made during the school years. By definition, of course, the adult with low intelligence who is making a satisfactory social adjustment is not retarded. Katz (1968) narrows the group to include *"only those adults with subaverage general intellectual functioning whose adaptive behavior is so impaired*

---

[1] The interested reader is directed to Cobb (1972), who has reviewed many of these studies.

Table 22-1   Descriptions of Former Special-class Pupils Living in New York City

Description	Percent (N = 348)
Interaction with family:	
Active, animated, helpful	27
Limited; converses; interested in surroundings	52
Very limited	10
Obeys commands only	8
Vegetative	2
Helping around house:	
Assumes major responsibility	19
Gives regular help	36
Gives sporadic help	22
Gives ineffectual or no help	22
Takes care of own physical needs completely	88
Can be left at home alone	80
Traveling in community:	
Takes bus, subway	35
Remains in immediate neighborhood	45
Never goes anywhere alone	20
Has own friends (by age of subject):	
17–25 years	62
26–30 years	50
Over 30 years	35
Interest in opposite sex:	
Sexual relations possible	5
Social contact only	21
Interested but no contact	15
None	59
Delinquent behavior:	
Getting lost; running away	4
Sex delinquency	3
Other offenses	4
None	89
Presently working for pay:	
Home or sheltered workshop	4
In the community	23
Not presently working	73

Source: Compiled from Saenger (1957).

that it comes to the attention of their families or social agencies, making it necessary to provide special services for them" (p. 5, author's italics). This approach has considerable practical utility and is in line with current practice.

One important longitudinal investigation, extending over a period of thirty years, followed samples of children who had been identified as retarded or mentally dull in the public schools of Lincoln, Nebraska. Many of them were no longer functionally retarded. In the first stage, Baller (1936) selected 206 former pupils with earlier IQs of 70 and below who had been unable to maintain satisfactory performance in regular

Fig. 22-1 This young man is in a postschool class which will prepare him for community living. *(University of Washington Child Development and Mental Retardation Center)*

classes. Later, Baller (1939) identified another group of 206 former pupils from regular classes (IQs 75-85) and matched them with normal controls (IQs 100-120). After intermediate follow-ups in 1951, 1961, and in 1964, Baller, Charles, and Miller (1967) located 109 of the original "low group," 138 of the "middle group," and 106 of the "high group."

By and large, the low group had made an increasingly satisfactory adjustment. By 1964, only 16 percent needed welfare support; 80 percent of the males and 77 percent of the females were "usually employed." The proportion with jobs had risen steadily over the years, although greater percentages of the middle and high groups attained complete self-sufficiency (93 percent and 96 percent respectively). Marital status was least favorable in the low group, who had "less success in getting, holding, or replacing a mate" (Cobb, 1972, p. 33). The low group had a mortality rate which was about twice the rate for their age group in the general population, a great many of the deaths being accidental.

Significant gains in IQ were noted on a subsample who were retested. Some of these gains may have been due to the fact that in the lower ranges, Wechsler IQs tend to be higher than scores on the Stanford-Binet, the original test. Baller, Charles, and Miller sorted fifty of the low group subjects into five categories:

1 Permanently retarded. In institutions or dependent on their families (seven subjects).

2 Low test scores (mostly 60–69) but "getting along," holding jobs, staying out of trouble, requiring little assistance (seven subjects).

3 Below average or borderline but useful and productive citizens (twenty-three subjects).

4 Average or better. Social adjustment indistinguishable from lower-class members of the general population (twelve subjects).

5 "Victim of circumstance" (originally misclassified) (one subject).

This is a remarkable state of affairs. Even though the low group had fared rather worse than the middle or high group, nearly three-quarters gave little cause for concern of any kind, and only 14 percent were actually dependent by the time they reached their middle years.

In another longitudinal study, Kennedy (1948, 1966) investigated adults who had attained school-age IQs of 45 to 75 and who had been selected from a census of "social inadequates" made some years before. She also studied a control group who had begun first grade with the retarded subjects, had progressed through school at a normal rate, and were of the same sex and race. Of the original groups of 256 retarded and 129 nonretarded subjects, Kennedy in 1960 located 179 of the retarded and 102 of the controls.

In the earlier follow-up Kennedy had found many similarities between the groups in marital and economic adjustment, though significantly more of the retarded adults were in laboring occupations, received lower job ratings from their employers, and failed to save money. On the whole, they were socially adequate and self-supporting. In the 1960 follow-up, Kennedy found considerable upward mobility, as did Baller et al. in Nebraska. By that time, 33 percent of the retarded subjects were skilled workers, though more of the controls had moved into jobs at higher levels and consequently had better incomes. Job stability was high in both groups; home ownership and quality of housing were also similar. Employer ratings revealed generally satisfactory job performance and actually showed less absenteeism and more promptness among the retarded workers, although in such qualities as learning, judgment, and efficiency they did not fare as well as the controls.

Job Success

Most of the studies which have followed retarded citizens into adult life have concentrated upon job success as an important criterion of adjustment. This is altogether reasonable in a society which values economic self-sufficiency. Furthermore, it is a much easier variable to rate than are the more elusive aspects of social adjustment, although "success" at a job may range from sheltered part-time employment to a truly competitive full-time career progression. As we have seen, both the Nebraska and the Connecticut studies found most retarded persons to be vocationally self-sufficient, their situations improving as they grew older. Kidd (1970) found 86 percent of former students in St. Louis, Missouri, EMR classes to be in full-time regular employment, and a twenty-year follow-up of twenty-one EMR males (Fitzgerald, 1968) found the majority to be self-supporting and maintaining an occupational status similar to that of their fathers although almost all had lost the academic skills they had acquired so laboriously in school. Not so optimistic was a study by Keeler (1964) of 116 former students in EMR classes in San Francisco, which found only 40 percent in full- or part-time employment.

Within this limited IQ range, there do not appear to be strong or at least consistent effects of intelligence on employment outcome, although in a broader sample such effects would be clear. Possession of specific work skills likewise appears to be relatively unimportant; most of the jobs retarded adults do obtain do not involve complex tasks.[2] Far more important tend to be qualities of personal adjustment and work habits, including initiative, perseverence, self-confidence, cooperation, cheerfulness, social mixing with other employees, respect for the supervisor, and undertanding and efficiency in work (Domino & McGarty, 1972; Neuhaus, 1967; Sali & Amir, 1971). Language and communication skills (Fiester & Giambra, 1972), production rate (Chafin, 1968), and manual dexterity (Sali & Amir, 1971) are also apparently related to job success. Poor social and occupational adjustment, on the other hand, has been associated with absenteeism and unacceptable social behavior (Research Utilization Branch, 1969) and with anxiety, jealousy, overdependency, poor self-evaluation, hostility, hyperactivity, emotionality, resistance, and failure to follow orders (Zigler & Harter, 1969).

Despite the general current against unnecessary labeling, there is some indication that employers who have purposefully hired retarded individuals tend to retain them even when economic conditions deteriorate (Halpern, 1973). Within the U.S. federal government, a program begun in 1964 to promote employment for the handicapped reported that 93 percent of the more than 6,000 retarded men and women had been considered successful in their jobs, even though two-thirds of them had not been previously employed (President's Committee on Employment of the Handicapped, 1970). Turnover rates compared favorably with other employees at the same grade (U.S. Civil Service Commission, 1972). Similarly, a special three-year training and placement project in Kansas City involved 164 employers in a commitment to hire and train retarded workers. Only 1 of 450 workers left the program during that time, and a follow-up study several months later found 95 percent of them still employed (Posner, 1970). Whether as many of these retarded individuals would independently have found or kept their jobs seems doubtful.

Conformity with the Law

Few facts are really known about mental retardation as it relates to lawbreaking, particularly criminal activity (Allen, 1968), but there is a recent awakening of interest in this question (Brown, 1972). It is, of course, important to distinguish retardation per se from impoverished circumstances and ethnic subgroup membership since the poor and members of some minority groups show an increased incidence of lawbreaking as well as mental retardation (Clark, 1970). Too, there is the possibility that mentally retarded offenders are less adept at escaping detection than are cleverer persons.

To cite one investigation, Jackson (1970) looked into the incidence of delinquency in 264 EMRs, ages eight to eighteen years, and found that almost 30 percent of the boys but none of the girls had delinquent records. This incidence is not very different from that found in many lower socioeconomic groups, nor is the sex difference unexpected. The reader will recall, however, that when retarded girls are discovered in sexual delinquencies, they are frequently sent to institutions. Jackson also found that family neglect and abnormal family structure were related to the incidence of delinquency in the boys.

Both the Nebraska study and the Connecticut study showed increased probabilities of arrests in their retarded groups, compared with the controls, but both also

---

[2] A useful set of job profiles suitable for retarded persons can be found in Peterson, Jones, Flanagan, and Nagin (1964).

showed a very marked decrease in this kind of behavior during adulthood. Most offenses were of a minor sort, and, furthermore, most subjects were law-abiding citizens and certainly no danger to their communities.

When one looks at prison populations, the picture is clouded by the fact that many retarded persons are sent not to prisons but to institutions for the retarded and by the confounding of social class/ethnic status with lawbreaking. Deutsch (Sternlicht & Deutsch, 1972) found that the mean IQ of a cross section of adult male inmates in Pennsylvania prisons was at or only slightly below the norm for the population at large. Yet in Allen's (1968) survey of correctional institutions housing approximately 200,000 offenders, nearly one in ten had IQs below 70. Among the retarded group, 72 percent had committed crimes against the person, including 36 percent imprisoned for homicide. Boslow and Kandel (1965) likewise found that retarded offenders had a higher proportion of sexual assaults and crimes than did the nonretarded. Even so, this of course represents a tiny fraction of the retarded population.

Intelligence

There is some evidence that not only personal-social adjustment but measured intelligence tends to improve in the mildly retarded after the school years. Retests of members of the low group in the Nebraska study by Charles (1953) and Baller et al. (1967) showed a rise from a mean of 53.0 on the 1916 Stanford-Binet administered in 1935 to a mean of 75.3 in 1950 and again to a mean of 81.6 in 1961, the latter two tests being the Wechsler-Bellevue. Some, but not all, of the initial rise may be accounted for by differences in the two scales. Chorus (1968) compared test scores of 275 Dutch adults ages twenty-five to twenty-six with scores obtained ten years earlier. Increments in IQ of 10 points or more were found in 100 subjects; decrements of the same magnitude were shown by only 48; scores of the rest changed less than 10 points. On the other hand, Rosen, Floor and Baxter (1974), who retested fifty EMRs approximately three years after discharge from an institution found an insignificant mean increment of less than 2 points on the Wechsler Adult Intelligence Scale with no change at all in academic performance on the Metropolitan Achievement Test. Shifting the focus to TMR adults, Saenger (1967) found that most of the employed adults demonstrated a gain of more than 5 points on retest, but the majority of the unemployed scored more than 5 points lower than they had during their school years, suggesting differences between the groups in stimulation and/or self-esteem. At this level, IQs tend to be quite stable. (See Chapter 17.)

Marriage

Although a relatively large number of mildly retarded adults do marry and apparently make a reasonable marital adjustment, they fare somewhat less well than comparable nonretarded groups, as the Nebraska and Connecticut studies revealed. Marriage is considerably more common for retarded women than retarded men. Retarded individuals tend to marry persons socially and intellectually more advanced than themselves, though the differences between husband and wife generally are not extreme (Edgerton, 1967; Scally, 1973).

Mattinson (1973) studied thirty-six British couples who had married following their release from an institution for the mentally retarded. Of the thirty-six marriages, only four were not being maintained. Although the couples varied greatly in social success and marital happiness, Mattinson judged that twenty-five marriages were af-

fectionate, that the partners both felt "better married than single." Most couples utilized their complementary skills. As one wife described it, "He doos the reading, and
I doos the writing" (p. 181). One husband told the investigator, "[I] cooked a chicken
last Sunday, roast potatoes, batter pudding . . . she ain't too good for cooking. She
never learned, I don't think" (p. 182). About these individuals, Mattinson concluded
that "paired, many of them were able to reinforce each other's strengths and established marriages which, in the light of what had happened to them previously, were no
more, no less, foolish than many others in the community, and which gave them
considerable satisfaction" (p. 185).

The Parental Role

Children are an added burden to a retarded couple, both economically and psychologically, and relatively few retarded parents are able to provide a really optimal
childrearing environment. Scally (1973), in Northern Ireland, found that nearly two-
thirds of the retarded mothers, many of them single, needed help with child care or
even removal of the child from the home. The birthrate among retarded individuals is
relatively low, however, primarily because so many remain unmarried and/or childless
(Reed & Anderson, 1973; Scally, 1973).

Prior to beginning an intensive educational program with infants of high-risk
families, Heber et al. (1973) surveyed the most deprived residential area in the city of
Milwaukee. They administered the Peabody Picture Vocabulary Test to all the mothers, fathers, and children over the age of two in 500 families with newborn infants.
There was striking congruence in the scores of the parents. (See Chapter 7.) When the
IQs of the forty older children of mothers with IQs of 80 and above were tallied, they
showed an irregular mean progression with age, remaining fairly constant in the 90-95
range. The forty-eight older children whose mothers scored below 80 showed a very
striking decline, however, from a mean of 95 for those below age three, to a mean of
60-65 for those age fourteen. "In other words, the generally acknowledged statement
that slum-dwelling children score lower on intelligence tests as they became older held
true only for the offspring of mothers whose IQs were below 80" (p. 5).

In a very large intergenerational study, Higgins, Reed, and Reed (1962) studied
7,778 children according to the intellectual status of their parents. Among the 7,035
children with neither parent retarded, the mean IQ was 107; of those 654 children with
one retarded parent, the mean IQ was 90; the 89 children with two retarded parents
attained a mean IQ of only 74. The risk of retardation was somewhat higher when the
retarded parent was the mother (Reed & Anderson, 1973), consistent with her more
important contribution to the child's upbringing. Even in children of normal intelligence born to retarded parents, investigators have found a high rate of academic
retardation and behavioral problems (Kennedy, 1966; Kohler, Brisson, & Charassin,
1970). Although the overall reproductive rate is relatively low among retarded individuals, then, the risk of retardation and poor achievement is relatively high among their
children.

These data all suggest that although there is no reason as a rule why a retarded
individual should be discouraged from marriage, parenthood is more problematic.
Both in terms of the extra demands with which the retarded parent may be unable to
cope, and even more cogently, in terms of the outlook for the children, responsible
professionals and family members need to help retarded adults think through the
situation very carefully. Of course, there are some individuals living in propitious

circumstances who make adequate parents. With proper training and sufficient resources, retarded women have much to give to a young child (Skeels, 1966). Limited verbal and intellectual capacities, inconsistencies born of coping with adverse circumstances and of limited foresight, and other handicaps are, however, likely to interfere with optimal childrearing, especially as the children grow older.

Voluntary sterilization and temporary contraceptive measures are now obtainable everywhere in the United States, although many retarded persons are unaware of their availability. Given time and help in understanding the long-range implications of parenthood, it is likely that most would opt to have no children. Without such help, however, Edgerton (1967) and Andron and Sturm (1973) found that most retarded adults say they do want children, though they give little thought to the consequences. Involuntary sterilization often has unacceptable ethical and legal implications (see end of chapter), but fortunately, there is hardly ever now the need to resort to such Draconian measures (LaVeck & de la Cruz, 1973).

PROGNOSIS FOR INDIVIDUALS RELEASED FROM INSTITUTIONS

In view of the changing roles of institutions and the expansion of other kinds of residential facilities, studies of persons released from institutions in the past predict little about the future. That is just as well, for as reviewers Cobb (1972), Eagle (1967), and Windle (1962) point out, the many existing studies reveal little aside from the fact that a high proportion of former residents, most of them among the institutional minority who are mildly retarded, do manage to stay in the community.

A sensitive account (Edgerton, 1967) of the daily lives of forty-eight former residents (IQs 47-85) reveals the important role of self-esteem in the individual's adjustment (see Chapter 9). Other persons tended to detect their retardation and to react negatively. Difficulties with space, time, and numbers intruded into their social interactions as well as their workaday affairs. These individuals experienced a great deal of loneliness and very little genuine social interaction. Most of them, however, found one or more benefactors on whom they could depend and without whose help they probably could not have successfully managed the complexities of independent living.

COMMUNITY SERVICES TO MEET THE NEEDS OF ADULTS[3]

Recent years have witnessed growth on a broad front of the kinds of community services which can enable retarded adults to enjoy a quality of life considerably better than the lonely and/or marginal adjustment so many have endured. As Edgerton (1967) discovered, almost without exception they need help in maintaining a reasonably satisfying adjustment, but finding such support is too often left to luck and coincidence. Provision of a broad variety of programs and personnel explicitly able to offer help seems essential.

Financial Assistance

Few people are aware of the amount of government assistance which is available to many retarded individuals. In fiscal year 1973, for example, income maintenance pay-

---

[3] The interested reader is referred to E. Katz (1968) for a comprehensive description of appropriate services.

ments accounted for approximately 39 percent of all U.S. government spending in behalf of the mentally retarded, or $341 million of a total of $879 million (Office of Mental Retardation Coordination [OMRC], 1972a). This does not include assistance under welfare programs for which the individuals may qualify for reasons other than their mental retardation.

An important resource for children of disabled, retired, or deceased parents is the Social Security Childhood Disability Allowance. Retarded offspring, whatever their ages, continue in the status of minors for the purposes of this program. They are due the same support as are normal children under the age of eighteen, including payments to mothers if they remain in their care. More than half the recipients of this allowance are retarded (OMRC, 1972b).

A variety of other assistance programs are also available. Under the Aid to the Permanently and Totally Disabled (APTD), approximately 20 percent of the recipients are diagnosed as retarded (OMRC, 1972b). Retarded persons are also eligible for Aid to the Blind and for Old-Age Assistance, as is everyone else who is blind or elderly. Mothers and children in financial need receive support under the program of Aid to Families with Dependent Children (AFDC). At least 5 percent of the children in this program are known to be retarded, and presumably mental retardation contributes to the lack of self-sufficiency of many of the mothers.

Vocational Rehabilitation and Sheltered Workshops[4]

A large part of one's status and self-image revolves around one's occupation, and of course for the common good, a contributing member of society is far preferable to a dependent one. A great deal of activity, consequently, revolves around preparing retarded individuals for gainful employment (see Chapter 15), finding them jobs, and if necessary providing continued guidance and/or sheltered working situations. For most retarded persons, this process begins during the schoolyears with some form of vocational preparation, often including a work-study schedule. Many school systems offer such opportunities to age twenty-one, but unfortunately only a small proportion of those eligible take advantage of the extended experience.

Government-supported vocational rehabilitation has grown rapidly. By 1971, state vocational rehabilitation agencies were annually serving about 35,700 retarded persons a year, approximately 12 percent of their total clientele. There had been increments every year since 1945, when a mere 0.3 percent of the clients had been retarded (OMRC, 1972b).

Vocational rehabilitation efforts vary according to the needs of the retarded client (Morgenstern & Michal-Smith, 1973). For some, a simplified assessment and brief counseling enable the individual to make the leap into the world of work. Others need more prolonged counseling, active help in finding a job, and continued contact among counselor, employee, and employer until stability is assured. Some need prevocational training and others temporarily need a sheltered situation in which they can practice appropriate job-related behavior before entering the competitive market.

For others, particularly those with unusual behavior, severe physical handicaps, and/or moderate to severe retardation, a sheltered workshop may provide a permanent and productive placement. There are few retarded adults who, given the right circumstances, cannot accomplish economically useful work. In fact, a wide discrepancy exists between what most retarded individuals actually do, vocationally, and what

---

[4] Conley (1973) discussed in detail the cost-benefit ratios of various rehabilitative services in relation to lifetime expected earnings of retarded workers.

Fig. 22-2 A sheltered workshop provides a worthwhile experience for this severely retarded adult. *(W. Barclay)*

they are both qualitatively and quantitatively capable of doing. (See Chapter 15.) Even very complex operations can be broken down into a series of simple tasks to be accomplished by a group working as a production line. The establishment of sheltered workshops, largely at the instigation of parents' groups but now taken over by numerous nonprofit and local organizations, has been a very positive phenomenon, but many more are needed. Participation in productive work, social interaction with other retarded and nonretarded employees, contacts with supervisory staff, and one's own paycheck all can play a potentially normalizing and salutory role.

Day Care and Activity Centers

Severely handicapped individuals sometimes cannot function even at the level of the usual sheltered workshop, but most of these individuals, too, can profit from out-of-home experience for part of the day. Many of those who live at home have working parents and must spend long, idle hours by themselves. Parents' groups have led the way in establishing centers providing day-care and simple training activities for this segment of the population. For a description of one lively and comprehensive program, see Olechnowicz (1973a).

Recreational and Social Activities

Recreational and social activities are lacking in the lives of many retarded adults, even those who function quite independently. Limited budgets, rejection by nonretarded individuals, restricted opportunities for social contacts, self-imposed isolation because of low self-esteem, and lack of skill in the use of leisure time, all reduce recreational participation and social relationships. Parents' groups, churches, scout troops, and other community organizations have undertaken recreational projects, but the supply is far from meeting the potential demand.

Services to the Elderly

An almost completely neglected group of retarded individuals is the elderly (Jones, 1972). Even those who have managed to get by with suitable employment and a reasonable adaptation during their productive years tend to experience marked deprivation in old age. Frequently they have no children, no pensions, and very low Social Security coverage because of their limited earnings. The age of retirement for nonretarded individuals is a time of crisis, and this is no less true of the retarded, who may indeed have fewer emotional and social resources to call upon. With very few exceptions have we even begun to consider these problems, much less do anything about them.

In summary, then, we can be optimistic that most retarded adults will "make it" in our society, in one way or another, but community services, now on the upswing, have a great deal to contribute. To the extent that they enable retarded individuals to become truly integrated citizens, as opposed to marginal hangers-on, the human benefits and economic returns can be enormous.

THE LAW AND THE MENTALLY RETARDED

During the 1960s, as an outgrowth of the movement to establish civil rights and equal justice under the law for all citizens, attention began to turn toward the plight of children and the mentally retarded. Many legal practices came to be seen in a new light. For example, court proceedings designed originally to maintain anonymity for juvenile and retarded offenders and to permit judges broad discretion in determining their best interests now could be seen as denying due process of law. "Offenses" such as running away, not viewed as criminal under adult law, could place a young or retarded individual in jeopardy.

Similarly, a great many other practices which had grown out of concern for the welfare of the mentally retarded were now seen as arbitrary, victimizing, and even inhumane (Allen, 1970). Extensive reexaminations of the legal system were undertaken in an effort to see that the basic rights of retarded children were respected. One of the first of these was the Report of the Task Force on Law of the President's Panel on Mental Retardation (Bazelon & Boggs, 1963), and many professional and voluntary groups have since given consideration to the rights of the mentally handicapped (e.g., AAMD, 1973a). In several areas, state and federal laws are being revised through legislation and/or court decisions.

The Right to Participate in Normal Activities

A number of state laws exclude retarded persons from participation in activities accessible to others. Most of these exclusions are gratuitous and inherently unfair.

Privacy, Dignity, and Liberty   Like other persons, retarded citizens should be accorded the right to respect and to as little interference as possible within the context of a supportive milieu. Explicitly, the individual should be guaranteed the rights to freedom of choice within his capacity to make decisions, to live in the least restrictive appropriate environment, to speak openly and fully, to practice a religion (or none at all), and to associate with peers (AAMD, 1973a).

Licenses and Contracts Where the determination of competence requires an examination, as in obtaining a driver's license, it is unnecessary to stipulate that the applicant not be retarded. Reasonable limitations on the right to enter independently into long-term major contracts such as bank loans can be judged by the earning power and credit history of the individual, as they would be for any other adult. Although retarded persons often need guidance to avoid being exploited, in this respect they are not very different from other naive consumers vulnerable to excessive advertising claims or fast-talking salesmen, so that the logical remedy is not special but general legislation for consumer protection.

The Right to Engage in Loving Relationships, Including Sexual Activity As human beings entitled to as normal a life as possible, mentally retarded citizens have the rights to engage in loving relationships and to sexual expression according to the same rules that govern other citizens. With control of the procreative consequences of sexual activity, social attitudes toward sexual practices in the United States among nonretarded persons have become considerably more permissive. The retarded, however, continue to live under rules and restrictions in residential facilities which are decidedly Victorian and to be judged by the community according to equally puritanical codes. Legal sanctions are seldom today applied to almost any form of sexual activity in private between consenting nonretarded adults, with the exception of prostitution. They are sometimes still applied to retarded individuals, however, and it is widely felt that prohibitions against homosexual or heterosexual activity are the responsibility of those who care for them. Yet, among professionals at least, "For the past several years there has been an increasing realization that the mentally retarded have the right . . . to develop and nurture a human relationship including sexual expression" (de la Cruz & LaVeck, 1973, p. xvi). There is little justification for a continuing double standard. The need for honest and explicit sexual education has become apparent, and a number of teaching programs are being developed (Bass, 1973).

Marriage A 1972 survey by Krischef found laws in at least a quarter of the states prohibiting marriage of retarded individuals. As we have seen, retardation need not be a barrier to successful marriage, and in fact the laws are seldom enforced. Their very existence, however, is an affront to the dignity of retarded citizens.

Sterilization and the Right to Bear Children Although questions of marriage and of childbearing are often intertwined, this need not and probably should not be the case. Considering the availability of voluntary sterilization, contraceptive measures, and early abortions, it is now possible to separate these questions much more easily than in the past. Although we have taken the position earlier that most retarded adults should be discouraged from having children, or at least from having large families, there of course will be exceptions to this rule of thumb. It is a matter probably best handled outside the law, through education and services ensuring that parenthood can be a matter of informed choice rather than of unplanned happenstance.

A proposed statement by the American Association on Mental Deficiency (1974) is worthy of note.

> Mentally retarded persons have the same basic rights as other citizens. Among these rights are the rights . . . to marry, to engage in sexual activity, to have children and to control one's own fertility by any legal means available. Since sterilization is a method of contraception available to most North American adults, this option should be open to most retarded citizens as well.
>
> However, recent reports on cases involving the sterilization of mentally retarded individuals without even the most elementary legal and procedural safeguards raise serious questions concerning the adequacy of current efforts to protect the human and constitutional rights of such citizens. Indications that retarded persons have been involuntarily rendered incapable of procreation because of presumed social irresponsibility, real or supposed genetic defects, or as a *quid pro quo* for release from an institution or receipt of financial assistance and social services are deeply disturbing, to say the least (p. 59).

Sterilization was a rather popular practice in the 1930s, as the result of the eugenics scare, and was often made a condition of parole from an institution (Goldstein, 1964). As of 1972, almost half the states had statutes permitting involuntary sterilization (Krischef, 1972), although the practice had been much reduced. This irreversible procedure is inconsistent with a view of mental retardation as a symptom which can change from time to time, and it sometimes appears later to have been a sad mistake (Tarjan, 1973). As the AAMD statement points out, abuses of this law in some cases have been flagrant and call into serious question the sterilization laws as presently formulated.

One unsettled question, however, has arisen very recently. The right to determine one's procreativity is a protected right, which cannot be waived by anyone but the individual himself, just as a parent or guardian cannot waive the right of a dependent person to be protected from self-incrimination. On the other hand, it is also held that, by reason of his limited intelligence, a retarded individual cannot give "informed consent" to sterilization or abortion procedures. An untenable, contradictory situation has thus been created, which essentially denies to retarded individuals their rights to such procedures. Surely this situation will soon be resolved.

Adoption   Some state laws make it difficult even for informed and willing prospective parents to adopt a retarded child. In some states, parents who unwittingly adopt a retarded child may seek annulment of the adoption as much as five years later. As Wolfensberger (1967) has suggested, to protect the rights of the child it is only fitting that adoptive parents be willing to take the same chances that natural parents do, especially after accepting a child whose retardation was not immediately apparent.

Guardianship

The appointment of a guardian for a child without parents, or for others incapable of acting effectively in their own behalf, is a time-honored practice which antedates the codification of formal laws (Martin, 1971). Usually the guardian is a member of the family, including a parent of a retarded person who has reached the age of majority and would otherwise no longer be under parental jurisdiction. Current concerns center around the notion of partial guardianship for retarded adults who can conduct their own day-to-day affairs but are unlikely to be able to handle major decisions and/or the management of their larger financial interests, such as a sizeable inheritance.

> Where legal guardianship of any kind is required, it should be carefully adapted to the specific requirements of the case. For some, of course, a comprehensive guardianship will be needed. But we urge that, as far as possible, mentally retarded adults be allowed freedom—even freedom to make their own mistakes. We suggest the development of limited guardianship of the adult person, with the scope of the guardianship specified in the judicial order. (Bazelon & Boggs, 1963, p. 25)

An innovative trusteeship program in England has been established by the National Society for Mentally Handicapped Children. It provides for the retarded through a trust fund of 500 pounds sterling donated by the parents, to take effect after the parents' deaths, and thereby guarantees a lifelong interest by the Society in the individual's well-being. In the United States, a few similar trusts, such as the Foundation for the Handicapped in the State of Washington, exist. Parents often make provision for a personal trust and guardianship to assure the child's support after their deaths. Some states have established protective services within appropriate state agencies.

Care and Custody

The authority to overcome the autonomy of the retarded adult in order to determine placement in a residential facility is a major issue. All fifty states have statutes providing for the commitment of retarded persons to state facilities, but only a minority likewise have statutes protecting the individual rights of those so committed (Newman, 1967). Retarded persons are frequently committed to institutions because of rather minor infractions of the law, but for many this means long-term placement without recourse to review (Kugel, Trembath & Sagar, 1968). In general, too, there has been a confounding of legal decisions about residential care with a determination of legal competency, and by this means many individuals have been denied control over their own affairs and eventual assumption of self-determination (Allen, Ferster & Weihofen, 1968).

Rights of Institutionalized Retarded Children

Within institutions, it is now clear that many rights are habitually violated. Among these are, for example:

> *The right to treatment and to education* (Mental Health Law Project, 1973)
> *The right to fair compensation for labor* (Mental Health Law Project, 1973; AAMD, 1973b)
> *The right to live in the least restrictive appropriate environment* (AAMD, 1973a)
> *The right to privacy and to protection against exploitation, demeaning treatment or abuse* (AAMD, 1973a)

As the doors of institutions have been opened to reveal sometimes frightful living conditions, enforced "peonage" of residents who furnish much of the unskilled maintenance and caretaking labor, and a lack of educational or training programs for the majority of residents, the public outcry has led to legal activity to enjoin such practices and to ameliorate the conditions. The parameters of the right to treatment and/or education are yet to be worked out in this context, but it seems clear that there will be considerable legal pressure to upgrade the developmental programs provided and to ensure that simple custodial containment no longer is deemed sufficient "treatment." Few people object to the fact that residents work within the institution. They do object, however, to the low or nonexistent pay, the frequently excessive hours, the lack of focus on the development of the retarded workers, and the occasional retention of a good worker who might be able to adapt effectively in a community. There are objections, too, to the quality of care rendered by some residents who are not prevented from engaging in hurried, harsh, and routinized care of persons younger and/or more severely handicapped than themselves.

The Rights to Education and Appropriate School Placement

These matters were discussed at length in Chapter 18 and constitute an active forefront in the establishment of the basic rights of retarded persons.

The Right to Appropriate Psychological Assessment[5]

Although educational placement provides the major occasion for psychological assessment and labeling (Mercer, 1973), these processes are by no means restricted to the schools. In view of the strong and long-lasting influence which professional appraisal may exert in the life of the child or adult, it is essential that the rights of the individual be safeguarded in such situations. Mercer (1974) lists several matters related to this issue, among them children's rights "to be evaluated within a culturally appropriate normative framework . . . to be assessed as multidimensional, many-faceted human beings . . . to be free of stigmatizing labels and . . . to cultural identity and respect" (p. 132). Individuals from ethnic minorities are particularly likely to be assessed by inappropriate instruments and by inappropriate standards. There is, too, a marked tendency to overlook adequate social behavior and to attach a label on the basis of IQ alone, violating a basic aspect of the definition of mental retardation.

It is difficult to reduce these matters to simple codes. How, for example, is one to avoid labeling individuals (no matter what the term employed) who do in fact need special assistance in school, even though their behavior outside of school may be quite adequate? How is one to justify an application for a special program of financial or vocational assistance? For individuals appropriately labeled mildly retarded at one point in their lives but not at another, how is one to prevent the evidence of the previous status from influencing admission to a training program or biasing a future employer who asks for evidence of successful completion of an academic high school program? Assumptions about the "incurability" of mental retardation may haunt the adult for the rest of his life. We would add to Mercer's list of rights, then, the right to be seen in the light of one's current status and competence, not one's history.

Rights of the Retarded under Criminal Law

The determination of competence plays an important role in establishing responsibility for criminal acts. Mental retardation is seen as a factor diminishing the ability to resist pressure to confess, and the decision of competence to stand trial, i.e., to participate in an adequate defense. There are complex questions centering, in addition, on

---

[5] Related issues are discussed in Chap. 2, 16, 17 and 18.

the right of the accused to be protected from incarceration when he is deemed incompetent to stand trial, especially when, if he had been tried, he probably would have been acquitted (Bazelon & Boggs, 1963).

The Right to Life

Considerable discussion has been given of late to the concept of euthanasia, particularly questions pertaining to advanced medical technology capable of keeping alive babies who are seriously deformed or damaged at birth. Many physicians feel that extraordinary lifesaving procedures may be withheld in some cases in which an infant is obviously doomed to gross retardation, which they see as an essentially meaningless existence, full of suffering. Indeed, an unknown but significant number probably act in accordance with this view. Others disagree, believing that it is dangerous to tamper with the most basic value of Western society, that human life is at all costs to be preserved.

> It is the position of the American Association on Mental Deficiency that the existence of mental retardation is no justification for the terminating of the life of any human being or for permitting such a life to be terminated either directly or through the withholding of life sustaining procedures (AAMD, 1973c).

We appreciate the excruciating dilemma this situation presents and can offer no easy solutions.

Summary

A wholesale review of the laws as they apply to retarded citizens is currently under way. Abuses have been many, although often those responsible have felt that they were acting in the best interests of those in their care. Inhumane treatment in institutions—or, rather, what amounts to no treatment at all—has been the inevitable result of inadequate funding by state legislatures beset by demands from their constituents for programs of many other kinds, and also from the fact that the constituency of the retarded has been unable to speak directly for itself. Equal protection under the law will, we hope, become a reality; there are already many signs of progress. But unless nonretarded citizens remain vigilant, abuses will continue, and retarded individuals will remain, in the eyes of many, something less than citizens deserving of the rights due all members our society.

REFERENCES

Abel, T. M., & Kinder, E. F. *The subnormal adolescent girl.* New York: Columbia University Press, 1942. Excerpts in Chap. 8 reprinted with the permission of the publisher.

Achenbach, T. M. Comparison of Stanford-Binet performance of nonretarded and retarded persons matched for MA and sex. *American Journal of Mental Deficiency,* 1970, **74,** 488-494.

Adams, J., McIntosh, E. I., & Weade, B. L. Ethnic background, measured intelligence, and adaptive behavior scores in mentally retarded children. *American Journal of Mental Deficiency,* 1973, **78,** 1-6.

Adelson, E., & Fraiberg, S. Gross motor development in infants blind from birth. *Child Development,* 1974, **45,** 114-126.

Aebli, H. *Didactique psychologique: Application à la didactique de la psychologie de Jean Piaget.* Neuchâtel, Switzerland: Delachaux et Niestlé, 1951.

Alabiso, F. Inhibitory functions of attention in reducing hyperactive behavior. *American Journal of Mental Deficiency,* 1972, **77,** 259-282.

Albizu-Miranda, C., & Stanton, H. R. The socioeconomics of mental retardation. In G. A. Jervis (Ed.), *Expanding concepts in mental retardation.* Springfield, Ill.: Charles C Thomas, 1968.

Aldrich, R. A., Holliday, A. R., Colwell, D. G., Jr., Johnson, B. J., Smith, E. M., & Sharpley, R. P. The mental retardation service delivery system project: A survey of mental retardation service usage and needs among families with retarded children in selected areas of Washington State. *Research Report,* 1971, **17**, No. 3.

Alexander, D., Ehrhardt, A. A., & Money J. Defective figure drawing, geometric and human in Turner's syndrome. *Journal of Nervous and Mental Disorders,* 1966, **142,** 161–167.

Alexander, D., & Money, J. Reading ability, object constancy, and Turner's syndrome. *Perceptual and Motor Skills,* 1965, **20**, 981–984.

Allan, L. D., Ferguson-Smith, M. A., Donald, I., Sweet, E. M., & Gibson, A. A. M. Amniotic-fluid alpha-feto-protein in the antenatal diagnosis of spina bifida. *Lancet,* 1973, **2**, 522–525.

Allen, G. Patterns of discovery in the genetics of mental deficiency. *American Journal of Mental Deficiency,* 1958, **62**, 840–849.

Allen, G., & Kallmann, F. J. Frequency and types of mental retardation in twins. *American Journal of Human Genetics,* 1955, **7**, 15–20.

Allen, M. K. Persistent factors leading to application for admission to a residential institution. *Mental Retardation,* 1972, **10**(4), 25–28.

Allen, R. C. The retarded offender: Unrecognized in court and untreated in prison. *Federal Probation,* 1968, **32**(3), 22–27.

Allen, R. C. Law and the mentally retarded. In F. J. Menolascino (Ed.), *Psychiatric approaches to mental retardation.* New York: Basic Books, 1970.

Allen, R. C., Ferster, E. Z., & Weihofen, H. *Mental impairment and legal incompetency.* Englewood Cliffs, N.J.: Prentice-Hall, 1968.

Alley, G. R., & Snider, B. Comparative perceptual motor performance of Negro and white young mental retardates. *Developmental Psychology,* 1970, **2**, 100–114.

Alper, A. E., & Horne, B. M. IQ changes of institutionalized mental defectives over two decades. *American Journal of Mental Deficiency,* 1959, **64**, 472–475.

Alpern, G. D., & Boll, T. J. *Developmental profile.* Indianapolis: Psychological Development Publications, 1972.

Altman, R., Talkington, L. W., & Cleland, C. C. Relative effectiveness of modeling and verbal instructions on severe retardates' gross motor performance. *Psychological Reports,* 1972, **31**, 695–698.

Amaria, R. P., Biron, L. S., & Leith, G. O. M. Individual versus co-operative learning. *Educational Research,* 1969, **11**, 95–103.

American Association on Mental Deficiency. Rights of mentally retarded persons. *Mental Retardation,* 1973, **11**(5), 56–58. (a)

American Association on Mental Deficiency. Guidelines for work by residents in public and private institutions for the mentally retarded. *Mental Retardation,* 1973, **11**(5), 59–62. (b)

American Association on Mental Deficiency. The right to life. *Mental Retardation,* 1973, **11**(6), 66. (c) Excerpt in Chap. 22 reprinted with the permission of the AAMD.

American Association on Mental Deficiency. Sterilization of persons who are mentally retarded: A statement. *Mental Retardation,* 1974, **12**(2), 59–60. Excerpt in Chap. 22 reprinted with permission of the AAMD.

American Psychiatric Association. *Diagnostic and statistical manual of mental disorders* (2d ed.) Washington, D.C.: American Psychiatric Association, 1968.

Ames, L. B. A low intelligence quotient often not recognized as the chief cause of many learning difficulties. *Journal of Learning Disabilities,* 1968, **1**, 735–739.

Anastasi, A. Heredity, environment, and the question "how?" *Psychological Review,* 1958, **65**, 197–208.

Anatov, A. N. Children born during the siege of Leningrad in 1942. *Journal of Pediatrics,* 1947, **30**, 250.

Anderson, J. E. The prediction of terminal intelligence from infant and preschool tests. *Yearbook of the National Society for the Study of Education,* 1940, **39**(1), 385-403.

Anderson, S., & Messick, S. Social competency in young children. *Developmental Psychology,* 1974, **10**, 282-293.

Anderson, V. E., Siegel, F. S., Tellegen, A., & Fisch, R. O. Manual dexterity in phenylketonuric children. *Perceptual and Motor Skills,* 1968, **26**, 827-834.

Andron, L., & Sturm, M. C. Is "I do" in the repertoire of the retarded? *Mental Retardation,* 1973, **11**(1), 31-34.

Angle, C. R., McIntire, M. S., & Meile, R. L. Neurologic sequelae of poisoning in children. *Journal of Pediatrics,* 1968, **73**, 531.

Apgar, V. Drugs in pregnancy. *American Journal of Nursing,* 1965, **65**(3), 104-105.

Apgar, V., Holaday, D. A., James, L. S., Berrien, C., & Weisbrot, I. M. Evaluation of the newborn infant: Second report. *Journal of the American Medical Association,* 1958, **168**, 1985-1988.

Apgar, V., & James, L. S. Further observations on the newborn scoring system. *American Journal of Diseases of Children,* 1962, **104**, 419-428.

Arnold, I. L., & Goodman, L. Homemaker services to families with young retarded children. *Children,* 1966, **13**, 149-152.

Aronson, S. M., & Volk, B. W. Genetic and demographic considerations concerning Tay-Sachs disease. In S. M. Aronson & B. W. Volk (Eds.), *Cerebral sphingolipidoses.* New York: Academic Press, 1962.

Arrighi, F. E., & Hsu, T. C. Localization of heterochromatin in human chromosomes. *Cytogenetics,* 1971, **10**, 81-86.

Arthur, G. A. *Point Scale of Performance Tests: Revised Form II. Manual for administering and scoring the tests.* New York: Psychological Corporation, 1947.

Asher, P., & Schonell, F. E. A survey of 400 cases of cerebral palsy in childhood. *Archives of Diseases of Childhood,* 1950, **52**, 360.

Atkinson, R. C., & Shiffrin, R. M. Human memory: A proposed system and its control processes. In K. W. Spence and J. T. Spence (Eds.), *The psychology of learning and motivation: Advances in research and theory* (Vol. 2). New York: Academic Press, 1968.

Ausman, J. O., & Gaddy, M. R. Reinforcement training for echolalia: Developing a repertoire of appropriate verbal responses in an echolalic girl. *Mental Retardation,* 1974, **12**(1), 20-21.

Axline, V. M. Some observations on play therapy. *Journal of Consulting Psychology,* 1948, **12**, 209-216.

Ayers, A. J. *Southern California Sensory Integration Tests.* Los Angeles: Western Psychological Services, 1972.

Azrin, N. H., Bugle, C., & O'Brien, F. Behavioral engineering: Two apparatuses for toilet training retarded children. *Journal of Applied Behavior Analysis,* 1971, **4**, 249-253.

Azrin, N. H., & Foxx, R. M. A rapid method of toilet training the institutionalized retarded. *Journal of Applied Behavior Analysis,* 1971, **4**, 89-99.

Babson, S. G., & Phillips, D. S. Growth and development of twins dissimilar in size at birth. *New England Journal of Medicine,* 1973, **289**, 937-940.

Bacher, J. H. The effect of special class placement on the self-concept, social adjustment, and reading growth of slow learners. *Dissertation Abstracts,* 1965, **25**(12), 7071.

Badt, M. I. Levels of abstraction in vocabulary definitions of mentally retarded school children. *American Journal of Mental Deficiency,* 1958, **63**, 241–246.

Baer, D. M. A case of the selective reinforcement of punishment. In C. Neuringer & J. L. Michael (Eds.), *Behavior modification in clinical psychology.* New York: Appleton-Century-Crofts, 1970.

Bailey, C. J., & Windle, W. F. Neurological, psychological, and neurohistological defects following asphyxia neonatorum in the guinea pig. *Experimental Neurology,* 1959, **1**, 467–482.

Baird, D., & Scott, E. M. Intelligence and childbearing. *Eugenics Review,* 1953, **45**, 139–154.

Baker, D., Telfer, M. A., Richardson, C. E., & Clark, G. R. Chromosome errors in men with antisocial behavior. *Journal of the American Medical Association,* 1970, **214**, 869–878.

Bakwin, H., & Bakwin, R. M. *Clinical management of behavioral disorders in children.* Philadelphia: Saunders, 1966.

Balla, D. A., Butterfield, E. C., & Zigler, E. Effects of institutionalization on retarded children: A longitudinal cross-institutional investigation. *American Journal of Mental Deficiency,* 1974, **78**, 530–549.

Balla, D., Styfco, S. J., & Zigler, E. Use of the opposition concept and outerdirectedness in intellectually average, familial retarded, and organically retarded children. *American Journal of Mental Deficiency,* 1971, **75**, 663–680.

Baller, W. R. A study of the present social status of a group of adults who, when they were in elementary schools, were classified as mentally deficient. *Genetic Psychology Monographs,* 1936, **18**, 165–244.

Baller, W. R. A study of the behavior records of adults who, when they were in school, were judged to be dull in mental ability. *Journal of Genetic Psychology,* 1939, **55**, 365–379.

Baller, W. R., Charles, D. C., & Miller, E. L. Mid-life attainment of the mentally retarded. *Genetic Psychology Monographs,* 1967, **75**, 235–329.

Balthazar, E. E. *Balthazar Scales of Adaptive Behavior, Section I: The scales of functional independence (BSAB-I).* Champaign, Ill.: Research Press, 1971.

Balthazar, E. E., Roseen, D. L., & English, G. E. *The Central Wisconsin Colony Scales of Adaptive Behavior: The Ambulant Battery.* Madison: Wisconsin State Department of Administration, 1968.

Bandura, A. Social learning through imitation. In N. R. Jones (Ed.), *Nebraska Symposium on Motivation.* Lincoln: University of Nebraska Press, 1962.

Bandura, A. *Principles of behavior modification.* New York: Holt, Rinehart & Winston, 1969.

Bandura, A., Ross, D. M., & Ross, S. A. A comparative test of the status of envy, social power, and secondary reinforcement theories of identificatory learning. *Journal of Abnormal and Social Psychology,* 1963, **67**, 527–534.

Bandura, A., & Walters, R. H. *Social learning and personality development.* New York: Holt, Rinehart & Winston, 1963.

Banham, K. *A social competence scale for adults.* Durham, N.C.: Family Life Publications, 1960.

Baratz. S. B., & Baratz, J. C. Early childhood intervention: The social science base of institutional racism. *Harvard Educational Review,* 1970, **40**, 29–50.

Barker, R. G., Dembo, T., & Lewin, K. Frustration and regression: An experiment with young children. *University of Iowa Studies in Child Welfare,* 1941, **18**, No. 1.

Barnard, K. *A program of stimulation for infants born prematurely.* Paper presented at the convention of the Society for Research in Child Development, Philadelphia, March 1973.

Barnes, A. C. *Intra-uterine development.* Philadelphia: Lea & Febiger, 1968.

Baroff, G. S. WISC patterning in endogenous mental deficiency. *American Journal of Mental Deficiency,* 1959, **64**, 482–485.

Barr, M. L. & Bertram, E. G. A morphological distinction between neurones of the male and female, and the behaviour of the nucleolar satellite during accelerated nucleoprotein syntheses. *Nature,* 1949, **163**, 676.

Barsch, R. H. *The parent of the handicapped child: The study of child rearing practices.* Springfield, Ill.: Charles C Thomas, 1968.

Bass, M. S. (Ed.) *Sexual rights and responsibilities of the mentally retarded.* Selected papers from AAMD Region IX Annual Conference, Newark, Delaware, October 1972. Ardmore, Penn.: 1973.

Bateman, B. Implications of a learning disability approach for teaching educable retardates. *Mental Retardation,* 1967, **5**, 23–25.

Bateman, B. "Clinically" obtained IQs versus "production line" IQs in a mentally retarded sample. *Journal of School Psychology,* 1969, **7**(1), 29–33.

Bateman, B. D. Educational implications of minimal brain dysfunction. *Annals of the New York Academy of Sciences,* 1973, **205**, 245–250.

Bath, K. E., & Smith, S. A. An effective token economy program for MR adults, *Mental Retardation,* 1974, **12**(4), 41–43.

Bauer, M. L. *Health characteristics of low-income persons.* DHEW publication No. (HSM) 73-1500. Rockville, Md.: National Center for Health Statistics, July 1972.

Baughman, E. E., & Dahlstrom, G. W. *Negro and white children.* New York: Academic Press, 1968.

Baumeister, A. A. Paired-associate learning by institutionalized and non-institutionalized retardates and normal children. *American Journal of Mental Deficiency,* 1968, **73**, 102–104.

Baumeister, A. A. The American residential institution: Its history and character. In A. A. Baumeister and E. C. Butterfield (Eds.), *Residential facilities for the mentally retarded.* Chicago: Aldine, 1970.

Baumeister, A. A., & Klosowski, R. An attempt to group toilet train severely retarded patients. *Mental Retardation,* 1965, **3**, 24–26.

Bayley, N. Factors influencing the growth of intelligence in young children. *Yearbook of the National Society for the Study of Education,* 1940, **39**(II), 49–79.

Bayley, N. Consistency and variability in the growth of intelligence from birth to eighteen years. *Journal of Genetic Psychology,* 1949, **75**, 165–196.

Bayley, N. On the growth of intelligence. *American Psychologist,* 1955, **10**, 805–818.

Bayley, N. A new look at the curve of intelligence. In *Proceedings of the 1956 Invitational Conference on Testing Problems.* Princeton, N.J.: Educational Testing Service, 1956.

Bayley, N. Value and limitations of infant testing. *Children,* 1958, **5**, 129–133.

Bayley, N. Comparisons of mental and motor test scores for ages 1–15 months by sex, birth order, race, geographical location, and education of parents. *Child Development,* 1965, **36**, 379–411.

Bayley, N. *Manual for the Bayley Scales of Infant Development.* New York: Psychological Corporation, 1969.

Bayley, N. Development of mental abilities. In P. H. Mussen (Ed.), *Carmichael's manual of child psychology* (Vol. 1). New York: Wiley, 1970.

Bayley, N., & Oden, M. H. The maintenance of intellectual ability in gifted adults. *Journal of Gerontology*, 1955, **10**, 91–107.

Bayley, N., Rhodes, L., Gooch, B., & Marcus, M. Environmental factors in the development of institutionalized children. In J. Hellmuth (Ed.), *Exceptional infant (Vol. 2): Studies in abnormalities*. New York: Brunner/Mazel, 1971.

Bayley, N., & Schaefer, E. S. Maternal behavior, child behavior, and their intercorrelations from infancy through adolescence. *Monographs of the Society for Research in Child Development*, 1963, **28**, No. 3.

Bazelon, D. L., & Boggs, E. M. *Report of the Task Force on Law, President's Panel on Mental Retardation*. Washington, D. C.: Government Printing Office, 1963. Excerpt in Chap. 22 reprinted with permission of the President's Committee on Mental Retardation.

Beals, R. K. Spastic paraplegia and diplegia. *Journal of Bone and Joint Surgery*, 1966, **48-A**, 827–846.

Beck, H. L. *Social Services to the Mentally Retarded*. Springfield, Ill.: Charles C Thomas, 1969.

Beck, H. L. *Group treatment for parents of handicapped children*. DHEW Publication No. (HSM) 73-5503. Washington, D.C.: U.S. Government Printing Office, 1973.

Beckwith, L. Relationships between attributes of mothers and their infants' IQ scores. *Child Development*, 1971, **42**, 1083–1097.

Bedger, J. E., Gelperin, A., & Jacobs, E. E. Socioeconomic characteristics in relation to maternal and child health. *Public Health Reports*, 1966, **81**, 829–833.

Bee, H. L., Van Egeren, L. F., Streissguth, A. P., Nyman, B. A., & Leckie, M. S. Social class differences in maternal teaching strategies and speech patterns. *Developmental Psychology*, 1969, **1**, 726–734.

Beier, D. C. Behavioral disturbances in the mentally retarded. In H. Stevens & R. Heber (Eds.), *Mental retardation: A review of research*. Chicago: University of Chicago Press, 1964.

Bell, R. Q. A reinterpretation of the direction of effects in studies of socialization. *Psychological Review*, 1968, **75**, 81–95.

Belmont, I., Belmont, L., & Birch, H. G. The perceptual organization of complex arrays by educable mentally subnormal children. *Journal of Nervous and Mental Disease*, 1969, **149**, 241–253.

Belmont, I., Birch, H. G., & Belmont, L. The organization of intelligence test performance in educable mentally subnormal children. *American Journal of Mental Deficiency*, 1967, **71**, 969–976.

Belmont, J. M. Long-term memory in mental retardation. In N. R. Ellis (Ed.), *International review of research in mental retardation* (Vol. 1). New York: Academic Press, 1966.

Belmont, J. M. Perceptual short-term memory in children, retardates, and adults. *Journal of Experimental Child Psychology*, 1967, **5**, 114–122.

Belmont, J. M. Medical-behavioral research in retardation. In N. R. Ellis (Ed.), *International review of research in mental retardation* (Vol. 5). New York: Academic Press, 1971.

Belmont, J. M., & Butterfield, E. C. The relations of short-term memory to development and intelligence. In L. P. Lipsitt and H. W. Reese (Eds.), *Advances in child development and behavior* (Vol. 4). New York: Academic Press, 1969.

Belmont, J. M. & Butterfield, E. C. Learning strategies as determinants of memory deficiencies. *Cognitive Psychology*, 1971, **2**, 411–420.

Belmont, J. M., & Ellis, N. R. Effects of extraneous stimulation upon discrimination learning in normals and retardates. *American Journal of Mental Deficiency,* 1968, **72**, 525–532.

Benda, C. E. *Mongolism and cretinism.* New York: Grune and Stratton, 1946. Excerpt in Chap. 4 reprinted with the permission of the author and the publisher.

Benda, C. E. Psychopathology of childhood. In L. Carmichael (Ed.), *Manual of child psychology* (2d ed.). New York: Wiley, 1954.

Bender, L. Principles of gestalt in copied form in mentally defective and schizophrenic persons. *Archives of Neurology and Psychiatry,* 1932, **27**, 661–680.

Bender, L. *A visual motor gestalt test and its clinical use.* American Orthopsychiatric Association Research Monograph No. 3, 1938.

Bender, L. Childhood schizophrenia—a clinical study of 100 schizophrenic children. *American Journal of Orthopsychiatry,* 1947, **17**, 40–56.

Bender, L. The life course of children with autism and mental retardation. In F. J. Menolascino (Ed.), *Psychiatric approaches to mental retardation.* New York: Basic Books, 1970.

Bender, L., & Andermann, K. Brain damage in blind children with retrolental fibroplasia. *Archives of Neurology,* 1965, **12**, 644–649.

Bender, L., & Faretra, G. Pregnancy and birth histories of children with psychiatric problems. *Proceedings Third World Congress on Psychiatry,* 1962, **11**, 1329–1333.

Benoit, E. P. Rationale of a social center for employed limited adults. In R. K. Eyman, C. E. Meyers, & G. Tarjan (Eds.), *Sociobehavioral studies in mental retardation.* Washington, D.C.: American Association on Mental Deficiency, 1973.

Bensberg, G. J., Jr. A test for differentiating endogenous and exogenous mental defectives. *American Journal of Mental Deficiency,* 1950, **54**, 502–506.

Bensberg, G. J., Jr. (Ed.) *Teaching the mentally retarded.* Atlanta: Southern Regional Education Board, 1965.

Benton, A. L. *The revised Visual Retention Test: Clinical and experimental applications.* New York: Psychological Corporation, 1955.

Benton, A. L. Behavioral indices of brain injury in school children. *Child Development,* 1962, **33**, 199–208.

Berfenstam, R., & William-Olsson, I. Early child care in Sweden. *International Monograph Series on Early Child Care* (Vol. 2). London: Gordon & Breach, 1973.

Berger, L., Bernstein, A., Klein, E., Cohen, J., & Lucas, G. Effects of aging and pathology on the factorial structure of intelligence. *Journal of Consulting Psychology,* 1964, **28**, 199–207.

Berger, R., Touati, G., Derre, J., Ortiz, M. A., & Martinette, J. "Cri du chat" syndrome with maternal insertional translocation. *Clinical Genetics,* 1974, **5**, 428–432.

Bergès, J., & Lézine, I. *The imitation of gestures.* (A. H. Parmelee, Jr., Trans.). London: William Heinemann Medical Books, 1965.

Bergsma, D. (Ed.) *Birth defects atlas and compendium.* Baltimore: National Foundation and Williams & Wilkins, 1973.

Bergsma, D., & Motulsky, A. G. (Eds.) *Symposium on intrauterine diagnosis.* Birth Defects Original Article Series 7, 1971, 1–36.

Berko, M. J. A note on "psychometric scatter" as a factor in the differentiation of exogenous and endogenous mental deficiency. *Cerebral Palsy Review,* 1955, **16**, 20.

Berlin, I. N. Consultation and special education. In I. Philips (Ed.), *Prevention and treatment of mental retardation.* New York: Basic Books, 1966.

Berman, J. L., Cunningham, G. C., Day, R. W., Ford, R., & Hsia, D. Y. Y. Causes for high phenylalanine with normal tyrosine in newborn screening programs. *American Journal of Diseases of Children,* 1969, **117**, 54-65.

Berman, J. L. & Ford, R. Intelligence quotients and intelligence loss in patients with phenylketonuria and some variant states. *Journal of Pediatrics,* 1970, **77**, 764-770.

Berman, M. I. Mental retardation and depression. *Mental Retardation,* 1967, **5**(6), 19-21.

Bernstein, B. Social class, linguistic codes and grammatical elements. *Language and Speech,* 1962, **5**, 221-240.

Bernstein, N. R., & Menolascino, F. J. Apparent and relative mental retardation. In F. J. Menolascino (Ed.), *Psychiatric approaches to mental retardation.* New York: Basic Books, 1970.

Bettelheim, B. *The empty fortress: Infantile autism and the birth of the self.* New York: Free Press, 1967.

Bialer, I. Conceptualization of success and failure in mentally retarded and normal children. *Journal of Personality,* 1961, **29**, 301-333.

Bialer, I. Psychotherapy and other adjustment techniques with the mentally retarded. In A. A. Baumeister (Ed.), *Mental retardation: Appraisal, education, and rehabilitation.* Chicago: Aldine, 1967.

Bialer, I. Emotional disturbance and mental retardation: Etiologic and conceptual relationships. In F. J. Menolascino (Ed.), *Psychiatric approaches to mental retardation.* New York: Basic Books, 1970. (a)

Bialer, I. Relationship of mental retardation to emotional disturbance and physical disability. In H. C. Haywood (Ed.), *Social-cultural aspects of mental retardation.* New York: Appleton-Century-Crofts, 1970. (b)

Bialer, I., & Cromwell, R. L. Task repetition in mental defectives as a function of chronological and mental age. *American Journal of Mental Deficiency,* 1960, **65**, 265-268.

Bialer, I., & Cromwell, R. L. Failure as motivation with mentally retarded children. *American Journal of Mental Deficiency,* 1965, **69**, 680-684.

Bierman, J. M., Connor, A., Vaage, M., & Honzik, M. P. Pediatricians' assessments of the intelligence of two-year-olds and their mental test scores. *Pediatrics,* 1964, **34**, 680-690.

Bijlsma, J. B., Wijffels, J. C. H. M., & Tegelaers, W. H. H. C8 trisomy mosaicism syndrome. *Helvetia Paediatrica Acta,* 1972, **27**, 281-298.

Bijou, S. W. A functional analysis of retarded development. In N. R. Ellis (Ed.), *International review of research in mental retardation* (Vol. 1). New York: Academic Press, 1966.

Bijou, S. W., Birnbrauer, J. S., Kidder, J. D., & Tague, C. Programmed instruction as an approach to teaching of reading, writing, and arithmetic to retarded children. *Psychological Record,* 1966, **16**, 505-522.

Bilsky, L., & Evans, R. A. Use of associative clustering techniques in the study of reading disability: Effects of list organization. *American Journal of Mental Deficiency,* 1970, **74**, 771-776.

Bilsky, L., Evans, R. A., & Gilbert, L. Generalization of associative clustering tendencies in mentally retarded adolescents: Effects of novel stimuli. *American Journal of Mental Deficiency,* 1972, **77**, 77-84.

Binet, A. La perception des longueurs et des nombres chez quelques petits enfants. *Revue Philosophique,* 1890, **30**, 68-81.

Binet, A. Nouvelles recherches sur la mesure du niveau intellectuel chez les infants d'ecole. *L'Année Psychologique,* 1911, **17**, 145-201.

Binet, A., & Henri, V. La psychologie individuelle. *L'Année Psychologique,* 1896, **2,** 411–463.

Binet, A., & Simon, T. Méthodes nouvelles pour le diagnostic du niveau intellectuel des anormaux. *L'Année Psychologique,* 1905, **11,** 191–244. (a)

Binet, A., & Simon, T. Sur la necessité d'établir un diagnostic scientifique des états inferieurs de l'intelligence. *L'Année Psychologique,* 1905, **11,** 1–28. (b)

Binet, A., & Simon, T. Le developpement de l'intelligence chez les enfants. L'Année Psychologique, 1908, **14,** 1–90; 245–366.

Binet, A., & Simon, T. La mesure du developpement de l'intelligence chez les jeunes enfants. *Bulletin de la Societe Libre pour l'Etude psychologique de L'Enfant,* 1911.

Birch, H. G. The problem of "brain damage" in children. In H. G. Birch (Ed.), *Brain damage in children: The biological and social aspects.* Baltimore: Williams & Wilkins, 1964.

Birch, H. G., & Belmont, I. Perceptual analysis and sensory integration in brain-damaged persons. *Journal of Genetic Psychology,* 1964, **105,** 173–179.

Birch, H. G., Belmont, I., & Karp, E. The prolongation of inhibition in brain-damaged patients. *Cortex,* 1965, **1,** 397–409.

Birch, H. G., & Belmont, L. Auditory-visual integration in brain-damaged and normal children. *Developmental Medicine and Child Neurology,* 1965, **7,** 135–144. (a)

Birch, H. G., & Belmont, L. Auditory-visual integration, intelligence and reading ability in school children. *Perceptual and Motor Skills,* 1965, **20,** 295–305. (b)

Birch, H. G., Belmont, L., Belmont, I., & Taft, L. Brain damage and intelligence in educable mentally subnormal children. *Journal of Nervous and Mental Disease,* 1967, **144,** 247–257.

Birch, H. G., & Bortner, M. Stimulus competition and concept utilization in brain-damaged children. *Developmental Medicine and Child Neurology,* 1967, **9,** 402–410.

Birch, H. G., & Cravioto, J. Infection, nutrition, and environment in mental development. In H. F. Eichenwald (Ed.), *Prevention of Mental Retardation Through Control of Infectious Diseases.* PHS Publication No. 1692. Washington, D.C.: U.S. Government Printing Office, 1968.

Birch, H. G., & Diller, L. Rorschach signs of organicity: A physiologic basis for perceptual disturbances. *Journal of Projective Techniques,* 1959, **23,** 184–197.

Birch, H. G., & Gussow, J. D. *Disadvantaged children: Health, nutrition and school failure.* New York: Grune & Stratton, 1970.

Birch, H. G., & Lefford, A. Intersensory development in children. *Monographs of the Society for Research in Child Development,* 1963, **28,** No. 5.

Birch, H. G., & Lefford, A. Two strategies for studying perception in "brain-damaged" children. In H. G. Birch (Ed.), *Brain damage in children: The biological and social aspects.* New York: Williams & Wilkins, 1964. Pp. 27–42.

Birch, H. G., Richardson, S. A., Baird, D., Horobin, G., & Illsley, R. *Mental subnormality in the community. A clinical and epidemiological study.* Baltimore: Williams & Wilkins, 1970.

Birnbrauer, J. S. Mental retardation. In H. Leitenberg (Ed.), *Handbook of behavior modification.* New York: Appleton-Century-Crofts, in press.

Birnbrauer, J. S., & Lawler, J. Token reinforcement for learning. *Mental Retardation,* 1964, **2**(5), 275–279.

Bjaanes, A. T., & Butler, E. W. Environmental variation in community care facilities for mentally retarded persons. *American Journal of Mental Deficiency,* 1974, **78,** 429–439.

Bjork, R. A. Positive forgetting: The non-interference of items intentionally forgotten. *Journal of Verbal Learning and Verbal Behavior,* 1970, **9**, 255-268.

Black, P., Jeffries, J. J., Blumer, D., Wellner, A., and Walker, A. E. The post-traumatic syndrome in children. In A. E. Walker, W. F. Caveness, & M. Critchley (Eds.), *The late effects of head injury.* Springfield, Ill.: Charles C Thomas, 1969.

Blackman, L. S., & Capobianco, R. J. An evaluation of programmed instruction with the mentally retarded utilizing teaching machines. *American Journal of Mental Deficiency,* 1965, **70**, 262-269.

Blackman, L. S., & Kahn, H. Success and failure as determinants of aspirational shifts in retardates and normals. *American Journal of Mental Deficiency,* 1963, **67**, 751-755.

Blank, C. E. Apert's syndrome (a type of acrocephalosyndactyly) observations on British series of thirty-nine cases. *Annals of Human Genetics,* 1960, **24**, 4-32.

Blanton, R. L. Historical perspectives on classification of mental retardation. In N. Hobbs (Ed.), *Issues in the classification of children* (Vol. 1). San Francisco: Jossey-Bass, 1975.

Blatman, S. Narcotic poisoning of children (1) through accidental ingestion of methadone and (2) in utero. *Pediatrics,* 1974, **54**, 329-332.

Blatt, A. Group therapy with parents of severely retarded children: A preliminary report. *Group Psychotherapy,* 1957, **10**, 133-140.

Blatt, B. The dark side of the mirror. *Mental Retardation,* 1968, **6**(5), 42-44.

Blatt, B., & Kaplan, F. *Christmas in Purgatory: A photographic essay on mental retardation.* Boston: Allyn and Bacon, 1966.

Block, J., Block, J. H., & Harrington, D. M. Some misgivings about the Matching Familiar Figures Test as a measure of reflection-impulsivity. *Developmental Psychology,* 1974, **10**, 611-632.

Block, R. A. Effects of instructions to forget in short-term memory. *Journal of Experimental Psychology,* 1971, **89**, 1-9.

Blodgett, H. E. *Mentally retarded children: What parents and others should know.* Minneapolis: University of Minnesota Press, 1971.

Bloom, B. S. *Stability and change in human characteristics.* New York: Wiley, 1964.

Bock, R. D., & Kolakowski, D. Further evidence of sex-linked major-gene influence on human spatial visualizing ability. *American Journal of Human Genetics,* 1973, **25**, 1-14.

Bodmer, W. F., & Cavalli-Sforza, L. L. Intelligence and race. *Scientific American,* 1970, **223**, 19-29.

Boehm, L. D. Conscience development in mentally retarded adolescents. *Journal of Special Education,* 1967, **2**, 98-103.

Boggs, E. M. Federal legislation. In J. Wortis (Ed.), *Mental retardation: An annual review. III.* New York: Grune & Stratton, 1971.

Boll, T. J. Conceptual vs. perceptual vs. motor deficits in brain damaged children. *Journal of Clinical Psychology,* 1972, **28**, 157-159.

Boll, T. J. Effect of age at onset of brain damage on adaptive abilities in children. *Proceedings of the 81st Annual Convention of the American Psychological Association, Montreal, Canada,* 1973, **8**, 511-512.

Böök, J. A. Genetical aspects of schizophrenic psychoses. In D. D. Jackson (Ed.), *The etiology of schizophrenia.* New York: Basic Books, 1960.

Borenzweig, H. Social group work in the field of mental retardation: A review of the literature. *Social Service Review,* 1970, **44**, 177-183.

Borg, W. R. *Ability grouping in the public schools.* Madison, Wis.: Dembar Educational Research Services, Inc., 1966.

Borginsky, M. E. *Provision of instruction to handicapped pupils in local public schools, Spring 1970.* Washington, D.C.: Office of Education, 1974.

Boring, E. G. Intelligence as the tests test it. *New Republic,* June 6, 1923, 35-37. Excerpt in Chap. 1 reprinted with the permission of the author.

Boring, E. G. *A history of experimental psychology* (2d ed.). New York: Appleton-Century-Crofts, 1950.

Borkowski, J. G., & Wanschura, P. B. Mediational processes in the retarded. In N. R. Ellis (Ed.), *International review of research in mental retardation* (Vol. 7). New York: Academic Press, 1974.

Bortner, M., & Birch, H. G. Patterns of intellectual ability in emotionally disturbed and brain-damaged children. *Journal of Special Education,* 1969, **3**, 351-369.

Bortner, M., & Birch, H. G. Cognitive capacity and cognitive competence. *American Journal of Mental Deficiency,* 1970, **74**, 735-744.

Boslow, H. M., & Kandel, A. Psychiatric aspects of dangerous behavior: The retarded offender. *American Journal of Psychiatry,* 1965, **122**, 646-652.

Bousfield, W. A. The occurrence of clustering in the recall of randomly arranged associates. *Journal of General Psychology,* 1953, **49**, 229-240.

Bousfield, W. A., Esterson, S., & Whitmarsh, G. A. A study of developmental changes in perceptual associative clustering. *Journal of Genetic Psychology,* 1958, **92**, 95-102.

Bovet, M. Piaget's theory of cognitive development, sociocultural differences, and mental retardation. In H. C. Haywood (Ed.), *Social-cultural aspects of mental retardation.* New York: Appleton-Century-Crofts, 1970.

Bowlby, J. *Attachment and loss* (Vol. 1). *Attachment.* New York: Basic Books, 1969.

Bowlby, J. *Attachment and loss* (Vol. 2). *Separation.* New York: Basic Books, 1973.

Bradway, K. P. Paternal occupational intelligence and mental deficiency. *Journal of Applied Psychology,* 1935, **19**, 527-542.

Bradway, K. P. Predictive value of Stanford-Binet preschool items. *Journal of Educational Psychology,* 1945, **36**, 1-16.

Bradway, K. P., & Robinson, N. M. Significant IQ changes in twenty-five years: A follow-up. *Journal of Educational Psychology,* 1961, **52**, 74-79.

Bradway, K. P., Thompson, C. W., & Cravens, R. B. Preschool IQs after twenty-five years. *Journal of Educational Psychology,* 1958, **49**, 278-281.

Brady, R. O. Sphingolipidoses. In R. W. Albers, G. J. Siegal, R. Katzman, & B. W. Agranoff (Eds.), *Basic neurochemistry.* Boston: Little, Brown, 1972.

Braginsky, D. D., & Braginsky, B. M. *Hansels and Gretels: Studies of children in institutions for the mentally retarded.* New York: Holt, Rinehart & Winston, 1971.

Braine, M. S. The ontogeny of certain logical operations: Piaget's formulation examined by nonverbal methods. *Psychological Monographs,* 1959, **73**, No. 5 (Whole No. 475).

Brandon, M. W. G., Kirman, B. H., & Williams, C. E. Microcephaly. *Journal of Mental Science,* 1959, **105**, 721-747.

Bray, N. W. Controlled forgetting in the retarded. *Cognitive Psychology,* 1973, **5**, 288-309.

Brenton, M. Mainstreaming the handicapped. *Today's Education,* March-April 1974, 20-25.

Bricker, W. A., Morgan, D. G., & Grabowski, J. G. Development and maintenance of a behavior modification repertoire of cottage attendants through T. V. feedback. *American Journal of Mental Deficiency,* 1972, **77**, 128-136.

Bridges, J. E. Philosophy and need for community living centres based on the experience of the Marbridge Foundation. *Deficience Mentale/Mental Retardation,* 1970, **20**(3), 8-11.

Brinson, D. W., & Bereiter, C. Acquisition of conservation of substances in normal, retarded, and gifted children. *Ontario Institute for Studies in Education, Educational Research Series,* 1967, **2**, 53–72.

Broadbent, D. E. A mechanical model for human attention and immediate memory. *Psychological Review,* 1957, **64**, 205–215.

Broadhead, G. D. Socioeconomic traits in mildly retarded children of differential diagnosis. *Rehabilitation Literature,* 1973, **34**, 104–107.

Broadhurst, P. L. Determinants of emotionality in the rat: III. Strain differences. *Journal of Comparative and Physiological Psychology,* 1958, **51**, 55–59.

Broca, A. Sur le siège de la faculté du langage articulé avec deux observations d'aphémie (perte de la parole). *Bulletin de la Societé d'Anatomie,* **6**, August 1861.

Bronfenbrenner, U. Socialization and social class through time and space. In E. E. Maccoby, T. M. Newcomb, & E. L. Hartley, *Readings in social psychology* (3d ed.). New York: Holt, 1958. Excerpts in Chap. 7 reprinted with the permission of the publisher.

Bronfenbrenner, U. Is early intervention effective? In S. Ryan (Ed.), *A report on longitudinal evaluations of preschool programs* (Vol. 2). Washington, D.C.: Office of Child Development, 1974.

Brookover, W. B., Erickson, E. L., & Joiner, L. M. *Self-concept and achievement* (Vol. 3). U.S. Office of Education, Cooperative Research Project No. 2831. East Lansing: Michigan State University, 1967.

Brown, A. L. Subject and experimental variables in the oddity learning of normal and retarded children. *American Journal of Mental Deficiency,* 1970, **75**, 142–151.

Brown, A. L. Proactive interference in the keeping track performance of retardates. Unpublished manuscript, University of Illinois, 1971.

Brown, A. L. A rehearsal deficit in retardates' continuous short-term memory: Keeping track of variables that have few or many states. *Psychonomic Science,* 1972, **29**, 373–376. (a)

Brown, A. L. Context and recency cues in the recognition memory of retarded children and adolescents. *American Journal of Mental Deficiency,* 1972, **77**, 54–58. (b)

Brown, A. L. Judgments of recency for long sequences of pictures: The absence of a developmental trend. *Journal of Experimental Child Psychology,* 1973, **15**, 473–480.

Brown, A. L. The role of strategic behavior in retardate memory. In N. R. Ellis (Ed.), *International review of research in mental retardation* (Vol. 7). New York: Academic Press, 1974.

Brown, A. L. The development of memory: Knowing, knowing about knowing, and knowing how to know. In H. W. Reese (Ed.), *Advances in child development and behavior* (Vol. 10). New York: Academic Press, 1975.

Brown, A. L., & Campione, J. C. Recognition memory for perceptually similar pictures in preschool children. *Journal of Experimental Psychology,* 1972, **95**, 55–62.

Brown, A. L., Campione, J. C., Bray, N. W., & Wilcox, B. L. Keeping track of changing variables: Effects of rehearsal training and rehearsal prevention in normal and retarded adolescents. *Journal of Experimental Psychology,* 1973, **101**, 123–131. Figures 14-2 and 14-3 copyright 1973 by the American Psychological Association. Reprinted by permission.

Brown, A. L., Campione, J. C., & Gilliard, D. M. Recency judgments in children: A production deficiency in the use of redundant background cues. *Developmental Psychology,* 1974, **10**, 303.

Brown, A. L., Campione, J. C., & Murphy, M. D. Keeping track of changing variables: Long-term retention of a trained rehearsal strategy by retarded adolescents. *American Journal of Mental Deficiency,* 1974, **78**, 446–453.

Brown, A. L., & Scott, M. S. Recognition memory for pictures in preschool children. *Journal of Experimental Child Psychology*, 1971, **11**, 410-412.

Brown, B. S., & Courtless, T. F. *The mentally retarded offender.* DHEW Publication No. (HSM) 72-9039. Washington, D.C.: Superintendent of Documents, U.S. Government Printing Office, 1972.

Brown, D., & Jones, E. Using the Bell Adjustment Inventory with the mentally retarded. *Rehabilitation Counseling Bulletin*, 1970, **13**, 288-294.

Brown, R., & McNeill, D. The tip-of-the-tongue phenomenon. *Journal of Verbal Learning and Verbal Behavior*, 1966, **5**, 325-337.

Brown, R. E., & Halpern, F. The variable pattern of mental development of rural black children. *Clinical Pediatrics*, 1971, **10**, 404-409.

Brown, R. I. The effect of visual distraction on perception in subjects of subnormal intelligence. *British Journal of Social and Clinical Psychology*, 1964, **3**, 30-38.

Bruckman, C., Berry, H. K., & Dasenbrock, R. J. Histidinemia in two successive generations. *American Journal of Diseases in Children*, 1970, **119**, 221-227.

Bruininks, R. H., Rynders, J. E., & Gross, J. C. Social acceptance of mildly retarded pupils in resource rooms and regular classes. *American Journal of Mental Deficiency*, 1974, **78**, 377-383.

Bruner, J. S. On perceptual readiness. *Psychological Review*, 1957, **64**, 123-152.

Bruner, J. S. The course of cognitive growth. *American Psychologist*, 1964, **19**, 1-15.

Bruner, J. S. On cognitive growth, I and II. In J. S. Bruner, R. R. Olver, & P. M. Greenfield (Eds.), *Studies in cognitive growth.* New York: Wiley, 1966.

Bruner, J. S., Olver, R. R., & Greenfield, P. M. *Studies in cognitive growth.* New York: Wiley, 1966.

Bucher, B., & Lovaas, O. Use of aversive stimulation in behavior modification. In M. R. Jones (Ed.), *Miami symposium on the prediction of behavior, 1967: Aversive stimulation.* Coral Gables, Fla.: University of Miami Press, 1968.

Bugelski, B. R. Presentation time, total time, and mediation in paired associates learning. *Journal of Experimental Psychology*, 1962, **63**, 409-412.

Bundey, S., Carter, C. O. & Soothill, J. F. Early recognition of heterozygotes for the gene for dystrophia myotonia. *Journal of Neurology, Neurosurgery, and Psychiatry*, 1970, **33**, 279.

Burks, B. S. The relative influence of nature and nurture upon mental development; a comparative study of foster parent-foster child resemblance and true parent-true child resemblance. *Yearbook of the National Society for the Study of Education*, 1928, **27**(1), 219-316.

Buros, O. (Ed.) *The seventh mental measurements yearbook.* Highland Park, N.J.: Gryphon Press, 1972.

Burt, C. The inheritance of mental ability. *American Psychologist*, 1958, **13**, 1-15.

Burt, C. The genetic determination of differences in intelligence: A study of monozygotic twins reared together and apart. *British Journal of Psychology*, 1966, **57**, 137-153.

Burton, T. A. Education for trainables: An impossible dream? *Mental Retardation*, 1974, **12**(1), 45-46.

Butler, N. R., & Alberman, E. D. (Eds.) *Perinatal problems: Second report of the 1958 British Perinatal Mortality Survey.* Edinburgh: E. S. Livingstone, 1969.

Butterfield, E. C. The role of environmental factors in the treatment of institutionalized mental retardates. In A. A. Baumeister (Ed.), *Mental retardation: Appraisal, education, and rehabilitation.* Chicago: Aldine, 1967. (a) Excerpt in Chap. 21 reprinted with the permission of the publisher and the author.

Butterfield, E. C. The characteristics, selection, and training of institution personnel. In A. A. Baumeister (Ed.), *Mental retardation: Appraisal, education, and rehabilitation.* Chicago: Aldine, 1967. (b)

Butterfield, E. C. Basic facts about public residential facilities for the mentally retarded. In R. B. Kugel & W. Wolfensberger (Eds.), *Changing patterns in residential services for the mentally retarded.* Washington, D.C.: President's Committee on Mental Retardation, 1969.

Butterfield, E. C., & Belmont, J. M. Assessing and improving the executive cognitive function of mentally retarded people. In I. Bialer & M. Sternlicht (Eds.), *Psychological issues in mental retardation.* Chicago: Aldine, 1975.

Butterfield, E. C., Wambold, C., & Belmont, J. M. On the theory and practice of improving short-term memory. *American Journal of Mental Deficiency,* 1973, **77,** 654-669.

Butterfield, E. C., & Zigler, E. The effects of success and failure on the discrimination learning of normal and retarded children. *Journal of Abnormal Psychology,* 1965, **70,** 25-31.

Cain, L. F., & Levine, S. *Effects of community and institutional school programs on trainable mentally retarded children.* NEA, CEC Research Monograph, Series B, No. B-1. Washington, D.C.: The Council for Exceptional Children, 1963.

Cain, L. F., Levine, S., & Elzey, F. F. *Manual for the Cain-Levine Social Competency Scale.* Palo Alto, Cal.: Consulting Psychologists Press, 1963.

Caldwell, B. M. *Cooperative preschool inventory* (Rev. ed.). Princeton, N.J.: Educational Testing Service, 1970.

Caldwell, B. M., & Richmond, J. B. Social class level and stimulation potential of the home. In J. Hellmuth (Ed.), *Exceptional infant, Vol. I. The normal infant.* Seattle: Special Child Publications, 1967.

Caldwell, B. M., Wright, C. M., Honig, A., & Tannenbaum, J. Infant day care and attachment. *American Journal of Orthopsychiatry,* 1970, **40,** 397-412.

Cameron, J., Livson, N., & Bayley, N. Infant vocalizations and their relationship to mature intelligence. *Science,* 1967, **157,** 331-333.

Campanelli, P. A. Sustained attention in brain damaged children. *Exceptional Children,* 1970, **36,** 317-324.

Campione, J. C., Hyman, L., & Zeaman, D. Dimensional shifts and reversals in retardate discrimination learning. *Journal of Experimental Child Psychology,* 1965, **2,** 255-263.

Cantor, G. N. A critique of Garfield and Wittson's reaction to the revised manual on terminology and classification. *American Journal of Mental Deficiency,* 1960, **64,** 954-956.

Cantor, G. N. Some issues involved in category VIII of the AAMD terminology and classification manual. *American Journal of Mental Deficiency,* 1961, **65,** 561-566.

Cantwell, D. P. Psychiatric illness in families of hyperactive children. *Archives of General Psychiatry,* 1972, **27,** 414.

Capobianco, R. J., & Knox, S. IQ estimates and the index of marital integration. *American Journal of Mental Deficiency,* 1964, **68,** 718-721.

Carlson, J. S., & Michalson, L. H. Methodological study of conservation in retarded adolescents. *American Journal of Mental Deficiency,* 1973, **78,** 348-353.

Carr, D. H. Chromosome studies in spontaneous abortions. *Obstetrics and Gynecology,* 1965, **26,** 308.

Carr, D. H. Chromosome studies in selected spontaneous abortions: polyploidy in man. *Journal of Medical Genetics,* 1971, **8,** 164-174.

Carr, G. L. Mosaic differences in non-institutionalized retarded children. *American Journal of Mental Deficiency,* 1958, **62**, 908–911.

Carr, J. Mental and motor development in young mongol children. *Journal of Mental Deficiency Research,* 1970, **14**(Part 3), 205–220.

Carroll, A. W. The effects of segregated and partially integrated school programs on self concept and academic achievement of educable mental retardates. *Exceptional Children,* 1967, **34**(2), 93–99.

Carson, N. A. J., & Neill, D. W. Metabolic abnormalities detected in a survey of mentally backward individuals in northern Ireland. *Archives of Diseases in Childhood,* 1962, **37**, 505.

Casati, I., & Lézine, I. *The stages of sensori-motor intelligence in the child from birth to two years.* Paris: Center of Applied Psychology, 1968. (E. V. Ristow, Trans., University of Washington, 1971, mimeographed.)

Casler, L. Maternal deprivation: A critical review of the literature. *Monographs of the Society for Research in Child Development,* 1961, **26**, (2, Serial No. 80).

Casler, L. Perceptual deprivation in institutional settings. In G. Newton & S. Levine (Eds.), *Early experience and behavior. The psychobiology of development.* Springfield, Ill.: Charles C Thomas, 1968.

Caspersson, T., Lomakka, G., & Zech, L. The 24 fluorescence patterns of the human metaphase chromosomes: Distinguishing characters and variability. *Hereditas,* 1971, **67**, 89–102.

Cassel, J. *Planning for public health: The case for prevention.* Paper presented at the Conference on Education of Nurses for Public Health, May 1973.

Castaneda, A., McCandless, B. R., & Palermo, D. S. The children's form of the manifest anxiety scale. *Child Development,* 1956, **27**, 317–326.

Cattell, J. McK. Mental tests and measurements. *Mind,* 1890, **15**, 373–381.

Cattell, P. Stanford-Binet IQ variations. *Schools and Society,* 1937, **45**, 615–618.

Cattell, R. B. The multiple abstract variance analysis equations and solutions: For nature-nurture research on continuous variables. *Psychological Review,* 1960, **67**, 353–372.

Cattell, R. B. *Personality and social psychology.* San Diego: Robert R. Knapp, 1964.

Cattell, R. B. Are IQ tests intelligent? *Psychology Today,* 1968, **2**, 56–62.

Cattell, R. B. *Abilities: Their structure, growth, and action.* Boston: Houghton Mifflin, 1971.

Centerwall, S. A., & Centerwall, W. R. A study of children with mongolism reared in the home compared to those reared away from the home. *Pediatrics,* 1960, **25**, 678–685.

Chaffin, J. D. Production rate as a variable in the job success or failure of educable mentally retarded adolescents. *Dissertation Abstracts,* 1968, **28A**(7), 2432–2433.

Chance, J. E. *Internal control of reinforcements and school learning process.* Paper presented at meetings of the Society for Research in Child Development, Minneapolis, March 1965.

Chandler, J. T., & Plakos, J. *Spanish-speaking pupils classified as educable mentally retarded.* Sacramento: California State Education Department, 1969.

Charles, D. C. Ability and accomplishment of persons earlier judged mentally deficient. *Genetic Psychology Monographs,* 1953, **47**, 3–71.

Chase, H. P. The effects of intrauterine and postnatal undernutrition on normal brain development. *Annals of the New York Academy of Sciences,* 1973, **205**, 231–244.

Chase, H. P., Dabiere, C. S., Welch, N. N., & O'Brien, D. Intrauterine undernutrition and brain development. *Pediatrics,* 1971, **47**, 491.

Chase, H. P., & Martin, H. P. Undernutrition and child development. *New England Journal of Medicine,* 1970, **282**, 933–939.

Chazan, M. The incidence and nature of maladjustment among children in schools for the educationally subnormal. *British Journal of Educational Psychology,* 1964, **34,** 292–304.

Chesley, L. C., & Annetto, J. E. Pregnancy in the patient with hypertensive disease. *American Journal of Obstetrics and Gynecology,* 1947, **53,** 372–381.

Chess, S., & Korn, S. The influence of temperament on the education of mentally retarded children. *Journal of Special Education,* 1970, **4,** 13–27.

Chess, S., Korn, S. J., & Fernandez, P. B. *Psychiatric disorders of children with rubella.* New York: Brunner/Mazel, 1971. Table 10-1 reprinted with permission of the publisher.

Chilman, C. S. Child-rearing and family relationship patterns of the very poor. *Welfare in Review,* 1965, 9–19.

Chorus, A. Types of retarded maturation in mental deficiency: A follow-up study in the Netherlands. In B. W. Richards (Ed.), *Proceedings of the First Congress of the International Association for the Scientific Study of Mental Deficiency* (held September 12-20, 1967, Montpellier, France). Surrey, England: Michael Jackson Publishing, 1968.

Chow, T. J., & Earl, J. L. Lead aerosols in the atmosphere: Increasing concentrations. *Science,* 1970, **169,** 577.

Christensen, D. E. *Reduction of hyperactive behaviors by conditioning procedures alone and combined with methylphenidate (Ritalin).* M. A. thesis, University of Illinois, Urbana, 1972. Figure 11-2 reprinted with permission of the author.

Christensen, D. E. Effects of combining methylphenidate and a classroom token system in modifying hyperactive behaviors. *American Journal of Mental Deficiency,* in press.

Churchill, D. W., Alpern, G. D., & DeMyer, M. K. (Eds.) *Infantile autism.* Springfield, Ill.: Charles C Thomas, 1971.

Churchill, J. A., Berendes, H. W., & Nemore, J. Neuropsychological deficits in children of diabetic mothers. *American Journal of Obstetrics and Gynecology,* 1969, **105,** 257–268.

Churchill, L. Sex differences among mildly retarded admissions to a hospital for the mentally retarded. *American Journal of Mental Deficiency,* 1964, **69,** 269–276.

Cieutat, V. J. Examiner differences with the Stanford-Binet IQ. *Perceptual Motor Skills,* 1965, **20,** 317–318.

City of Birmingham (England) Education Committee. *Report of the Special Services After-care Sub-Committee,* 1956.

Clark, A. D., & Richards, C. J. Auditory discrimination among economically disadvantaged and nondisadvantaged preschool children. *Exceptional Children,* 1966, **33,** 259–262.

Clark, R. *Crime in America.* New York: Simon & Schuster, 1970.

Clarke, A. D. B. *Assets and deficits in imbecile learning.* Paper read at the XVIIth International Congress of Psychology, Washington, D.C., 1963.

Clarke, A. D. B., & Clarke, A. M. Cognitive changes in the feeble-minded. *British Journal of Psychology,* 1954, **45,** 173–179.

Clarke, A. D. B., Clarke, A. M., & Reiman, S. Cognitive and social changes in the feeble-minded—three further studies. *British Journal of Psychology,* 1958, **49,** 144–157.

Clarke, C. A. The prevention of Rh isoimmunization. In V. A. McKusick & R. Clairborne (Eds.), *Medical genetics.* New York: Hospital Practice Publishing Co., 1973.

Clarke-Stewart, K. A. Interactions between mothers and their young children: Characteristics and consequences. *Monographs of the Society for Research in Child Development,* 1973, **38**(6–7, Serial No. 153).

Clausen, J. A., & Clausen, S. R. The effects of family size on parents and children. In J. Fawcett (Ed.), *Psychological perspectives on fertility.* New York: Basic Books, 1973.

Cleary, T. A. Test bias: Prediction of grades of Negro and white students in integrated colleges. *Journal of Educational Measurement,* 1968, **5**, 115-124.

Cleary, T. A., Humphreys, L. G., Kendrick, S. A., & Wesman A. Educational uses of tests with disadvantaged students. *American Psychologist,* 1975, **30**, 15-42.

Cleland, C. C., Patton, W. F., & Seitz, S. The use of insult as an index of negative reference groups. *American Journal of Mental Deficiency,* 1967, **72**, 30-33.

Cleland, C. C., & Swartz, J. D. *Mental retardation: Approaches to institutional change.* New York: Grune & Stratton, 1969.

Cobb, H. V. *The forecast of fulfillment.* New York: Teachers College Press, 1972.

Cochran, I. L., & Cleland, C. C. Manifest anxiety of retardates and normals matched as to academic achievement. *American Journal of Mental Deficiency,* 1963, **67**, 539-542.

Coleman, J. S. *The adolescent society.* Glencoe, Ill.: Free Press, 1961.

Coleman, J. S., et al. *Equality of educational opportunity.* Washington, D.C.: U.S. Government Printing Office, 1966.

Coleman, M. (Ed.) *Serotonin in Down's syndrome.* London: North-Holland, 1973.

Collaborative Study of Children Treated for Phenylketonuria, Preliminary Report No. 8. Principal Investigator: Richard Koch. Presented at the Eleventh General Medical Conference, Stateline, Nevada, February 1975.

Collins, H. A., & Burger, G. K. The self concepts of adolescent retarded students. *Education and Training of the Mentally Retarded,* 1970, **5**, 23-30.

Collins, H. A., Burger, G. K., & Koherty, D. Self-concept of EMR and nonretarded adolescents. *American Journal of Mental Deficiency,* 1970, **75**, 285-289.

Collmann, R. D., & Newlyn, D. Changes in Terman-Merrill IQs of mentally retarded children. *American Journal of Mental Deficiency,* 1958, **63**, 307-311.

Collmann, R. D., & Stoller, A. Shift of childbirth to younger mothers, and its effect on the incidence of mongolism in Victoria, Australia, 1959-1964. *Journal of Mental Deficiency Research,* 1969, **13**, 13-19.

Colm, H. The value of projective methods in the psychological examination of children: The Mosaic Test in conjunction with the Rorschach and Binet tests. *Rorschach Research Exchange and Journal of Projective Techniques,* 1948, **12**, 216-233.

Colvin, S. S. Intelligence and its measurement: A symposium. *Journal of Educational Psychology,* 1921, **12**, 136-139.

Comings, D. E. The structure and function of chromatin. *Advances in Human Genetics,* 1972, **3**, 237.

Committee on Nomenclature, American Psychiatric Association. *Diagnostic and statistical manual of mental disorders* (2d ed.). Washington, D.C.: American Psychiatric Association, 1968.

Congdon, D. M. The adaptive behavior scales modified for the profoundly retarded. *Mental Retardation,* 1973, **11**(1), 20-21.

Conger, J. J. The meaning and measurement of intelligence. *Rocky Mountain Medical Journal,* June 1957. Excerpt in Chap. 1 reprinted with the permission of the author.

Conley, R. W. *The economics of mental retardation.* Baltimore: Johns Hopkins, 1973.

Conners, C. K. Psychological assessment of children with minimal brain dysfunction. *Annals of the New York Academy of Sciences,* 1973, **215**, 283-302.

Conners, C. K., & Barta, F., Jr. Transfer of information from touch to vision in brain-injured and emotionally disturbed children. *Journal of Nervous and Mental Diseases,* 1967, **145**, 138-141.

Conway, E., & Brackbill, Y. *Effects of obstetrical medication on infant sensorimotor behavior.*

Paper presented at the meeting of the Society for Research in Child Development, Santa Monica, Calif., 1969.

Cook, J. J. Dimensional analysis of child-rearing attitudes of parents of handicapped children. *American Journal of Mental Deficiency,* 1963, **68**, 354–361.

Cooper, G. D., York, M. W., Daston, P. G., & Adams, H. B. The Porteus Test and various measures of intelligence with southern Negro adolescents. *American Journal of Mental Deficiency,* 1967, **71**, 787–792.

Cooper, L. Z., & Krugman, S. Diagnosis and management: Congenital rubella. *Pediatrics,* 1966, **37**, 335.

Cornwell, A. C. Development of language, abstraction, and numerical concept formation in Down's syndrome children. *American Journal of Mental Deficiency,* 1974, **79**, 179–190.

Cornwell, A. C., & Birch, H. G. Psychological and social development in home-reared children with Down's syndrome (Mongolism). *American Journal of Mental Deficiency,* 1969, **74**, 341–350.

Corte, H. E., Wolf, M. M., & Locke, B. J. A comparison of procedures for eliminating self-injurious behavior of retarded adolescents. *Journal of Applied Behavior Analysis,* 1971, **4**, 201–213.

Covington, M. V. Stimulus discrimination as a function of social-class membership. *Child Development,* 1967, **38**, 607–613.

Cowen, E., Zax, M., Klein, R., Izzo, L., & Trost, M. The relation of anxiety in school children to school record, achievement, and behavioral measures. *Child Development,* 1965, **36**, 685.

Cowie, V. A. *A study of the early development of mongols.* Institute for Research into Mental Retardation Monograph No. 1. New York: Pergamon Press, 1970.

Coyte, M. J. A real "love-in": Foster grandparents and the retarded. *Welfare Reporter,* 1969, **20**(3), 29–33.

Craft, M., & Miles, L. *Patterns of care for the subnormal.* Oxford, England: Pergamon Press, 1967.

Craik, F. I. M., & Lockhart, R. S. Levels of processing: A framework for memory research. *Journal of Verbal Learning and Verbal Behavior,* 1972, **11**, 671–684.

Crandall, V. C., Katkovsky, W., & Crandall, V. J. Children's beliefs in their own control of reinforcements in intellectual-academic achievement situations. *Child Development,* 1965, **36**, 91–109.

Cravioto, J. Nutrition and learning in children. In N. S. Springer (Ed.), *Nutrition and mental retardation.* Ann Arbor: Institute for the Study of Mental Retardation and Related Disabilities, 1972.

Cravioto, J., Birch, H. G., & Gaona, C. E. Early malnutrition and auditory-visual integration in school-age children. *Journal of Special Education,* 1967, **2**, 75.

Creak, M. Schizophrenic syndrome in childhood. Further progress report of a working party. *Developmental Medicine and Child Neurology,* 1964, **6**, 530–535.

Crick, F. H. C. The genetic code. *Scientific American,* 1962, **207**, 66–74.

Cromwell, R. L. Personality evaluation. In A. A. Baumeister (Ed.), *Mental retardation: Appraisal, education, rehabilitation.* Chicago: Aldine, 1967. (a)

Cromwell, R. L. Success-failure reactions in mentally retarded children. In J. Zubin & G. A. Jervis (Eds.), *Psychopathology of mental development.* New York: Grune & Stratton, 1967. (b)

Cromwell, R. L., Baumeister, A., & Hawkins, I. F. Research in activity level. In N. R. Ellis (Ed.), *Handbook of mental deficiency.* New York: McGraw-Hill, 1963.

Cromwell, R. L., & Foshee, J. G. Studies in activity level: IV. Effects of visual stimulation during task performance in mental defectives. *American Journal of Mental Deficiency,* 1960, **65**, 248-251.

Cronbach, L. J. *Essentials of psychological testing* (2d ed.). New York: Harper & Row, 1960.

Cronbach, L. J. Five decades of public controversy over mental testing. *American Psychologist,* 1975, **30**, 1-14.

Crosby, K. G. Attention and distractibility in mentally retarded and intellectually average children. *American Journal of Mental Deficiency,* 1972, **77**, 46-53.

Crossen, P. E. Giemsa banding patterns of human chromosomes. *Clinical Genetics,* 1972, **3**, 169-179.

Crosson, J. E. A technique for programming sheltered workshop environments for training severely retarded workers. *American Journal of Mental Deficiency,* 1969, **73**, 814-818.

Crosson, J. E., & deJung, J. E. The experimental analysis of vocational behavior in severely retarded males. Final Report. Eugene: University of Oregon, February 1967.

Crowe, F. W. Axillary freckling as a diagnostic aid in neurofibromatosis. *Annals of Internal Medicine,* 1964, **61**, 1142-1143.

Crowe, F. W., Schull, W. J., & Neel, J. V. *A clinical, pathological, and genetic study of multiple neurofibromatosis.* Springfield, Ill.: Charles C Thomas, 1956.

Cruickshank, W. M. Development of education for exceptional children: current educational practices with exceptional children. In W. M. Cruickshank & G. O. Johnson (Eds.), *Education of exceptional children and youth.* Englewood Cliffs, N.J.: Prentice-Hall, 1958.

Cruickshank, W. M. *The brain injured child in home, school, and community.* Syracuse, N.Y.: Syracuse University Press, 1967.

Cruickshank, W. M., Bentzen, F., Ratzeberg, F. H., & Tannhauser, M. T. *A teaching method for brain-injured and hyperactive children.* Syracuse, N.Y.: Syracuse University Press, 1961.

Cruickshank, W. M., Bice, H. B., Wallen, N. E., & Lynch, K. S. *Perception and cerebral palsy* (2d ed.). Syracuse, N.Y.: Syracuse University Press, 1965.

Cruickshank, W. M., & Johnson, G. O. *Education of exceptional children and youth.* Englewood Cliffs, N.J.: Prentice-Hall, 1958.

Culliton, B. Patients' rights: Harvard is site of battle over X and Y chromosomes. *Science,* 1974, **186**, 715-717.

Cummings, S. T., Bayley, H. C., & Rie, H. E. Effects of the child's deficiency on the mother: A study of mothers of mentally retarded, chronically ill and neurotic children. *American Journal of Orthopsychiatry,* 1966, **36**, 595-608.

Cundick, B. P., & Robison, L. R. Performance of medically diagnosed brain-damaged children and control subjects. *Perceptual and Motor Skills,* 1972, **34**, 307-310.

Cushner, I. M., & Mellits, E. D. The relationship between fetal outcome and the gestational age and birth weight of the fetus. *Hopkins Medical Journal,* 1971, **128**, 252-260.

Dale, P. S. *Language development: Structure and function.* Hinsdale, Ill.: Dryden Press, 1972.

Dallman, P. R., & Spirito, R. A. Brain response to protein undernutrition: Mechanism of preferential protein retention. *Journal of Clinical Investigation,* 1972, **51**, 2175-2180.

Dancis, J., & Levitz, M. Abnormalities of branched-chain amino acid metabolism: Hypervalinemia, branched-chain ketonuria (maple syrup urine disease), isovaleric acidemia. In J. B. Stanbury, J. B. Wyngaarden, & D. S. Fredrickson (Eds.), *The metabolic basis of inherited disease* (3d ed.). New York: McGraw-Hill, 1972.

Dangel, H. L. Biasing effect of pretest referral information on WISC scores of mentally retarded children. *American Journal of Mental Deficiency,* 1972, **77**, 354-359.

Dasen, P. R. Preliminary study of sensorimotor development in Baoule children. *Early Child Development and Care,* 1973, **2**, 345-354.

Datta, L. E. *A report on evaluation studies of Project Head Start.* Paper presented at the 1969 American Psychological Association Convention, Washington, D.C., September 1969.

Datta, L. E. *New directions for early child development programs.* Invited address: Child Development and Child Psychiatry Conference, University of Missouri, October 1972.

Datta, L. E., Mitchell, S., & McHale, C. *The effects of Head Start programs on some aspects of child development: A summary.* Washington, D.C.: Office of Child Development, October 1972.

Davenport, R. K., Rogers, C. M., & Rumbaugh, D. M. Long-term cognitive deficits in chimpanzees associated with early impoverished rearing. *Developmental Psychology,* 1973, **9**, 343-347.

David, M., & Appell, G. *Loczy ou le Maternage Insolite.* Paris: Éditions du Scarabée, 1973.

David, M., & Lézine, I. Early child care in France. *International Monograph Series on Early Child Care* (Vol. 6). London: Gordon & Breach, 1974.

David, O. J. *The association between lower level lead concentrations and hyperactivity in children.* Proceedings of the International Symposium on Health Effects of Environmental Pollution, Paris, June 24-28, 1974. (Abstract 167)

Davids, A., Spencer, D., & Talmadge, M. Anxiety, pregnancy, and childbirth abnormalities. *Journal of Consulting Psychology,* 1961, **25**, 74-77.

Davie, R., Butler, N., & Goldstein, H. *From birth to seven.* London: Longman/National Children's Bureau, 1972. Excerpt in Chap. 7 reprinted with the permission of the publisher.

Davis, J. The effects of early environment on later development. *Developmental Medicine and Child Neurology,* 1970, **12**, 98-99. (Annotation)

Day, E. J. The development of language in twins. I. A comparison of twins and single children. *Child Development,* 1932, **3**, 179-199.

Dayan, M. I., & McLean, J. The Gardner Behavior Chart as a measure of adaptive behavior of the mentally retarded. *American Journal of Mental Deficiency,* 1963, **67**, 887-892.

Décarie, T. G. *Intelligence and affectivity in early childhood.* New York: International Universities Press, 1965.

DeFries, J. C. Quantitative aspects of genetics and environment in the determination of behavior. In. L. Ehrman, G. S. Omenn, & F. Caspari (Eds.), *Genetics, environment and behavior: Implications for educational policy.* New York: Academic Press, 1972.

deGrouchy, J., Royer, P., Salmon, C., & Lamy, M. Deletion partielle du bras long du chromosome 18. *Pathologie et Biologie,* 1964, **12**, 579.

de la Cruz, F. F., & LaVeck, G. D. (Eds.) *Human sexuality and the mentally retarded.* New York: Brunner/Mazel, 1973.

Delp, H. A., & Lorenz, M. Follow-up of 84 public school special class pupils with IQs below 50. *American Journal of Mental Deficiency,* 1953, **58**, 175-182.

DeMyer, M. K., Pontius, W., Norton, J. A., Barton, S., Allen, J., & Steele, R. Parental practices and innate activity in normal, autistic, and brain-damaged infants. *Journal of Autism and Childhood Schizophrenia,* 1972, **2**, 49-66.

Dennis, W. (Ed.) *Readings in the history of psychology.* New York: Appleton-Century-Crofts, 1948.

Dennis, W. Causes of retardation among institutional children: Iran. *Journal of Genetic Psychology,* 1960, **96**, 47-59.

Dennis, W., & Najarian, P. Infant development under environmental handicap. *Psychological Monographs,* 1957, **71**, No. 7.

Dentler, R. A., & Mackler, B. Effects on sociometric status of institutional pressure to adjust among retarded children. *British Journal of Social and Clinical Psychology,* 1964, **3**, 81-89.

Des Lauriers, A., & Halpern, F. Psychological tests in childhood schizophrenia. *American Journal of Orthopsychiatry,* 1947, **17**, 57-67.

Desmond, M. M., Wilson, G. S., Verniaud, W. M., Melnick, J. L., & Rawls, W. E. The early growth and development of infants with congenital rubella. In *Advances in Teratology* (Vol. IV). New York: Academic Press, 1970.

Deutsch, C. P. Auditory discrimination and learning: Social factors. *Merrill-Palmer Quarterly,* 1964, **10**, 277-296.

Deutsch, C. P. Social class and child development. In B. M. Caldwell & H. N. Ricciuti (Eds.), *Review of Child Development Research* (Vol. III). Chicago: University of Chicago Press, 1973.

Deutsch, C. P., & Schumer, F. *Brain-damaged children: A modality-oriented exploration of performance.* New York: Brunner/Mazel, 1970.

Deutsch, M. The role of social class in language development and cognition. *American Journal of Orthopsychiatry,* 1965, **35**, 78-88.

Deutsch, M. Happenings on the way back to the Forum. *Harvard Educational Review,* 1969, **39**, 523-557.

DeVries, R. Relationships among Piagetian, IQ, and achievement assessments. *Child Development,* 1974, **45**, 746-756.

Dewan, J. G. Intelligence and emotional stability. *American Journal of Psychiatry,* 1948, **104**, 548-555.

Dicks-Mireaux, M. J. Mental development of infants with Down's syndrome. *American Journal of Mental Deficiency,* 1972, **77**, 26-32.

Dinger, J. C. *Testimony before the Select Subcommittee on Education of the Committee on Education and Labor,* House of Representatives, March 9, 1973. Washington, D.C.: U.S. Government Printing Office, 1973.

Dingman, H. F. Some uses of descriptive statistics in population analysis. *American Journal of Mental Deficiency,* 1959, **64**, 291-295.

Dingman, H. F., & Tarjan, G. Mental retardation and the normal distribution curve. *American Journal of Mental Deficiency,* 1960, **64**, 991-994. Figure 2-3 reprinted with permission of publisher.

Dittmann, L. L. The family of the child in an institution. *American Journal of Mental Deficiency,* 1962, **66**, 759-765.

Dobbs, V. The effect of non-promotion on the achievement of matched groups of once-retained first graders as compared with never-retained second graders. In *Abstracts of Peabody Studies in Mental Retardation 1962-1964,* **3**, (Abstract No. 47). Unpublished Ed.S. study, George Peabody College, 1963.

Dodge, M. R., & Harris, F. R. *Use of reinforcement principles with autistic children.* Proceedings of the ninth annual research meeting, Olympia, Washington, 1969. *Research Report,* 1969, **2**(2), 82-84.

Dolgoborodova, N., & Danilkina, G. La defectologie en U.R.S.S. (Deficiencies in the U.S.S.R.). *Nos Enfants Anadaptes,* 1968, **27**(3), 29-31.

Doll, E. A. *The Vineland Social Maturity Scale: Revised condensed manual of directions.* Vineland, N.J.: The Training School, 1936.

Doll, E. A. The essentials of an inclusive concept of mental deficiency. *American Journal of Mental Deficiency,* 1941, **46**, 214–219.

Doll, E. A. Influence of environment and etiology on social competence. *American Journal of Mental Deficiency,* 1945, **50**, 89–94.

Doll, E. A. *Vineland Scale of Social Maturity.* Minneapolis: American Guidance Service, 1964.

Doll, E. A. *Preschool attainment record* (Research ed.). Circle Pines, Minn.: American Guidance Service, 1966.

Doll, E. E. Trends and problems in the education of the mentally retarded: 1800–1940. *American Journal of Mental Deficiency,* 1967, **72**, 175–183. Excerpt in Chap. 18 reprinted with the permission of the publisher and author.

Doll, E. E. A historical view of the private residential facility in the training and study of the mentally retarded in the United States, *Mental Retardation,* 1970, **8**(5), 3–8.

Doman, R. J., Spitz, E. B., Zucman, E., Delacato, C. H., & Doman, G. Children with severe brain injuries: Neurological organization in terms of mobility. *Journal of the American Medical Association,* 1960, **174**, 257–262.

Domino, G., Goldschmid, M., & Kaplan, M. Personality traits of institutionalized mongoloid girls. *American Journal of Mental Deficiency,* 1964, **68**, 498–502.

Domino, G., & McGarty, M. Personal and work adjustment of young retarded women. *American Journal of Mental Deficiency,* 1972, **77**, 314–321.

Domino, G., & Newman, D. Relationship of physical stigmata to intellectual subnormality in mongoloids. *American Journal of Mental Deficiency,* 1965, **69**(4), 541–547.

Dony, M., & Deegener, G. [The performance of brain-damaged and nonbrain-damaged children.] *Diagnostica,* 1973, **19**(3), 97–106.

Douglas, M. E. Some concrete contributions to occupational education in the academic classroom. *American Journal of Mental Deficiency,* 1944, **48**, 288–291.

Down, L. J. Observations on ethnic classification. *London Hospital Reports,* 1866, **3**, 259–262.

Drage, J., Berendes, H. W., & Fisher, P. D. The Apgar scores and four-year psychological performance. In *Perinatal Factors Affecting Human Development.* Washington, D. C.: Pan American Health, 1969.

Dreger, R. M., & Miller, K. S. Comparative psychological studies of Negroes and whites in the United States: 1959–1965. *Psychological Bulletin,* 1968, **70**, 1–58.

Drets, M. E., & Shaw, M. W. Specific banding patterns of human chromosomes. *Proceedings of the U. S. National Academy of Sciences,* 1971, **68**, 2073–2077.

Drews, E. M. *The effectiveness of homogeneous and heterogeneous ability grouping in ninth grade English classes with slow, average, and superior students.* Unpublished manuscript, Michigan State University, 1962.

Drews, E. M. The slow learner, grouping patterns, and classroom communications. In R. L. Schiefelbusch, R. H. Copeland, & J. O. Smith (Eds.), *Language and mental retardation: Empirical and conceptual considerations.* New York: Holt, 1967.

Drillien, C. M. The social and economic factors affecting the incidence of premature birth. Part I: Premature birth without complications of pregnancy. *Journal of Obstetrics and Gynaecology of the British Commonwealth,* 1957, **64**, 161–184.

Drillien, C. M. *The growth and development of the prematurely born infant.* Baltimore: Williams & Wilkins, 1964.

Drillien, C. M. The incidence of mental and physical handicaps in school age children of very low birth weight. II. *Pediatrics,* 1967, **39,** 238–247.

Drillien, C. M. Complications of pregnancy and delivery. In J. Wortis (Ed.), *Mental retardation: An annual review.* (Vol. 1). New York: Grune & Stratton, 1970.

Drillien, C. M., Jameson, S., & Wilkinson, E. M. Studies in mental handicap. Part I: Prevalence and distribution by clinical type and severity of defect. *Archives of Disease in Childhood,* 1966, **41**(219), 528–538.

Drotar, D. Outerdirectedness and the puzzle performance of nonretarded and retarded children. *American Journal of Mental Deficiency,* 1972, **77,** 230–236.

Druker, J., & Hagen, J. W. Developmental trends in the processing of task-relevant and task-irrelevant information. *Child Development,* 1969, **40,** 371–382.

Duckworth, S. V., Ragland, G. G., Sommerfeld, R. E., & Wyne, M. D. Modification of conceptual impulsivity in retarded children. *American Journal of Mental Deficiency,* 1974, **79,** 59–63.

Dugdale, R. L. *The Jukes: A study of crime, pauperism, disease, and heredity.* New York: Putnam, 1877.

Dunn, L. M. Special education for the mildly retarded—is much of it justifiable? *Exceptional Children,* 1968, **35**(1), 5–24. Excerpt in Chap. 18 reprinted with permission of the publisher.

Dunn, L. M. Small, special-purpose residential facilities for the retarded. In R. B. Kugel & W. Wolfensberger (Eds.), *Changing patterns in residential services for the mentally retarded.* Washington, D.C.: President's Committee on Mental Retardation, 1969.

Dunn, L. M. Children with moderate and severe general learning disabilities. In L. M. Dunn (Ed.), *Exceptional children in schools* (2d ed.). New York: Holt, 1973.

Durham Educational Improvement Program, Annual Report. Durham, N.C.: Duke University, 1966–1967.

Dybwad, R. F. The international scene: Patterns of organization and development in member associations of the International League of Societies for the Mentally Handicapped. *Mental Retardation,* 1973, **11**(1), 3–5.

Dykman, R. A., Peters, J. E., & Ackerman, P. T. Experimental approaches to the study of minimal brain dysfunction: A follow-up study. *Annals of the New York Academy of Sciences,* 1973, **205,** 93–108.

Eagle, E. Prognosis and outcome of community placement of institutionalized retardates. *American Journal of Mental Deficiency,* 1967, **72,** 232–243.

Earhart, R. H., & Warren, S. A. Long-term constancy of Binet IQ in retardation. *Training School Bulletin,* 1964, **61**(3), 109–115.

Eaves, L. C., Nuttall, J. C., Klonoff, H., & Dunn, H. G. Developmental and psychological test scores in children of low birth weight. *Pediatrics,* 1970, **45**(1), 9–20.

Eayrs, J. T. *Thyroid and central nervous development. Scientific basis of medicine annual reviews.* London: University of London and Athlone Press, 1966.

Edelson, R. I., & Sprague, R. L. Conditioning of activity level in a classroom with institutionalized retarded boys. *American Journal of Mental Deficiency,* 1974, **78,** 384–388.

Edgerton, R. B. *The cloak of competence: Stigma in the lives of the mentally retarded.* Berkeley: University of California Press, 1967.

Edgerton, R. B., & Dingman, H. F. Good reasons for bad supervision: "Dating" in a hospital for the mentally retarded. *Psychiatric Quarterly Supplement,* 1964, **38,** 221–233.

Edgerton, R. B., & Edgerton, C. R. Becoming mentally retarded in a Hawaiian school. In

R. K. Eyman, C. E. Meyers, & G. Tarjan (Eds.), *Sociobehavioral studies in mental retardation.* Washington, D.C.: American Association on Mental Deficiency, 1973.

Edwards, J. H., Harnden, D. G., Cameron, A. H., Crosse, V. M., & Wolff, O. H. New trisomic syndrome. *Lancet,* 1960, **1**, 787-790.

Eells, K. W., Davis, A., Havighurst, R. J., Herrick, V. E., & Tyler R. W. *Intelligence and cultural differences: A study of cultural learning and problem-solving.* Chicago: University of Chicago Press, 1951.

Egan, R. Should the educable mentally retarded receive driver education? *Exceptional Children,* 1967, **33**, 323.

Egg, M. *When a child is different: A basic guide for parents and friends of mentally retarded children.* New York: John Day, 1964.

Ehlers, W. H. *Mothers of retarded children: How they feel, where they find help.* Springfield, Ill.: Charles C Thomas, 1966.

Ehrman, L., Omenn, G. S., Caspari, E. (Eds.) *Genetics, environment and behavior: Implications for educational policy.* New York: Academic Press, 1972.

Eichenwald, H. F., & Fry, P. C. Nutrition and learning: Inadequate nutrition in infancy may result in permanent impairment of mental function. *Science,* 1969, **163**, 644-648.

Eimas, P. D. Information processing in problem-solving as a function of developmental level and stimulus saliency. *Developmental Psychology,* 1970, **2**, 224-229.

Eisenberg, L. Emotional determinants of mental deficiency. *American Medical Association Archives of Neurology and Psychiatry,* 1958, **80**, 114-121.

Eisenberg, L. Strengths of the inner city child. *Baltimore Bulletin of Education,* 1963, **41**(2), 10-16.

Eldridge, R. The torsion dystonias: Literature review, genetic and clinical studies. *Neurology,* 1970, **20**, Suppl. Part 2, 63-65.

Eldridge, R., O'Meara, K., & Kitchin, D. Superior intelligence in sighted retinoblastoma patients and their families. *Journal of Medical Genetics,* 1972, **9**, 331-335.

Elkind, D. Quantity conceptions in junior and senior high school students. *Child Development,* 1961, **32**, 551-560.

Ellis, M. J., Witt, P. A., Reynolds, R., & Sprague, R. L. Methylphenidate and the activity of hyperactives in the informal setting. *Child Development,* 1974, **45**, 217-220.

Ellis, N. R. The stimulus trace and behavioral inadequacy. In N. R. Ellis (Ed.), *Handbook of mental deficiency.* New York: McGraw-Hill, 1963.

Ellis, N. R. Memory processes in retardates and normals. In N. R. Ellis (Ed.), *International review of research in mental retardation* (Vol. 4). New York: Academic Press, 1970.

Ellis, N. R., Barnett, C. D., & Pryer, M. W. Operant behavior in mental defectives: Exploratory studies. *Journal of Experimental Analysis of Behavior,* 1960, **3**, 63-69.

Elmer, E. *Children in jeopardy.* Pittsburgh: University of Pittsburgh Press, 1967.

Elmer, E., & Gregg, G. S. Developmental characteristics of abused children. *Pediatrics,* 1967, **40**, 596-602.

Emanuel, I. Some preventive aspects of abnormal intrauterine development. *Postgraduate Medicine,* 1972, **51**, 144-149.

Emanuel, I. Problems of outcome of pregnancy: Some clues from the epidemiologic similarities and differences. In S. Kelly, E. B. Hook, D. T. Janerich, & I. H. Porter (Eds.), *Birth defects: Risks and consequences.* New York: Academic Press, in press.

Emanuel, I., & Sever, L. E. Questions concerning the possible association of potatoes and neural-tube defects, and an alternative hypothesis relating to maternal growth and development. *Teratology,* 1973, **8**, 325-331.

Epstein, C. J., Schneider, E. L., Conte, F. A., & Friedman, S. Prenatal detection of genetic disorders. *American Journal of Human Genetics,* 1972, **24**, 214-226.

Epstein, H. T. Phrenoblysis: Special brain and mind growth periods. I. Human brain and skull development. *Developmental Psychology,* 1974, **7**, 207-216. (a)

Epstein, H. T. Phrenoblysis: Special brain and mind growth periods. II. Human mental development. *Developmental Psychology,* 1974, **7**, 217-224. (b)

Epstein, R., & Komorita, S. S. Self-esteem, success-failure, & locus of control in Negro children. *Developmental Psychology,* 1971, **4**, 2-8.

Erickson, M. T. The predictive validity of the Cattell Infant Intelligence Scale for young mentally retarded children. *American Journal of Mental Deficiency,* 1968, **72**, 728-731.

Erickson, M. T. MMPI profiles of parents of young retarded children. *American Journal of Mental Deficiency,* 1969, **73**, 728-732.

Erikson, E. *Childhood and society.* New York: Norton, 1950.

Erlenmeyer-Kimling, L., & Jarvik, L. F. Genetics and intelligence: A review. *Science,* 1964, **142**, 1477-1478. Table 3-1 reprinted with permission of the publisher.

Escalona, S. K. Some considerations regarding psychotherapy with psychotic children. *Bulletin of the Menninger Clinic,* 1948, **12**, 126-134.

Estabrook, A. H. *The Jukes in 1915.* Washington, D.C.: Carnegie Institution, 1916.

Estes, W. K. *Learning theory and mental development.* New York: Academic Press, 1970.

Estes, W. K. Learning theory and intelligence. *American Psychologist,* 1974, **29**, 740-749.

Evans, G. W., & Spradlin, J. E. Incentives and instructions as controlling variables of productivity. *American Journal of Mental Deficiency,* 1966, **71**, 129-132.

Evans, H. J., Buckton, K. E., Sumner, A. T. Cytological mapping of human chromosomes: Results obtained with quinacrine fluorescence and acetic saline-Giemsa techniques. *Chromosoma,* 1971, **35**, 301-325.

Eveloff, H. H. The autistic child. *American Medical Association Archives of General Psychiatry,* 1960, **3**, 66-79.

Eyl, T. B., Wilcox, K. R., Jr., & Reizen, M. S. Mercury, fish, and human health. *Michigan Medicine,* 1970, **69**, 873.

Eyman, R. K. Profile at Pacific State Hopsital as of 3/1/74. (Mimeographed)

Falender, C. *Mother-child interaction and the child's participation in the Milwaukee Project: An experiment in the prevention of cultural-familial mental retardation.* Paper presented at the Convention of the Society for Research in Child Development, Philadelphia, March 1973.

Farber, B. Effects of a severely mentally retarded child on family integration. *Monographs of the Society for Research in Child Development,* 1959, **24** (Whole No. 71).

Farber, B. Family organization and crisis: Maintenance of integration in families with a severely mentally retarded child. *Monographs of the Society for Research in Child Development,* 1960, **25** (1, Serial No. 75). (a)

Farber, B. Perceptions of crisis and related variables in the impact of a retarded child on the mother. *Journal of Health and Human Behavior,* 1960, **1**, 108-118. (b)

Farber, B. *Mental retardation: Its social context and social consequences.* Boston: Houghton Mifflin, 1968.

Farber, B., & Blackman, L. S. Marital role tensions and number and sex of children. *American Sociological Review,* 1956, **21**, 596-601.

Farber, B., & Jenné, W. C. Family organization and parent-child communication: Parents and siblings of a retarded child. *Monographs of the Society for Research in Child Development,* 1963, **28**, No. 7, (Whole No. 91).

Farber, B., & Ryckman, D. B. Effects of severely retarded children on family relationships. *Mental Retardation Abstracts,* 1965, **2**, 1–17.

Fechter, J. V., Jr. Modeling and environmental generalization by mentally retarded subjects of televised aggressive or friendly behavior. *American Journal of Mental Deficiency,* 1971, **76**, 266–267.

Feldhusen, J. F., & Klausmeier, H. J. Anxiety, intelligence, and achievement in children of low, average, and high intelligence. *Child Development,* 1962, **33**, 403–409.

Feldman, L. Retardation, poverty, and jobs. *Manpower,* 1969, **1**(8), 30–32.

Ferguson-Smith, M. A. Karyotype-phenotype correlations in gonadal dysgenesis and their bearing on the pathogenesis of malformations. *Journal of Medical Genetics,* 1965, **2**, 142.

Ferster, C. B. Positive reinforcement and behavioral deficits of autistic children. *Child Development,* 1961, **32**, 437–456.

Ferster, C. B., & DeMyer, M. K. The development of performances in autistic children in an automatically controlled environment. *Journal of Chronic Diseases,* 1961, **13**, 312–345.

Ferster, C. B., & Skinner, B. F. *Schedules of reinforcement.* New York: Appleton-Century-Crofts, 1957.

Fessard, C. Cerebral tumors in infancy: 66 clinicoanatomical case studies. *American Journal of Diseases of Children,* 1968, **115**, 302–308.

Fialkow, P. J. Thyroid antibodies, Down's syndrome, and maternal age. *Nature,* 1967, **214**, 1253–1254.

Fialkow, P. J. Genetic aspects of autoimmunity. *Progress in Medical Genetics,* 1969, **7**, 117.

Fiester, A. R., & Giambra, L. M. Language indices of vocational success in mentally retarded adults. *American Journal of Mental Deficiency,* 1972, **77**, 332–337.

Fine, M. J. Attitudes of regular and special class teachers toward the educable mentally retarded child. *Exceptional Children,* 1967, **33**, 429–430.

Fischhoff, J., Whitten, C. F., & Pettit, M. G. A psychiatric study of mothers of infants with growth failure secondary to maternal deprivation. *Journal of Pediatrics,* 1971, **79**, 209–215.

Fisher, G. M. A note on the validity of the Wechsler Adult Intelligence Scale for mental retardates. *Journal of Consulting Psychology,* 1962, **26**, 391. (a)

Fisher, G. M. Further evidence of the invalidity of the WAIS for the assessment of intelligence of mental retardates. *Journal of Mental Deficiency Research,* 1962, **6**, 41–43. (b)

Fisher, M. A., & Zeaman, D. Growth and decline of retardate intelligence. In N. R. Ellis (Ed.), *International review of research in mental retardation* (Vol. 4). New York: Academic Press, 1970.

Fisher, M. A., & Zeaman, D. An attention-retention theory of retardate discrimination learning. In N. R. Ellis (Ed.), *International review of research in mental retardation* (Vol. 6). New York: Academic Press, 1973.

Fishler, K., Graliker, B. V., & Koch, R. The predictability of intelligence with Gesell Developmental Scales in mentally retarded infants and young children. *American Journal of Mental Deficiency,* 1964, **69**, 515–525.

Fitzgerald, D. E. A generation follow-up of some former public school mentally handicapped students. *Dissertation Abstracts,* 1968, **28a**(8), 2892.

Flavell, J. H. *The developmental psychology of Jean Piaget.* Princeton, N.J.: Van Nostrand, 1963. Excerpts in Chap. 12 reprinted with the permission of the publisher.

Flavell, J. H. Developmental studies of mediated memory. In H. W. Reese & L. P. Lipsitt

(Eds.), *Advances in child development and behavior* (Vol. 5). New York: Academic Press, 1970.

Flavell, J. H. What is memory development the development of? *Human Development,* 1971, **14,** 272–278.

Flavell, J. H., Beach, D. R., & Chinsky, J. M. Spontaneous verbal rehearsal in a memory task as a function of age. *Child Development,* 1966, **37,** 283–299.

Flavell, J. H., Friedrichs, A. G., & Hoyt, J. D. Developmental changes in memorization processes. *Cognitive Psychology,* 1970, **1,** 324–340.

Følling, A. Über Ausscheidung von Phenylbrenztraubensäure in den Harn als Stoffweckselanomalie in Verbindung mit Imbezillität. *Atschrift für physiolische Chemistrie,* 1934, **227,** 169–176.

Fomon, S. J., & Anderson, T. A. (Eds.) *Practices of low-income families in feeding infants and small children.* DHEW Publication No. (HSM) 72-5605. Rockville, Md.: Maternal and Child Health Service, 1972.

Forbes, A.P., & Engel, E. The high incidence of diabetes mellitus in 41 patients with gonadal dysgenesis and their close relatives. *Metabolism,* 1963, **12,** 428.

Forbes, L. Some psychiatric problems related to mental retardation. *American Journal of Mental Deficiency,* 1958, **62,** 637–641.

Forehand, R., & Baumeister, A. A. Effect of frustration on stereotyped body rocking: Follow-up. *Perceptual and Motor Skills,* 1970, **31,** 894. (a)

Forehand, R., & Baumeister, A. A. Effects of variations in auditory-visual stimulation on activity levels of severe mental retardates. *American Journal of Mental Deficiency,* 1970, **74,** 470–474. (b)

Forness, S. R., & MacMillan, D. L. The origins of behavior modification with exceptional children. *Exceptional Children,* 1970, **37,** 93–100.

Forssman, H., & Akesson, H. O. Mortality of the mentally deficient: A study of 12,903 institutionalized subjects. *Journal of Mental Deficiency Research,* 1970, **14,** 276–296.

Fotheringham, J. B. Retardation, family adequacy and institutionalization. *Canada's Mental Health,* 1970, **18**(1), 15–18.

Fotheringham, J. B., Skelton, M., & Hoddinott, B. A. *The retarded child and his family: The effects of home and institution.* Toronto: Ontario Institute for Studies in Education, 1971.

Fowle, C. M. The effect of the severely mentally retarded child on his family. *American Journal of Mental Deficiency,* 1968, **73,** 468–473.

Fowler, W. Problems of deprivation and developmental learning. *Merrill-Palmer Quarterly of Behavior and Development,* 1970, **16,** 2.

Foxx, R. M., & Azrin, N. H. Restitution: A method of eliminating aggressive-disruptive behavior of mentally retarded and brain damaged patients. *Behaviour Research and Therapy,* 1972, **10,** 15–27.

Foxx, R. M., & Azrin, N. H. The elimination of autistic self-stimulatory behavior by overcorrection. *Journal of Applied Behavior Analysis,* 1973, **6,** 1–14.

Frank, H. S., & Rabinovitch, M. S. Auditory short-term memory: Developmental changes in rehearsal. *Child Development,* 1974, **45,** 397–407.

Franks, D. J. Ethnic and social status characteristics of children in EMR and LD classes. *Exceptional Children,* 1971, **37,** 537–538.

Fraser, F. C. Genetic background of congenital malformations. In *23rd Ross Pediatric Research Conference.* Columbus, Ohio: Ross Lab., 1956.

Freeman, F. N., Holzinger, K. J., & Mitchell, B. S. The influence of environment on the intelligence, school achievement, and conduct of foster children. *Yearbook of the National Society for the Study of Education,* 1928, **27**(1), 103-217.

Freeman, F. S. *Theory and practice of psychological testing* ((2nd ed.). New York: Holt, 1955. (3rd ed., 1962)

Freeman, R. D. Psychopharmacology and the retarded child. In F. J. Menolascino (Ed.), *Psychiatric approaches to mental retardation.* New York: Basic Books, 1970.

Freud, S. *Lecture to the College of Physicians.* Vienna, Austria, 1904.

Freud, S. *An outline of psychoanalysis.* New York: Norton, 1949.

Freyberg, P. S. Concept development in Piaget's terms in relation to school attainment. *Journal of Educational Psychology,* 1966, **57**, 164-168.

Friedman, E. C., & Barclay, A. The discriminative validity of certain psychological tests as indices of brain damage in the mentally retarded. *Mental Retardation,* 1963, **1**, 291-293.

Friedman, J., Strochak, R. D., Gitlin, S., & Gottsgen, M. Koppitz Bender scoring system and brain injury children. *Journal of Clinical Psychology,* 1967, **23**, 179-182.

Friedsam, H. J., & Dick, H. R. A note on the facilitation of early institutional adjustment of retarded children. *Mental Retardation,* 1968, **6**(3), 15-17.

Friend, R. M., & Neale, J. M. Children's perception of success and failure: An attributional analysis of the effects of race and social class. *Developmental Psychology,* 1972, **7**, 124-128.

Frimpter, G. W. Cystathioninuria, sulfite oxidase deficiency and beta-mercaptolactate-cysteine disulfiduria. In J. B. Stanbury, J. B. Wyngaarden, & D. S. Fredrickson (Eds.), *The metabolic basis of inherited disease* (3d ed.). New York: McGraw-Hill, 1972.

Frith, U., & Hermelin, B. The role of visual and motor cues for normal, subnormal and autistic children. *Journal of Child Psychology and Psychiatry,* 1969, **10**, 153-163.

Froesch, E. R. Essential fructosuria and hereditary fructose intolerance. In J. B. Stanbury, J. B. Wyngaarden, & D. S. Fredrickson (Eds.), *The metabolic basis of inherited disease* (3d ed.). New York: McGraw-Hill, 1972.

Frostig, M., Lefever, D. W., & Whittlesey, J. R. B. A developmental test of visual perception for evaluating normal and neurologically handicapped children. *Perceptual and Motor Skills,* 1961, **12**, 383-394.

Frostig, M., Lefever, D. W., & Whittlesey, J. R. B. *The Marianne Frostig developmental test of visual perception.* Palo Alto, Calif.: Consulting Psychologists Press, 1964.

Fuller, J. L., & Scott, J. P. Heredity and learning ability in infrahuman mammals. *Eugenics Quarterly,* 1954, **1**, 28-43.

Fuller, R., & Schuman, J. Treated phenylketonuria: Intelligence and blood phenylalanine levels. *American Journal of Mental Deficiency,* 1971, **75**, 539-545.

Furth, H. G. *Piaget for teachers.* Englewood Cliffs, N.J.: Prentice-Hall, 1970.

Gallagher, J. Rejecting parents? *Exceptional Children,* 1956, **22**, 273-276, 294. Excerpt in Chap. 20 reprinted with permission of the publisher.

Gallagher, J. J. A comparison of brain-injured and nonbrain-injured mentally retarded children on several psychological variables. *Monographs of the Society for Research in Child Development,* 1957, **22**(2, Serial No. 65).

Gallagher, J. J. The special education contract for mildly handicapped children. In R. L. Jones & D. L. MacMillan (Eds.), *Special education in transition.* Boston: Allyn and Bacon, 1974.

Gallien, J. J. The achievement discrepancy of educable mentally retarded as affected by the use of achievement test data. *Dissertation Abstracts,* 1968, **28A**(8), 3070-3071.

Galton, F. *Hereditary genius.* London: MacMillan, 1869.

Galton, F. Supplementary notes on "prehension" in idiots. *Mind,* 1887, **12**, 79-82.

Gampel, D. H., Gottlieb, J., & Harrison, R. H. Comparison of classroom behavior of special-class EMR, integrated EMR, low IQ, and nonretarded children. *American Journal of Mental Deficiency,* 1974, **79**, 16-21.

Gampel, D. H., Harrison, R. H., & Budoff, M. *An observational study of segregated and integrated EMR children and their nonretarded peers: Can we tell the difference by looking?* Unpublished manuscript, Research Institute for Educational Problems, 1972.

Garai, J. E., & Scheinfeld, A. Sex differences in mental and behavioral traits. *Genetic Psychology Monographs,* 1968, **77**, 169-299.

Gardner, J. M., & Selinger, S. Trends in learning research with the mentally retarded. *American Journal of Mental Deficiency,* 1971, **75**, 733-738.

Gardner, L. I. Deprivation dwarfism. *Scientific American,* July 1972.

Gardner, W. I. Social and emotional adjustment of mildly retarded children and adolescents: Critical review. *Exceptional Children,* 1966, **33**, 97-105.

Gardner, W. I. Occurrence of severe depressive reactions in the mentally retarded. *American Journal of Psychiatry,* 1967, **124**, 386-388.

Gardner, W. I. Use of punishment procedures with the severely retarded: A review. *American Journal of Mental Deficiency,* 1969, **74**, 86-103.

Gardner, W. I. Use of behavior therapy with the mentally retarded. In F. J. Menolascino (Ed.), *Psychiatric approaches to mental retardation.* New York: Basic Books, 1970. Excerpt in Chap. 19 reprinted with permission of the publisher.

Gardner, W. I., Cromwell, R. L., & Foshee, J. G. Studies in activity level: II. Effects of visual stimulation in organics, familials, hyperactives, and hypoactives. *American Journal of Mental Deficiency,* 1959, **63**, 1028-1033.

Garfield, J. C. Motor impersistence in normal and brain-damaged children. *Neurology,* 1964, **14**, 623-630.

Garfield, J. C., Benton, A. L., & MacQueen, J. C. Motor impersistence in brain-damaged and cultural-familiar defectives. *Journal of Nervous and Mental Disease,* 1966, **142**, 434-440.

Garfield, S. L. Abnormal behavior and mental deficiency. In N. R. Ellis (Ed.), *Handbook in mental deficiency: Psychological theory and research.* New York: McGraw-Hill, 1963.

Garfield, S. L. & Affleck, D. C. A study of individuals committed to a state home for the retarded who were later released as not mentally defective. *American Journal of Mental Deficiency,* 1960, **64**, 907-915.

Garfield, S. L., & Wittson, C. Some reactions to the revised "Manual on terminology and classification in mental retardation." *American Journal of Mental Deficiency,* 1960, **64**, 951-952. (a)

Garfield, S. L., & Wittson, C. Comments on Dr. Cantor's remarks. *American Journal of Mental Deficiency,* 1960, **64**, 957-959. (b)

Garrod, A. E. Inborn errors of metabolism (Croonian Lectures). *Lancet,* 1908, **2**, 1, 73, 142, 214.

Gartler, S. M., Liskay, R. M., Campbell, B. K., Sparkes, R., & Gant, N. Evidence for two functional X chromosomes in human oocytes. *Cell Differentiation,* 1972, **1**, 215-218.

Gartler, S. M., Liskay, R. M., & Gant, N. Two functional X chromosomes in human fetal oocytes. *Experimental Cell Research,* 1973, **82**, 464-466.

Gaudia, G. Race, social class, and age of achievement of conservation on Piaget's tasks. *Developmental Psychology,* 1972, **5**, 158-165.

Gayton, W. F., & Bassett, J. E. The effect of positive and negative reaction tendencies on receptive language development in mentally retarded children. *American Journal of Mental Deficiency,* 1972, **76**, 499-508.

Gelb, A., & Goldstein, K. Psychologische Analysen hirnpathologischer Faelle. *Ambr. Barth,* Leipzig, 1920. Partially trans. in *Source book of Gestalt psychology.* New York: Harcourt, Brace & World, 1938.

Gelinier-Ortigues, M. C., & Aubry, J. Maternal deprivation, psychogenic deafness and pseudo-retardation. In G. Caplan (Ed.), *Emotional problems of early childhood.* New York: Basic Books, 1955.

Gellis, S. S., & Feingold, M. *Atlas of mental retardation syndromes.* DHEW, Rehabilitation Services Administration, Division of Mental Retardation. Washington, D.C.: U.S. Government Printing Office, 1969.

Gellner, L. *A neurophysiological concept of mental retardation and its educational implications.* Chicago: J. Levinson Research Foundation, 1959.

Gelof, M. Comparisons of systems of classifications relating degrees of retardation to measured intelligence. *American Journal of Mental Deficiency,* 1963, **68**, 297-317.

Gerjuoy, I. R., & Spitz, H. Associative clustering in free recall: Intellectual and developmental variables. *American Journal of Mental Deficiency,* 1966, **70**, 918-927.

Gerjuoy, I. R., & Winters, J. J., Jr. Development of lateral and choice-sequence preferences. In N. R. Ellis (Ed.), *International review of research in mental retardation* (Vol. 3). New York: Academic Press, 1968.

Gerjuoy, I. R., Winters, J. J., Jr., Pullen, M., & Spitz, H. Subjective organization by retardates and normals during forced recall of visual stimuli. *American Journal of Mental Deficiency,* 1969, **73**, 791-797.

Germeraad, P. When parents age. In *Stress on families of the mentally handicapped.* Proceedings of the Third International Congress, Paris, March 21-26, 1966. Brussels, Belgium: International League of Societies for the Mentally Handicapped, 1966.

Gerst, M. S. *Symbolic coding operations in observational learning.* Unpublished doctoral dissertation, Stanford University, 1968.

Gesell, A., et al. *Gesell Developmental Schedules.* New York: Psychological Corporation, 1949.

Getman, G. N., Kane, E. R., Halgren, M. R., & McKee, G. W. *The physiology of readiness, an action program for the development of perception for children.* Minneapolis: Programs to Accelerate School Success, 1964.

Getman, G. N., & Kephart, N. C. *The perceptual development of retarded children.* Lafayette, Ind.: Purdue University, 1956.

Gewirtz, J. L. A learning analysis of the effects of normal stimulation, privation and deprivation, on the acquisition of social motivation and attachments. In B. M. Foss (Ed.), *Determinants of infant behaviour.* New York: Wiley, 1961.

Gibson, D. Intelligence in the mongoloid and his parent. *American Journal of Mental Deficiency,* 1967, **71**, 1014-1016.

Gibson, E. J. *Principles of perceptual learning and development.* New York: Appleton-Century-Crofts, 1969.

Gil, D. *Violence against children.* Cambridge, Mass.: Harvard University Press, 1971.

Gilhool, T. K. The uses of litigation: The right of retarded citizens to a free public education. In D. J. Stedman (Ed.), *Current issues in mental retardation and human development.* Washington, D.C.: Office of Mental Retardation Coordination, 1972.

Ginsburg, H. *The myth of the deprived child.* Englewood Cliffs, N.J.: Prentice-Hall, 1972.

Ginsburg, H., & Opper, S. *Piaget's theory of intellectual development: An introduction.* Englewood Cliffs, N.J.: Prentice-Hall, 1969. Excerpt in Chap. 12 reprinted with permission of the publisher.

Girardeau, F. L., & Spradlin, J. E. Token rewards in a cottage program. *Mental Retardation,* 1964, **2**(6) 345–351.

Gittelman, M., & Birch, H. G. Childhood schizophrenia: Intellect, neurologic status, perinatal risk, prognosis, and family pathology. *Archives of General Psychiatry,* 1967, **17,** 16–25.

Glaser, R. Instructional technology and the measurement of learning outcomes. *American Psychologist,* 1963, **18,** 519–521.

Glaser, R., & Nitko, A. J. Measurement in learning and instruction. In R. L. Thorndike (Ed.), *Educational measurement* (2d ed.). Washington, D.C.: American Council on Education, 1971.

Glick, B. S., & Margolis, R. A study of the influence of experimental design on clinical outcome in drug research. *American Journal of Psychiatry,* 1962, **118,** 1087.

Goddard, H. H. *The Kallikak family.* New York: Macmillan, 1912.

Goddard, H. H. *Human efficiency and levels of intelligence.* Princeton, N.J.: Princeton University Press, 1920.

Gold, M. W. Stimulus factors in skill training of the retarded on a complex assembly task: Acquisition, transfer and retention. *American Journal of Mental Deficiency,* 1972, **76,** 517–526.

Gold, M. W. Research on the vocational habilitation of the retarded: The present, the future. In N. R. Ellis (Ed.), *International review of research in mental retardation* (Vol. 6). New York: Academic Press, 1973.

Goldberg, B., & Soper, H. Childhood psychosis or mental retardation: A diagnostic dilemma. I. Psychiatric and psychological aspects. *Canadian Medical Association Journal,* 1963, **89,** 1015–1019.

Goldberg, F. H. The performance of schizophrenic, retarded, and normal children on the Bender-Gestalt test. *American Journal of Mental Deficiency,* 1957, **61,** 548–555.

Goldberg, I. I. Trainable but noneducable, a debate with W. M. Cruickshank. *National Education Association Journal,* 1958, **47,** 622–623.

Golden, M., & Birns, B. Social class and cognitive development in infancy. *Merrill-Palmer Quarterly,* 1968, **14,** 139–149.

Golden, M., Birns, B., Bridger, W., & Moss, A. Social-class differentiation in cognitive development among black preschool children. *Child Development,* 1971, **42,** 37–45.

Goldfarb, W. The effects of early institutional care on adolescent personality. *Journal of Experimental Education,* 1943, **12,** 106–129.

Goldfarb, W. Psychological privation in infancy and subsequent adjustment. *American Journal of Orthopsychiatry,* 1945, **15,** 247–255.

Goldfarb, W. Rorschach test differences between family-reared, institution-reared, and schizophrenic children. *American Journal of Orthopsychiatry,* 1949, **19,** 624–633.

Goldfarb, W. Emotional and intellectual consequences of psychologic deprivation in infancy: A reevaluation. In P. H. Hoch & J. Zubin (Eds.), *Psychopathology of childhood.* New York: Grune & Stratton, 1955.

Goldfarb, W. *Childhood schizophrenia.* Cambridge, Mass.: The Commonwealth Fund and Harvard University Press, 1961.

Goldfarb, W., Braunstein, P., & Scholl, H. An approach to the investigation of child schizophrenia: The speech of schizophrenic children and their mothers. *American Journal of Orthopsychiatry,* 1959, **29,** 481–490.

Goldfarb, W., Goldfarb, N., & Pollack, R. C. Changes in IQ of schizophrenic children during residential treatment. *Archives of General Psychiatry,* 1969, **21**, 673-690.

Goldman, H. I., Goldman, J. S., Kaufman, I., & Liebman, O. B. Late effects of early dietary protein intake on low-birth-weight infants. *Journal of Pediatrics,* 1974, **85**, 764-769.

Goldschmidt, R. *Physiological genetics.* New York: McGraw-Hill, 1938.

Goldstein, A. P. *Structured learning therapy: Toward a psychotherapy for the poor.* New York: Academic Press, 1973.

Goldstein, A. P., Martins, J., Hubbins, J., Van Belle, H. A., Schaaf, W., Wiersma, H., & Goodhart, A. The use of modeling to increase independent behavior. *Behavior Research and Therapy,* 1973, **11**, 31-42.

Goldstein, H. Social and occupational adjustment. In H. A. Stevens & R. Heber (Eds.), *Mental retardation.* Chicago: University of Chicago Press, 1964.

Goldstein, H., Moss, J. W., & Jordan, L. J. *The efficacy of special class training on the development of mentally retarded children.* Urbana: University of Illinois, Institute for Research on Exceptional Children, 1965.

Goldstein, K. Die localization in der grosshirnrinde. *Handbuch vor normalische und pathologische Physiologie,* 1927, **10**, 600.

Goldstein, K. Concerning rigidity. *Character and Personality,* 1942-1943, **11**, 209-226.

Goodenough, F. L. *Exceptional children.* New York: Appleton-Century-Crofts, 1956.

Goodman, H., Gottlieb, J., & Harrison, R. H. Social acceptance of EMRs integrated into a nongraded elementary school. *American Journal of Mental Deficiency,* 1972, **76**, 412-417.

Goodman, J., & Cameron, J. IQ constancy in preschool mentally retarded children: Why? *American Journal of Mental Deficiency,* in press.

Goodnow, J. J., & Bethon, B. Piaget's tasks: The effects of schooling and intelligence. *Child Development,* 1966, **37**, 573-582.

Goodwin, D. W., Schulsinger, F., Moller, N., Hermansen, L., Guze, S. B., & Winokur, G. Alcohol problems in adoptees raised apart from alcoholic biological parents. *Archives of General Psychiatry,* 1973, **28**, 238-243.

Gordon, D. A., & Baumeister, A. A. The use of verbal mediation in the retarded as a function of developmental level and response availability. *Journal of Experimental Child Psychology,* 1971, **12**, 95-105.

Gordon, I. J. *Parent involvement in compensatory education.* Champaign: University of Illinois Press, 1970.

Gorham, K. A., Timberg, E. E., & Moore, C. B. *Selected reading suggestions for parents of mentally retarded children.* Washington, D.C.: Office of Child Development, 1970.

Gorlow, L., Butler, A., & Guthrie, G. M. Correlates of self-attitudes of retardates. *American Journal of Mental Deficiency,* 1963, **67**, 549-555.

Gottlieb, J., & Budoff, M. Social acceptability of retarded children in nongraded schools differing in architecture. *American Journal of Mental Deficiency,* 1973, **78**, 15-19.

Gottlieb, J., & Davis, J. E. Social acceptance of EMR children during overt behavioral interactions. *American Journal of Mental Deficiency,* 1973, **78**, 141-143.

Goulet, L. R. Verbal learning and memory research with retardates: An attempt to assess developmental trends. In N. R. Ellis (Ed.), *International review of research in mental retardation* (Vol. 3). New York: Academic Press, 1968.

Goulet, L. R., & Barclay, A. Guessing behavior of normal and retarded children under two random reinforcement conditions. *Child Development,* 1967, **38**, 545-552.

Graham, F., & Berman, P. W. Current status of behavior tests for brain damage in infants and preschool children. *American Journal of Orthopsychiatry,* 1961, **31**, 713–727.

Graham, F. K., Ernhart, C. B., Craft, M., & Berman, P. W. Brain injury in the preschool child: Some developmental considerations. *Psychological Monographs,* 1963, **77**, 573–574.

Graliker, B. V., Koch, R., & Henderson, R. A. A study of factors influencing placement of retarded children in a state residential institution. *American Journal of Mental Deficiency,* 1965, **69**, 553–559.

Gramm, E. P. Peter Beautiful: The story of an enchanted child. *American Journal of Mental Deficiency,* 1951, **56**, 271–274. Excerpt in Chap. 20 reprinted with permission of the publisher.

Graves, W. L., Freeman, M. G., & Thompson, J. D. Culturally related reproductive factors in mental retardation. In H. C. Haywood (Ed.), *Social-cultural aspects of mental retardation.* New York: Appleton-Century-Crofts, 1970.

Gray, R. M., & Kasteler, J. M. The effects of social reinforcement and training on institutionalized mentally retarded children. *American Journal of Mental Deficiency,* 1969, **74**, 50–56.

Graziano, A. M. (Ed.) *Behavior therapy with children.* Chicago: Aldine, 1971.

Great Britain, Department of Education and Science. *Reports on Education,* No. 69. London: HM Stationery Office, 1971.

Grebler, A. M. Parental attitudes toward mentally retarded children. *American Journal of Mental Deficiency,* 1952, **56**, 475–483.

Green, C., & Zigler, E. Social deprivation and the performance of retarded and normal children on a satiation type task. *Child Development,* 1962, **33**, 499–508.

Green, J. D. The hippocampus. *Physiological Review,* 1964, **44**, 561.

Green, R. F. Age-intelligence relationship between ages sixteen and sixty-four: A rising trend. *Developmental Psychology,* 1969, **1**, 618–627.

Greene, F. M. Programmed instruction techniques for the mentally retarded. In N. R. Ellis (Ed.), *International review of research in mental retardation* (Vol. 2). New York: Academic Press, 1966.

Greenfield, P. M. On culture and conservation. In J. S. Bruner, R. R. Oliver, and P. M. Greenfield (Eds.), *Studies in cognitive growth.* New York: Wiley, 1966.

Gregg, G. S., & Elmer, E. Infant injuries: Accident or abuse? *Pediatrics,* 1969, **44**, 434–439.

Gregg, N. M. Congenital cataract following German measles in the mother. *Transactions of the Ophthalmological Society of Australia,* 1941, **3**, 35.

Griggs, R. C., Sunshine, I., Newhill, V. A., Newton, B. W., Buchanan, S., & Rasch, C. A. Environmental factors in childhood lead poisoning. *Journal of the American Medical Association,* 1964, **187**, 703.

Grosneck, J. K. Academic, social and sociometric behaviors involved in the integration of primary aged males from a special class into a regular class. *Dissertation Abstracts International,* 1969, **30**(6-A), 2400–2401.

Grossman, F. K. *Brothers and sisters of retarded children: An exploratory study.* Syracuse, N.Y.: Syracuse University Press, 1972.

Grossman, H. (Ed.) *Manual on terminology and classification in mental retardation, 1973 revision.* Washington, D.C.: American Association on Mental Deficiency, 1973. Excerpts in Chaps. 2 and 17 and Tables 2-2 and 17-6 reprinted with permission of the publisher.

Gruelich, W. W. The rationale of assessing the developmental status of children from roentgenograms of the hand and wrist. *Child Development,* 1950, **21**, 33–44.

Gruen, G. E. Memory, IQ, and transitive inference in normals and retardates. *Developmental Psychology*, 1973, **9**, 436.

Gruen, G. E., & Korte, J. Information processing in familially retarded and nonretarded children. *American Journal of Mental Deficiency*, 1973, **78**, 82–88.

Gruen, G. E., & Vore, D. A. Development of conservation in normal and retarded children. *Developmental Psychology*, 1972, **6**, 146–157.

Gruen, G. E., & Zigler, E. Expectancy of success and the probability learning of middle-class, lower-class, and retarded children. *Journal of Abnormal Psychology*, 1968, **73**, 343–352.

Gruenwald, P. Growth of the human fetus. I. Normal growth and its variation. *American Journal of Obstetrics and Gynecology*, 1966, **94**, 1112–1119.

Gubbay, S. S., Elles, E., Walton, J. N., & Court, S. D. M. Clumsy children. A study of apraxic and agnosic defects in 21 children. *Brain*, 1965, **88**, 295–312.

Guertin, W. H. Mental growth in pseudo-feebleminded. *Journal of Clinical Psychology*, 1949, **5**, 414–418.

Guess, D. The influence of visual and ambulation restrictions on stereotyped behavior. *American Journal of Mental Deficiency*, 1966, **70**, 542–547.

Guilford, J. P. The structure of intellect. *Psychological Bulletin*, 1956, **53**, 267–293.

Guilford, J. P. Three faces of intellect. *American Psychologist*, 1959, **14**, 469–479.

Guilford, J. P. *The nature of human intelligence.* New York: McGraw-Hill, 1967.

Guilford, J. P. Intelligence has three facets. *Science*, 1968, **160**, 615–620.

Guilford, J. P., & Hoepfner, R. The analysis of intelligence. New York: McGraw-Hill, 1971.

Gumz, E. J., & Gubrium, J. F. Comparative parental perceptions of a mentally retarded child. *American Journal of Mental Deficiency*, 1972, **77**, 175–180.

Gunzburg, H. C. *Social competence and mental handicap.* London: Baillere, Tindall, & Cassell, 1968.

Guskin, S. L., Bartel, N. R., & MacMillan, D. L. Perspective of the labeled child. In N. Hobbs (Ed.), *Issues in the classification of children* (Vol. 2). San Francisco: Jossey-Bass, 1975.

Guskin, S. L., & Spicker, H. H. Educational research in mental retardation. In N. R. Ellis (Ed.), *International review of research in mental retardation* (Vol. 3). New York: Academic Press, 1968.

Gussow, J. D. *Nutrition and mental development.* ERIC/IRCD Urban Disadvantaged Series, No. 36. New York: ERIC Information Retrieval Center on the Disadvantaged, 1974.

Guthrie, E. R., & Horton, G. P. *Cats in a puzzle box.* New York: Rinehart Press, 1946.

Guthrie, G. M., Butler, A., & Gorlow, L. Personality differences between institutionalized and non-institutionalized retardates. *American Journal of Mental Deficiency*, 1963, **67**, 543–548.

Guthrie, R. Mass screening for genetic disease. In V. A. McKusick & R. Claiborne (Eds.), *Medical Genetics.* New York: Hospital Practice Publishing Company, 1973.

Guthrie, R., & Susi, A. A simple phenylalanine method for detecting phenylketonuria in large populations of newborn infants. *Pediatrics*, 1963, **32**, 338–343.

Gutride, M., Goldstein, A. P., & Hunter, G. F. The use of modeling and role playing to increase social interaction among asocial psychiatric patients. *Journal of Consulting and Clinical Psychology*, 1973, **40**, 408–415.

Gutshall, R. W., Harper, C., & Burke, D. An exploratory study of the interrelations among driving ability, driving exposure, and socioeconomic status of low, average, and high intelligence males. *Exceptional Children,* 1968, **35**, 43–47.

Haddad, H. M., & Wilkins, L. Congenital anomalies associated with gonadal aplasia, review of 55 cases. *Pediatrics,* 1959, **23**, 885.

Haeussermann, E. *Developmental potential of preschool children.* New York: Grune & Stratton, 1958.

Hagen, J. W. The effect of distraction on selective attention. *Child Development,* 1967, **38**, 685–694.

Hagen, J. W., & Hale, G. A. The development of attention in children. In A. Pick (Ed.), *Minnesota Symposium on Child Development* (Vol. 7). Minneapolis: University of Minnesota Press, 1973.

Hagen, J. W., & Huntsman, N. Selective attention in mental retardates. *Developmental Psychology,* 1971, **5**, 151–160.

Hagen, J. W., Jongeward, R. H., Jr., & Kail, R. V., Jr. Cognitive perspectives on the development of memory. In H. Reese (Ed.), *Advances in child development and behavior* (Vol. 10). New York: Academic Press, 1975.

Hagen, J. W., Meacham, J. A., & Mesibov, G. Verbal labeling, rehearsal, and short-term memory. *Cognitive Psychology,* 1970, **1**, 47–58.

Hall, C. S. The inheritance of emotionality. *Sigma Xi Quarterly,* 1938, **26**, 17–27.

Hallahan, D. P. & Cruickshank, W. M. *Psycho-educational foundations of learning disabilities.* Englewood Cliffs, N.J.: Prentice-Hall, 1973.

Hallahan, D. P., Stainback, S., Ball, D. W., & Kauffman, J. M. Selective attention in cerebral palsied and normal children. *Journal of Abnormal Child Psychology,* 1973, **1**, 280–291.

Halpern, A. S. Some issues concerning the differential diagnosis of mental retardation and emotional disturbance. *American Journal of Mental Deficiency,* 1970, **74**, 796–800.

Halpern, A. S. General unemployment and vocational opportunities for EMR individuals. *American Journal of Mental Deficiency,* 1973, **78**, 123–127.

Halpern, A. S., & Equinozzi, A. M. Verbal expressivity as an index of adaptive behavior. *American Journal of Mental Deficiency,* 1969, **74**, 180–186.

Halstead, W. C. Brain and intelligence: *A quantitative study of the frontal lobes.* Chicago: University of Chicago Press, 1947.

Hamilton, C. R., Moldawer, M. Y., Rosenberg, H. S. Hashimoto's thyroiditis and Turner's syndrome. *Archives of Internal Medicine,* 1968, **122**, 69.

Hamilton, J., & Standahl, J. Suppression of stereotyped screaming behavior in a profoundly retarded institutionalized female. *Journal of Experimental Child Psychology,* 1969, **7**, 114–121.

Hannaway, P. J. Failure to thrive: A study of 100 infants and children. *Clinical Pediatrics,* 1970, **9**, 96–99.

Hanson, E. H. Do boys get a square deal in school? *Education,* 1959, **79**, 597–598.

Hardy, H. A. The relationship between self-attitudes and performance on a paired-associates learning task in educable retardates. *Dissertation Abstracts,* 1967, **27**, 1657.

Hardy, J. B., McCracken, G. H., Jr., Gilkeson, M. R., & Sever, J. L. Adverse fetal outcome following maternal rubella after the first trimester of pregnancy. *Journal of the American Medical Association,* 1969, **207**, 2414–2420.

Haring, N., & Kunzelmann, H. The finer focus of therapeutic behavioral management. In J. Hellmuth (Ed.), *Educational therapy* (Vol. 1). Seattle, Wash.: Special Child Publications, 1966.

Haring, N. G., & Phillips, E. L. *Analysis and modification of classroom behavior.* Englewood Cliffs, N.J.: Prentice-Hall, 1972.

Harlem Youth Opportunities Unlimited, Inc. *Youth in the ghetto.* New York: Author, 1964.

Harlow, H. F. The formation of learning sets. *Psychological Review,* 1949, **56**, 51-65.

Harlow, H. F. Learning and satiation of response in intrinsically motivated complex puzzle performance by monkeys. *Journal of Comparative and Physiological Psychology,* 1950, **43**, 289-294.

Harlow, H. F. The development of affectional patterns in infant monkeys. In B. M. Foss (Ed.), *Determinants of infant behaviour.* New York: Wiley, 1961.

Harlow, H. F. The maternal affectional system. In B. M. Foss (Ed.), *Determinants of infant behaviour II.* New York: Wiley, 1963.

Harlow, H. F., & Griffin, G. Induced mental and social deficits in rhesus monkeys. In S. F. Osler & R. E. Cooke (Eds.), *The biosocial basis of mental retardation.* Baltimore: Johns Hopkins, 1965.

Harper, P. S., & Dyken, P. R. Early onset dystrophia myotonica: Evidence supporting a maternal environmental factor. *Lancet,* 1972, **2**, 53-55.

Harris, D. B., & Roberts, J. *Intellectual maturity of children: Demographic and socioeconomic factors,* DHEW Publication No. (HSM) 72-1059. Washington, D.C.: U.S. Government Printing Office, 1972.

Harris, H. Development of moral attitudes in white and Negro boys. *Developmental Psychology,* 1970, **2**, 376-383. (a)

Harris, H. *Principles of human biochemical genetics.* New York: American Elsevier, 1970. (b)

Harrison, R. H., & Budoff, M. A factor analysis of the Laurelton Self-Concept Scale. *American Journal of Mental Deficiency,* 1972, **76**, 446-459. (a)

Harrison, R. H., & Budoff, M. Demographic, historical, and ability correlates of the Laurelton Self-Concept Scale in an EMR sample. *American Journal of Mental Deficiency,* 1972, **76**, 460-480. (b)

Hart, N. W. M. Academic progress in relation to intelligence and motivation in the opportunity school. *Slow Learning Child,* 1964, **11**, 40-46.

Harter, S. Discrimination learning set in children as a function of IQ and MA. *Journal of Experimental Child Psychology,* 1965, **2**, 31-43.

Harter, S. Mental age, IQ, and motivational factors in the discrimination learning set performance of normal and retarded children. *Journal of Experimental Child Psychology,* 1967, **5**, 123-141.

Harter, S., & Zigler, E. Effectiveness of adult and peer reinforcement on the performance of institutionalized and noninstitutionalized retardates. *Journal of Abnormal Psychology,* 1968, **73**, 144-149.

Harter, S., & Zigler, E. The assessment of effectance motivation in normal and retarded children. *Developmental Psychology,* 1974, **10**, 169-180.

Hausman, R. M. Assessment of the learning potential of exceptional children. *IMRID (Institute on Mental Retardation and Intellectual Development) Papers and Reports,* 1969, **6**(3).

Hawkins, R. P., Peterson, R. F., Schweid, E., & Bijou, S. W. Behavior therapy in the home: Amelioration of problem parent-child relations with the parent in a therapeutic role. *Journal of Experimental Child Psychology,* 1966, **4**, 99-107.

Hayden, A., & Dmitriev, V. *New perspectives on children with Down's syndrome.* Paper presented at Down's Syndrome Congress, Milwaukee, September 1974.

Haywood, H. C. Discrimination and following behavior in chicks as a function of early environmental complexity. *Perceptual and Motor Skills,* 1965, **21**, 299-304.

Haywood, H. C. Experiential factors in intellectual development: The concept of dynamic intelligence. In J. Zubin & G. Jervis (Eds.), *Psychopathology of mental development.* New York: Grune & Stratton, 1967.

Haywood, H. C. Motivational orientation of overachieving and underachieving elementary school children. *American Journal of Mental Deficiency,* 1968, **75**, 661–667.

Haywood, H. C., & Tapp, J. T. Experience and adaptive behavior. In N. R. Ellis (Ed.), *International review of research in mental retardation* (Vol. 1). New York: Academic Press, 1966.

Haywood, H. C., & Weaver, S. J. Differential effects of motivational orientations and incentive conditions on motor performance in institutionalized retardates. *American Journal of Mental Deficiency,* 1967, **72**, 459–467.

Head, H. *Aphasia and kindred disorders of speech.* Cambridge: Cambridge University Press, 1926.

Heal, L. W., Bransky, M. L., & Mankinen, R. L. The role of dimensional preference in reversal and non-reversal shifts of retardates. *Psychonomic Science,* 1966, **6**, 509–510.

Heal, L. W., & Johnson, J. T., Jr. Inhibition deficits in retardate learning and attention. In N. R. Ellis (Ed.), *International review of research in mental retardation* (Vol. 4). New York: Academic Press, 1970.

Hebb, D. O. The effect of early and late brain injury upon the test scores, and the nature of adult intelligence. *Proceedings of the American Philosophical Society,* 1942, **85**, 275–292.

Hebb, D. O. The organization of behavior. New York: Wiley, 1949.

Hebb, D. O. Drives and the conceptual nervous system. *Psychology Review,* 1955, **62**, 243–253.

Heber, R. F. A manual on terminology and classification in mental retardation. *American Journal of Mental Deficiency,* 1959, **64**, Monogr. Suppl. (Rev. ed.), 1961. Excerpt in Chap. 8 reprinted with permission of the publisher.

Heber, R. Personality. In H. A. Stevens & R. Heber (Eds.), *Mental retardation: A review of research.* Chicago: University of Chicago Press, 1964.

Heber, R. *Epidemiology of mental retardation.* Springfield, Ill.: Charles C Thomas, 1970.

Heber, R. F., Dever, R. B., & Conry, J. The influence of environmental and genetic variables on intellectual development. In H. J. Prehm, L. A. Hamerlynck, & J. E. Crosson (Eds.), *Behavioral research in mental retardation.* Eugene: University of Oregon, 1968.

Heber, R., Garber, H., & Falender, C. *The Milwaukee Project: An experiment in the prevention of cultural-familial retardation.* September 1973. (Mimeographed)

Hecht, F., Bryant, J., Gruber, D., & Townes, P. L. The nonrandomness of chromosomal abnormalities. Association of trisomy 18 and Down's syndrome. *New England Journal of Medicine,* 1964, **271**, 1081–1086.

Hecht, F., & MacFarlane, J. P. Mosaicism in Turner's syndrome reflects the lethality of XO. *Lancet,* 1969, **2**, 1197.

Heilbrun, A. B., Jr., Harrell, S. N., & Gillard, B. J. Perceived maternal child-rearing patterns and the effects of social nonreaction upon achievement motivation. *Child Development,* 1967, **38**, 267–281.

Hellman, L. M., & Pritchard, J. A. *Williams obstetrics* (14th ed.). New York: Appleton-Century-Crofts, 1971.

Helsel, E. D. Residential services. In J. Wortis (Ed.), *Mental retardation: An annual review.* New York: Grune & Stratton, 1971.

Henmon, V. A. C. Intelligence and its measurement: A symposium. *Journal of Educational Psychology,* 1921, **12**, 195–198.

Hereford, S. M., Cleland, C. C., & Fellner, M. Territoriality and scent-marking: A study of profoundly retarded enuretics and encopretics. *American Journal of Mental Deficiency,* 1973, **77**, 426–430.

Hermann, A. *Értelmi elmaradas: Értelmi fejlödes az óvodás otthonokban (Mental retardation: Mental development in preschool homes).* Budapest: Tankönyvkiadó, 1967.

Hermann, A., & Komlósi, S. Early child care in Hungary. *International Monograph Series on Early Child Care* (Vol. 1). London: Gordon & Breach, 1972.

Hernandez, J. Unpublished manuscript. Chapel Hill, N.C.: Frank Porter Graham Child Development Center, 1968.

Heron, W. T. The inheritance of brightness and dullness in maze learning ability in the rat. *Journal of Genetic Psychology,* 1941, **59**, 41–49.

Herrnstein, R. J. IQ. *The Atlantic Monthly,* September 1971, 43–64.

Herrnstein, R. J. *IQ in the meritocracy.* Boston: Little, Brown, 1973.

Hertzig, M. E., & Birch, H. G. Longitudinal course of measured intelligence in preschool children of different social and ethnic backgrounds. *American Journal of Orthopsychiatry,* 1971, **41**, 416–426.

Hertzig, M. E., Birch, H. G., Thomas, A., & Mendez, O. A. Class and ethnic differences in the responsiveness of preschool children to cognitive demands. *Monographs of the Society for Research in Child Development,* 1968, **33**(1, Serial No. 117).

Hess, E. H. Imprinting. *Science,* 1959, **130**, 133–141.

Hess, R. D. *Maternal teaching styles and the socialization of educability.* Paper presented at the meeting of the American Psychological Association, Los Angeles, September 1964. Excerpt in chap. 8 reprinted with permission of the author.

Hess, R. D. Parental behavior and children's school achievement: Implications for Head Start. In E. Grotberg (Ed.), *Critical issues in research related to disadvantaged children.* Princeton: Educational Testing Service, 1969.

Hess, R. D. Class and ethnic influences upon socialization. In P. H. Mussen (Ed.), *Carmichael's manual of child psychology* (3d ed.), (Vol. 2). New York: Wiley, 1970.

Hess, R. D., & Shipman, V. C. Early experience and the socialization of cognitive modes in children. *Child Development,* 1965, **36**, 869–886.

Hess, R. D., Shipman, V. C., Brophy, J. E., & Bear, R. M. *The cognitive environments of urban preschool children follow-up phase.* Chicago: The Graduate School of Education, University of Chicago, 1969.

Higgins, J. V., Reed, E. W., & Reed, S. C. Intelligence and family size: A paradox resolved. *Eugenics Quarterly,* 1962, **9**, 84–90.

Hilgard, E. R. *Introduction to psychology* (2d ed.). New York: Harcourt, Brace, 1957.

Hilgard, E. R., & Bower, G. H. *Theories of learning* (4th ed.). Englewood Cliffs, N.J.: Prentice-Hall, 1974.

Hinton, G. Childhood psychosis or mental retardation: A diagnostic dilemma. II. Pediatric and neurological aspects. *Canadian Medical Association Journal,* 1963, **89**, 1020–1024.

Hintzman, D. L., & Block, R. A. Repetition and memory: Evidence for a multiple-trace hypothesis. *Journal of Experimental Psychology,* 1971, **88**, 297–306.

Hirsch, I., & Walder, L. Training mothers in groups as reinforcement therapists for their own children. *Proceedings of the 77th Annual Convention of the American Psychological Association,* 1969, **4**(Part 2), 561–562.

Hiskey, M. S. Nebraska Test of Learning Aptitude. Lincoln, Neb.: Author, 1941–1955.

Hobbs, N. (Ed.) *Issues in the classification of children* (2 vols.). San Francisco: Jossey-Bass, 1975. (a)

Hobbs, N. *The futures of children.* San Francisco: Jossey-Bass, 1975. (b)

Hodgson, W. R. Misdiagnosis of children with hearing loss. *Journal of School Health*, 1969, **39**, 570-575.

Hoe, B. Educating the retarded in USSR. *Instructor*, 1969, **79**, 99-101.

Hoeltke, G. M. Effectiveness of special class placement for educable mentally retarded children. *Dissertation Abstracts*, 1967, **27** (10-A), 3311.

Hofstaetter, P. R. The changing composition of "intelligence": A study of T technique. *Journal of Genetic Psychology*, 1954, **85**, 159-164.

Holden, R. H. Prediction of mental retardation in infancy. *Mental Retardation*, 1972, **10**(1), 28-30.

Hollingshead, A. B., & Redlich, F. C. *Social class and mental illness: A community study.* New York: Wiley, 1958.

Holroys, J., & Wright, F. Neurological implications of WISC verbal-performance discrepancies in a psychiatric setting. *Journal of Consulting Psychology*, 1965, **29**, 206-212.

Holt, K. S. The home care of severely retarded children. *Pediatrics*, 1958, **22**, 746-755.

Holt, S. *The genetics of dermal ridges.* Springfield, Ill.: Charles C Thomas, 1968.

Holzman, M. The verbal environment provided by mothers for their very young children. *Merrill-Palmer Quarterly*, 1974, **20**, 31-42.

Honig, W. K. *Operant behavior: Areas of research and application.* New York: Appleton-Century-Crofts, 1966.

Honzik, M. P. Environmental correlates of mental growth: Prediction from the family setting at 21 months. *Child Development*, 1967, **38**, 337-364.

Honzik, M. P., Macfarlane, J. W., & Allen, L. The stability of mental test performance between two and eighteen years. *Journal of Experimental Education*, 1948, **17**, 309-324.

Hood, C. Social and cultural factors in health of children of immigrants. *Archives of Disease in Childhood*, 1971, **46**, 371-375.

Hook, E. W. Behavioral implications of the human XYY genotype. *Science*, 1973, **179**, 139-150.

Horn, J. L. Organization of abilities and the development of intelligence. *Psychological Review*, 1968, **75**, 242-259.

Horn, J., Loehlin, J., & Willerman, L. *Nature, nurture and intelligence: Twin and adoption studies agree.* Paper presented at the First International Congress of Twin Studies, Rome, October 1974.

House, B. J., Brown, A. L., & Scott, M. S. Children's discrimination learning based on identity or difference. In H. W. Reese (Ed.), *Advances in child development and behavior* (Vol. 9). New York: Academic Press, 1974.

House, B. J., & Zeaman, D. A comparison of discrimination learning in normal and mentally defective children. *Child Development*, 1958, **29**, 411-416.

Hsia, D. Y., & Gelles, S. S. Studies on eryshroblastosis due to ABO incompatibility. *Pediatrics*, 1954, **13**, 503-510.

Hubbard, J. E. *Results of team evaluations in 134 state residential institutions in the U. S.* Final project report to the Division of Mental Retardation, 1969.

Hubel, D. H. Effects of distortion of sensory input on the visual system of kittens. *The Physiologist*, 1967, **10**, 17-45.

Huber, W. G. The relationship of anxiety to the academic performance of institutionalized retardates. *American Journal of Mental Deficiency*, 1965, **69**, 462-466.

Hudson, W. Pictorial depth perception in African groups. *Journal of Social Psychology*, 1960, **52**, 183-208.

Huessy, H. R. Study of the prevalence and therapy of the choreatiform syndrome of hyper-kinesis in rural Vermont. *Acta Paedopsychiatrica,* 1967, **34,** 130–135.

Hulicka, I. M. The socially unmotivated. In J. S. Roucek (Ed.), *The slow learner.* New York: Philosophical Library, 1969.

Hull, C. L. *Principles of behavior.* New York: Appleton, 1943.

Hulzinga, R. J. The relationship of the ITPA to the Stanford-Binet, Form L-M, and the WISC. *Journal of Learning Disabilities,* 1973, **6**(7), 53–58.

Hume, P. B. Direct and indirect mental health services for the mentally retarded. In E. Katz (Ed.), *Mental health services for the mentally retarded.* Springfield, Ill.: Charles C Thomas, 1972.

Hungerford, R. H., DeProspo, C. J., & Rosenzweig, L. E. *The non-academic pupil.* New York: Association of New York City Teachers of Special Education, 1948.

Hunt, E., Frost, N., & Lunneborg, C. Individual differences in cognition: A new approach to intelligence. In G. H. Bower (Ed.), *The psychology of learning and motivation* (Vol. 7). New York: Academic Press, 1973.

Hunt, E., Lunneborg, C., & Lewis, J. What does it mean to be high verbal? *Cognitive Psychology,* 1975, in press.

Hunt, J. McV. *Intelligence and experience.* New York: Ronald Press, 1961.

Hunt, J. McV. Intrinsic motivation and its role in psychological development. In D. Levine (Ed.), *Nebraska symposium on motivation, 1965.* Lincoln: University of Nebraska Press, 1965.

Hunt, J. McV. Transcript of discussion. Conference on the nature of intelligence, University of Pittsburgh, March 1974. (Mimeographed)

Hunt, J. McV., & Kirk, G. E. Social aspects of intelligence: Evidence and issues. In R. Cancro (Ed.), *Intelligence: Genetic and environmental influences.* New York: Grune & Stratton, 1971.

Hunt, J. McV., & Kirk, G. E. *Criterion-referenced tests of semantic mastery in school readiness: A paradigm with illustrations.* Urbana: University of Illinois Psychological Development Laboratory, May 1973. (Mimeographed)

Hunt, J. McV., Paraskevopoulos, J., Schickedanz, D., & Uzgiris, I. C. Variations in the mean ages of achieving object permanence under diverse conditions of rearing. In B. L. Friedlander, G. E. Kirk, & G. M. Sterritt (Eds.), *Exceptional infant* (Vol. 3). New York: Brunner/Mazel, 1974.

Hunt, N. *The world of Nigel Hunt: The diary of a mongoloid youth.* New York: Garrett Publishing, 1967.

Hutchison, A. Stress on families of the mentally handicapped. In *Stress on families of the mentally handicapped.* Proceedings of the Third International Congress, Paris, March 21–26, 1966. Brussels, Belgium: International League of Societies for the Mentally Handicapped, 1966.

Hutt, C. *Males and females.* London: Penguin, 1972.

Hutt, C., & Hutt, S. J. Biological studies of autism. *Journal of Special Education,* 1969, **3,** 3–11.

Iano, R. P. Social class and parental evaluation of educable retarded children. *Education and Training of the Mentally Retarded,* 1970, **5**(2), 62–67.

Iano, R. P., Ayers, D., Heller, H. B., McGettigan, J. F., & Walker, V. S. Sociometric status of retarded children in an integrative program. *Exceptional Children,* 1974, **40,** 267–271.

Illingworth, R. S. Assessment for adoption, a follow-up study. *Acta Paediatrica Scandinavia*, 1969, **58**, 33–36.

Individualized Data Base Project, Report No. 1. Pomona, Calif.: Pacific State Hospital, 1974.

Ingbar, S. F., & Woeber, K. A. The thyroid gland. In R. H. Williams (Ed.), *Textbook of endocrinology* (5th ed.). Philadelphia: Saunders, 1974.

Inhelder, B. *The diagnosis of reasoning in the mentally retarded* (2d ed.). (W. B. Stephens and others, Trans.) New York: Chandler Publishing, 1968. Excerpt in Chap. 12 reprinted with permission of The John Day Co.

Inhelder, B., & Piaget, J. *The growth of logical thinking from childhood to adolescence.* New York: Basic Books, 1958.

Inhelder, B., & Piaget, J. *The early growth of logic in the child.* New York: Harper & Row, 1964.

Insley, J. Syndrome associated with a deficiency of part of the long arm of chromosome No. 18. *Archives of Diseases in Childhood, 1967,* **42**, 140.

Institute of Medicine, National Academy of Sciences. *Infant death: An analysis by maternal risk and health care.* ISBN No. 0-309-02119-7. Washington, D.C.: National Academy of Sciences, 1973.

Ireton, H., Thwing, E., & Gravem, H. Infant mental development and neurological status, family socioeconomic status, and intelligence at age four. *Child Development,* 1970, **41**, 937–945.

Irwin, O. Infant speech: The effect of systematic reading of stories. *Journal of Speech and Hearing Research,* 1960, **3**, 187–190.

Itard, J. M. G. *The wild boy of Aveyron.* (George & Muriel Humphrey, Trans.) New York: Appleton-Century-Crofts, 1932.

Jackson, D. D. (Ed.) *The etiology of schizophrenia.* New York: Basic Books, 1960.

Jackson, M. S. Reactions of some Australian mothers to the birth of their mentally handicapped child. *Slow Learning Child,* 1969, **16**, 37–43.

Jackson, N. Educable mental handicap and delinquency. *Educational Research,* 1970, **12**, 128–134.

Jackson, R. N. Urban distribution of educable mental handicap. *Journal of Mental Deficiency Research,* 1968, **12**, 312–316.

Jacobs, J. F., & Pierce, M. L. The social position of retardates with brain damage associated characteristics. *Exceptional Children,* 1968, **34**, 677–681.

Jacobs, P. A., Brunton, M., Melville, M. M., Brittain, R. P., & McClement, W. F. Aggressive behavior, mental subnormality and the XYY male. *Nature,* 1965, **208**, 1351–1352.

Jacobs, P. A., & Strong, J. A. A case of human intersexuality having a possible XXY sex-determining mechanism. *Nature,* 1959, **183**, 302.

James, W. *The principles of psychology.* New York: Henry Holt, 1890.

Jasper, H. H., Ward, A. A., Jr., & Pope, A. (Eds.) *Basic mechanisms of the epilepsies.* Boston: Little, Brown, 1969.

Jedrysek, E., Pope, L., Klapper, Z., & Wortis, J. *Psychoeducational evaluation of the preschool child.* New York: Grune & Stratton, 1972.

Jencks, C. *Inequality: A reassessment of the effect of family and schooling in America.* New York: Basic Books, 1972.

Jensen, A. R. Rote learning in retarded adults and normal children. *American Journal of Mental Deficiency,* 1965, **69**, 828–834.

Jensen, A. R. Social class and verbal learning. In M. Deutsch, I. Katz, & A. R. Jensen (Eds.), *Social class, race, and psychological development.* New York: Holt, 1968.

Jensen, A. R. How much can we boost IQ and scholastic achievement? *Harvard Educational Review,* 1969, **39**, 1–123. (a)

Jensen, A. R. Intelligence, learning ability and socioeconomic status. *Journal of Special Education,* 1969, **3**, 23–35. (b)

Jensen, A. R. A theory of primary and secondary familial mental retardation. In N. R. Ellis (Ed.), *International review of research in mental retardation* (Vol. 4). New York: Academic Press, 1970. (a)

Jensen, A. R. IQs of identical twins reared apart. *Behavioral Genetics,* 1970, **1**, 133–148. (b)

Jensen, A. R. Can we and should we study race differences? In J. Hellmuth (Ed.), *Disadvantaged child (Vol. 3): Compensatory education—a national debate.* New York: Brunner/Mazel, 1970. (c)

Jensen, A. R. The role of verbal mediation in mental development. *Journal of Genetic Psychology,* 1971, **118**(First half), 39–70.

Jensen, A. R. Cumulative deficit: A testable hypothesis? *Developmental Psychology,* 1974, **10**, 996–1019.

Jensen, A. R., & Rohwer, W. D., Jr. The effect of verbal mediation on the learning and retention of paired associates by retarded adults. *American Journal of Mental Deficiency,* 1963, **68**, 80–84.

Jervis, G. A. The genetics of phenylpyruvic oligophrenia. *Journal of Mental Science,* 1939, **85**, 719.

Jervis, G. A. Studies of phenylpyruvic oligophrenia: The position of the metabolic error. *Journal of Biological Chemistry,* 1947, **169**, 651.

Jinks, J. L., & Fulker, D. W. A comparison of the biometrical, genetical, MAVA and classical approaches to the analysis of human behavior. *Psychological Bulletin,* 1970, **73**, 311–349.

Johansen, W. L. *Elemente der exacten Erblichkeitslehre* (2d ed.). Jena: G. Fischer, 1912.

Johnson, D. L. The influences of social class and race on language test performance and spontaneous speech of preschool children. *Child Development,* 1974, **45**, 517–521.

Johnson, G. O. A study of the social position of mentally handicapped children in the regular grades. *American Journal of Mental Deficiency,* 1950, **55**, 60–89.

Johnson, G. O. Special education for the mentally retarded—A paradox. *Exception Children,* 1962, **29**, 62–69.

Johnson, O. G., & Bommarito, J. W. *Tests and measurements in child development: A handbook.* San Francisco: Jossey-Bass, 1971.

Johnson, R. C. Prediction of independent functioning and of problem behavior measures of IQ and SQ. *American Journal of Mental Deficiency,* 1970, **74**, 591–593.

Johnson, R. C., & Abelson, R. B. The behavioral competence of mongoloid and non-mongoloid retardates. *American Journal of Mental Deficiency,* 1969, **73**, 856–857.

Jones, H. E. The environment and mental development. In L. Carmichael (Ed.), *Manual of child psychology* (2d ed.). New York: Wiley, 1954.

Jones, H. E., & Conrad, H. S. The growth and decline of intelligence: A study of a homogeneous group between the ages of ten and sixty. *Genetic Psychology Monographs,* 1933, **13**, 223–298.

Jones, K. L., & Smith, D. W. Recognition of the fetal alcohol syndrome in early infancy. *Lancet,* 1973, **ii**, 999–1101.

Jones, K. L., Smith, D. W., Streissguth, A. P., & Myrianthopoulos, N. C. Outcome in offspring of chronic alcoholic women. *Lancet,* 1974, **i**, 1076–1078.

Jones, K. L., Smith, D. W., Ulleland, C. N., & Streissguth, A. P. Pattern of malformation in offspring of chronic alcoholic mothers. *Lancet,* 1973, **i**, 1267–1271.

Jones, L. H. The problems of aging and protective services for the retarded adult. In D. J. Stedman (Ed.), *Current issues in mental retardation and human development.* Washington, D.C.: Office of Mental Retardation Coordination, 1972.

Jones, L. V. A factor analysis of the Stanford Binet at four age levels. *Psychometrika,* 1949, **14**, 299-331.

Jones, L. V. Primary abilities in the Stanford Binet, age 13. *Journal of Genetic Psychology,* 1954, **84**, 125-147.

Jones, R. W. Cross-sectional views of visual reproduction and the effects of distraction on visual reproduction by brain-damaged retardates, familial retardates, and normal children. *Dissertation Abstracts,* 1964, **25**(3), 2068.

Jordan, T. E. Early developmental adversity and classroom learning: A prospective inquiry. *American Journal of Mental Deficiency,* 1964, **69**, 360-371.

Juel-Nielsen, N. Individual and environment. A psychiatric-psychological investigation of monozygotic twins reared apart. *Acta Psychiatrica Scandinavia,* 1965, Suppl. 183.

Justice, R. S., O'Connor, G., & Warren, N. Problems reported by parents of mentally retarded children—who helps? *American Journal of Mental Deficiency,* 1971, **75**, 685-691.

Kaback, M. M., & O'Brien, J. S. Tay-Sachs Prototype for prevention of genetic disease. In V. A. McKusick & R. Claiborne (Eds.), *Medical genetics.* New York: Hospital Practice Publishing, 1973.

Kadis, A. L. *Psychotherapy with mental defectives.* Paper read at meetings of the American Association on Mental Deficiency, May 1951.

Kaelber, C. T., & Pugh, T. F. Influence of intrauterine relations on the intelligence of twins. *New England Journal of Medicine,* 1969, **280**, 1030-1034.

Kagan, J. Impulsive and reflective children: Significance of conceptual tempo. In J. D. Krumboltz (Ed.), *Learning and the educational process.* Chicago: Rand McNally, 1965. (a)

Kagan, J. Reflection-impulsivity and reading ability in primary grade children. *Child Development,* 1965, **36**, 609-628. (b)

Kagan, J. Developmental studies in reflection and analysis. In A. H. Kidd & J. H. Rivoire (Eds.), *Perceptual development in children.* New York: International Universities Press, 1966.

Kagan, J., Henker, B., Hen-Tov, A., Levine, J., & Lewis, M. Infants' differential reactions to familiar and distorted faces. *Child Development,* 1966, **37**, 519-530.

Kagan, J., & Moss, H. A. *Birth to maturity: A study in psychological development.* New York: Wiley, 1962.

Kagan, J., & Tulkin, S. R. Social class differences in child rearing during the first year. In H. R. Schaffer (Ed.), *The origins of human social relations.* New York: Academic Press, 1971.

Kalckar, H. M., Kinoshita, J. H., & Donnell, G. N. Galactosemia: Biochemistry, genetics, pathophysiology and developmental aspects. *Biology of Brain Dysfunction,* 1973, **1**, 31-88.

Kamin, L. J. *The science and politics of I.Q.* Potomac, Md.: Lawrence Erlbaum Associates, 1974.

Kangas, J., & Bradway, K. Intelligence at middle age: A 38-year follow-up. *Developmental Psychology,* 1971, **5**, 333-337. Table 17-2 reprinted with the permission of the publisher.

Kanner, L. Autistic disturbance of affective contact. *Nervous Child,* 1943, **2**, 217-250.

Kanner, L. Feeblemindedness, absolute, relative, and apparent. *Nervous Child,* 1948, **7,** 365-397.

Kanner, L. Problems of nosology and psychodynamics of early infantile autism. *American Journal of Orthopsychiatry,* 1949, **19,** 416-426.

Kanner, L. *Child psychiatry* (3d ed.). Springfield, Ill.: Charles C Thomas, 1957.

Kanner, L. *A history of the care and study of the mentally retarded.* Springfield, Ill.: Charles C Thomas, 1964.

Kanner, L., & Eisenberg, L. Notes on the follow-up studies of autistic children. In P. H. Hoch & J. Zubin (Eds.), *Psychopathology of childhood.* New York: Grune & Stratton, 1955.

Kaplan, A. R. *Genetic factors in "schizophrenia."* Springfield, Ill.: Charles C Thomas, 1972.

Kappauf, W. E. Studying the relation of task performance to the variables of chronological age, mental age, and IQ. In N. R. Ellis (Ed.), *International review of research in mental retardation* (Vol. 6). New York: Academic Press, 1973.

Karp, L., Smith, D. W., Omenn, G. S., Johnson, S., & Jones, K. The use of ultrasound in the prenatal exclusion of primary microcephaly. *Gynecologic Investigation,* 1975, in press.

Katz, E. *The retarded adult in the community.* Springfield, Ill.: Charles C Thomas, 1968.

Katz, E. Introduction. In E. Katz (Ed.), *Mental health services for the mentally retarded.* Springfield, Ill.: Charles C Thomas, 1972.

Katz, I. A new approach to the study of school motivation in minority group children. In V. Allen (Ed.), *Psychological factors in poverty.* Chicago: Markham, 1970.

Kaufman, M. E. The formation of a learning set in institutionalized and noninstitutionalized mental defectives. *American Journal of Mental Deficiency,* 1963, **67,** 601-605.

Kaufman, M. E. The effects of institutionalization on development of stereotyped and social behaviors in mental defectives. *American Journal of Mental Deficiency,* 1967, **71,** 581-585.

Kaufman, M. E. Long-term retention of a learning set in mentally retarded children. *American Journal of Mental Deficiency,* 1971, **75,** 752-754.

Kaufman, M. E., & Levitt, H. A study of three stereotyped behaviors in institutionalized mental defectives. *American Journal of Mental Deficiency,* 1965, **69,** 467-473.

Kaufman, M. E., & Prehm, H. J. A review of research on learning sets and transfer of training in mental defectives. In N. R. Ellis (Ed.), *International review of research in mental retardation* (Vol. 2). New York: Academic Press, 1966.

Keane, V. E. Incidence of speech and language problems in the mentally retarded. *Mental Retardation,* 1972, **10**(2), 3-8.

Keasey, C. T., & Charles, D. C. Conservation of substance in normal and mentally retarded children. *Journal of Genetic Psychology,* **111**(2), 1967, 271-279.

Keeler, K. F. Post-school adjustment of educable mentally retarded youth educated in San Francisco. *Dissertation Abstracts,* 1964, **25**(2), 936-937.

Keleske, L., Solomons, G., & Opitz, E. Parental reactions to phenylketonuria in the family. *Journal of Pediatrics,* 1967, **70,** 793-798.

Kellaghan, T., & MacNamara, J. Family correlates of verbal reasoning ability. *Developmental Psychology,* 1972, **7,** 49-53.

Kelley, T. L. *Crossroads in the mind of man.* Stanford, Calif.: Stanford University Press, 1928.

Kelley, W. N., & Wyngaarden, J. B. The Lesch-Nyhan syndrome. In J. B. Stanbury, J. B. Wyngaarden, & D. S. Fredrickson (Eds.), *The metabolic basis of inherited disease* (3d ed.). New York: McGraw-Hill, 1972.

Kendler, T. S. Development of mediating responses in children. *Monographs of the Society for Research in Child Development,* 1963, **28**(1, Serial No. 86).

Kennedy, C., Drage, J. S., & Schwartz, B. K. *Preliminary data with respect to the relationships between Apgar score at one and five minutes and fetal outcome.* Paper presented the spring scientific meeting of the Collaborative Perinatal Project, National Institute of Neurological Diseases and Blindness, Washington, 1963.

Kennedy, R. J. The social adjustment of morons in a Connecticut city. Hartford, Conn.: State Office Building, 1948.

Kennedy, R. J. *A Connecticut community revisited: A study of the social adjustment of a group of mentally deficient adults in 1948 and 1960.* Hartford: Connecticut State Department of Health, Office of Mental Retardation, 1966.

Kennedy, W. A. A follow-up normative study of Negro intelligence and achievement. *Monographs of the Society for Research in Child Development,* 1969, **34**(2, Serial No. 126).

Kennedy, W. A., Van de Riet, V., & White, J. C., Jr. A normative sample of intelligence and achievement of Negro elementary school children in the southeastern United States. *Monographs of the Society for Research in Child Development,* 1963, **28**(6, Serial No. 90).

Kennedy, W. S. Cultural deprivation: Its role in central nervous system functioning. In J. Khanna (Ed.), *Brain damage and mental retardation.* Springfield, Ill.: Charles C Thomas, 1968.

Keogh, B. K., & Birch, H. G. Relation between birth condition and neuro-behavioral organization in the neonate. *Pediatric Research, 1968,* **2**, 243-249.

Kephart, N. C. *The slow learner in the classroom* (2d ed.). Columbus, Ohio: Charles E. Merrill, 1971.

Kermode, G. O. Food additives. *Scientific American,* 1972, **226** (March), 15-21.

Kershner, J. R. Intellectual and social development in relation to family functioning: A longitudinal comparison of home vs. institutional effects. *American Journal of Mental Deficiency,* 1970, **75**, 276-284.

Kershner, J. R. Conservation of vertical-horizontal space perception in trainable retarded children. *American Journal of Mental Deficiency,* 1973, **77**, 710-716.

Kessler, J. W., Ablon, G., & Smith, E. Separation reactions in young, mildly retarded children. *Children,* 1969, **16**, 2-7.

Kety, S. S., Rosenthal, D., Wender, P. H., & Schulsinger, F. Mental illness in the biological and adoptive families of adopted schizophrenics. *American Journal of Psychiatry,* 1971, **128**, 302.

Kidd, J. W. The "adultated" mentally retarded. *Education and Training of the Mentally Retarded,* 1970, **5**(2), 71-72.

King, R. D., Raynes, N. V., & Tizard, J. *Patterns of residential care: Sociological studies in institutions for handicapped children.* London: Routledge and Kegan Paul, 1971.

King, W. L., & Seegmiller, B. Performance of 14- to 22-month-old black, firstborn male infants on two tests of cognitive development. *Developmental Psychology,* 1973, **8**, 317-326.

Kirk, S. A. *Early education of the mentally retarded: An experimental study.* Urbana: University of Illinois Press, 1958.

Kirk, S. A., McCarthy, J. J. & Kirk, W. D. *Examiner's manual: Illinois Test of Psycholinguistic Abilities* (Rev. ed.). Urbana: University of Illinois Press, 1968.

Kirk, W. D. Correlation between arithmetic achievement and performance on Piaget tasks. *Slow Learning Child,* 1968, **15**, 89-101.

Kirkendall, D. R., & Ismail, A. H. The ability of personality variables in discriminating among three intellectual groups of preadolescent boys and girls. *Child Development,* 1970, **41**, 1173-1181.

Kirkland, M. H. Institutions for the retarded: Their place in the continuum of services. *Mental Retardation,* 1967, **5**(2), 5-8. Excerpt in chap. 21 reprinted with permission of the publisher and the author.

Klaber, M. M. Parental visits to institutionalized children. *Mental Retardation,* 1968, **6**(6), 39-41.

Klaber, M. Institutional programming and research: A vital partnership in action. In A. A. Baumeister & E. C. Butterfield (Eds.), *Residential facilities for the mentally retarded.* Chicago: Aldine, 1970.

Klaber, M. M., & Butterfield, E. C. Stereotyped rocking—A measure of institution and ward effectiveness. *American Journal of Mental Deficiency,* 1968, **73**, 13-20.

Klaber, M. M., Butterfield, E. C., & Gould, L. J. Responsiveness to social reinforcement among institutionalized retarded children. *American Journal of Mental Deficiency,* 1969, **73**, 890-895.

Klapper, Z. S. Developmental psychology. In J. Wortis (Ed.), *Mental retardation: An annual review* (Vol. 1). New York: Grune & Stratton, 1970.

Klaus, R. A., & Gray, S. W. The early training project for disadvantaged children: A report after five years. *Monographs of the Society for Research in Child Development,* 1968, **33**(4, Serial No. 120).

Klausmeier, H. J., & Wiersma, W. The effects of IQ level and sex on divergent thinking of seventh grade pupils of low, average, and high IQ. *Journal of Educational Research,* 1965, **58**, 300-302.

Klinefelter, H. F., Jr., Reifenstein, E. C., Jr., & Albright, F. Syndrome characterized by gynecomastia, aspermatogenesis with aleydigism and increased excretion of follicle-stimulating hormone. *Journal of Clinical Endocrinology,* 1942, **2**, 615.

Knight, D., Ludwig, A. J., Strazzulla, M., & Pope, L. The role of varied therapies in the rehabilitation of the retarded child. *American Journal of Mental Deficiency,* 1957, **61**, 508-515.

Knight, O. B. *The self concept of educable mentally retarded children in special and regular classes.* Unpublished doctoral dissertation, *Dissertation Abstracts* 28-4483A. University of North Carolina, Chapel Hill, 1967.

Knobloch, H., & Pasamanick, B. The developmental behavioral approach to the neurologic examination in infancy. *Child Development,* 1962, **33**, 181-198.

Knobloch, H., & Pasamanick, B. Prospective studies on the epidemiology of reproductive causality: Methods, findings, and some implications. *Merrill-Palmer Quarterly, 1966,* **12**, 27-43.

Knobloch, H., & Pasamanick, B. Prediction from the assessment of neuromotor and intellectual status in infancy. In J. Zubin & G. A. Jervis (Eds.), *Psychopathology of mental development.* New York: Grune & Stratton, 1967.

Knox, W. E. Phenylketonuria. In J. B. Stanbury, J. B. Wyngaarden, D. S. Frederickson (Eds.), *The metabolic basis of inherited disease.* New York: McGraw-Hill, 1972.

Koch, R. A longitudinal study of 143 mentally retarded children (1955-1961). *The Training School Bulletin,* 1963, **1**, 4-11.

Koch, R., & Dobson, J. C. (Eds.) *The mentally retarded child and his family: A multidisciplinary handbook.* New York: Brunner/Mazel, 1971.

Kogan, K. L., & Tyler, N. Mother-child interaction in young physically handicapped children. *American Journal of Mental Deficiency,* 1973, **77**, 492-497.

Kogan, K. L., Wimberger, H. C., & Bobbitt, R. A. Analysis of mother-child interaction in young mental retardates. *Child Development,* 1969, **40**, 799-812.

Kohen-Raz, R. Mental and motor development of kibbutz, institutionalized, and home-reared infants in Israel. *Child Development,* 1968, **39**, 489-504.

Kohler, C., Brisson, S., & Charassin, R. Enquete sur la nuptialité et la descendance d'adultes debiles mentaux moyen suivis depuis leur enfance (Survey on the marriage rate and the lineage of adult mental defectives who have been followed since childhood). *Revue d'Hygiene et de Medecine Sociale,* 1970, **18**, 73-88.

Köhler, W. *The mentality of apes.* (E. Winter, Trans.) New York: Harcourt, Brace & World, 1925.

Kolvin, I., Humphrey, M., & McNay, A. Cognitive factors in childhood psychosis. *British Journal of Psychiatry,* 1971, **118**, 415-419.

Komai, T., Kishimato, K., & Ozaki, Y. Genetic study of microcephaly based on Japanese material. *American Journal of Human Genetics,* 1955, **7**, 51-65.

Komisar, D. D. Community care for retarded: A caution from Great Britain. *Rehabilitation Record,* 1965, **6**(3), 38-40.

Köng, E. Very early treatment of cerebral palsy. In J. M. Wolf (Ed.), *The results of treatment in cerebral palsy.* Springfield, Ill.: Charles C Thomas, 1969.

Korkes, L. *A study of the impact of mentally ill children upon their families.* Trenton: New Jersey Department of Institutions and Agencies, 1955. (Mimeographed)

Korner, A. F. Early stimulation and maternal care. *Early Child Development & Care,* 1973, **2**, 307-327.

Kounin, J. S. Intellectual development and rigidity. In R. G. Barker, J. S. Kounin, & H. F. Wright (Eds.), *Child behavior and development.* New York: McGraw-Hill, 1943.

Kramm, E. R. *Families of mongoloid children.* Children's Bureau Publication No. 401. Washington, D.C.: U.S. Government Printing Office, 1963.

Kraus, P. E. *Yesterday's children: A longitudinal study of children from kindergarten into the adult years.* New York: Wiley-Interscience, 1973.

Krech, D., Rosenzweig, M. R., & Bennett, E. L. Dimensions of discrimination and level of cholinesterase activity in the cerebral cortex of the rat. *Journal of Comparative and Physiological Psychology,* 1956, **49**, 261-268.

Krechevsky, I. Hereditary nature of "hypotheses." *Journal of Comparative Psychology,* 1933, **16**, 99-116.

Kreutzer, M. A., Leonard, C., & Flavell, J. H. *An interview study of children's knowledge about memory.* Unpublished manuscript, University of Minnesota, 1974.

Krischef, C. H. State laws on marriage and sterilization of the mentally retarded. *Mental Retardation,* 1972, **10**(3), 36-38.

Krumboltz, J. D., & Krumboltz, H. B. *Changing children's behavior.* Englewood Cliffs, N.J.: Prentice-Hall, 1972.

Kubaiko, J. H., & Kokaska, C. J. Driver education for the educable mentally retarded: Is our instruction adequate? *Training School Bulletin,* 1969, **66**, 111-114.

Kugel, R. B., & Parsons, M. H. *Children of deprivation: Changing the course of familial retardation.* Washington, D.C.: Children's Bureau, 1967.

Kugel, R. B., Trembath, J., & Sagar, S. Some characteristics of patients legally committed to a state institution for the mentally retarded. *Mental Retardation* 1968, **6**(4), 2-8.

Kuhlmann, F. *Tests of mental development.* Minneapolis: Educational Test Bureau, 1939.

Kuralt, W. H. Homemaker service in a public agency for families with a mentally retarded member. In *Homemaker home health aide-service for families with a mentally retarded member.* New York: National Council for Homemaker Services, 1966.

Kurland, L. T., Faro, S. N., & Siedler, H. Minimata disease: The outbreak of a neurologic disorder in Minimata, Japan, and its relationship to the ingestion of seafood contaminated by mercuric compounds. *World Neurology,* 1960, **1**, 370.

Kurtz, R. A. Comparative evaluations of suspected retardates. *American Journal of Diseases of Children,* 1965, **109**, 58-65.

Kurtz, R. A., & Wolfensberger, W. Separation experiences of residents in an institution for the mentally retarded: 1910-1959. *American Journal of Mental Deficiency.* 1969, **74**, 389-396.

Kushlick, A. Paper No. 1. In E. Stephen (Ed.), *Residential care for the mentally retarded.* Oxford, England: Pergamon Press, 1970.

LaCrosse, J. E. *A study of examiner reliability on the Stanford-Binet Intelligence Scale (Form L-M) employing white and Negro examiners as subjects.* Unpublished M. A. thesis, University of North Carolina, 1964.

LaDu, B. N. Histidinemia. In J. B. Stanbury, J. B. Wyngaarden, & D. S. Fredrickson (Eds.), *The metabolic basis of inherited disease* (3d ed.). New York: McGraw-Hill, 1972.

Lagos, J. C., & Gomez, M. R. Tuberous sclerosis: Reappraisal of a clinical entity. *Mayo Clinic Proceedings,* 1967, **42**, 26-49.

Lambert, N. M., Wilcox, M. R., & Gleason, W. P. *The educationally retarded child.* New York: Grune & Stratton, 1974.

Landsteiner, K., & Wiener, A. S. An agglutinable factor in human blood recognized by immune sera for Rhesus blood. *Proceedings of the Society for Experimental Biology and Medicine,* 1940, **43**, 223.

Langman, J. *Medical embryology: Human development—normal and abnormal.* Baltimore: Williams & Wilkins, 1969.

Lapouse, R., & Monk, M. A. An epidemiologic study of behavior characteristics in children. *American Journal of Public Health,* 1958, **48**, 1134-1144.

Laufer, M. W., & Gair, D. S. Childhood schizophrenia. In L. Bellak & L. Loeb (Eds.), *The schizophrenic syndrome.* New York: Grune & Stratton, 1969.

Laurendeau, M., & Pinard, A. *Causal thinking in the child.* New York: International Universities Press, 1962.

Laurendeau, M., & Pinard, A. *The development of the concept of space in the child.* New York: International Universities Press, 1970.

Laurent, C., & Robert, J. M. Etude génétique et clinique d'une famille de sept enfants dan laquelle trois sujets son atteints de la "maladie du cri-du chat." *Année Genetique,* 1966, **9**, G113.

LaVeck, G. D., & de la Cruz, F. F. Contraception for the mentally retarded: Current methods and future prospects. In F. F. de la Cruz & G. D. LaVeck (Eds.), *Human sexuality and the mentally retarded.* New York: Brunner/Mazel, 1973.

Lawson, D., Metcalfe, M., & Pampiglione, G. Meningitis in childhood. *British Medical Journal,* 1965, **1**, 557-562.

Leahy, A. M. Nature-nurture and intelligence. *Genetic Psychology Monographs,* 1935, **17**, 241-305.

Lee, E. S. Negro intelligence and selective migration: A Philadelphia test of the Klineberg hypothesis. *American Sociological Review,* 1951, **16**, 227-233.

Lefford, A., Birch, H. G., & Green, G. The perceptual and cognitive bases for finger localization and selective finger movement in preschool children. *Child Development,* 1974, **45**, 335-343.

Lejeune, J., Berger, R., Laforcade, J., & Réthoré, M. O. La délétion partielle du bras long du chromosome 18. Individualisation d'un nouvel état morbide. *Année Gentique,* 1966, **9,** 32.

Lejeune, J., Gautier, M., & Turpin, R. Le mongolisme. Premier example d'aberration autosomique humaine. *Année Genetique,* 1959, **1,** 41.

Lejeune, J., Laforcade, J., Berger, R., Vialatte, J., Boeswillwald, M., Seringe, P., & Turpin, R. Trois cas de délétion partielle du bras court du chromosome 5. *Comples Rendus Academie des Sciences,* 1963, **257,** 3098.

Leland, H., Nihira, K., Foster, R., Shellhaas, M., & Kagin, E. *Conference on measurement of adaptive behavior, III.* Parsons, Kansas: Parsons State Hospital and Training Center, 1968. Excerpt in Chap. 17 reprinted with permission of the publisher.

Leland, H., Shellhaas, M., Nihira, K., & Foster, R. Adaptive behavior: A new dimension in the classification of the mentally retarded. *Mental Retardation Abstracts,* 1967, **4,** 359-387.

Leland, H., & Smith, D. E. Unstructured material in play therapy for emotionally disturbed, brain damaged, mentally retarded children. *American Journal of Mental Deficiency,* 1962, **66,** 621-628.

Leland, H., & Smith, D. E. *Play therapy with mentally subnormal children.* New York: Grune & Stratton, 1965. Excerpt in Chap. 19 reprinted with permission of the publisher and the senior author.

Leland, H., & Smith, D. E. Psychotherapeutic considerations with mentally retarded and developmentally disabled children. In I. Katz (Ed.), *Mental health services for the mentally retarded.* Springfield, Ill.: Charles C Thomas, 1972.

Lemkau, P. V., & Imre, P. D. Results of a field epidemiologic study. *American Journal of Mental Deficiency,* 1969, **73,** 858-863.

Lemli, L., & Smith, D. W. The XO syndrome: A study of the differential phenotype in 25 patients. *Journal of Pediatrics,* 1963, **63,** 577.

Lempp, R., & Vogel, B. Untersuchungen zur kindlichen Schizophrenie (Research into childhood schizophrenia). *Acta Paedopsychiatria,* 1966, **33**(10), 322-331.

Lenkowsky, R. S., & Blackman, L. S. The effect of teachers' knowledge of race and social class on their judgments of children's academic competence and social acceptability. *Mental Retardation,* 1968, **6**(6), 15-17.

Lenneberg, E. H. *Biological foundations of language.* New York: Wiley, 1967.

Lenneberg, E. H. The effect of age on the outcome of central nervous system disease in children. In R. L. Isaacson (Ed.), *The neuropsychology of development.* New York: Wiley, 1968.

Lenneberg, E. H., Nichols, I. A., & Rosenberger, E. F. Primitive stages of language development in Mongolism. *Disorders of Communication,* 1962, **VVL-1,** 119-137.

Leonard, M. F., Landy, G., Ruddle, F. H., & Lubs, H. A. Early development of children with abnormalities of the sex chromosomes: A prospective study. *Pediatrics,* 1974, **54,** 208-212.

Lesch, M., & Nyhan, W. L. A familial disorder of uric acid metabolism and central nervous system function. *American Journal of Medicine,* 1964, **36,** 561.

Levenstein, P. *A message from home: A home-based intervention method for low-income preschoolers.* Paper presented at conference on "The Mentally Retarded and Society: A Social Science Perspective." Niles, Michigan, April 18, 1974.

Levine, M. N. Hypothesis behavior by humans during discrimination learning. *Journal of Experimental Psychology,* 1966, **71,** 331-338.

Levine, M. N., & Elliott, C. B. Toilet training for profoundly retarded with a limited staff. *Mental Retardation,* 1970, **8**(3), 48–50.

Levitt, E. A., Rosenbaum, A. L., Willerman, L., & Levitt, M. Intelligence of retinoblastoma patients and their siblings. *Child Development,* 1972, **43**, 939–948.

Levy, D. M. *Maternal overprotection.* New York: Columbia University Press, 1943.

Levy, E. Z. Long-term follow-up of former inpatients at the Children's Hospital of the Menninger Clinic. *American Journal of Psychiatry,* 1969, **125**, 1633–1639.

Levy, H. L., Madigan, P. M., Shih, V. E. Massachusetts metabolic disorders screening program. I. Techniques and results of urine screening. *Pediatrics,* 1972, **49**, 825–836.

Levy, H. L., Shih, V. E., & Madigan, P. M. Routine newborn screening for histidinemia: Clinical and biochemical results. *New England Journal of Medicine,* 1974, **291**, 1214–1219.

Lewin, K. *A dynamic theory of personality.* New York: McGraw-Hill, 1935.

LeWinn, E. B., Doman, G., Doman, R. J., Delacato, C. H., Spitz, E. B., & Thomas, E. W. Neurological organization: The basis for learning. In J. Hellmuth (Ed.), *Learning disorders* (Vol. 2). Seattle, Wash.: Special Child Publications, 1966.

Lewis, E. D. Types of mental deficiency and their social significance. *Journal of Mental Science,* 1933, **79**, 298–304.

Lewis, M. Infants' responses to facial stimuli during the first year of life. *Developmental Psychology,* 1969, **1**, 75–86.

Lewis, M. Individual differences in the measurement of early cognitive growth. In J. Hellmuth (Ed.), *Exceptional infant* (Vol. 2). New York: Brunner/Mazel, 1971. (a)

Lewis, M. *Infant development in lower-class American families.* Paper presented at the meeting of the Society for Research in Child Development, Minneapolis, 1971. (b)

Lewis, M. (Ed.) *The effect of the infant on its caregiver.* New York: Wiley-Interscience, 1974.

Lewis, M., Goldberg, S., & Rausch, M. Attention distribution as a function of novelty and familiarity. *Psychonomic Science,* 1967, **7**, 227–228.

Lewis, M., Kagan, J., & Kalafat, J. Patterns of fixation in infants. In J. S. Seidman (Ed.), *The child: A book of readings.* New York: Holt, 1967.

Lewontin, R. C. Race and intelligence. *Bulletin of the Atomic Scientists,* 1970, **26**, 2–8.

Lilienfeld, A. M., & Parkhurst, E. A study of the association of factors of pregnancy and parturition with the development of cerebral palsy: A preliminary report. *American Journal of Hygiene,* 1951, **53**, 262–282.

Lilienfeld, A. M., & Pasamanick, B. The association of maternal and fetal factors with the development of mental deficiency: II. *American Journal of Mental Deficiency,* 1956, **60**, 557–569.

Lillie, D. L. The effects of motor development lessons on mentally retarded children. *American Journal of Mental Deficiency,* 1968, **72**, 803–808.

Linde, T. F., & Kopp, T. *Training retarded babies and pre-schoolers.* Springfield, Ill.: Charles C Thomas, 1973.

Lindsjö, A. Down's syndrome in Sweden: An epidemiological study of a three-year material. *Acta Paediatrica Scandinavia,* 1974, **63**, 571–576.

Lindsley, D. C. Psychopathology and motivation. In M. Jones (Ed.), *Nebraska symposium on motivation* (Vol. 5). Lincoln: University of Nebraska Press, 1966.

Lindsten, J. Source of the X in XO females: The evidence of Xg. *Lancet,* 1963, **1**, 558.

Lipman, R. S. The use of psychopharmacological agents in residential facilities for the retarded. In F. J. Menolascino (Ed.), *Psychiatric approaches to mental retardation.* New York: Basic Books, 1970.

Lipman, R. S., & Griffith, B. C. Effects of anxiety level on concept formation: A test of drive theory. *American Journal of Mental Deficiency,* 1960, **65,** 342–348.

Lippman, L., & Goldberg, I. I. *Right to education: Anatomy of the Pennsylvania case and its implications for exceptional children.* New York: Teachers College Press, 1973.

Lister, C. M. The development of a concept of weight conservation in E. S. N. children. *British Journal of Educational Psychology,* 1969, **39,** 245–252.

Litrownik, A. J., Franzini, L. R., & Harvey, S. *Acceleration of identity and equivalence conservation in moderately retarded children via film-mediated modeling.* Paper presented at meetings of the American Psychological Association, New Orleans, September 1974.

Littell, W. M. The Wechsler Intelligence Scale for Children: Review of a decade of research. *Psychological Bulletin,* 1960, **57,** 132–156.

Little, W. J. On the influence of abnormal parturition, difficult labor, premature birth, and asphyxia neonatorum on the mental and physical condition of the child, especially in relation to deformities. *Transactions of the London Obstetrical Society,* 1862, **3.**

Liverant, S. Intelligence: A concept in need of re-examination. *Journal of Consulting Psychology,* 1960, **24,** 101–110.

Lloyd-Still, J. D., Hurwitz, I., Wolff, P. H., & Shwachman, H. Intellectual development after severe malnutrition in infancy. *Pediatrics,* 1974, **54,** 306–311.

Lockyer, L., & Rutter, M. A five- to fifteen-year follow-up study on infantile psychosis: IV. Patterns of cognitive ability. *British Journal of Social and Clinical Psychology,* 1970, **9,** 152–163.

Lodge, A., & Kleinfeld, P. B. Early behavioral development in Down's syndrome. In M. Coleman (Ed.), *Serotonin in Down's syndrome.* London: North-Holland, 1973.

Logan, H. My child is mentally retarded. In Wolfensberger & Kurtz (Eds.), *Management of the family of the mentally retarded.* New York: Follett Educational Corp., 1969. pp. 363–369.

Lorber, J., & Bassi, U. The aetiology of neonatal hydrocephalus (excluding cases with spina bifida). *Developmental Medicine and Child Neurology,* 1965, **7,** 289–294.

Lorenz, K. Z. The companion in the bird's world. *The Auk,* 1937, **54,** 245–273.

Lotter, W. Services for a group of autistic children in Middlesex. In J. K. Wing (Ed.), *Early childhood autism.* Oxford: Pergamon Press, 1966.

Lovaas, O. I. Behavioral treatment of autistic children. *University Programs Modular Studies.* Morristown, N.J.: General Learning Press, 1973.

Lovaas, O. I., Berberich, B. F., Perloff, B. F., & Schaeffer, B. Acquisition of imitative speech by schizophrenic children. *Science,* 1966, **10,** 705–707.

Lovaas, O. I., & Bucher, B. D. *Perspectives in behavior modification with deviant children.* Englewood Cliffs, N.J.: Prentice-Hall, 1974.

Lovaas, O. I., Freitas, I., Nelson, K., & Whalen, C. The establishment of imitation and its use for the development of complex behavior in schizophrenic children. *Behavior Research and Therapy,* 1967, **5,** 171–181.

Lovaas, O. I., Schreibman, L., Koegel, R., & Rehm, R. Selective responding by autistic children to multiple sensory input. *Journal of Abnormal Psychology,* 1971, **77,** 211–212.

Lovaas, O. I., & Simmons, J. Q. Manipulation of self-destruction in three retarded children. *Journal of Applied Behavior Analysis,* 1969, **2,** 143–157.

Lovell, K. The developmental approach of Jean Piaget: Open discussion. In M. Garrison, Jr. (Ed.), Cognitive Models and development in mental retardation. *American Journal of Mental Deficiency,* 1966, **70**(Monogr. Suppl.), 84–95.

Lowenfeld, M. The Mosaic Test. *American Journal of Orthopsychiatry,* 1949, **19**, 537-550.

Lowenfeld, M. *The Lowenfeld Mosaic Test.* London: Newman Neame, Ltd., 1954.

Lubchenco, L. O., Hansman, C., Dressler, M., et al. Intrauterine growth as estimated from liveborn birth-weight data at 24 to 42 weeks of gestation. *Pediatrics,* 1963, **32**, 793-800.

Lucito, L. J. Independence-conformity behavior as a function of intellect: Bright and dull children. *Exceptional Children,* 1964, **31**, 5-13.

Lucker, W. G. *The effects of environmental stimulation on the perceptual thresholds of high active and low active mentally retarded persons.* Institution on Mental Retardation and Intellectual Development, Monograph No. 15, August 1970.

Ludkins-Katz, F. Creative art expression of the mentally retarded. In E. Katz (Ed.), *Mental health services for the mentally retarded.* Springfield, Ill.: Charles C Thomas, 1972.

Lunneborg, P. Relations among social disability, achievement, and anxiety measures in children. *Child Development,* 1964, **35**, 169-182.

Luria, A. R. Experimental study of the higher nervous activity of the abnormal child. *Journal of Mental Deficiency Research,* 1959, **3**, 1-22.

Luria, A. R. *The role of speech in the regulation of normal and abnormal behavior.* New York: Pergamon Press, 1961.

Luria, A. R. Psychological studies of mental deficiency in the Soviet Union. In N. R. Ellis (Ed.), *Handbook of mental deficiency.* New York: McGraw-Hill, 1963.

Lüscher, K. K., Gross, P., & Ritter, V. Early child care in Switzerland. *International Monograph Series on Early Child Care* (Vol. 4). London: Gordon & Breach, 1973.

Luszki, W. A. Application of deprivation concepts to the deaf retarded. *Mental Retardation,* 1964, **2**(3), 164-170.

Lutkus, A., & Trabasso, T. Transitive inferences by preoperational, retarded adolescents. *American Journal of Mental Deficiency,* 1974, **78**, 599-606.

Lyle, J. G. The effect of an institution environment upon the verbal development of imbecile children. (ii) Speech and language. *Journal of Mental Deficiency Research,* 1960, **4**, 1-13.

Lynn, D. B. Determinants of intellectual growth in women. *School Review,* 1972, **80**, 240-260.

Lyon, M. F. Sex chromatin and gene action in the mammalian X-chromosome. *American Journal of Human Genetics,* 1962, **14**, 135.

Lyon, R., & Bland, W. The transfer of adult mental retardates from a state hospital to nursing homes. *Mental Retardation,* 1969, **7**(5), 31-36.

McAllister, R. J., Butler, E. E., & Jen-lei, T. Patterns of social interaction among families of behaviorally retarded children. *Journal of Marriage and the Family,* 1973, **35**, 93-100.

MacAndrew, C., & Edgerton, R. B. IQ and the social competence of the profoundly retarded. *American Journal of Mental Deficiency,* 1964, **69**, 385-390.

McCall, R. B. Intelligence quotient pattern over age: Comparisons among siblings and parent-child pairs. *Science,* 1970, **170**, 644-648.

McCall, R. B., Appelbaum, M. I., & Hogarty, P. S. Developmental changes in mental performance. *Monographs of the Society for Research in Child Development,* 1973, **38**, (Serial No. 150).

McCartin, Sister R. A., Dingman, H. F., Meyers, C. E., & Mercer, J. R. Identification and disposition of the mentally handicapped in the parochial school system. *American Journal of Mental Deficiency,* 1966, **71**, 202-206.

McClearn, G. E., & DeFries, J. C. *Introduction to behavioral genetics.* San Francisco: W. H. Freeman, 1973.

Maccoby, E. E. Developmental psychology. *Annual Review of Psychology,* 1964, **15,** 203-250.

Maccoby, E. E. *The development of sex differences.* Stanford, Calif.: Stanford University Press, 1966.

Maccoby, E. E. Impressions from China. *Newsletter of the Society for Research in Child Development,* Fall 1974, 5, 8.

Maccoby, E. E., & Hagen, J. W. Effects of distraction upon central versus incidental recall: Developmental trends. *Journal of Experimental Child Psychology,* 1965, **2,** 280-289.

Maccoby, M., & Modiano, N. On culture and equivalence. In J. S. Bruner, R. R. Olver, & P. M. Greenfield (Eds.), *Studies in cognitive growth.* New York: Wiley, 1966.

McConnell, O. L. Koppitz's Bender-Gestalt scores in relation to organic and emotional problems in children. *Journal of Clinical Psychology,* 1967, **23,** 370-374.

McConnell, T. R. Outerdirectedness in normal and retarded children as a function of institutionalization. In *Abstracts of Peabody studies in mental retardation, 1962-1964,* 1965, **3,** (Abstract no. 80).

McDonald, A. Children of very low birth weight. *M.E.I.U. research monograph* No. 1. London: Medical Education and Information Unit of the Spastics Society and Heinemann Medical Books, 1967.

McGavern, M. L., Cleland, C. C., & Swartz, J. D. "Locating" the profoundly mentally retarded. *Mental Retardation,* 1974, **12**(2), 49-50.

McGuire, L., & Omenn, G. S. Congenital adrenal hyperplasia (adrenogenital syndrome). I. Family studies in IQ. *Behavior Genetics,* 1975, in press.

Mackay, H. A., & Sidman, M. Instructing the mentally retarded in an institutional environment. In G. A. Jervis (Ed.), *Expanding concepts in mental retardation: A symposium.* Springfield, Ill.: Charles C Thomas, 1968, pp. 164-169.

McKeown, T., & Leck, I. Institutional care of the mentally subnormal. *British Medical Journal,* 1967, **3**(5565), 573-576.

Mackie, R. P., & Robbins, P. P. Exceptional children in local public schools. *School life,* 1960, **43,** 15.

McKinney, J. D. Developmental study of the acquisition and utilization of conceptual strategies. *Journal of Educational Psychology,* 1972, **63,** 22-31.

McKusick, V. A. *Mendelian inheritance in man: Catalogs of autosomal dominant, autosomal recessive, and X-linked phenotypes* (3d ed.). Baltimore: Johns Hopkins, 1971.

McKusick, V. A. *Heritable disorders of connective tissue* (4th ed.). St. Louis: Mosby, 1972. Chaps. 4 and 11.

McKusick, V. A., & Chase, G. A. Human genetics. *Annual Review of Genetics,* 1973, **7,** 435-473.

McKusick, V. A., Hall, J. G., & Char, F. The clinical and genetic characteristics of homocystinuria. In N. A. J. Carson & D. N. Raine (Eds.), *Inherited disorders of sulphur metabolism.* London: J & A Churchill, 1971.

McLaughlin, B. *Learning and social behavior.* New York: Free Press, 1971.

McLaughlin, J. A., & Stephens, B. Interrelationships among reasoning, moral judgment, and moral conduct. *American Journal of Mental Deficiency,* 1974, **79,** 156-161.

McLean, J. E., Yoder, D. E., & Schiefelbusch, R. E. (Eds.). *Language intervention with the retarded: Developing strategies.* Baltimore: University Park Press, 1972.

McManis, D. L. Relative thinking by retardates. *American Journal of Mental Deficiency,* 1968, **73,** 484-492.

McManis, D. L. Comparisons of gross, intensive, and extensive quantities by normals and retardates. *Child Development,* 1969, **40**, 237-244. (a)

McManis, D. L. Conservation and transitivity of weight and length by normals and retardates. *Developmental Psychology,* 1969, **1**, 373-382. (b)

McManis, D. L. Conservation of identity and equivalence of quantity by retardates. *Journal of Genetic Psychology,* 1969, **115**, 63-69. (c)

McManis, D. L. Conservation, seriation, and transitivity performance by retarded and average individuals. *American Journal of Mental Deficiency,* 1970, **74**, 784-791.

McManis, D. L., Bell, D. R., & Pike, E. O. Performance of reward-seeking and punishment-avoiding retardates under reward and punishment. *American Journal of Mental Deficiency,* 1969, **73**, 906-911.

MacMillan, D. L. Paired-associate learning as a function of explicitness of mediational set by EMR and nonretarded children. *American Journal of Mental Deficiency,* 1972, **76**, 686-691.

MacMillan, D. L. The problem of motivation in the education of the mentally retarded. In R. L. Jones & D. L. MacMillan (Eds.), *Special education in transition.* Boston: Allyn and Bacon, 1974.

MacMillan, D. L., & Forness, S. R. Behavior modification: Savior or savant? In R. K. Eyman, C. E. Meyers, & G. Tarjan (Eds.), *Sociobehavioral studies in mental retardation.* Washington, D.C.: American Association on Mental Deficiency, 1973.

MacMillan, D. L., Jones, R. L., & Aloia, G. F. The mentally retarded label: A theoretical analysis and review of research. *American Journal of Mental Deficiency,* 1974, **79**, 241-261.

MacMillan, D. L., & Keogh, B. K. Normal and retarded children's expectancy for failure. *Developmental Psychology,* 1971, **4**, 343-348.

McNemar, Q. *The revision of the Stanford-Binet Scale.* Boston: Houghton Mifflin, 1942.

McNemar, Q. Lost: Our intelligence? Why? *American Psychologist,* 1964, **19**, 871-882.

McReynolds, P., Ferguson, J. T., & Ballachey, E. L. *Hospital adjustment scale.* Palo Alto, California: Consulting Psychologists Press, 1953.

Madden, J., Levenstein, P., & Levenstein, S. *Longitudinal IQ outcomes of the mother-child home program, 1967-1973.* Freeport, N.Y.: Verbal Interaction Project, 1974. (Mimeographed)

Madsen, M. C., & Connor, C. Cooperative and competitive behavior of retarded and nonretarded children of two ages. *Child Development,* 1973, **44**, 175-178.

Mahaney, E. J., Jr., & Stephens, B. Two year gains in moral judgment by normals and retardates. *American Journal of Mental Deficiency,* 1974, **79**, 134-141.

Mahoney, K., Van Wagenen, R. K., & Meyerson, L. Toilet training of normal and retarded children. *Journal of Applied Behavioral Analysis,* 1971, **4**, 173-182.

Mahoney, S. C. Observations concerning counseling with parents of mentally retarded children. *American Journal of Mental Deficiency,* 1958, **63**, 81-86.

Malone, C. A. Safety first: Comments on the influence of external danger in the lives of children of disorganized families. *American Journal of Orthopsychiatry,* 1966, **36**, 3-12. (Copyright, 1966, the American Orthopsychiatric Association, Inc.). Excerpt in Chap. 8 reproduced by permission.

Malpass, L. F., Hardy, M. W., Gilmore, A. S., & Williams, C. G. Automated instruction for retarded children. *American Journal of Mental Deficiency,* 1964, **69**, 405-412.

Malpass, L. F., Mark, S., & Palermo, D. S. Responses of retarded children to the Children's Manifest Anxiety Scale. *Journal of Educational Psychology,* 1960, **51**, 305-308.

Mamula, R. A. The use of developmental plans for mentally retarded children in foster family care. *Children,* 1971, **18**, 65-68.

Mandler, G., & Sarason, S. A study of anxiety and learning. *Journal of Abnormal and Social Psychology,* 1952, **47**, 166-173.

Maney, A. C., Pace, R., & Morrison, D. F. A factor analytic study of the need for institutionalization: Problems and populations for program development. *American Journal of Mental Deficiency,* 1964, **69**, 372-384.

Mann, J. B., Alterman, S., & Hills, A. G. Albright's hereditary osteodystrophy comprising pseudohypoparathyroidism and pseudopseudohypoparathyroidism: With report of two cases representing the complete syndrome occurring in successive generations. *Annals of Internal Medicine,* 1962, **56**, 315.

Mann, P. H. Modifying the behavior of Negro educable mentally retarded boys through group counseling procedures. *Journal of Negro Education,* 1969, **38**, 135-142.

Manosevitz, M., Prentice, N. M., & Wilson, F. Individual and family correlates of imaginary companions in preschool children. *Developmental Psychology,* 1973, **8**, 72-79.

Markman, E. M. *Factors effecting the young child's ability to monitor his memory.* Unpublished Ph.D. dissertation, University of Pennsylvania, 1973.

Marshall, N. R., Hegrenes, J. R., & Goldstein, S. Verbal interactions: Mothers and their retarded children vs. mothers and their nonretarded children. *American Journal of Mental Deficiency,* 1973, **77**, 415-419.

Martin, A. S. *The effect of the novelty-familiarity dimension of discrimination learning by mental retardates.* Unpublished Ph.D. thesis, University of Connecticut, 1970.

Martin, A. S., & Tyrrell, D. J. Oddity learning following object-discrimination learning in mentally retarded children. *American Journal of Mental Deficiency,* 1971, **75**, 504-509.

Martin, C. J., Boersma, F. J., & Bulgarella, R. Verbalization of associative strategies by normal and retarded children. *Journal of General Psychology,* 1968, **78**, 209-218.

Martin, E. W., Jr. Breakthrough for the handicapped: Legislative history. *Exceptional Children,* 1968, **34**, 493-503.

Martin K. Guardianship. In J. Wortis (Ed.), *Mental retardation: An annual review* (Vol. 3). New York: Grune & Stratton, 1971.

Masland, R. L. Comment. In W. F. Windle (Ed.), *Neurological and psychological deficits of asphyxia neonatorum.* Springfield, Ill.: Charles C Thomas, 1958.

Masling, J. The effects of warm and cold interaction on the administration and scoring of an intelligence test. *Journal of Consulting Psychology,* 1959, **23**, 336-341.

Mason, H. H., & Turner, M. E. Chronic galactosemia. Report of case with studies on carbohydrates. *American Journal of Diseases of Children,* 1935, **50**, 359-374.

Matarazzo, J. E. *Wechsler's measurement and appraisal of adult intelligence.* (5th ed.). Baltimore: Williams & Wilkins, 1972. Table 17-3 reprinted by permission of the author and the publisher.

Matejcek, Z., Doutlik, S., & Janda, V. The evaluation of neuro-psychiatric sequelae in children after parainfectious encephalitis. *Acta Paedopsychiatrica,* 1964, **31**, 301-309.

Matejcek, Z., & Langmeier, J. New observations on psychological deprivation in institutional children in Czechoslovakia. *Slow Learning Child,* 1965, **12**, 20-37.

Matsunaga, E. Possible genetic consequences of family planning. *Journal of the American Medical Association,* 1966, **198**, 533-540.

Mattinson, J. Marriage and mental handicap. In F. F. de la Cruz & G. D. LaVeck (Eds.), *Human sexuality and the mentally retarded.* New York: Brunner/Mazel, 1973.

Mayer, C. L. The relationship of early special class placement and the self-concepts of mentally handicapped children. *Exceptional Children,* 1966, **33**, 77-81.

Meeker, M. N. *The structure of intellect.* Columbus, Ohio: Charles C. Merrill, 1969.

Mehler, J., & Bever, T. G. Cognitive capacity of very young children. *Science,* 1967, **158,** 141–142.

Mehlman, B. Group play therapy with mentally retarded children. *Journal of Abnormal And Social Psychology,* 1953, **48,** 53–60.

Mehr, H. M. The application of psychological tests and methods to schizophrenia in children. *Nervous Child,* 1952, **10,** 63–93.

Melton, A. W., & Martin, E. *Coding processes in human memory.* New York: Wiley, 1972.

Melzack, R. Early experience: A neuropsychological approach to heredity-environment interactions. In G. Newton, & S. Levine (Eds.), *Early experience and behavior: The psychobiology of development.* Springfield, Ill.: Charles C Thomas, 1968, pp. 65–82.

Melzack, R., & Scott, T. H. The effect of early experience and response to pain. *Journal of Comparative and Physiological Psychology,* 1957, **50,** 155–161.

Menkes, J. H., Hurst, P. L., & Craig, J. M. A new syndrome: Progressive familial infantile cerebral dysfunction associated with an unusual urinary substance. *Pediatrics,* 1954, **14,** 462.

Menkes, M. M., Rowe, J. S., & Menkes, J. H. A twenty-five year follow-up study on the hyperkinetic child with minimal brain dysfunction. *Pediatrics,* 1967, **39,** 393–399.

Menolascino, F. J. Emotional disturbance and mental retardation. *American Journal of Mental Deficiency,* 1965, **70,** 248–256. (a)

Menolascino, F. J. Psychiatric aspects of mongolism. *American Journal of Mental Deficiency,* 1965, **69,** 653–660. (b)

Menolascino, F. J. Parents of the mentally retarded: An operational approach to diagnosis and management. *Journal of the American Academy of Child Psychiatry,* 1968, **7,** 589–602.

Menolascino, F. J. Emotional disturbances in mentally retarded children. *American Journal of Psychiatry,* 1969, **126,** 168–176.

Menolascino, F. J. (Ed.) *Psychiatric approaches to mental retardation.* New York: Basic Books, 1970.

Menolascino, F. J. Primitive, atypical, and abnormal behaviors. In E. Katz (Ed.), *Mental health services for the mentally retarded.* Springfield, Ill.: Charles C Thomas, 1972.

Mental Health Law Project. *Basic rights of the mentally handicapped.* Washington, D.C.: Author, 1973.

Menzel, E. W., Jr., Davenport, R. K. Jr., & Rogers, C. M. The effects of environmental restriction upon the chimpanzee's responsiveness to objects. *Journal of Comparative and Physiological Psychology,* 1963, **56,** 78–85.

Mercer, J. R. Patterns of family crisis related to reacceptance of the retardate. *American Journal of Mental Deficiency,* 1966, **71,** 19–32.

Mercer, J. R. Sociological perspectives on mild mental retardation. In M. C. Haywood (Ed.), *Socio-cultural aspects of mental retardation.* New York: Appleton-Century-Crofts, 1970.

Mercer, J. R. *Labelling the mentally retarded.* Berkeley: University of California Press, 1973. Excerpts in chap. 2 reproduced by permission of the publisher.

Mercer, J. R. A policy statement on assessment procedures and the rights of children. *Harvard Educational Review,* 1974, **44,** 125–141.

Mermelstein, E., & Shulman, L. Lack of formal schooling and acquisition of conservation. *Child Development,* 1967, **38,** 39–52.

Merrill, M. A. On the relation of intelligence to achievement in the case of mentally retarded children. *Comparative Psychological Monographs,* 1924, **2,** (Whole No. 10).

Metrakos, J. D., & Metrakos, K. Genetic studies in clinical epilepsy. In H. H. Jasper, A. A. Ward, Jr., & A. Pope (Eds.), *Basic mechanisms of the epilepsies.* Boston: Little, Brown, 1969.

Metz, A. S. *Number of pupils with handicaps in local public schools, Spring, 1970,* DHEW Publication No. (OE) 73-11107. Washington, D.C.: National Center for Educational Statistics, 1973.

Meyen, E. L., & Hieronymus, A. N. The age placement of academic skills in curriculum for the EMR. *Exceptional Children,* 1970, **36**, 333-339.

Meyer, W. J. Cerebral dysfunction. In G. O. & H. D. Blank (Eds.), *Exceptional children research review.* Washington, D.C.: The Council for Exceptional Children, 1968.

Meyerowitz, J. H. Parental awareness of retardation. *American Journal of Mental Deficiency,* 1967, **71**, 637-643. (a)

Meyerowitz, J. H. Peer groups and special classes. *Mental Retardation,* 1967, **5**(5), 23-26. (b)

Meyers, C. E., & Dingman, H. F. Factor analytic and structure of intellect models in the study of mental retardation. In M. Garrison, Jr. (Ed.), Cognitive models and development in mental retardation. *American Journal of Mental Deficiency,* 1966, **70**, (Monogr. Suppl.). 7-25.

Meyers, C. E., Dingman, H. F., Attwell, A. A., & Orpet, R. E. Comparative abilities of normals and retardates of M.A. 6 years on a factor-type test battery. *American Journal of Mental Deficiency,* 1961, **66**, 250-258.

Meyers, C. E., & Lombardi, T. P. Definition of the mentally retarded: Decision time for AAMD. *Mental Retardation,* 1974, **12**(2), 43.

Michaels, J., & Schucman, H. Observations on the psychodynamics of parents of retarded children. *American Journal of Mental Deficiency,* 1962, **66**, 568-573.

Mikkelsen, M., & Stene, J. Genetic counseling in Down's syndrome. *Human Heredity,* 1970, **20**, 457-464.

Miles, C. C., & Miles, W. R. The correlation of intelligence scores and chronological age from early to late maturity. *American Journal of Psychology,* 1932, **44**, 44-78.

Milgram, N. A. IQ constancy in disadvantaged Negro children. *Psychological Reports,* 1971, **29**, 319-326.

Milgram, N. A. MR and mental illness: A proposal for conceptual unity. *Mental Retardation,* 1972, **10**(6), 29-31.

Milgram, N. A., & Riedel, W. Verbal context and visual compound in paired-associate learning of mental retardates. *American Journal of Mental Deficiency,* 1969, **73**, 755-761.

Milkovich, L., & van den Berg, B. J. Effects of prenatal meprobamate and chlordiazepoxide hydrochloride on human embryonic and fetal development. *New England Journal of Medicine,* 1974, **291**, 1268-1271.

Miller, G. A. The magical number seven, plus or minus two: Some limits on our capacity for processing information. *Psychological Review,* 1956, **63**, 81-97.

Miller, G. A., Galanter, E., & Pribram, K. H. *Plans and the structure of behavior.* New York: Holt, 1960.

Miller, M. B. *Locus of control, learning climate, and climate shift in serial learning with mental retardates.* Ann Arbor, Michigan: University Microfilms, 1961.

Miller, R. M. Prenatal origins of mental retardation. *Journal of Pediatrics,* 1967, **71**, 455.

Miller, R. W. Delayed radiation effects in atomic-bomb survivors. *Science,* 1969, **166**, 569-574.

Miller, S. A., Shelton, J., & Flavell, J. H. A test of Luria's hypotheses concerning the development of verbal self-regulation. *Child Development,* 1970, **41**, 651-665.

Millichap, J. G. Drugs in management of minimal brain dysfunction. *Annals of the New York Academy of Sciences,* 1973, **205**, 321-334.

Miranda, S. B., & Fantz, R. L. Visual preferences of Down's syndrome and normal infants. *Child Development,* 1973, **44**, 555-561.

Miranda, S. B., & Fantz, R. L. Recognition memory in Down's syndrome and normal infants. *Child Development,* 1974, **45**, 651-660.

Miron, N. B. Behavior problems of the mentally retarded. In E. Katz (Ed.), *Mental health services for the mentally retarded.* Springfield, Ill.: Charles C Thomas, 1972.

Mirsky, A. F., Primac, D. W., Stevens, J. R., & Cosimo, A. A comparison of patients with focal and non-focal epilepsy on a test of attention. *Electroencephalography and Clinical Neurophysiology,* 1958, **10**, 206-207.

Mitchell, A. C., & Smeriglio, V. Growth in social competence in institutionalized mentally retarded children. *American Journal of Mental Deficiency,* 1970, **74**, 666-673.

Mitchell, S. K. *Life changes, help from others, and the outcomes of pregnancy.* Unpublished manuscript, University of Washington, 1974.

Mittler, P. E. (Ed.). *Aspects of autism: Some approaches to childhood psychoses.* London: British Psychological Society, 1968.

Mittler, P. Biological and social aspects of language development in twins. *Developmental Medicine and Child Neurology,* 1970, **12**, 741-757. (a)

Mittler, P. (Ed.). *The psychological assessment of mental and physical handicap.* London: Methuen, 1970. (b)

Mittwoch, U. Sex differences in cells. *Scientific American,* 1963, **209**, 54-62.

Money, J. Impulse, aggression and sexuality in the XYY syndrome. *St. John's Law Review,* 1970, **44**, 220-235.

Money, J., & Lewis, V. IQ, genetics, and accelerated growth: Adrenogenital syndrome. *Bulletin of Hopkins Hospital,* 1966, **118**, 365-373.

Montessori, M. [*Montessori method*] (A.E. George, Trans.). New York: Frederick A. Stokes Co., 1912.

Moore, C. L., & Retish, P. M. Effect of the examiner's race on black children's Wechsler Preschool and Primary Scale of Intelligence IQ. *Developmental Psychology,* 1974, **10**, 672-676.

Moore, G., & Stephens, B. Two year gains in moral conduct by normals and retardates. *American Journal of Mental Deficiency,* 1974, **79**, 147-153.

Moore, T. Language and intelligence: A longitudinal study of the first 7 years. *Human Development,* 1968, **11**, 1-24.

Mooring, I. M. Planning as a tool of prevention for the mentally retarded. *Mental Retardation,* 1969, **7**(2), 41-45.

Moreno, J. L. *Psychodrama* (Vol. 1). New York: Beacon House, 1946.

Morgenstern, M., LowBeer, H., & Morgenstern, F. [*Practical training for the severely handicapped child*] (F. Morgenstern, Trans.). Tadworth, Surrey, England: Spastics Society Medical Education and Information Unit in association with William Heinemann Medical Books, Ltd., 1966.

Morgenstern, M., & Michal-Smith, H. *Psychology in the vocational rehabilitation of the mentally retarded.* Springfield, Ill: Charles C Thomas, 1973.

Morris, P. *Put away: A sociological study of institutions for the mentally retarded.* New York: Atherton, 1969.

Morrison, D., & Pothier, P. Two different remedial motor training programs and the development of mentally retarded preschoolers. *American Journal of Mental Deficiency,* 1972, **77**, 251–258.

Morrison, J. R., & Stewart, M. A. A family study of the hyperactive child syndrome. *Biological Psychiatry,* 1971, **3**, 189.

Morrissey, J. R. Status of family-care programs. *Mental Retardation,* 1966, **4**(5), 8–11.

Mosher, L. R., & Feinsilver, D. *Special report on schizophrenia.* Washington, D.C.: U.S. Department of Health, Education, and Welfare, 1970.

Moss, J. W. *Failure-avoiding and success-striving behavior in mentally retarded and normal children.* Unpublished doctoral dissertation. George Peabody College, 1958.

Mowatt, M. H. Group therapy approach to emotional conflicts of the mentally retarded and their parents. In F. J. Menolascino (Ed.), *Psychiatric approaches to mental retardation.* New York: Basic Books, 1970.

Moyles, F. W., & Wolins, M. Group care and intellectual development. *Developmental Psychology,* 1971, **4**, 370–380.

Moynahan, E. D. The development of knowledge concerning the effect of categorization upon free recall. *Child Development,* 1973, **44**, 238–246.

Mueller, J. B., & Porter, R. Placement of adult retardates from state institution in community care facilities. *Community Mental Health,* 1969, **5**, 289–294.

Mumpower, D. L. Sex ratios found in various types of referred exceptional children. *Exceptional Children,* 1970, **36**, 621–622.

Murphy, D. P. Ovarian irradiation: Its effect on the health of subsequent children. *Surgery, Gynecology, and Obstetrics,* 1928, **47**, 201–215.

Mussen, P., & Rosenzweig, M. R. *Psychology: An introduction.* Lexington, Massachusetts: D. C. Heath, 1973. Figure 14-1 reprinted by permission of the publisher.

Myers, D. G., Sinco, M. E., & Stalma, E. S. *The right-to-education child (A curriculum for the severely and profoundly mentally retarded).* Springfield, Ill.: Charles C Thomas, 1973.

Myklebust, H. R., & Burchard, E. M. L. A study of the effects of congenital and adventitious deafness of the intelligence, personality, and social maturity of school children. *Journal of Educational Psychology,* 1945, **36**, 321–343.

Nadler, H. L., & Gerbie, A. Role of amniocentesis in the intrauterine detection of genetic disorders. *New England Journal of Medicine,* 1970, **282**, 596–599.

Nadler, H. L., Inouye, T., & Hsia, D. Y. Y. Classical galactosemia. In D. Y. Y. Hsia (Ed.), *Galactosemia.* Springfield, Ill.: Charles C Thomas, 1969.

Naeye, R. L., & Blanc, W. A. Relation of poverty and race to antenatal infection. *New England Journal of Medicine,* 1970, **283**, 555–560.

Needleman, H. L., Davidson, I., Sewall, E. M., & Shapiro, I. M. Subclinical lead exposure in Philadelphia schoolchildren. Identification by dentine lead analysis. *New England Journal of Medicine,* 1974, **290**, 245–248.

Needleman, H. L., Tuncay, O. C., & Shapiro, I. M. Lead levels in deciduous teeth of urban and suburban American children. *Nature,* 1972, **235**, 111.

Neimark, E. D., & Lewis, N. The development of logical problem-solving strategies. *Child Development,* 1967, **38**, 107–117.

Neman, R., Roos, P., McCann, B. M., Menolascino, F. J., & Heal, L. W. Experimental evaluation of sensorimotor patterning used with mentally retarded children. *American Journal of Mental Deficiency,* 1975, **79**, 372–384.

Neufeld, E. F., & Barton, R. W. Genetic Disorders of mucopolysaccharide metabolism. In G. E. Gaull (Ed.), *Biology of Brain Dysfunction* (Vol. 1). New York: Plenum Press, 1973.

Neufeld, E. F., & Fratatoni, J. C. Inborn errors of mucopolysaccharide metabolism. *Science,* 1970, **169**, 141.

Neuhaus, E. C. Training the mentally retarded for competitive employment. *Exceptional Children,* 1967, **33**, 625–628.

Newland, T. E. *The severely mentally handicapped child: A non-public school responsibility.* Paper presented at the convention of the International Council on Exceptional Children, Boston, March 1953.

Newman, H. G., & Doby, J. T. Correlates of social competence among trainable mentally retarded children. *American Journal of Mental Deficiency,* 1973, **77**, 722–732.

Newman, R. W. (Ed.). *Institutionalization of the mentally retarded.* New York: National Association for Retarded Children, 1967.

New York City Board of Education. *Let's Look at Children.* Princeton, N.J.: Educational Testing Service, 1965.

Niebuhr, E. Localization of the deleted segment in the Cri-du-chat syndrome. *Human Genetics,* 1972, **16**, 357–358.

Nielsen, H. H. Psychological appraisal of children with cerebral palsy: A survey of 128 reassessed cases. *Developmental Medicine and Child Neurology,* 1971, **13**, 707–720.

Nielsen, J. [Klinefelter's syndrome and the XYY syndrome. A genetical, endocrinological and psychiatric-psychological study of thirty-three severely hypogonadal male patients and two patients with the XYY syndrome]. *Acta psychiatrica Scandinavia,* 1969, **209** (suppl.).

Nielsen, J. Criminality among patients with Klinefelter's syndrome and XYY syndrome. *British Journal of Psychiatry,* 1970, **117**, 365–369.

Nielsen, J., Sørensen, A., Theilgard, A., Frøland, A. & Johnsen, S. G. A psychiatric-psychological study of 50 severely hypogonadal male patients, including 34 with Klinefelter's syndrome, 47,XXY. *Acta Jutlandica,* 1969, **41**, 1–183.

Nihira, K., Foster, R., Shellhaas, M., & Leland, H. *Adaptive behavior scales: Manual.* Washington, D.C.: American Association on Mental Deficiency, 1969.

Nirje, B. The normalization principle and its human management implications. In R. B. Kugel & W. Wolfensberger (Eds.), *Changing patterns in residential services for the mentally retarded.* Washington, D.C.: President's Committee on Mental Retardation, 1969.

Nisbet, J. K., & Entweistle, N. J. Intelligence and family size, 1949–1965. *British Journal of Educational Psychology,* 1967, **37**, 188–193.

Niswander, K. R., & Gordon, M. *The women and their pregnancies* (Vol. 1). Philadelphia: Saunders, 1972.

Noel, B., Duport, J. P., Revil, D., Dussuyer, I., & Quack, B. The XYY syndrome: Reality or myth? *Clinical Genetics,* 1974, **5**, 387–394.

Noonan, J. R., & Barry, J. R. Performance of retarded children. *Science,* 1967, **156**, 171.

Nordoff, P., & Robbins, C. *Music therapy in special education.* New York: John Day, 1971.

North, A. F., Jr. Small-for-dates neonates. 1: Maternal, gestational, and neonatal characteristics. *Pediatrics,* 1966, **38**, 1013–1019.

North, A. F., Jr. Project Head Start and the pediatrician. *Clinical Pediatrics,* 1967, **6**, 191–194.

Northcutt, M. P. *The comparative effectiveness of classroom and programmed instruction in the teaching of decimals to fifth-grade students.* Ann Arbor, Michigan: University Microfilms, 1963.

Nuckolls, K. B., Cassel, J., & Kaplan, B. H. Psychosocial assets, life crisis, and the prognosis of pregnancy. *American Journal of Epidemiology,* 1972, **95**, 431–441.

Nye, W. C., McManis, D. L., & Haugen, D. M. Training and transfer of categorization by retarded adults. *American Journal of Mental Deficiency,* 1972, **77**, 199-207.

Nyhan, W. L. Disorders of nucleic acid metabolism. In G. E. Gaull (Ed.), *Biology of Brain Dysfunction.* New York: Plenum Press, 1973.

Oberle, M. W. Lead poisoning: A preventable childhood disease of the slums. *Science,* 1969, **165**, 991.

O'Connor, N., & Hermelin, B. Discrimination and reversal learning in imbeciles. *Journal of Abnormal and Social Psychology,* 1959, **59**, 409-412.

O'Connor, N., & Hermelin, B. *Speech and thought in severe subnormality.* New York: Pergamon Press, 1963.

O'Connor, N., & Hermelin, B. The selective visual attention of psychotic children. *Journal of Child Psychology and Psychiatry,* 1967, **8**(3/4), 167-179.

O'Dell, S. Training parents in behavior modification: A review. *Psychological Bulletin,* 1974, **81**, 418-433.

Office of Mental Retardation Coordination. *Mental retardation activities of the Department of Health, Education, and Welfare,* March 1972 (DHEW Publication No. OS-72-27). Washington, D.C.: U.S. Government Printing Office, 1972. (a).

Office of Mental Retardation Coordination. *Mental retardation source book* (DHEW Publication No. OS 73-81). Washington, D.C.: Department of Health, Education, and Welfare, 1972. (b) Table 21-1 reproduced by permission of the Office for the Handicapped.

O'Gorman, G. *The nature of childhood autism.* London: Butterworths, 1967.

Okada, S., & O'Brien, J. Tay-Sachs disease: Generalized absence of a beta D-N-acetylhexosaminidase component. *Science,* 1969, **165**, 698.

Oki, T., Sakai, T., Kizu, M., Higashi, H., Otsuka, F., & Asano, N. A psychological study on the personality traits of the organic and the subnormal mental deficiency. The result of the Marble Gestalt Test. *Bulletin of the Osaka Medical School,* 1960, **6**, 84-91.

O'Leary, K. D., & Drabman, R. Token reinforcement programs in the classroom: A review. *Psychological Bulletin,* 1971, **75**, 379-398.

Olechnowicz, H. *Patterns of personal-social development in severely mentally defective children.* Pruszków, Poland: Psychoneurological Institute, 1973. (a)

Olechnowicz, H. (Ed.) *Studies in the socialization of the severely and profoundly retarded.* Warsaw, Poland: Nasza Ksiegarnia, 1973. (b)

Olshansky, S. Chronic sorrow: A response to having a mentally defective child. *Social Casework,* 1962, **43**, 191-194.

Olshansky, S. Parent responses to a mentally defective child. *Mental Retardation,* 1966, **4**(4), 21-23.

Olshansky, S., & Schonfield, J. Institutionalization of preschool retardates. *Mental Retardation,* 1964, **2**, 109-115.

Olson, D. R. On conceptual strategies. In J. S. Bruner, R. R. Olver, & P. M. Greenfield (Eds.), *Studies in Cognitive Growth.* New York: Wiley, 1966.

Olson, D. R. Language acquisition and cognitive development. In H. C. Haywood (Ed.), *Social-cultural aspects of mental retardation.* New York: Appleton-Century-Crofts, 1970.

Olson, M. I., & Shaw, C. M. Presenile dementia and Alzheimer's disease in mongolism. *Brain,* 1969, **92**, 147-156.

Omari, I. M., & MacGinitie, W. H. Some pictorial artifacts in studies of African children's pictorial depth perception. *Child Development,* 1974, **45**, 535-539.

Omenn, G. S. Genetic engineering: Present and future. In R. H. Williams (Ed.), *To live and to die: When, why, and how.* New York: Springer-Verlag, 1973. (a)

Omenn, G. S. Genetic issues in the syndrome of minimal brain dysfunction. *Seminars in Psychiatry,* 1973, **5**, 5-17. (b)

Omenn, G. S. Alcoholism: A pharmacogenetic disorder. *Modern Problems of Pharmacopsychiatry,* 1974, **10**, in press.

Omenn, G. S., & Motulsky, A. G. Eco-genetics: Genetic variation in susceptibility to environmental agents. In B. Cohen (Ed.), *Genetic issues in public health.* New York: Johns Hopkins, 1974. (a)

Omenn, G. S., & Motulsky, A. G. Intrauterine diagnosis and genetic counseling implications for psychiatry in the future. In S. Arieti (Ed.), *American Handbook of Psychiatry* (2d ed.). New York: Basic Books, 1974. (b)

Oppel, W. C., & Royston, A. B. Teen-age births: Some social, psychological, and physical sequelae. *American Journal of Public Health,* 1971, **61**, 751-756.

Orlando, R., & Bijou, S. W. Single and multiple schedules of reinforcement in developmentally retarded children. *Journal of the Experimental Analysis of Behavior,* 1960, **3**, 339-348.

Ornitz, E. M., & Ritvo, E. R. Perceptual inconstancy in early infantile autism. *Archives of General Psychiatry,* 1968, **2**, 389-399.

Orshansky, M. Who's who among the poor: A demographic view of poverty. *Social Security Bulletin,* July 1965, 3-32.

Osgood, C. E. A behavioristic analysis. In C. E. Osgood (Ed.), *Contemporary approaches to cognition, a behavioristic analysis.* Cambridge, Mass.: Harvard University Press, 1957. (a)

Osgood, C. E. (Ed.). *Contemporary approaches to cognition, a behavioristic analysis.* Cambridge, Mass.: Harvard University Press, 1957. (b)

Osgood, C. E., & Miron, M. S. *Approaches to the study of aphasia.* Urbana: University of Illinois Press, 1963.

Osofsky, J. E., & Danzger, B. Relationships between neonatal characteristics and mother-infant interaction. *Developmental Psychology,* 1974, **10**, 124-310.

Ounsted, C., & Taylor, D. *Gender differences: Their ontogeny and significance.* Baltimore: Williams & Wilkins, 1972.

Owens, W. A. Age and mental abilities: A second adult follow-up. *Journal of Educational Psychology,* 1966, **57**, 311-325.

Pacella, M. J. The performance of brain damaged mental retardates on successive trials of the Bender-Gestalt. *American Journal of Mental Deficiency,* 1965, **69**, 723-728.

Palmer, F. H. Socioeconomic status and intellectual performance among Negro preschool boys. *Developmental Psychology,* 1970, **3**, 1-9.

Pandey, C. Popularity, rebelliousness, and happiness among institutionalized retarded males. *American Journal of Mental Deficiency,* 1971, **76**, 325-331.

Papez, J. W. A proposed mechanism of emotion. *Archives of Neurology and Psychiatry,* 1937, **38**, 725.

Paraskevopoulos, J. N., & Hunt, J. McV. Object construction and imitation under differing conditions of rearing. *Journal of Genetic Psychology,* 1971, **119**, 301-321.

Paraskevopoulos, J. N., & Kirk, S. A. *The development and psychometric characteristics of the Revised Illinois Test of Psycholinguistic Abilities.* Urbana: University of Illinois Press, 1969.

Parsons, L. B., McLeroy, N., & Wright, L. Validity of Koppitz's developmental score as a measure of organicity. *Perceptual and Motor Skills,* 1971, **33**, 1013-1014.

Patau, K., Smith, D. W., Therman, E., Inhorn, S. L., & Wagner, H. P. Multiple congenital anomaly caused by an extra chromosome. *Lancet,* 1960, **1**, 790.

Patten, B. M. *Foundations of embryology* (3d ed.). New York: McGraw-Hill, 1968.

Patterson, G. R. Behavioral intervention procedures in the classroom and the home. In A. E. Bergin, & S. L. Garfield (Eds.), *Handbook of psychotherapy and behavior change: An empirical analysis.* New York: Wiley, 1971.

Patterson, G. R., Jones, R., Whittier, J., & Wright, M. A. A behavior modification technique for the hyperactive child. *Behavior Research and Therapy,* 1965, **2**, 217-226.

Patton, R. G. & Gardner, L. I. Short stature associated with maternal deprivation syndrome: Disordered family environment as cause of so-called idiopathic hypopituitarism. In L. I. Gardner (Ed.), *Endocrine and genetic diseases of childhood.* Philadelphia: Saunders, 1969.

Paulson, M. J., & Stone, D. Specialist-professional intervention: An expanding role in the care and treatment of the retarded and their families. In R. K. Eyman, C. E. Meyers, & G. Tarjan (Eds.), *Sociobehavioral studies in mental retardation.* Washington, D.C.: American Association on Mental Deficiency, 1973.

Pavlov, I. P. *Conditioned reflexes.* London: Oxford University Press, 1927.

Payne, D., Johnson, R. C., & Abelson, R. B. *Comprehensive description of institutionalized retardates in the Western United States.* Boulder, Colo.: Western Interstate Commission for Higher Education, 1969.

Payne, J. E. The effect of institutionalization on educable mentally retardates' expectancy of failure. *Training School Bulletin,* 1971, **68**, 77-81.

Pearson, K. On the laws of inheritance in man: II. On the inheritance of the mental and moral characters in man, and its comparison with the inheritance of physical characters. *Biometrika,* 1904, **3**, 131-190.

Peck, H. B., Rabinovitch, R. D., & Kramer, J. B. A treatment program for parents of schizophrenic children. *American Journal of Orthopsychiatry,* 1949, **19**, 592-598.

Peckham, C. *Mentally handicapped children. National Children's Bureau tenth annual review.* London: National Children's Bureau, 1974.

Penchaszadeh, V. B., Hardy, J. B., Mellits, E. D., et al. Growth and development in an "inner city" population: An assessment of possible biological and environmental factors. I. Intra-uterine growth. *Johns Hopkins Medical Journal,* 1972, **130**, 384-397.

Penney, R. K., & Willows, D. M. Mediational deficiency of mentally retarded children: III. Effect of length of institutionalization. *American Journal of Mental Deficiency,* 1970, **74**, 780-783.

Penrose, L. S. *Mental defect.* New York: Farrar and Rinehart, 1934.

Penrose, L. S. Observations on the aetiology of mongolism. *Lancet,* 1954, **1**, 505-509.

Penrose, L. S. Genetics of growth and development of the foetus. In L. S. Penrose (Ed.), *Recent advances in human genetics.* London: J & A Churchill, 1961.

Penrose, L. S. The effects of change in maternal age distribution upon the incidence of mongolism. *Journal of Mental Deficiency Research,* 1967, **11**(2), 54-57.

Pense, A. W., Patton, R. E., Camp, J. L., & Kebalo, C. A cohort study of institutionalized young mentally retarded children. *American Journal of Mental Deficiency,* 1961, **66**, 18-22.

Perlstein, M. A. Infantile cerebral palsy. *Advances in Pediatrics,* 1955, **7**, 209-248.

Perlstein, M. A., & Attala, R. Neurologica sequelae of plumbism in children. *Clinical Pediatrics,* 1966, **5**, 292.

Peterson, R. O., Jones, E. M., Flanagan, R. C., & Nagin, E. F. *Guide to jobs for the mentally retarded.* Pittsburgh: American Institute for Research, 1964.

Philips, I. Children, mental retardation, and emotional disorder. In I. Philips (Ed.), *Prevention and treatment of mental retardation.* New York: Basic Books, 1966.

Piaget, J. *The language and thought of the child.* New York: Harcourt, Brace, 1926.

Piaget, J. *Classes, relations et nombres: essai sur les "groupements" de la logistique et la réversibilité de la pensée.* Paris: Vrin, 1942.

Piaget, J. *Traité de logique.* Paris: Colin, 1949.

Piaget, J. *The psychology of intelligence.* New York: Harcourt, Brace, 1950.

Piaget, J. *Play, dreams and imitation in childhood.* New York: Norton, 1951.

Piaget, J. *The origins of intelligence in children* (2d ed.). New York: International Universities Press, 1952.

Piaget, J. *The construction of reality in the child.* New York: Basic Books, 1954.

Piaget, J. *Logic and psychology.* New York: Basic Books, 1957.

Piers, E. V., & Harris, D. B. Age and other correlates of self-concept in children. *Journal of Educational Psychology,* 1964, **55**, 91-95.

Pilkey, L., Goldman, M., & Kleinman, B. Psychodrama and empathic ability in the mentally retarded. *American Journal of Mental Deficiency,* 1961, **65**, 595-605.

Pinard, A. *An experimental study of mental development based on Piaget's theory.* Paper presented to the Department of Psychology, Yale University, December 1959. Excerpt in Chapter 12 reprinted by permission of the author.

Pincus, J. G., & Tucker, G. *Behavioral neurology.* New York: Oxford University Press, 1974.

Pinneau, S. R. *Changes in intelligence quotient, infancy to maturity.* Boston: Houghton Mifflin, 1961.

Piotrowski, Z. A comparison of congenitally defective children with schizophrenic children in regard to personality structure and intellectual type. *Proceedings of the American Association on Mental Deficiency,* 1937, **61**, 78-90.

Pollack, M. Brain damage, mental retardation, and childhood schizophrenia. *American Journal of Psychiatry,* 1958, **415**, 422-428.

Pollack, M. Comparison of childhood, adolescent, and adult schizophrenias. Etiologic significance of intellectual functioning. *Archives of General Psychiatry,* 1960, **2**, 652-660.

Pollack, M. Mental subnormality and childhood schizophrenia. In J. Zubin & G. A. Jervis (Eds.), *Psychopathology in mental development.* New York: Grune & Stratton, 1967.

Porteus, S. D. *Guide to Porteus Maze Test.* Vineland, N.J.: The Training School, 1924.

Porteus, S. D. *The maze test and clinical psychology.* Palo Alto, California: Pacific Books, 1959.

Posner, B. Why employers say "yes" in Kansas City. *Special Report: Fresh Views on Employment of the Mentally Handicapped.* Washington, D.C.: President's Committee on Employment of the Handicapped, August 1970.

Postman, L. Short-term memory and incidental learning. In A. W. Melton (Ed.), *Categories of human learning.* New York: Academic Press, 1964.

Potts, J. T., Jr. Pseudohypoparathyroidism. In J. B. Stanbury, J. B. Wyngaarden, & D. S. Fredrickson (Eds.), *Metabolic basis of inherited disease* (3d ed.). New York: McGraw-Hill, 1972.

Powell, L. F. The effect of extra stimulation and maternal involvement on the development of low-birth-weight infants and on maternal behavior. *Child Development,* 1974, **45**, 106-113.

Prechtl, H. F. R. The mother-child interaction in babies with minimal brain damage (a follow-up study). In B. M. Foss (Ed.), *Determinants of infant behaviour: II.* New York: Wiley, 1963.

Prehm, H. J. Rote learning in retarded children: Some implications for the teaching-learning process. *Journal of Special Education,* 1967, **1**, 397-399.

President's Committee on Employment of the Handicapped. *Nine years of progress: Employment of the mentally retarded and mentally restored (1961-1970).* Washington, D.C.: U.S. Government Printing Office, 1970.

President's Committee on Mental Retardation. *Residental Services for the Mentally Retarded. An action policy proposal.* Washington, D.C.: U.S. Government Printing Office, 1970. (a)

President's Committee on Mental Retardation. *The six-hour retarded child.* Washington, D.C.: U.S. Government Printing Office, 1970. (b)

President's Panel on Mental Retardation. *A proposed program for national action to combat mental retardation.* Washington, D.C.: U.S. Government Printing Office, 1962. (a)

President's Panel on Mental Retardation. *Report of the mission to Denmark and Sweden.* Washington, D.C.: U.S. Government Printing Office, August 1962. (b)

President's Panel on Mental Retardation. *Report of the mission to the Netherlands.* Washington, D.C.: U.S. Government Printing Office, July 1962. (c)

President's Task Force on Manpower Conservation. *One-third of a nation.* Washington, D.C.: U.S. Government Printing Office, 1964.

Pressey, S. L. Intelligence and its measurement: A symposium. *Journal of Educational Psychology,* 1921, **12**, 144-147.

Price-Williams, D. R. A study concerning concepts of conservation of quantities among primitive children. *Acta Psychologica,* 1961, **18**, 297-305.

Pringle, M. L. K., & Bossio, V. A study of deprived children; Part I: Intellectual, emotional, and social development; Part II: Language development and reading attainment. *Vita Humana,* 1958, **1**, 142-170.

Pringle, M. L. K., & Naidoo, S. Early child care in Britain. *International Monograph Series on Early Child Care* (Vol. 5). London: Gordon & Breach, 1974.

Prugh, D. G., & Harlow, R. G. *Masked deprivation in infants and young children* (Public Health Paper No. 14). Geneva, Switzerland: World Health Organization, 1962, 9-29.

Quay, L. C. Academic skills. In N. R. Ellis (Ed.), *Handbook of Mental Deficiency.* New York: McGraw-Hill, 1963.

Quay, L. C. Language dialect, age, and intelligence-test performance in disadvantaged black children. *Child Development,* 1974, **45**, 463-468.

Rabin, A. I., & Haworth, M. R. *Projective techniques with children.* New York: Grune & Stratton, 1960.

Raivio, K. O., & Seegmiller, J. E. Genetic diseases of metabolism. *Annual Review of Biochemistry,* 1972, **41**, 543-576.

Rajalakshmi, R. The psychological status of under-privileged children reared at home and in an orphanage in South India. *Indian Journal of Mental Retardation,* 1968, **1**, 53-61.

Rapier, J. L. Learning abilities of normal and retarded children as a function of social class. *Journal of Educational Psychology,* 1968, **59**, 102-110.

Record, R. G., McKeown, T., & Edwards, J. M. An investigation of the difference in measured intelligence between twins and single births. *Annals of Human Genetics,* 1970, **34**, 11-20.

Reed, E. W., & Phillips, V. P. The Vale of Siddem revisited. *American Journal of Mental Deficiency,* 1959, **63**, 699-702.

Reed, E. W., & Reed, S. C. *Mental retardation: A family study.* Philadelphia: Saunders, 1965.

Reed, J. C., & Reitan, R. M. Verbal and performance differences among brain-injured children with lateralized motor deficits. *Perceptual and Motor Skills,* 1969, **29**, 747-752.

Reed, S. C. *Counseling in medical genetics* (2d ed.). Philadelphia: Saunders, 1963. Excerpts in Chap. 21 reproduced by permission of the author and the publisher.

Reed, S. C., & Anderson, V. E. Effects of changing sexuality on the gene pool. In F. F. de la Cruz and G. D. LaVeck (Eds.), *Human sexuality and the mentally retarded.* New York: Brunner/Mazel, 1973.

Reger, R. Reading ability and CMAS scores in educable mentally retarded boys. *American Journal of Mental Deficiency,* 1964, **68**, 652-655.

Reiss, P. Implications of Piaget's developmental psychology for mental retardation. *American Journal of Mental Deficiency,* 1967, **72**, 361-369.

Reitan, R. M. A research program on the psychological effects of brain lesions in human beings. In N. R. Ellis (Ed.), *International review of research in mental retardation* (Vol. 1). New York: Academic Press, 1966.

Reitan, R. M., & Boll, T. J. Neuropsychological correlates of minimal brain dysfunction. *Annals of the New York Academy of Sciences,* 1973, **205**, 65-88.

Report to the Medical Research Council of the Conference on Phenylketonuria, 1963. Treatment of phenylketonuria. *British Medical Journal,* 1963, **1**, 1691.

Research Utilization Branch, Division of Research and Demonstration Grants, Office of Research, Demonstrations, and Training, Social and Rehabilitation Service, Department of Health, Education and Welfare. A special program to place mentally retarded persons in federal employment. *BRIEF,* 1969, **2**, No. 9.

Restle, F. The selection of strategies in cue learning. *Psychological Review,* 1962, **69**, 11-19.

Reynolds, M. C., & Balow, B. Categories and variables in special education. In R. L. Jones & D. L. McMillan (Eds.), *Special education in transition.* Boston: Allyn and Bacon, 1974.

Rheingold, H. L. Interpreting mental retardation to parents. *Journal of Consulting Psychology,* 1945, **9**, 142-148.

Rheingold, H. L. The modification of social responsiveness in institutional babies. *Monographs of the Society for Research in Child Development,* 1956, **21**(2, Serial No. 63).

Rheingold, H. L. The measurement of maternal care. *Child Development,* 1960, **31**, 565-575.

Rheingold, H. L. The effect of environmental stimulation upon social and exploratory behaviour in the human infant. In B. M. Foss (Ed.), *Determinants of infant behaviour.* New York: Wiley, 1961.

Rheingold, H. L., & Bayley, N. The later effects of an experimental modification of mothering. *Child Development,* 1959, **30**, 353-372.

Richards, B. W. Mongolism: The effect of trends in age at childbirth on incidence and chromosomal type. *Journal of Mental Subnormality,* 1967, **13**, 3-13.

Richardson, S. A. Family components in mental retardation—some findings. In National Institute of Child Health and Human Development, *The Social Sciences and Mental Retardation: Family Components.* Report of a conference held at Bethesda, Maryland, January 1968. Washington, D.C.: Public Health Service, 1968.

Ricker, L. H., & Pinkard, C. M., Jr. Three approaches to group counseling involving motion pictures with mentally retarded adults. *Proceedings of the International Copenhagen Congress on the Scientific Study of Mental Retardation,* 1964, **2**, 714-717.

Riesen, A. H. The development of visual perception in man and chimpanzee. *Science,* 1947, **106**, 107-108.

Riesen, A. H. Effects of stimulus deprivation on the development and strophy of the visual sensory system (Brain and behavior: Session I, Symposium, 1959). *American Journal of Orthopsychiatry,* 1960, **33**, 23-56.

Riesen, A. H. Effects of early deprivation of photic stimulation. In S. F. Osler & R. F. Cooke, *The biosocial basis of mental retardation.* Baltimore: Johns Hopkins, 1965.

Rimland, B. *Infantile autism.* New York: Appleton-Century-Crofts, 1964.

Rimoin, D. L., & Schimke, R. N. *Genetic disorders of the endocrine glands.* St. Louis: Mosby, 1971.

Risley, T. R. The effects and side effects of punishing the autistic behaviors of a deviant child. *Journal of Applied Behavior Analysis,* 1968, **1**, 21-34.

Risley, T. R., & Wolf, M. Established speech in echolalic children. *Behavioral Research and Therapy,* 1967, **5**, 73-88.

Robbins, M., & Glass, G. V. The Doman-Delacato rationale: A critical analysis. In J. Hellmuth (Ed.), *Educational therapy* (Vol. 2). Seattle: Special Child Publications, 1969.

Roberts, J. A. F. The genetics of mental deficiency. *Eugenics Review,* 1952, **44**, 71-83.

Roberts, J. *Intellectual development of children by demographic and socioeconomic factors.* DHEW Publication No. (HSM) 72-1012. Washington, D.C.: U.S. Government Printing Office, 1972.

Roberts, J., & Engel, A. Family background, early development, and intelligence of children 6-11 years. *Vital and Health Statistics* (Series 11, No. 142). Washington, D.C.: Health Resources Administration, 1974.

Robinson, A. M. *Remotivation technique* (Rev. ed.). Philadelphia: APA/Smith Kline and French Laboratories, Remotivation Project, 1964.

Robinson, C. Error patterns in level 4 and level 5 object permanence training. *American Journal of Mental Deficiency,* 1974, **78**, 389-396.

Robinson, H. B. An experimental examination of the size-weight illusion in young children. *Child Development,* 1964, **35**, 91-108.

Robinson, H. B., & Robinson, N. M. Longitudinal development of very young children in a comprehensive day care program: The first two years. *Child Development,* 1971, **42**, 1673-1683.

Robinson, N. M. Bender-Gestalt performances of schizophrenics and paretics. *Journal of Clinical Psychology,* 1953, **9**, 291-293.

Robinson, N. M., & Robinson, H. B. A follow-up study of children of low birth weight and control children at school age. *Pediatrics,* 1965, **35**, 425-433.

Robinson, N. M., & Robinson, H. B. Staff studies and planning cross-national research. Final report to Office of Child Development. Grant No. CB-191, 1974.

Rodriques, J., & Lombardi, T. P. Legal implications of parental prerogatives for special class placements of the MR. *Mental Retardation,* 1973, **11**(5), 29-31.

Rogers, A. C., & Merrill, M. A. *Dwellers in the Vale of Siddem.* Boston: Richard G. Badger, Gorham Press, 1919.

Rogers, C. R. *Client-centered therapy.* Boston: Houghton Mifflin, 1951.

Rohwer, W. D., Jr. Elaboration and learning in childhood and adolescence. In H. W. Reese (Ed.), *Advances in child development and behavior* (Vol. 8). New York: Academic Press, 1973.

Roos, P. Human rights and behavior modification. *Mental Retardation,* 1974, **12**(3), 3-6.

Rosen, D., & Bruno, M. *Trends: Residential services for the mentally retarded.* Madison, Wisc.: National Association of Superintendents of Public Residential Facilities, 1971.

Rosen, E., Fox, R. E., & Gregory, I. *Abnormal psychology* (2d ed.). Philadelphia: Saunders, 1972.

Rosen, H. G., & Rosen, S. Group therapy as an instrument to develop a concept of self-worth in the adolescent and young adult mentally retarded. *Mental Retardation,* 1969, **7**(5), 52-55.

Rosen, L. Selected aspects in the development of the mother's understanding of her mentally retarded child. *American Journal of Mental Deficiency,* 1955, **59**, 522.

Rosen, M., Diggory, J. C., Floor, L., & Nowakiwska, M. Self-evaluation, expectancy and performance in the mentally subnormal. *Journal of Mental Deficiency Research,* 1971, **15**, 81-95.

Rosen, M., Diggory, J. C., & Werlinsky, B. E. Goal setting and expectancy of success in institutionalized and non-institutionalized mental subnormals. *American Journal of Mental Deficiency,* 1966, **71**, 249-255.

Rosen, M., Floor, L., Baxter, D. IQ, academic achievement and community adjustment after discharge from the institution. *Mental Retardation,* 1974, **12**(2), 51-53.

Rosenbaum, A. L. Neuropsychologic outcome of children born via the occiput posterior position. In C. R. Angle & E. A. Bering, Jr. (Eds.), *Physical trauma as an etiological agent in mental retardation.* Washington, D.C.: Superintendent of Documents, U.S. Government Printing Office, 1970.

Rosenberg, B. Q., & Sutton-Smith, B. Sibling age spacing effects upon cognition. *Developmental Psychology,* 1969, **1**, 661-665.

Rosenthal, D. *Genetic theory and abnormal behavior.* New York: McGraw-Hill, 1970.

Rosenthal, D., & Kety, S. S. (Eds.). *The transmission of schizophrenia.* New York: Pergamon Press, 1968.

Rosenzweig, M. R., Krech, D., Bennett, E. L., & Diamond, M. C. Modifying brain chemistry and anatomy by enrichment or impoverishment of experience. In G. Newton & S. Levine (Eds.), *Early experience and behavior.* Springfield, Ill.: Charles C Thomas, 1968.

Ross, A. O. Conceptual issues in the evaluation of brain damage. In J. Khanna (Ed.), *Brain damage and mental retardation.* Springfield, Ill.: Charles C Thomas, 1968.

Ross, D. M. Effect on learning of psychological attachment to a film model. *American Journal of Mental Deficiency,* 1970, **74**, 701-707. (a)

Ross, D. M. The relationship between intentional learning, incidental learning, and type of reward in preschool, educable mental retardates. *Child Development,* 1970, **41**, 1151-1158. (b)

Ross, D. M. Incidental learning of number concepts in small group games. *American Journal of Mental Deficiency,* 1970, **74**, 718-725. (c)

Ross, D. M. Retention and transfer of mediation set in paired-associate learning of educable retarded children. *Journal of Educational Psychology,* 1971, **62**, 322-327.

Ross, D. M., & Ross, S. A. The efficacy of listening training for educable mentally retarded children. *American Journal of Mental Deficiency,* 1972, **77**, 137-142.

Ross, D. M., & Ross, S. A. Cognitive training for the EMR child: Situational problem solving and planning. *American Journal of Mental Deficiency,* 1973, **78**, 20-26. (a)

Ross, D. M., & Ross, S. A. Storage and utilization of previously formulated mediators in educable mentally retarded children. *Journal of Educational Psychology,* 1973, **65**, 205-210. (b)

Ross, D. M., & Ross, S. A. *Pacemaker primary curriculum.* Belmont, Calif.: Fearon Publishers, 1974.

Ross, D. M., Ross, S. A., & Downing, M. L. Intentional training vs. observational learning of mediational strategies in EMR children. *American Journal of Mental Deficiency,* 1973, **78**, 292-299.

Ross, D. M., Ross, S. A., & Evans, T. A. The modification of extreme social withdrawal by modeling with guided participation. *Journal of Behavior Therapy and Experimental Psychiatry,* 1971, **2**, 273-279.

Ross, L. E., & Ross, S. M. Classical conditioning and intellectual defect. In D. K. Routh (Ed.), *The experimental psychology of mental retardation.* Chicago: Aldine, 1973.

Ross, R. T. IQ changes in hospitalized retardates. *California Mental Health Research Digest,* 1971, **9**, 30-31. (a)

Ross, R. T. A preliminary study of self-help skills and age in hospitalized Down's syndrome patients. *American Journal of Mental Deficiency,* 1971, **76**, 373-377. (b)

Ross, R. T. Behavioral correlates of levels of intelligence. *American Journal of Mental Deficiency,* 1972, **76**, 545-549.

Ross, R. T., & Boroskin, A. Are IQ's below 30 meaningful? *Mental Retardation,* 1972, **10**(4), 24.

Ross, R. T., Boroskin, A., & Giampiccolo, J. S., Jr. *Fairview Behavior Evaluation Battery for the mentally retarded* (5 scales). Costa Mesa, Calif.: Fairview State Hospital, Research Department, 1970-1974.

Ross, S. A. Effects of intentional training in social behavior on retarded children. *American Journal of Mental Deficiency,* 1969, **73**, 912-919.

Ross, S. A. Modeling and imitation. In B. B. Wolman (Ed.), *International encyclopedia of psychiatry, psychoanalysis, and psychology.* New York: Basic Books, 1975.

Rössle, R. I. *Wachstum und Altern.* Münich, 1922.

Rosvold, H. E., Mirsky, A. F., Sarason, I., Bransome, E. D., Jr., & Beck, L. H. A continuous performance test for brain damage. *Journal of Consulting Psychology,* 1956, **20**, 343-350.

Rotter, J. B. *Social learning and clinical psychology.* New York: Prentice-Hall, 1954.

Routh, D. K., Schroeder, C. S., & L'Tuama, L. A. Development of activity level in children. *Developmental Psychology,* 1974, **10**, 163-168.

Rowley, V. N. Analysis of the WISC performance of brain damaged and emotionally disturbed children. *Journal of Consulting Psychology,* 1961, **25**, 553.

Rubin, S. S. A reevaluation of figure-ground pathology in brain damaged children. *American Journal of Mental Deficiency,* 1969, **74**, 111-115.

Rubin, T. I. *Jordi.* New York: Macmillan, 1960. Excerpt in Chap. 10 reprinted with permission of the publisher.

Rucker, C. N., Howe, C. E., & Snider, B. The participation of retarded children in junior high academic and nonacademic regular classes. *Exceptional Children,* 1969, **35**, 617-623.

Rundquist, E. A. Inheritance of spontaneous activity in rats. *Journal of Comparative Psychology,* 1933, **16**, 415-438.

Rutter, M. The influence of organic and emotional factors on the origins, nature and outcome of childhood psychosis. *Developmental Medicine and Child Neurology,* 1965, **7**, 518-528.

Rutter, M. Concepts of autism: A review of research. *Journal of Child Psychology and Psychiatry,* 1968, **9**, 1-25.

Rutter, M. Psychological development—Predictions from infancy. *Journal of Child Psychology and Psychiatry,* 1970, **11**, 49–62.

Rutter, M. L. Psychiatry. In J. Wortis (Ed.), *Mental Retardation: An annual review* (Vol. 3). New York: Grune & Stratton, 1971.

Rutter, M. The development of infantile autism. *Psychological Medicine,* 1974, **4**, 147–163.

Rutter, M., Graham, P. J., & Yule, W. A neuropsychiatric study in childhood. *Clinics in Developmental Medicine* (No. 35–36). London: S.I.M.P. with Heinemann, 1970.

Rutter, M., Greenfield, D., & Lockyer, L. A five to fifteen year follow-up study of infantile psychosis: II. Social and behavioral outcome. *British Journal of Psychiatry,* 1967, **113**, 1183–1199.

Rutter, M., & Hemming, M. Individual items of deviant behavior: Their prevalence and clinical significance. In M. Rutter, J. Tizard, & K. Whitmore, *Education, health, and behavior.* London: Longman, 1970. Table 9-1 reproduced by permission of Longman Group, Ltd., and John Wiley, Inc.

Rutter, M., Lebovici, S., Eisenberg, L., Sneznevskij, A. V., Sadoun, R., Brooke, E., & Lin, T. A tri-axial classification of mental disorders in childhood. *Journal of Child Psychology and Psychiatry,* 1969, **10**, 41–61.

Rutter, M., Tizard, J., & Whitmore, K. (Eds.). *Education, health and behavior.* London: Longmans, 1970.

Ryckman, D. B. A comparison of information processing abilities of middle and lower class Negro kindergarten boys. *Exceptional Children,* 1967, **33**, 545–553.

Ryckman, D. B., & Wiegerink, R. The factors of the Illinois Test of Psycholinguistic Abilities: A comparison of 18 factor analyses. *Exceptional Children,* 1969, **36**, 107–113.

Ryle, A., Pond, D. A., & Hamilton, M. The prevalence and patterns of psychological disturbance in children of primary age. *Journal of Child Psychology and Psychiatry,* 1965, **6**, 101–113.

Sabagh, G., Dingman, H. F., Tarjan, G., and Wright, S. W. Social class and ethnic status of patients admitted to a state hospital for the retarded. *Pacific Sociological Review,* 1959, **2**, 76–80.

Sackett, G. P. Some persistent effects of different rearing conditions on preadult behavior of monkeys. *Journal of Comparative and Physiological Psychology,* 1967, **64**, 263–265.

Sacks, E. L. Intelligence scores as a function of experimentally established social relationships between child and examiner. *Journal of Abnormal and Social Psychology,* 1952, **47**, 354–358.

Saenger, G. *The adjustment of severely retarded adults in the community.* Albany: Interdepartmental Health Resources Board, 1957. Table 22-1 compiled and reprinted with permission of the publisher.

Saenger, G. *Factors influencing the institutionalization of mentally retarded individuals in New York City.* Albany: Interdepartmental Health Resources Board, 1960.

Saenger, G. Social and occupational adjustment of the mentally retarded. In J. Zubin & G. A. Jervis (Eds.), *Psychopathology of mental development.* New York: Grune & Stratton, 1967.

Sali, J., & Amir, J. Personal factors influencing the retarded person's success at work: A report from Israel. *American Journal of Mental Deficiency,* 1971, **76**, 42–47.

Saltz, R. Effects of part-time "mothering" on IQ and SQ of young institutionalized children. *Child Development,* 1973, **44**, 166–170.

Sanchez, O., & Junis, J. J. Partial trisomy 8 (8q24) and the trisomy-8 syndrome. *Humangenetik,* 1974, **23**, 297-303.

Sandberg, A. A., Koepf, G. F., Ishihara, T., & Hauschka, T. S. An XYY human male. *Lancet,* 1961, **2**, 488-489.

Sanders, H. J. Food additives: Part I. *Chemical and Engineering News,* October 10, 1966, 100.

Sandgrund, A., Gaines, R. W., & Green, A. H. Child abuse and mental retardation: A problem of cause and effect. *American Journal of Mental Deficiency,* 1974, **79**, 327-330.

Sarason, I. G., & Sarason, B. R. *Constructive classroom behavior: A teacher's guide to modeling and role-playing techniques.* New York: Behavioral Publications, 1974.

Sarason, S. B., Davidson, K. S., Lighthall, F. F., Waite, R. R., & Ruebush, B. K. *Anxiety in elementary school children.* New York: Wiley, 1960.

Satter, G., & McGee, E. Retarded adults who have developed beyond expectation; Part I: Intellectual functions. *Training School Bulletin,* 1954, **51**, 43-55.

Sattler, J. M. *Assessment of children's intelligence.* Philadelphia: Saunders, 1974.

Savage, M. H., Weltman, R., and Zarfas, D. E. Short-term care for the mentally retarded. *Mental Retardation,* 1967, **5**, 9-14.

Scally, B. G. Marriage and mental handicap: Some observations in Northern Ireland. In F. F. de la Cruz and G. D. LaVeck (Eds.), *Human sexuality and the mentally retarded.* New York: Brunner/Mazel, 1973.

Scanlon, J. Intellectual development of youths as measured by a short form of the Wechsler Intelligence Scale. (U.S. DHEW Publication No. HRA 74-1610). Washington, D.C.: U.S. Government Printing Office, 1973.

Scarr, S. Effects of birth weight on later intelligence. *Social Biology,* 1969, **16**, 249-256.

Scarr-Salapatek, S. Race, social class and IQ. *Science,* 1971, **176**, 1285-1295.

Scarr-Salapatek, S., & Williams, M. L. The effects of early stimulation on low-birth-weight infants. *Child Development,* 1973, **44**, 94-101.

Schaefer, E. S. Need for early and continuing education. In V. H. Denenberg (Ed.), *Education of the infant and young child.* New York: Academic Press, 1970.

Schaefer, E. S. Parents as educators: Evidence from cross-sectional, longitudinal and intervention research. *Young Children,* April 1972, 227-239.

Schaffer, H. R. Some issues for research in the study of attachment behavior. In B. M. Foss (Ed.), *Determinants of infant behaviour II.* New York: Wiley, 1963.

Schaffer, H. R., & Emerson, P. E. Patterns of response to physical contact in early human development. *Journal of Child Psychology and Psychiatry,* 1964, **5**, 1-13.

Schaie, K. W., Labouvie, G. V., & Buech, B. V. Generational and cohort-specific differences in adult cognitive functioning. *Developmental Psychology,* 1973, **9**, 151-166.

Schain, R. J., & Yannet, H. Infantile autism. *Journal of Pediatrics,* 1960, **57**, 560-567.

Scheerenberger, R. C. *Estimated incidence of mental retardation in the State of Illinois for 1966.* Springfield: Division of Mental Retardation Services, 1966.

Scheerenberger, R. C. Methodology: General principles based on psychological research. In R. C. Scheerenberger (Ed.), *Training the severely and profoundly mentally retarded. Mental Retardation in Illinois;* monogr. suppl. #3. Springfield, Ill.: Department of Mental Health, 1967.

Schein, J. Cross-validation of the Continuous Performance Test for brain damage. *Journal of Consulting Psychology,* 1962, **26**, 115-118.

Schlesinger, K., & Griek, B. J. The genetics and biochemistry of audiogenic seizures. In G. Lindzey & D. D. Thiessen (Eds.), *Contributions to behavior-genetic analysis: The mouse as a prototype.* New York: Appleton-Century-Crofts, 1970.

Schmid-Kitsikis, E. Piagetian theory and its approach to psychopathology. *American Journal of Mental Deficiency,* 1973, **77,** 695-705.

Schmidt, F. L., & Hunter, J. E. Racial and ethnic bias in psychological tests: Divergent implications of two definitions of test bias. *American Psychologist,* 1974, **29,** 1-8.

Schmidt, L. J., & Nelson, C. C. The affective/cognitive attitude dimension of teachers of educable mentally retarded minors. *Exceptional Children,* 1969, **35,** 695-701.

Schmitt, F. O. (Ed.). *The neurosciences: Second study program.* New York: Rockefeller University Press, 1970.

Schopler, E. Early infantile autism and receptor processes. *Archives of General Psychiatry,* 1965, **13,** 327-335.

Schopler, E., Brehm, S. S., Kinsbourne, M., & Reichler, R. J. Effect of treatment structure on development in autistic children. *Archives of General Psychiatry,* 1971, **24,** 415-421.

Schopler, E., & Reichler, R. J. Psychobiological referents for the treatment of autism. In D. W. Churchill, G. D. Alpern, & M. K. DeMeyer (Eds.), *Infantile autism.* Springfield, Ill.: Charles C Thomas, 1971.

Schroeder, S. R. Automated transduction of sheltered workshop behaviors. *Journal of Applied Behavior Analysis,* 1972, **4,** 106-109. (a)

Schruber, F. Neurologic sequelae of paranatal asphyxia. *Journal of Pediatrics,* 1940, **16,** 297-309.

Schreibman, L., & Lovaas, O. I. Overselective response to social stimuli by autistic children. *Journal of Abnormal Child Psychology,* 1973, **1,** 152-168.

Schrott, H. G., Karp, L., & Omenn, G. S. Prenatal prediction in myotonic dystrophy: Guidelines for genetic counseling. *Clinical Genetics,* 1973, **4,** 38-45.

Schurr, K. T., & Brookover, W. *The effect of special class placement on the self-concept of ability of the educable mentally retarded child.* U.S. Office of Education. East Lansing: Michigan State University, 1967.

Schurr, K. T., Joiner, L. M., & Towne, R. C. Self-concept research on the mentally retarded: A review of empirical studies. *Mental Retardation,* 1970, **8**(5), 39-43.

Schuster, S. O., & Gruen, G. E. Success and failure as determinants of the performance predictions of mentally retarded and non-retarded children. *American Journal of Mental Deficiency,* 1971, **76,** 190-196.

Schusterman, R. J. Strategies of normal and mentally retarded children under conditions of uncertain outcome. *American Journal of Mental Deficiency,* 1964, **69,** 66-75.

Schwarz, R. H., & Cook, J. J. Mental age as a predictor of academic achievement. *Education and Training of the Mentally Retarded,* 1971, **6,** 12-15.

Schwarz, R. H., & Flanigan, P. J. Evaluation of examiner bias in intelligence testing. *American Journal of Mental Deficiency,* 1971, **76,** 262-265.

Schwarz, R. H., & Jens, K. G. The expectation of success as it modifies the achievement of mentally retarded adolescents. *American Journal of Mental Deficiency,* 1969, **73,** 946-949.

Schwarz, R. H., & Shores, R. E. The academic achievement of EMR students and social class. *American Journal of Mental Deficiency,* 1969, **74,** 338-340.

Scott, J. P. Genetic differences in the social behavior of inbred strains of mice. *Journal of Heredity,* 1942, **33,** 11-15.

Scott, J. P., & Marston, M. Critical periods affecting the development of normal and maladjustive social behavior of puppies. *Journal of Genetic Psychology,* 1950, **77,** 25-60.

Scott, K. G. Engineering attention: Some rules for the classroom. *Education and Training of the Mentally Retarded,* 1966, **1,** 125-129.

Seagoe, M. V. *Yesterday was Tuesday, all night and all day.* Boston: Little, Brown, 1964.

Searle, L. V. The organization of heredity maze-brightness and maze-dullness. *Genetic Psychology Monographs,* 1949, **39**, 279-325.

Sechzer, J. A., Faro, M. D., & Windle, W. F. Studies of monkeys asphyxiated at birth: Implications for minimal cerebral dysfunction. *Seminars in Psychiatry,* 1973, **5**, 19-34.

Seeley, M. S. An experimental evaluation of sociodrama as a social habilitation technique for mentally retarded adolescents. *Dissertation Abstracts International,* 1971, **32**, 3040.

Seguin, E. *Idiocy and its treatment by the physiological method.* (1866) Clifton, N.J.: Augustus M. Kelley, 1971.

Seitz, S., & Hoekenga, R. Modeling as a training tool for retarded children and their parents. *Mental Retardation,* 1974, **12**(2), 28-31.

Sells, C. J., West, M. A., & Reichert, A. Reducing the institutional waiting lists for the mentally retarded. *Clinical Pediatrics,* 1974, **13**, 740-745.

Selye, H. *The stress of life.* New York: McGraw-Hill, 1956.

Selye, H. *The physiology and pathology of exposure to stress.* Montreal: Acta, Inc., 1950.

Sever, J. L. Infectious agents and fetal disease. In H. A. Waisman & G. R. Kerr (Eds.), *Fetal growth and development.* New York: McGraw-Hill, 1970.

Severy, L. J., & Davis, K. E. Helping behavior among normal and retarded children. *Child Development,* 1971, **42**, 1017-1031.

Shaffer, D. Psychiatric aspects of brain injury in childhood: A review. *Developmental Medicine and Child Neurology,* 1973, **15**, 211-220.

Shaffer, D., McNamara, N., & Pincus, J. H. Controlled observations on patterns of activity, attention, and impulsivity in brain-damaged and psychiatrically disturbed boys. *Psychological Medicine,* 1974, **4**, 4-18.

Shafter, A. J. The needs of the mentally retarded in rural settings. In R. C. Scheerenberger (Ed.), *Nonmetropolitan planning for the mentally retarded.* Springfield, Ill.: Mental Health Department, 1968.

Shapiro, A. Delinquent and disturbed behavior within the field of mental deficiency. In A. V. S. DeRueck & R. Porter (Eds.), *The mentally abnormal offender.* Boston: Little, Brown, 1968.

Sharlin, S. A., & Polansky, N. A. The process of infantilization. *American Journal of Orthopsychiatry,* 1971, **42**, 92-102.

Sharp, S. E. Individual psychology: A study in the psychological method. *The American Journal of Psychology,* 1899, **10**, 329-391.

Shellhaas, M. D., & Nihira, K. Factor analytic comparison of reasons retardates are institutionalized in two populations. *American Journal of Mental Deficiency,* 1970, **74**, 626-632.

Shepard, T. H. Teratogenicity from drugs—an increasing problem. *Disease-a-Month.* Chicago: Yearbook Medical Publishers, June 1974.

Shepp, B. E., & Turrisi, F. D. Learning and transfer of mediating responses in discriminative learning. In N. R. Ellis (Ed.), *International review of research in mental retardation* (Vol. 2). New York: Academic Press, 1966.

Sherman, M., & Key, C. B. The intelligence of isolated mountain children. *Child Development,* 1932, **3**, 279-290.

Shields, J. *Monozygotic twins brought up apart and brought up together.* London: Oxford University Press, 1962.

Shields, J. Heredity and psychological abnormality. In H. J. Eysenck (Ed.), *Handbook of abnormal psychology.* London: Pitman Medical Publishers, 1973.

Shif, Z. I. Development of children in schools for the mentally retarded. In M. Cole &

I. Maltzman (Eds.), *A handbook of contemporary Soviet psychology*. New York: Basic Books, 1969.

Shipe, D. Impulsivity and locus of control as predictors of achievement and adjustment in mildly retarded and borderline youth. *American Journal of Mental Deficiency*, 1971, **76**, 12-22.

Shipe, D., & Shotwell, A. M. Effects of out-of-home care on mongoloid children: A continuation study. *American Journal of Mental Deficiency*, 1965, **69**, 649-652.

Shotwell, A., & Lawrence, E. Mosaic patterns of institutionalized mental defectives. *American Journal of Mental Deficiency*, 1951, **56**, 161-168.

Shuey, A. M. *The testing of Negro intelligence* (2d ed.). New York: Social Science Press, 1966.

Shultz, T., & Zigler, E. Emotional concomitants of visual mastery in infants. The effects of stimulus movement on smiling and vocalizing. *Journal of Experimental Child Psychology*, 1970, **10**, 390-402.

Shuman, R. M., Leech, R. W., & Alvord, E. C., Jr. Neurotoxicity of hexachlorophene in the human: I. A clinicopathologic study of 248 children. *Pediatrics*, 1974, **54**, 689-695.

Shuman, R. M., Leech, R. W., & Alvord, E. C., Jr. Neurotoxicity of hexachlorophene in the human: II. A clinicopathologic study of 46 premature infants. *Archives in Neurology*, 1975, **32**, 320-325.

Siegel, P. S., & Foshee, J. G. Molar variability in the mentally defective. *Journal of Abnormal and Social Psychology*, 1960, **61**, 141-143.

Silberberg, D. H. Maple syrup urine disease metabolites studied in cerebellum cultures. *Journal of Neurochemistry*, 1969, **16**, 1141.

Silverstein, A. B. Anxiety and the quality of human-figure drawings. *American Journal of Mental Deficiency*, 1966, **70**, 607-608.

Silverstein, A. B. An alternative factor analytic solution of Wechsler's intelligence scales. *Educational and Psychological Measurement*, 1969, **29**, 763-767. (a)

Silverstein, A. B. Changes in the measured intelligence of institutionalized retardates as a function of hospital age. *Developmental Psychology*, 1969, **1**, 125-127. (b)

Silverstein, A. B. The measurement of intelligence. In N. R. Ellis (Ed.), *International review of research in mental retardation* (Vol. 4). New York: Academic Press, 1970.

Simches, G., & Bohn, R. Issues in curriculum: Research and responsibility. *Mental Retardation*, 1963, **1**, 84-87.

Simpson, N. E. Diabetes in the families of diabetics. *Canadian Medical Association Journal*, 1968, **98**, 427.

Singer, J. E., Westphal, M., & Niswander, K. R. Sex differences in the incidence of neonatal abnormalities and abnormal performance in early childhood. *Child Development*, 1968, **39**, 103-112.

Skeels, H. M. Adult status of children with contrasting early life experiences. *Monographs of the Society for Research in Child Development*, 1966, **31**(3, Serial No. 105).

Skeels, H. M., & Dye, H. B. A study of the effects of differential stimulation on mentally retarded children. *Proceedings and Addresses of the American Association on Mental Deficiency*, 1939, **44**, 114-136.

Skeels, H. M., Updegraff, R., Wellman, B. L., & Williams, H. M. A study of environmental stimulation, an orphanage preschool project. *University of Iowa Studies in Child Welfare*, 1938, **15**, 129-145. Excerpt in Chap. 21 reprinted with permission of the publisher.

Skinner, B. F. *The behavior of organisms*. New York: Appleton-Century-Crofts, 1938.

Skinner, B. F. *Verbal behavior*. New York: Appleton-Century-Crofts, 1957.

Skinner, B. F. Operant behavior. In W. K. Honig (Ed.), *Operant behavior: Areas of research and application.* New York: Appleton-Century-Crofts, 1966.

Skodak, M. Children in foster homes. *University of Iowa Studies in Child Welfare,* 1939, **16**, 1–156.

Skodak, M., & Skeels, H. M. A final follow-up study of one hundred adopted children. *Journal of Genetic Psychology,* 1949, **75**, 85–125.

Slater, E., Beard, A. W., & Glithero, E. The schizophrenia-like psychosis of epilepsy. *British Journal of Psychiatry,* 1963, **109**, 95–150.

Slater, E., & Cowie, V. *The genetics of mental disorders.* London: Oxford University Press, 1971.

Slavson, S. R. *Analytic group psychotherapy, with children, adolescents, and adults.* New York: Columbia University Press, 1950.

Slivkin, S. E., & Bernstein, N. R. Group approaches to treating retarded adolescents. In F. J. Menolascino (Ed.), *Psychiatric approaches to mental retardation.* New York: Basic Books, 1970.

Sloan, H. R., & Fredrickson, D. S. Gangliosidoses: Tay-Sachs disease. In J. B. Stanbury, J. B. Wyngaarden, & D. S. Fredrickson (Eds.), *The metabolic basis of inherited disease* (3rd ed.). New York: McGraw-Hill, 1972.

Sloan, W. The Lincoln-Oseretsky Motor Development Scale. *Genetic Psychology Monographs,* 1955, **51**, 183–252.

Sluckin, W. (Ed.). *Early learning and early experience: Selected readings.* Baltimore: Penguin Books, 1971.

Smedslund, J. The acquisition of conservation of substance and weight in children. *Scandinavian Journal of Psychology,* 1961, **2**, 11–20, 71–87, 153–160, 203–210.

Smiley, S. S., & Weir, M. W. Role of dimensional dominance in reversal and non-reversal shift behavior. *Journal of Experimental Child Psychology,* 1966, **4**, 296–307.

Smirnov, A. A., & Zinchenko, P. I. Problems in the psychology of memory. In M. Cole & I. Maltzman (Eds.), *A handbook of contemporary Soviet psychology.* New York: Basic Books, 1969.

Smith, A. C., Flick, G. L., Ferriss, G. S., & Sellman, A. H. Prediction of developmental outcome at seven years from prenatal, perinatal, and postnatal events. *Child Development,* 1972, **43**, 495–507.

Smith, C. A. Effects of maternal under-nutrition upon the newborn infant in Holland (1944–1945). *Journal of Pediatrics,* 1947, **30**, 229–243.

Smith, D. C., Decker, H. A., Herberg, E. N., & Rupke, L. K. Medical needs of children in institutions for the mentally retarded. *American Journal of Public Health,* 1969, **59**, 1376.

Smith, D. W. Autosomal abnormalities. *American Journal of Obstetrics and Gynecology,* 1964, **90**, 1055.

Smith, D. W. *Recognizable patterns of human malformation.* Philadelphia: Saunders, 1970.

Smith, D. W., Patau, K., Therman, E., & Inhorn, S. L. A new autosomal trisomy syndrome. *Journal of Pediatrics,* 1960, **57**, 338.

Smith, D. W., & Wilson, A. A. *The child with Down's syndrome (mongolism).* Philadelphia: Saunders, 1973. Figures 4-1 through 4-7, 18-1, and 20-1 reprinted with the permission of the publisher and the senior author.

Smith, E. D. *Spina bifida and total care of spinal myelomeningocele.* Springfield, Ill.: Charles C Thomas, 1965.

Smith, R. M. Creative thinking abilities of educable mentally handicapped children in the regular grades. *American Journal of Mental Deficiency,* 1967, **71**, 571–575.

Smith, S., & Guthrie, E. R. *General psychology in terms of behavior.* New York: Appleton-Century-Crofts, 1921.

Smolev, S. R. Use of operant techniques for the modification of self-injurious behavior. *American Journal of Mental Deficiency,* 1971, **76**, 295–305.

Snyder, R. D. Congenital mercury poisoning. *New England Journal of Medicine,* 1971, **284**, 1014.

Snyder, R. T. Personality adjustment, self attitudes, and anxiety differences in retarded adolescents. *American Journal of Mental Deficiency,* 1966, **71**, 33–41.

Snyder, R. T., Jefferson, W., & Strauss, R. Personality variables as determiners of academic achievement of the mentally retarded. *Mental Retardation,* 1965, **3**, 15–18.

Snyder, S. H., & Meyerhoff, J. L. How amphetamine acts in minimal brain dysfunction. *Annals of the New York Academy of Sciences,* 1973, **205**, 310–320.

Snyderman, S. E., Norton, P. M., Roitman, E., & Holt, L. E., Jr. Maple syrup urine disease with particular reference to dietotherapy. *Pediatrics,* 1964, **34**, 454.

Solitaire, G. B., & Lamarche, J. B. Alzheimer's disease and senile dementia as seen in mongoloids: Neuropathological observations. *American Journal of Mental Deficiency,* 1966, **70**, 840–848.

Solnit, A., & Stark, M. Mourning and the birth of a defective child. In F. J. Menolascino (Ed.), *Psychiatric aspects of the diagnosis and treatment of mental retardation.* Seattle, Wash.: Special Child Publications, 1971.

Solomons, G. Drug therapy: Initiation and follow-up. *Annals of the New York Academy of Sciences,* 1973, **205**, 335–344.

Sontag, L. W. The possible relationship of prenatal environment to schizophrenia. In D. D. Jackson (Ed.), *The etiology of schizophrenia.* New York: Basic Books, 1960.

Sontag, L. W., Baker, C. T., & Nelson, V. L. Personality as a determinant of performance. *American Journal of Orthopsychiatry,* 1955, **25**, 555–562.

Sontag, L. W., Baker, C. T., & Nelson, V. L. Mental growth and personality development: A longitudinal study. *Monographs for the Society of Research in Child Development,* 1958, **23**(2, Serial No. 68).

Sorcher, M., & Goldstein, A. P. A behavior modeling approach in training. *Personnel Administration,* 1972, **35**, 35–41.

Spearman, C. General intelligence objectively measured and determined. *American Journal of Psychology,* 1904, **15**, 201–293.

Spence, K. W. *Behavior theory and conditioning.* New Haven: Yale University Press, 1956.

Spiker, C. C., & McCandless, B. R. The concept of intelligence and the philosophy of science. *Psychological Review,* 1954, **61**, 255–266.

Spitz, H. H. Field theory in mental deficiency. In N. Ellis (Ed.), *Handbook of mental deficiency.* New York: McGraw-Hill, 1963.

Spitz, H. H. The role of input organization in the learning and memory of mental retardates. In N. R. Ellis (Ed.), *International review of research in mental retardation* (Vol. 2). New York: Academic Press, 1966.

Spitz, H. H. The channel capacity of educable mental retardates. In D. K. Routh (Ed.), *The experimental psychology of mental retardation.* Chicago: Aldine, 1973. (a)

Spitz, H. H. Consolidating facts into the schematae of learning and memory of mental retardates. In N. R. Ellis (Ed.), *International review of research in mental retardation* (Vol. 6). New York: Academic Press, 1973. (b)

Spitz, H. H., Goettler, D. R., & Webreck, C. A. Effects of two types of redundancy on visual digit span performance of retardates and varying aged normals. *Developmental Psychology,* 1972, **6**, 92–103.

Spitz, H. H., & Nadler, B. T. Logical problem solving by educable retarded adolescents and normal children. *Developmental Psychology,* 1974, **10**, 404-412. Figure 13-4 copyright 1974 by the American Psychological Association. Reprinted with permission of the publisher and the senior author.

Spitz, H. H., & Webreck, C. A. Effects of spontaneous vs. externally-cued learning on the permanent storage of a schema by retardates. *American Journal of Mental Deficiency,* 1972, **77**, 163-168.

Spitz, R. A. Hospitalism; an inquiry into the genesis of psychiatric conditions in early childhood. *Psychoanalytic studies of the child* (Vol. 1). New York: International Universities Press, 1945.

Spitz, R. A. Hospitalism: A follow-up report. *Psychoanalytic studies of the child* (Vol. 2). New York: International Universities Press, 1947.

Spradlin, J. E., Cromwell, R. L., & Foshee, J. G. Studies in activity level. III. Effects of auditory stimulation in organics, familials, hyperactives and hypoactives. *American Journal of Mental Deficiency,* 1960, **64**, 754-757.

Spradlin, J. E., Girardeau, F. L., & Corte, E. Fixed ratio and fixed interval behavior of severely and profoundly retarded subjects. *Journal of Experimental Child Psychology,* 1965, **2**, 340-353.

Sprague, R. L. Minimal brain dysfunction from a behavioral point of view. *Annals of the New York Academy of Sciences,* 1973, **205**, 349-361.

Sprigle, H. A. The learning to learn program. In S. Ryan (Ed.), *A report of longitudinal evaluations of preschool programs.* Washington, D.C.: Office of Child Development, 1972.

Srole, L., Langner, T. S., Michael, S. T., Opler, M. K., Rennie, T. A. C. *Mental health in the metropolis: The midtown Manhattan study.* New York: McGraw-Hill, 1962.

Stacey, C. L., & DeMartino, M. F. *Counseling and psychotherapy with the mentally retarded: A book of readings.* Glencoe, Ill.: The Free Press, 1957.

Stanbury, J. B. Familial goiter. In J. B. Stanbury, J. B. Wyngaarden, & D. S. Fredrickson (Eds.), *The metabolic basis of inherited disease* (3d ed.). New York: McGraw-Hill, 1972.

Stanton, J. E., & Cassidy, V. M. Effectiveness of special classes for educable mentally retarded. *Mental Retardation,* 1964, **2**, 8-13.

Stedman, D. J., & Eichorn, D. H. A comparison of the growth and development of institutionalized and home-reared mongoloids during infancy and early childhood. *American Journal of Mental Deficiency,* 1964, **69**, 391-401.

Stein, J. F., & Longenecker, E. D. Patterns of mothering affecting handicapped children in residential treatment. *American Journal of Mental Deficiency,* 1962, **66**, 749-758.

Stein, Z., Susser, M., Saenger, G., & Marolla, F. Nutrition and mental performance. Prenatal exposure to the Dutch famine of 1944-1945 seems not related to mental performance at age 19. *Science,* 1972, **178**, 708-713.

Steisel, I. M., Katz, K. S., & Harris, S. L. The controlling behavior of mothers of children with phenylketonuria. *Pediatric Research,* 1973, **7**, 293.

Stephan, C., Stephano, S., & Talkington, L. W. Use of modeling in survival skill training with educable mentally retarded. *The Training School Bulletin,* 1973, **70**, 63-68.

Stephens, B., & McLaughlin, J. A. Two year gains in reasoning by normals and retardates. *American Journal of Mental Deficiency,* 1974, **79**, 116-126.

Stephens, B., Mahaney, E. J., & McLaughlin, J. A. Mental ages for achievement of Piagetian reasoning assessments. *Education and Training of the Mentally Retarded,* 1972, **7**, 124-127.

Stern, C. Model estimates of the number of gene pairs involved in pigmentation variability of the Negro-American. *Human Heredity,* 1970, **20**, 165-168.

Stern, C. *Principles of human genetics* (3d ed.). San Francisco: Freeman, 1973.

Sternlicht, M. Fantasy aggression in delinquent and nondelinquent retardates. *American Journal of Mental Deficiency,* 1966, **70**, 819-821. (a)

Sternlicht, M. Psychotherapeutic procedures with the retarded. In N. R. Ellis (Ed.), *International review of research in mental retardation* (Vol. 2). New York: Academic Press, 1966.

Sternlicht, M. *Adolescent retardates' values as gleaned from sentence-completion responses.* Paper presented at the meeting of the Eastern Psychological Association, Boston, April 1967.

Sternlicht, M., & Deutsch, M. R. *Personality development and social behavior in the mentally retarded.* Lexington, Mass.: Lexington Books, 1972.

Sternlicht, M., Pustel, G., & Siegel, L. Comparison of organic and cultural-familial retardates on two visual-motor tasks. *American Journal of Mental Deficiency,* 1968, **72**, 887-889.

Sternlicht, M., & Siegel, L. Institutional residence and intellectual functioning. *Journal of Mental Deficiency Research,* 1968, **12**, 119-127.

Sterns, K., & Borkowski, J. The development of conservation and horizontal vertical space perception in mental retardates. *American Journal of Mental Deficiency,* 1969, **73**, 785-791.

Sterritt, G. M., & Rudnick, M. Auditory and visual rhythm perception in relation to reading ability in fourth-grade boys. *Perceptual and Motor Skills,* 1966, **22**, 859-864.

Stevenson, H. W., Friedrichs, A. G., & Simpson, W. E. Learning and problem solving by the mentally retarded under three testing conditions. *Developmental Psychology,* 1970, **3**, 307-312.

Stevenson, H. W., Hale, G. A., Klein, R. E., & Miller, L. K. Interrelations and correlates in children's learning and problem solving. *Monographs of the Society for Research in Child Development,* 1968, **33**(7, Serial No. 123).

Stewart, M. A. Hyperactive children. *Scientific American,* 1970, **222**(4), 94-98.

Stewart, M. A., Pitts, F. N., Craig, A. G., & Dieruf, W. The hyperactive child syndrome. *American Journal of Orthopsychiatry,* 1966, **36**, 861-867.

Stoch, M. B., & Smythe, P. M. Does undernutrition during infancy inhibit brain growth and subsequent intellectual development? *Archives of Diseases of Childhood,* 1963, **38**, 546-552.

Stone, N. D. Family factors in willingness to place the mongoloid child. *American Journal of Mental Deficiency,* 1967, **72**, 16-20.

Stott, D. H. *The social adjustment of children: Manual to the Bristol Social Adjustment Guides.* London: University of London Press, 1963.

Stott, D. H. Follow-up study from birth effects of prenatal stresses. *Developmental Medicine and Child Neurology,* 1973, **15**, 770-787.

Strauss, A. A. Beitraege zur Einteilung, Entstehung und Klinik der schwersten Schwachsinnsformen. *Archiv fur Psychiatrie,* 1933, **99**, 693-708.

Strauss, A. A., & Kephart, N. C. Behavior differences in mentally retarded children as measured by a new behavior rating scale. *American Journal of Psychiatry,* 1940, **96**, 1117-1123.

Strauss, A. A., & Kephart, N. C. *Psychopathology and education of the brain-injured child.* New York: Grune & Stratton, 1955.

Strauss, A. A., & Lehtinen, L. E. *Psychopathology and education of the brain-injured child.* New York: Grune & Stratton, 1947.

Strauss, A. A., & Werner, H. The mental organization of the brain-injured mentally defective child. (The mentally crippled child.) *American Journal of Psychiatry,* 1941, **97,** 1194-1203.

Streissguth, A., & Bee, H. L. Mother-child interactions and cognitive development in children. *Young Children,* February 1972, 154-173.

Strichart, S. S. Effects of competence and nurturance on imitation of nonretarded peers by retarded adolescents. *American Journal of Mental Deficiency,* 1974, **78,** 665-673.

Strother, C. R. Minimal cerebral dysfunction: An historical overview. *Annals of the New York Academy of Sciences,* 1973, **205,** 6-17.

Stuck, G. B., & Wyne, M. D. Study of verbal behavior in special and regular elementary school classrooms. *American Journal of Mental Deficiency,* 1971, **75,** 463-469.

Struwe, F. Histopathologische Untersuchungen uber Entstehung und Wessen der senilen Plaques. *Zeitschrift des Neurologia Psychiatrica,* 1929, **122,** 291-307.

Sulzbacher, S. I. Psychotropic medication with children: An evaluation of procedural biases in results of reported studies. *Pediatrics,* 1973, **51,** 513-517.

Sulzbacher, S. I. Chemotherapy with learning disabled children. In H. F. Eichenwald & A. Talbot (Eds.), *The L-D child.* Dallas: University of Texas Health Sciences Center, 1974.

Suppes, P. The semantics of children's language. *American Psychologist,* 1974, **29,** 103-114.

Switzky, H. N., & Haywood, H. C. Conjugate control of motor activity in mentally retarded persons. *American Journal of Mental Deficiency,* 1973, **77,** 567-570.

Talkington, L. W., & Altman, R. Effects of film-mediated aggressive and affectual models on behavior. *American Journal of Mental Deficiency,* 1973, **77,** 420-425.

Talkington, L. W., Hall, S. M., & Altman, R. Use of peer modeling procedure with severely retarded subjects on a basic communication response skill. *The Training School Bulletin,* 1973, **69,** 145-149.

Talkington, L. W., & Hutton, W. O. Hyperactive and nonhyperactive institutionalized retarded residents. *American Journal of Mental Deficiency,* 1973, **78,** 47-50.

Tallan, H. H., Moore, S., & Stein, W. H. L-Cystathionine in human brain. *Journal of Biological Chemistry,* 1958, **230,** 707-716.

Tallman, I. Spousal role differentiation and the socialization of severely retarded children. *Journal of Marriage and the Family,* 1965, **27,** 37-42.

Tarjan, G. Sex: A tri-polar conflict in mental retardation. In R. K. Eyman, C. E. Meyers, & G. Tarjan (Eds.), *Sociobehavioral studies in mental retardation.* Washington, D.C.: American Association on Mental Deficiency, 1973.

Tarjan, G., Eyman, R. K., & Miller, C. P. Natural history of mental retardation in a state hospital, revisited: Releases and deaths in two admission groups, ten years apart. *American Journal of Diseases of Children,* 1969, **117,** 609-620.

Tarjan, G., Wright, S. W., Eyman, R. K., & Keeran, C. V. Natural history of mental retardation: Some aspects of epidemiology. *American Journal of Mental Deficiency,* 1973, **77,** 369-379. Table 21-2 reproduced by permission of the publisher and the senior author.

Tate, B. G., & Baroff, G. S. Aversive control of self-injurious behavior in a psychotic boy. *Behavioral Research and Therapy,* 1966, **4,** 281-287.

Tate, B. G., & Baroff, G. S. Training the mentally retarded in the production of a complex product: A demonstration of work potential. *Exceptional Children,* 1967, **27,** 405-408.

Tavormina, J. B. Basic models of parent counseling: A critical review. *Psychological Bulletin,* 1974, **11**, 827-835.

Tawadros, S. M. Spontaneity training at the Dorra Institute, Alexandria, Egypt. *Group Psychotherapy,* 1956, **9**, 164-167.

Taylor, E. M. *Psychological appraisal of children with cerebral defects.* Cambridge, Mass.: Harvard University Press, 1959.

Taylor, J. F. Role playing with borderline and mildly retarded adolescents in an institutional setting. *Exceptional Children,* 1969, **36**, 205-208.

Terman, L. M. *The measurement of intelligence.* Boston: Houghton Mifflin, 1916.

Terman, L. M. Expert testimony in the case of Alberto Flores. *Journal of Delinquency,* 1918, **3**, 145-164. Excerpts in Chap. 16 reprinted with permission of the publisher.

Terman, L. Intelligence and its measurement: A symposium. *Journal of Educational Psychology,* 1921, **12**, 127-133.

Terman, L. M., & Merrill, M. A. *Measuring intelligence.* Boston: Houghton Mifflin, 1937.

Terman, L. M., & Merrill, M. A. *The Stanford-Binet Intelligence Scale, third revision.* (With 1972 tables by R. L. Thorndike) Boston: Houghton Mifflin, 1973. Tables 2-1, 17-1, and 17-5 reprinted with permission of the publisher.

Teuber, H. L. Mental retardation after early trauma to the brain: Some issues in search of facts. In C. R. Angle & E. A. Bering, Jr. (Eds.), *Physical trauma as an etiological agent in mental retardation.* Washington, D.C.: U.S. Government Printing Office, 1970.

Thalhammer, O., Scheibenreiter, S., & Pantilitschko, M. Histidinemia: detection by routine newborn screening and biochemical observations on three unrelated cases. *Z. Kinderheilk,* 1971, **109**, 279-292.

Thomas, A., Chess, S., & Birch, H. G. *Temperament and behavior disorders in children.* New York: New York University Press, 1968.

Thomas, A., Chess, S., Birch, H. G., Hertzig, M. E., & Korn, S. *Behavioral individuality in early childhood.* New York: New York University Press, 1963.

Thomas, A., Hertzig, M. E., Dryman, I., & Fernandez, P. Examiner effect in IQ testing of Puerto Rican working-class children. *American Journal of Orthopsychiatry,* 1971, **41**, 809-821.

Thomas, C. A. The genetic organization of chromosomes. *Annual Review of Genetics,* 1971, **5**, 237-256.

Thompson, C. W., & Magaret, A. Differential test responses of normals and mental defectives. *Journal of Abnormal Social Psychology,* 1947, **42**, 284-293.

Thompson, J. J., & Thompson, M. W. *Genetics in medicine* (2d ed.). Philadelphia: Saunders, 1973.

Thompson, T., & Grabowski, J. (Eds.) *Behavior modification of the mentally retarded.* New York: Oxford University Press, 1972.

Thompson, W. R., & Grusec, J. Studies of early experience. In P. H. Mussen (Ed.) *Carmichael's manual of child psychology* (Vol. I). New York: Wiley, 1970.

Thomson, G. H. A hierarchy without a general factor. *British Journal of Psychology,* 1916, **8**, 271-281.

Thomson, G. H. *The factorial analysis of human ability* (3d ed.). Boston: Houghton Mifflin, 1948.

Thomson, G. H. *The factorial analysis of human ability* (5th ed.). London: University of London Press, 1951.

Thomson, G. H. Chapter in C. Murchison (Ed.), *A history of psychology in autobiography* (Vol. 4). Worcester, Mass.: Clark University Press, 1952.

Thong, Y. H., Steele, R. W., Vincent, M. M., Hensen, S. A., & Bellanti, J. A. Impaired in vitro cell-mediated immunity to Rubella virus during pregnancy. *New England Journal of Medicine,* 1973, **289**, 604-606.

Thorndike, E. L. Animal intelligence: An experimental study of the associative processes in animals. *Psychological Review,* Monograph Supplement, 1898, **2**(8).

Thorndike, E. L. *The psychology of learning.* New York: Teachers College, 1913.

Thorndike, E. L. *The measurement of intelligence.* New York: Columbia Teachers College, 1925.

Thorndike, R. L. Concepts of culture fairness. *Journal of Educational Measurement,* 1971, **8**, 63-70.

Thorne, F. Counseling and psychotherapy with mental defectives. *American Journal of Mental Deficiency,* 1948, **52**, 263-271.

Thurston, D., Graham, F. K., Ernhart, C. B., Eichman, P. L., & Craft, M. Neurologic status of three-year-old children originally studied at birth. *Neurology,* 1960, **10**, 680-690.

Thurstone, L. L. The vectors of mind. *Psychological Review,* 1934, **41**, 1-32.

Thurstone, L. L. *Primary mental abilities.* Chicago: University of Chicago Press, 1938.

Thurstone, L. L. *Multiple-factor analysis.* Chicago: University of Chicago Press, 1947.

Thurstone, T. G. An evaluation of educating mentally handicapped children in special classes and in regular classes. U.S. Office of Education, Cooperative Research Project No. OE-SAE 6452. Chapel Hill: University of North Carolina, 1959.

Tilton, J. R., & Ottinger, D. R. Comparison of the toy play behavior of autistic, retarded, and normal children. *Psychological Reports,* 1964, **15**, 967-975.

Tizard, B., & Rees, J. A comparison of the effects of adoption, restoration to the natural mother, and continued institutionalization on the cognitive development of four-year-old children. *Child Development,* 1974, **45**, 92-99.

Tizard, J. *Community services for the mentally handicapped.* London: Oxford University Press, 1964.

Tizard, J., & Grad, J. C. *The mentally handicapped and their families: A social survey.* Institute of Psychiatry, Maudsley Monographs No. 7. London: Oxford University Press, 1961.

Tizard, J., & Tizard, B. The social development of two-year-old children in residential nurseries. In H. R. Schaffer (Ed.), *The origins of human social relations.* London: Academic Press, 1971.

Tjio, J. A., & Levan, A. The chromosome number of man. *Hereditas,* 1956, **42**, 1-6.

Tobias, J., & Gorelick, J. The Porteus Maze Test and the appraisal of retarded adults. *American Journal of Mental Deficiency,* 1962, **66**, 600-606.

Tolman, E. C. *Purposive behavior in animals and men.* New York: Appleton-Century, 1932.

Tolman, E. C. Cognitive maps in rats and men. *Psychological Review,* 1948, **55**, 189-208.

Torrance, E. P. *Rewarding creative behavior.* Englewood Cliffs, N.J.: Prentice-Hall, 1965.

Towne, R. C., Joiner, L. M., & Schurr, T. *The effect of special class placement on the self concept of academic ability of the mentally retarded. A time series experiment.* Paper presented at meetings of the Council for Exceptional Children, St. Louis, 1967.

Tredgold, A. F. *A textbook of mental deficiency* (6th ed.). Baltimore: William Wood & Co., 1937.

Tredgold, R. F., & Soddy, K. *A textbook of mental deficiency* (9th ed.). London: Bailliere, Tindall & Cox, 1956. Excerpt in Chap. 5 reprinted with permission of the publisher.

Treffert, D. A. Epidemiology of infantile autism. *Archives of General Psychiatry,* 1970, **22**, 431-438.

Trippi, J. A. Special-class placement and suggestibility of mentally retarded children. *American Journal of Mental Deficiency,* 1973, **78**, 220-222.

Tryon, R. C. A theory of psychological components—an alternative to mathematical factors. *Psychological Review,* 1935, **42**, 425-454.

Tryon, R. C. Genetic differences in maze learning in rats. *Yearbook of the National Society for the Study of Education,* 1940, **39**(1), 111-119.

Tryon, R. C. Domain formulation of cluster and factor analysis. *Psychometrika,* 1959, **24**, 113-136.

Tsuang, M. T., & Lin, T. Y. A clinical and family study of Chinese mongol children. *Journal of Mental Deficiency Research,* 1964, **8**, 84-91.

Tsuchiya, K. Causation of Ouch-Ouch disease. (Itai-Itai Byō) I. Nature of the disease. II. Epidemiology and evaluation. *Keio Journal of Medicine,* 1969, **18**, 181-211.

Tuddenham, R. D. The nature and measurement of intelligence. In L. Postman (Ed.), *Psychology in the making.* New York: Alfred A. Knopf, 1962.

Tuddenham, R. D. A 'Piagetian' test of cognitive development. In W. B. Dockrell (Ed.), *On intelligence: Contemporary theories and educational implications.* London: Methuen, 1970.

Tulving, E., & Pearlstone, Z. Availability versus accessibility of information in memory for words. *Journal of Verbal Learning and Verbal Behavior,* 1966, **5**, 381-391.

Turkewitz, G., & Birch, H. G. Neurobehavioral organization of the human newborn. In J. Hellmuth (Ed.), *Exceptional infant, studies in abnormalities* (Vol. 2). New York: Brunner/Mazel, 1971.

Turner, H. H. A syndrome of infantilism, congenital webbed neck and cubitus valgus. *Endocrinology,* 1938, **23**, 566.

Turnure, J. E. Distractibility in the mentally retarded: Negative evidence for an orienting inadequacy. *Exceptional Children,* 1970, **37**, 181-186.

Turnure, J. E. Outerdirectedness in EMR boys and girls. *American Journal of Mental Deficiency,* 1973, **78**, 163-170.

Turnure, J. E., & Thurlow, M. L. Verbal elaboration and the promotion of transfer of training in educable mentally retarded children. *Journal of Experimental Child Psychology,* 1973, **15**, 137-148.

Turnure, J., & Zigler, E. Outerdirectedness in the problem solving of normal and retarded children. *Journal of Abnormal and Social Psychology,* 1964, **69**, 427-436.

Tustin, F. *Autism and childhood psychosis.* New York: Aronson, 1973.

Tyler, L. E. *The psychology of human differences* (3d ed.). New York: Appleton-Century-Crofts, 1965.

Tymchuk, A. J. Personality and sociocultural retardation. In R. L. Jones & D. L. MacMillan (Eds.), *Special education in transition.* Boston: Allyn and Bacon, 1975.

Ullmann, L. P., & Krasner, L. *A psychological approach to abnormal behavior.* (2d ed.). Englewood Cliffs, N.J.: Prentice Hall, 1975.

U.S. Civil Service Commission, Bureau of Recruiting and Examining. *An 8 1/2-year record: Mentally retarded workers in the federal service.* Washington, D.C.: U.S. Government Printing Office, 1972.

U.S. Department of Labor. *Employment of women.* Washington, D.C.: U.S. Government Printing Office, 1975.

U.S. Office of Education. *Statistics of special education for exceptional children.* Biennial survey of education in the United States, 1952-1954. Washington, D.C.: U.S. Department of Health, Education and Welfare, 1954.

Uzgiris, I. C. Sociocultural factors in cognitive development. In H. C. Haywood (Ed.),

Social-cultural aspects of mental retardation. New York: Appleton-Century-Crofts, 1970.

Uzgiris, I. C., & Hunt, J. McV. *Assessment in infancy: Ordinal scales of psychological development.* Urbana: University of Illinois Press, 1975.

Vandenberg, S. G. *Methods and goals in human behavior genetics.* New York: Academic Press, 1965.

Vandenberg, S. G. Primary mental abilities or general intelligence? Evidence from twin studies. In J. M. Thoday & A. S. Parkes (Eds.), *Genetic and environmental influences on behavior.* Edinburgh: Oliver & Boyd, 1968.

Vandenberg, S. G. The future of human behavior genetics. In L. Ehrman, G. S. Omenn, E. Caspari (Eds.), *Genetics, environment and behavior; implications for educational policy.* New York: Academic Press, 1972.

Vandenberg, S. G. Possible hereditary factors in minimal brain dysfunction. *Annals of the New York Academy of Sciences,* 1973, **205**, 223-230.

Vandenberg, S. G., Stafford, R. E., & Brown, A. M. The Louisville twin study. In S. G. Vandenberg (Ed.), *Progress in human behavior genetics.* Baltimore: Johns Hopkins Press, 1968.

VanderVeer, B., & Schweid, E. Infant assessment: Stability of mental functioning in young retarded children. *American Journal of Mental Deficiency,* 1974, **79**, 1-4.

Van Krevelen, A. Autismus infantum. *Acta Paedopsychiatrica,* 1960, **27**, 97-107.

Van Osdol, B. M., & Carlson, L. A. study of developmental hyperactivity. *Mental Retardation,* 1972, **10**(3), 18-24.

Van Wagenen, R. K., Meyerson, L., Kerr, N. J., & Mahoney, K. Field trials of a new procedure for toilet training. *Journal of Experimental Child Psychology,* 1969, **8**, 147-159.

Vaughan, R. W. Community, courts, and conditions of special education today: Why? *Mental Retardation,* 1973, **11**(2), 43-47.

Vernon, McC. *Multiply handicapped deaf children: Medical, educational and psychological considerations.* Washington, D.C.: Council for Exceptional Children, 1969.

Viggiani, J. C. Educating the mentally retarded in England. *Child Study Center Bulletin,* 1969, **5**(2), 29-35.

Vinh-Bang. Elaboration d'une échelle de développement du raisonnement. *Proceedings of the 15th International Congress on Psychology,* 1957, 333-334.

Vinh-Bang. Evolution des conduites et apprentissage. In A. Morf, J. Smedslund, Vinh-Bang, & J. F. Wohlwill (Eds.), *L'apprentissage des structures logiques. Etudes d'épistémologie génétique* (Vol. 9). Paris: Presses University, 1959.

Vitello, S. J. Facilitation of class inclusion among mentally retarded children. *American Journal of Mental Deficiency,* 1973, **78**, 158-162.

Vogel, F. ABO blood groups and disease. *American Journal of Human Genetics,* 1970, **22**, 464-475. (a)

Vogel, F. The genetics of the normal human electroencephalogram. *Humangenetik,* 1970, **10**, 91-114. (b)

Vogt, D. K. *Literacy among youths 12-17 years.* U.S. DHEW Publication No. (HRA) 74-1613. Washington, D.C.: U.S. Government Printing Office, 1973.

Von Senden, M. *Raum- und Gestaltauffassung bei Operierten Blindgeborenen vor und nach der Operation.* Leipzig: Barth, 1932.

Vygotsky, L. S. *Thought and language.* (E. Hanfmann & G. Vakar, Trans.). Cambridge, Mass.: M.I.T. Press, 1962.

Wachs, T. D. Report on the utility of a Piaget-based infant scale with older retarded children. *Developmental Psychology,* 1970, **2**, 449.

Wachs, T. D., & Cromwell, R. L. Perceptual distortions by mentally retarded and normal children in response to failure information. *American Journal of Mental Deficiency,* 1966, **70**, 803–806.

Wachs, T. D., Uzgiris, I. C., & Hunt, J. McV. Cognitive development in infants of different age levels and from different environmental backgrounds. An explanatory investigation. *Merrill-Palmer Quarterly,* 1971, **17**, 283–317.

Wagner, P. Children tutoring children. *Mental Retardation,* 1974, **12**(5), 52–55.

Waldrop, M. F., & Halverson, C. F., Jr. Minor physical anomalies and hyperactive behavior in young children. In J. Hellmuth (Ed.), *Exceptional infant* (Vol. 2). New York: Brunner/Mazel, 1971.

Walker, K. P., & Gross, F. L. IQ stability among educable mentally retarded children. *Training School Bulletin,* 1970, **66**, 181–187.

Wallace, R. A., Fulkerson, W., Shults, W. D., & Lyon, W. S. *Mercury in the environment: The human element.* Oak Ridge National Laboratory, National Science Foundation Environmental Program, 1971.

Wallace, S. J., & Michie, E. A. A follow-up study of infants born to mothers with low oestriol excretion during pregnancy. *Lancet,* 1966, **2**, 560–563.

Wallach, M., & Kogan, N. *Modes of thinking in young children: A study of the creativity-intelligence distinction.* New York: Holt, 1965.

Wallin, J. E. Prevalence of mental retardates. *School and Society,* 1958, **86**, 55–56.

Wallin, J. E. Training of the severely retarded, viewed in historical perspective. *Journal of General Psychology,* 1966, **74**, 107–127.

Wanderer, Z. W., & Sternlicht, M. Alternative guidance: A psychotherapeutic approach to mental deficiency. *International Mental Health Review Research Newsletter,* 1964, **7**, 13–15.

Wanschura, P. B., & Borkowski, J. G. The development and transfer of mediational strategies by retarded children in paired-associate learning. *American Journal of Mental Deficiency,* 1974, **78**, 631–639.

Warburg, M., & Mikkelsen, M. A case of 13–15 trisomy or Bartholin-Pataux's syndrome. *Acta Ophthalmologica,* 1963, **41**, 321.

Warkany, J. *Congenital malformations: Notes and comments.* Chicago: Year Book Medical Publishers, 1971.

Warkany, J., Passarge, E., & Smith, L. B. Congenital malformations in autosomal trisomy syndromes. *American Journal of Diseases in Children,* 1966, **112**, 502.

Watson, J. D. *Molecular biology of the gene* (2d ed.). New York: W. A. Benjamin, Inc., 1970.

Watson, L. S., Jr. Application of operant conditioning techniques to institutionalized severely and profoundly retarded children. *Mental Retardation Abstracts,* 1967, **4**, 1–18.

Watson, L. S., Jr. Behavior modification of residents and personnel in institutions for the mentally retarded. In A. A. Baumeister & E. C. Butterfield (Eds.), *Residential facilities for the mentally retarded.* Chicago: Aldine, 1970.

Watson, L. S., Jr., & Bassinger, J. F. Parent training technology. *Mental Retardation,* 1974, **12**(5), 3–10.

Waugh, N. C., & Norman, D. A. Primary memory. *Psychological Review,* 1965, **72**, 89–104.

Weaver, S. J. *Effects of motivation-hygiene orientations and interpersonal reaction tendencies in intellectually subnormal children.* Ann Arbor, Mich.: University Microfilms, 1966.

Weber, W. W. Survival and sex ratio in trisomy 17-18. *American Journal of Human Genetics,* 1967, **19**, 369.

Webster, T. G. Unique aspects of emotional development in mentally retarded children. In F. J. Menolascino (Ed.), *Psychiatric approaches to mental retardation.* New York: Basic Books, 1970.

Wechsler, D. *The measurement of adult intelligence.* Baltimore: Williams & Wilkins, 1939.

Wechsler, D. *Wechsler Intelligence Scale for Children: Manual.* New York: Psychological Corporation, 1949.

Wechsler, D. Cognitive, conative, and non-intellective intelligence. *American Psychologist,* 1950, **5**, 78-83.

Wechsler, D. *Wechsler Adult Intelligence Scale, manual.* New York: Psychological Corporation, 1955. Table 2-1 reprinted with permission of the publisher and the author.

Wechsler, D. *Manual for the Wechsler Preschool and Primary Scale of Intelligence.* New York: Psychological Corporation, 1967.

Wechsler, D. *Wechsler Intelligence Scale for Children—revised.* New York: Psychological Corporation, 1974.

Weener, P., Barritt, L. S., & Semmel, M. I. A critical evaluation of the Illinois Test of Psycholinguistic Abilities, *Exceptional Children,* 1967, **27**, 373-380.

Wei, T. T. D., Lavatelli, C. B., & Jones, R. S. Piaget's concept of classification: A comparative study of socially disadvantaged and middle-class young children. *Child Development,* 1971, **42**, 919-927.

Weikart, D., et al. The Ypsilanti-Carnegie Infant Education Project. *Bulletin of the High/Scope Foundation,* Spring 1974, No. 1.

Weisberg, P. Operant procedures with the retardate: An overview of laboratory research. In N. R. Ellis (Ed.), *International review of research in mental retardation* (Vol. 5). New York: Academic Press, 1971.

Weise, P., Koch, R., Shaw, K. N. F., & Rosenfeld, M. J. The use of 5HTP in the treatment of Down's syndrome. *Pediatrics,* 1974, **54**, 165-168.

Weiss, G., Minde, K., Werry, J. S., Douglas, V., & Nemeth, E. Studies on the hyperactive child. VIII. Five-year follow-up. *Archives of General Psychiatry,* 1971, **24**, 409-414.

Weiss, W., & Jackson, C. E. *Maternal factors affecting birthweight. Perinatal factors affecting human development* (PASBS Publication No. 185). Washington, D.C.: Pan American Health Organization, 1969.

Wender, P. H. Some speculations concerning a possible biochemical basis of minimal brain dysfunction. *Annals of the New York Academy of Sciences,* 1973, **205**, 18-28.

Wepman, J. M., Cruickshank, W. M., Deutsch, C. P., Morency, A., & Strother, C. R. Learning disabilities. In N. Hobbs (Ed.), *Issues in the classification of children* (Vol. 1). San Francisco: Jossey-Bass, 1975.

Werner, E. E., Bierman, J. M., & French, F. E. *The children of Kauai.* Honolulu: University of Hawaii Press, 1971.

Werner, E. E., Honzik, M. P., & Smith, R. S. Prediction of intelligence and achievement at ten years from twenty months pediatric and psychologic examinations. *Child Development,* 1968, **39**, 1063-1075.

Werner, E., Simonian, K., Bierman, J. M., & French, F. E. Cumulative effect of perinatal complications and deprived environment on physical, intellectual, and social development of preschool children. *Pediatrics,* 1967, **39**, 490-505.

Werner, H., & Strauss, A. A. Types of visuo-motor activity in their relation to low and high performance ages. *Proceedings of the American Association on Mental Deficiency,* 1939, **44**, 163-168.

Werner, H., & Strauss, A. A. Pathology of figure background relation in the child. *Journal of Abnormal and Social Psychology,* 1941, **36**, 58-67.

Werner, H. Abnormal and sub-normal rigidity. *Journal of Abnormal and Social Psychology,* 1946, **41**, 15-24.

Wertelcki, W., Schindler, A. M., & Gerald, P. S. Partial deletion of chromosome 18. *Lancet,* 1966, **2**, 641.

Westall, R. G., Dancis, J., & Miller, S. Maple sugar urine disease. *American Medical Association Journal of Diseases in Children,* 1957, **94**, 571.

Whalen, C. K., & Henker, B. A. Creating therapeutic pyramids using mentally retarded patients. *American Journal of Mental Deficiency,* 1969, **74**, 331-337.

Whalen, C. K., & Henker, B. A. Pyramid therapy in a hospital for the retarded: Methods, program evaluation, and long term effects. *American Journal of Mental Deficiency,* 1971, **75**, 414-434.

White, B. L., & Held, R. Plasticity of sensorimotor development in the human infant. In J. Rosenblith & W. Allinsmith (Eds.), *The causes of behavior* (2d ed.). Boston: Allyn and Bacon, 1966.

White, B. L., & Watts, J. C. *Experience and environment: Major influences on the development of the young child* (Vol. 1). Englewood Cliffs, N.J.: Prentice-Hall, 1973. Excerpt in Chap. 7 reprinted with permission of the publisher.

White, R. The effects of teacher personality variables as measured by the achievement of mentally retarded students. *Education and Training of the Mentally Retarded,* 1970, **5**, 194-202.

White, R. W. Motivation reconsidered: The concept of competence. *Psychological Review,* 1959, **66**, 297-333.

White, R. W. Competence and the psychosexual stages of development. In M. R. Jones (Ed.), *Nebraska symposium on motivation, 1960.* Lincoln: University of Nebraska Press, 1960.

White, S. H. Evidence for a hierarchical arrangement of learning processes. In L. P. Lipsitt & C. C. Spiker (Eds.), *Advances in child development and behavior* (Vol. 2). New York: Academic Press, 1965.

Whitman, M. A., & Sprague, R. L. Learning and distractibility in normals and retardates. *Training School Bulletin,* 1968, **65**, 89-101.

Wiener, G., Crawford, E. E., & Snyder, R. T. Some correlates of overt anxiety in mildly retarded patients. *American Journal of Mental Deficiency,* 1960, **64**, 735-739.

Wiener, G., Rider, R. V., & Oppel, W. C. Some correlates of IQ changes in children. *Child Development,* 1963, **34**, 61-68.

Wiener, G., Rider, R. V., Oppel, W. C., Fischer, L. K., & Harper, P. A. Correlates of low birth weight: Psychological status at six to seven years of age. *Pediatrics,* 1965, **35**, 434-444.

Wilcox, P. H. The Gardner Behavior Chart. *American Journal of Psychiatry,* 1942, **98**, 874-880.

Willerman, L. Fetal head positions during delivery and intelligence. In C. R. Angle & E. A. Bering, Jr. (Eds.), *Physical trauma as an etiological agent in mental retardation.* Washington, D.C.: U.S. Government Printing Office, 1970. (a)

Willerman, L. Maternal pelvic size and neuropsychological outcome. In C. R. Angle & E. A. Bering, Jr., (Eds.), *Physical trauma as an etiological agent in mental retardation.* Washington, D.C.: U.S. Government Printing Office, 1970. (b)

Willerman, L. Biosocial influences on human development. *American Journal of Orthopsychiatry,* 1972, **42**, 452-462.

Willerman, L., Broman, S. H., & Fiedler, M. Infant development, preschool IQ, and social class. *Child Development,* 1970, **41**, 69-77.

Willerman, L., & Churchill, J. A. Intelligence and birth weight in identical twins. *Child Development,* 1967, **38**, 623-629.

Willerman, L., Naylor, A. F., & Myrianthopoulos, N. C. Intellectual development of children from interracial matings. *Science,* 1970, **170**, 1329-1331.

Williams, F. (Ed.) *Language and poverty: Perspectives on a theme.* Chicago: Markham Publishing, 1970.

Williams, J. R., & Scott, R. B. Growth and development of Negro infants: IV. Motor development and its relationship to child rearing practices in two groups of Negro infants. *Child Development,* 1953, **24**, 103-121.

Wilson, J. G. *Environment and birth defects.* New York: Academic Press, 1973.

Wilson, P. D., & Riesen, A. H. Visual development in rhesus monkeys neonatally deprived of patterned light. *Journal of Comparative and Physiological Psychology,* 1966, **61**, 87-95.

Wilson, R. S. Twins: Mental development in the preschool years. *Developmental Psychology,* 1974, **10**, 580-588.

Wilson, W. Social psychology and mental retardation. In N. R. Ellis (Ed.), *International review of research in mental retardation* (Vol. 4). New York: Academic Press, 1970.

Wilton, K. M., & Boersma, F. J. Conservation research with the mentally retarded. In N. R. Ellis (Ed.), *International review of research in mental retardation* (Vol. 7). New York: Academic Press, 1974.

Windle, C. Prognosis of mental subnormals. *American Journal of Mental Deficiency,* 1962, **66**(Monogr. suppl.)

Windle, C. What's in a name? In R. K. Eyman, C. E. Meyers, & G. Tarjan (Eds.), *Sociobehavioral studies in mental retardation.* Washington, D.C.: American Association on Mental Deficiency, 1973.

Winick, M. Nutrition and nerve cell growth. *Federation Proceedings,* 1970, **29**, 1510-1515.

Winick, M., & Rosso, P. Effects of malnutrition on brain development. *Biology of Brain Dysfunction,* 1973, **1**, 301-317.

Wink, C. F. Mental retardation and learning under symbolic reinforcement in view of self-acceptance. *Dissertation Abstracts,* 1963, **23**, 2430-2431.

Witmer, L. Orthogenic cases, XIV—Don: A curable case of arrested development due to a fear psychosis the result of shock in a three-year-old infant. *Psychological Clinic,* 1919-22, **13**, 97-111.

Witkop, C. J., Jr., & Henry, F. V. Sjogren-Larson syndrome and histidinemia: Hereditary biochemical diseases with defects of speech and oral functions. *Journal of Speech and Hearing,* 1963, **28**, 109-123.

Witkowski, T. Investigations on the moral sensitivity of subnormal children. *Annales de Philosophie,* 1967, **15**(4), 95-106.

Wohlwill, J. F. From perception to inference: A dimension of cognitive development. In W. Kessen and C. Kuhlman (Eds.), *Thought in the young child.* Chicago: University of Chicago Press, 1962.

Wohlwill, J. F. Piaget's theory of the development of intelligence in the concrete operations period. In M. Garrison, Jr. (Ed.), *Cognitive models and development in mental retardation. American Journal of Mental Deficiency,* 1966. (Monogr. Suppl.)

Wolf, J. M. (Ed.) *The results of treatment in cerebral palsy.* Springfield, Ill.: Charles C Thomas, 1969.

Wolf, M. M., Risley, T., & Mees, H. L. Application of operant conditioning procedures to the behaviour problems of an autistic child. *Behaviour Research and Therapy,* 1964, **1,** 305-312.

Wolfensberger, W. Embarrassments in the diagnostic process. *Mental Retardation,* 1965, **3**(3), 29-31.

Wolfensberger, W. Counseling the parents of the retarded. In A. A. Baumeister (Ed.), *Mental retardation: Appraisal, education, and rehabilitation.* Chicago: Aldine, 1967.

Wolfensberger, W. The origin and nature of our institutional models. In R. B. Kugel & W. Wolfensberger (Eds.), *Changing patterns in residential services for the mentally retarded.* Washington, D.C.: President's Committee on Mental Retardation, 1969.

Wolfensberger, W., & Kurtz, R. A. (Eds.) *Management of the family of the mentally retarded.* New York: Follett Educational Corp., 1969.

Wolfensberger, W., & Kurtz, R. A. Measurement of parents' perceptions of their children's development. *Genetic Psychology Monographs,* 1971, **83,** 3-92.

Wolfensberger, W., with Nirje, B., Olshansky, S., Perske, R., & Roos, P. *The principle of normalization in human services.* Ontario, Canada: National Institute on Mental Retardation, 1972.

Wolff, P. H. The developmental psychologies of Jean Piaget and psychoanalysis. *Psychological Issues,* 1960, **2,** Monograph No. 5. New York: International Universities Press, 1960.

Wood, A. C., Jr., Friedman, C. J., & Steisel, I. M. Psychosocial factors in phenylketonuria. *American Journal of Orthopsychiatry,* 1967, **37,** 671-679.

Wood, J. W., Johnson, K. G., & Omori, Y. In utero exposure to the Hiroshima atomic bomb. An evaluation of head size and mental retardation twenty years later. *Pediatrics,* 1967, **39,** 385-392.

Woodburne, L. S. *The neural basis of behavior.* Columbus, Ohio: Merrill, 1967.

Woodrow, H. Intelligence and its measurement: A symposium. *Journal of Educational Psychology,* 1921, **12,** 207-210.

Woodward, K. F., Brown, D., & Bird, D. Psychiatric study of mentally retarded preschool children. *American Medical Association Archives on General Psychiatry,* 1960, **2,** 156-170.

Woodward, K. F., Siegel, M. G., & Eustis, M. J. Psychiatric study of mentally retarded children of preschool age: Report on first and second years of a three-year project. *American Journal of Orthopsychiatry,* 1958, **28,** 376-393.

Woodward, K. F., Jaffe, N., & Brown, D. Psychiatric program for very young retarded children. In F. J. Menolascino (Ed.), *Psychiatric aspects of the diagnosis and treatment of mental retardation.* Seattle, Wash.: Special Child Publications, 1971.

Woodward, M. The behavior of idiots interpreted by Piaget's theory of sensori-motor development. *British Journal of Educational Psychology,* 1959, **29,** 60-71.

Woodward, M. Concepts of space in the mentally subnormal studied by Piaget's method. *British Journal of Social and Clinical Psychology,* 1962, **1,** 25-37.

Woodward, M. The application of Piaget's theory to research in mental deficiency. In N. R. Ellis (Ed.), *Handbook of mental deficiency.* New York: McGraw-Hill, 1963.

Woodworth, R. S. Heredity and environment. A critical survey of recently published material on twins and foster children. *Social Science Research Council Bulletin,* 1941, **47.**

Wooster, A. D. Formation of stable and discrete concepts of personality by normal and mentally retarded boys. *Journal of Mental Subnormality,* 1970, **16**(30), 24-28.

World Health Organization. *International classification of diseases* (8th rev.). New York: WHO, 1968.

Wortis, H. Poverty and retardation: Social aspects. In J. Wortis (Ed.), *Mental retardation: An annual review* (Vol. 1). New York: Grune & Stratton, 1970.

Wortis, H., Bardach, J. L., Cutler, R., Rue, R., & Freedman, A. Child-rearing practices in a low socio-economic group. *Pediatrics,* 1963, **32**, 298-307.

Wortis, H., Jedrysek, E., & Wortis, J. Unreported defect in the siblings of retarded children. *American Journal of Mental Deficiency,* 1967, **72**, 388-392.

Wortis, J. A note on the concept of the "brain-injured child." *American Journal of Mental Deficiency,* 1956, **61**, 204-206.

Wortis, J. Prevention of mental retardation. *American Journal of Orthopsychiatry,* 1965, **35**, 886-895.

Wortis, J. Successful family life for the retarded child. In *Stress on families of the mentally handicapped.* Proceedings of the Third International Conference, Paris, March 21-26, 1966. Brussels, Belgium: International League of Societies of the Mentally Retarded, 1966.

Wortis, J. Poverty and retardation: Biosocial factors. In J. Wortis (Ed.), *Mental retardation: An annual review* (Vol. 1). New York: Grune & Stratton, 1970.

Wright, L. *The performance of overachieving males on certain measures of efficiency and divergence: A study in personality integration.* Ann Arbor, Mich.: University Microfilms, 1964.

Wright, S. W., & Tarjan, G. Phenylketonuria. *American Journal of Diseases of Children,* 1957, **93**, 405-419.

Wright, S. W., Tarjan, G., & Eyer, L. Investigation of families with two or more mentally defective siblings. Clinical observations. *American Journal of Diseases of Children,* 1959, **91**, 4, 445-456.

Wright, T., & Nicholson, J. Physiotherapy for the spastic child: An evaluation. *Developmental Medicine and Child Neurology,* 1973, **15**, 146-163.

Wrightsman, L., Jr. The effects of anxiety, achievement motivation, and importance upon performance on an intelligence test. *Journal of Educational Psychology,* 1962, **52**, 150-156.

Yando, R., & Zigler, E. Outerdirectedness in the problem-solving of institutionalized and noninstitutionalized normal and retarded children. *Developmental Psychology,* 1971, **4**, 277-288.

Yannet, H. Mental deficiency due to prenatally determined factors. *Pediatrics,* 1950, **5**, 328-336.

Yarrow, L. J. The etiology of mental deprivation: The deprivation model. In J. Hellmuth (Ed.), *Cognitive studies: Volume I.* New York: Brunner/Mazel, 1970.

Yarrow, L. J., Rubenstein, J. L., & Pedersen, F. A. *Dimensions of early stimulation: Differential effects on infant development.* Presented at the meeting of the Society for Research in Child Development, Minneapolis, April 1971.

Yates, F. A. *The art of memory.* London: Routledge & Kegan Paul, 1966.

Yendovitskaya, T. V. Development of memory. In A. V. Zaporozhets & D. B. Elkonin (Eds.), *The psychology of pre-school children.* Cambridge, Mass.: M.I.T., 1971.

Yntema, D. B., & Meuser, G. E. Keeping track of variables that have few or many states. *Journal of Experimental Psychology,* 1962, **63**, 391-395.

Yoder, P., & Forehand, R. Effects of modeling and verbal cues upon concept acquisition of nonretarded and retarded children. *American Journal of Mental Deficiency,* 1974, **78**, 566-570.

Younghusband, E., Birchall, D., Davie, R., & Kellmer Pringle, M. L. (Eds.) *Living with handicap.* London: The National Bureau for Co-operation in Child Care, 1970.

Zamenhof, S., Van Marthens, E., & Margolis, F. L. DNA (cell number) and protein in neonatal brain: Alteration by maternal dietary protein restriction. *Science,* 1968, **160**, 322–330.

Zaporozhets, A. V. *Development of voluntary movements.* Moscow: The Publishing House, Academy of Pedagogical Sciences, 1960.

Zausmer, E., Pueschel, S., & Shea, A. A sensori-motor stimulation program for the young child with Down's syndrome: Preliminary report. *MCH Exchange,* 1972, **2**(4), 1–4.

Zeaman, D. One programmatic approach to retardation. In D. K. Routh (Ed.), *The experimental psychology of mental retardation.* Chicago: Aldine, 1973.

Zeaman, D. *Experimental psychology of mental retardation: Some states of the art.* Invited address to meetings of the American Psychological Association, New Orleans, August 31, 1974.

Zeaman, D., & House, B. J. Approach and avoidance in the discrimination learning of retardates. *Child Development,* 1962, **33**, 355–372.

Zeaman, D., & House, B. J. The role of attention in retardate discrimination learning. In N. R. Ellis (Ed.), *Handbook of Mental Deficiency.* New York: McGraw-Hill, 1963. Figures 13-1 and 13-2 reprinted with permission of the publisher.

Zeaman, D., & House, B. J. The relation of IQ and learning. In R. M. Gagne (Ed.), *Learning and individual differences.* Columbus, Ohio: Charles E. Merrill, 1966.

Zigler, E. Research on personality structure in the retardate. In N. R. Ellis (Ed.), *International review of research in mental retardation* (Vol. 1). New York: Academic Press, 1966.

Zigler, E. Familial mental retardation: A continuing dilemma. *Science,* January 20, 1967, **155**, 292–298. (a)

Zigler, E. Mental retardation, technical comment. *Science,* 1967, **157**, 578. (b)

Zigler, E. Developmental versus difference theories of mental retardation and the problem of motivation. *American Journal of Mental Deficiency,* 1969, **73**, 536–555.

Zigler, E. The retarded child as a whole person. In H. E. Adams & W. K. Boardman (Eds.), *Advances in experimental clinical psychology.* New York: Pergamon Press, 1971.

Zigler, E. The retarded child as a whole person. In D. K. Routh (Ed.), *The experimental psychology of mental retardation.* Chicago: Aldine, 1973.

Zigler, E., & Balla, D. A. Luria's verbal deficiency theory of mental retardation and performance on sameness, symmetry, and opposition tasks: A critique. *American Journal of Mental Deficiency,* 1971, **75**, 400–413.

Zigler, E., Balla, D. A., & Butterfield, E. C. A longitudinal investigation of the relationship between preinstitutional social deprivation and social motivation in institutionalized retardates. *Journal of Personality and Social Psychology,* 1968, **10**, 437–445.

Zigler, E., & Butterfield, E. C. Motivational aspects of changes in IQ test performance of culturally deprived nursery school children. *Child Development,* 1968, **39**, 1–14.

Zigler, E., Butterfield, E. C., & Capobianco, F. Institutionalization and the effectiveness of social reinforcement: A five- and eight-year follow-up study. *Child Development,* 1970, **3**, 253–263.

Zigler, E., Butterfield, E. C., & Goff, G. A measure of preinstitutional social deprivation for institutionalized retardates. *American Journal of Mental Deficiency,* 1966, **70**, 873–885.

Zigler, E. F., & Harter, S. The socialization of the mentally retarded. In D. A. Goslin (Ed.), *Handbook of socialization theory and research.* Chicago, Ill.: Rand McNally, 1969.

Zigler, E., Hodgen, L., & Stevenson, H. W. The effect of support and nonsupport on the performance of normal and feebleminded children. *Journal of Personality,* 1958, **26,** 106–122.

Zigler, E., Levine, J., & Gould, L. Cognitive processes in the development of children's appreciation of humor. *Child Development,* 1966, **37,** 507–518.

Zimmerman, E. H., Zimmerman, J., & Russell, D. Differential effects of token reinforcement on instruction-following behavior in retarded students instructed as a group. *Journal of Applied Behavior Analysis,* 1969, **2,** 101–118.

Zimmerman, J., Stuckey, T., Garlick, B., & Miller, M. Effects of token reinforcement on productivity in multiple handicapped clients in a sheltered workshop. *Rehabilitation Literature,* 1969, **30,** 34–41.

Zito, R. J., & Bardon, J. I. Achievement motivation among Negro adolescents in regular and special education programs. *American Journal of Mental Deficiency,* 1969, **74,** 20–26.

Zwilling, E. Teratogenesis. In B. H. Willier (Ed.), *The analysis of development.* Philadelphia: Saunders, 1955.

NAME INDEX

SUBJECT INDEX

Funds, governmental, 44
  (*See also* Government)

G factor, 7-8, 345
Galactosemia, 96-97
Gametes, 55, 58, 62
Garden-variety deficiency, 34, 167
General-adaptation syndrome, 148
General factor, 7-8, 345
General intelligence, 7-8, 22-23
Generalization, 245
  memory and, 296
Genes, 55-57
  dominant, 59-60, 93-96
  heterozygous, 60
  homozygous, 60
  mutant, 63-64
  recessive, 60-61, 96-97
  (*See also* Genetic factors)
Genetic factors, 51, 53-107
  Albright's osteodystrophy, 96
  alternative forms and, 65
  animal studies, 67-68
  Apert's syndrome, 96
  behavioral influences, 66-67
  biochemistry and physiology, 68
  biology of living cells, 54-59
  brain damage and, 217
  carbohydrate metabolism and,
    96-97, 104
  cell division, 57-59
  cerebral angiomatosis, 95
  chromosomes, 54-55
    (*See also* Autosomal
      chromosomes;
      Chromosomes)
  code messages and letters, 56
  color blindness and, 62
  concordance, 69
  continuum of indirectness, 66
  correlational methods, 71
  cranial anomalies, 96
  dominance, 59-60
  disorders due to, 93-96
  Down's syndrome, 77-88
  environmental interaction with,
    53-54
  epidemiology and, 68
  in epilepsy, 66, 138
  expressivity, 64-65
  fructose intolerance, 97
  fundamental processes, 54
  galactosemia, 96-97
  genotype, 60, 64-65
  gonadal dysgenesis, 90-92
  histidinemia, 101-102
  homocystinuria, 102-103
  Hunter syndrome, 104
  Hurler syndrome, 104
  hyperactivity and, 231
  intelligence and, 71-75
  IQ higher than normal and,
    106-107
  Klinefelter's syndrome, 92
  Lesch-Nyhan syndrome, 105-106
  lipid storage disease, 104-105
  maple syrup urine disease, 101

Genetic factors:
  Mendelian traits, 62
  metabolic disorders, 96-106
  microcephaly, 65, 106
  microscopic units, 55-57
  mucopolysaccharide storage
    disease, 104
  mutation, 63-64
  myotonic dystrophy, 95
  neurofibromatosis, 95
  nucleic acid disorder, 105-106
  partial deletions, 89-90
  pedigree analysis, 68-69
  penetrance, 64-65
  phenocopy, 65
  phenotype, 60, 64-65
  phenylketonuria, 97-101
  polygenic inheritance, 62-63
  primary form, 65
  protein and amino acid
    metabolism and, 97-103
  pseudohypoparathyroidism, 96
  psychosocial disadvantage and,
    168-169
  recessive genes, 60-61
  disorders due to, 96-97, 105
  sex chromosomes, 61-62, 90-93
  study methods, 67-71
  Sturge-Weber syndrome, 95
  susceptibility and, 65
  syndromes, 76-107
  Tay-Sachs disease, 104-105
  thyroid hormone synthesis and,
    103-104
  transmission, modes of, 59-65
  trisomy 13 and 18, 89
  trisomy 21, 77-88
  tuberous sclerosis, 94-95
  Turner's syndrome, 90-92
  twin studies, 69-70, 73
Genotype, 60, 64-65
Geographic region, retardation
  and, 41-42
Germ cells, 55, 58, 62
Glial cells, 110, 113
Global capacity, 6
Goitrous hypothyroidism, 65, 103
Gonadal dysgenesis, 90-92
Government, 47, 368, 369
  adult aid by, 466
  institutions and, 449
  labeling and, 44
Grade, retention in, 381
Gradients, embryonic, 109-110
Grand mal seizures, 139
Gray matter, 110, 112
Group factor theory, 8-9
Group homes, 452-453
Group tests versus individual tests,
  21-22
Group therapy, 401-403
  with parents, 402-403
Grouping:
  cognitive functioning and,
    250-251
  memory and, 295-296

Growth, physical: malnutrition
  and, 131
  psychological development
    and, 150
Guardianship laws, 470-471
Guidance, alternative, 400
Guided learning, 305
Guilford's three-dimensional
  theory, 9-10

Habituation, 229
Halfway houses, 452
Handling of infants, 443-444
Harlem Youth Opportunities
  Unlimited, 154
Head injury:
  at birth, 128-129
  postnatal, 129
Head Start, 368, 385-386
Health, physical, socioeconomic
  status and, 172-173
Health professionals, mental (*see*
  Psychotherapy)
Hedonist, intact, 190
Helpfulness, 191-193
Hemiplegia, cerebral palsy and,
  135
Heredity (*see* Genetic factors)
Herpes virus hominis, 118-119
Heterozygous genes, 60
Hexachlorophene, neurotoxicity
  from, 127-128
Higher-order structures, acquisition
  of, 271
Hindbrain, 110
Hippocampus, 112, 139-140
Histidinemia, 101-102
Home:
  care, support for, 454
  environment, 173-175
  variables in, institutionalization
    and, 444
  (*See also* Family; Parents)
Homes:
  foster, 453-454
  group, 452-453
  nursing, 453
Homocystinuria, 102-103
Homogeneous grouping, 379, 381
Homologous chromosomes, 55
Homozygous genes, 60
Hospitals, custodial, 433-434
Hostels, 452
Hullian theory, 266-267
Hunger, 131-132
Hunter syndrome, 104
Hurler syndrome, 104
Hydrocephalus, 142, 143
Hygiene-oriented individual, 189
Hyperactivity, 229-235
  drugs and, 233
  etiology, 230-232
  management, 233-235
  measurement, 232-233
Hyperbilirubinemia, 120
Hypertension, pregnancy and, 120
Hypogonadism, 92